HERO

HERO

THE LIFE AND LEGEND OF

LAWRENCE
OF ARABIA

MICHAEL KORDA

JR
BOOKS

First published in Great Britain in 2011 by
JR Books, 10 Greenland Street, London NW1 0ND
www.jrbooks.com

ISBN 978-1-907532-29-0

3 5 7 9 10 8 6 4

Printed by the MPG Books Group

For Margaret, again and always

And not by eastern windows only,
When daylight comes, comes in the light,
In front the sun climbs slow, how slowly,
   But westward, look, the land is bright.

          —Arthur Hugh Clough,
            "Say Not the Struggle Naught Availeth"

I do not pretend to have understood T. E. Lawrence fully, still less to be able to portray him; there is no brush fine enough to catch the subtleties of his mind, no aerial viewpoint high enough to bring into one picture the manifold of his character. . . . I am not a tractable person or much of a hero-worshipper, but I could have followed Lawrence over the edge of the world. I loved him for himself, and also because there seemed to be reborn in him all the lost friends of my youth. . . . If genius be, in Emerson's phrase, "a stellar and undiminishable something," whose origin is a mystery and whose essence cannot be defined, then he was the only man of genius I have ever known.

—John Buchan (Lord Tweedsmuir),
Pilgrim's Way

The will is free;
Strong is the soul, and wise and beautiful;
The seeds of godlike power are in us still;
Gods are we, bards, saints, heroes, if we will!

—Matthew Arnold,
written in a copy of Emerson's *Essays*

He was indeed a dweller upon mountain tops where the air is cold, crisp and rarefied, and where the view on clear days commands all the Kingdoms of the world and the glory of them.

—Winston S. Churchill,
on Lawrence

Oh! If only he had died in battle! I have lost my son, but I do not grieve for him as I do for Lawrence. . . . I am counted brave, the bravest of my tribe; my heart was iron, but his was steel. A man whose hand was never closed, but open. . . . Tell them. . . . Tell them in England what I say. Of manhood, the man, in freedom, free; a mind without equal; I can see no flaw in him.

—Sheikh Hamoudi,
on being told of Lawrence's death

Contents

List of Maps

Preface

I t has been ninety-two years since the end of World War I, known until September 1939 as the Great War. Of the millions who fought in it, of the millions who died in it, of its many heroes, perhaps the only one whose name is still remembered in the English-speaking world is T. E. Lawrence, "Lawrence of Arabia."

There are many reasons for this—even during his own lifetime Lawrence was transformed into a legend and a myth, the realities of his accomplishments overshadowed by the bright glare of his fame and celebrity—and it is the purpose of this book to explore them, as objectively, and sympathetically, as possible, for Lawrence was from the beginning a controversial figure, and one who very often did his best to cover his tracks and mislead his biographers.

Since the British government began to open its files and release what had hitherto been secret documents in the 1960s, Lawrence's feats have been confirmed in meticulous detail. What he wrote that he did, he did—if anything he underplayed his role in the Arab Revolt, the 1919 Paris Peace Conference that followed the Allies' victory, and the British effort to create a new Middle East out of the shards of the defeated Ottoman

Empire in 1921 and 1922. Many of the problems that confront us in the Middle East today were foreseen by Lawrence, and he had a direct hand in some of them. Today, when the Middle East is the main focus of our attention, and when insurgency, his specialty, is the main weapon of our adversaries, the story of Lawrence's life is more important than ever.

As we shall see, he was a man of many gifts: a scholar, an archaeologist, a writer of genius, a gifted translator, a mapmaker of considerable talent. But beyond all that he was a creator of nations, of which two have survived; a diplomat; a soldier of startling originality and brilliance; an authentic genius at guerrilla warfare; an instinctive leader of men; and above all, a hero.

We have become used to thinking of heroism as something that simply happens to people; indeed the word has been in a sense cheapened by the modern habit of calling everybody exposed to any kind of danger, whether voluntarily or not, a "hero." Soldiers—indeed all those in uniform—are now commonly referred to as "our heroes," as if heroism were a universal quality shared by everyone who bears arms, or as if it were an accident, not a vocation. Even those who die in terrorist attacks, and have thus had the bad luck to be in the wrong place at the wrong time, are described as "heroes," though given a choice most of them would no doubt have preferred to be somewhere else when the blow was struck.

Lawrence, however, was a hero in the much older, classical sense—it is surely no accident that he decided to translate Homer's *Odyssey*—and like the heroes of old he trained himself, from early childhood, for the role. Without the war, Lawrence might never have accomplished his ambition, but once it came he was prepared for it, both morally and physically. He had steeled himself to an almost inhuman capacity to endure pain; he had studied the arts of war and of leadership; he had carefully honed his courage and his skill at leading men—like the young Napoleon Bonaparte he was ready to assume the role of hero when fate presented him with the opportunity. He seized it eagerly with both hands in 1917, and like Ajax, Achilles, Ulysses, he could never let go of it. No matter how hard he tried to escape from his own legend and fame later on, they stuck to him to the very end of his life, and beyond: seventy-five years after his death he remains as famous as ever.

This book, therefore, is about the creation of a legend, a mythic figure, and about a man who became a hero not by accident, or even by one single act of heroism, but who made himself a hero by design, and did it so successfully that he became the victim of his own fame.

"His name will live in history," King George V wrote on Lawrence's death in 1935.

And it has.

HERO

CHAPTER ONE

"Who Is This Extraordinary Pip-Squeak?"

In the third summer of the world's greatest war a small garrison of Turkish soldiers still held the port of Aqaba, on the Red Sea, as they had from the beginning—indeed since long before the beginning of this war, for Aqaba, the site of Elath during biblical times, and later garrisoned during the Roman era by the Tenth Legion, had been part of the Ottoman Empire for centuries, steadily declining under Turkish rule into a small, stiflingly hot place hardly bigger than a fishing village, reduced by 1917 to a few crumbling houses made of whitewashed dried mud brick and a dilapidated old fort facing the sea. Its site was on the flat, narrow eastern shore amid groves of date palms, in the shadow of a jagged wall of mountains as sharp as a shark's teeth and a steep plateau that separated it from the great desert stretching to Baghdad in the east, north to Damascus and south to Aden, more than 1,200 miles away.

Today a busy, thriving resort city and the principal port of Jordan, a nation which did not then exist, Aqaba is famous for its beaches and its coral reefs, which attract scuba divers from all over the world. It is situated at the head of the Gulf of Aqaba, which is separated from the Gulf of Suez by the spade-shaped southern tip of the Sinai. At the narrow mouth of the Gulf of Aqaba, some archaeologists believe, lies a shallow "land bridge" over which Moses led the Jews across the Red Sea on their flight from Egypt. From the first days of the war, Aqaba had attracted the attention of British strategists in the Middle East, starting with no less imposing a figure than that remote and awe-inspiring military and diplomatic potentate, the victor of Omdurman, *sirdar*, or commander in chief, of the Egyptian army and British agent and consul general in Egypt,* Field Marshal the Earl Kitchener, KG, KP, OM, GSCI, GCMG, GCIE.

It was not that Aqaba itself was such a valuable prize, but a rough dirt road, or track, ran northeast from it to the town of Maan, some sixty miles away as the crow flies, and a major stop on the railway line the Turks had built with German help before the war from Damascus to Medina. From Maan it seemed possible—at any rate to those looking at a map in Cairo or London rather than riding a camel over a waterless, rocky desert landscape—to threaten Beersheba and Gaza from the east, thus at one stroke cutting off the Turks' connection with their Arabian empire, eliminating once and for all the Turkish threat to the Suez Canal and making possible the conquest of Jerusalem and the Holy Land. Seen on the map, the Gulf of Aqaba was like a knife blade aimed directly at Maan, Amman, and Damascus. With Aqaba as a supply base, it might be feasible to attack the richest and most important part of the Ottoman Empire, whose inhabitants, divided though they might be by tribe, religion, tradition, and prejudice, could perhaps be encouraged, if only out of self-interest, to rise against the Turks.

Three years of war did not shift the Turks; nor did anything seem likely to. The Turkish garrison in Aqaba was so weak, dispirited and isolated that small British naval landing parties had managed to get onshore and take a few prisoners, but the prisoners only confirmed what anybody on a naval vessel could tell from the sea with a pair of binoculars—a single narrow, winding passage, what we might call a canyon and the Arabs a wadi, cut through the steep mountains to the north of the town, and

* This was the equivalent of the viceroy in India, a post to which Kitchener aspired, but never attained.

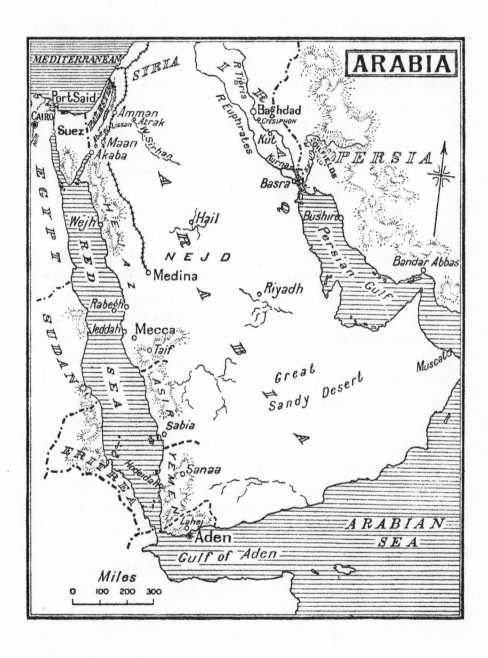

the Turks had spent the last three years fortifying the rugged, rocky high ground on either side of it with trenches that overlooked the beaches. The high ground rose sharply, in the form of natural rocky terraces, like giant steps, providing defensive positions for machine gunners and riflemen. It would be easy enough for the Royal Navy to land troops on the beaches at Aqaba, assuming troops could be made available for that purpose, but once ashore they would have to fight their way uphill against a stubborn and well-entrenched enemy, in a landscape whose chief feature, apart from blistering, overwhelming heat, was a lack of drinking water, except for the few wells forming the strongpoints of the Turkish defense system.

Many British officers underrated, even despised the Turkish army—the general opinion was that Turkish soldiers were poorly trained and poorly armed, as well as slovenly, cruel, and reluctant to attack, while their officers were effete, poorly educated, and corrupt. This opinion persisted despite the fact that when a combined British, Australian, and New Zealander army landed at Gallipoli in April 1915, in an attempt to take Constantinople and open up a year-round warm-water route through the Dardanelles to Allied shipping (without which the beleaguered Russian Empire seemed certain to collapse), it was fought to a standstill by an inferior number of Turks. The British were obliged to evacuate after eight months of fighting, leaving behind 42,957 dead—in addition to 97,290 men seriously wounded and 145,000 gravely ill, mostly from dysentery. The failure at Gallipoli briefly ended the hitherto charmed political career of Winston Churchill, the first lord of the admiralty, who had been a prime mover of the campaign. The defeat also ensured the collapse of the Russians' army and their monarchy, and ought to have taught the British that in a defensive role Turkish soldiers were as stubborn and determined as any in the world. Further proof was not lacking. Twice, the unfortunate General Sir Archibald Murray, GCB, GCMG, CVO, DSO, who commanded the Egyptian Expeditionary Force, tried to break through the Turkish lines in front of Gaza, and twice British troops were driven back with heavy losses by the unyielding, entrenched Turkish infantry.

As for the corruption of the Turkish officer class and politicians, while it was notoriously widespread, here, too, there were exceptions. When a British army advancing from the port city of Basra, in what was then Mesopotamia and is now Iraq, in an attempt to capture Baghdad, was trapped and surrounded less than 100 miles from its goal in the town of Kut al-Amara in December 1915, the British government tried to bribe the Turkish commander to lift the siege. A twenty-eight-year-old temporary second-lieutenant and acting staff captain named T. E. Lawrence, on the intelligence staff of General Murray's predecessor in Cairo, was sent by ship from Suez to Basra with instructions from Kitchener himself, then secretary of state of war, to offer the Turkish commander, Khalil Pasha, up to £1 million (about $90 million in contemporary terms) to allow the British forces in Kut to retreat back to Basra.

On the morning of April 29, 1916, Lawrence and two companions—one of them Aubrey Herbert, a member of Parliament and an expert on Turkey—walked out of the British lines with a white flag and, after being blindfolded, were led to Khalil's quarters, where, following lengthy negotiations in French, he firmly but politely turned the offer down, even when it was doubled at the last minute. Since it was by then too late for the three British officers to go back to their own lines, Khalil offered them his hospitality for the night, and gave them, according to Lawrence, "a most excellent dinner in Turkish style." Of the 13,000 British and Indian soldiers who had survived the 147-day siege and were still alive to surrender at Kut, more than half would die in Turkish prisoner-of-war camps—from disease; starvation; malnutrition; the effects of a harsh climate; and Turkish incompetence, indifference, and cruelty with regard to prisoners of war.

In the autumn of 1916, less than six months after the dinner with Khalil Pasha behind the Turkish lines at Kut, Aqaba was very much on Lawrence's mind. He was perhaps the only officer in Cairo who had actually been in Aqaba before the war, swum in its harbor, and explored the countryside behind it. He had not been at all surprised when he was picked out, as a mere acting staff captain, to offer a Turkish general a £1 million bribe—among his character traits was supreme self-confidence—since his knowledge of the Turkish army was appreciated at the highest level, both in Cairo and in London. Unmilitary in appearance he might be—he often neglected to put on his Sam Browne belt, and he wore leather buttons, rather than shiny brass ones, on his tunic—but few people disputed his intelligence, his attention to detail, or his capacity for hard work. His manner was more that of an Oxford undergraduate than a staff officer, and many people below the rank of field marshal or full general were offended by it, or dismissed him as an eccentric poseur and show-off who did not belong in the army at all—not only did Lawrence not "fit in," but he was a nonsmoker, a teetotaler, and, when he bothered to eat at all, by inclination a vegetarian, except on occasions when he was obliged to please his Arab hosts by sharing their mutton. Neither his sense of humor nor his unmistakable air of intellectual superiority appealed to more conventional spirits, and his short stature (he was five feet five inches tall), a head that seemed disproportionately large for his body, and unruly blond hair set him apart from fellow junior officers. One of his companions on the trip behind Turkish lines described him as "an odd gnome, half cad—with a touch of genius," and a superior at headquarters in Cairo may have summed up the general opinion there of Lawrence when he asked, "Who is this extraordinary pip-squeak?"

To those who judged him by his quirky manner and his ill-fitting, wrinkled, off-the-rack uniform, the cuffs of his trousers always two or three inches above his boots, the badge sometimes missing from his peaked cap, Lawrence did not cut a soldierly figure, so most of them failed to notice the intense, ice-blue eyes and the unusually long, firm, determined jaw, a facial structure more Celtic than English. It was the face of a nonreligious ascetic, capable of enduring hardship and pain beyond what most men would even want to contemplate, a true believer in other people's causes, a curious combination of scholar and man of action, and, most important of all, a dreamer.

Lawrence was also somebody who, however improbable it might seem to those around him in Cairo, aspired to be both a leader of men and a hero. He claimed that when he was a boy his ambition had been "to be a general and knighted by the time he was thirty," and both goals would come close to being within his grasp at that age, had he still wanted them. Lawrence's duties in Cairo seemed tailor-made for his talents. After an initial period of mapmaking, at which he was something of a self-taught expert, he soon turned himself into a kind of liaison between military intelligence (which came under the War Office) and the newly formed Arab Bureau (which came under the Foreign Office), a situation that gave him a certain independence. He became, largely through interviewing Turkish prisoners of war, the leading expert on the battle order of the Turkish army—which divisions were where, who commanded them, and how reliable their troops were—and sometimes edited the *Arab Bulletin*, a kind of secret magazine or digest that gathered every kind of intelligence about the Arab world and the Turkish army for the benefit of senior officers. Lawrence wrote a lot of the *Arab Bulletin* himself (published between 1916 and 1919, it would eventually run to over 100 issues and many hundreds of pages); and not only was it lively and well written (unlike most intelligence documents), combining the virtues of a gossip column and an encyclopedia, but it also reflected his own point of view, and had a considerable influence on British policy, both in Cairo and in London. Since Lawrence's mentor from his undergraduate days at Oxford, the archaeologist and Oxford don D. G. Hogarth (repackaged, for wartime purposes, as a commander in the Royal Navy Volunteer Reserve) was a major figure in the Arab Bureau, Lawrence was naturally drawn more toward the bureau than toward military intelligence; but in both departments he found a certain number of kindred souls who were able to appreciate his keen mind despite his eccentricities and unmilitary behavior.

One of these was Ronald Storrs, Oriental secretary of the British Agency in Cairo, a civil servant and Foreign Office official whose job it was to advise the British high commissioner, Sir Henry McMahon—the de facto ruler of Egypt, the position Kitchener had held until he joined the war cabinet in 1914—on the subtleties of Arab politics. It is remarkable but very typical of Lawrence that he and Storrs, though very different creatures, became friends on first meeting, and remained friends to the end of Lawrence's life—Storrs would be one of his pallbearers. Storrs was sociable, ambitious, fond of the good things of life, an eminently "clubbable man," to borrow a phrase from Dr. Johnson, and would go on after the war to become military governor of Jerusalem—a post once held by Pontius Pilate, as Storrs himself pointed out with good humor—and to a happy and contented marriage. Storrs regarded Lawrence with something like affectionate awe—"Into friendship with T. E. Lawrence I know not how I entered," he would write in his memoir, *Orientations*; "then suddenly it seemed I must have known him for many years." For his part, Lawrence would later describe Storrs in *Seven Pillars of Wisdom* with backhanded affection: "The first of us was Ronald Storrs . . . the most brilliant Englishman in the Near East, and the deepest, though his eyelids were heavy with laziness, and his eyes dulled by care of self, and his mouth made unbeautiful by hampering desires." Storrs's ambitions were realistic, and he pursued them sensibly and zealously—indeed, *Orientations* sometimes reminds the reader of Samuel Pepys's diaries in its frank admission of a civil servant's determination to climb the ladder of success—and they would eventually be achieved by marriage and a knighthood. By contrast, Lawrence sensibly concealed from Storrs his own more schoolboyish daydreams of being a knight and a general before the age of thirty, let alone of being a hero, in the full classical sense of the word, as well as a founder of nations. Nobody, least of all Storrs, could ever accuse Lawrence of "laziness," "care of self," or "hampering desires." He loved to spend time in Storrs's apartment in Cairo, borrowing books in Greek or Latin, which he was always careful to return, listening to Storrs play the piano, and talking about music and literature; but even so, Storrs seems to have detected early on that Lawrence was more than an Oxonian archaeologist in an ill-fitting uniform—that behind the facade was a man of action.

When, in mid-October 1916, Lawrence accompanied Storrs on a journey to Jidda in the Hejaz, the Red Sea port closest to Mecca, to negotiate with the infinitely difficult and obstinate Sharif Hussein ibn Ali-el-Aun about British support for the Arab Revolt, Storrs's postprandial naps and his reading of Henry James's *The Ambassadors* and H. G. Wells's *Mr. Britling* in the stifling privacy of his cabin on board a British steamer were interrupted by Lawrence's "revolver practice on deck at bottles after lunch," which "tore my ears and effectually ruined my siesta." Had Storrs but known it, weapons had always played a significant part in Lawrence's life—he was taught by his father to be an excellent shot, and on his journeys through the Middle East before the war as an undergraduate and an apprentice archaeologist he had always gone armed; on one occasion, he had fired back at an Arab peasant who fired at him, either wounding his assailant or startling the Arab's horse; and on another he was beaten badly on the head with his own automatic pistol by a robber who, fortunately for Lawrence, was unable to fathom how to release its safety catch.

In later years Lawrence liked to say that he made himself so difficult in the role of a superior young know-it-all that military intelligence was only too happy to let him go to the Arab Bureau, which had more the atmosphere of a Senior Common Room at Oxford than of the army. He boasted of making himself "quite intolerable to the Staff. . . . I took every opportunity to rub into them their comparative ignorance and inefficiency (not difficult!) and irritated them further by literary airs, correcting split infinitives and tautologies in their reports." Perhaps as a result, nobody objected when Lawrence took a few days' leave in Storrs's company, and Storrs was happy enough to have him as a travel companion.

Lawrence may have been the only person in Cairo who would have thought of a journey to Jidda as a lark. A stifling, dusty rail journey from Cairo to Suez was followed by a sea journey of almost 650 miles on board a slow steamer taken over by the Royal Navy, the heat made bearable only by the breeze of the ship's movement. "But when at last we anchored in the outer harbor," Lawrence wrote of his first sight of Jidda, "off the white town hung between the blazing sky and its reflection in the mirage that swept and rolled over the wide lagoon, then the heat of Arabia came out like a drawn sword and smote us speechless."

10 · H E R O ·

For Storrs, the journey to Jidda—it was his third—however tedious and hot, was part of his job; the notion of an Arab revolt against the Turks had been an idée fixe with British strategists in the Middle East since long before the war. Indeed Kitchener and Storrs had discussed the possibility with Emir (Prince) Abdulla—one of the sons of Hussein, sharif and emir of Mecca—before it was even certain that Turkey would join the Germans and the Austro-Hungarians against the British, the French, and the Russians. In October 1914, three months after war had broken out, and only a few days after Turkey had finally (and fatally) joined the Central Powers, Kitchener sent a grandiloquent message to Sharif Hussein from London, with an open proposal to back an Arab revolt: "Till now we have defended and befriended Islam in the person of the Turks: henceforth it shall be in that of the noble Arab. It may be that an Arab of true race will assume the Caliphate at Mecca or Medina, and so good may come by the help of God out of all the evil which is now occurring."

This pious hope, fortified by Kitchener's tactfully phrased suggestion that with British help and support the sharif might replace the sultan of Turkey as caliph, the spiritual leader of Islam, eventually led both to a revolt, so far mostly sporadic and unsuccessful, and to spirited bargaining, in which Storrs was one of the chief players—hence, his sea voyage to a place where Christians, even when bearing gifts, or the promise thereof, were still regarded as infidels. The Hejaz, the mountainous coastal region of Arabia bordering the Red Sea, contained two of the three holiest cities of Islam: Mecca and Medina. (The third, soon to be a source of serious disagreement between the British and the Arabs, and later of course between the Jews and the Arabs, is Jerusalem.) It was only with great reluctance that the Arabs had allowed the British to open a consulate in Jidda (the Union Jack flying there was a particular grievance, since it consists of a cross in three different forms), and on the occasions when it was necessary for the sharif's sons to meet with an Englishman, they rode down from Mecca to Jidda, a distance of about forty-five miles, to do so. Mecca was, and remains today, a city closed to infidels. As for their father, the sharif preferred to remain in Mecca whenever possible, communicating with his British ally by long, opaque, and often bewildering letters in Arabic, and from time to time by telephone to Jidda, for surprisingly there was a telephone system in the holy city; his own number was, very appropriately, Mecca 1.

After a walk from the harbor through the fly-infested open stalls of the food market in the oppressive heat, Storrs and Lawrence were happy enough to be shown into a shaded room in the British consulate, where they were awaited by the British representative in Jidda, Lieutenant-Colonel Cyril Wilson, who disliked both his visitors: he did not trust Storrs, and he had argued with Lawrence in Cairo about the appropriateness of British officers' wearing Arab clothing. "Lawrence wants kicking and kicking *hard* at that," Wilson wrote, adding, "He was a bumptious young ass," though Wilson would soon change his mind, and become one of Lawrence's supporters. Lawrence's opinion of Wilson, though he would tone it down in later years when writing *Seven Pillars of Wisdom*, was at first equally critical—critical enough so that Storrs prudently censored it out of his account of the meeting. Part of Wilson's resentment at Lawrence's presence was that it was unclear to him what Lawrence was doing there; the rest no doubt was a result of Lawrence's personality, which older and more conventional officers found trying at the best of times.

In fact Lawrence's presence was not, as he later suggested, "a holiday and a joy-ride," a pleasant way of using up a few days of leave sightseeing in the congenial company of Storrs. Management and control of the Arab Revolt were shared among a bewildering number of rival agencies and personalities, each with its own policy: the British high commissioner in Egypt, the commander in chief of the Egyptian Expeditionary Force, and the Arab Bureau, in Cairo; military intelligence in Ismailia, halfway between Port Said and Suez; the War Office, the Foreign Office, and the Colonial Office, in London; the government of India, in Delhi (the largest body of Muslims in the world was in India and what is now Pakistan); and the governor-general of the Sudan, in Khartoum, since the shortest supply route to the Hejaz was across the narrow Red Sea, from Port Sudan to Jidda. Colonel Wilson was, in fact, the representative in Jidda of a larger-than-life imperial figure, General Sir Reginald Wingate Pasha, GCB, GCVO, GBE, KCMG, DSO, the fiery governor-general of the Sudan, an old and experienced Arab hand who had fought under Kitchener and had known Gordon of Khartoum. Storrs, a diplomat, was the adviser of Sir Henry McMahon, the high commissioner of Egypt. Lawrence's immediate superior was Brigadier-General Gilbert Clayton, who, like Wingate and Storrs, was another of Kitchener's devoted disciples. Until recently Clayton had been serving as director of all military intelligence in Egypt, and as Wingate's liaison with the Egyptian Expeditionary Force and chief of the newly formed Arab Bureau.

Lawrence admired Clayton, and would later describe him as "like water, or permeating oil, soaking silently and insistently through everything," which is probably the best description of how an intelligence chief ought to operate. Clayton appears to have had no great confidence in the ability of Storrs, a mere civil servant, to judge men and events, especially in the military sphere; but he had come to respect Lawrence's judgment, and to rely on his well-informed reports about affairs in the Ottoman Empire. It was not therefore Storrs who was "babysitting" Lawrence, but Lawrence who was babysitting Storrs, though Storrs may not at first have realized the fact.

Given the number of conflicting agencies involved in the Arab Revolt, it is hardly surprising that British policy was inconsistent. Most of the older members of the war cabinet in London were, or had been, by instinct and habit Turcophiles; for throughout the eighteenth and nineteenth centuries support for the Ottoman Empire—however devious, corrupt, and incompetent the sultans may have been—was a cornerstone of British foreign policy. Turkey was the indispensable buffer between imperial Russia and the Mediterranean—Russia's undisguised ambition to seize Constantinople and dominate the Near East and the Balkans concerned British statesmen almost as much as its relentless advance south toward Afghanistan. In the west, Russia's ambition would threaten the Suez Canal; in the south it threatened India, still the "jewel in the crown," the largest and most valuable of British colonial possessions. Hence, propping up Turkey, the "sick man of Europe," as Czar Nicholas I* is said to have referred to the Ottoman Empire, was thought to be a vital British interest. Those who still believed this—and there were many— were not well pleased by the fact that bumbling diplomacy on the part of Great Britain in 1914, and greed and duplicity on the part of Turkey, had brought Turkey into the war on the side of the Central Powers, while Russia was now an ally of the British. Enthusiasm for an Arab revolt was, as a result, always equivocal in London, while in Delhi there was outright opposition and obstructionism for fear that a successful Arab revolt would inspire similar ambitions among the hundreds of millions of Muslims in India. Support for an Arab revolt centered on the powerful figure of Field Marshal Kitchener until his death at sea in June 1916, but survived among those of his acolytes who remained in the Middle East, and also a few powerful political figures in London, particularly David Lloyd George, who had replaced Kitchener as secretary of state for war and would shortly replace an exhausted Asquith as prime minister. The actual Arab Revolt had been going on since the summer of 1916, but Storrs, who was deeply involved in the diplomatic side, was not alone in criticizing the "incoherent and spasmodic" quality of the leadership to date, or in longing for "a supreme and independent control of the campaign," which he had hoped to find in Aziz Ali Bey el Masri, Sharif Hussein's chief of staff.

Years later, after Lawrence had died, Storrs wrote in *Orientations*: "None of us realized then that a greater than Aziz was already taking charge."

---

* What the czar actually said, during a conversation reported by the British ambassador in Saint Petersburg in 1853—in the course of which the czar raised the possibility that Russia and Great Britain might split up the Ottoman Empire between them— was: "We have a sick man on our hands, a man gravely ill; it will be a great misfortune if one of these days he slips through our hands, especially before the necessary arrangements are made."

That Lawrence might be the leader Storrs had in mind was certainly not immediately evident, at any rate to Wilson, but rapidly became more so with the arrival in Jidda, from Mecca, of Emir Abdulla, mounted on a magnificent white Arabian mare, and accompanied by a large and colorful retinue. Abdulla, the object of Storrs's visit, was short, rotund, and animated, but an impressive figure all the same, wearing "a yellow silk *kuffiya*, heavy camel's hair *aba*, white silk shirt,"* the whole effect spoiled only, in Storrs's opinion, by ugly Turkish elastic-sided patent leather boots. Abdulla was a good part of the reason for the tension between Storrs and Wilson, apart from the natural mistrust between a civil servant and a professional soldier, for they were obliged to inform him that many, indeed most, of the things his father had been promised would not be forthcoming, a task that was uncongenial to them both. The most important among these was a flight of fighter aircraft from the Royal Flying Corps (RFC) to deal with the Turkish aircraft, which had been supplied by Germany and, like most modern war equipment, were having a disproportionate effect on the morale of the Bedouin tribesmen who made up the majority of the Arab forces. The plan had been to station the RFC aircraft about seventy-five miles north of Jidda in Rabegh, with a brigade of British troops to guard them. This plan was reversed at the last minute by General Wingate in Khartoum—the RFC would not send the planes without British troops, but the question of stationing a British brigade in the Hejaz was a political hot potato, since the Arabs were likely to resent the presence of foreign Christian troops in their Holy Land as much as they resented that of the Turks—or possibly more, since the Turks were at least Muslims.

In the course of the lengthy discussions—Abdulla was a born diplomat, who would go on to become the first king of Jordan, and would die in the Dome of the Rock mosque in Jerusalem in 1951, assassinated by a Palestinian fanatic who believed the king was planning to make a separate peace with Israel—both Wilson and Storrs seem to have allowed the

---

*A *kufiyya* (spellings differ in English transliterations of Arabic) is the Arab head cloth; and an *aba* is a long cloak.

young staff captain to take over, since he clearly knew his facts. "When Abdallah* quoted Feisal's telegram," Storrs wrote, "saying that unless the two Turkish aeroplanes were driven off the Arabs would disperse: 'Lawrence remarked that very few Turkish aeroplanes last more than four or five days. . . . ' 'Abdallah was impressed with Lawrence's extraordinary detailed knowledge of enemy dispositions' which, being . . . temporarily sub-lieutenant in charge of 'maps and marking of Turkish Army distribution,' he was able to use with masterly effect. As Syrian, Circassian, Anatolian, Mesopotamian names came up, Lawrence at once stated exactly which unit was in each position, until Abdallah turned to me in amazement: 'Is this man God, to know everything?' "

Despite Lawrence's dazzling display of knowledge, at the same time he took the opportunity to carefully appraise Abdulla. In fact, the primary purpose of his "holiday" was to report back to General Clayton in Cairo on Sharif Hussein's sons, and to give a firsthand appraisal of which one of them the British should back as the military leader of the revolt. Secondarily, he was to appraise Storrs and Wilson for Clayton's benefit, a function of which his two hosts were happily unaware. Lawrence had a certain respect for Wilson as an administrator, and a trusted link with Sharif Hussein, but he soon came to the conclusion that Abdulla, although superficially charming, was not the leader the British were looking for, still less the man that Lawrence himself was searching for. Abdulla, he would write, "was short, strong, fair-skinned, with a carefully trimmed brown beard, a round smooth face, and full short lips. . . . The Arabs thought Abdulla a far-seeing statesman, and an astute politician. Astute he certainly was, but I suspected some insincerity throughout our talk. His ambition was patent. Rumor made him the brain of his father, and of

---

*Except when quoting from other sources, as I do here from Storrs, I have elected to use whenever possible Lawrence's own spelling for Arab names and places, which is relatively phonetic, but not necessarily systematic. "Abdullah," "Abdulla," and "Abdallah" are all possible spellings, and of course refer to the same person. Since the maps in the book come from various sources, the transliteration of place-names in them is not necessarily consistent, but it is easy enough to follow.

the Arab Revolt, but he seemed too easy for that. . . . My visit was really to see for myself who was the yet unknown master-spirit of the affair, and if he was capable of carrying the revolt to the distance and greatness I had conceived for it: and as our conversation proceeded I became more and more sure that Abdulla was too balanced, too cool, too humorous to be a prophet, especially the armed prophet whom history assured me was the successful type in such circumstances."

No doubt Abdulla, who, behind a jovial and good-natured facade, was a shrewd judge of men, divined something of Lawrence's reservations about him, both in Wilson's hot little room at the consulate and later on, in Abdulla's sumptuously appointed tent outside Jidda. The interior of this tent was decorated with brightly colored silk-embroidered birds, flowers, and texts from the Koran; it was placed near the green-domed shrine that was reputed to be the burial place of Mother Hawa, as Muslims call Eve, where Abdulla had pitched his camp in the hope of avoiding the fever that was reported in town. He may also have been sensitive enough to guess that young Lawrence was not only a potential man of action, but something even more dangerous: a man of destiny.

In any case, the relationship between the two men, while polite, would never be close. Even though Lawrence was at least partly responsible for securing for Abdulla after the war the throne of what was then called Trans-Jordan, Abdulla in his memoirs—published in 1950, only a year before his own assassination—belittled Lawrence's role in the Arab Revolt, and complained of "the general dislike of Lawrence's presence" among the tribes. Rather reluctantly, however, he eventually agreed to Lawrence's request to venture inland to meet two of Abdulla's brothers, Emir Ali and Emir Feisal, though Storrs had to call their father, Sharif Hussein, in Mecca before Abdulla was authorized to prepare the necessary letter. The hesitation was less from a desire to prevent this inquisitive and well-informed young Englishman from observing the real state of the sharif's armies in the field—though this thought may have crossed Abdulla's mind—than from the sensible fear that once Lawrence was out of Jidda, as a European and Christian he was very likely to be murdered, or that in his khaki uniform he could be mistaken for a Turkish officer, and murdered on that account. On Storrs's first trip to the Hejaz in 1914 one of the sharif's aides had offered to sell him for £1 the severed heads of seven Germans who had been murdered that week in the hinterland, and strong feelings on the subject of infidels near the holy places had not lessened since then among the Bedouin, despite the fact that the British and the French were now their allies.

Such stories as these merely spurred Lawrence on. It is unclear from the somewhat conflicting accounts of Storrs and Lawrence why Storrs was willing to deploy on Lawrence's behalf his considerable powers of persuasion against the sharif to make possible a journey of considerable danger that, so far as he knew, nobody in Cairo had ordered or authorized Lawrence to make, but very likely he bowed to what he already recognized was a stronger will. Besides, nobody at Jidda or in Cairo seemed to know what was going on at Rabegh, let alone in the desert beyond it, and Lawrence's proposal to go and find out for himself may have seemed daring, but sensible. As for Lawrence, he did not bother asking for permission; he simply sent a telegram to Clayton that began: "Meeting today: Wilson, Storrs, Sharif Abdallah, Aziz el-Masri, myself. Nobody knows real situation Rabugh so much time wasted. Aziz al-Masri going Rabugh with me tomorrow."*

So began the adventure.

Lawrence traveled to Rabegh by ship with Storrs and Aziz el Masri, on a rusty, wallowing old tramp steamer; there they transferred to a more comfortable Indian liner anchored in the harbor. On board the liner they were joined by Emir Ali, the sharif's eldest son, for three days of discussion in a comfortably carpeted tented enclosure on deck, during the course of which Ali repeated at great length the same requests for more gold, guns, and modern equipment that his brother had made at Jidda,

---

* Lawrence's spelling of Arabic names and places is erratic, and so is Storrs's, but I have preferred to quote from letters and documents as they were written, rather than imposing on them a false conformity.

but with less force and less humor. Closer to the fighting, his view of the situation was less optimistic than Abdulla's—his brother Feisal, with the bulk of the Arab army, was about 100 miles to the northeast, encamped in the desert, still licking his wounds from the failure of the attack on Medina, and hoping, if possible, to prevent a Turkish advance on Mecca or Rabegh. Ali reported that "considerable" Turkish reinforcements were arriving in Medina from Maan, that the Arab army needed artillery like that of the Turks, and that his brother Feisal was hard pressed; but as Storrs was to note later, there was in fact no reliable means of passing intelligence from Feisal in the field to Ali in Rabegh or from there to Jidda and Mecca, let alone anybody to assess the reliability of the information, and act on it.

Lawrence liked Ali at once, in fact "took a great fancy" to him and praised his dignified good manners, but at the same time reached the conclusion that Ali was too bookish, lacked "force of character," and had neither the health nor the ambition to be the "prophet" Lawrence was looking for. As for Ali, he was "staggered" by his father's instruction to send Lawrence up-country, but once having expressed his doubts about the wisdom of it, he gave in gracefully. To all Sharif Hussein's sons, their father's word was law. By the time Storrs departed on the same hideous, crowded tramp steamer that had brought them—it had no refrigerator, electric lights, or radio, and on board the principal food was tinned tripe—for the long, slow return journey to Suez, often into a "very fierce" gale, Lawrence's arrangements were already made. Ali had graciously offered Lawrence his own "splendid riding camel," complete with his own beautiful, highly decorated saddle and its elaborate trappings, and had chosen, to accompany Lawrence, a reliable tribesman, Obeid el Raashid, together with Obeid's son. Years later, Storrs could still remember the sight of Lawrence standing on the shore in the pitiless sun, "waving grateful hands" as Storrs's tramp steamer raised anchor.

Lawrence's decision to travel into the interior of the Hejaz was undertaken at a critical moment for the Arab Revolt. Ever since June 1916, when

Sharif Hussein, after much hesitation and endless bargaining with the British, had finally made the decision to rebel against the Turkish government, he had relied on two separate forces. The first force (usually referred to as "the regulars") consisted of Arab prisoners of war or deserters from the Turkish army, more or less disciplined and uniformed, and commanded by Arabs who for the most part had been officers in the Turkish army. Of these officers, the two most prominent for the moment were Aziz el Masri, an experienced professional soldier who was the sharif's chief of staff; and Nuri as-Said, an Arab nationalist from Baghdad who was both a political and a military workhorse. The second, and much larger and more colorful, armed force was drawn from those Bedouin tribes that had been moved by British gold, the hope of plunder, loyalty, or blood ties (however slender) to the sharif of Mecca—or, more rarely, by nascent Arab nationalism—to join in the struggle. Some of these Bedouin were under the more or less lackadaisical command of Emir Ali at Rabegh, but the majority were under the command of Ali's younger and more inspiring brother, Emir Feisal. Since the beginning of the revolt the British had contributed quantities of small arms and gold sovereigns (the Arabs, from the sharif himself down to the lowliest tribesman, would do nothing without advance payment in gold), machine guns, ammunition, naval support, food supplies, and military advice, without much to show for it so far, except the sharif's refusal to join the jihad. Sharif Hussein had managed to capture and hold on to Mecca, and after a siege had taken nearby Taif. But the Arab attack on Medina, the last station on the railway line from Damascus, 280 miles to the north of Mecca, had failed dismally; the Arabs were driven back by the steady discipline of the entrenched Turks and by well-sited modern artillery.

Medina had made it apparent that the Bedouin levies were unprepared for modern warfare, and easily panicked by modern weapons like artillery and airplanes; nor did they lend themselves to the discipline and organization of a modern army. If they obeyed anyone, the men obeyed their tribal leader, or sheikh, and all the men were equal—they had no concept of a chain of command, no such thing as noncommissioned

officers, and no understanding of *Kadavergehorsam*,* the reflexive obedience to an order that was pounded into trained infantry on the parade
ground in every army in Europe. Since their primary loyalty was to tribe,
clan, and family, the heavy casualties of modern warfare were unacceptable to the tribesmen—they were brave enough, and could be inspired
(though never ordered) to perform daring acts; but each death in their
ranks was a grievous personal loss, not a statistic, and they came and
went as they pleased. If a man felt the need to go home and tend to his
camels or goats, he would leave and perhaps send back a son or a brother
with his rifle to take his place. It was not, in brief, an army that could
stand up to the Turks on equal terms in sustained attack on fixed positions; nor was it an army that British officers understood or trusted.

Since the British were paying for the Arab armies by the head, there
was also a natural tendency on the part of Sharif Hussein and his sons to
inflate the number of their troops, aggravated by the Arabic tendency to
use the word "thousands" as a synonym for "many"; thus to this day the
number of Arabs actually fighting in the revolt is unclear. Hussein
claimed he had 50,000 fighters but admitted that only about 10,000 of
them were armed; the Arab "regulars" may have numbered 5,000. Feisal's
army in 1917 consisted of about 5,000 men mounted on camels, and
another 5,000 on foot. (A good many of these men on foot may have been
unarmed servants, or slaves, for slaves, mostly blacks from the Sudan,
were still commonplace throughout Arabia; indeed there was a rumor
that one member of the French mission to Jidda had bought *une jeune
négresse*, or a fair-skinned Circassian, "for a very reasonable price.") In
the Hejaz the Arabs certainly outnumbered the Turks, of whom there
were about 15,000; but the Turks were by comparison a disciplined, modern force, with trained NCOs and an officer corps (aided by German and
Austro-Hungarian advisers and military specialists), for the most part
holding well-fortified strongpoints—a position not so very different
(terrain and climate apart) from that of the U.S. Army in Vietnam.

---

* The "corpse-like obedience" much prized in the German army.

Two keys to warfare in the region were the single-line Hejaz railway, the vital supply line connecting Medina to Damascus; and the location of wells, which determined the line of any advance in the desert.

A third and most indispensable key—and the only one over which the British had any direct control—consisted of the ports along the Red Sea, which rose like the rungs of a ladder one by one up the coast of the Hejaz from Jidda in the south to Aqaba in the north. Rabegh, which was in British hands, was about seventy-five miles north of Jidda by sea; Yenbo, more precariously in Arab hands, about 100 miles north of Rabegh; Wejh (still in Turkish hands) about 200 miles north of Rabegh; and Aqaba nearly 300 miles north of Wejh. Inland, past Aqaba to Yenbo, the Hejaz railway ran about fifty miles distant from and more or less parallel to the coastline behind a formidable barrier of rugged mountains, until it ended in Medina. This configuration made the railway vulnerable to small parties who knew their way through the mountains, but also meant that the Turks had the means to quickly transfer troops from Medina or from Maan to threaten any of the ports held by the British and the Arabs. It was the guns of British warships that made such an attack risky; and the support of the Royal Navy (as well its ability to bring in a constant stream of supplies, equipment, and gold) was the major factor keeping the Arab Revolt alive.

For all that, the war in the Middle East was going badly. Attempts by the British to break through the Turkish line at Gaza had failed; the Arabs' attempt to take Medina had led merely to a protracted and humiliating defeat; and the Arabs' hostility toward any European presence inland meant that nobody in Cairo had a clear picture of just what Feisal's men were doing, or what was taking place in the vast, empty desert beyond the few small ports on the Red Sea in the possession of the Allies.

Emir Ali insisted that Lawrence leave after dark, so none of the tribesmen camped in Rabegh would know that an Englishman was riding into the interior; for the same reason, he provided Lawrence with an Arab head cloth and cloak as a disguise. The *kufiyya*, or head cloth, held around the head by a knotted *agal* of wool, or in the case of persons of great importance finely braided gold and colored silk thread, was (and remains) the most distinctive item of Bedouin clothing. The pattern of the cloth and the color of the *agal* usually identify one's tribe, so they also serve to identify friend and foe. The Bedouin disliked the sight of European peaked caps and sun helmets, finding them at once blasphemous and comic. The sun helmets seemed all the more comic because the few British officers who adopted the *kufiyya* (which was convenient and protective in the desert) usually wore it *over* the bulky khaki solar topee, making a grotesque and ludicrous display of themselves before the natives. What looked like a huge cloth-covered beehive on the head was funnier still when the wearer was bobbing up and down on a camel. Lawrence avoided this from the first, in the interest of providing an identifiably Arab silhouette in the moonlight—besides, he had often worn a *kufiyya* while working in the desert as a young archaeologist before the war, and found nothing strange about it. It was cool and sensible: it protected the wearer from the sun, the loose ends could be tied around the face against wind and sandstorms, and it did not provoke the hostility of the tribesmen.

Emir Ali and his half brother Emir Zeid, the youngest of Hussein's sons, came down to see Lawrence off, in a date palm grove on the outskirts of the camp. No doubt they had mixed emotions: neither of them can have relished being responsible for Lawrence's safe journey. Ali also disliked from the start the whole idea of Lawrence's journey to see Feisal, which offended his strong religious sensibilities. However, Zeid, still a "beardless" young man, was not shocked or outraged at all—his mother was Turkish, and as the third of Hussein's three wives was a relative newcomer to the harem, so Zeid had neither Ali's intense religious feelings, nor his father's and half brothers' attachment to the Arab cause; indeed Lawrence at once judged him insufficiently Arab for his purposes.

Neither Obeid nor his son carried any food with them—the first stage of their journey was to Bir el Sheikh, where Ali said they might pause for a meal, about sixty miles away; no Arab thought a journey of such a short distance required food, rest, or water. As for riding a camel, though it was not Lawrence's first attempt, he made no pretense of being a good or experienced rider. Unlike most Englishmen of his class and age, he was not an experienced horseman—his family's budget had not extended to riding lessons; he and his brothers had excelled at bicycling, not horsemanship. Nor had he ever covered this kind of distance on a finely bred camel, which paced, in long, undulating strides, while the rider sat erect as in a sidesaddle, with the right leg cocked over a saddle post, and the left in the stirrup. Two years of desk work in Cairo had not prepared Lawrence for the fatigue, the saddle sores on legs unused to riding, the backache, the suffocating heat, or the monotony of riding by night, often over rough ground. Sometimes he dozed off—neither Obeid nor his son was a talker—and woke with a start to find himself slipping sideways, saved from a fall only by grabbing the saddle post quickly.

He had no fears about his companions—it was an extension of the Arab belief in the obligation of hospitality toward a guest as an absolute duty that those charged with conveying a stranger must protect him with their lives, whatever they thought of him. But Obeid was a Hawazim Harb, and the Harbs surrounding Rabegh were hardly more than lukewarm on the subject of the sharif of Mecca; also, their sheikh was known to be in touch with the Turks. Then too, as Lawrence knew from his experiences traveling, mostly on foot, through Palestine, the Sinai, and what is now Lebanon, Iraq, and Syria—where, as a young archaeologist he had separated armed, warring factions among the workers at the dig—the blood feud was an unavoidable part of Arab life. It involved not just tribe against tribe, but feuding within clans and families and between individuals—no matter how peaceful a situation might seem, you could never be protected from sudden, unexpected violence that might also engulf the stranger.

Empty, vast, and unprofitable as the desert looked to Europeans, every barren square foot of it, every wadi, every steep rocky hill, every sparse patch of thornbush, every well—however disgusting the water—was claimed by some tribe or person and would be defended to the death against trespassers. Nor was "the desert" a romantic, endless landscape of windblown sand dunes: much of it was jagged, broken, black volcanic rock, as sharp as a razor, and fields of hardened lava that even camels had difficulty crossing. Steep valleys zigzagged to nowhere; towering, knife-edged hills rose from the sand; flat patches of bleached, glassy sand, the size of some European countries, reflected the harsh sunlight like vast mirrors at 125 degrees Fahrenheit or more, and stretched to the horizon, broken only by sudden sandstorms appearing out of nowhere. Except for remote areas where a green fuzz of short, rough grass in the brief "rainy season" was counted as rich pasturage for the great herds of camels that were the principal source of wealth for the Bedouin tribes, this was the landscape, or close to it, of Cain and Abel, of Joseph sold into slavery by his brothers, of Job—it was not a safe or kindly place to be.

Lawrence's mind was on the fact that the path they were following was the traditional route by which pilgrims traveled from Medina to Mecca—indeed, in the Hejaz a large part of the Arabs' feeling against the Turks came from the building of the railway from Damascus to Medina, since the Bedouin earned money by providing guides, camels, and tented camps for the pilgrims along the desert route (and also from robbery and shameless extortion at their expense). It was the local Bedouin's ferocious hostility to this modern encroachment that had so far prevented the Turks from building a planned 280-mile extension of the railway from Medina all the way to Mecca. Lawrence, as his camel paced in the moonlight from the flat sand of the coast into the rougher going of scrub-covered sand dunes marred by potholes and tangled roots, meditated on the fact that the Arab Revolt, in order to succeed, would have to follow the "Pilgrim Road" in reverse, as he was doing, moving north toward Syria and Damascus, bringing faith in Arab nationalism and an Arab nation as they advanced, as the pilgrims brought their faith in Islam yearly to Mecca.

Perhaps in deference to the fact that he was an Englishman, not an Arab, his guides called a halt at midnight, and allowed Lawrence a few hours of sleep in a hollow in the sand, then woke him before dawn to continue, the road now climbing the length of a great field of lava, against which pilgrims for untold generations had left cairns of rocks on their way south, then across a wide area of "loose stone," then on and upward until at last they reached the first well of their journey. They were now in territory controlled by the local tribes, who favored the Turks, or whose sheikhs received payment from the Turks, and reported on the movement of strangers.

No well on a much-used route like this one was ever likely to be deserted—a well was the Arab equivalent of a New England village store—and with good reason Ali had warned Lawrence strictly against talking to anyone he might meet along the way. Neither then nor later did Lawrence ever try to pass himself off as a native—his Arabic was adequate, but in each area of the Ottoman Empire, and beyond, it was spoken differently, and both his speech and his appearance marked him out as a stranger—not necessarily an Englishman, because his fair coloring and straight, sharp nose were not uncommon among Circassians, but certainly not a Bedouin.

Anything but a lush oasis, the well was a desolate place, surrounded by the remains of a stone hut, some rude "shelters of branches and palm leaves," and a few shabby, ragged tents. A small number of Bedouin watched after their camels from a distance as Obeid's son Abdullah climbed down into the well and brought up water in a goatskin, while his father and Lawrence rested in the shade.

Lawrence seems to have attracted no attention, even when a group of Harb tribesmen driving a large herd of camels arrived, followed, perhaps more dangerously, by two richly dressed young men riding thoroughbred camels: a sharif and his cousin disguised as a master and servant to pass through the country of a hostile tribe undisturbed. This pair might at least have been expected to express some curiosity about the presence of a stranger at the well, but Lawrence seems to have possessed a natural gift for remaining silent and motionless, without betraying himself—he had always been fearless; from boyhood on he had deliberately cultivated indifference to danger and hardship, as well as emotional independence, as if rehearsing for the role he was about to play, and his lack of fear somehow communicated itself to others in the sense that they felt he belonged where he was, whoever he might be.

In some ways, this was more effective than a vulgar disguise—the real Lawrence was actually less noticeable than if he had tried to darken his skin and pretend to be an Arab, like Sandy Arbuthnot, a character in John Buchan's classic adventure novel *Greenmantle*, who many believe was based in part on Lawrence. It was something of a skill, the equivalent of camouflage or protective coloration. As a junior staff officer Lawrence had sat unnoticed among vastly more senior officers in meetings where he had no business to be, without attracting attention to his presence until he spoke (at which point, he usually dominated the conversation); he did the same among the Bedouin. His individualism—and later his curious combination of fame and shyness—gave people the impression that he never "belonged" anywhere, but he had the great actor's gift for playing whatever role was presented to him. It was then not yet apparent that the role of a hero would come to him more easily—and stick to him much longer—than any other.

In any case, unquestioned, Lawrence and his guides continued on through an increasingly difficult and barren landscape, which gradually gave way to fine white sand that radiated the heat and the glare of the sun until he had to close his eyes against it. In the distance were fantastic rock formations and jagged mountains. They had left the roadway, such as it was, to track across country for hours, and rejoined it just as the sun began to set. Bir el Sheikh, when they reached it, proved to be nothing more than a tiny cluster of "miserable" rock huts on either side of the way, from which the smoke of cooking fires arose. Obeid dismounted and bought flour; and this was the end of the first stage of their journey.

Lawrence describes, with the eye of a good travel writer, how Obeid mixed the flour with a little water and patted and pulled it into a disk about "two inches thick, and six inches across," which he plunged into the embers of a brushwood fire to bake, and which the three of them shared after Obeid had clapped it between his hands to knock the cinders off. Lawrence's indifference to food was notorious, and he had no difficulty surviving on the usual Bedouin rations of flour and dates. (It was their rare feast that made him queasy: a whole sheep—cooked with head, innards, and all—served on an enormous copper tray in a thick bed of rice moistened with hot grease.)

An hour to cook and eat their meal, an hour of rest, and they were on their way again, in pitch darkness, on fine sand so soft that Lawrence at first found the silence oppressive. Along the way, perhaps because Lawrence blended in so well with the Bedouin way of life and made none of the complaints and demands that might be expected from a British officer, Obeid had become more talkative, and even gave Lawrence a few tactful hints about how to get the best out of his camel. Obeid had already indicated to Lawrence the existence of a small village of date farmers only a few hours from Rabegh, and of another settlement farther on along a valley that would give the Turks an opportunity of flanking Feisal's army and attacking Rabegh, or, alternatively, marching south from well to well to isolate Rabegh and attack Mecca. Neither Emir Abdulla nor Emir Ali had thought to mention this interesting feature of the topography around Rabegh, which Lawrence instantly realized made the idea of placing a British brigade there both risky and pointless. Hitherto, whenever Sharif Hussein had been alarmed by signs of a Turkish advance, he had requested the immediate dispatch of a brigade, while the British had hesitated, unwilling to commit troops when so many were needed elsewhere; but whenever the British, alarmed by events in the Hejaz, had offered a brigade, the sharif had always turned it down at the last minute, saying that his people would object to the presence of Christian soldiers. Now it was clear to Lawrence that placing a British brigade in Rabegh would be useless, even in the unlikely event that General Wingate agreed to provide one, and at the same time, Sharif Hussein agreed to accept it.

Adding to Lawrence's vast store of knowledge was his long-standing passion for military history, tactics, and strategy. Castles had fascinated him since his childhood, and as a boy he had visited, sketched, and measured the remains of most of the great castles in Britain and France, traveling phenomenal distances by bicycle. As an undergraduate at Oxford he visited the great crusader castles of the Near East; indeed his thesis at Oxford, which won him a "first"—so brilliant a success that his tutor at Jesus College gave a lavish "dinner to the examiners to celebrate it"—was *The Influence of the Crusades on European Military Architecture— to the End of the XIIth Century*, with maps, architectural plans, and photographs by himself (it would eventually be published as a book).

Lawrence never did things by half. His interest in medieval fortifications and armor led him naturally to a broader study of military thinking. His friend and biographer in later life, the distinguished British military historian and philosopher of war B. H. Liddell Hart, would praise Lawrence's "astonishingly wide" reading of military texts. That reading began when Lawrence was only fifteen, with what he himself dismissed as such "schoolboy stuff" as "Creasy's *Fifteen Decisive Battles of the World*, Napier's *History of the War in the Peninsula*, Coxe's *Marlborough*, Mahan's *Influence of Sea-Power on History*, Henderson's *Stonewall Jackson*." He went on to Procopius and Vegetius, and from there to the Germans: Clausewitz, Moltke, Freiherr von der Goltz; then, working backward, to Jomini and Napoleon. He "browsed" his way, as he put it, through all thirty-two volumes of Napoleon's correspondence, then moved on to the earlier French writers on war: Bourcet (of whose book there was said to be only one copy in England, in the War Office library), and de Saxe.

Liddell Hart would compare Lawrence to Napoleon* (favorably), though Lawrence himself never made such a claim. In part this was because his admiration for Napoleon as a general would eventually be eclipsed by his admiration for Marshal Maurice de Saxe, the great eighteenth-century French general (though he was in fact of German and Polish descent), and author of a remarkable work on the art of war, *Mes Rêveries*, which was to have a great effect on Lawrence (and later, in World War II, on Field Marshal Montgomery).

---

*Liddell Hart also compared Lawrence to Sherlock Holmes for "his extraordinary perceptiveness of details which other men missed."

The generals in Cairo may be forgiven for not noticing that they had a budding military genius in their midst in the person of Temporary Second-Lieutenant and Acting Staff Captain T. E. Lawrence. But even before the war he had begun quite consciously to develop as a kind of sideline to archaeology and literature what Napoleon called *le coup d'oeil de génie*, the rare and elusive "quick glance of genius" that enables a great commander to see at once, on a map or from the landscape in front of him, the point at which an enemy is weakest, and where an attack will throw the enemy off balance. Years of studying castles had given Lawrence an instinctive feel for topography—it was no accident that he had entered the army through the back door as a mapmaker—and a real gift for visualizing how geographical features determine the movement of armed forces, and inexorably govern both attack and defense.

Generals Murray and Wingate, as well as the emirs Abdulla and Ali, might not appreciate how Obeid's chance remark about date palm villages east of Rabegh brought Lawrence to the conclusion that a British brigade would be "quite useless there to save Mecca from the Turks," but Lawrence understood it instantly. His ability to think in three dimensions, his keen eye for even the smallest details of the landscape, and his remarkable visual memory were all formidable assets for a soldier, though as yet untested in battle. Freud's famous comment that "biology is destiny" has its equivalent in military terms—geography determines strategy; it is the inescapable foundation of the whole art of war. Lawrence was already working out, by a process of rational observation, a new way of thinking about how the Arabs might win their war against the Turks—indeed a new way of thinking about war altogether.

His heirs would include such unusual British officers as Major-General Orde Wingate, who would put Lawrence's ideas to use in the Sudan, Palestine, and Abyssinia between the wars, and in Burma during World War II; and Colonel David Stirling, a leader of the Long Range Desert Group in North Africa in World War II. He also influenced several even more successful, unconventional, and revolutionary soldiers, including Mao Zedong in China, Ho Chi Minh in Vietnam, and Fidel

Castro in Cuba, and in our day both sides in conflicts such as those in Iraq and Afghanistan. Lawrence is now studied with just as much attention by those trying to put down a guerrilla insurgency as by those trying to lead one. The roadside bomb, the unexpected attacks by relatively small numbers of fighters who strike hard, then vanish back into the trackless wastes of the desert (or the jungle, or the slums), the use of high explosives as a political statement, the ability of a guerrilla leader to turn his army's weaknesses into strength—these are all legacies from Lawrence's study of warfare as a young man.

Lawrence and his two Arab escorts rode on through the moonlit night and into the glare of day, crossing a valley so wide that it seemed like a plain, down which the Turks, had they chosen to, could have descended to the southwest from Medina in strength to take Rabegh, and past a village, where they were joined by "a garrulous old man" on a camel, who plied them with questions and offered them "the unleavened dough cake of yesterday, crumbled while still warm between the fingers, and moistened with liquid butter till its particles would only fall apart reluctantly." Sprinkled with sugar, this was a delicacy of the Hejaz, which Obeid and his son ate greedily, but which Lawrence compared to eating "damp sawdust."

The old man was not only garrulous but inquisitive, and full of news— Feisal "had been beaten out of Kheif in the head of the Wadi Safra," with some casualties, and had fallen back on Hamra, which was nearby, or possibly Wasta, which was nearer. Lawrence suspected—and it would soon be confirmed—that the old man was in the pay of the Turks, and was careful not to say anything that might confirm he himself was English. They rode on through harsh though magnificent scenery—rising from the desert floor were steep hills 2,000 feet high formed of bands of brilliantly colored rock—and then through the welcome change of green groves of thorn trees and acacias. They paused at a genuine desert oasis, with clear water surrounded by a narrow strip of grass and wildflowers, and went on into Wasta, one of the numerous date-growing villages of the Beni Salem in Wadi Safra. Obeid led Lawrence to the courtyard of a low, mud-roofed house, and into a small guest house, where he instantly fell asleep on a palm-frond mat.

He woke to find a meal prepared for him of fresh dates and bread—the entire village, it seemed, was inhabited at the moment by black Sudanese slaves, who tended to the date palms and looked after the houses while their masters were away herding camels or, now, fighting in Emir Feisal's forces. The Arabs' wives and children were far away in the desert too, camped out in black goat's hair tents in the wilderness, pasturing the camel herds while the man of the household fought the Turks.

Even in peacetime the tribal Arabs were seldom in their houses more than three months a year. The desert was the world they lived in, and they preferred their tents to houses. The Beni Salem of Wadi Safra had a life that revolved around camel breeding and dates, the latter a primitive form of international commerce. In Mecca the Arabs purchased slaves brought across the Red Sea from the Sudan; in Wadi Safra, the slaves raised and harvested the dates, which were shipped back to the Sudan for a tidy profit. It was a pattern that went back 1,000 years, and even Sherif Hussein's decision to fight the Turks did not completely interrupt it.

Before long, as soon as the worst heat of the day was past, Lawrence and his guides were off again, this time without their inquisitive friend, crossing a wide stretch of desert scoured by yearly flash floods (like those in Texas and New Mexico), which in good years brought to Wadi Safra a low tide of mud and water that made agriculture possible, and in bad years washed away houses, palm trees, and irrigation systems with a swift-moving wall of water eight feet deep. Lawrence noted it all, every detail, like a geologist; and three years later, when he sat down to write *Seven Pillars of Wisdom*, he was able to re-create the landscape of Wadi Safra with amazing and minute exactitude. Beyond the village of Wasta lay Kharma; and soon after it, across a jagged but more fertile landscape, they reached Hamra, the object of their three days of travel, with about 100 houses surrounded by palm groves. As they approached it the emptiness of the desert gave way to a widespread, casual encampment of Feisal's soldiers, grazing their camels or sheltering from the sun beneath stunted thorn trees or under rock ledges. Obeid, who had relapsed into silence, greeted those he knew, then led Lawrence to a low house on a hillock, where his camel knelt down in a courtyard before a doorway guarded by a black slave with a sword, who led him into a second, inner courtyard. There he saw, "standing framed between the posts of a black doorway, a white figure waiting tensely for me."

Lawrence was a born hero-worshipper*—it is ironic, but entirely appropriate, that he would become an object of intense hero worship in his own lifetime—but at this moment he was also a man in *search* of a hero: the leader and prophet in arms without whom the Arab Revolt, he was convinced, would fail. It was at once a psychological and a practical need. On the practical level, he was looking for a man behind whom the many different (and often mutually hostile) Arab tribes might unite, a man who had the dignity and physical impact of a leader, and last but not least one who would also satisfy the British that their money was being wisely spent—not a mere figurehead, but something much greater: a historical figure. The emirs Ali, Abdulla, and Zeid had disappointed him. Now, he instantly recognized in their brother Feisal everything he had been searching for, not only politically, but personally. If it was not love at first sight, it was something very much like that.

He would later comment that Feisal was "almost regal in appearance ... Very much like the monument of Richard I at Fontevraud," which Lawrence had seen during his bicycling tours of French castles and cathedrals. This comparison to the brave but pious king, an inspired leader of men and the supreme warrior of the Middle Ages, who fought his own father and brothers for the throne and who has passed into English history as Richard the Lionheart, was high praise indeed, for he was a figure Lawrence admired greatly. It was also, perhaps, something of a political daydream, for Feisal, courageous and inspiring as he may have been,

---

* Others to whom he had a similarly intense initial reaction included his archaeological mentor D. G. Hogarth; the English explorer of Arabia Charles Doughty; Field Marshal Lord Allenby; Winston Churchill; Marshal of the Royal Air Force Lord Trenchard, founder of the RAF; George Bernard Shaw; and Thomas Hardy.

would have been the last person to take arms against his father and his brothers to become sharif of Mecca himself. (He and his brothers still signed their letters to their father as "Your Slave.")

Later, in *Seven Pillars of Wisdom*, Lawrence would write: "I felt at the glance that now I had found the man whom I had come to Arabia to seek. . . . He looked very tall and pillar-like, very slender, dressed in long white silk robes and a brown headcloth bound with a brilliant scarlet and gold cord. His eyelids were drooped, and his close black beard and colourless face were like a mask against the strange still watchfulness of his body. His hands were loosely crossed in front of him on his dagger."

Feisal ushered Lawrence into a small dark room, in which Lawrence, whose eyes were still accustomed to the outside glare, could only just distinguish the presence of a crowd of people seated on the floor. Feisal and Lawrence sat down on the carpet—Lawrence comments that Feisal stared down at his hands, "which were twisting slowly about his dagger," without drawing our attention to the fact that for Arabs the eye-to-eye stare, which among Britons and Americans signifies an honest man-to-man approach, is instead either a challenge or sheer bad manners by someone who doesn't know any better—a European, for example.

In a soft voice, speaking Arabic, Feisal asked Lawrence, "And do you like our place here in Wadi Safra?"

To which, after a pause, Lawrence replied, "Well; but it is far from Damascus."

To quote Lawrence, his words fell "like a sword into their midst," and all those in the room held their breath for a silent moment. Damascus was their dream—the capital of an Arab state, or nation, that would stretch from the Mediterranean to the Persian Gulf.

Then Feisal smiled, and said, "Praise be to God, there are Turks nearer us than that."

What Feisal thought of Lawrence was—and would always be—harder to know. The bond between them would grow stronger than either of them could have foreseen that day, but Feisal's personality was of necessity far

more opaque than Lawrence's—he was a prince, of a great and proud ruling family trapped between its Arab rivals in the desert (of whom the
most dangerous was the future king of Saudi Arabia, ibn Saud*), and its
Turkish overlords in Constantinople. Feisal was a politician, a man skilled
at hiding his emotions and veiling his thoughts, hardly one to trust a
stranger, and certainly not one who would imagine that a British officer
might put Arab interests before those of his own country. At their very
first meeting, Feisal took in Lawrence's admiration for his own person,
his unusual knowledge of Arab ways, his lack of racial prejudice toward
Arabs, and his undisguised enthusiasm for the Arab cause; but Feisal
was cautious by nature, not impulsive, except in the heat of battle, and he
cannot initially have been sure why this young Englishman had been
sent to him. Yet Feisal came quickly to feel affection, trust, and respect
for Lawrence, and from the first instant was encouraged by his arrival at
Wadi Safra, as might not have been the case had Lawrence been a more
conventional British officer. The British were powerful friends and allies,
but that is not to say Feisal trusted them completely, any more than he
trusted any other European colonial power with ambitions in the Near
East—France, for example.

The two men were close in age—Lawrence was twenty-eight, Feisal
thirty-three—but Feisal had grown up in a world of cruelty, treachery,
and deceit, where the penalty for anti-Turkish activity ranged from exile
to torture and public hanging. He had been educated in Constantinople,
sat as a member in the Turkish parliament, served as his father's emissary to the Turkish government, and been a combination of guest and
hostage for his father's good behavior to Ahmed Jemal Pasha, one of the
triumvirate that ruled Turkey, as well as the Turkish overlord of Syria
and all those parts of the Ottoman Empire in which the Arabs were a
majority. (Jemal Pasha was known among Arabs as *al-Saffah*—the blood
shedder, or the butcher.) Feisal had seen his friends and coconspirators,
fellow members of Arab secret societies proscribed by the Turks, executed

* Abd al-Aziz ibn Abd ar-Rahman ibn Faysal ibn Turki Abd Allah ibn Muhammad Al
Saud (c. 1880–1953), referred to as ibn Saud.

in mass hangings carried out in public by Jemal's order, and had been obliged to watch them die without shedding a tear or letting his expression betray his emotions.* His was neither a simple nor a transparent character.

Nor, of course, was Lawrence's; this is perhaps why they got on well from the beginning. Even to somebody as congenitally suspicious as Feisal, it was at once obvious that Lawrence was not a spy in any conventional meaning of the word. He was there to report what he saw, certainly, but his sympathy was already for the Arabs, and his attitude was supportive. A more professional military man might have dwelled on the fact that Feisal's army had been retreating ever since its humiliating failure to take Medina, which—together with the devastating effects of Turkish artillery, machine guns, and aircraft on poorly armed mounted tribesmen with no experience of the power of modern weapons and high explosives†—had deeply shaken the morale and self-confidence of Feisal's troops. Lawrence, on the contrary, was sympathetic rather than critical. He understood that supplies were slow to reach Feisal's army partly because neither Abdulla in Mecca nor Ali in Rabegh had any sense of urgency or any professional supply officers to organize efficiently the flow of flour, ammunition, and gold; and that because Feisal lacked machine guns, mortars, and mountain artillery (which could be broken down into pieces, and carried by camels), he could hardly hope to meet the Turks on equal terms. Had Lawrence himself been a spit-and-polish regular, the state of the Arab army might have dismayed or appalled him, but he was not.

---

* This was in part because the French consul in Beirut, François Georges-Picot, had fled from the consulate at the outbreak of war between the Ottoman Empire and France, leaving behind him in his desk drawer the names of Arab notables in Lebanon and Syria who had been in touch with him about Arab independence in the event Turkey entered the war. For many of those on his list it was a sentence of death—twenty-one of them were hanged in 1916, many after months of terrible torture.

† Lawrence was foremost among the British officers who would teach the Arabs everything there was to know about dynamite, gun cotton, and more modern high explosives, thus preparing the way for the roadside bomb and the suicide vest as a means of political statement or revenge in the Middle East.

In fact, the only signs of spit and polish in sight were the profession-
ally neat rows of tents of an Egyptian army unit sent from the Sudan by
General Wingate to support the Arabs with machine guns and some
antiquated short-range light artillery, no match for the Turks' modern
German field guns and howitzers. The Egyptians had been picked because
they were Muslims and it was thought that the Arabs would resent their
presence less than that of British troops, but in fact the Arabs thought
them effete townsmen, over-disciplined by their officers, and too easily
upset when Arabs stole from them,* for the Egyptians received ample
British army rations. For their part, the Egyptian regulars greatly preferred the Turks to the desert vagabonds, whom they held in contempt.
The Egyptians' esprit de corps was not improved by the fact that the
Turks had a reputation for cutting the throat of any wounded left behind
by Feisal's army, without necessarily discriminating between Egyptians
and Arabs.

Lawrence took careful notes of everything he saw—the unhappiness
of the Egyptians; the shortage of rice, barley, and flour; the number of
men still armed with ancient muzzle loaders or single-shot rifles rather
than modern bolt-action British Lee-Enfields or Turkish Mausers. Had
he been educated at Sandhurst instead of Jesus College, Oxford, his eye
for military detail and deficiencies could hardly have been sharper. He
got from Feisal and Feisal's officers a detailed account of the failed attack
on Medina, including the fact—which Feisal did not mention, but those
around him did—that when the Turkish artillery had opened fire, driving the Arabs into retreat, Feisal himself had ridden up and down through
the barrage trying to rally the fleeing tribesmen, a gesture worthy of
Bonaparte's at the crossing of the Rivoli, but in this case unsuccessful.
The attack on Medina had been "a desperate measure," Lawrence concluded, more desperate than was appreciated in Cairo and London.

---

* The voracious thievery of the Arabs against friend and foe alike was a complaint of
all foreign troops in Arab lands, shared by the German, British, and American armies
in North Africa during World War II. Another complaint was the Arabs' indifference
toward digging sanitation trenches and carrying out other basic hygiene routines
common to all European-trained armies in the field.

When one of the local tribes, the Beni Ali, discouraged by the Turkish artillery fire, had offered to surrender "if their villages were spared," the Turkish commander, Fakhri Pasha, had heard them out patiently, carrying on a long, polite, slow negotiation in the eastern manner, while in the meantime his troops assaulted one of the Beni Ali villages, raped the women, murdered "everything within its walls"—men, women, and children—then set fire to the houses and threw the bodies of the hundreds they had killed into the flames.

Fakhri Pasha and his troops had played a significant role in the bloody Turkish genocide of the Armenians; they were now determined to teach an equally harsh lesson to the Arabs. Though the Arabs were capable of great cruelty, it was a strict rule of desert warfare that the women and children of your enemy were spared. This was a new kind of war to them.

Feisal talked strategy to Lawrence, and found that their minds worked as one. Like Lawrence, he could see very clearly the routes the Turks could use to isolate Rabegh and advance on Mecca, once they concentrated their forces. Neither Lawrence nor Feisal was a professional soldier, but Lawrence had a good knowledge of strategy; and Feisal was a realistic judge of what his own troops could do (as well as what they could not), and knew how to lead and to keep together the different tribes who would otherwise have been at one another's throat. Feisal was confident that, given better weapons and modern artillery, he could stop the Turks from taking Mecca, but he still imagined that if he moved in concert with Ali from Rabegh and Abdulla from Mecca, Medina could be taken by a three-pronged attack. Lawrence already doubted the wisdom of this, and would soon think of Medina not as a danger spot to be eliminated, but as a fatal trap for the Turks.

The two days that Lawrence spent with Feisal's army in Wadi Safra were of critical importance both to him and to the future of the Arab Revolt. First, he was the only British officer who had actually seen Feisal's Arab army "in the field"; second, he had made his mind up about Feisal— here was the prophetlike figure he had been searching for and had failed to find in Feisal's brothers. Perhaps most important, Lawrence had established himself in Feisal's mind as the one man who could and would persuade the British to send the equipment, supplies, and instructors that the Arab army so desperately needed. Lawrence was very frank about what he thought could (and could not) be had from Cairo, but he also, rather recklessly, took on himself the responsibility for artillery, light machine guns, and so on to the Arabs—an amazingly bold commitment for a temporary second-lieutenant and acting staff captain.

Despite the fact that the two men got along well together, there were still areas of difficulty that lay unplumbed between them. Feisal, for example, wished aloud somewhat wistfully that Britain was not such a "disproportionate" ally, and remarked that while the Hejaz might look barren, so did the Sudan, yet the British had taken it anyway. "They hunger," he said, "for desolate lands." The Arabs, he pointed out, had no desire to exchange being Turkish subjects for becoming British subjects. There also hovered between them the much thornier subject of British, French, and Russian ambitions in the Middle East.

Lawrence already knew of the existence of the Sykes-Picot agreement. Although it was supposedly secret, it was the kind of thing that was impossible to hide in the close world of military and political intelligence in Cairo, where everybody knew everyone else and the atmosphere was that of a Senior Common Room at Oxford. Lawrence may not, at this stage, have known every detail of the agreement, but he certainly knew that in May 1916 Sir Mark Sykes, a wealthy Conservative member of Parliament who was something of a passionate traveler in the Ottoman Empire, and François Georges-Picot, a French diplomat who at the outbreak of war was the French consul in Beirut, had negotiated a Franco-British agreement apportioning to their respective countries large areas of the Ottoman Empire. France was to get an area (the Blue Zone) consisting of what is now Lebanon and a "zone of influence" including Syria and extending eastward to include Mosul, in what is now Iraq, and a large area to the north; Britain was to get an area (the Red Zone) that would include the rest of what is now Iraq, from Baghdad to Basra, as well as the Persian Gulf sheikhdoms and a "zone of influence" extending westward to include what is now Jordan.

Once Sykes and Picot brought the agreement to Petrograd for the approval of the czarist government, they found themselves obliged to cut the Russians in on the deal—imperial Russia insisted on fulfilling its old ambition of annexing Constantinople and the Turkish Straits, as well as much of Armenia, and also insisted that control of the Holy Land—i.e., Palestine—be shared among the three powers, so as to place the Christian holy sites under the protection of France (nominally Catholic), Russia (representing the Russian, Greek, and Serbian Orthodox churches), and Great Britain (Protestant) and thus to satisfy religious opinion in the three major Christian faiths. In November 1917 the situation would be further complicated by two events. First, immediately after the Bolsheviks seized power in Russia, they published all of imperial Russia's secret treaties, to the great embarrassment of the French and the British. Second, in London the *Times* published Foreign Secretary Arthur Balfour's letter to Lord Rothschild, stating publicly that the British government would "view with favour the establishment in Palestine of a national home for the Jewish people." This letter injected a further religious and racial element into an area which also contained Muslim holy sites and a largely Muslim population, and which most Arabs believed was part of the territory they were fighting for.

Though both Lawrence and Feisal would later claim ignorance of the Sykes-Picot agreement, this was certainly not true of the former, and probably not true of the latter. The British, in their endless negotiations with Sharif Hussein, had always been careful to avoid agreeing to any specific frontiers for "the Arab nation," and had pointed out, though without much emphasis or detail, that France and Britain had certain "historic" claims to territory in the Ottoman Empire that would have to be respected. This insistence that the division of the spoils should come after the Allies' victory was intended in part to get the Arabs fighting. The idea left floating delicately in the air, and expressed with exquisite diplomatic tact by Kitchener, Wilson, Storrs, and others, was that the harder the Arabs fought, the more they might hope to claim at the peace table; but it was also a reaction to Sharif Hussein's breathtaking and meticulously detailed demand to be made king of an Arab nation stretching from the Mediterranean to the Persian Gulf, and including all of what is now Palestine, Lebanon, Syria, Saudi Arabia, and Iraq.

Eager to get the Arabs to start fighting the Turks, the British did not deny the sharif's claims; they merely cautioned him that they and the French would have to be satisfied, and that discussion of the exact frontiers of an Arab nation would have to wait until the peace conference following the Allies' victory. In the meantime, Britain had already taken and occupied a sizable part of Mesopotamia, including Basra and Baghdad, in part to ensure a steady supply of oil for the Royal Navy, and also wanted control of the approaches to the Suez Canal; France had, or claimed, strong historic ties with Lebanon and Syria going back to the days of the Crusades; and neither country wished to see Jerusalem in Arab hands.

The sharif of Mecca was only too well aware of the fact that Britain, France, and Russia would have to be satisfied, as was his son Abdulla, who had been directly involved in the negotiations, so it seems likely that some hint of the problem would have made its way to Feisal, though the sharif's policy toward his allies and his sons was to simply ignore what he didn't want to hear. In much the same way, the sharif affected to ignore the fact that his rivals in the Arabian Peninsula, particularly ibn Saud, as well as the educated and highly politicized elite in Damascus, were hardly likely to accept him as their king.

Lawrence's guilt at encouraging the Arabs to fight even though he knew they were not going to get what they wanted (and what they thought they had been promised) would become increasingly severe as the war went on and as his place in the Arab Revolt increased in importance. It was the reason why he would refuse to accept any of the honors and decorations he was awarded; it was at the root of his self-disgust and shame;

it would eventually make him follow a strategy of his own, urging Feisal and the Arabs on in an effort to reach Damascus before the British or the French entered the city, and declare an independent Arab nation whose existence could not be denied at the peace conference—a grand, sublime gesture would, he hoped, render the Sykes-Picot agreement null and void in the eyes of the world.

Lawrence's mention of Damascus when he first met Feisal was thus both a challenge and the equivalent of a knowing wink: an indication that here, at least, was one Englishman who understood what Feisal really wanted—a so-called "Greater Syria," long the ambition of Arab nationalists, which would include Lebanon (and its ports) as its Mediterranean seacoast and, of course, Damascus as its capital. Attacking Medina, even taking it, would hardly get Feisal any nearer to Damascus than he was at Wadi Safra. Medina was more than 800 miles from Damascus, and so long as Feisal's army was stuck in the desert halfway between Medina and Mecca, with no roads or railway to supply it, Damascus might as well have been on the moon. The British—accompanied by just enough French officers and French Muslim North African specialist units to stake out France's claim to Lebanon and Syria when they got there—were still trying to break through the Turkish lines at Gaza, which was only 175 miles away from Damascus as the crow flies. It was not enough for Feisal and his brothers merely to defend Mecca against Fakhri Pasha. If the Arab army, whatever its deficiencies, could not move north, leapfrogging past Medina, and win some highly publicized victories along the way, Hussein's claim to a kingdom and the hopes of Arab nationalists would both be stillborn.

Lawrence and Feisal understood each other on this point, but it was not yet clear to Feisal how to accomplish the goal with the ill-armed and unreliable forces at his command. It was Lawrence's strategic imagination, and his determination to make the British high command in Cairo not only accept his vision but finance and support what most of this command thought was unlikely or impossible, that would make himself and Feisal famous within a year and start Feisal on a path that would reshape the Middle East and lead to the creation of new nations and frontiers that are still in place today, for better or for worse.*

At the end of their second long talk together, Lawrence promised to return, if he was allowed to, after he had seen to Feisal's needs, and requested from Feisal an escort to take him to Yenbo, rather than back to Rabegh. This was an interesting decision, since it shows how Lawrence's mind worked. The port of Yenbo was in Arab hands, though lightly and precariously held, but it was more than 100 miles north of Rabegh, and in fact actually *behind* Medina. The ride to Yenbo was considerably longer and more difficult than the ride back to Rabegh, but it was at Yenbo that he had arranged to be picked up by the Royal Navy.

He left Hamra at sunset, accompanied by an escort of fourteen hand-picked tribesmen; rode down the Wadi Safra back to the village of Kharma in the darkness; then turned right and climbed up a steep "side valley," full of thorn and brushwood, onto an ancient stone causeway, an old pilgrim route, until they reached a well and a ruined fort, where they rested. At daylight they moved on again through a lunar landscape of hardened lava, "huge crags of flowing surface but with a bent and twisted texture, as though it had been played with oddly while soft," set in a sea of shifting sand dunes. They began riding quickly—to Lawrence's great discomfort, for he was not yet accustomed to the motions of a swiftly moving camel—onward into the intense heat of the day over "glassy sand mixed with shingle," where the reflected sunlight soon became unbearable, and each drop of sweat coursing down his face was a torture.

From there they traveled on to Wadi Yenbo, a deep, wide valley, scoured by flash floods, where heat mirages shimmered before their eyes. They rested during the worst heat of the day under the sparse branches of

---

* It should be understood that neither Lawrence nor Feisal imagined the present-day frontiers. Feisal had in mind a much larger, unitary Arab state, with his father as its king. Lawrence knew that the Arabs would have to give up some of the places they wanted, in order to satisfy British and French ambitions in the area; but his own map of the Middle East after victory, which he drafted in 1918 for the British cabinet, also shows a far larger state than the Arabs got in the shape of Jordan and Iraq.

an acacia tree, then rode on through sand and shingle until they halted for the night, and felt at last like a balm "a salt wind from the sea blowing over our chafed faces." After baking bread and boiling coffee, they rested until two in the morning, then moved on over rough country—hard, slow going until they arrived at a salt flat, which they raced over, reaching the gates of Yenbo, perched high above the salt flat on a coral cliff, at six in the morning.

Here Lawrence spent four days in the "picturesque, rambling house" of Sheikh Abd el Kader el Abdo, Feisal's "agent" here—at this point Yenbo was by no means safe, since the local sharif and emir was known to be pro-Turk. While waiting for the Royal Navy to appear, Lawrence wrote down everything he had seen. His reports were remarkable documents, long (in this case 17,000 words), detailed, full of trenchant and well-expressed military and political opinions, and containing a wealth of invaluable information and observations on everything from the position of wells to the most minute topographical observations. This was to be an important factor in Lawrence's swift rise—even those who did not much like him, or agree with him about the importance and the direction of the Arab Revolt, were often persuaded by his written reports, which reached the very highest levels of the War Office and even the war cabinet, and confirmed that here, at any rate, was a uniquely well informed and self-confident young officer, with strong opinions formed on the spot, rather than in an office in Cairo 800 miles from the fighting.

However, when Captain William ("Ginger") Boyle, RN, appeared at last with HMS *Suva*, a former Australian freighter, on November 1, Lawrence failed to make a good initial impression; he was "travel-stained," he had abandoned his luggage, and he wore a native head cloth instead of his uniform cap, which he had lost during his arduous days of desert travel. Boyle, the senior officer of the Red Sea Naval Patrol, was a large, bluff, hearty, quick-tempered naval type (he would go on to a long career, ending as Admiral of the Fleet the Twelfth Earl of Cork and Orrery, GCB, GCVO). He had been a fervent supporter of the Arab Revolt from its beginning—and generous with supplies, ammunition, and offshore bombardments of Turkish positions—but not to the point of wishing to see a British officer dressed like a native, or sauntering casually onto the bridge of HMS *Suva* with his hands in his pockets, as if the vessel were a cab he had just hailed on the Strand. Lawrence's unmilitary appearance, his failure to salute, and his strongly expressed opinions on every subject under the sun, including the Royal Navy, sent Boyle's temper soaring; but despite Lawrence's diminutive height, improper attire, and irritating habit of omniscience, his combination of enthusiasm, sincerity, and practical common sense eventually put Boyle at ease, and by the time they reached Jidda they were friends, and would remain so for life. Boyle had discovered the most striking thing about Lawrence: however far-fetched his ideas might seem at first, he usually knew what he was talking about.

In Jidda they found HMS *Euryalus*, the flagship, with the commander in chief of the Egyptian Squadron, Vice-Admiral Sir Rosslyn Wemyss, GCB, CMG, MVO, on board, on his way to Port Sudan to meet with General Sir Reginald Wingate, governor-general of the Sudan and *sirdar* of the Egyptian army, at Khartoum. This was fortunate for Lawrence: Wemyss—a widely respected naval figure and a friend of King George V—combined impeccable connections with a fervent belief in the possibilities of the Arab Revolt. Indeed, a visit on board Wemyss's flagship had been one factor clinching the Arabs' decision to revolt: they were awed by the size of its guns, and indeed astonished that a vessel so big and heavy could float at all.

Wemyss was no stranger to odd behavior—he kept in his day cabin on board *Euryalus* a gray parrot trained to cry out, in a pronounced Oxford accent, "Damn the kaiser!"—and he liked Lawrence, whatever headgear Lawrence wore. Wemyss, who would come to Lawrence's help again, always appearing at the right moment unexpectedly like a wizard in a pantomime, took him across the Red Sea to Port Sudan, and from there to Wingate's headquarters in Khartoum, where Wingate—the original and firmest supporter of the Arab Revolt—read his reports and listened to his opinion that the situation in the Hejaz was not dire, as many people in Cairo supposed, but "full of promise." What the Arabs needed, Lawrence said, was not British troops, whose appearance at Rabegh would cause the tribesmen to give up the fight and return to their herds, but merely a few Arabic-speaking British technical advisers, explosives, and a modest number of modern weapons.

As it happened, this was exactly the message that the chief of the imperial general staff (CIGS) in London most wanted to receive, for the terrible battles on the western front in 1916 made manpower a crucial question. Verdun had cost the French nearly 500,000 casualties, and the first Battle of the Somme, launched by the British to support the French at Verdun, would cost them more than 600,000 casualties, 60,000 on the first day alone; and General Murray, the commander in chief of the Egyptian Expeditionary Force in Cairo, was under constant pressure from the CIGS in London to squeeze every possible division, brigade, and person out of his army for immediate dispatch to France.

Lawrence was perhaps the only person in the world who would have described his three or four days at Wingate's palace in Khartoum—on the steps of which Lawrence's predecessor in the imagination of the British public as a desert adventurer, General Gordon, had been murdered— as "cool and comfortable." Everybody else who had visited Khartoum at any time of year described it as hellishly hot, though certainly Wingate's palace was plush and lavish after the desert, and surrounded by beautiful gardens. When Lawrence was not conferring with Wingate and Wemyss, he spent his time reading Malory's *Morte d'Arthur,* a pleasure interrupted by the kind of event that seldom failed to occur at the right moment in Lawrence's career. His host, Sir Reginald Wingate, was abruptly informed that Sir Henry McMahon had been recalled from Cairo to Britain, and Wingate was to take McMahon's place as British high commissioner in Egypt. Thus supreme control of Egypt would pass from the hands of a civilian into the firmer hands of a soldier who supported the revolt passionately, who would be in direct command of the British end of it, and who knew Lawrence well. At the same time the change would bring to an end a curious division: political responsibility for the Arab Revolt had been in Cairo and military responsibility in Khartoum, and this had been a source of delay and confusion to all concerned.

Both senior officers read and were impressed by Lawrence's reports from the Hejaz. They were still more impressed by Lawrence himself; and it must be noted that, as was so often the case with Lawrence, though still a temporary second-lieutenant he was conferring as an equal with an admiral and with his excellency the governor-general of the Sudan and *sirdar* of the Egyptian army. This easy access to the most senior officers and officials was due not to Lawrence's social position, which was less than negligible, but to his acute mind; to his strong opinions, which were based on facts he had personally observed; and to his view of policy and strategy, which was far broader and more imaginative than that of most junior officers—or, indeed, most senior ones.

In short, part of the reason for Lawrence's success was that he knew what he was talking about, and could make his points succinctly even among men far senior to him in age, experience, and rank. Even the busiest of officials made time to listen to what Lawrence had to say: generals, admirals, high commissioners, and princes now, and in the not very distant future, also artists, scholars, prime ministers, presidents, kings, and giants of literature. Lawrence himself, though reasonably respectful of rank unless provoked, seemed almost unconscious of it, treated others as if they were all equals and was himself treated as an equal by many of the highest figures in the world. He may have been the only person in twentieth-century Britain who was just as much at ease with King George V as with a hut full of RAF recruits. Certainly, he eventually won Wingate over completely, and Wingate was not an easy man for a temporary second-lieutenant without a proper cap or uniform to win over.

Unlike McMahon, whom he was to replace, Wingate was fiery, hot-tempered, and impulsive. One only needs to look at Wingate's portrait in *Seven Pillars of Wisdom* to read his character: a square, bulky face straight out of Kipling, the expression angry and challenging, the eyes piercing, the sharp tips of the ferocious waxed mustache pointing straight out like horns—all this suggests the human equivalent of a Cape buffalo bull about to put its head down and charge. In the end, Wingate was too much so for his own good; but this was exactly the spirit that was called for at the top if the Arab Revolt was to survive and prosper. Lawrence tended to describe the senior officers who crossed his path with distant and sometimes stinging irony, but he showed Wingate a rare degree of respect, despite serious differences of opinion between them on the subject of a British presence and—even less welcome to Lawrence—a French presence in Rabegh. Wingate no doubt terrified other junior officers, but it can have done Lawrence no harm that he, like Wingate, was a man of the desert. Wingate had fought in the Sudan and Ethiopia, had conquered the final remnant of the Mahdi's Dervish army, and was at the same time a man of refined tastes and sensibility, who spoke and read Arabic fluently.

Lawrence therefore traveled back to Cairo by train with far greater confidence in his future than he had felt leaving it for Jidda with Storrs a month ago, though his optimism was to prove short-lived. In Cairo confusion reigned, stirred up in part by the impending departure of McMahon, and in part by concern for what was happening at Rabegh, owing to rumors that the Turks were about to attack. If the Turks were able to take Rabegh, they could outflank Feisal's army and recapture Mecca, in which case the Arab Revolt would be over.

Wingate.

Happily, Lawrence, having just returned from the Hejaz and met Feisal, was in a position to calm these concerns. He was not alone in attributing them to Colonel Édouard Brémond, the head of the French military mission, who was as anxious to place a French military presence—in the form of North African Muslim soldiers and specialists—in Rabegh as most of the British were to keep them away. In the first place, the equivalent of a French brigade in Rabegh would mean that the British had to send one as well, and this the CIGS was unwilling to do. In the second place, the British were anxious to keep the French out of what was regarded as a British "sphere of interest." Lawrence knew Brémond, a big and energetic man, a fluent Arabist with a wealth of experience in commanding Muslim troops in desert warfare; they behaved toward each other with exquisite courtesy but a complete lack of trust. Brémond reported to Paris on Lawrence's anti-French sentiments, and Lawrence made no secret of his hope "to biff the French out of" the territory they coveted. The French colonial system, which operated so efficiently in Algeria and French Morocco, was exactly what Lawrence wanted to spare the Arabs: French settlers; a Europeanized native army with French officers; and the rule of French law, culture, and the French language imposed on those of the native elite who wanted something more for themselves and their families than looking after their herds, flocks, and fields in the desert. Lawrence had no great enthusiasm for the British colonial system, especially in India, but the French were undoubtedly more determined to impose French ideas and interests on the natives in their Arab colonies than the British were in theirs, and the result was that Lawrence often seemed more anxious to defeat France's ambitions in the Near East than to defeat the Turks.

Lawrence's future was already being discussed at the highest level before he was even back in Cairo. The CIGS himself suggested to Wingate by cable on November 11 that Lawrence be dispatched to Rabegh "to train Arab bands," while in Cairo Clayton had finally succeeded in getting Lawrence transferred full-time to the Arab Bureau, to handle propaganda aimed at the Arabs. Having secured Lawrence, Clayton was unwilling to give him up, and there followed a brief, polite tug-of-war between Wingate and Clayton over him, complicated by the fact that if he was sent to Rabegh he would be under the command of Colonel Wilson in Jidda (who had referred to Lawrence as "a bumptious ass").

By this time the fear that Rabegh might fall had made its way up to the war cabinet in London, along with considerable pressure from the French government to place French "technical" units there to prevent this. Clayton ordered Lawrence to write a strong memorandum expressing his opinion that Allied troops sent to Rabegh would cause the Arab Revolt to collapse, which Clayton then cabled, unexpurgated, to the cabinet and to the CIGS. Thus, Lawrence's views, which sensibly dismissed the possibility that Rabegh might be taken by the Turks so long as Feisal and his army were given the support he had requested, were accepted with relief in London, and quickly transformed into policy. Lawrence articulately presented his argument against sending the French units, as well as his belief that Yenbo, not Rabegh, was the important place, since it was nearer to Feisal's army, and urged that every effort should be made to cut the railway line linking Damascus and Medina, rather than attempting to take Medina.

Neither the Foreign Office nor the CIGS seems to have been taken aback by the fact that diplomatic policy and military strategy were being formulated by a second-lieutenant in Cairo, perhaps because Lawrence's opinions were so forcefully presented (and corresponded, in large part, with what everybody in London wanted to hear), and perhaps because Lawrence was the only person who had ridden out into the desert to see for himself what Feisal was doing. In any case, the result was—to Colonel Wilson's great annoyance—that Lawrence was ordered back to the Hejaz to serve as a liaison officer with Feisal. On paper, he would be reporting directly to Wilson, but he would also be serving as Clayton's eyes and ears in Feisal's camp.

In *Seven Pillars of Wisdom*, Lawrence makes a grand show of his unwillingness to go, alleging that it "was much against my grain," but this must be taken with a pinch of salt. In fact it seems more likely that what Lawrence objected to was going to Rabegh, since this would place him too close to Wilson for comfort, whereas in Yenbo he would enjoy considerable independence, even more so once he journeyed inland and joined Feisal.

In any case, whether Lawrence went willingly or not, it was the first step on the road that would eventually turn him into perhaps the most celebrated, exotic, and publicized hero of World War I.

CHAPTER TWO

Aqaba, 1917: The Making of a Hero

Lawrence left Cairo on November 25, 1916, and arrived back in Yenbo early on December 2, having spent no more than ten days in Cairo while his future was being decided. He was pleased to be nearly 200 miles away from Colonel Wilson in Jidda, and to discover that Wilson had already sent Major H. G. Garland to Yenbo to teach the Arabs how to handle explosives, and to keep track of incoming supplies. Lawrence was ambivalent regarding Garland, whose expertise about explosives was vital if the railway to Medina was to be cut, but whose attitude toward the Arabs distressed him. Garland was a former metallurgist, caustic and quick tempered, but his joy in setting off large, destructive explosions fortunately communicated itself to the Arabs. He took the time to teach Lawrence the rudiments of demolition, which Garland approached rather in the spirit of enthusiastic amateur than in the cautious, step-by-step manner of the Royal Engineers, who, Lawrence complained, treated explosives like the "sacrament." Garland stuffed volatile detonators, fuses, and primers carelessly into his pockets; tossed explosives around as if they were tennis balls; and encouraged in Lawrence a similar fearlessness on the subject. He taught Lawrence not only how to use high explosives but how to inflict the maximum damage to the railway, by blowing up culverts and bridges and by taking the time and trouble to destroy as many rails as possible, especially the curved rails—which, because they were in short supply, were harder for the Turks to replace than straight ones. Garland, as it turned out, was a jack-of-all-trades, who could repair machine guns, improvise an artillery plan, lay out a defense perimeter, supervise the digging of trenches, and give lessons in the use of grenades, one pattern of which he had invented himself. He was hardworking and efficient, so much so that Lawrence was able without great trouble to shift onto Garland's shoulders the uncongenial job of being a glorified supply officer at Yenbo.

In some ways, the situation seemed better than it had when Lawrence had traveled to Rabegh less than two months earlier. The Royal Flying Corps (RFC) had finally overcome its nervousness about stationing aircraft in Rabegh; there was now a flight of four British aircraft, under the command of an officer who spoke Arabic, and guarded by 300 Egyptian soldiers who were more alarmed by their Arab allies than by the threat of a Turkish attack. The RFC flight was more important, at the moment, for carrying out aerial reconnaissance than for attacking Turkish warplanes, but its presence was heartening to the Arabs. General Wingate had scraped up from the Sudan whatever he could in the way of light artillery—most of it antiquated, some of it French—and sent it over, as a sop to Colonel Brémond. The mere sight of these guns was encouraging to the Arabs, and the sound of them was even more so. Lawrence could feel that the promises he had rashly made to Feisal were being kept, and it was therefore with some confidence that he rode with a guide up to the broadest part of Wadi Yenbo, where Feisal and his army were reported to be. As night fell they heard the noise of a sizable force in front of them. Lawrence's guide dismounted and moved forward, cocking his rifle, fearing that they might have stumbled into a Turkish force, but he soon came back with the news that Feisal's army was spread out from one side of the wadi to the other; the size of the force was indicated by the discontented roar and grumbling of hundreds of camels and by the number of tiny fires flickering in the dark.

Unfortunately, the numerous fires had been lit because it was cold and wet—a recent rain had turned the floor of Wadi Yenbo into slimy mud, and men and animals were uncomfortable and disgruntled. Amid all the confusion and noise—the Arabs tended to waste ammunition firing off shots into the night sky to keep their spirits up, or to greet late arrivals—Lawrence finally located Feisal seated calmly on a carpet spread on the rocks, surrounded by baggage camels, while one of his secretaries read reports aloud to him by the light of a lantern held above his head by a slave. Meanwhile, Arab tribal leaders and notables waited in the dark to complain to him. Around Feisal was incredible disorder—camels everywhere, filling the night with their noise and the smell of their dung; the mules of the Egyptian gunners braying and kicking; men spread out in the mud next to the animals, trying to sleep with their cloaks wrapped around them—the perfect picture of an army on the run. The Turks, Feisal explained, had outflanked his army and sent it flying headlong in retreat toward Yenbo, opening up the way to Rabegh and Mecca, and taking the area around Hamra, with its wells, where Lawrence had first met Feisal only a few weeks ago. Feisal's half brother Zeid had been forced to flee, leaving much of his baggage behind and abandoning a key position, while many of Feisal's tribal contingents had faded into the hills. Feisal had thought it best to cut his losses and retreat far enough so that he could fall back on Yenbo if the Turks continued to attack. It was exactly the kind of debacle that British doubters had always predicted would happen if the Turks attacked the Arab irregulars, and that Lawrence had convinced Wingate, Murray, Clayton, and the CIGS in London would not. It was not as if the Turks had inflicted serious losses; the Arabs had fled before any serious fighting took place.

Yet during the course of a long, cold, uncomfortable night, made even more miserable by a white mist that drenched everybody to the skin, Lawrence saw signs that kindled his optimism. The Arabs had failed again, certainly, just as they had outside Medina, but Feisal's spirits were high, he was cheerful and patient with those who brought him complaints, and he seemed unsurprised, even amused, by what had happened. Feisal's sense of humor ("that invariable magnet of Arab good will," as Lawrence put it) as he chaffed those who had fled first or fastest, taught Lawrence how to handle the tribesmen: they responded poorly to criticism or reproof but enjoyed a good story even when it was at their own expense.

After a breakfast of dates, Feisal decided to move the army, partly to get it out of the mud and onto higher, drier ground; partly no doubt to take the men's minds off their position, and off the danger they would be in if the Turks pursued them. The great drums were beaten; men mounted their camels and formed up in two wings, leaving a wide central alley, down which Feisal rode, followed by flag bearers, the intimates of his household, and the 800 men of his bodyguard. Lawrence rode close to Feisal, a privileged position, and was impressed by the savage splendor of the moment, and by Feisal's instinctive majesty. Daylight—and his presence—had transformed a fleeing mob back into the semblance of an army. Feisal rode ahead and picked out a new encampment on high ground, near the village of Nakhl Mubarak, hidden among groves of date palms, less than forty miles from Yenbo. He raised his tents on a hill overlooking the camp, surrounded by his bodyguard, with the neat rows of the Egyptian gunners' tents below him, and the Arab army spread out in its usual chaotic disorder beyond them.

It was here that Feisal asked Lawrence to wear Arab clothes, since these would be more acceptable to the tribesmen than his khaki uniform, which reminded them of a Turkish officer, and would also enable him "to slip in and out of his tent without making a sensation which he had to explain away each time to strangers." To make sure that Lawrence would be recognized as a privileged member of the inner circle, Feisal presented him with the white and gold-threaded robes of a sharifian bridegroom, sent to Feisal by an aunt—perhaps as a hint, Lawrence wondered—that would become Lawrence's trademark, both in the field and, much to the annoyance or amusement of other British officers, off it. Feisal also gave Lawrence his own British Short Lee-Enfield rifle, the standard .303-caliber weapon of the British army. This one had a very special history; marked as having been issued to the Essex Regiment, it had been captured at Gallipoli by the Turks. Enver Pasha, leader of the ruling Turkish triumvirate, had it polished, reblued, and inlayed with a boastful but beautiful flowing Arabic inscription in gold on the receiver: "Part of our booty in the battles for the Dardanelles." He gave it to Sharif Hussein as a present, and also as a tactful reminder of Turkey's victory over the British. Hussein had passed it on to Feisal at the beginning of the revolt. Lawrence would carry it all through the war; he carved his own initials on the stock, and initially cut a notch in the stock above the magazine for each Turk he killed, a practice he gave up in self-disgust when he reached number four.*

In the two days he spent with Feisal before returning to Yenbo to help organize its defense, Lawrence had an opportunity to judge the strength and the weaknesses of Feisal's forces. He used the Egyptian gunners, who, unlike the Arab tribesmen, did not consider themselves above menial labor, to clear an emergency landing strip for the RFC aircraft, and sat in on all of Feisal's meetings with the disputatious tribal leaders, noting how Feisal gently led them to do what in any other army would be normal practice, such as posting a guard at night in exposed positions, or sending out patrols. It was an army without rules and without noncommissioned officers, in which each man had to have his say (often at length), and in which an enormous amount of time and patience had to be spent—wasted, in the eyes of most British officers—to accomplish anything.

It was also an army in which religion was ever-present, from the moment the imam climbed to the top of a little hill overlooking the camp before dawn and called the faithful for prayers to the last call for prayer at dusk—even though most of the men did not seem to Lawrence particularly religious. Feisal, for example, was casually observant, but not, it appeared, from any deep belief or interest; he simply felt obliged as a leader to set a good example. He was a chain-smoker, although tobacco was forbidden to Muslims; he had a certain amused contempt for the narrow-minded puritanism of his father's desert rival ibn Saud and his Wahhabi followers, and no enthusiasm at all for his father's efforts to

---

*Lawrence brought the rifle home with him after the war, and presented it to King George V. It is now displayed prominently in the arms collection of the Imperial War Museum in London.

reintroduce sharia law to Mecca in place of the secular Turkish legal code, which was based on France's Code Napoléon. Religion among the tribesmen was simply a given, something they all shared; few of them, in fact, had ever met anyone who was *not* a Muslim. Drawing from this experience, Lawrence would write the "Twenty-Seven Articles," as a guide for British officers working with the Arabs, a work so full of common sense and tolerance that it is still relevant today. What is extraordinary is how well Lawrence fitted into Feisal's entourage and camp life without any attempt at disguising who he was. He shared the routine, the food, the harsh living conditions, the obligatory long-drawn-out exchange of compliments so alien to a westerner, living among them without complaint or special treatment, and always careful to ensure that he was never seen "advising" Feisal or, worse yet, contradicting him.

For all of Feisal's superhuman calm and patience, it was clear to Lawrence that his position at Nakhl Mubarak was hazardous and exposed. It became even more critical when Feisal learned that a Turkish column had surprised his half brother Zeid and Zeid's 800 tribesmen while they were preparing their morning coffee. Zeid had of course not bothered to post any guards or send out any patrols while he and his force slept, and they were now in full retreat, having abandoned much of their baggage and equipment, including their coffeepots. From everywhere came reports that the Turks were concentrating rapidly on Feisal's position. Lawrence sent a messenger off to Yenbo asking the RFC to make a reconnaissance flight and determine where the Turks were and in what strength, and asked that an urgent message be telegraphed to "Ginger" Boyle for naval support. He then rode to Yenbo himself on "a magnificent bay camel" with an escort provided by Feisal. There, he found that the indefatigable and inventive Garland had already been preparing defensive positions, on the optimistic assumption that the Arabs would man them.

Lawrence himself does not seem to have made any such assumption. He had already reached the conclusion that while "man by man" the Arabs were good, "as a mass they are not formidable, since they have no corporate spirit or discipline, or mutual confidence." His report to Clayton recommended using them in the smallest possible units, and keeping them busy by making raids on Turkish outposts and the railway, rather than letting them "sit still"; sitting still made them "get nervous, and anxious to return home," a trait that Feisal himself shared. In short, Lawrence had already made up his mind that the Arabs needed to fight an altogether different kind of war—guerrilla warfare was, he thought, the best way to use them effectively. He was familiar with Colonel C. E. Callwell's classic *Small Wars*, the British army's bible on fighting guerrillas, in which Callwell, who had fought in the Boer War, wrote: "Guerrilla warfare is what the regular armies always have to dread, and when this is directed by a leader with a genius for war, an effective campaign becomes well-nigh impossible."

Lawrence believed the very qualities that made the tribesmen such poor material for conventional warfare could help them defeat the Turks: swift mobility, hit-and-run tactics, a gift for long-range sniping, and a tradition of mounted raids that took an enemy by surprise, after which the raiders vanished back into the desert with their plunder. Fighting as guerrillas in small numbers they could deliver an endless series of pinpricks rather than a smashing blow, and over time the pinpricks might prove fatal for the enemy. As for the "leader with a genius for war," there seems little doubt from Lawrence's reports that he already saw himself in that role.

The next morning Lawrence was disagreeably surprised to learn that it was not just Zeid who had been defeated. Feisal and his army had clashed with the Turks too, in exactly the kind of conventional battle that Lawrence believed the Arabs should avoid, and had been badly beaten. Zeid's sudden defection had exposed Feisal's untrained and poorly organized tribesmen to a determined Turkish attack. Feisal tried to get his men to stand and fight at Nakhl Mubarak, but they were overcome by Turkish artillery, as well as by the fact that their antiquated guns (Lawrence called these guns "old rubbish" left over from the Boer War) proved not to have the range of the Turkish artillery—nor had they been supplied with sights, range tables, or even reliable ammunition. As a result the men of the Juheina tribe, on Feisal's left, lost heart quickly and fled the battlefield. The Juheina would later claim that they had merely been tired and thirsty and had needed a coffee break, but in any case their flight led to the rapid collapse of the rest of Feisal's line and a disorderly rout as the entire army raced back toward Yenbo and the protection of the British naval guns.

For a western army this would have been a disgrace, and would have been followed by severe disciplinary measures and perhaps courts-martial for the senior officers; but when Lawrence reached Feisal's house in Yenbo, he found the emir and his commanders in a jolly mood, trading insults, and taunting Zeid in a good-natured way for the speed with which he and his men had run away from the battle. Zeid and his men were "quiet, but in no other way mortified by their shame," Lawrence remarked; nor did Feisal seem dismayed by the collapse of his army in the face of only three battalions of Turks—in numbers, less than half the fighting men Feisal had. This incident fully justified Colonel Callwell's firmly expressed opinion in *Small Wars*: "While all goes well, irregular forces hold together and obey their chiefs, but in the hour of trial the bonds which keep the mass intact are apt to snap, and then the whole dissolves and disappears."

Feisal's only concern was that the Juheina tribesmen on his left, who had fled from the battlefield when the fragile bonds that tied them to him snapped, might have gone over to the enemy. But when this turned out not to be the case—they were guilty of cowardice, but not betrayal—the Juheina were given a chance to make up for their ignominious flight by going forward to harass the Turks' line of communications with sniper fire, a logical decision, since this was their country and they knew the best places to shoot from.

Hoping that this might at least slow the Turks, Feisal and Lawrence went out to see how the town might be saved. Yenbo, fortunately, lent itself to defense—the town was built on a coral reef that rose some twenty feet above sea level, surrounded on two sides by water, and on the other two sides by wide, flat stretches of glistening sand and salt, with no drinkable water to be had on them. The Arabs' dislike of manual labor did not need to be confronted, since the ground was coral, and far too hard to dig in—instead Lawrence and Garland reinforced the existing walls, and placed the Egyptian gunners and naval machine gun parties at the crucial points. Boyle had managed to produce five naval ships and anchored them close inshore; they included the modern, powerful shallow-draft monitor *M 31*, whose six-inch guns would surely stop any Turkish attempt to rush the town across the salt flats. Navy signalers were placed in the minaret of the mosque, with Feisal's blessing on this intrusion by infidels, to direct the fire of the ships' guns.

At dusk, silence fell on the town as Feisal's men waited for the attack—by that time the Turks were only three miles away—but none came. After darkness had fallen, the ships turned on their searchlights and aimed them at the wide salt flats, illuminating the flats harshly in a careful crisscross pattern through the night. The commander of the Turkish advance hesitated at the sight of the brightly lit landscape, and lost heart at the prospect of advancing across brilliantly lit open ground as flat as a billiard table, toward an enemy holding the high ground. The night passed without a Turkish attack, or a gun's being fired.

Lawrence was sufficiently confident of the outcome—and exhausted—that he went aboard the *Suva* and fell asleep. He would later conclude that the Turks' failure to rush Yenbo that night "and stamp out Feisal's army once and for all" had cost them the war.

For the moment, however, the Turks still held Gaza on their right and Medina on their left, and threatened Mecca. The Arab army had been saved, but the Arab cause was in as precarious a situation as ever. Feisal—with the help of lavish supplies of British gold—had kept his army together, but only under the protection of British warships; what it needed was a strategy, and Lawrence was about to provide one.

Until now, Lawrence's role had been that of an observer and a liaison officer, but those limits were about to be changed rapidly. At home, the energetic David Lloyd George had replaced the exhausted Asquith as prime minister. Lloyd George was by instinct an "easterner": he deeply distrusted the idea that the war could be won only by breaking through the German lines on the western front whatever the cost in British and French lives, and his notoriously devious mind was attracted to the notion of knocking Germany's weakest ally out of the war and rearranging the Middle East. In London, Cairo, and Khartoum the decision was finally made that the Arabs simply could not be allowed to fail. In Mecca Sharif Hussein still vacillated, alternately calling Colonel Wilson in Jidda to request British troops and then changing his mind and refusing permission for them to land, while Colonel Brémond schemed to get his French North African troops into the Hejaz. With the sharifian forces more or less bottled up on the coast in Rabegh and Yenbo under the protection of the Royal Navy there seemed nothing much they could do to keep the tribes from deserting, one by one.

Lawrence was among those who saw that it was necessary to go on the offensive, rather than sit and defend coastal enclaves. As long ago as October 1916 Feisal had considered moving the Arab base of operations to Wejh, 180 miles north of Yenbo, but he had hesitated, reluctant to put too much distance between his army and Mecca. In addition, moving the Arab army out of one tribal area to another produced endless difficulties, and exposed it to attacks from the Turkish garrison in Medina. Lawrence dismissed such doubts; he was determined to launch the Arab army out into the desert and cut it free from its own bases on the Red Sea. He came up with a strategy, leading Liddell Hart to declare that "the military art was one in which [Lawrence] attained creativeness" and to compare Lawrence to Marlborough, Napoleon, Sherman, and Stonewall Jackson. Lawrence wanted Abdulla to take his army of 5,000 men deep into the desert fifty miles north of Medina, and base it there around the wells of the fertile Wadi Ais, from which position he could threaten the railway line to Medina and at the same time cut off caravans arriving from central Arabia. This would deflect the attention of the Turkish commander Fakhri Pasha from any attempt to take Rabegh or Mecca, and also screen from him Feisal's line of march as Feisal took his army north to Wejh. Instead of being spread out south of Medina but unable to take it, the Arabs would then be well to the north of Medina, able to cut off its supply line at any time. If they could take Aqaba as well, they would be free to move farther north across the empty desert toward Amman and Damascus, and the huge political prize that Syria represented.

Given Lawrence's ambitions for the Arabs—and his own carefully concealed desire for leadership and military glory—it is perhaps fitting, as Liddell Hart points out, that he and Feisal set out on the 200-mile flank march up the Red Sea coast exactly 121 years after an audacious young general named Napoleon Bonaparte, at the age of twenty-six, began the flank march along the Riviera, which would make him famous. Lawrence was only two years older than Bonaparte (but five steps inferior to him in rank); he took his own first step toward fame on January 2, when, to conceal Feisal's departure with 10,000 men into the desert from Yenbo, he personally led a raiding party of thirty-five tribesmen in the opposite direction, climbed over steep "knife-sharp" rocks in the dark and then down into the crevices of a precipice to attack an encampment of Turks at first light, shooting up their tents and taking two prisoners. This was a far cry from making maps or writing intelligence reports at a desk in Cairo, or even acting as a liaison officer to Feisal. It was the first raid that Lawrence personally commanded, and marks his sudden emergence not only as a strategist but as a guerrilla leader whom the Arabs would respect and follow.

The next day he rode north with Feisal and the bodyguards; he was already considered one of Feisal's own household, with a place close enough to Feisal to take several snapshots of him leading the bodyguard, followed by a camel rider bearing his standards, wrapped around long poles topped with a gilded orb and spear point—iconic photographs of hundreds of armed camel riders advancing in line across the rock-strewn, featureless desert, the vanguard of an army that, as Lawrence had predicted, grew while it moved north. For it was above all action that legitimized the Arab Revolt—the sense of being part of a great historical event was a vital factor in persuading Arabs to join, and this required stagecraft, and a gift for propaganda as well as gold and weapons. Lawrence's photographs* are like those of a skilled director; they have the purposeful look of the films of early Soviet directors such as Eisenstein and Pudovkin, a sense of vast numbers irresistibly on the move, which prompted one tribal leader to remark to Lawrence, "We are no longer Arabs, but a people."

Feisal's dignity and his gift for showmanship were powerful factors in securing the adherence of the tribes—almost as important as the British gold he paid out to them. At the beginning of the march he and his bodyguard, now numbering more than 1,000 dashing, colorful tribesmen mounted on splendid camels, rode in silence through the massed contingents of his army, which formed up to provide a broad alley lined by Arabs on foot, each beside his camel. To each contingent, as he passed it, Feisal gave a grave greeting, bowing his head and murmuring in his "rich, melodic voice," *"Salaam aleikum,"* "Peace upon you"; then, when he had passed through the whole army, the men mounted to the sound of drummers, and burst into songs in praise of Feisal and his family.

Once the column was on its way—"It looked like a river of camels," Lawrence wrote later, "for we filled up the Wadi to the tops of its banks, and poured along in a quarter of a mile long stream"—he rode back to Yenbo to supervise the loading of the stores there on board one of the British ships (these stores included 8,000 rifles, 3 million rounds of small arms ammunition, two tons of high explosive, and many tons of foodstuff), for there was a real danger that the Turks might take the opportunity to seize the now almost undefended port. Feisal's brother Ali, prodded into action by his father, Sharif Hussein, and by Colonel Wilson, made a feint attack on Medina, while Abdulla, also set in motion by numerous threats and entreaties, successfully surprised and defeated a Turkish battalion camped south of Medina, then attacked and captured

---

*Lawrence was the first military hero to carry a camera with him into battle, as well as a dagger, a pistol, and a rifle. A gifted and enthusiastic amateur photographer, he also played a role in the development of aerial photography, and most of the good (and genuine) photographs of the Arab Revolt are by him.

a Turkish supply column. This happy outcome had unfortunate results, however, since the Turks were carrying a large quantity of gold—like the British, the Turks understood that tribal loyalty required payment in advance—and once the tribesmen had looted it, many of them rode straight for home with as much of it as they could carry. Still, Abdulla's successful march brought him new followers to replace the old, and by January 19 he had reached the wells at Wadi Ais, having dominated Fakhri Pasha's attention for nearly three crucial weeks.

March by march, Feisal led his army northward, staying close to the sea, and using the hills and mountains to screen his movement from the Turks for as long as possible, so that they would suppose he was still within easy reach of Yenbo, and able to fall back and defend it. In the meantime, Lawrence proceeded up the coast by sea to Um Lejj, a small port halfway between Yenbo and Wejh, and arrived on January 15 to meet Feisal. He was joined the next day by Major Charles Vickery; this was the first appearance of the "official" British military mission to Emir Feisal and the Arab army. Vickery was a professional soldier, a gunner, who had served many years in the Sudan, and spoke Arabic fluently. He was one of the two staff officers of Colonel Stewart Newcombe, who had been designated to command British military support, and one of the first of those British regular officers who would be, to use a slightly later term, upstaged by T. E. Lawrence in Arabia.

Newcombe himself was an old friend of Lawrence's—he had been in command when Lawrence, then a scholar-archaeologist, with a companion, had been assigned by Kitchener before the war to complete a map-making survey of the Sinai—a military mission, since it involved tracing the routes by which the Turkish army might attack the Suez Canal. This daring desert adventure was concealed under the auspices of the Palestine Exploration Fund, dedicated to retracing the exact route of Moses and the Jews. Lawrence had actually reached Aqaba and swum in the shark-infested gulf to an island offshore where he had been forbidden to go—infuriating the Turkish governor, who assumed, not unreasonably, that what was going on was espionage, not scholarship.

Newcombe, though he was a professional soldier to the core, knew Lawrence well, and liked him. Vickery, almost instantly, did not; he and Lawrence got off on the wrong foot from the very beginning. He was offended by Lawrence's unmilitary ways and, more important, by Lawrence's easy assumption that Feisal and Feisal's Arab army would reach Damascus, when, so far as Vickery could see, they were hard pressed to reach Wejh on time and in good order. Matters were not helped when Vickery stubbornly insisted on wearing his Arab head cloth over his pith helmet, prompting one of the Arabs to exclaim, "*Mashallah*, the head of an ox!" This set all the Arabs laughing, and Lawrence joined in. Vickery was both offended and humiliated, and did not forgive Lawrence. Good as Vickery's Arabic was, he was of the pukka sahib type, believing strongly that Englishmen should stick together and maintain their distance and their dignity when dealing with "natives." This was just the kind of attitude Lawrence was determined to eliminate in dealing with the Arabs.

Lawrence, Vickery, and Boyle journeyed inland a few miles to Owais, where Feisal and his army were encamped. They were greeted by Feisal with a lavish meal, which Boyle described as "a greasy stew" poured over rice and topped with ladles of boiling mutton fat, into which each guest reached with the fingers of his right hand to select chunks of innards and diced fat. Both Vickery and Boyle had been shocked and disgusted by "the absence of any sanitary precautions around the camp," and by the sight and smell everywhere of both human and camel feces drying in the blazing sun, which did nothing to improve their appetite. Vickery—one can sympathize with him—took a long swig from a large pocket flask full of whiskey, then offered it around; Lawrence and Boyle thought this was disrespectful to their Muslim host, though Feisal seems to have been more amused than not.

Plans were made for taking Wejh and its garrison. Boyle would take 500 of Feisal's Arabs aboard one of his ships and land them on the north side of the town, to prevent the Turks from escaping, while Feisal's army would simultaneously attack the south side of the town. Fortunately for Lawrence, Vickery wisely chose to proceed to Wejh by ship.

On January 18, Feisal's army was on the move again; Feisal was gambling that Wejh would fall, for there were few reliable wells or springs along the way, nor was there any certainty that the local tribes would rally to him. It was like marching into the unknown with 10,000 men, half of them mounted, the other half on foot. Shortly after midday, Newcombe himself appeared, arriving by horse from Um Lejj. In theory, his arrival should have ended Lawrence's adventure. Newcombe was not only Lawrence's commanding officer, but also Feisal's senior British adviser—unlike Vickery, though, he seems to have recognized at once that replacing Lawrence would be a mistake. "What do you want me to do?" was his first question to Lawrence, to which he added that "seniority didn't matter a damn." This was exactly what Lawrence wanted to hear. Vickery had made Lawrence acutely aware of both his junior rank and his anomalous position, leading Lawrence to believe that he would have to return to his desk job in Cairo as soon as Newcombe's British mission was firmly in place.

Newcombe was soon aware that Feisal's army moved at a ponderous pace, with no sense of urgency. Endless time was spent while Feisal met with local tribal leaders and tried to persuade them to join him, each meeting dragging on with time-wasting compliments, ceremonious politeness, and the obligatory cups of coffee and mint tea. Then there were all the difficulties of moving a large army across rough terrain with little or no water, compounded by the Arabs' lack of time sense, and the difficulty of sending and acknowledging orders in an army that was largely illiterate. The men were already two days behind schedule by the time they reached Wadi Hamdh, where they were joined by the energetic young Sharif Nasir of Medina and his men, and where many of the local Billi tribes "came to swell the advancing host, and to consume more time in talk." Newcombe rode ahead impatiently to see if he could reach the fleet about twenty miles south of Wejh, where the navy was supposed to unload goatskins full of water, but by the time he got there Boyle had lost patience and had already landed his 500 Arabs as well. Their lack of any habits of sanitation and their unfamiliarity with toilets and urinals had made them unwelcome passengers. Boyle then quickly engaged the Turks at Wejh with the guns of his six ships.

When the army approached Wejh on January 24, Lawrence was surprised to hear distant firing. This news galvanized the Arabs, who had worried that they might arrive too late to participate in looting the town. They plunged ahead to find only a few Turks still resisting. Vickery had commanded the assault, and with his 500 Arabs and the big guns of the navy vessels had successfully taken the town. This led to further bad blood between himself and Lawrence. Vickery was outraged by the slowness of Feisal's army and the fact that it arrived too late to join in the assault; Lawrence was upset that twenty of Vickery's Arabs had been killed. The fact that Vickery dismissed these as light losses and expressed his satisfaction with the result angered Lawrence, who felt that each Arab life was precious, and that in any case the whole fight had been unnecessary, since the Turkish garrison could have been surrounded and would have surrendered in two days without any loss of life on either side. In the meantime, the town had been looted by the Arabs (its inhabitants were mostly Egyptian and pro-Turk) and smashed to bits by the British naval bombardment. As a result, much rebuilding would have to be done before it could be used as a base.

Lawrence's concern about the loss of twenty Arabs may seem odd during a war in which British war dead would exceed 750,000, but he felt strongly that "Our men were not materials, like soldiers, but friends of ours, trusting in our leadership." Vickery had used the tribesmen for a formal assault, which Lawrence criticized as "silly," since the Arabs were not trained for that, nor had it been necessary.

However it was won, the taking of Wejh transformed the Arab Revolt overnight. Although it was 150 miles from the railway line, the presence of a secure base and Feisal's army so far north of Medina made the Turks aware of how fragile the link was between Medina and Maan. Far from being a dagger aimed at Mecca, Fakhri Pasha's force at Medina now looked increasingly like marooned fugitives, separated from the main body of the Turkish army. To keep them supplied, special detachments had to be formed to guard the railway line, eventually rising to more than 12,000 men spread out for hundreds of miles along the line, the equivalent of a full division. Together with Fakhri Pasha's troops at Medina, they made up three divisions of infantry that would be missing from the Turkish lines from Gaza to Beersheba when the British attacked there again.

Lawrence paid a flying visit to Cairo, where his stock was now higher, in pursuit of mountain guns, machine guns, and instructors, all of which Feisal would need if he was to make any real headway against the Turks. Although machine guns, instructors, and even mortars and armored cars were provided rapidly, the guns presented problems. The British, it turned out, had no modern artillery that could be disassembled and carried by camels; the French were well supplied with just such weapons, but Brémond was determined to demand a price for them—they must be handled and served by his French North African troops (whose officers were French), and protected by a British brigade, rather than by the Arabs. Since the British, on Lawrence's advice, were unwilling to send a brigade, and Feisal was unwilling to accept French officers, the guns sat at Suez, unused.

Although the date was January 1917, it was apparent to the farsighted—and nobody was more farsighted and realistic than Lawrence—that putting artillery of any kind in the hands of the Arabs might make it very much harder to impose the terms of a settlement for the Middle East on them after the war. Nobody wanted to talk about the Sykes-Picot agreement, but the knowledge of its terms was already beginning to determine the Allies' policy, even though the bear's hide was being shared out before the bear had been killed. Brémond's attempts to persuade Lawrence, and later Feisal, that British forces (with the help of the French) should take Aqaba made it obvious that the French hoped to reach Damascus and stake their claim to Syria before Feisal did. Brémond was already reporting back to Paris on Lawrence's anti-French sentiments as if he were an enemy rather than an ally, although he would recommend Lawrence twice for a Croix de Guerre and to be made a *chevalier* of the Légion d'Honneur. Lawrence refused to acknowledge both honors or wear the decorations.

The capture of Wejh changed the nature of the Arab struggle. It brought Feisal new Bedouin allies from the vast desert area to the north of Medina, including what is now Jordan, and stretching into Syria and as far to the west as Lebanon and Palestine on the Mediterranean coast. The possibility of transforming a localized revolt in the Hejaz into a broader pan-Arab revolt that might be supported by Arabs in cities like Damascus, Aleppo, Beirut, and Jerusalem made Feisal, quite suddenly, a more important figure than his brothers, who remained behind with the thankless task of either besieging Medina or assaulting it, neither of which they ever succeeded in doing. It also increased Lawrence's importance, since he was the Englishman who was closest to Feisal, and the only one who might reasonably claim to know what was on Feisal's mind.

Perhaps Feisal's two most important acquisitions after the taking of Wejh were in the persons of Jaafar Pasha and Auda Abu Tayi. Jaafar, an Arab from Baghdad, was a senior career officer in the Turkish army, a well-trained professional soldier who had fought the British with distinction in Libya, had been captured, had escaped, was recaptured, and was finally converted to the Arab cause. Jaafar would take command of the "regular" troops, a small and somewhat disheveled group of Arab prisoners of war from the Turkish army—at this point they numbered around 600—who were overshadowed by the more glamorous (and numerous) Bedouin. Jaafar conveyed to British officers a respectable and reliable military presence, despite the small size of his "army" and its tattered uniforms.

The second adherent was very different indeed. Auda Abu Tayi was a tribal leader of the Howeitat, "a tall, strong figure with a haggard face, passionate and tragic," a warrior and bandit chieftain of fearsome reputation, "who had married twenty-eight times, and had been wounded thirteen times," and who had killed with his own hands in battle seventy-five men, all Arabs, for he did not dignify the Turks he had slain by bothering to count them. Most of Auda's life had been spent in raids and in blood feuds, the principal feud being against a cousin, during the course of which he had seen his own favorite son and half his own tribe killed.

Auda was a bigger-than-life figure out of a desert saga from some other age: lean, hawk-nosed, with sharply pointed whiskers and beard, and flashing dark eyes that could change instantly from radiating good humor to furious menace. He was a hero who, had he not been a Bedouin and a Muslim, might have seemed at home beside such legendary figures as Ajax and Achilles, cunning, ruthless, violent, physically strong, a born leader and utterly without fear. He was known as a savage fighter and feared throughout northern Arabia, Syria, and Lebanon. The Turks had put a price on his head (among the Turks he had murdered was a tax collector) many times, without result. It was not just admiration for Auda that kept him safe—anybody who gave him up to the Turks would have to live in fear of revenge from Auda's extended family, his tribe, and their allies. Even the Turks found it more expedient to bribe him than to attempt to hunt him down.

Close as was the relationship between Lawrence and Feisal, Lawrence's intense admiration for Auda is a constant theme in *Seven Pillars of Wisdom*, not surprisingly, since they had many traits in common: physical courage, hardiness, cool judgment under fire, indifference to danger, a flamboyant gift for the theatrical side of warfare, and a magnetic attraction that drew hero-worshippers to them and made them natural leaders. Auda was the more bloodthirsty of the two; he reveled in killing his enemies, and had been known in his younger days to cut out the heart of someone he had killed and take a bite out of it while it was still beating—though, as James Barr points out in *Setting the Desert on Fire*, in that respect Auda was merely an old-fashioned traditionalist, since this had been, in the good old days, an accepted custom in desert blood feuds.

Lawrence's description of Feisal's camp at Wejh during February and early March 1917 makes it clear that the majority of his men were doing nothing except lounge around, while Feisal sought to resolve blood feuds and to win the loyalty (or at least the neutrality) of the sheikhs of the tribes and clans to the north. This involved endless negotiations and the exchange of "presents," which in practice meant payment in gold sovereigns, and promises of more to come. The British supplied the gold, and also, to the great amusement of the Arabs, two armored cars, and a variety of other vehicles, as well as drivers from the Army Service Corps, and a naval wireless station powered by a generator. The encampment was spread out and enormous, since each tribe and clan wanted its tents to be as far away from the others as possible, and included at its center a tented bazaar, or marketplace. Lawrence made a point of walking everywhere barefoot, so as to toughen the soles of his feet. He lived in comparative opulence in Feisal's camp, on a raised "coral shelf" about a mile from the sea, where Feisal maintained "living tents, reception tents, staff tents, guest tents," and the tents of the numerous servants. It was not only with gold and honeyed words that Feisal sought to impress the tribal leaders, but also with his impressive surroundings, as befitted a prince and a son of the sharif of Mecca. The number and size of his tents, the layers of priceless carpets, and the endless banquets—these were all necessary accompaniments if he was to move his army north toward Damascus.

For the moment, neither Jaafar's "regulars" nor Auda's tribesmen had much to do. Such action as was taking place consisted largely of raids inland to damage the railway line to Medina, and these were carried out by Newcombe, Garland, and Lawrence, accompanied by small numbers of tribesmen to engage the Turks if they appeared. The Turks were determined to repair the railway line whenever it was broken—and since the line had originally been intended to run all the way to Mecca, they had no shortage of rails stored in Medina with which to repair it.

Medina continued to be the focus of everybody's attention. The Turks were determined to hold on to it; the army of Abdulla was ensconced to the north of the city in Wadi Ais; Feisal still harbored thoughts of advancing from Wejh to attack it in collaboration with Abdulla; Colonel Brémond was being urged on by cables from Paris to persuade the Arabs to attack Medina at once. Early in March, the partial interception of a message from Jemal Pasha to Fakhri Pasha, which seemed to call for the evacuation of Medina and the transfer of the troops there to Gaza and Beersheba, set off a panic. General Murray, in Cairo, had been informed it was Prime Minister David Lloyd George's personal wish that he should attack Gaza again, and he was preparing to do so with some reluctance, since he was also warned at the same time not to expect any additional troops, and even that he might have to send more of his units to France. The addition of two or three more Turkish divisions on the Gaza-Beersheba line would almost certainly prevent an attack, so it became imperative that either Medina should be taken, or the railway should be cut off once and for all so no Turkish troops could be transferred north.

Since his nominal superior Colonel Newcombe was away dynamiting railway tracks, Lawrence decided to ride from Wejh to Wadi Ais to inform Abdulla of what was happening—and, perhaps more important, what was expected of him, since, in Lawrence's words, "he had done nothing against the Turks for the past two months." Lawrence was ill with dysentery, "feeling very unfit for a long march," but despite this he set off, with Feisal's approval and a handpicked escort of tribesmen, for Wadi Ais, a distance of about 100 miles as the crow flies, but more on the ground. His traveling party might have made him feel uneasy had he not been too sick to think about it, since it was ill-assorted, consisting of men from different tribes. He was unable to ride more than four or five hours at a stretch; the pools of water and the few wells on the way had turned salty, a cause for some concern; boils on his back were giving him considerable pain when he rode; and the landscape, which was rugged, hilly, and flinty, made it necessary from time to time to dismount and walk the camels up zigzagging slippery trails of worn stone. In the distance, huge and fantastic rock formations loomed. Finally, the landscape changed: there was grass for the camels in a narrow valley, and the men camped for the night under the lee of a "steep broken granite" cliff. Lawrence was suffering from a headache, a high fever, occasional fainting fits, and attacks of dysentery that left him light-headed and exhausted.

He was woken by a shot, but thought nothing of it at first, since there was game in the valley; then one of the party roused him and led him to a hollow in the cliff, where the body of one of the Ageyl camel men lay. The man had been shot in the head, at close range. After some initial confusion and discussion of the ethics of blood feuds, it was agreed that he had been shot by another of the party, Hamed the Moor, following a brief quarrel between them. Lawrence crawled back to where he had been lying, beside the baggage, "feeling that this need not have happened this day of all days when I was in pain." A noise made him open his eyes, and he saw Hamed, who had put his rifle down to pick up his saddlebags, no doubt preparing to run away. Lawrence drew his pistol, and Hamed confessed to the murder. At this point the others arrived, and the Ageyl's fellow tribesmen demanded, as was their right, blood for blood. Lawrence, whose head was pounding, gave some thought to this. There were many Moors in the army, descendants of Moroccans who had fled to the Hejaz when the French took over their country, and if the remaining two Ageyl shot Hamed there would inevitably be a blood feud between the Moors and the Ageyl. Lawrence decided that as a stranger, a non-Muslim, and a man without a family, he could execute the Moor without creating a blood feud that might spread through the army. His traveling companions, after some discussion, agreed.

He marched Hamed at gunpoint into a narrow crevice in the cliff, "and gave him a few moments' delay, which he spent crying on the ground," then "made him rise and shot him through the chest." Hamed fell to the ground, but was still alive and "shrieking," as blood spurted from his wound, so Lawrence shot him again. By that time, Lawrence's hand was shaking so badly that the bullet struck the dying man only in the wrist. Lawrence regained control of himself, moved closer, put the muzzle of his pistol to Hamed's neck, under the jaw, and pulled the trigger.

That did it. The remaining Ageyl, for whose benefit Lawrence had carried out the execution, buried Hamed's body, and after a sleepless night Lawrence was so ill that they had to lift him up into his saddle at daybreak.

Lawrence devotes only four paragraphs to Hamed's execution in *Seven Pillars of Wisdom*, and some of his biographers give the incident less space or even leave it out altogether; but despite the brevity, the obvious restraint, and the total lack of self-pity, his account clearly represents a turning point in the life of the former Oxford archaeologist and aesthete turned mapmaker and intelligence officer. He does not mention it again, perhaps because—as with so many things that happen in war—leaving it behind and moving on seemed more sensible. The prose in which Lawrence describes the experience, despite a tendency toward a certain florid and archaic quality when he is trying too hard to create the literary masterpiece that he hoped would take its place beside such great books as *Moby-Dick, Thus Spoke Zarathustra,* and *The Brothers Karamazov,* is in this instance notably spare and lean. Indeed it is one of the places in *Seven Pillars of Wisdom* where Lawrence succeeds in striking exactly the tone that Ernest Hemingway spent his life perfecting: a shocking event is described in the bare minimum of words, and with no attempt to convey Lawrence's feelings at killing another human being at close range. It is unlikely that he had none, but whatever they may have been, he does not share them with the reader. In the words of W. B. Yeats, he "cast a cold eye on life, on death," and passed by.

Perhaps his own illness, and the greater importance in the grand scheme of things of reaching Emir Abdulla as soon as possible with the message about Medina (which, ironically, turned out to be false), helped Lawrence to put the incident out of his mind. But whatever the case, Hamed's death marks the point at which Lawrence gave up the moral comfort of being a liaison officer, observing events from a distance, and transformed himself into a man of action, leading other men, sometimes to their death; killing Turks when he had to kill them; exposing himself to danger with a lack of fear, or even of caution, that astonished both the Bedouin and the British; and accepting unthinkable pain without complaint.

Shock finally set in, for Lawrence's description of the next two days of his journey to Wadi Ais has a quality of desert hallucination. His meticulous description of the landscape conveys in its wealth of details a cumulative horror, which reaches a peak when during a rest he throws a rock at one of the party's camels in disgust at its self-satisfied mastication. At one point Lawrence's party stumbles across a Bedouin encampment and instead of letting him sleep outside, his host—"with the reckless equality" and hospitality "of desert men"—insists that Lawrence share his tent, so that Lawrence leaves in the morning with his "clothes stinging-full of fiery points feeding on us," because of the lice and fleas. On the third day, crossing a "broken river of lava," one of his camels breaks a leg in a pothole—the bones strewn around are mute testimony to the frequency with which this occurs—and Lawrence feels so sick that he fears some well-meaning tribesman will try to cure him, for the only method the Bedouin know is to burn a hole or holes in the patient's body in a spot which is assumed to be opposite the site of the illness, a treatment often more painful than the disease, or to have a boy urinate into the wound.

At last he found Abdulla, in the process of setting up a new camp in a pleasant grove of acacia trees—as was always the case with Bedouin camps, the men and animals had fouled the old one by paying no attention at all to sanitary arrangements. Lawrence handed over the letters he had been carrying from Feisal, and explained the problem of Medina to Abdulla in his luxurious tent, although Abdulla did not seem much disturbed by or interested in it. Then, Lawrence collapsed in the adjacent tent that was pitched for him.

Lawrence spent about ten days in his tent "suffering a bodily weakness that made my animal self crawl away and hide till the shame was passed." This surely refers to dysentery, a common enough illness among Europeans living with the Bedouin and unaccustomed to tainted water and unhygienic surroundings. Lawrence's symptoms may also have been intensified by some degree of what we would now call post-traumatic stress disorder, brought about by the execution of Hamed. In any event, for ten days he rested and tried to recuperate in his stifling tent, drowsing, plagued by flies, and thinking about military strategy. Eventually, he came to the conclusion that any attempt to take Medina would be a mistake. As Lawrence himself put it, he "woke out of a hot sleep, running with sweat and pricking with flies, and wondered what on earth was the good of Medina to us?" In *Colonel Lawrence*, Liddell Hart bases his claim for Lawrence as a military genius on these sickbed musings in Abdulla's camp. Indeed the conclusions that Lawrence reached about war, as he set them out in *Seven*

Pillars of Wisdom five years later, define very well the kinds of warfare that big western armies found it so hard to win against through much of the twentieth century, and the first decade of the twenty-first. First of all, Lawrence reached the conclusion that in "irregular warfare" it made no sense to hold or to seize a specific point. The goal was to strike the enemy where he least expected to be attacked, then vanish back into the desert, and to avoid, so far as possible, big battles in which the enemy could put to use his superior firepower and military discipline.

The object, he decided, should be to keep the Turks bottled up in Medina, where they could do no harm, and therefore to restrict, not cut, the railway that was their only line of communication with the rest of the Turkish

TURKEY'S LIFELINE

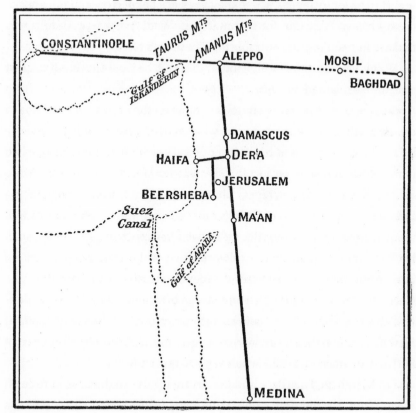

army. Half-starved and reduced to eating their own transport animals, which were useless to them without forage, the Turks would no longer present a serious danger to Mecca, and could be reduced to exhaustion and impotence by frequent attacks on the railway, which they would constantly have to repair and defend—they would, in fact, be "all flanks and no front." Once Lawrence rose from his sickbed, he had a simple strategy for beating the Turks, not by fighting battles to take the fortresses and towns they held, but by destroying what they could neither easily replace nor defend: locomotives, railway cars, telegraph wires, bridges, and culverts. The Turks would have to spread themselves thin to defend these targets, and it would then be easier to attack and kill small Turkish parties. In short, a war of mobility was needed, a war in which the Arabs would use to the full their possession of camels and the protection of the desert in order to appear where they were least expected, and not anchor themselves in Wejh—or for that matter in Wadi Ais, where Abdulla was making himself too comfortable for Lawrence's taste.

When Lawrence was well enough to stand, he went to Abdulla's great tent and explained his plans, without eliciting any enthusiasm from Abdulla, who was no more anxious to blow up the railway than he was to attack Medina. A cultivated man who enjoyed poetry and hunting, he had come to Wadi Ais at his brother Feisal's request, but having reached it and made himself comfortable, he was not about to be prodded into action, least of all by Lawrence, whom he disliked. However, recognizing in Lawrence a reflection of Feisal's more spirited view of the war (as well as an altogether superior will), he allowed Lawrence to gather a group of his tribesmen, a quantity of explosives, two of the antiquated mountain guns Abdulla had received from General Wingate in Khartoum, and a German Maxim machine gun on a sledge drawn by a long-suffering donkey, and to go out to put his ideas into practice. Abdulla's cousin Sharif Shakir, an altogether more warlike figure, promised to collect a force of 800 fighting men, to attack whatever Lawrence liked.

On March 26, Lawrence and his advance party of thirty men rode off down Wadi Ais and undertook a three-day march across the desert to a

600-foot hill of sand that overlooked the railway station at Aba el Naam. It consisted of two buildings and a water tank, and like most of the Turkish stations, was as stoutly built of stone as a fortress, and garrisoned by nearly 400 troops; but also, like most of them, it had the disadvantage of being surrounded by higher ground, since any railway must be laid when possible on flat ground, and take advantage of valleys. Lawrence was therefore able to approach very close to the station without being seen. Shakir turned up as night fell, but with only 300 men instead of the 800 he had promised; as Lawrence soon discovered, any Arab promises of numbers were best taken with a grain of salt. Still, he was determined to go ahead, and rode on in the dark to the south of the station, where, for the first time in the war, he "fingered the rails . . . thrillingly," and planted "twenty pounds of blasting gelatine" under the track, with one of Garland's improvised trigger fuses, made from the lockwork of an old British army single-shot Martini rifle, with the trigger exposed so that pressure would release it. He put his two guns in position, and placed the Maxim to kill the locomotive's crew, if they survived the explosion. At daybreak, he started shelling the station, doing considerable damage, especially to the all-important water tank. The crew of the locomotive uncoupled it from the train and began to back it southward toward safety until it ran over the mine and vanished in a cloud of sand and smoke. Although Lawrence's Maxim gunners had apparently lost interest or patience and abandoned their post, in this first effort thirty Turkish prisoners were taken, and about seventy Turks were killed or wounded; nine more were killed when they tried to surrender and the Arabs shot them anyway. The station and the train caught fire, the locomotive was seriously damaged, and a part of the track was destroyed. For three days all traffic to and from Medina was stopped. Only one of Lawrence's Bedouin was slightly hurt, so the attack demonstrated his theory about inflicting the maximum damage with the minimum of losses.

Lawrence's detractors, then and now, still argue that this was merely a "pinprick," in "a sideshow of a sideshow" compared with the western front, but it in fact was a modest first effort at a new kind of warfare—in which an organized, modern, occupying army was forced to deal with small but lethal attacks by an enemy who appeared suddenly out of nowhere, struck hard, and vanished again; in which the ambush, the roadside or railway "improvised explosive device," the grenade thrown onto a busy café terrace, the destruction of rolling stock, even the "suicide bomber," would take the place of battle; and in which it was almost impossible to distinguish enemy combatants from the surrounding civilian population.

Lawrence rode back to Abdulla's camp, where a huge celebration took place, and set off the next morning with about forty tribesmen and a machine gun platoon to mine the tracks again. He seems to have regained his health and equilibrium. Mechanical devices and gadgets, whether in the form of bombs, fuses, cameras, or motorcycles, always seemed to cheer Lawrence up, even at the worst of times, and his description of the landscape is, as always, detailed and fascinating. He had the gifts of a great nature writer and presents with a kind of detached objectivity the hardships of desert travel: a fierce sandstorm, which sends pebbles and whole small trees flying at his party like projectiles, followed by heavy rain and a sudden drop in the temperature that leaves him and his party shivering. The wind is so strong that Lawrence's robes get in his way as he climbs a rocky crag, so he strips and makes his way naked up the sharp, slippery rocks—one of the servants falls headfirst to his death—and finally arrives at kilometer 1,121 (measured from Damascus) of the railway at ten at night, close to a small station with a Turkish garrison.

Lawrence was eager to experiment with a more complicated mine; its trigger would fire two separate charges at the same time, placed about ninety feet apart. It took him four hours to lay the mine; then he crawled back to "a safe distance" to wait for dawn. "The cold was intense," he wrote later, "and our teeth chattered, and we trembled and hissed involuntarily, while our hands drew in like claws." Only the day before, the heat had been so oppressive that Lawrence had been unable to walk barefoot, to the amusement of the tribesmen "whose thick soles were proof even against slow fire." It is worth noting that the desert provides every kind of torment—heat, cold, rain, flash floods, windstorms, biting insects, and sandstorms, sometimes all on the same day.

At dawn a trolley with four men and a sergeant passes over the mine, but luckily it is too light to set off the explosive—Lawrence doesn't want to waste his explosives and firing mechanism on so small a target. Later a patrol of Turkish soldiers on foot examines the area around the mine—it has been impossible to hide the tracks because the rain has turned the sand to mud—but finds nothing; then, a heavy train, fully loaded with civilians, many of them women and children, being evacuated from Medina runs over the mine but fails to explode it, infuriating the "artist" in Lawrence—he has already begun to think of demolition as a kind of art form—but relieving "the commander" and, more important, the human being, who has no wish to kill women and children. By now the Turkish garrison is aware of the presence of Lawrence and the others, and opens fire from a distance; Lawrence and his men hide until night-fall. Then he makes his way back to kilometer 1,121 and slowly, carefully, with infinite caution feels up and down the line in the dark for the buried hair trigger, finds it, and raises it one-sixteenth of an inch higher. After-ward, to confuse the Turks, Lawrence and his men blow up a small rail-way bridge, cut about 200 rails, and destroy the telegraph and telephone lines, then head for home, having already sent on ahead of them the machine gunners and their donkey. The next morning, they hear a great explosion, and learn from a scout left behind that a locomotive with trucks of spare rails and a gang of laborers set off the mine in front of it and behind it, effectively blocking the track for days.

Quite apart from his boyish excitement at blowing things up—one of Lawrence's endearing qualities is a kind of innocent delight in pyrotech-nics, and throughout his life he retained some of the more attractive characteristics of an adolescent—Lawrence had every reason to be pleased. He had blocked the line to Medina for days, and rendered Turk-ish troops all the way up and down the line nervous and on full alert, at the cost of a little blasting gelatine and the accidental death of one ser-vant with a fear of heights.

Lawrence could easily imagine the effect of doing this on a grand scale, and he was eager to get away from Abdulla, whose generosity did not compensate in Lawrence's eyes for his lack of fighting spirit.

Each of them misjudged the other. When Abdulla fought, he fought well—he had led the force that captured Taif, the summer resort of Mecca, in the autumn of 1916 and took more than 4,000 Turkish prisoners, the only real victory of the Arab forces to date—and in some ways he was a better leader than Feisal, more flexible, and with a superficial layer of charm, worldly wisdom, and good humor that would keep him on his throne in Amman for over thirty years once Lawrence had helped him secure it. As for Lawrence, Abdulla's distrust of him as a subversive British agent was unfounded—in fact, Lawrence wanted more for the Hashemite family than they were able to manage, and would use his status as a hero again and again in their support. No doubt Abdulla and his brothers resented the way Lawrence took the limelight—as he still does take it—in the world's view of the Arab Revolt, but in the end Abdulla and Feisal would never have had their thrones without his help, and their victory was in part his invention.

Lawrence rode back to Wejh, changed his travel-stained clothing, and went immediately to pay his respects to Feisal, happy, one senses, to be back in a more martial atmosphere. His arrival coincided with that of Auda Abu Tayi and Auda's eleven-year-old son Mohammed—Auda's entrance into Feisal's tent is in fact one of the best set pieces of *Seven Pillars of Wisdom*: "I was about to take my leave when Suleiman the guest-master hurried in and whispered to Feisal, who turned to me with shining eyes, trying to be calm, and said 'Auda is here.' I shouted, 'Auda Abu Tayi,' and at that moment the tent-flap was drawn back and a deep voice boomed salutations to our lord, the Commander of the Faithful: and there entered a tall strong figure with a haggard face, passionate and tragic. . . . Feisal had sprung to his feet. Auda caught his hand and kissed it warmly, and they drew aside a pace or two, and looked at each other: a splendid pair, as unlike as possible, but typical of much that was best in Arabia, Feisal the prophet, and Auda the warrior, each looking his part to perfection."

Lawrence saw in Auda the means of taking Aqaba, and moving the Arab Revolt north into Syria—for Auda was the preeminent desert warrior of his time, who could never be satisfied just with blowing up sections of railway track: his mind was set on a fast-moving war of sudden raids; he "saw life as a saga," in which he was determined to be at the center. A visit to the English part of the camp, laid out in neat lines near the beach, was enough to warn Lawrence that the British were still determined to push the Arabs into attacking Medina, an objective that he had already concluded was probably impossible, and in any case pointless. Confident that the railway destruction could be continued in his absence, he returned to Feisal's encampment and began to talk with Auda about the best way to move north, raise the Howeitat and some of the smaller tribes, and attack Aqaba from the direction the Turks would least expect. Auda, who had a natural sense of strategy, was enthusiastic; and Feisal, better than anyone else, understood the enormous importance of an unexpected Arab victory won without the help of the British—or even without their knowledge, for Lawrence had already made up his mind to take Aqaba as a kind "private venture," drawing on Feisal for men, camels, and money.

Lawrence's time at Wejh was marked by many warning signs that his own plans and those of his superiors were beginning to diverge sharply. He was in Wejh for just over three weeks, from April 14, 1917, to May 9, a period during which it was becomingly increasingly clear to Feisal that the French intended to claim Lebanon and Syria for themselves after the war, and that it suited them and to a lesser degree the British to direct the Arab armies toward taking Medina, rather than moving north into Syria and Palestine. During this period Sir Mark Sykes paid two short visits to Wejh. The first visit was to meet with Feisal while Lawrence was away; he had tried to present the content of the Sykes-Picot agreement to Feisal in the vaguest and most benevolent terms, without revealing that the British, French, and Russians had already agreed on a map that divided up the Ottoman Empire among them and excluded the Arabs from most of the cities and areas the Arabs wanted. Charming though Sykes was, the effect of his vagueness about details was to heighten rather than decrease Feisal's shrewd and well-informed suspicions about Anglo-French policy in the Near East. Sykes returned to Wejh after a journey to Jidda for an even more trying and difficult meeting with Feisal's father; and on May 7, accompanied by Colonel Wilson, he met with Lawrence, who, like most of the British officers in the Hejaz, now including even Wilson himself, strongly objected to urging the Arabs to fight while at the same time negotiating "behind their backs." Lawrence was particularly outspoken on this subject, and it clearly played a role in his decision "to go [his] own way," and ride deep into Syria with Auda, then take Aqaba from the undefended east.

He wrote an apologetic letter to General Clayton in Cairo. Then, without receiving orders or even bothering to inform his superior officers— he took advantage of the fact that Newcombe, who would certainly have tried to talk him out of it, was away attacking the railroad—Lawrence left with his Arab followers.

Lawrence's many critics in later years have tried to belittle the risk of what he was proposing to do, but in fact it was a daring decision. Liddell Hart describes it as a "venture . . . in the true Elizabethan tradition—a privateer's expedition," across some of the harshest and most difficult terrain in the world, led by a man who already had a price on his head. It involved a desert march of more than 600 miles, a long "turning movement" that would take Lawrence to Damascus, then down through difficult terrain and unreliable tribes "to capture a trench within gunfire of our ships."

Lawrence left Wejh early on May 9, with fewer than fifty tribesmen, accompanied by Auda Abu Tayi; Sharif Nasir, who would be Feisal's spokesman to the tribes and the nominal commander; and Nesib el Bekri, a Syrian nationalist politician who hoped to make contact with Feisal's supporters in the north. Lawrence took with him a train of baggage camels carrying ammunition; packs of blasting gelatine, fuses, and wire so he could continue his demolition work; a "good" tent in which Nasir could receive visitors; sacks of rice, tea, and coffee for entertaining distinguished guests; and spare rifles to give away as presents. Each man carried on his own saddle forty-five pounds of flour intended to last him for six weeks, and the men shared among them the load of 22,000 gold sovereigns from Feisal's treasury, weighing more than 800 pounds, to pay salaries and use where required as presents or bribes.

Lawrence was not, of course, the first person to think about taking Aqaba. Kitchener had had his eye on the port even before 1914, and Feisal had brought it up often in the years since. Admiral Wemyss was interested enough in Aqaba to order regular naval reconnaissance, and even two landings by naval parties, since the Royal Navy feared the Turks might use Aqaba as a base from which to float mines down into the Red Sea, or even station a German submarine there to threaten the approach to Port Suez and the Suez Canal. Lawrence saw it, more realistically, as the way to leapfrog over the Turkish forces in the Hejaz, and bring the Arab Revolt within striking distance of Damascus and Jerusalem. He had the advantage over almost everybody else that he had been in Aqaba in 1914, working for the Survey of Palestine Exploration Committee, and indirectly for Kitchener, drawing up a map of the Sinai, and had left Aqaba, expelled by the *kaimakam* (police chief) and escorted by policemen, on the same route by which he proposed to attack it now. He had even made a map of it, based on aerial photographs, in Cairo—a daring innovation at the time.

Even Lawrence's spirit of adventure would be sorely tried by the hardships of the route, and his goals were already compromised by Mark Sykes's visit, which had brought him face-to-face with a moral dilemma: leading the Arabs into battle for lands that the Allied powers had already decided they were not going to get. The notes in his diaries confirm his moral revulsion and his guilt, and it is perhaps no accident that he was soon troubled by the same boils and fevers that had given him so much pain on the way to Abdulla's camp at Wadi Ais. "The weight is bearing me down now," he wrote on May 13; ". . . pain and agony today." It seems

possible that Lawrence's physical agony was at least in part psychoso-
matic, and far more bearable to him than the spiritual agony of knowing
that his government had no intention of respecting its promises to the
Arabs, let alone his.

The journey was an epic one—a glance at the map Lawrence made
later for *Seven Pillars of Wisdom* shows both its length and the fact that
Lawrence and Auda set their course over some of the most barren and
difficult desert in Arabia, in order to avoid running into Turkish patrols,
or tribes that were hostile to the sharifian cause. Even for a hardened
Bedouin hero like Auda it was a daunting journey—with a high risk of
dying from thirst or starvation along the way, or being killed by hostile
tribesmen.

They set out "on the old pilgrim route from Egypt," and after two hours
took a short rest (Lawrence was already feeling ill), then rode on through
the night and through the next day over white, hard-packed sand that
reflected the sun's rays like a mirror. Even Lawrence, who is usually indifferent to suffering, remarks that the bare rocks on either side of their
path "were too hot to touch and threw off waves of heat in which our
heads ached and reeled." They were unable to increase the pace because
their baggage camels were weakened by mange, and Auda feared to press
them too hard. They rested briefly, at Lawrence's request, each man seeking relief from the sun by squatting on the burning sand in the shade
from a cloak or a folded saddle blanket thrown over the branches of a
thornbush. Finally they reached an oasis, where, typically of the strange
coincidences of desert life, they found a rugged, independent-minded old
farmer, who sold them fresh vegetables to go with their cans of army-issue
beef stew. They rested for two nights, much to Auda's distress, for he preferred the empty vistas of the desert to an oasis and vegetable gardens.

Also typically of desert travel, they were no sooner out of sight of the
oasis than it seemed like an illusion; they were forced to dismount and
climb "a precipitous cliff" by a steep goat track of razor-sharp stones,
leading their camels, two of which fell and broke a leg, and were instantly
slaughtered and butchered by the Bedouin, who shared out the meat.

They rested again when they reached the encampment of Sharif Sharraf, set deep in the steep-sided valley of Wadi Jizil, with its walls of wind-shaped stone and of fiery-red rock that ran down from here to Petra, the land once inhabited by the Nabateans, while waiting for Sharraf's return with news of what was happening to the north. During this time Lawrence acquired, more out of pity than need, two servants—Daud and Farraj—who were about to be whipped for unruly behavior.

The farther north Lawrence and his companions rode, the less sure it was that they would meet tribes who favored Sharif Hussein and the Arab Revolt, and the more likely that they might be attacked or betrayed to the Turks. Lawrence had in mind two objectives: the first was to pursue the roundabout way to capture Aqaba by surprise; the second was to try to win the loyalty of the tribes as far north as Damascus and the mountains of Lebanon for the sharif of Mecca and his sons, a task bound to infuriate the French.

After two days, Sharraf finally appeared, preceded by celebratory volleys of rifle shots: an elderly, powerful man, with a shrewd and sinister face, he was a major figure in Sharif Hussein's court in Mecca, and drew a certain respect even from so proud a figure as Auda, who put on his best clothes and elastic-sided boots to pay his respects. Over a large meal of rice and mutton in Sharraf's tent, Lawrence managed to persuade the old man to let him have nineteen warriors to add to their own—Sharraf was in a good mood, having blown up a piece of the railway line and captured numerous Turkish prisoners. Except for officers, Turkish prisoners were not in themselves very valuable, having nothing much on them to take except their rifles, but Sharif Feisal paid so much a head in English gold for each Turkish prisoner brought in alive.* Lawrence also heard

---

* The Geneva Conventions were not observed in the desert. Arab wounded were normally tortured, then killed by the Turks, either by being bayoneted or by having their throats cut. As a result, the Arabs usually killed their own wounded, rather than leaving them to the mercy of the Turks. The Arabs had in any case no way to transport or care for Turkish wounded or their own. The British paid for Turkish prisoners by the head, since many of them were Arabs who had been conscripted into the Ottoman army and who might be persuaded into fighting the Turks. On both sides, the level of cruelty was high.

from Sharraf the good news that there were pools of rainwater in the dry, barren country ahead. This mattered because there had been no water skins to buy at Wejh "for love or money," so Lawrence's party was left woefully short and dependent on the wells along the way.

The next day they resumed their march, over the seemingly endless expanse of a lava field, on which the camels could walk only with great difficulty, and it was not until they were eleven days out of Wejh that they reached the railway, near Dizad, about sixty miles to the south of the railway station at Tebuk. Here, they paused to blow up some of the line and pulled down the telegraph poles and wires. Then they rode on into the furnace of El Houl ("the desolate place"), where the superheated desert wind cracked and parched their lips and skin, and across which they rode for three days and nights before they reached a well. They were now on the edge of the great Nefudh, the rolling, lifeless dunes that stretched to the horizon like a billowing ocean of sand. Lawrence, in a spirit of adventure, suggested to Auda that they cut across the Nefudh, but Auda replied gruffly that it was their business to reach Arfaja alive, not to play at being explorers, and steered them across polished mudflats from which the reflected heat almost made Lawrence faint. They were now two days out in the desert, with the nearest water a day's march farther and their camels growing weaker with every mile. They had dismounted to lead their beasts when Lawrence suddenly noticed that one of the camels was riderless.

The missing rider was Gasim, a "surly . . . stranger from Maan," about whom nobody seemed to care much. Lawrence, however, little as he liked Gasim, felt an obligation to go back for him. He mounted his own tired, thirsty camel and turned and rode back alone into the empty, desolate wilderness. It was an act of folly, but also an act of will. He had no use for Gasim, and knew that he himself, as a foreigner, would not be blamed for "shirking his duty," but that was precisely the excuse he refused to use. As "a Christian and a sedentary person" he would find it impossible to lead "Moslem nomads" if he made himself an exception to their rules.

His camel's reluctance to march away from the herd was matched by

Lawrence's own loneliness and sense of the absurdity of risking his own life for a man he had planned to get rid of as soon as he could. Improbably, after an hour and a half he saw an object move, dismissed it as a mirage, then realized it was Gasim, "nearly blinded," and stammering incoherently. He seated Gasim behind himself, and set off on the long ride back, using his army compass to retrace his steps. Gasim continued to scream and babble, so Lawrence hit him, and threatened to throw him off and ride on by himself, eventually quieting the terrified man. The camel, sensing the presence nearby of her herd mates, picked up her pace, and Auda appeared out of the heat mirages, grumbling that had he been present, he would not have let Lawrence go. "For that thing, not worth a camel's price," he shouted in a fury, striking out at Gasim, but in fact, as Lawrence had calculated, the episode soon became part of the legend of "Aurens" (as the Arabs pronounced his name). To his execution of Hamed the Moor, his unquestioned physical courage and powers of endurance, his daring use of explosives, and his lavish generosity with British gold coins was now added his rescue of the worthless Gasim, confirming his status as a hero. Indeed, by rescuing Gasim he had lived up to the ideals of courage the Bedouin admired most, but by no means always followed themselves, particularly when those ideals involved the rescue of a stranger, or a man of another tribe.

Even when they finally reached water at the wells of Arfaja, the desert still proved to be dangerous. That night, while they were drinking coffee around the fire, unseen assailants shot at them until Auda's cousin kicked sand over the fire, putting it out, at which point they drove their attackers away with a fusillade of rifle shots, though not before one of their own was killed. They rode on the next morning, and on their twentieth day since leaving Wejh they reached the tents of the Howeitat, Auda's own tribe, where they were feasted with one of those lavish meals that Lawrence loathed so much: hot grease and pieces of mutton on a bed of rice, decorated with the singed heads of the slaughtered sheep.

Here, they hastened to send six bags of gold coins in Auda's care, as a tribute to Emir Nuri Shaalan, who led the desert tribes in Syria and the Lebanon mountains and was one of the four great men ruling the Arabian desert. The others were Feisal's father, Emir Hussein of Mecca, whose control over the Hejaz, the holy city of Mecca, and the Red Sea ports made him formidable; his greatest rival, ibn Saud, emir of the Rashids, a ferocious and implacable warrior who controlled the vast desert space to the east of Hejaz, with his capital at Riyadh, and whose followers were Wahhabis, fierce Muslim puritans and fundamentalists; and the *idrisi*, Sayid Mohammed ibn Ali, who controlled the region south of the Hejaz. The competition between the four desert rulers was intense, and in many ways more important to them than any quarrel they might have with Turkey. As to their loyalties to outsiders, Hussein was of course now the ally of Britain and France, supported by the Foreign Office in London and the Arab Bureau in Cairo, though he remained always aware of the growing power of ibn Saud. Ibn Saud received support and backing from the government of India and the Colonial Office in London. The *idrisi* took money from both sides and was notoriously unreliable; and Nuri Shaalan was in the pay of the Turks, though open to higher bids from the Allied Powers. British policy, as can be seen, was confused— indeed, when open warfare finally broke out between Hussein and ibn Saud after the end of World War I, the Foreign Office and Cairo backed and supported Hussein, while the Colonial Office and New Delhi backed and supported ibn Saud, so the British taxpayer ended up paying for both sides in that war. None of the four was a Jeffersonian idealist of course— Hussein's enemies in Mecca were kept in chains in the dungeons beneath his palace, ibn Saud punished infringements of sharia with public beheadings, and both the *idrisi* and Nuri Shaalan were feared despots.

Lawrence had already taken the precaution of sending one of Nuri's men on ahead with a message making it clear that they came in peace and sought his hospitality, but, in typical desert fashion, the messenger failed to arrive, and was later found lying in the desert, a desiccated corpse—a victim of thirst or murder—with the remains of his camel beside him. The Howeitat were on the move, as they sought grazing for the camels, heading northwest along Wadi Sirhan in the direction of Azrak, which was less than 120 miles from Jerusalem to the west, and from Damascus to the north, and fell within Nuri's sphere of influence. Lawrence was now deep behind the Turkish lines, where a large part of the population favored the Ottoman Empire, or was in its pay.

When Auda returned, bringing with him more tribesmen as well as the somewhat ambiguous blessing of Nuri Shaalan, Lawrence's relief was quickly ruffled by a burst of overoptimism from Sharif Nasir and Auda, who now proposed to change the objective of the attack from Aqaba to Damascus itself, and raise the tribes of Syria and Lebanon to make an army. Lawrence was alarmed by this. The Turks had more than enough troops in Syria to put down such a rising; besides, Aqaba would become, from the British point of view, a more important conquest than Damascus, since it would ensure that as the Arab forces moved north they would provide the desert right wing of any British advance through the Holy Land to Jerusalem. However attached Lawrence was to the Arab cause and to Feisal, he could never altogether forget the demands of British strategy. Like any man who has two masters with opposing interests, he was torn between them.

Lawrence's position was equivocal. In theory, at any rate, Sharif Nasir was in command of the expedition, with Auda as his coequal military leader. Lawrence had already found out that neither of them was willing to accept an order from the other, and that his best policy was to win over one at a time to what he wanted to do, playing each man off skillfully against the other, and both of them against Nesib el Bekri, whose only interest was in reaching Damascus. It was obvious to Lawrence that even if all of Syria could be raised against the Turks, which was doubtful, trying to take Damascus before the British broke through the Turkish lines at Gaza and while Aqaba remained in Turkish hands would lead to a disaster. By suggesting to Auda that an advance on Damascus would make Sharif Nasir the man of the hour, and to Nasir that raising the local tribes to advance on Damascus would put Auda in effective control of the expedition, Lawrence managed to stave off the change in plans.

Secure now that Auda would raise enough men to take Aqaba, Lawrence felt free to pursue the last and most dangerous part of his plan. He rode off alone on a 400-mile journey through enemy territory, both to test for himself the degree of support that could be expected from the Syrian tribes once Aqaba was taken, and to attract the attention of the Turks. He wanted them looking anxiously toward the approaches to Damascus, while he turned south to take Aqaba. The danger involved, and his state of mind, can be gauged by the words he scribbled for General Clayton, which he left behind in a notebook at Nebk, close to Azrak: "Clayton, I've decided to go off alone to Damascus, hoping to get killed on the way: for all sakes try and clear this show up before it goes further. We are calling them to fight for us on a lie, and I can't stand it."

The farther Lawrence was from the calming presence of Feisal and of those British officers whom he respected, like Newcombe, Boyle, and Wilson, the more alone and desperate he felt. It was one thing to take on the responsibility for leading an expedition to capture Aqaba, but quite another to come close to provoking, with whatever misgivings, a full-scale Syrian uprising, which would certainly have led to thousands of deaths, all the while knowing that the French were going to get Damascus in the end. Lawrence was willing to accept blood on his hands, but not in unlimited quantity for no purpose. He was still weighed down by what Sykes had told him, and what he already knew or guessed about the Sykes-Picot agreement.

He was also fed up with the bickering and political machinations of his nearest companions—even Auda, with his unquenchable greed for loot and his prodigious vanity, had begun to get on Lawrence's nerves, as had the wily and ambitious Sharif Nasir; and the Syrians in his party ("pygmies," in Lawrence's opinion) were weaving improbable and complicated political fantasies, and were anxious to seize power for themselves. He felt tainted, corrupted, embittered. "Hideously green, unbearable, sour, putrid smelling," he wrote of Wadi Sirhan, where the Howeitat were encamped for the moment in an ugly, pitiless landscape, rich only in poisonous snakes. "Salt and snakes of evil doing. Leprosy of the world!"

These were the ravings of a man who was not only physically exhausted, but tortured by his own guilt, and by a sense that things were passing out of his control into the hands of scheming politicians. Lawrence seems to have convinced himself that it was his duty to seek out Feisal's friends and supporters in Syria, dangerous as this was for him and for them, and for the best part of two weeks he rode from tribe to tribe, at the mercy of anybody who wanted to claim a reward by betraying him to the Turks. The journey convinced him, correctly, that Syria was not yet ripe for revolt, and that it would take news of solid victories by the British and the Arabs to win over Syrian politicians and tribal leaders. Here in the north, Mecca seemed far away, and the notion of Sharif Hussein as the self-proclaimed "king of the Arabs" was regarded with considerable skepticism. In Syria, what people wanted was the arrival of the British army, and all the riches (and political possibilities) it would bring, but so long as General Murray was unable to break through the Turkish lines at Gaza, there seemed no point in risking torture and hanging at the hands of the Turks.

Lawrence himself describes his journey as "reckless," which it certainly was, since the Turks had already put a price on his head; but it was not entirely fruitless. At one point he was warned that his host for the night had sent word to the Turks that he was there, and he swiftly slipped out through the back of the tent, mounted his camel, and rode away. At another point, he had a secret meeting with Ali Riza Pasha, the Turkish army commander in Damascus, outside the city walls. Ali Riza was an Arab, and Lawrence took the risk of meeting with him face-to-face to ask him to prevent an uprising in the city until the British army was close enough to prevent a massacre. On the way back to Nebk, Lawrence met with Nuri Shaalan, in the old man's camp near Azrak. He described Nuri's frightening appearance five years later in *Seven Pillars of Wisdom*: "he was very old, livid and worn. . . . Over his coarse eyelashes the eyelids wrinkled down, sagging in tired folds, through which, from the overhead sun, a red light glittered in his eyes and made them look like fiery pits in which the man was slowly burning."

Not only was Nuri frightening to look at it and ruthless enough to earn the respect of Auda; he was also shrewd and well informed, and questioned Lawrence closely about the intentions of the British and French in Syria. Lawrence dismissed the documents Nuri showed him, in which Britain's promises to the Arabs over the past three years contradicted each other, and advised him to believe only the latest promise and forget the rest. This cynicism seemed to satisfy Nuri, or perhaps represented his own realistic view of the matter, and he let Lawrence go on his way. Lawrence cheerfully advised Nuri to secure his own position with the Turks by telling them he had been in the area.

Lawrence accomplished what he set out to do. He spread the news of his presence throughout Syria, even going to the trouble of blowing up a railway bridge at Ras Baalbek, on the Aleppo-Damascus line—final proof, if any were needed, that he was in Syria, and that the force he was gathering in Wadi Sirhan was intended for an attack in the direction of Damascus, not Aqaba.

Lawrence arrived back at Nebk on June 16, 1917, to find Auda and Nasir "quarrelling." He managed to settle the quarrel by the time they set out on June 19 with the 500 men Auda had gathered. Their first march (of two days) was to Beir, in what is now Jordan, where they discovered that the Turks had dynamited the wells. They managed to clear one, but Auda was now wary about what they would find at El Jefer, fifty miles to the southwest across difficult desert terrain, where, if the wells were destroyed, their camels would die. They camped at Beir and sent a scout ahead, while Lawrence rode to the north with more than 100 tribesmen, among them Zaal, "a noted raider," to attack the railway and ensure that the Turks would be looking in the wrong direction. They rode hard, in "six hour spells," with only one or two hours of rest between spells. They reached the railway north of Amman and, after watering the camels, moved on hoping to destroy a bridge, only to find that the Turks were busy repairing it. Since Lawrence's objective was to make the Turks believe he was going toward Azrak, his raiding party continued on and found a curved stretch of the railway near Minifir. Although hunted by tribesmen in the pay of the Turks and by Turkish infantrymen mounted on mules, Lawrence and his party managed to blow up the railway and leave behind a buried mine to damage or destroy the locomotive when the Turks sent a repair train down from Damascus. They took two Turkish prisoners, deserters, who died of their wounds—there was nothing the raiding party could do for them, though Lawrence left behind, attached to a telegraph pole he had torn down, a letter he wrote in French and German indicating where they could be found.

The party moved on by night and the next day captured a young Circassian* cowherd. This posed a problem—it seemed to Lawrence unfair to kill him, but at the same time they could neither take him with them nor turn him loose, since he would certainly tell the Turks of their presence. They were unable to tie him up, since they had no rope to spare, and in any case if he was tied to a tree or a telegraph pole in the desert he would die hideously of thirst. Finally he was stripped of his clothes, and one of the tribesmen cut him swiftly across the soles of his feet with a dagger. The man would have to crawl naked on his hands and knees an hour or two to his home, but the wounds would heal eventually and he would survive.

The incident gives one a picture of Lawrence's curious mixture of practicality and humanitarianism. Unlike the Arabs he rode with, he was constantly torn between his own system of ethics and their more savage instincts. The tribesmen had no compunction about cutting the throat of a terrified captive after robbing and stripping him. As if to prove this, Zaal led the party, maddened by the sight of a herd of fat sheep—they had been living off a diet of hard dried corn kernels for days—in a raid on a Turkish railway station at Atwi, about fifty miles east of the Dead Sea,

---

* Circassians were a Caucasian people, many of whom were sent into exile in the Ottoman Empire after the Russian army finally conquered their mountain homeland. Many of them were blond, blue-eyed, and fair-skinned, though Muslim. Their women were exceptionally beautiful, and much prized in the harems of wealthy Turks. It may have been Lawrence's ability to pass as a Circassian that would save his life later on, when he was taken prisoner at Deraa (see page 342).

where Zaal sniped at and killed a fat railway official on the platform. The tribesmen exchanged rifle fire with the Turks, then plundered an unde-fended building; drove off the herd of sheep; shot and killed four men who, unluckily for them, arrived on a hand trolley in the middle of all this; set fire to the station; and rode off. The raiding party slaughtered the stolen sheep, gorging on mutton, and even feeding it to their camels, "for the best riding camels were taught to like cooked meat," as Lawrence notes, adding, with his usual precision, that "one hundred and ten men . . . ate the best parts of twenty-four sheep." Then he blew up a stretch of track and they set out on the long journey back to Beir.

Raids like this kept the Turks on edge, while satisfying the Bedouin's taste for plunder and action. They also acclimatized Lawrence to the ways of the Bedouin, which most British officers found infuriating. The Bedouin had no sense of time; they did not accept orders; they would break off fighting to loot, then ride home with what they had stolen; they thought nothing of stripping and killing enemy wounded; they wasted ammunition by firing *feux de joie* into the air to announce their comings and goings; when there was food they gorged on it, instead of thinking ahead; when there was water, they drank until their bellies were swollen, instead of rationing it out sensibly; they stole shamelessly, from friend and foe alike; their tribal quarrels and blood feuds made it difficult to rely on them when they were formed up in large numbers; by British standards they were cruel to animals; and they were distrustful of Euro-peans and Christians, even as allies. In order to lead them, Lawrence had to learn to accept their ways, to share their ribald and teasing sense of humor and their extravagant emotions and love of tall tales, to embrace the extreme hardships of their life, and to understand that because they were intense individualists any attempt to give a direct order to them would be treated as an insult. This was a difficult task— even such great explorers and pro-Arabists as Richard Burton and Charles Doughty had never managed to lead the Bedouin, or be accepted by them as equals—yet Lawrence succeeded, though in doing so, he gave up some part of himself that he never recovered, eventually becoming a stranger among his own countrymen. Nobody understood this better than Lawrence himself, who wrote: "A man who gives himself to the possession of aliens leads a Yahoo life. . . . He is not one of them. . . . In my case my effort for these years to live in the dress of Arabs, and to imitate their mental foundation, quitted me of my English self, and let me look at the West and its conventions with new eyes, and destroyed it all for me. At the same time I could not sincerely take on the Arab skin: it was an affectation only."

That was written years later, when his intense fame, and his disappointment at his own failure to get for the Arabs what he had promised them, had embittered Lawrence about the role he played in the war. But there is no reason to believe that he felt this way as he rode back into Beir "without casualty, successful, well-fed, and enriched, at dawn." He was fêted by Auda and Nasir, and found the rest of the party cheered by a message from the wily Nuri Shaalan that a force of 400 Turkish cavalrymen was hunting for Lawrence's party in Wadi Sirhan, guided by his own nephew, whom Nuri had instructed to take them by the slowest and hardest of routes.

On June 28 Lawrence set out for El Jefer, despite news that the Turks had destroyed the wells. This turned out to be true, but Auda, whose family property these wells were on and who knew them well, searched out one well the enemy had failed to destroy. Lawrence organized his camel drivers to act as sappers, digging in the unbearable midday heat until they were able to expose the masonry lining of the well, and open it. The Ageyl camel drivers, less resistant to manual labor than the Bedouin tribesmen, then formed a kind of bucket brigade to bring up enough water to take the camels over the next fifty barren miles.

Lawrence sent word ahead to a friendly tribe to attack the Turkish blockhouse guarding the approach from the north to Abu el Lissal, the gateway to the wadi that led down to Aqaba, some fifty miles away. The attack was timed to stop the weekly caravan that carried food and supplies from Maan to all the outposts on the way to Aqaba, and to Aqaba itself. The taking of the blockhouse turned out to be a bloody, botched affair, during which the Turks slaughtered Arab women and children in their tents nearby; in retaliation the infuriated Arabs took no prisoners after the blockhouse fell to them, then sent word sent to Lawrence it was in their hands. He set out for Abu el Lissal on July 1, pausing when his party reached the railway line to blow up a long section of track, and sending a small party to Maan to stampede the Turkish garrison's camels in the night. Despite these precautions, however, a Turkish column advanced on Abu el Lissal, reoccupying the blockhouse.

As Liddell Hart points out, this was Lawrence's first exposure to the vicissitudes of war—a Turkish relief battalion had arrived in Maan just as the news came that the blockhouse at Abu el Lissal had been attacked. It was an accident, a coincidence, but the result was that the Arab tribesmen abandoned the blockhouse, which they had pillaged and destroyed, and the Turkish battalion set up camp at the well. Lawrence had foreseen this possibility and had an alternative plan in mind—already, he was thinking like generals he admired. It would take time and involve splitting his forces, and possibly serious losses, one part of his strength attacking the Turkish battalion to hold it in position, the other taking an alternative but slower route behind the Turks to Aqaba.

Either way, Lawrence had placed himself in a position from which no retreat was possible. There was no chance that he could take his forces back to Wejh, which was nearly 300 miles south as the crow flies, and more than twice that by any route he could take over the desert. The Turks were already in Wadi Sirhan, and could bring in reinforcements from Maan and Damascus. If they were successful Lawrence and his men would be cut off, surrounded, and killed, the Arabs as traitors to the Ottoman Empire. Lawrence himself, a British officer caught out of uniform in Arab clothing, was sure to be tortured, then hanged as a spy. He had no option but to move forward and seek battle.

It requires a very special kind of courage to advance and attack a larger, well-positioned force when one's lines of communication and path of retreat have been cut. Much as Lawrence would dislike Marshal Foch when he met Foch at the Peace Conference in Paris in 1919—and rejected

AQABA-MAAN ZONE

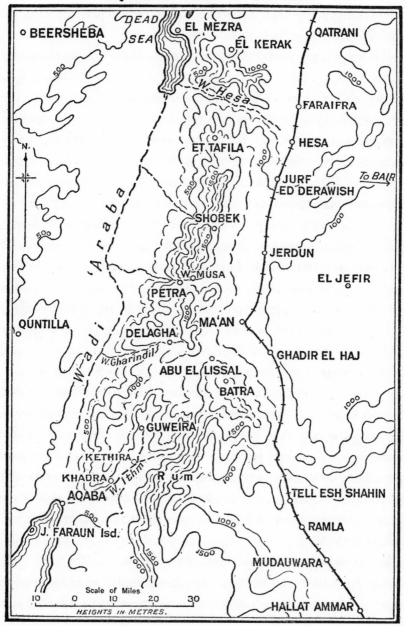

BEERSHEBA

DEAD SEA

EL MEZRA

EL KERAK

QATRANI

W. Hesa

FARAIFRA

N.

ET TAFILA

HESA

JURF ED DERAWISH

To BAIR

SHOBEK

'Araba

JERDUN

EL JEFIR

Wadi

W. MUSA

PETRA

QUNTILLA

DELAGHA

MA'AN

W. Gharindil

GHADIR EL HAJ

ABU EL LISSAL

BATRA

GUWEIRA

KETHIRA

KHADRA

W. Ithm

R u m

TELL ESH SHAHIN

AQABA

J. FARAUN Isd.

RAMLA

MUDAUWARA

HALLAT AMMAR

Scale of Miles

10   0   10   20   30

HEIGHTS IN METRES.

the kind of massed frontal attack that had already led to so many million deaths on the western front—he would have agreed with Foch's most famous military apothegm: *"Mon centre cède, ma droite recule; situation excellente. J'attaque!"**

Through a day of heat that produced waves of mirages, Lawrence led his party toward Abu el Lissal, pausing only to blow up ten railway bridges and a substantial length of the track. At dusk they stopped to bake bread and rest for the night, but the arrival of messengers with the news that a Turkish column had arrived spurred Lawrence on. His men remounted their camels—"Our hot bread was in our hands and we ate it as we went," he wrote—and rode through the night, stopping at first light on the crest of the hills that surrounded Abu el Lissal to greet the tribesmen who had taken the blockhouse and lost it. Just as there was no going back, Lawrence realized, there was no going forward so long as a Turkish battalion held Abu el Lissal. Even if they could make their way around it, Lawrence's force would still be bottled up in a valley with Turks at either end. The Arab force dismounted and spread out on the hills around the Turkish campsite, while Lawrence sent someone to cut the telegraph line to Maan. The Turks were, literally, caught napping. From higher ground the Arabs began to shoot down on the Turks, in a firefight that lasted all day. The men kept continually on the move over the rocky, thorny ground, so as not to offer the Turks a fixed target, until their rifles were too hot to touch, and the stone slabs they lay down upon to fire were so superheated by the sun that whatever patch of skin touched them peeled off in great strips, while the soles of their feet, lacerated by thorns and burned by the hot rock, left bloody footprints whenever they moved. Short of water because of the haste in which they had left, the tribesmen suffered agonies of thirst.

By late afternoon Lawrence himself was so parched that he lay down in a muddy hollow and tried to filter the moisture out of the mud by sucking at the dirt through the fabric of his sleeve. There, he was found

---

* "My center is giving way, my right is in retreat; situation excellent, I shall attack!"

by an angry Auda, "his eyes bloodshot, and staring, his knotty face working with excitement," in Lawrence's words. "Well, how is it with the Howeitat?" Auda asked, grinning. "All talk and no work?"—throwing Lawrence's earlier criticism of Auda's tribe back in his face.

"By God indeed," Lawrence replied tauntingly, "they shoot a lot and hit little."

Auda was not one to take criticism (or sarcasm) lightly. Turning pale with rage, he tore off his headdress and threw it to the ground (since as Muslims the Bedouin never go uncovered, this was a significant indicator of Auda's anger), and ran up the steep slope of the hill calling to his tribesmen to come to him. At first Lawrence thought that Auda might be pulling the Howeitat out of the battle, but the old man stood up despite the constant Turkish rifle fire, glaring at Lawrence, and shouted, "Get your camel, if you wish to see the old man's work."

Lawrence and Nasir made their way to the other side of the slope, where their camels were tethered. Here, sheltered from the gunfire, were 400 camel men, mounted and ready. Auda was not in sight. Hearing a sudden, rapid intensification of the firing, Lawrence rode forward to a point from which he could look down the valley, just in time to see Auda and his fifty Howeitat horsemen charging directly down at the Turkish troops, firing from the saddle as they rode. The Turks were forming up for an attempt to fight their way back to Maan when Auda's bold cavalry charge hit them in the rear.

With Nasir at his side, Lawrence waved to his 400 camel men, who charged toward the Turkish flank, riding into a volley of rifle fire. The Turks were poorly prepared to deal with the surprise of a dense charge over rough ground of 400 camel riders. Lawrence, who was riding a racing camel that was faster than the rest, led the charge, firing his revolver, and smashed into the Turkish ranks, at which point his camel collapsed suddenly in a heap, sending Lawrence flying out of the saddle. He was knocked senseless by the fall, but luckily the bulk of his camel prevented him from being trampled to death by the force following him, which swept to either side of his camel like the sea sweeping around a rock.

When he regained consciousness and stood up, he found that he had accidentally shot his own camel in the back of the head, and that the battle was over. The sheer velocity of the two charges had broken the Turks' formation and degenerated into a brief massacre as the riders shot and hacked away with their curved sabers at small, isolated groups of soldiers. Three hundred Turks had been killed—"slaughtered," Lawrence wrote, with a hint of self-disgust—and 160 were seriously wounded, for a loss of only two Arabs.

Auda appeared, "his eyes glazed over with the rapture of battle," muttering incoherently, "Work, work, where are words?"—surely a rebuke to Lawrence for his disparaging comment about Howeitat marksmanship. Auda's robes, his holster, his field-glass case, and his sword scabbard had all been pierced by bullets, and his mare had been killed under him, but he was unharmed. Having learned from a Turkish prisoner that Maan was garrisoned by only two companies, he was eager to take the town and loot it; but Lawrence's sense of strategic priorities was undiminished by his fall, and he managed after much difficulty to persuade Auda and the tribesmen that they must move down the wadi toward Aqaba instead. Taking Maan would certainly look like a triumph, but it would be a temporary one at best, since the Turks would quickly assemble a force big enough to recapture it. Taking Aqaba would bring Feisal's army into Palestine, Syria, and Lebanon, and would give the Arabs not only a place in the strategic "big picture," but—he hoped—one at the peace conference.

In the meantime, there seemed no alternative to spending the night on the battlefield, surrounded by the bodies of the enemy, until Auda, who was superstitiously afraid of the presence of so many corpses, and tactically concerned lest the Turks attack them during the night, or lest other Howeitat clans with whom he had a blood feud use the opportunity to kill them on the pretext of mistaking them for Turks, persuaded Lawrence to move on. Wrapped in his cloak against the damp, chilly evening, Lawrence felt the inevitable reaction to victory "when it became clear that nothing was worth doing, and that nothing worthy had been done."

The Arabs, as was their custom, had stripped the clothes off the bodies of their enemies, and now wore bloodstained Turkish tunics over their robes. The more seriously wounded of the Turks would have to be left behind, so Lawrence looked around for blankets or discarded pieces of uniform to cover them from the day's brutal sun. This had been a battalion of young Turkish conscripts. "The dead men," Lawrence noted, "looked wonderfully beautiful. The night was shining down, softening them into new ivory." He found himself envying the dead, and feeling disgust at the noise of the Arabs behind him, quarreling over the spoils; the dead were spread out in low heaps or singly where they had fallen, and Lawrence began mechanically in the moonlight to rearrange them in rows, at once a lunatic attempt to impose western ideas of neatness on the chaos of death, and a kind of self-punishing atonement for having led the attack that had killed them.

Lawrence had managed to persuade the Arabs to spare some of the Turkish officers, including a former policeman whom he persuaded to write letters in Turkish to each of the commanders of the three major outposts between Abu el Lissal and Aqaba, urging them to surrender, and promising them that if they and their men did so they would reach Egypt alive as prisoners. Considering the mood of the moment, this was a farsighted tactical move. The ground was rough and water scarce between here and Aqaba, and men and animals were by now almost completely played out. It was by no means sure that the Arabs would prevail if one of the Turkish posts offered serious resistance.

The path ahead of them was as twisted as a corkscrew—a determined team of machine gunners in the right spot could have held up an army many times larger than Lawrence's until thirst overcame them, but fortunately his letters did the trick. The first outpost, of 120 men, surrendered immediately, opening up "the gateway to the gorge of the Wadi Itm," which in turn led directly to Aqaba. The next day, the garrison at Kethera, about eighteen miles farther on, proved more hesitant to surrender, but after prolonged negotiations, the Arabs managed to take the place in a surprise night attack, without losses. Lawrence knew from his pocket diary that it was the night of a full lunar eclipse, and had counted on the Turks' being superstitiously distracted by it, as well as its providing the total darkness that made the attack possible.*

Wadi Itm, as they descended it, got narrower and steeper, demonstrating convincingly how impossible it would have been for the British to fight their way up it from the sea. The garrison at Aqaba had marched inland to reinforce the last Turkish post at Khedra four miles away, but this was in fact a fatal move, for all the fortifications faced the sea, from which any attack was expected to come. Nothing had been prepared for an attack down Wadi Itm. Lawrence had sent messages on ahead to tell the local tribes to harass the Turks, and when he arrived they were already firing on the Turkish lines. The last thing Lawrence wanted was an all-out assault, which would certainly be costly in lives, and he twice repeated his offer of taking the Turks prisoner. At last, as the Turkish commander took in the number of Arabs assembled against him, he ordered his men to cease firing and surrendered on the morning of July 6, less than two months after Lawrence's departure from Wejh.

One of the prisoners was a German army well-borer, standing out among the Turks with his red hair, blue eyes, and field-gray uniform. Lawrence paused to chat with him in German, and eased his mind by saying he would be sent to Egypt, where food and sugar were plentiful, not to Mecca. Then, while the Arabs looted the camp, Lawrence raced his camel four miles on to Aqaba, and plunged it headlong into the sea.

He had achieved the impossible—successfully carried out a dangerous, long maneuver behind enemy lines, covering hundreds of miles over what everybody else assumed was impassable terrain to capture a critical port, and killed or captured more than 1,200 Turks for a loss of only two of his own men.

---

* Liddell Hart remarks admiringly that this is an early example of Lawrence's genius for strategy taking over virtually without a pause from the tactical ability he had shown in the battle, and perhaps it is. Lawrence was as precocious in his military abilities as he was in almost everything else he put his hand to, and like Odysseus, the future translator of the *Odyssey* was at once a bold warrior, a brilliant planner, and a man with an infinite capacity for craft and deceit. Lawrence was both a hero and "Odysseus of the many wiles," to quote from his own translation, and using his pocket diary as a weapon—in this case more potent than mortars or mountain guns, neither of which he possessed—is an early example of the kind of unexpected thinking that made him a formidable guerrilla leader.

Photograph by T. E. Lawrence of the Arab advance on Aqaba.

—

Aqaba was in ruins, "dirty and contemptible"; and now that the regular supply caravan, which meandered every two weeks from Maan down past the Turkish outposts carrying rations, had been cut off, there was no food for either victors or vanquished. Lawrence had more than 500 men, 700 prisoners, and 2,000 hungry and demanding men from the local tribes to feed. Of his Turkish prisoners forty-two were officers, and indignant at not being housed any better than their men. There were fish in the Red Sea, of course, but Lawrence had no hooks or lines, and the desert tribesmen had no knowledge of fishing—nor had they any desire to eat fish. The town was surrounded by groves of date palms, but at this season the dates were still raw, and produced violent stomach cramps and diarrhea when boiled and eaten. The Arabs could slaughter and eat their camels, of course, but eventually this would immobilize the entire force.

With his usual indifference to food, Lawrence himself did not suffer, or feel much sympathy for his prisoners—it was his general view that people ate too much anyway—but at the same time he realized that the capture of Aqaba would be of no use to the Egyptian Expeditionary Force unless they heard of it, and that sooner or later the Turks would give some thought to retaking the port. A British armed tug had paid one of its regular visits, lobbed a few shells into the hills, and sailed on without paying any attention to the Arabs' signals from the shore. It would be at least a week before this tug, or another ship of the Royal Navy, returned. The small force Lawrence now had assembled at Aqaba needed not just food, but modern weapons, ammunition, tents, and above all gold, since gold was the only thing that could guarantee the tribesmen's loyalty.

Lawrence had not bothered to inform Cairo where he was going, or with what object, and he had no idea what was happening in the rest of the war. He did not therefore know that General Murray's second attack on Gaza had failed, like the first. Gaza was no easy nut to crack—with the help of the Germans, the Turks had fortified their trenches, taking advantage of every piece of high ground and of the impenetrably thick hedges and clumps of cactus (considered worse by the troops than barbed wire), in which they had carefully sited machine gun nests. On the British side, despite huge efforts to build a small-gauge railway line to bring supplies and ammunition forward and to lay a water line, neither had been completed. Murray's plan of attack was therefore hamstrung, since he required more than 400,000 gallons of water a day for men, animals, and vehicles. He had a large mounted force of about 11,000 sabers, and an overwhelming superiority of numbers in infantry, as well as an artillery strength of more than 170 guns (as well as a naval bombardment of Gaza from the sea, and the first use of tanks and poison gas in the Middle East); but the Turks still managed to hold their ground, and since the only way of securing water was to take Gaza, the British, having failed to do so, were obliged to break off the battle. Murray had inflicted 1,300 casualties on the Turks, at the cost of 3,000 British and Commonwealth casualties. Both Lawrence and Liddell Hart would later point out that Lawrence's tiny force had inflicted almost the same number of casualties on the Turks for a loss of only two men!

The resulting stalemate—a miniature reproduction of the situation on the western front—was made worse by Murray's overoptimistic dispatches home during the first battle of Gaza, which had produced first jubilation, then consternation in the war cabinet as the facts became known. The prime minister remained determined to knock Turkey out of the war, and looked for a stronger commander for the Egyptian Expeditionary Force. It was decided to replace Murray with General Sir Edmund Allenby, GCB, GCMG, GCVO, a powerful, impatient, hard-thrusting cavalryman, know as "the bull" to men who served under him, because of both his size and his fearsome temper. Allenby had fought brilliantly in the Boer War, but quarreled badly there with Douglas Haig, who was now the commander in chief of the British Expeditionary Forces in France. Allenby, who violently disagreed with Haig's tactics, had promptly crossed him again, and as a result it was thought wise to give Allenby a command as far away from France as possible. It was also hoped that as a cavalryman who had chafed at trench warfare he would bring a new level of energy and drive to the Egyptian Expeditionary Force (EEF).

When Allenby took his leave of Lloyd George in London, the prime minister told him "that he wanted Jerusalem as a Christmas present for the British people." Considering that the British army had been stuck outside Gaza for two years, this was a tall order, but Allenby, his spirits and self-confidence buoyed by being released from Haig's command and given a show of his own, set to work immediately to breathe new life into the EEF. A consummate professional soldier, he moved his headquarters forward to Rafah,* only nineteen miles from the front line at Gaza, instead of trying to command the army from Cairo, where General Murray had preferred to remain. Allenby immediately set out to see everything he could with his own eyes, instead of relying on his staff officers for information, another failing of Murray's. He knew he could expect no reinforcements, given the pressure on the western front, and would have to make do with what he had. He also understood at once that advancing up the coast to attack Gaza for the third time would get him nowhere. He

---

*Now the site of a major border crossing from Egypt into Gaza.

would need to surprise the Turks with a new strategy, one that made use of the vast, empty desert area to the east to go around the Turkish lines and fortifications that stretched from Gaza on the Turkish right to Beer-sheba on their left. But what kind of army could travel great distances over a waterless desert?

Meanwhile, in Aqaba Lawrence faced two urgent problems: the first was feeding his men and his prisoners; the second was defending Aqaba against a Turkish attack, which Lawrence estimated would take about ten days. To protect Aqaba, Lawrence made use of his skill at creating maps to pick four independent strongpoints, each of which the Turks would have to attack separately if they were going to advance down Wadi Itm. He put Auda in command of one of them, and chose carefully from among the tribes to man the others. To obtain food and supplies, there was only one course open to him—to leave Aqaba and ride 150 miles across the Sinai desert to the Suez Canal. The terrain is some of the harshest in the world, with only one well between Aqaba and the Suez Canal, and the Bedouin tribes of the Sinai had the reputation of being predatory and pro-Turk.

Taking only seven men with him—one of them would have to drop out and return to Aqaba because his camel was unfit—Lawrence set off on July 7 to bring the news of the Arab victory to Cairo. Riding continuously at a walk with only short intervals of rest, in order not to exhaust their camels, the small party arrived at Shatt, on the canal, on July 9, a journey of forty-nine hours, which pushed both men and camels to their limit, crossing over Mitla Pass* and then across the shifting, rolling dunes to the east bank of the canal. Occasional heaps of rusting, empty army-ration bully beef cans in the desert marked the approach to civilization.

There, the natural lethargy of army administration took over, as if to mark Lawrence's passage from Asia and the Arabs back to the world of uniforms, regulations, and orders. The lines at Shatt, it turned out, had

---

* Mitla Pass would be the site of major tank battles between the Israelis and the Egyptians in 1956, 1967, and 1973.

been abandoned because of an outbreak of plague. Lawrence picked up a telephone in an abandoned office hut and found it still working. He rang general headquarters at Suez and asked for a boat to take him across the canal, but was told that this was no business of the army's, and that he would have to call Inland Water Transport. Though he explained the importance of his mission, Inland Water Transport was indifferent. It might try to send a boat tomorrow, to take him to the Quarantine Department. He called again, and argued his case more vehemently, but this did no good—he was cut off. Finally, "a sympathetic northern accent from the military exchange" came on the line: "It's no bluidy good, Sir, talking to them fooking water boogars: they're all the same." The kindly operator finally managed to put Lawrence through to Major Lyttleton at Port Tewfik. Lyttleton handled cargo shipments for the Arab forces at Jidda, Yenbo, and Wejh, and promised to have his launch at Shatt in half an hour. Once Lawrence reached Port Tewfik, Lyttleton took one look at him in his verminous, filthy robes, and brought him straight to the Sinai Hotel, where Lawrence had a hot bath, his first in months, iced lemonades, dinner, and a real bed, while his men were sent northward to "the animal camp on the Asiatic side" in Kubri, and provided with rations and bedding.

The next morning, on the train to Cairo via Ismailia, Lawrence played a game of hide-and-seek for his own amusement, in the true Oxford undergraduate tradition, with the Royal Military Police. There was nothing he enjoyed more than confronting puzzled and vexed minor authorities with the unfamiliar contrast of his blue-eyed face and upper-class accent and his present costume of Arab robes and bare feet. Although he carried a special pass issued to him by Major Lyttleton, identifying him as a British officer, Lawrence wanted to go as far as he could before showing it, and no doubt to annoy as many people on the way as possible. This kind of thing—combining a perverse schoolboy fondness for practical jokes with a flamboyant flaunting of his unmilitary ways and special privileges—was to become something of a specialty of Lawrence's as his fame increased.

After numerous minor adventures with the authorities, Lawrence changed trains at Ismailia for Cairo, and found his friend Admiral Wemyss in conversation with a large, intimidating, and unfamiliar general, pacing up and down the platform waiting to board their private carriage on the train to Cairo. The general was Allenby, on one of his inspection tours, and his presence, together with that of the admiral, froze everyone to attention except Lawrence, who, recognizing one of Wemyss's aides, Captain Rudolf Burmester, RN, walked forward and explained who he was and why he was there. At first Burmester was unable to recognize Lawrence, whose weight had dropped to less than ninety-eight pounds, and who was standing before him barefoot in Arab robes, but he immediately realized the significance of what Lawrence told him, and promised to load a naval ship up with "all the food in Suez" and send it to Aqaba at once. He also informed Lawrence that the unfamiliar general was Allenby, who had replaced Murray; and it was there, on the platform, that Lawrence and Allenby first set eyes on each other.

Lawrence on the railway platform after Aqaba, as Allenby strides by.

Lawrence boarded the train, arrived in Cairo at noon, and went straight to the Savoy Hotel, where the Arab Bureau was located. He walked past the sleeping sentry to General Clayton's rooms; Clayton was hard at work, and merely glanced up at the small robed figure, and waved him away with a quick *"Mush fadi,"* Anglo-Egyptian slang that can mean anything from "Not now; I'm busy" to "Bugger off!"

Clayton, who supposed that Lawrence was still somewhere around Maan blowing up railway bridges, was astonished, but not vexed, to see his protégé standing barefoot on his doorsill. Clayton confirmed with one call that HMS *Dufferin* was already loading food at Suez for an emergency trip to Aqaba. Then, at Lawrence's request, he drew £16,000 in gold from the bank and sent it under guard to Suez to make good the promises Lawrence had written out on army telegraph forms and left with the tribal sheikhs when the gold he was carrying ran out. It was, Lawrence said, imperative for his reputation that these notes, accepted with great reluctance—since Arabs had no faith in paper money of any kind—be redeemed as soon as possible.

Lawrence found that his uniform had been eaten by moths in his absence—or at any rate so he says in *Seven Pillars of Wisdom*, but it is also possible that he had already decided he was more of a sensation in his Arab robes than he would be in uniform. After all, were there no servants in the hotel to look after such things? For that matter, was he the only junior officer in Cairo to have no soldier as servant? Come to that, Cairo was well known for tailors who could whip up a suit or a tropical uniform to order in a few hours. If Clayton could produce £16,000 in gold coins at the drop of a hat, it seems unlikely that with all the resources of the Arab Bureau at his disposal he could not get Lawrence into uniform in a couple of hours if he had wanted to. It seems more probable that Clayton, like Lawrence, realized that the Arab regalia was an asset. This is, in fact, the first moment at which Lawrence can be seen consciously creating the "Lawrence legend"—a creation that, like Frankenstein's monster, would shortly take on a life of its own.

In any case, Lawrence appeared before his commander in chief just as he had been on the platform at Ismailia, barefoot, clothed in his white sharifian robes and his headdress with the golden *agal*. Since Allenby was, among other things, famous as a stickler for perfection in every detail of military uniform, regardless of rank, there is no doubt that he too saw in Lawrence and this unusual garb an opportunity, rather than merely a young staff officer in need of a stern lecture on the dangers of "going native." As for Lawrence, though he had not been greatly impressed by generals Maxwell and Murray, and occasionally even made fun of them when he thought he could get away with it, he was instantly impressed, even overawed, by Allenby.

"Allenby was physically large and confident," he wrote, "and morally so great that the comprehension of our littleness was not easy to him. He sat in his chair looking at me—not straight, as his custom, but sideways, puzzled." Lawrence felt that Allenby was trying to decide how much of what he was seeing was "genuine actor and how much charlatan," and this was probably true enough, since Allenby was still turning that question over in his mind toward the end of his own life: "He [Lawrence] thinks himself a hell of a soldier and loves posturing in the limelight." But Allenby was by then retired, a field marshal, and a viscount, whereas in 1917 he apparently came quickly to the opinion that Lawrence was, to use his own word, "an actor" (by which Lawrence meant "a man of action") as opposed to a mere charlatan.

Allenby was not an easy man to impress, but Lawrence succeeded in impressing him, as he explained what he had done, what he intended to do in Syria now that he had captured Aqaba, and what he needed to do it, "offering to hobble the enemy by preaching, if given stores and arms and a fund of two hundred thousand sovereigns to convince and control the converts." In fact, it would require close to £200,000 in gold sovereigns *a month* to fund the Arab Revolt, but even at that price the revolt was cheap. Allenby listened calmly, studied the map as Lawrence explained about the tribes, the wadis, the desert—subjects about which he was a masterful lecturer—and asked an occasional trenchant question.

Though no two people could look less alike, Allenby and Lawrence got along famously from the beginning, partly because Lawrence knew what he was talking about, and partly because Allenby and Lawrence had many unseen similarities. They were both brilliant soldiers and at the same time intellectuals; Allenby had commanded a flying column of horsemen in the Boer War and understood the mechanics of a guerrilla war; above all Allenby was a cavalryman, who hated the brutal, wasteful head-on attacks on the western front and wanted to open up a war of movement. Like Lawrence, he sought unconventional and imaginative solutions to military problems and rejected the conventional ones, and also like Lawrence, he relished his independence. He instinctively respected Lawrence's courage and intellect, and was willing to put up with his unorthodox behavior if it brought results, as it already had. Moving Feisal's army north from Wejh to Aqaba would isolate the three Turkish divisions at Medina while at the same time turning Feisal's forces loose in the Syrian desert to smash trains and railway lines, cut the Turks' communications, and keep their attention focused in the wrong direction. Allenby saw at once that he needed a fast-moving mobile force on his right as he advanced to take Beersheba, one that could go for long periods of time without food or water in extreme heat—and here it was, ready made, with a base from which it could be supplied. He did not expect the Arab army to fight conventional battles any more than Lawrence did, but a glance at Lawrence's map told Allenby that he could feint at Gaza while aiming his main blow at Beersheba, with its vital wells, while all the time the Turks would be looking out toward the empty desert in the northeast, wondering where the Bedouin were.

After a moment's thoughtful silence, Allenby said to Lawrence, "Well, I will do for you what I can," and that was that. He would prove as good as his word. Not only would the Arabs receive gold in huge amounts— which Lawrence would disburse, thus confirming his authority—they would eventually get food, small arms, ammunition, Lewis guns and instructors, Stokes mortars and instructors, armored cars, flights of British aircraft, enormous amounts of high explosives, and even camels and mules. Allenby grudged Lawrence nothing. He was even willing to put up with the political consequences—for the taking of Aqaba, once it was properly exploited, would put the Arab army, funded and armed by the British, only 120 miles from Jerusalem and 240 miles from Damascus— which is to say, far from the Hejaz and at the very center of British and French ambitions in the Middle East. Lawrence had set in motion what would rapidly become huge changes in one of the most volatile areas of the world—ones that are still being fought over today.

Whatever Lawrence might think of them, the honors he had earned were not neglected. Colonel Wilson, who only a few months ago had referred to him as "a bumptious young ass," recommended Lawrence for the Distinguished Service Order (DSO), a decoration for bravery for offi- cers that is only one step below the Victoria Cross (VC), and praised his "personality, gallantry and grit." General Sir Reginald Wingate was even more impressed by Lawrence's secret journey through Syria than by the taking of Aqaba. Wingate praised Lawrence to the chief of the imperial general staff (CIGS) in London, and going one step beyond Colonel Wilson, asked for "special recognition" of "this gallant and successful adventure"—the Victoria Cross.*

Despite this recommendation, Lawrence was ineligible for the Victo- ria Cross, since there were no British witnesses to his feats; but the DSO was not considered a sufficient reward, so instead Lawrence was made a Companion of the Order of the Bath (CB), the Military Division of which was then limited to 750 members. This was an extraordinary and unprec- edented honor for a man of only twenty-eight, and one that Lawrence shared with such illustrious predecessors as Nelson and the duke of Wel- lington. Since a CB could not be awarded to an officer below field rank, Lawrence was instantly promoted to major to make him eligible.

Lawrence never acknowledged or accepted the award; nor did he, as he later claimed, turn it down, since he was unable to. Once an award has

---

* The Victoria Cross has been awarded only 1,353 times since it was created on Janu- ary 29, 1856, by Queen Victoria as Britain's highest award for valor and gallantry in the face of the enemy. It can be awarded both to officers and to other ranks, and takes precedence over all other British military awards.

been made, on the basis of recommendations by the recipient's superior officers, it is published in the *London Gazette*, the official newspaper of the crown, which, among other things, publishes all military postings, promotions, and awards. The moment the award has been "gazetted," it is official. So far as the army and the crown were concerned, Lawrence was now Temporary Second-Lieutenant and Acting Major T. E. Lawrence, CB, and always would be, whether he accepted the actual decoration itself from the hand of the king or not. He was henceforth entitled to put the initials after his name, and to wear the ribbon of the CB on his uniform, though he never did. This is an important point because Lawrence believed that he had turned the award down, while the fact was that he could not do so, however much he may have wanted to.

He would write to his father later of the award: "Tell Mother they asked for that twopenny thing* she likes [the Victoria Cross], but fortunately didn't get it. All these letters & things are so many nuisances afterwards, & I'll never wear or use any of them. Please don't either. My address is simply T.E.L., no titles please."

Lawrence was already famous within the British army in the Middle East, and at his ease with figures as important as the CIGS, but even he could not have imagined that within a year he would be world famous as the "prince of Mecca," the "uncrowned king of Arabia," and, more permanently, as "Lawrence of Arabia," a phrase he could never get rid of.

But who, exactly, was he?

---

* The Victoria Cross is made of bronze from Russian cannons captured at Sebastopol, during the Crimean War, and was popularly supposed to cost only twopence to manufacture.

CHAPTER THREE

"The Family Romance"

These consciously remembered mental impulses of childhood embody the factor which enables us to understand the nature of hero-myths. . . . The later stage . . . begun in this manner might be described as "the neurotic's family romance."

—Sigmund Freud, *Collected Papers*

S hortly before the outbreak of World War I, a tall, lean, slightly stooped gentleman of distinguished appearance sat down in the small study of his modest Oxford home to write a letter to his five sons, to be opened and read only after his death. Whether he had some apprehension—unfounded, as it turned out—about his own health, or whether like many intelligent people he sensed the storm clouds of war upon the horizon, and knew that those of his sons who were old enough to do so would want to serve king and country, it is impossible to guess. In any event, he briefly, and with great dignity, outlined for them what he and their mother had never been able to share with them during all their years together as a family.

On the envelope, once he had sealed it, he wrote in his firm handwriting, "To my sons—But not to be opened except mother and I are dead—OR when mother desires to—"

My dear sons—I know this letter will be a cause of great sorrow and sadness to you all as it is to me to write it. The cruel fact is this, that yr Mother and I were never married.

When I first met Mother, I was already married. An unhappy marriage without love on either side—tho' I had four young daughters. Yr Mother and I unfortunately fell in love with each other and when the exposé came, thought only of getting away and hiding ourselves with you Bob, then a Baby. There was no divorce between my wife and myself. How often have I wished there had been! Then I drank and mother had a hard time but happily I was able to cure myself of that. You can imagine or try to imagine how yr. Mother and I have suffered all these years not knowing what day we might be recognized by someone and our sad history published far and wide. You can think of what delight we saw each of you growing up to manhood for men are valued for themselves and not for their family history, except of course under particular circumstances. My real name when I met yr Mother was Thomas Robert Tighe Chapman Bart but needless to say I have never taken the Title. There is one little ray of sunshine in the sad history, namely, that my sister who married my cousin Sir Montagu Chapman, & my brother Francis Vansittart Chapman of South Hill (my father's place; the life interest of which I agreed to sell) were always loving to me & it is thro' their goodness that I have been able to leave you the greater part of the sum I have left. My brother at his death left me £25000. & my sister in her Will has bequeathed me £20000, but owing to the wording of her Will I shall not receive this £20000 if I die before her. She is alive but a great invalid & no fresh Will of hers wld be valid tho' I know she intended and wished this £20000 to go to you all, if I should die before her. She for many years gave me £300 a year, which, with my own fortune, enabled us all to live very comfortably & saved Mother and me great pinching to make ends meet & also kept me from drawing on my Capital for every day expenses.

Bob's name was registered in Dublin (near St. Stephen's Green) as "Chapman"; hence his name in my Will. I shld recommend him to retain his name of Lawrence; a man may change his sirname [*sic*] anytime & need not take legal steps to do so, except he is expecting to inherit places or moneys from others, who know him by his former name.

I can say nothing more, except that there was never a truer saying than "the ways of transgressors are hard." Take warning from the terrible anxieties & sad thoughts endured by both yr Mother and me for now over thirty years; I know not what God will say to me (yr Mother is the least to be blamed) but I say most distinctly that there is no happiness in this life, except you abide in Him thro' Christ & oh I hope you all will.

Father

Readers of Victorian fiction will recognize here the essential elements and tone of Dickens's greatest novels, particularly in all these details about wills, money, the invalid sister, and the family secret, as well as the pious exhortation at the end of the letter. It is hard to think of Lawrence as a latter-day Pip or Oliver Twist, but it is in this light that we must see him and his four brothers, who grew up in the shadow of their loving parents' secret. There is no evidence that any of them ever read their father's letter, or even knew of its existence. Two of them, Frank and Will, would be killed early on in the war; one of them would survive the war to become perhaps its most famous hero; and of the other two, Bob, the eldest, and Arnold, the youngest, eventually made their peace with their parents' relationship, though late in life and reluctantly. T. E. Lawrence, known in his family as Ned, seems, perhaps because he was the most sensitive and imaginative of the boys, to have guessed early on in his childhood that something was "irregular" about his parents, and apparently came by himself to the conclusion that his parents were not married. He mistakenly imagined, however, that his mother had had a relationship with an older man and had given birth to her three eldest sons by him, then met "Mr. Lawrence," who befriended her, adopted her sons, and fathered two more. Thus he recognized himself as his mother's son, but instinctively denied his father's paternal role, a textbook example of Freud's Oedipus complex. At any rate, Ned faced—earlier than the other boys—the fact that he was illegitimate, in an age when this still mattered very much indeed, and learned the truth about his parents' relationship long before his brothers.

For those interested in heredity, it is curious to note that Ned's father shared with his second son the altogether mistaken belief that a British title, award, or decoration can be turned down, or not "taken." Until 1963, when the Peerage Act was amended to allow Tony Benn to renounce his title as the second viscount Stangate and thereby retain his seat in the House of Commons,* a person who inherited a peerage was obliged to accept it. Ned's father was a baronet (a hereditary knighthood, ranked just below a peerage) whether he wanted to be or not. He could and did change his name, refuse to use his title, give up his properties, and so on, but so far as the crown and the law of Great Britain were concerned, he remained Sir Thomas Chapman, the seventh baronet. Indeed his wife, Lady Chapman, would very correctly write to the Home Office to confirm her husband's death in 1919 to the Registrar of the Baronetage, after which the title became extinct for lack of a legitimate male heir.

The facts of T. E. Lawrence's birth did not become widespread public knowledge until 1953,† when word leaked out about Richard Aldington's hostile "biographical inquiry" into Lawrence's life. This inquiry created alarm and indignation both in what remained of the Lawrence family and among those—much more numerous—who fiercely resented an attack on a British national hero, as well as concern for the feelings of Lawrence's mother, who was then still alive.

There is no doubt that this background played a major role in forming Lawrence's character and shaping his desire to become a hero. A powerful

---

* Sir Alec Douglas-Home would take advantage of the change in the law to renounce his place in the peerage as the fourteenth earl of Home and become prime minister the same year.

† Although they had been revealed in a French biography of Lawrence as early as 1941.

combination of shame, guilt, and ambition drove him to seek a fame brilliant enough to make the name Lawrence more worthy than the name Chapman, and thus to offer his father, the aristocrat who had put aside his title and wealth to run away with his daughters' governess, a hero for a son.

In 1932, when the Irish Academy of Letters was founded, the poet William Butler Yeats wrote to Lawrence, then serving in the Royal Air Force as an aircraftman first class under the name Shaw, to tell him that he had been proposed as an associate member. Lawrence, who was reluctant to join clubs and associations of any kind—for example, he had given up his prestigious fellowship at All Souls College, Oxford, and declined an honorary doctorate from the University of St. Andrews—nevertheless sent Yeats a gracious letter of acceptance, in which he remarked, "I am Irish, and it has been a chance to admit it publicly."

Like many things about Lawrence's view of his family, this was not altogether the truth. His father, Thomas Robert Tighe Chapman, was a descendant of William Chapman, of Hinckley, in Leicestershire, England, a distant cousin of the Elizabethan adventurer Sir Walter Raleigh. William, together with his brother John, received a substantial grant of land in County Kerry, Ireland, at the expense of the Irish inhabitants, who either were cleared away or became tenants. William's son Benjamin was a Roundhead, who served as an officer in a troop of horse raised for Parliament during the Civil War, rose to the rank of captain, and was rewarded by Oliver Cromwell with several estates in County Westmeath, Ireland. Three generations later, in 1782, Benjamin Chapman III was made a baronet, and six baronets followed over the next 137 years, each of them staunchly English and firmly Protestant. They were, in fact, members of what came to be called the "Protestant Ascendancy," those English families that were granted huge estates from the land of the defeated and despised native Irish. The simple historical fact is that Ireland was ruled for several centuries by the English; the major landowners, of whom Sir Thomas Chapman was one, were English; and the Anglo-Irish, as the small, dominant class was called, held sway over a resentful, dispossessed, disenfranchised Catholic majority. The Chapmans, from generation to generation, lived off the income of their estates in Ireland, sent their sons to be educated in England, and married young women from families of a similar background.

T. E. Lawrence himself was born in Wales, and so far as is known never visited Ireland; thus neither his birth nor his ancestry qualified him to claim he was Irish. However, he may have been moved by a sentimental regard for his friends Mr. and Mrs. Bernard Shaw, or he may have felt an increasing sense of guilt over Britain's imperial role.

Thomas Robert Tighe Chapman, Lawrence's father, was perhaps the most mysterious personality in the Lawrence "family romance." We know that he went to Eton, the foremost of England's famous public schools (which are of course expensive, exclusive, and private), and that instead of going on to Oxford or Cambridge, he attended the Royal Agricultural College, in Cirencester, in England—no doubt a more suitable education for a landed gentleman farmer, for the Chapmans' family land in Ireland "totaled over 1,230 acres," which required a practical knowledge of farm management from its owner if it was to remain profitable. Since the estate was valued at £120,296 in 1915 (approximately the equivalent of at least $10 million today), there is no question that it was farmed well, or that the Chapmans were a family of considerable landed wealth, connected by marriage with other wealthy and prominent Anglo-Irish families like the Vansittarts (T. E. Lawrence's grandmother was a Vansittart, and the distinguished diplomat Lord Vansittart, GCB, GCMG, was his second cousin).

How much active interest Thomas Chapman took in farming is hard to determine. He seems to have lived as a wealthy sportsman, hunting, shooting (he was reputed to be the best snipe and pheasant shot in Ireland), and yachting. He was an enthusiastic amateur photographer at a time when photographers developed and printed their own pictures in an improvised darkroom at home, and when the camera was still a bulky object that used glass plates and required a tripod; and he eventually became an accomplished bicycle enthusiast, at a time when bicycling was all the rage. Judging from his letters to his sons, he had a firm, sensible, and practical knowledge of business, although Lawrence would later claim that his father never wrote a check himself—perhaps because he was used to having "a man of business" to do that for him. Chapman admits that he drank, in his letter to his sons, but how much he drank is unclear. In Ireland toward the end of the Victorian era the pole was set pretty high, and none of Chapman's neighbors in later years remembered him as a heavy drinker. Since the woman he married and the woman he left his wife for were both teetotalers who objected to any consumption of wine, beer, or spirits, it would not have been necessary for Chapman to be a drunk to stir up complaints about his drinking at home; but in the hunting and shooting world of Anglo-Irish landowners in those days a man would have had to drink very hard indeed to qualify as a drunkard.

Three things are absolutely clear about Chapman: he was a gentleman, in every meaning of that word; he was an enthusiastic sportsman, more interested in foxhunting and shooting birds than in farming; and he was a caring, wonderful father. In 1873 he married Edith Sarah Hamilton, a cousin, and between 1874 and 1881 they had four daughters. Whether this was a love match or a practical union between two related landowning Protestant families is hard to judge at this distance in time, but it seems clear enough that Edith and Thomas were not well suited to each other. She was fiercely religious; she was known to the local villagers as "the Vinegar Queen" because of her sour expression; and she earned considerable dislike by her practice of slipping Protestant religious tracts under the doors of her Catholic tenants and neighbors. Their home, South Hill, near Delvin, built by Benjamin Chapman, the first baronet, is one of those big eighteenth-century stone country houses that look more solid than beautiful, though a visitor in the 1950s commented on the beauty of the landscaping and the gardens, and on the Georgian grace of the interior, with its pillared hall, fine moldings, marble fireplaces, and ornamental ceilings. Edith Chapman (who became Lady Chapman when her husband inherited the baronetcy in 1914) held frequent prayer meetings; she also insisted that her husband get up in the middle of the night to read the Bible aloud to her, and had an alarm clock by the bed to wake him for that purpose. To what extent, if any, the fact that Edith had four daughters in a row played a part in the deterioration of their marriage is hard to guess. At that time, Thomas could not have had any realistic expectation of inheriting the title. Until 1870 his elder brother William was first in the line of succession, should their cousin Sir Benjamin die or fail to have a male heir.* He therefore didn't need a son to inherit it after him, but that does not necessarily mean, much as he may have loved his daughters, that he didn't hope for a son, with whom he might have shared his love of horses, sailing, hunting, and shooting.

At some point between 1878 and 1880, Thomas Chapman sought a governess for his daughters, and hired a young woman from Scotland named Sarah Lawrence. Edith Chapman's religious zeal was increasing rapidly, and it may be that she was unwilling to hire an Irish Catholic woman. If this is the case she must have been pleased by the choice, since Sarah Lawrence was deeply religious, as firmly opposed to liquor as Mrs. Chapman herself, and a fervent Protestant. Sarah was short, energetic, intelligent, and despite a very determined jaw, quite pretty. The Chapman girls adored her, and she quickly took over managing the house as well, leaving Edith Chapman to her prayers. Thomas Chapman's drinking (and Edith's objection to it) had by then reached the stage where he was obliged to hide liquor bottles in odd places around the house, while his wife devoted herself, when she was not holding prayer meetings, to hunting them down and emptying them. It does not sound like a happy house-hold, but the daughters may have been shielded from much of this—or perhaps like many people, once they grew up they remembered only the happier moments and repressed the rest.

As to why Sarah was called a governess, instead of a nanny, it is hard to say. She may have been in charge of the education, moral welfare, and upbringing of the Chapman girls, with an "Irish girl" to do the heavy work of cleaning, bathing, cooking, making beds, etc.; or perhaps calling her a

---

*In fact, William died in 1870 without issue, and Sir Benjamin would die in 1914, also without issue, at which point Thomas succeeded to the title.

governess was intended put her in a higher station than that of the rest of the servants, who were, of course Irish and Catholic. In any case, her role soon became that of governess, and in later life, when she was keeping a house of her own, her five sons would all comment on her fanatical zeal, energy, and eagle eye.

Sometime in 1885 a crisis occurred. Sarah Lawrence became pregnant and was obliged to leave in disgrace and settle in Dublin. The Chapman girls were deeply distressed and upset by her departure—the second of them, Rose, could still describe, nearly seventy years later, a spiral-shaped crystal scent bottle with a silver top which Sarah had given her on leaving, and which her mother took away from her. It is clear that there was a deep affection between the girls and Sarah. Rose would describe her years later as "so gay and pretty."

A Catholic neighbor of the Chapmans would comment, decades later, that Edith Chapman "was the sort of woman who was terribly pious, and would go to church at all hours of the day, and then if a wretched kitchen maid got into trouble, would cast her out without a character [reference]. Where did Christianity come [into] that?" It seems likely that Edith would have been even less forgiving of a governess who became pregnant than a mere kitchen maid, but in this case there was worse to come. Several months after Sarah's departure, a family servant happened to see Sarah and Thomas Chapman together in Dublin, and—perhaps having been jealous of Sarah's privileged place in the household—reported the fact to Edith. After an angry confrontation, Thomas "eloped," which is to say that he walked out of his home and his marriage and went to join Sarah, who had given birth to his child, in lodgings "over an oyster bar, near the Abbey or the Gaiety theater," in Dublin.

The scandal was enormous—the wealthy sportsman and landowner had abandoned his wife and children for the daughters' governess, having gotten her pregnant under his own roof, challenging every assumption of a class society: the sanctity of marriage, the place of servants, the privileges and obligations of birth and wealth—all perhaps best expressed in the words of that favorite, richly complacent Victorian hymn: "The rich man in his castle, the poor man at the gate, He made them high or lowly, and ordered their estate."

The oyster bar is a wonderful touch too, of course—there is something truly Dickensian about Chapman's instant descent from South Hill with its eighteenth-century pillared hallway to lodgings in a back street of Dublin. A neighbor remembered that the day Chapman left South Hill he had one of his horses tacked up to take a last ride over his property at five-thirty in the morning, saying good-bye not so much to his family, perhaps, as to his land and the life of a wealthy sportsman that went with it. Despite this, one of his foxhunting companions, named Magan, commented gruffly that it was "The only sensible thing that Tommy ever did—can't think why he didn't do it sooner."

Sarah Lawrence, who would present Thomas Chapman with five sons, of which T. E. Lawrence was the second, lived until 1959, dying at the age of ninety-eight. She was, even in her youth, a woman of firm principles and amazing determination. Her most famous son, T. E. Lawrence, spent a lifetime trying to fathom his relationship with his mother, and never quite succeeded. He saw in her much of himself—one friend of his (a woman) remarked, "T. E. got his firm chin and the piercing blue eyes from his mother, his strength of character and ability to martyr himself in the desert. She had those martyr qualities. . . . She forced herself." Lawrence himself would write of Sarah, "No trust ever existed between my mother and myself. . . . I always felt that she was laying siege to me, and would conquer, if I left a chink unguarded." Almost everybody who met Sarah commented on the intensity of her personality, and on her indomitable will, as well as her refusal to compromise on most moral issues.

Sarah's unflinching sense of right and wrong and her moral certainty were no doubt made a more painful burden for her by the fact that she not only bore Thomas Chapman five illegitimate sons—for his wife would never agree to a divorce—but was illegitimate herself, as her own mother had been. Sarah was born in 1861, in the north of England; her birth name was Junner, and her mother, Elizabeth Junner, had been a servant in the household of an insurance surveyor, Thomas Lawrence, in Sunderland, County Durham. A case has been made, very convincingly, that Sarah was the child of "Thomas Lawrence's eldest son, John," and this certainly does seem possible—it is a reflection of a well-known social problem during the Victorian age, when female servants were often made pregnant by the master of the house (as was the case with Sarah) or by one of his sons (as was apparently the case with her mother). Almost invariably in such circumstances, the young woman paid the price, being sacked without a letter of reference, and the illegitimate babies that resulted often ended up in orphanages.

Elizabeth Junner apparently died of alcoholism (not an uncommon fate for such women). Her daughter Sarah seems to have been taken in by a grandfather and to have spent her childhood in Spartan conditions on his farm in Perthshire, Scotland, where she had to walk six miles back and forth to school five days a week. The death of her grandmother made it necessary to place Sarah in the care of an aunt, who may have been the servant of the rector of "a low church" parish. Sarah spent several unhappy years there, subjected to a strong and unforgiving religious upbringing, apparently unalleviated by any warmth or affection. Typically of Scotland, she received a good education, however. At some point she was sent to Skye, an island of bleak and barren beauty, where she may have done housework; and at the age of eighteen she was selected by the agent for the Chapman estate, who had been searching for a reliably Protestant Scottish nanny or governess to look after the Chapmans' daughters. Sarah shortly journeyed to Ireland to join the household at South Hills, with consequences we already know. She seems to have adopted the surname Lawrence along the way, borrowing it no doubt from whatever her mother had told her about the man who had been her father; but like her son T. E. Lawrence she changed her surname often, and on the birth certificates of her sons she is variously identified as "Sarah Chapman (formerly Laurence) [sic]," "Sarah Maden," and "Sarah Jenner." Some of this variation may be due to inattention or careless spelling by busy clerks, but it is still unusual, and perhaps reveals a certain anxiety about her ambiguous position as an unmarried mother.

In an age when reliable contraception was largely unavailable, illegitimacy was a widespread consequence of placing young single women as domestic employees in large households, where they were exposed to temptation and were at the mercy of their employers or older male servants; hence, the housemaid "in the family way" is a stock figure in Victorian melodrama and music hall.

Unlike her mother, Sarah Junner managed to create a better life for herself by the sheer strength of her personality and her good education. It may be that once she was fired, Thomas Chapman's first instinct had been to keep her in lodgings in Dublin and visit her on his frequent trips there. If so, he underestimated her determination, and perhaps also the strength of his feelings for her. In the event, he continued living at home and visiting Sarah in Dublin until their son Montagu Robert (always known in the family as "Bob") was born in December 1885. It was only then, when they were already illicit parents, that they were observed by a servant, and that Edith Chapman confronted her husband.

It is testimony to Sarah's strength of character that Thomas Chapman not only gave up his own name but also adopted for himself what he assumed was Sarah's surname. He did not do this by deed poll or any other legal document—he simply started calling himself Lawrence, and that was that. It is not clear whether he took the name voluntarily, or whether this was one of Edith's demands for their separation, but in any case changing his name does not seem to have bothered him. Between Sarah's various surnames and Thomas's change of name, it is hardly surprising that T. E. Lawrence found it so easy to adopt different names for his own service in the army and the RAF.

In 1885 the modern need for official documents about one's identity hardly existed. There were of course no computers, no credit cards, and no driver's licenses; the idea of attaching a photograph to a document was still in its infancy; birth and death certificates were more likely to be kept in parish archives than in government files, and were therefore subject to the perils of poor spelling, bad handwriting, hearsay evidence, and a pious concern to tidy up the written record and gloss over small human failings among the parishioners.

Still, even under his new name, Thomas Lawrence could hardly expect to go unnoticed in a small city like Dublin in the 1880s. The scandal of his departure from home certainly was public knowledge. A shopkeeper in Delvin said many years later that from the moment of Thomas's departure, Edith refused to "go out in society," and fell back on the support of her numerous relatives.

Perhaps inevitably, the newly named Lawrence family soon took up a rootless and wandering existence outside Ireland, in remote places where Thomas was unlikely to be recognized. First they moved to the village of Tremadoc, in Carnarvon, North Wales, where Sarah gave birth to their second child, Thomas Edward Lawrence, on August 16, 1888; then to a house in Kirkcudbright, Scotland, where Sarah gave birth to their third son, William George, in December 1889; then briefly to the Isle of Man, then to Saint Helier in Jersey, in the Channel Islands; then to Dinard, a seaside resort in Brittany, where there were many English visitors and residents—perhaps too many, for they moved again, first to a rented house on an estate in New Forest, in Hampshire, and finally to a large, comfortable redbrick house of their own in Oxford, at 2 Polstead Road.

A photograph taken of Sarah with four of her sons (Arnold was not yet born) in the summer 1894 at Langley Lodge, in the New Forest, is interesting. First, the picture shows Sarah in an elegant ruffled blouse and a fashionably tight skirt, holding baby Frank, and makes it clear that despite giving birth to four children she still had a remarkably trim figure and a tiny waist, as well as a very pretty face. Second, the house looks rather grand, with big columns on the porch, and carefully tended greenery. The boys look healthy, are blond, and are all dressed in sailor suits, with straw hats. Next to Ned's bare knees sits an alert small dog, apparently a terrier, its doubts about being photographed mirrored by the expression on Ned's face. The boys' little shoes are brightly polished—evidence, one suspects, of a nanny or maid behind the scenes hard at work. It does not look exactly like the penurious background that the grown-up T. E. Lawrence describes when writing about his childhood; and judging from the expression on Sarah's face it rather bears out his rare, and somewhat baffled, admiring description of his parents' relationship as "a real love match."

Although Thomas Chapman—now Thomas Lawrence—had left behind most of his wealth, he received a modest but comfortable yearly income, and had some limited access to capital—they were by no means penniless exiles. What is more, there was a certain pattern to their moves. All these places were near enough to Ireland to make it easy for Thomas to go back to Dublin on "family business" connected with the estate when necessary; and the Isle of Man, the Channel Islands, and Dinard were well placed to give him the maximum opportunity to indulge his love of sailing. The eventual move back to England, first to a house in Hampshire, then to one in suburban Oxford, reflects both a concern that if one of their boys was born in France he would become subject to military service there, and a desire to have the boys educated at home in their own language. By the time they reached Oxford in 1896, they had four children: Bob, Ned, Bill, and Frank. (The fifth boy, Arnold, was born in Oxford in 1900. In addition, Sarah gave birth to three other sons, two stillborn and one who lived for only a few hours.)

If one reason for the deterioration of the Chapmans' marriage was that Edith Chapman produced four girls in succession and no son, Thomas can only have been satisfied by his decision to leave her for Sarah, who bore him eight boys, of whom five lived and thrived. In fact, by all accounts, Thomas, though not an ebullient personality, seems to have become far more cheerful than he had been when he was living with Edith. He enjoyed the company of his sons, and was anything but remote or diffident where they were concerned; indeed no detail of what they were doing seems to have been too small to interest him, and his letters to them when they were older are models of a what a parent's letters ought to be—full of practical advice and commonsense suggestions, as well as letting the boys, particularly Ned, explore their own limits without nagging or scolding. Thomas remained an enthusiastic shot, though now on a smaller scale, having given up his estates, and he taught the older boys to shoot well, although they did not share his enthusiasm for shooting game birds. He also taught them how to sail, enjoyed bicycling with them, conveyed to them his own skill at carpentry and photography, and imparted, at least to Ned, his interest in church architecture. In an age when upper-class parents were often distant, and left the upbringing of their children to nannies and tutors, he was quite the reverse, deeply involved in everything they did.

There is no doubt that Sarah was the driving force in the family, however. She was always in motion, a whirlwind of energy, the family disciplinarian. People who did not know her well thought her "overpowering and terrifying," and she pushed her sons relentlessly and ruled their lives with alarming strictness. Many who met Sarah found her charming, but her blunt outspokenness and fiercely held opinions could also be disconcerting to strangers. On the other hand, since these are exactly the characteristics that the English admire in the Scots, and that the Scots themselves believe set them apart from the distant politeness and hypocrisy of the English, the wiliness of the Welsh, and the charm-laden duplicity of the Irish, many people found this side of Sarah endearing too.

T. E. Lawrence himself, even when he was older and a national hero, still found his mother terrifying, and as soon as he could, he carefully arranged his life to see as little of her as possible. From the beginning, he seems to have attracted her attention like a lightning rod, unlike the other boys. During the war, Auda Abu Tayi would refer to Lawrence as "the world's imp," and impishness seems to have been a permanent part of his character even when he was an infant—certainly his mother seems to have come down much harder on him than on his brothers, for naughtiness, disobedience, and a general failure to live by her strict and unforgiving rules.

Against this picture of Sarah as a domestic tyrant is the fact that the Lawrences were in their own way a happy family,* in which both parents

---

* They may have been an exception to the famous first line of Tolstoy's *Anna Karenina*: "Happy families are all alike; each unhappy family is unhappy in its own way." The Lawrences constituted a very happy family, but one that hardly resembled anyone else's.

arranged their lives around the needs of their children—although to a degree that may, at any rate to Ned, often have felt suffocating. Thomas Lawrence had no work or job, and apart from his infrequent visits to Dublin on "family business" and his occasional day in the field with a few shooting companions, he was often at home. Sarah, with or without "help," was a constant presence, cleaning, tidying, polishing, and keeping the whole household up to her very high standards of perfection. They must have made an odd-looking couple: he very tall, courtly, stooped, and thin; she tiny, much younger, and continuously in motion. Socially, they were even odder, by turn-of-the-century English standards. Thomas was, despite his change of name, recognizably a member of the upper class, in the way he dressed, in his speech, and in his polite but detached relationship to workmen and others of "the lower classes." Sarah's accent was unmistakably Scottish; her firm, direct way of dealing with people was very different from his; and she was comfortable with members of what was then still called "the working class." People who met them instantly thought that there was something strange about them as a couple, a mismatch between the languid politeness of the Old Etonian and the alarming energy of the former governess. Some even noticed that Sarah never referred to Thomas as "my husband," but instead always spoke of him as "Mr. Lawrence," or "the boys' father."

Though in later life T. E. Lawrence would remark, half in complaint, half in admiration, that his parents lived on a "workman's salary" of not more than £400* a year, and had to pinch pennies to make ends meet with five sons, in fact they seem to have lived comfortably enough, and not to have wanted for anything. Doubtless it was a big step down in income for a man who had been born to considerable wealth, but in late Victorian and Edwardian England £400 a year was the income of a member of the middle or "professional" class, not of a workman, and its cur-

---

* This is T. E. Lawrence's estimate, but Jeremy Wilson, the author of *The Authorized Biography of T. E. Lawrence*, estimates that it was, including interest from capital at his disposal, more like £1,000 per year, which would be equivalent to about $125,000 a year today.

rent equivalent would be at least $100,000, if we bear in mind that in 1890 taxation was very low. It is also clear enough that from time to time Thomas Lawrence had access to capital: hence his ability to buy bicycles for his sons and himself, to continue sailing and shooting, and to fund Ned's bicycling tours in France and a walking tour in Syria when Ned was older. On the other hand, Sarah was certainly always aware of the need to scrimp and save—it was part of her character, implanted by her own impoverished childhood.

T. E. Lawrence would inherit both parents' attitudes toward money: on the one hand, like his mother, he reduced his expenses to the absolute minimum; but like his father's, his attitude toward money was "lordly" when it came to things like his custom-made Brough motorcycles (the Brough was a two-wheeled equivalent of a Rolls-Royce). He spent a fortune by any standards paying artists to do the paintings and the drawings for *Seven Pillars of Wisdom*, and having the copies individually bound in leather by the finest bookbinders in England. His generosity to friends was lavish to the point of impoverishing himself.

Naturally, the elder Lawrences' lives were conditioned to a certain degree by the need to maintain their secret, but that apparently did not prevent them from having friends, from going out, or from having visitors—indeed everybody who knew them remarked on what good company the Lawrences were. During the years when they lived in Dinard, they had many friends among the British residents—the area around Dinard, in Normandy, was an inexpensive place for Britons to live or retire—and the family of their landlord, the Chaignons, not only became friends, but would maintain the contact when the boys were grown up.

The same was true during the time the Lawrences spent in the New Forest, when Bob, Ned, and Will had many friends, one of whom, Janet Laurie, would be a friend of Ned's for life—so far as we know the only girl to whom he ever proposed marriage. This was the case in Oxford too. The "isolation" of the Lawrence family has certainly been exaggerated, especially when it came to the friends of the boys, who were constantly in and out of the house.

The eventual choice of Oxford was sensible, both because it offered excellent opportunities for education—the parents were determined to give the boys the best possible education—and because in a university town, which was essentially middle-class, there were fewer people who would have heard their story, or who might recognize Thomas Lawrence as Thomas Chapman. In London, by contrast, the story of Thomas Chapman's running off with his daughters' governess was well known among people of his class, a kind of scandalous object lesson in how not to conduct an affair; he would certainly have been recognized at his club, whereas in Oxford he could use the Oxford Union as a club without being bothered—the dons, wrapped up in their own insular world, were unlikely to have heard the gossip about him, or to care.

Another reason for choosing Oxford was that it was then a lively religious center. Sarah's religious feelings had always been strong, and they grew stronger still as she took on herself the responsibility for the sin of breaking up Thomas's marriage and giving him five illegitimate children. She was not a religious zealot like Edith Chapman, but she wanted a place to bring up her children in a religious atmosphere, and Oxford certainly was that. Hardly a day passed in Oxford without the sound of choral singing, organs, and bells somewhere. Not that Sarah was a High Church Anglican, or would have approved of the pomp and circumstance of religion as it was practiced at the university. She was a strict follower of the evangelical movement, and attended Sunday service at St. Aldates Church, in the center of Oxford, planted firmly opposite Christ Church College and Cathedral, in stubborn opposition to High Anglicanism, with its "Roman" rites and elaborate services. The evangelicals, or Low Church Anglicans, then as now, preferred simpler services, emphasized the personal relationship between the communicant and Jesus, and believed that the Bible should be taken literally. The Lawrence family met for prayers and Bible reading every morning before the older children left for school, as well as on Sundays, with the boys kneeling beside their father as he led the service, and he or Sarah read aloud to them from the Bible.

Of course this kind of religious home life was more common in the late Victorian era than it is now, but even by late Victorian standards religion played a large role in the lives of the Lawrence family, and was certainly a bond between Sarah and Thomas. She was fervent in her belief, and Thomas seems to have been too, though in the polite and unobtrusive manner of his class. He was a gentleman in religion as in everything else, whereas Sarah was consumed by a need to save him, to compensate by the intensity of her faith for the sin into which she had led him, and to atone for it by ensuring that her sons' religious feelings were as strong as her own. To some extent, she succeeded—her eldest son, Bob, would eventually accompany her to China as a missionary; Frank and Will seem to have retained throughout their short lives a certain degree of religious feeling. But Arnold was much less religious; and with her second son, Ned, she failed completely, and therefore, throughout his life, fought all the harder to save him.

The problem went far beyond the fact that Ned was the "Peck's bad boy" of the Lawrence family, an incorrigible rule-breaker and mischievous practical joker, with a gift for spinning imaginative tales—Sarah recognized that in other ways Ned was the child who most resembled her. He had her determination; her features; her piercing, bright blue eyes; and, as he grew older, her stature, though the other boys all took after the father in height as well as coloring. Frank, for example, was tall, lean, a good scholar, but also brilliant at exactly those team sports that are generally taken to indicate character in England: rugby and cricket. Will was described by a contemporary as "really an Adonis to look at, beautiful in body," tall, graceful, a prizewinning gymnast. As striking as Ned's face was, and as physically strong as he became, he hated competitive sports and avoided as much as he could all forms of organized games—not an easy thing to do in an English school, nor one that made for popularity, either with the masters or with the other boys.

Because of T. E. Lawrence's fame, few families have been subjected to such intense scrutiny as the Lawrences, or have been the subject of so much retroactive psychoanalysis. The fact that his mother was the disciplinarian of the household, and that she carried out herself whatever physical punishment she decided was needed, has been given an exaggerated role in the development of Lawrence's admittedly complex personality. In keeping with her very literal view of Christianity, Sarah had an equally simple faith in the old adage "Spare the rod, and spoil the child." In her old age, when T. E. Lawrence became a friend of Lady Astor,* his mother remarked that "one of the reasons that Lord Astor's horses never won is because he wouldn't whip them." On the other hand, descriptions of Sarah as a sadistic mother are wildly overdrawn. Using a whip or a switch on children was more the rule than the exception at all levels of society in the late nineteenth century, and none of the Lawrence children, when they were grown, seem to have complained about it. She never had to whip Bob or Frank, and Arnold remembered being whipped only once, but she was obliged to whip Ned on his buttocks frequently, for fairly routine misbehavior, or for refusing to learn to play the piano. It seems likely that there was a clash of wills between Ned and Sarah—T. E. Lawrence would sum it up by writing that "we do rub each other up the wrong way"—which did not develop between her and the other boys. Her youngest son, Arnold, would later say that his mother wanted "to break T. E.'s will," but this is merely to say that throughout her life she wanted all her sons to be obedient, pious, and truthful, and that Ned, unlike his brothers, was not necessarily or consistently any of those things. Biographers have speculated about the extent to which T. E. Lawrence's strong streak of masochism in later life, as well as his extraordinary ability to endure pain and deprivation, was a product of the beatings he received from his mother, but this seems doubtful. Sarah loved her sons, was loved

---

* This was an unlikely friendship, but T. E. Lawrence and Lady Astor got along famously. Forceful and vivacious, she bullied and protected him like a mother hen, and so far as is known she was the only woman he ever allowed to ride pillion on his motorcycle. Nancy Astor, whose birth name was Langehorne, was a native of Danville, Virginia; she was married to the enormously wealthy Viscount Astor, and was the first woman ever elected to a seat in Parliament. In later life, she was an appeaser, and the Astors' great country house Cliveden was the social and spiritual center of those who sought peace with Germany and conciliation with Hitler. She once told Winston Churchill, "If I were your wife, I'd put poison in your coffee," to which he replied, "And if I were your husband, I'd drink it."

by them, and took an interest and great pride in everything they did. At all times, there were present in the house a full-time nanny and other servants, as well as Thomas Lawrence, so it is unlikely that the whippings were in any way cruel or unusual punishment, or carried out in such a way as to leave deep psychic scars. As in most English families of their class, the nannies were a calming and beloved presence—one of them stayed for several years, and when she left to join her sister in Canada, she was replaced by another with whom T. E. Lawrence was still in correspondence many years later, when he was famous.

As to the question of why such whippings were carried out by Sarah rather than Thomas, this may merely reflect the fact that he himself must have been caned by older boys ("prefects") and by masters during his years at Eton, a practice which was then common in public schools. Thomas was not the only nineteenth-century Englishman of his class to leave school with a marked distaste for corporal punishment. Winston Churchill, who was beaten at Harrow (Eton's rival) and much resented it, did not blame his father (whom he idolized) for sending him there, but as a result never laid his hand on his own son Randolph, whose behavior might have persuaded even the most benevolent of fathers to pick up a whip. All the Lawrence boys agree that their father retained a "quiet authority" in the family, and that he could be "very firm when necessary," sometimes intervening when he thought Sarah was being "unduly harsh," and invariably making the bigger decisions that affected their lives.

The biggest of these, of course, was deciding where the boys should go to school. It is impossible to guess whether Thomas regretted not being able to send his sons to Eton, but in any case there was no way that he could have afforded to send five boys there; nor, despite the fact that he was an Old Etonian himself, would Eton have accepted them in the knowledge that they were illegitimate. It also may be that having been sent to a boarding school, Thomas did not want to subject his sons to the same experience, but it is more likely that neither parent wished to send the boys away. The boys were the center of their lives, the main justification for their illicit union, the clearest sign that it had been "blessed," and the greatest source of their happiness. The first thing any outsider ever noticed about the Lawrences was how close they were to each other— indeed when Ned went "up" to Oxford, to a college that was only a few minutes away from his home by bicycle, he came home every night, despite the fact that undergraduates were supposed to spend their first two years living in their college. The boys were not afraid to leave home; nor did their parents discourage them from doing so, even in the case of Ned, whose journeys on foot would take him through some of the most dangerous country in the world; but for different reasons neither Thomas nor Sarah shared the enthusiasm of the English upper class for sending children away to school as early as possible.

The school they chose was the City of Oxford High School, whose elaborate Victorian facade still stands on George Street, close by Jesus College, where Ned would spend his undergraduate years, and the Ashmolean Museum, where his interest in archaeology was first kindled. The school was a high-minded hybrid, founded in 1888 by Thomas Hill Green, fellow of Balliol College and White's Professor of Moral Philosophy. It was originally intended to provide Oxford dons, now that they were allowed to marry and reside outside their college, with a school for their children that would form a kind of educational ladder leading them to Oxford University on their graduation, while also admitting children of Oxford's growing middle class. Much admired in its time, the school's architecture was in Victorian high Gothic style, and was eccentric and lavish even by the standards of Oxford, with a glazed domed tower of vaguely Turkish appearance, surmounted by an elaborate weather vane, and below it a wonderful clock with gilt hands set against a golden sunburst on a bright blue background. The cornerstone was laid by Prince Leopold, the youngest son of Queen Victoria, and the school was unusual in that it was a joint enterprise of the university and the city of Oxford. The fact that the City of Oxford High School did not attempt to imitate such great public schools as Eton, Harrow, Rugby, and Winchester was something of an asset for Oxford dons, many of whom would have been uncomfortable with the atmosphere of snobbery and the bullying that went on in the famous boarding schools of England. The school's staff, curriculum, and seriousness of purpose were second to none; its fees were reasonable; and no embarrassing or difficult questions were raised about accepting the sons of "Mr. and Mrs. Lawrence" as pupils.

Until the move to Oxford, Ned had had little in the way of formal schooling, except for an hour a day at the École Sainte-Marie in Dinard, and no experience of English school life, though he already showed signs of alarming precocity, and a voracious appetite for learning as much as he could about a wide variety of subjects. Both in France and in England he was taught by a governess, as well as by his mother and father, and it was clear to everyone that Ned was both enormously intelligent and naturally diligent. As to his precocity, Sarah claimed that Ned had learned the alphabet by the age of three, and his eldest brother, Bob, recalled that Ned could read the newspaper upside down at the age of five (though it is hard to gauge the usefulness of this feat). He spoke French fluently by the age of six, and started to learn Latin at age five. (Ned, who seems early on to have shown an aptitude for languages, learned French quickly as a second language; and in later life he would address the Council of Four at the Paris Peace Conference in fluent French.) His interests included the architecture of castles, armor, weapons, heraldry, old coins, medieval glassware, the geography and history of the Holy Land, and military tactics, as well as photography and carpentry. Ned, like many gifted children, paid more attention to what interested him than to the formal curriculum of the school, and on the subjects he cared about he was so well-informed and opinionated as to alarm even the most learned adults. A voracious reader, he went through books at a rapid rate, most of them outside his assigned reading, and although he would later claim to be able to extract the gist of a book quickly, the truth seems to be that like many bright children he skipped the parts he found dull, or disagreed with. All his brothers were intelligent, dutiful students, but Ned was in an entirely different category—a slightly unfocused prodigy.

It must be said that the masters at the City of Oxford High School recognized almost instantly that Ned was special. This might not have been the case at a boarding school, for it was clear from the beginning that he would never "fit in" conventionally, and that he was resolutely determined to avoid team sports of every kind, hanging on the sidelines with a knowing grin on his face—not an easy thing to get away with in any English school. Years later one of his masters would remark that "he knew no fear and we wondered why he did not play games." This was a shrewd comment, for Ned was already almost totally fearless, and determined to build up his strength and put it to a test, but at the same time he disliked all forms of organized competition. He became, like his father, a bicycle enthusiast, and always had the latest kind of racing bike—another indication that Thomas Lawrence had access to money when he wanted it, and never stinted his boys on anything. Ned often tinkered with his bikes to make them faster, and at an early age he pushed himself to amazing speeds and distances. Other boys seem to have respected him, rather than being outraged by his peculiar sense of humor and by the fact that he was an unapologetic "loner," perhaps because he was also a self-taught wrestler.

The fact that Lawrence was "different" from the two brothers nearest him in age, both of whom were enthusiastic about games and good "team players," has sometimes been attributed to the fact that he knew early on about his parents' secret whereas they did not. Lawrence claimed to have overheard, when he was four and a half years old, a conversation between his father and a solicitor about Thomas Lawrence's estates in Ireland, and although he drew the wrong conclusion, it is not impossible that a very bright child might have managed to overhear enough of the conversation to deduce that there was something irregular about his parents' situation. Lawrence would not have been the first child to pay an unhappy price for eavesdropping, and learning thereby something he did not want to know, and in his case he felt he must keep it a secret from his brothers. It would also, no doubt, have contributed to his resistance toward his mother's strong religious exhortations and her insistence on complete obedience, knowing that her own behavior had been less than perfect. At any rate, whatever significance young Ned's knowledge of the family secret may have had, it did not prevent him from feeling a strong, protective, and often touching affection for his brothers. The fact that the Lawrence boys were so close must also have helped protect Ned from the kind of bullying that a boy who won't play organized games might expect to attract in any school.

Although one of the "houses" of the City of Oxford High School would be named after T. E. Lawrence, he does not seem to have enjoyed his school years there. He disliked being forced to follow the curriculum, rather than devoting his time to his own interests, and he would complain, once he was grown up, that he had lived in morbid fear of being punished by the masters, even though there is little or no evidence that he was ever in fact disciplined severely in school. He wrote several essays for the school magazine, and these already demonstrated his ability as a writer—for he was as anxious to make his name as a respected author as he was to be a military hero. The ferocious, almost photographic attention to detail and the love of landscape that make *Seven Pillars of Wisdom* a great piece of nature writing as well as a war memoir are already evident in his essay on a family cycling tour in the countryside, as is the mocking, mordant tone that occasionally surfaces in his youthful satires on cricket and on the relentless pursuit of scholarships, neither of which can have pleased the masters who read them.

It would be a mistake, however, to see Ned as a misfit at the City of Oxford High School. He seems to have had plenty of friends, and he was not above ordinary rough horseplay—indeed, in the autumn of 1904 his leg was broken just above the ankle in "a playground scuffle." This accident would not normally have been of any great consequence, but in Ned's case, as is so often true of episodes in the life of T. E. Lawrence, there are certain mysteries about it. The break was apparently slow to heal, and kept Ned out of school for the rest of the term. This is odd—it was not a compound fracture, and if the leg was in a cast, there seems no good reason why he should have been kept at home. Some biographers have suggested that the break itself, or the slow mending of the bone, may have been caused by Ned's preference for a vegetarian diet, but this too seems unlikely: a diet of bread, milk, cheese, vegetables, and fruit would have been high in calcium and might even have speeded the healing process better than the usual British diet of starchy foods and overcooked meat. Also, both Ned and his mother believed that the accident halted his growth.* His mother may have preferred to imagine that the broken bone was the reason why he stopped growing, rather than accepting the more likely possibility that his shortness was a genetic gift from her.

In any event, Ned stopped growing after the schoolyard accident, and he would always be rather sensitive about his height, though he masked his sensitivity by occasional self-mockery. Even his friend Storrs refers to him as "a gnome," and his fellow officers in the Middle East during the war often referred to him as "little Lawrence," though not necessarily without affection. Usually, in group photographs nearly everybody towers over him, except Emir Abdulla and Gertrude Bell. His shortness was certainly accentuated by his very large head, though this effect was somewhat disguised when he wore long, flowing Arab robes and a headdress. That may have been one reason he continued to wear Arab clothing for portraits and official occasions even after the war was over.

The fact that Ned was out of school for the best part of one term did not prevent him from earning the prizes and scholarships he had mocked so cleverly in the school magazine. In the same year as the accident, at the age of sixteen, he took the Junior Oxford Local Examinations, which included tests in religious knowledge, arithmetic, history, English (language and literature), geography, Latin, Greek, French, and mathematics,

---

* Three doctors—Maurice Carter, MD; Avodah Offit, MD; and Thomas Murray, MD—have expressed strong doubt that a broken bone in an otherwise healthy boy could possibly halt or impede growth. In any case, there is considerable controversy about T. E. Lawrence's adult height. His American biographer Lowell Thomas puts his height at five feet five and a half inches; one of his British biographers, the poet Robert Graves, puts it at five feet six inches; some people put it as low as five feet three inches; Lawrence's medical records during his service in the RAF put it at five feet five inches. At the time the average height of an Englishman of his age was five feet six inches. Height was then something of a class matter—the upper classes, given a better diet, tended to be taller than the "working class," so Lawrence was certainly short for somebody of his class, though not very much shorter than, say, the Prince of Wales (the future King Edward VIII, afterward the duke of Windsor), or Winston Churchill.

and "was placed in the First Class." His weakest marks were in arithmetic and mathematics, but "he gained a distinction in Religious Knowledge," perhaps not surprisingly after all those prayer meetings and daily Bible readings.

During the year he continued his strong interest in archaeology. Together with a similarly inclined friend, C. F. C. Beeson, he toured Oxford and the surrounding areas, making brass rubbings of medieval tombs in churches and tipping workmen for old glass fragments and pottery in building sites. Beeson was somewhat awed by the intensity of Ned's interest in archaeology, but the two boys seem to have gotten along well enough. Oxford was a good place for apprentice archaeologists at that time, owing to the numerous new buildings and enlargements being made to various colleges, and the boys brought most of their "finds" to Oxford's Ashmolean Museum—indeed they brought so many interesting sixteenth- and seventeenth-century finds to the museum, many of which were accepted for the Ashmolean's collection, that the two schoolboys were praised by name in the Annual Report of the Museum for 1906, an unusual distinction. It is typical of Lawrence's lifelong ability to attract the admiring attention of powerful older men that he eventually came to the attention of David G. Hogarth, keeper of the Ashmolean Museum, who would become his mentor in archaeology and would make possible the years Lawrence spent in the Ottoman Empire as an archaeological assistant before the war. Indeed Hogarth was the first and by far the most important of Lawrence's many surrogate father figures.

In *The Hero with a Thousand Faces*, Joseph Campbell, a student of myths, examines the psychology of the hero, and perfectly describes the part that David Hogarth would play in Ned Lawrence's life: "His role is precisely that of the Wise Old Man of the myths and fairy tales whose words assist the hero through the trials and errors of the weird adventure. He is the one who points to the shining magic sword that will kill the dragon-terror . . . applies healing balm to the almost fatal wounds, and finally dismisses the conqueror back into the world of normal life, following the great adventure into the enchanted night."

High-flown as these words may seem, they might serve as an apt description of Lawrence's life—and his hold on our imagination. Ned may have had no idea where or how far the objects he and his friend Beeson dug up from the ground would eventually lead him, but like so much else in his life, they drew him inexorably toward the path of a hero, a first small step away from maternal protection and domination.

As mentioned, biographers of T. E. Lawrence have tended to focus on his mother as the source of his many problems, including a general aversion to women (with some notable exceptions); a morbid fear of sexual contact, even of physical touch; a self-punishing spirit; and a refusal to accept the rewards that he had earned. Lawrence himself certainly expressed the somewhat extreme opinion that it would have been better for his parents if he and his brothers had never been born. "They should not have borne children" was his final judgment on the matter, based on the deep psychological and social gulf between them, which, he supposed, was responsible for the painful conflict he felt within himself.

It is understandable that Sarah has received greater attention (and blame) than Thomas from those who have written about T. E. Lawrence— she lived for nearly a quarter of a century after her famous son's death, and for forty years after Thomas Lawrence's death, so that many of Lawrence's friends met her, and were impressed by her strength of character. Lawrence's father, by contrast, died before his son had achieved a kind of apotheosis as a hero and a worldwide celebrity, and has therefore been relegated to an offstage role in the Lawrence family drama.

Of course to become a fully functioning adult any son must break free from his emotional dependence on his mother, a task made more difficult when the mother is as strong-willed as Sarah, and as reluctant to let her children go. In Ned's case there is another, and perhaps more powerful, influence at work: the desire to be heroic; and that is, inevitably, centered on the father.

Although Thomas (Chapman) Lawrence's presence in most books about T. E. Lawrence is ghostly, that was by no means the case in life. This is, perhaps unconsciously, partly Ned's doing; at fifteen he was already a master dissimulator. In Lawrence's own accounts of his childhood—the most important sources being his letters to Charlotte Shaw, wife of Bernard Shaw; and to Lionel Curtis, who became something of a soul mate of Lawrence's after the war, when they were both fellows of All Souls College, Oxford—it is his mother toward whom he directs attention, both for forcing her strict religious ideas on her sons and for taking their father away from the lordly status he had enjoyed as a wealthy landowner and baronet. The fact that his father had willingly given up wealth and status for love, and may have been happy with his decision, was not one that Lawrence wanted to contemplate; nor did he wish to consider the fact that his mother exchanged life as a domestic servant for a lifelong relationship with a gentleman (admittedly living under a false name), a huge leap upward in status.

That is not to deny that it was a love match; it clearly was, and the fact that Sarah bore Thomas eight children argues for a fairly intense erotic attachment on both sides, however much guilt Sarah had to struggle with as a result—indeed she is said to have believed that she was risking damnation for herself in order to save him, and that their five living sons were proof that God might forgive her. Toward the end of her long life, she is said to have murmured over and over again, "God hates the sin, but loves the sinner." This summed up her faith in salvation for herself, and it pained her deeply that Ned did not share her faith.

Even though Ned may have believed, from what he had overheard and misunderstood as a child, that Thomas Lawrence was not his real father, it was nevertheless not his mother's approval that he sought. It was always approval from his father, and from the alternative father figures he would collect along the way—hence his briskly dismissing in advance the pride his mother would feel when she learned that he had been recommended for the Victoria Cross. His suggestion in his letter home was unmistakably that the Victoria Cross was exactly the kind of sentimental and popular tribute to valor his mother would like, but that his father, as a gentleman of superior education and breeding, would despise it as much as Lawrence did.

As Ned gained greater freedom to move about on his own, or with friends like Beeson, and took advantage of the latest racing bicycle to increase the distance he could travel and the amount of time he spent away from home, his interests became those that would appeal to Thomas Lawrence, rather than to his mother. His father—whose closest friend was the learned H. T. Inman, author of *The Churches of Oxford*—was after all far more likely than his mother to appreciate Ned's brass rubbings and archaeological finds. Church architecture, medieval warfare, the classics—these were all areas in which Ned's father was knowledgeable; and in some pursuits, like bicycling, woodworking, carpentry, and photography, Thomas was a patient instructor and quick to appreciate and praise Ned's considerable abilities. In later life T. E. Lawrence would play a large part in building a house for his fellow archaeologists at Carchemish (in what is now Iraq), and carry out not only wood carving but quite elaborate and ambitious stone carving that convinced experts it was Hittite rather than his own work; he also took remarkable photographs under the most difficult conditions imaginable. Thus, Ned not only learned from his father but worked hard to please him. Indeed, his first effort at carpentry and woodcarving was a finely finished book case he made for his father. Thomas Lawrence was not at all a distant offstage observer of the continuing dramatic confrontation between Sarah and Ned; instead he was a constant and much-admired presence in Ned's life.

It is not uncommon for an adolescent boy to fantasize that he is the offspring of somebody far more impressive than his putative father and that one day he will be recognized, by his noble and valorous feats, and restored to his rightful place—indeed this fantasy is the basis for many myths and children's stories in every culture. In Ned's case, this natural fantasy was made more intense by the suspicion that Thomas Lawrence might, in fact, *not* be his father. To this suspicion was no doubt added, later, the painful fact that Thomas had given up the station in society which would have enabled Ned and his brothers to go to Eton, like their father, rather than attend the City of Oxford High School as day boys, and would have confirmed them as "gentlemen," members by birth of the upper class, unlike their mother.

As an adolescent, Ned had two contradictory but not uncommon reactions. One was to build up and even to exaggerate his father's previous social status, emphasizing Thomas's "lordly" ways and former wealth. The other was to impress his father by beating him at his own games. If Thomas Lawrence rode 100 miles in a day on his bicycle, Ned would ride (or claim to have ridden) 200. He would practice endlessly to become not just as good a shot as his father, but a *better* one; would become not just an amateur interested in church and castle architecture, but an expert, who claimed to have visited, studied, and sketched *every* significant castle in Britain and France. Clearly, part of this is familiar: the adolescent boy's driving hunger for his father's approval and praise. But there is also an element of rivalry, which Ned carried to enormous lengths, and which he clearly won, though it brought him no pleasure, and no release from his feelings.

That these feelings were strong and impossible for Ned to reconcile is demonstrated by a mysterious episode in which he ran away from home and joined the army. It is placed by different biographers as occurring sometime between 1904 and 1906, though 1904 seems more probable, since Ned would then have been sixteen, a more likely age for a boy to run away from home. Lawrence alluded to this episode several times in later life, but tried to keep it out of the biographies that were written during his lifetime, probably so as not to cause his mother more pain. Since Ned had no relatives to run away to—his mother's relatives were unknown to him, and his father's lived under a different name—he did perhaps the only thing he could think of to escape from what had become intolerable to him. Joining the army was a drastic and perhaps desperate decision, and almost certainly a cry for help.

In the Victorian-Edwardian era, service in the ranks of the British army was almost as low as you could fall on the social ladder; the "Tommy," in his red coat, was still regarded, in the duke of Wellington's famous words about his troops two generations earlier, as "the scum of the earth, recruited for drink!" The popular view of signing on as a soldier was captured by one working-class mother who remarked that she would rather see her son dead "than wearing the red coat!"

As a result, the British army was something less than scrupulous in accepting recruits. The recruiting sergeant seems to have been willing to overlook Ned's height and obvious immaturity, and signed him up as a boy soldier in the Royal Garrison Artillery. This antiquated branch of the Royal Artillery was similar to the U.S. Coast Artillery and served in forts built to protect major ports and naval facilities from attack. Boy soldiers were trained as trumpeters and buglers, but no special precautions were taken to separate them from adult soldiers in the barracks. Ned may have served in the Falmouth Garrison, on the south coast of Cornwall, but for how long is hard to know. He would later claim that he was there six to eight months, but this is very unlikely—his school friends did not remember any such long absence; nor did his surviving brothers. A more likely version is that he spent six to eight weeks there, or possibly only six to eight days. However short a time Ned served in the army, though, it was not an experience he would ever forget. The brutality, the foul language, the rough banter about sex, the fistfights, the drunken brawling on weekends—none of these can have been easy for a child of Sarah's to endure, even for a few days. Interestingly enough, he claimed not to have minded the discipline, which in those days was rough-and-ready at the hands of noncommissioned officers of the old school.

His father, possibly at Ned's urgent pleading, moved quickly to buy him out of his enlistment, a recognized practice in those days. Thomas Lawrence not only managed to get Ned out of the army but may also have managed to erase the whole episode from the army's files. Thomas demonstrated more skill at facing down the army bureaucracy than he gets credit for, and obviously knew how to resume the role of a gentleman with friends in high places when he had to.

This family crisis—no other word will do—evidently also led Thomas and Sarah, however reluctantly, to reconsider how to deal with their brilliant and difficult second son, who, it was now quite evident, was going to require very different treatment from the other four boys. It is not hard to see here too the evidence of the father's quiet authority in persuading Sarah that this particular colt needed to be ridden on a lighter rein. Over the next two years, a number of changes were made, all of them intended to give him greater freedom. His bicycling trips became longer and more extended; the peculiarities of his vegetarian diet became a pretext for his skipping family meals; he would eventually be allowed to switch from preparation for a mathematics scholarship at the university, which he hated, to history, which was more to his liking; and finally, less than two years after he had run off to join the army, his parents built him a small cottage in the garden at 2 Polstead Road, which allowed him to live separately from the rest of the family.

This was obviously a large concession to a son who had demonstrated just how far he was willing to go in placing himself beyond his mother's reach. T. E. Lawrence later claimed that he had actually built the cottage himself, but his account was contradicted by his mother, and seems unlikely—the cottage (which still stands) not only is attractive but shows every evidence of skilled professional construction, especially in the steeply countered cathedral roof, rising to a solid central brickwork chimney. Given his own skills, Ned surely helped with the woodwork and the interior; the lines of the exterior woodwork are very elaborate and fanciful indeed for a simple cottage, and may show his hand and imagination at work. Although the cottage was explained away as a place for Ned to study in once he had switched to history and become an undergraduate at Oxford, it seems in fact to have been designed from the outset for him to live in, with a fireplace, a stove, running water, electric light, and "a house telephone." It is impossible not to see this arrangement as a victory over his mother, giving him the ability to come and go without supervision, freeing him from her insistence on knowing what he was doing at all times, and giving him complete privacy—an unusual, indeed enviable situation for a boy of eighteen or nineteen living at home at that time!

Ned's decision to switch from mathematics to history is probably a case of following his own growing interests—but more than that, it reflects his impatience with abstract learning, and with any subject having clearly defined rules. He appears to have learned languages, for example, instinctively, by talking and by trial and error, but without making any attempt to master and memorize tedious grammatical rules, which bored him. He was a familiar and difficult figure in academic life: the brilliant young man with rather too many interests, who resists learning the basics of anything thoroughly, and who skates by at examination time on a combination of omnivorous reading, strong opinions, and verbal dexterity. As a result, Ned's entrance to Oxford was neither as easy nor as automatic as it might have been.

In the summer of 1906, when Ned was eighteen and had only one more year to spend in school, he made his first trip abroad, with his friend Beeson—another big step in the untying of his mother's apron strings, though he would try to make up for that by the length and detail of his letters home. After taking the Oxford Local Examinations, a prerequisite for entering Oxford University, he set off on a two-week cycling tour of Brittany, using Dinard, where the Lawrence family was still remembered with fond feelings, as his home base. In the end, his friend Beeson (whose nickname was "Scroggs") went home before Ned did, so he spent almost two weeks more touring by himself.

Ned's letters home are remarkable, and not just for their length and their amazingly descriptive detail, but also for his evident determination to hide his own feelings from his mother. The letters were meant to be read by the whole family, and are affectionate enough in tone, but they also exude a certain steely detachment and distance, which may not have escaped his mother's notice. Certainly they are very unlike the monosyllabic, dutiful letters that most schoolboys send home, and while the intelligence, power of observation, and insight they demonstrate would astonish and even alarm most parents, they are also a bit chilling. A single surviving earlier letter from Ned to his mother, from Colchester, when he and his father were on a cycling trip in 1905, is signed, "Love to yourself," but perhaps significantly the letters from the 1906 trip, with a couple of exceptions, are mostly signed, "With love to all," or, "With love to everybody," or they simply end without any closing at all.

Two other things are noticeable in the letters. The first is that Ned's commitment to a vegetarian diet was apparently rather less strict abroad than at home, since he boasts of having tried some of everything on the prix fixe luncheon menu at the Grand Hôtel de l'Europe in Dinan, which included sardines, fowl, cold meats, and hash. Second, he was scrupulously careful about accounting for every penny (and, indeed, halfpenny) he spent.

A longish letter, written on August 14 to his mother, runs to some 1,400 words, and includes two excellent architectural drawings. Almost all of it is about the Château de Tonquédec, with minute attention to the interesting details of the latrines, and it reveals an astonishing knowledge of medieval building techniques. (In some respects, his letters home were notes for future works.) He also mentions that he has reached his highest speed to date on a bicycle—thirty miles an hour in high gear on the sand of a nearby beach—and feels he is fit enough to ride 100 miles a day for months. All this must have been of interest to his father (and is perhaps intended to impress him) but probably not to his mother, to whom the letter is addressed. Another letter, 2,300 words long, is mostly about the Château de la Hunaudaye; it reads like a learned guidebook, and contains a full-page detailed plan of the fortress, one of two in this series of letters home, done in pen and ink by Ned, which could hardly be improved on by a professional architect, and which illustrate not only his thorough knowledge of medieval architecture at this early age, but even more his understanding of medieval warfare. He knows why the fortress was built the way it was, and what its strengths and weaknesses were—in short, his is an expert's view of how to defend or attack a fortified place, and how to make the best use of the topography in siting and building one.

It would be a mistake to leap from this to comparisons to the young Napoleon, who is said to have relied on his tactical instincts to win schoolyard fights; but much that is contained in young Ned's letters to his family reads like a brilliant and insightful essay on medieval fortifications and warfare by a particularly gifted cadet at Sandhurst or West

Point, and makes it easy to understand why T. E. Lawrence's notes and dispatches from the field were read with such interest even at the level of the chief of the imperial general staff. His observation and grasp of significant details, his broad overview, and his crisply expressed conclusions are all in evidence here—the schoolboy demonstrates the same skill in writing reports and drawing maps as the temporary second-lieutenant and acting staff captain would demonstrate eight years later, though one guesses that none of it is what his mother wanted to hear.

His knowledge of medieval clothing and armor is, if anything, even more impressive, perhaps even daunting. The unfamiliar words flow by on page after page: maniple, chausable, dalamtic, stoles, alb (but no tunic, Ned observes), on a bishop's effigy; jupon, *genouillières*, jambs, sollerets, on the effigy of Tiphaine du Guesclin, widow of Jean V de Beaumanoir, which exhibits a rare combination of fifteenth-century haute couture and armor—Ned meticulously counts the twenty-two round buttons on her jupon, notes that her spurs have rowels, and describes her face and hairstyle in detail. These letters seem very serious and almost self-consciously erudite, as if Ned was already practicing to write essays for his tutor, or to write his thesis, which would also be on the subject of medieval military architecture, with plans, drawings, and photographs by himself.

One letter, addressed to one of his younger brothers, Will, in reply to Will's letter describing his rather tentative exploration of a Roman or Celtic camp and possible burial mound at home, is very much *du haut en bas*, full of detailed suggestions and warnings, and ends with a reminder that digging is good exercise. It is not exactly supercilious in tone, but close to it. Another, to his older brother Bob, also deals with Will's excavations, but in a bossier way—nothing more is to be done until Ned comes home, and until Woolley, an assistant keeper of the Ashmolean, with whom Ned is already on close terms, has been consulted. Ned also notes that he has received a letter from Scroggs informing him that he has received "a first with distinction in Scripture & English" in the Oxford Local Examinations, but with no other results. A fuller letter describing his results arrived from his mother a few days later. "The result is on the whole not as good as I had hoped," he replied, "although I am quite satisfied with the Eng." He does not seem to have been much disturbed.

As Jeremy Wilson notes in his authorized biography of T. E. Lawrence, Ned "had been placed in the First Class; of 4,645 candidates, only twelve had achieved a higher total." His worst results were in algebra and geometry, and for a future translator of *The Odyssey* he did rather poorly in Greek and Latin, but one might guess that the examiners of schoolboys were more interested in grammar—not one of Ned's strong points in any language—than in fluency, style, and literary knowledge.

It is usually difficult to read much into the letters home of eighteen-year-olds, but as in so many other things, T. E. Lawrence is an exception. The later T. E. Lawrence is perfectly apparent in these letters written in 1906: the urge to push himself as hard as he could physically; the astonishing accumulation of knowledge, and the mastery of every detail of any subject that interested him; the curious combination of extreme aesthetic sensibility and a fascination with the art of warfare; the fear that his mother's will, stronger even than his own, will prevail over him unless he keeps his guard up at all times; the determination to win his father's approval, as well as to beat him at those things Thomas cares most about; the instinctive position of leadership he takes toward his brothers, even Bob, the firstborn. All these traits would remain true of T. E. Lawrence for the rest of his life. Not only was the child (as Wordsworth put it) "father of the Man"; he *was* the man.

Ned's "First" did not guarantee him entry to the Oxford college of his choice. With the aid of a private tutor (called a crammer in England), L. Cecil Jane, who was to become an admirer and friend throughout Ned's years at Oxford, and for many years beyond, he prepared to take the examination for a scholarship at St. John's College, his older brother Bob's college, in December 1906, but he was unsuccessful.

A month later, in January 1907, further crammed by the indefatigable Jane, Ned tried, this time successfully, for a scholarship at Jesus College, where his birth in Wales would work to his advantage. The college's founder, Hugh Price (or Aprice), who lived during the reign of Elizabeth I, was a Welshman, and over the centuries the college had developed strong links to Wales. Considering that Lawrence would later claim to be Irish, it is ironic to note that his birth in Wales secured him not only a place at Jesus but a scholarship of £50 a year. Ned was, of course, no more Welsh than Irish, but the fact apparently passed unnoticed at Jesus. Perhaps with this in mind, Ned went on a cycling tour of Welsh castles over the Easter vacation, and found the Welsh "rather inquisitive," but apparently honest. Once again he tested his limit in terms of speed and endurance on a bicycle, and sent home long, detailed, but curiously impersonal letters about castle architecture.

In the autumn of 1907 Ned would "go up" to Jesus College at the age of nineteen, for three years—years which, in many ways, would be the most influential of his life. In later life he would complain—rather unfairly, one would judge—about his school days, which he described as "miserable sweated years of unwilling work," but about Oxford he had no such feelings. He remarked in a letter to Liddell Hart, "When . . . I suddenly went to Oxford, the new freedom felt like Heaven."

CHAPTER FOUR

Oxford, 1907–1910

Noon strikes on England, noon on Oxford town. . . .
  Proud and godly kings hath built her, long ago,
  With her towers and tombs and statues all arow,
With her fair and floral air and the love that lingers there,
  And the streets where the great men go.

> —James Elroy Flecker, "The Dying Patriot"

I was a modest, good-humoured boy.
It is Oxford that has made me insufferable.

> —Sir Max Beerbohm, "Going Back to School"

I n Britain one "goes up" to Oxford or to Cambridge; conversely, if dismissed or expelled, one is "sent down." Lawrence, of course, did not so much "go up" as go sideways—his home in Oxford was only a few minutes from Jesus College by bicycle. For most of his fellow undergraduates, Oxford was the first great adventure of their young lives, away from home and boarding school at last, in a place where they were treated as adults, and expected to behave like adults—with a certain allowance always made, of course, for the follies of young men of the upper classes letting off steam. For Lawrence it was slightly less of an adventure—he had already run away from home and experienced life in barracks with scores of older recruits in an age when each metal cot was exactly two feet away from the next. Still, it was a huge change in status.

Oxford University was and remains a nebulous institution, more of a gas than a solid, as T. E. Lawrence would later describe the Arab Revolt, and guerrilla warfare in general. In order to join it young men (and now of course young women) apply to the colleges of their choice, take an examination, and undergo a firm and probing interview. If accepted, they will spend three academic years at their college, during which the university into which they have been matriculated will seldom touch their lives, except in the form of the "proctor" and his bowler-hatted "bulldogs," enforcers of the university regulations while undergraduates are outside their own college in the streets of Oxford. The university's buildings are spread through the town—among them are such architectural landmarks as the Bodleian Library, the Sheldonian Theatre, and the Ashmolean Museum—but the life of the university and much of its teaching take place within the thirty-odd walled-in colleges. When asked where they "went to university" Oxonians are more likely to give the name of their old college than that of Oxford: Magdalen, Christ Church, Jesus, Balliol, etc., each college being, effectively, a world in itself. For both the undergraduates and the fellows (known as "dons"—a hangover from the days when the older colleges were still Catholic ecclesiastical institutions), their college is their home, the center of their world, as the regiment is for officers and senior NCOs in the British army. They eat there; they study there (for the most part); the undergraduates live there for the first two of their three years, as do bachelor dons; and the undergraduates' academic career is centered on their once-a-week meeting with their tutor, often a fellow of their college, who usually sets them an essay to write, and listens to it at the next tutorial, giving his opinions afterward and setting a direction for further reading, sometimes over a glass of sherry. Much of the benefit of an Oxford education is derived from the undergraduate's relationship with the tutor—if the personalities dovetail, if there is a bond of mutual sympathy and interest, much can be attained. In the absence of these things, disenchantment can quickly set in.*

Lawrence, as so often in his life, was a special case. Unlike his classmates, he did not live at his college. They had assigned "rooms," usually a sitting room–study and a bedroom; there were several rooms to a staircase, with "a scout"—a combination of valet, butler, and housemaid—to look after the residents. Rooms ranged from medieval discomfort to palatial grandeur, according to the students' ability to pay, and according to an indecipherable social code in the office of the bursar, who made the assignments. In Lawrence's day, it was quite common for undergraduates to be served breakfast, lunch, or tea in their rooms, and for those who could afford it, full dinner parties, with a special menu and wines chosen from the college's cellar. The entrance to each set of rooms (usually two to a landing) was through a pair of doors, and when the outer one was closed (this was called "sporting one's oak") it was a sign that one did not wish to be disturbed. Thus the undergraduates had a degree of privacy that few of them could have enjoyed at boarding school or, for the most part, at home.

Lawrence's principal tutor, Reginald Lane Poole, was actually at his older brother's college, St. John's, rather than at Jesus. Poole was not perhaps the ideal tutor for such a rara avis as Lawrence—he was keeper of the archives and lecturer of diplomacy at Oxford, the author of 151 scholarly works, a forbiddingly conventional historian who preferred solidly based research to brilliant insight, and who was described by one of Lawrence's friends at Oxford as looking "as if he descended from a long line of maiden aunts." In fact, Lawrence seems to have found two much more interesting and (perhaps interested) unofficial tutors: his crammer, L. C. Jane, whom he continued to visit, often at odd hours of the night; and David Hogarth, the keeper of the Ashmolean Museum, who, until

---

* A typical case of the latter kind was the dislike between the future poet laureate and television celebrity John Betjeman and his tutor at Magdalen College, C. S. Lewis, author of, among other things, *The Narnia Chronicles*. Lewis called Betjeman an "idle prig" and was instrumental in sending him down, and Betjeman later described Lewis as arid, unsympathetic, and uninspiring, and blamed his failure at Oxford on Lewis.

his death in 1927, remained one of the most powerful influences in Lawrence's life.

Except for one term in 1908, Lawrence continued to live at home throughout his years at Jesus, and since he seldom ate dinner "at Hall"—indeed, he seldom participated in any conventional meal, except that he had a fondness for tea (among his few self-indulgences was a sweet tooth)—his contact with his fellow undergraduates was minimal. He did not take part in team sports or frequent the Junior Common Room or join any of the undergraduate clubs and societies that are deemed to be an essential part of the Oxford experience. In short, he managed to attend Oxford on his own terms. The only exception was his service in the Oxford University Officers' Training Corps. Lawrence was one of the first to volunteer, no doubt in part because as a schoolboy he had been in a similar organization, the St. Aldate's Church Lads' Brigade, and perhaps because he thought he might as well put to some use his brief service in the army. In addition, he was made a signaler, a position that in those days involved cycling, his passion. Besides, his enthusiasm for military matters was genuine, and not necessarily confined to reading books on strategy and tactics.

Lawrence was never friendless, despite his Cheshire cat–like invisibility at Jesus. "Scroggs" Beeson was up, though not at the same college, and Lawrence made friends with several undergraduates at Jesus, including an American Rhodes Scholar from Kansas, W. O. Ault; and Vyvyan W. Richards, a "Welsh-American," with whom Lawrence had a more intimate friendship than with any other contemporary. Ault's tutor was also Reginald Lane Poole, and as Ault was also studying medieval history he saw quite a lot of Lawrence, who introduced him to the art of taking brass rubbings. Lawrence seems to have been the only person at Jesus who did not treat Ault as an outsider because he was American.

Vyvyan Richards was rather more of a soul mate than Scroggs or Ault, a sensitive young man who shared Lawrence's medieval interests and, like Lawrence, was a passionate devotee of William Morris, the Victorian aesthete and founder of a school of arts and crafts. Much of Morris's work was in the Gothic revival mode—indeed, the curious roof design of

Lawrence's cottage in the garden at 2 Polstead Road looks very much as if it had been inspired by the cupolas of the famous "Red House" Morris had designed and built for himself and his wife Jane.* Lawrence and Richards shared Morris's passionate commitment to designing and printing beautiful books, when possible by hand, with hand-set type, eschewing altogether the modern linotype and the machine press, in favor of medieval printing methods and hand-painted illumination.

They even discussed setting up a hand press of their own somewhere in the English countryside, and devoting themselves to printing limited or single-copy editions of the great books—a plan that elicited a rare degree of disapproval from Lawrence's usually silent father. It is not altogether clear whether Thomas Lawrence disapproved of the fantasy that a hand press could be made into a paying proposition, or whether he realized immediately, unlike his son, that Richards was a homosexual and deeply attracted to Ned. On the first point Thomas was a sound judge of business schemes—he had, after all, once managed a very large estate, and was still involved in it—and on the second he was worldly enough to recognize the nature of Richards's affection for Ned immediately, even if Ned did not. It had been only thirteen years since Oscar Wilde's conviction for "gross indecencies," in what had been one of the most publicized scandals of the age, and homosexuality not only was on every parent's mind but was punishable by social disgrace and even imprisonment.

Vyvyan Richards may have summed up the nature of their friendship best when he said, much later in life, "Quite frankly, for me it was love at first sight," and went on to regret that Lawrence "had neither flesh nor carnality of any kind. He received my affection, my sacrifice, in fact, eventually my total subservience, as though it was his due. He never gave even the slightest sign that he understood my motives, or fathomed my desire. . . . I realize now that he was sexless—at least that he was unaware of sex." This may or may not be true—perhaps Lawrence was more aware of the nature of Richards's interest than he let on, but at the same time

---

* At Bexleyheath, south of London.

was unwilling to respond to it, and since he nevertheless liked Richards, solved the problem by simply ignoring it. It may have consoled Richards to suppose that Lawrence was "sexless," but it seems more likely that Lawrence was, from an early age, determined to suppress any sexual feelings, whether toward Richards or anyone else. It is possible, of course, that he might have been homosexual had he allowed his sexual instincts to emerge, but since he was a master of self-control, this never happened until much later in his life, and even then in a very strange form.

At the time he met Richards, Lawrence was in the process, common to most undergraduates, of testing his limits. Richards reported that his friend went swimming at night in the winter, plunging through a gap in the ice into a river (probably the Cherwell). Lawrence also went without food or sleep for protracted periods of time, and spent many hours at the Oxford University Officers' Training Course pistol range, practicing with both the strong and the weak hand to the point of exhaustion. It is possible that Lawrence was already preparing himself for some great feat—military glory and heroism were never far from his mind—but he may also have been submitting himself to a punishing and demanding regime intended to subdue and control just those urges which Vyvyan Richards hoped to arouse in him. In those days it was believed that ejaculation of any kind weakened the body, and athletes were sternly warned against sexual relationships and masturbation. Lawrence, as one who always carried things too far, invented for himself the most punishing physical routine he could stand.

Whether or not he recognized the nature of Richards's affection, Lawrence was held back from any sexual activity by a naturally abstemious nature, a lack of any sensible sexual education, and his extreme religious upbringing at home. In addition, Lawrence never experienced the sexual curiosity that develops between boys in boarding school, and he had had what may have been a frightening experience as a boy in a barracks full of grown men. The result, perhaps intensified by self-consciousness over his short stature, was to produce a personality that was not so much "sexless" as armored against sexual temptation, and the longer he avoided any kind of sexual relationship, the more difficult it became for him to have one. His youngest brother, Arnold, was of the opinion that Lawrence died a virgin, and he was surely right.

It is very significant that at the same time Lawrence was gently deflecting Vyvyan Richards's advances, while retaining Richards as a friend—and actually making plans for the two of them to share a William Morris–inspired country cottage where they would hand-print aesthetically satisfying volumes, a cottage complete with separate "shut beds" marked "Meum" and "Tuam"—Lawrence made the mistake of proposing marriage to a young woman.

Lawrence's first sight of Janet Laurie has a certain innocent sexual ambivalence to it. In the spring of 1894, when the Lawrences moved to New Forest, the Lauries were neighbors. Apparently, Janet's parents had wanted a son, and therefore had the little girl's hair cut short, and dressed her in a boy's clothes—one of those strange decisions that, at the time, often made otherwise quite ordinary English families seem bizarre to foreigners. One Sunday morning, when the Lawrences were attending church, Ned saw Janet sitting in a pew in front of him, and said to his nanny, "What a naughty little boy to keep his hat on in church." Janet turned around, stuck her tongue out at him, and said, "I'm not a boy, I'm a girl." "And a very rude little girl," Nanny said predictably, but a friendship had been struck, and Janet soon became a frequent visitor at Langley Lodge. Although Sarah was generally dismissive of girls—"We could never be bothered with girls in our house," she would tell the poet Robert Graves, when he came to write a biography of T. E. Lawrence after the war—she seems to have made an exception for Janet, whom Ned particularly liked, since Janet was something of a tomboy.

Over the years, Janet became a friend of all the Lawrence boys; for a time, she was at a boarding school in Oxford, and although she went home after the death of her father, she continued to pay frequent visits to 2 Polstead Road, and "sometimes stayed there." She seems to have played the role of a sister to all the boys, and to have been accepted by their parents almost as one of the family.

A photograph of Janet taken when she might have been about seventeen shows an attractive young woman, with a striking profile, very lively eyes, and a full mouth, dressed in a white blouse rather like a man's shirt, with a tie, possibly the summer uniform of her school. She manages to look severe and sensual at the same time. Everybody who met her agreed that she was "a lovely girl," as well as being good-natured and fun. Sarah went so far as to hope that her eldest son, Bob, might marry Janet one day, and no doubt did what she could to encourage that, but Bob was too serious and easily shocked to attract Janet. Ned would later say of his older brother, who would become a missionary doctor, "He is illuminated from inside, not from out. His face very often shines like a lamp." Janet set her cap at the taller and better-looking Will instead, incurring Sarah's displeasure, since Sarah disliked having her plans thwarted.

Ned was "more than two years younger" than Janet, and considerably shorter. She saw him as a beloved and mischievous younger brother, always up to such tricks as sneaking her into his room at Jesus for tea, or egging her on to toss a sugar cube through the open window of a don. She was therefore surprised when Ned abruptly proposed to her one evening after dinner, though she might have guessed that something was up when Ned waited until everybody else had left the dining room, then carefully bolted the door. Given Ned's taste for practical jokes, she very likely assumed that she was about to become the victim of one, and was therefore understandably astonished when he asked her to marry him, without even a preliminary kiss, indeed without even looking her in the eye. Although she would later say she realized at once that he was serious, her immediate reaction, perhaps out of shock, was to laugh. A moment of dreadful embarrassment followed—there they were, locked in the dining room, with the rest of the Lawrence family no doubt wondering what had become of them. Ned was deeply hurt, but he confined himself to saying, "Oh, I see," and seems afterward never to have held it against her.

It is a scene straight out of an English farce, but it must have been an awful moment for Lawrence. Some of those who have written about him have raised the possibility that Janet's refusal to marry him was what drove him to spend years in the Middle East in the company of men, but that may be attaching too much importance to the incident. It seems more likely that Lawrence was attempting to sort out his problems with Vyvyan Richards's increasing emotional dependency by abruptly proposing to Janet—he was always one for the big, dramatic, life-changing gesture. Whatever the case, Lawrence was never as ill at ease with women as has been claimed. Many of them, like Janet, were close friends, but in the end, Lawrence no more wanted a sexual relationship with a woman than he did with Richards.

It may be true that Lawrence "worshipped Janet from afar," in later years, or that he referred to her to a friend as "the girl I adore," but one should not read too much into this. His feelings for Clare Sydney Smith, the wife of his commanding officer toward the end of his life, were amiable enough, but there is no hint of any sexual interest on Lawrence's part;* he was comfortable enough with women who had the capacity and patience to break through his rather brittle defenses, and yet respected his privacy and the orderly way he isolated himself when he felt a need for isolation. Except for the impulsive marriage proposal, he preferred to keep his distance, and cannot ever have imagined that he could live within the confines of marriage. One suspects that apart from the momentary damage to his amour propre, Lawrence was probably more relieved than upset when Janet turned him down.

Despite his peculiarities Lawrence, like other undergraduates, sought fun in breaking rules and regulations, and in the kind of pranks that seem daring and hilarious at the time, but may not necessarily seem so many years later when they are retold. Lawrence, like many undergraduates over the centuries, became an expert at climbing the walls and towers of the Oxford colleges, by day to take photographs and by night for his own amusement. One of his biographers, Robert Graves, claimed that

---

* This may not have been true, however, on Clare's part, to Lawrence's great embarrassment.

Lawrence invented "the now classic climb from Balliol College to Keble College," and it may be so.* His mother vigorously denied that Ned ever left his cottage in the garden to crawl around the roofs of Oxford at night; she said that he was always home by midnight. But since he often visited his friend the crammer, L. C. Jane, between midnight and four in the morning, this may be just another example of parental self-delusion. One friend told of Lawrence's turning up in his rooms one evening, exhausted after having studied for forty-five hours nonstop without food or sleep, and firing a revolver loaded with blank cartridges out the window. This friend also told of Lawrence's nearly drowning when he insisted on canoeing on the Cherwell during a winter flood. A famous feat of Lawrence's was to lead a canoe trip at night down the Trill Mill stream, the sewer that runs under the streets of Oxford, firing blank cartridges up through the gratings in the streets above. Whether this was a first or not is hard to say—it has certainly been done again since.

Despite his eccentricities regarding nourishment and sleep, Lawrence's years at Jesus do not seem all that different from the usual undergraduate experience. In those days, there was a deep social divide between "exhibitioners"—bright young men who had won a partial scholarship and were expected to work hard and earn a "First"—and young men from well-to-do families and public schools, for whom Oxford was more likely to be a social experience. Lawrence and his friends were clearly in the former group: basically serious, hardworking, and determined to do well, but not averse to the occasional prank—indeed Lawrence's taste for practical jokes and for pulling the legs of people naive enough to believe him was apparently already fully developed, and would not invariably seem among his most endearing qualities.

In one way, however, Lawrence was very different from most undergraduates. He already had a very firm sense of what he wanted to do, and

---

*Although Graves too was an Oxonian, there is some doubt that he got this right. Mark Blandford-Baker, the home bursar of Magdalen College, Oxford, points out, "Balliol is surrounded by Trinity plus a bit of St. John's." Lawrence may have been pulling Graves's leg.

remarkable skill in meeting, and winning over, those who might one day be of use to him. It was also clear to Lawrence what he did *not* want to do, which was to become a don himself. This was just as well, since even the admiring Jane did not consider him "a scholar by temperament." He still had Byronic fantasies of becoming a hero and of liberating a people—it was not yet clear which people he had in mind—and something more than a layman's interest in military history, strategy, and tactics; but his interest in archaeology and medieval buildings was the strongest focus of his work at Oxford. Revealingly, Lawrence chose to write a thesis on medieval fortifications, about which he already knew a good deal, indeed perhaps more than his examiners. This subject would have the further advantage of allowing him to make use of his growing skill as a photographer and a cartographer, as well as providing a good reason for spending the vacations away from home. Warfare was never far from his mind, despite his other interests.

In preparation for his thesis, Lawrence did another of his marathon bicycle tours of France, sending home long letters, which often read as if he intended to incorporate them into the thesis later on. In the summer of 1907 he had taken a bicycle tour through northern France, traveling part of the route in the company of his father, who was on the way to join the rest of the Lawrence family on Jersey, in the Channel Isles, where they were spending their summer holiday. In the summer of 1908 he went alone on a much more ambitious 2,400-mile tour of France to examine the castles and fortresses he had not already seen. Once again, his letters (mostly to his mother) are formidably detailed, evincing Lawrence's lifelong struggle to create a literary style of his own. His interest in the Middle East is clearly strong and growing. In his first letter he asks his mother to send him all the information she can get from the newspapers about political events in Turkey, where the sultan was under pressure from the "Young Turks" to grant a constitution. Lawrence refers to "the rubbish here that they call newspapers," exhibiting exactly the same tone of impatience with the French that he would show toward them during the war, and afterward at the peace conference.

Ten days later, when he writes from Aigues-Mortes, in Provence, the fact that his attention is moving toward the Middle East is repeated, in a kind of poetic vision that prefigures his travels there: "I rode to Les Baux, a queer little ruined & dying town upon a lonely 'olive sandalled' mountain. Here I had a most delightful surprise. I was looking from the edge of a precipice down the valley far over the plain, watching the green changing into brown, & the brown into a grey line far away on the horizon, when suddenly the sun leaped from behind a cloud, & a sort of silver shiver passed over the grey: then I understood, & instinctively burst out with a cry of 'Θάλασσα, Θάλασσα' [Thalassa, Thalassa], that echoed down the valley & startled an eagle from the opposite hill." The shout of the Greeks in Xenophon's *Anabasis* when they at last glimpsed the Black Sea shining in front of them after their 1,000-mile retreat from what is now Iraq came naturally to a young man steeped in the classics, as Lawrence was; but, more important, it was his first distant glimpse of the Mediterranean.

Today, we can have no idea of what it then meant to a well-educated young Englishman—the Mediterranean is now just a few hours away by plane, and its shores are an endless array of tourist destinations—but in the first decade of the twentieth century, it was still the focal point of European imagination, culture, and respect for the past, a world at once classical and deeply romantic.

A day later, Lawrence reached the sea and bathed in it, writing afterward to his mother, "I felt at last that I had reached the way to the South, and all the glorious East: Greece, Carthage, Egypt, Tyre, Syria . . . they were all there, and all within reach. . . . I would accept a passage for Greece tomorrow."

Perhaps fortunately, no such passage was offered, and Lawrence bicycled off to Nîmes, and from there by stages to Narbonne and Carcassonne. He was bronzed, thin, and fit, and he amazed the French by his feats of endurance and his diet—he ate 126 green plums in one day, or so he claimed. He was plagued only by dense clouds of mosquitoes (which, as any tourist to the region can attest, are still a problem today) and by

Americans who overtipped tourist guides at the major sites. Perhaps in deference to his mother, Lawrence spent more time writing home about churches than castles. On this trip, as on all future ones, Lawrence carried a camera—whether his own or his father's is not clear—and although he depreciates his own pictures, and says he expects to have to burn them, they are, like his drawings, far beyond the usual work of amateur photographers.

He arrived back at Oxford in the first week of September, having assembled a good part of what he needed in terms of his thesis, though he had not as yet decided what the exact theme would be—it would not be enough to have examined a large number of English and French fortresses and describe them in detail; he would need to develop a theory about them and demonstrate it convincingly. This was provided for him by C. F. Bell of the Ashmolean, when Lawrence was showing him the drawings and photographs from the summer trip. Bell suggested that Lawrence might study the question whether the earliest crusaders had brought back to Europe from the Middle East the pointed arch and vault that are the trademarks of medieval Gothic architecture, or whether instead they had brought these ideas with them to the Middle East, thus introducing those architectural elements into the Arab world. To Lawrence, one of the major attractions of his friend Bell's idea lay in the fact that the distinguished Oxford scholar Charles Oman, author of *The Art of War in the Middle Ages*, took the latter point of view, which was therefore the orthodox answer. Nothing would be more likely to pique the examiners' interest than an undergraduate's attacking accepted or conventional wisdom, particularly when it was held by such a formidable figure as Oman, who was virtually a one-man historical industry. In fact, Lawrence could hardly have chosen a more tempting person to contradict than Professor Oman, whose influence was enormous in just those areas where Lawrence intended to make his career: history and archaeology. The "imp" in Lawrence must have been instantly aroused. And as if that were not temptation enough, it was immediately apparent to Lawrence that in order to write his thesis, he would need to journey to the

Middle East and survey the crusaders' castles for himself. Since this was exactly where he dreamed of going, the attraction was irresistible.

Bell's boss D. G. Hogarth was an experienced traveler who had worked on archaeological digs in Syria, Egypt, Cyprus, and Crete, and Lawrence sensibly consulted him. Hogarth was discouraging—the summer was the wrong time of year to go; Lawrence would need money to hire a guide and servants to look after his tent and animals. Lawrence replied firmly that he was going, and intended to walk, not to ride, and do without a tent or servants altogether. "Europeans don't walk in Syria," Hogarth said; "it isn't safe or pleasant." Lawrence replied, "Well, I do," and thus a lifelong friendship began.

Feeling that he had failed to convey the dangers facing travelers to the Middle East, Hogarth suggested that Lawrence write for advice to C. M. Doughty, the famous explorer of Arabia and author of the book *Arabia Deserta*, which would play an influential role in Lawrence's life. Hogarth may not at this point have realized the degree to which danger and physical hardship constituted a challenge for Lawrence, or that testing his powers of endurance was as irresistible as taking a potshot at Professor Oman's theories. Doughty's reply was even more discouraging than Hogarth's well-intentioned advice. In Doughty's opinion, the heat in July and August would be unbearable; he described Syria as "a land of squalor," considered travel on foot "out of the question," warned of "ill-will" toward Europeans on the part of the local population, and suggested that at a minimum a mule or a horse and its owner were necessary.

Coming from a man who had taken the pilgrim route to Mecca under appalling conditions, and gone on to reach some of the most remote cities in central Arabia, it was advice that any sensible person would have taken; but Lawrence cheerfully replied that his "little pleasure trip" promised to be more interesting than he had bargained for, and proceeded to read Doughty's book, which was nearly 600,000 words long and one of those great classics more talked about than read. Lawrence was strongly influenced by Doughty's idiosyncratic, convoluted, somewhat antiquarian style, and by Doughty's courage in following the

Bedouin through the desert from Damascus to Jidda without any of the privileges and comforts of a European traveler. Doughty, like Hogarth, would become a friend and admirer of Lawrence, always eager to hear of his young acolyte's adventures.

Lawrence prepared himself methodically for the journey—first, he found an instructor in Arabic, a half-Irish, half-Arab Protestant clergyman. He also found, in the person of E. H. New, somebody who could improve his architectural drawings. In both cases he benefited from the fact that in Oxford there is always somebody, somewhere who is an expert on *any* subject, however abstruse—it is just a question of digging him or her out. Lawrence also dug out C. H. C. Pirie-Gordon, who had actually visited some of the castles Lawrence was interested in, and who lent Lawrence his own maps, on which he had made many useful notations.

Lawrence planned to wear "a lightweight suit with many pockets," into which he put two thin shirts, a spare pair of socks, the all-important camera, and film packs. He also carried what his biographers describe as "a revolver," but which may in fact have been a Mauser C96 7.63-millimeter automatic pistol,* with adjustable sights, which he mentions in one of his letters. His father gave him either £100 or £200 for the journey—it is hard to know which, but either way it represented a considerable sum of money at the time, $10,000 at least in contemporary terms. From this, Lawrence paid his passage, and bought what was then an expensive pistol and a camera that cost £40.

His father's generosity was matched by that of the Earl Curzon,† who was a former viceroy of India and then chancellor of the University of Oxford (and with whom Lawrence would clash bitterly after the war, when Curzon was foreign secretary). At the urging of the head of Lawrence's

---

* Lawrence is fairly specific about this, though he seems to have carried several different kinds of pistols over the years. If his reference to the Mauser is true, then it is exactly the same kind of pistol which the young Winston Churchill carried when he charged with the Twenty-First Lancers at the Battle of Omdurman in the Sudan, Kitchener's great victory, in 1898, and with which he shot several Mahdist tribesmen.

† He was created marquess of Curzon in 1921.

college, Curzon persuaded the Ottoman government to issue the necessary *irades*—essentially letters of safe conduct to be shown to the local
authorities—without which travel in the more remote parts of the Ottoman
Empire was very difficult.

In our own age, when a journey to even the most faraway places is measured in hours and when young people backpack all over the world and
keep in touch by cell phone, it is hard to imagine just how isolated and
primitive the Ottoman Empire once was. The Turkish railway system,
most of it financed and built by the Germans, was still makeshift and
primitive, and whole sections had yet to be built. To travel from Haidar
Pasha, on the Asian shore opposite Constantinople, the starting point of
the Baghdad Railway, to Baghdad, nearly 900 miles away, it was necessary to leave the train and take to donkey, horse, or mule twice, since two
important tunnels remained uncompleted; and the lines to the south
were of different gauges, so that passengers and goods had to be unloaded
and reloaded at several points. In addition, there were still only single-line
tracks, which enormously complicated the task of moving rail traffic in
two directions. This alone made travel in the Ottoman Empire a daunting
proposition.

Hospitals were few, far between, and primitive; diseases such as cholera and malaria were rife; sanitation was lacking outside hotels *de grand
luxe* in the major cities; roads were mostly dirt tracks; and south and east
of Damascus the Arabs made a practice of robbing strangers. Except for
Constantinople, a big and cosmopolitan city, life in most of the Ottoman
Empire was still ruled by family, clan, or tribe; and much of the empire
was inhabited by rival or warring nationalities and ethnic groups. The
"Young Turks" who had taken power in 1908 were determined to modernize the country, but progress was slow, and deeply resisted. Over the
decades, the Ottoman Empire had been driven out of Europe, and subjected
to any number of humiliating concessions. Under one such concession,
foreigners were tried according to the laws of their own country, rather
than those of Turkey; as a result, both the Turks who ruled the empire

and the Arabs who resented the presence of all foreigners were deeply hostile to the western powers.

Still, all this must be set against the spontaneous generosity of all the ethnic groups in the empire, especially the Arabs, to whom hospitality to a stranger was (and remains) both a religious obligation and a matter of honor. They managed, however, to combine this with a voracious appetite for theft—so long as you were not a guest under their roof, or in their tent, you were fair game. Thus it was that Lawrence received food and a night's lodging, however poor his host, but was also shot at, robbed, and badly beaten. Missionaries of numerous denominations and nationalities, including Americans, Scots, and Jews, also offered him hospitality. In all his lengthy letters home Lawrence benefited from the fact that the British and most of the major European powers ran their own post offices and postal services in the Ottoman Empire, the Turkish post office being notoriously unreliable. His letters give no hint of homesickness, fear, complaint, or self-doubt. He walked more than 1,000 miles, mostly on rough, rocky paths, for up to thirteen hours a day in temperatures ranging from ninety to 107 degrees, and visited the sites of thirty-six crusader castles—an extraordinary achievement.

He left England on June 18, 1909, on board the P&O liner SS *Mongolia*. It made only two short stops, at Gibraltar and Marseille, then went on to Port Said, where he was stuck for five nights in one of the most raucous and sordid ports on earth waiting for a berth on a ship to Beirut. He spent most of his time on board studying Arabic, and although he dismissed the voyage as "a monstrous waste of time," he seems to have enjoyed the variegated company at his table on the *Mongolia*: "a French girl & a German male, a Swede, two Spaniards, an Indian of some sort, an Italian, an Arab, and a Greek. Swede, & Hindu talk English." He reached Port Said on June 30, and reported home by letter that he enjoyed good bathing on the beach; had seen the Suez Canal; and was eating melons, peaches, apricots, and grapes—and that nevertheless Port Said was "a horrible place" (few travelers will disagree). He did not arrive in Beirut until July 6—eighteen days for a journey that would now take six hours.

From the beginning, he set himself a demanding pace, averaging about twenty miles on foot a day. Although he is usually portrayed as an instinctive loner, he had actually made plans in Beirut to go with a party of five American tutors at the American College there, but one of them fell ill, so they dropped out and he went on alone. He had no trouble finding places to stay, either in native homes or at missions, though he remarks on the number of flea bites he picked up—inevitably, since most Palestinian houses were built on two levels, the higher end for the family, and the lower one for the animals, both under one roof. He praised the food even in the most modest homes: *leben*, a kind of thin yogurt, eaten by dipping a piece of rolled-up bread into the bowl; two kinds of bread, one small and dusted with sesame seeds and cumin, which he liked, and the other a very thin, flat, round bread, sometimes three feet in diameter and very dry and brittle, which he didn't. He always offered to pay; sometimes money was accepted, but mostly it was not. His letters home could serve as models for anybody writing about travel and adventure off the beaten path, and there is in them, though he seldom gets credit for it, a certain sweetness toward people, a desire to believe the best of them until they proved otherwise. He always radiated a powerful, even incandescent enthusiasm and curiosity that seemed to light up everything he saw, however weary, footsore, or sick he was.

And sick he was, quite often—he had already contracted malaria on his bike trip through the south of France, and now he contracted a different and more serious strain; his feet gave him endless trouble; his face and hands were burned and chapped by the heat and the wind; he was covered with insect bites from head to foot; and he clearly didn't care.

Those who have not read Lawrence's letters home, to his parents and to his brothers, can have no idea of just how *likable* he was, and how far removed from the neurotic figure, obsessed by his own illegitimacy, whom some of his biographers and critics have described. What is more, his letters reveal an enviable family picture—there is not a hint of jealousy between the brothers, and his parents are interested in every single thing that Ned does. However fierce the psychological tug-of-war was between Sarah and her second son—a contest that Ned could never win, but that he learned to avoid by putting as much distance as he could between himself and his mother—their concern for each other and his efforts to please her are clear. Simply by being in the Holy Land, of course, he was pleasing her as he could never have done by traveling in France, no matter how many miles he rode a day, or how few shillings a day he spent on himself.

It is, one assumes, largely for her benefit that his letters are not just about local customs and crusaders' fortresses, but are shot through with biblical references: "From Dan we passed to the site of Abel-Beth-Maachah, where Sheba was finally run to earth by Joab." Lawrence never neglects to point out each of the biblical sites he visits, though these sites are not his primary interest, of course; and he displays throughout his letters an amazing amount of biblical knowledge—perhaps not so extraordinary for somebody brought up in a family with daily Bible readings. He notes that he has stood on the place where the Arabs believe Jonah was cast ashore, and describes a beautiful spring dedicated by the Greeks to Pan in the village of Banias (on the Golan Heights), which "Mother will remember from Matthew xvi or Mark viii and other places."

Given Lawrence's enthusiasm for the Arab cause, it is interesting that he remarks about Palestine: "The sooner the Jews farm it all the better: their colonies are bright spots in a desert." After describing the primitive farming methods of the Arabs, he notes by contrast that he has just heard the news of Louis Blériot's first crossing of the Channel by airplane. Lawrence has great sympathy for the Arabs, but a brisk impatience with the Turks, whom he sees, correctly, as retarding political development and education, and imposing on all subject races of the empire a bureaucracy that is slow moving, corrupt, and punitive. Although he has yet to meet the Bedouin, or even to see the desert—for he is trudging up and down the stony hills of what is now Israel, Syria, and Lebanon, climbing, as he remarks wearily (and with pardonable exaggeration), the height of Mont Blanc every day—he notes with approval the farmers "ploughing in their fields" with a revolver on their belt or a rifle over their shoulder, and the occasional appearance of a desert Arab in a *kufiyya*. As if it were a premonition of many a page in *Seven Pillars of Wisdom*, he writes of the heat in northern Palestine: "Inland, up the mountains, it is cooler, though when one gets among the large rocks one is stifled: they seem almost to give off a vapour, or heat-breath, that is horrible; add to that a sirocco, a wind that shrivels every green thing it meets, that blisters one's face & hands, & makes one feel that one is walking towards some gigantic oven; and you get an idea of the vast possibilities." Since he adds that the shaded hallway of the hotel in Tiberias, even though cooled by a large block of ice, was over 106 degrees, and that it felt "quite cool" compared with the temperature outside in the sun, gives some idea of what Lawrence had in mind by unbearable heat.

It was not only heat that didn't bother Lawrence—he was also exposed to the sudden violence of the Middle East, and took a certain delight in the experience. His attitude was similar to that of the young Winston Churchill: "Nothing in life is more exhilarating than to be shot at without result." Lawrence, who was destined to form with Churchill both an effective team at the Colonial Office and a lifelong mutual admiration society, took much the same delight in the crack of bullets whipping past his head, and had his first experience of it near Aleppo, in what is now Syria. More remarkably, while he tried to pass the incident off with lighthearted good humor in a letter to his mother, he made no attempt to hide what had happened from her, when it would presumably have been very easy to do so by simply not mentioning it.

In Latakia, he had spent the night in the house of a young Arab nobleman, Abdul Kerim, who had just acquired a Mauser pistol similar to Lawrence's, and amused himself by blazing away from his fortresslike house on a hill at the surrounding villages. A few days later, while Lawrence was on his way to Aleppo, over "the worst road on the face of the globe," "an ass with an old gun" on a horse took a shot at him from about 200 yards. Since Lawrence was wearing a suit and shoes, and on foot, it would have been obvious that he was a European—the man with the gun may have felt it was his religious duty to take a potshot at an infidel, or perhaps intended more practically to rob Lawrence, or perhaps both. Lawrence fired back and grazed the horse, which bolted and carried its rider about 800 yards away (not a bad snap shot with a pistol at 200 yards). Lawrence then carefully put up his rear sight as high it would go and fired a shot right over the man's head,* prompting him to gallop away as fast as he could ride, astonished that "a person with nothing but a pistol could shoot so far."

Lawrence complained to the governor of the district, who sent all his police out to search for the man, with (of course) no results; one thinks of the police chief's weary order in *Casablanca*: "Round up the usual suspects." The consensus was that Lawrence's assailant had hoped to bluff him into paying for a safe passage; if so, that was certainly a misreading of Lawrence's character.

Lawrence was intending to walk to Damascus, but a succession of events persuaded him to end his journey in Aleppo. He wrote home to explain that one of the newspapers in Aleppo had reported his murder, in a village where he had never been, so that he was treated "like a ghost" by the hotel staff and the local missionaries; then his boots had given up the ghost at last, exposing his feet to "cuts & chafes & blisters" which seemed unlikely to heal in this climate; finally, his camera was stolen (more trouble for the unfortunate police, who now had on their hands a British subject who had been shot at by a native, was reported to have been murdered, and had lodged a complaint about a stolen camera). In the circumstances, it seemed to Lawrence best to go home. He was in any case down to the last of his money, he had just recovered from his fourth bout of malaria, and the rainy season was about to begin, so he left with few regrets. He prudently sent a letter to Sir John Rhys, the principal of Jesus

---

* This pretty much confirms that the pistol he carried was a Mauser C96—no other pistol had adjustable sights calibrated for up to 1,000 meters, which made sense because the pistol could be carried in a wooden holster that clipped to the butt serving as a stock, thus allowing it to be fired like a carbine. It was, however, a bulky and heavy weapon, not easily concealable, and would seem to prove that Lawrence must have carried more than what he could stuff into his pockets.

College, to explain that he would be returning late, while also very wisely asking his father to go to Jesus and explain matters to the authorities in person. (*"Sir John does not like to be bothered with college matters,"* Lawrence warned his father.)

In his letter to Sir John Rhys, however, Lawrence mentioned that he had been "robbed and rather smashed up," something which he had neglected to tell his parents, and which may have been the deciding factor in persuading him to return home, rather than the state of his shoes. Apparently, the shooting incident had not been the only attack on Lawrence: while trying to purchase Hittite seals on Hogarth's behalf in a village near the Euphrates, he was followed and set upon by an importunate beggar, who had been attracted by Lawrence's cheap copper watch. Thinking that it was gold, the man stalked Lawrence and hit him on the head with a rock on the deserted road, knocking him down. He then robbed Lawrence and tried to shoot him with the Mauser. Fortunately for Lawrence, the operation of the cocking bolt and the safety catch of a Mauser C96 are confusing even to experienced owners of the pistol, so the thief was unable to shoot. Instead, Lawrence's assailant bashed him about the head again and made off with all his possessions, biting his hand severely in the fight, and leaving him for dead. Lawrence recovered enough to walk five miles to the next town, where the local authorities and (perhaps more important) the "village elders" quickly found the guilty man—no doubt they already knew who he was—and returned to Lawrence his watch, his seals, his pistol, and his money. Lawrence thanked Rhys for having helped procure the *irades* (safe-conduct letters) from the Ottoman government, without which the shooting incident and the attack on him might have been far more difficult to resolve, and also asked Rhys not to mention his injuries to his father.

The robbery has caused considerable difficulty for biographers, since Lawrence wrote or told several variants of it to different people. Thus, in Robert Graves's biography of Lawrence the Mauser becomes a Colt, the safety catch of which the robber didn't know how to move; in Liddell

Hart's biography it becomes an old Webley revolver,* which the robber inadvertently rendered unfireable by pulling out the trigger guard; and in both these versions the robber is interrupted by a passing shepherd before he can finish Lawrence off. However it happened, it must have been a frightening experience, even for somebody as stoic and fatalistic as Lawrence, and would explain both why he decided to go home and why he went all the way back by ship, instead of much more quickly by ship to Marseille and then by train: he would have wanted his wounds to heal as much as possible before his family saw him. This attack may have been the one reported, in garbled form, in the Aleppo newspaper, causing people to believe he was dead. That it *did* happen is certain. Apart from the fading scars, when Lawrence returned C. H. C. Pirie-Gordon's annotated map to him, he apologized for the bloodstain on it, and in any case there is nothing intrinsically unlikely about the attack.

Lawrence may or may not have worked as a coal checker in Port Said to help pay for his way home, and may or may not have sold his Mauser in Beirut for the same reason (though if he did sell it, as has been claimed, for only £5, he made a very poor deal for such an expensive weapon); but somehow he managed to reach home in one piece and, most important of all, with his enthusiasm for the Middle East undiminished.

What might have seemed to most travelers two lucky escapes, and a good reason not to repeat the experience, merely whetted Lawrence's appetite. Already it was clear to him that he did not want to become a don, or spend his life cataloging potsherds and glass fragments at the Ashmolean; he wanted both the freedom that only an alien world could offer him, and the adventurous life of a man of action. Just as hardship, physical challenge, and self-discipline had developed from habits into addictions, danger too became addictive. Of course to the would-be hero every assault and life-threatening encounter is merely a challenge to be overcome, a step forward in his apprenticeship—the more frightening

---

* In the Lowell Thomas version the pistol becomes a Colt .45 Peacemaker, which the robber doesn't realize has to be cocked with the thumb before firing; but this may be a sop to American readers—Lawrence clearly identifies it as a Mauser.

and the more physically punishing, the better, provided he survives. Per-haps without realizing it, Lawrence had taken his first steps on that path, as if he had already heard, in the words of Joseph Campbell, "a cry (if not from the housetops, then—more miserably—within every heart): a cry for the redeeming hero, the carrier of the shining blade, whose blow, whose touch, whose existence, will liberate the land."

That land was not to be found among the gray spires of Oxford.

The college raised no difficulties about Lawrence's return a week late—an unusual and physically demanding journey through the Holy Land by an undergraduate would have seemed more important than his arriving home on time; and even the dons could hardly fail to notice that he was emaciated and toughened by his experiences. One of them described Lawrence's face as "thinned to the bone by privation." He settled back into the routine of college life, but he was infected by more than malaria—henceforth, Lawrence's mind was firmly fixed on the Middle East, and on finding a way to get back there for a longer time. He may not have wanted to break the news yet to Richards, but hand-printing beautiful books in a William Morris cottage in the woods (or a windmill by the sea, an alter-native version of this plan) was no longer Lawrence's goal.

After his journey, life in the tiny cottage in the garden of 2 Polstead Road too must have seemed more cramped and confining than before, and Oxford a place of narrow vistas, gray sky, and penetrating cold. Many undergraduates stumble through their third and last year at Oxford dazed by the ordeal of the final examination that lies ahead of them, and still more by the question of what they are going to do with themselves when they leave Oxford, but Lawrence was already determined to find a way back to the Middle East, and merely saw his finals as a necessary step on the way. He needed not only a "First," but more: an interesting and provocative First; and he reenlisted his patient crammer L. C. Jane to en-sure that he was well prepared. He had until the Easter vacation of 1910 to hand in his thesis, and though he boasted later of preparing it at the very last minute, the evidence seems to be that he prepared very carefully indeed. He had it typed (typing was rare at the time), and it included a large number of maps, plans, drawings, photographs, and even postcards, which backed up his view that the crusaders had brought their architecture to the Middle East, rather than being influenced by what they found there.

He had persuaded Hogarth to write a letter of introduction to C. M. Doughty, who was to become another of Lawrence's father figures, and now it bore fruit. The meeting between Lawrence and the old man was a success, and, in Hogarth's words, "in no way diminished the disciple's fervor." In fact it served to increase Lawrence's determination to follow in Doughty's footsteps.

Lawrence did not seem to have had any doubts about his thesis, except for the fear that it might be too ambitious and too long for the examiners. Indeed, the material in it was so new and challenging that there was at first some doubt that anybody at Oxford was competent to judge it. In the event, Lawrence "took a most brilliant First Class," according to his crammer L. C. Jane, so brilliant that Lawrence's tutor gave a dinner party to the examiners to celebrate the achievement. This rare, and possibly unique, event in Oxford demonstrates the respect in which Lawrence was held, despite doubt that he was "a natural scholar."

Afterward, Lawrence set off on a cycling tour in France with his brother Frank, who appears not to have shared Ned's interest in castles and fortifications. Ned wrote to his mother that he was busy reading *Petit Jehan de Saintré*, "a xv Cent. Novel of knightly manners," of which he had been trying to find a well-printed copy, as well as the work of "Molière & Racine & Corneille & Voltaire," an ambitious reading program for somebody bicycling almost fifty miles a day. He pauses to explain to his mother his passion for reading, and for beautiful books. "Father won't know all this—but if you can get the right book at the right time you taste joys—not only bodily, physical, but spiritual also, which pass one out above and beyond one's miserable self, as it were through a huge air, following the light of another man's thought. And you can never be quite the old self again."

What Sarah made of all this is hard to know—as so often with Lawrence's letters home, it reads as if he were trying out ideas and phrases that he intended to develop, refine, and use later, perhaps in this case for a letter to his friend Vyvyan Richards, who still expected Lawrence to join him in the hand-printing venture; or perhaps Lawrence was merely trying to persuade his mother that the plan for printing books with Richards was a better one than his father thought.

On his return to Oxford Lawrence was persuaded by C. F. Bell to go for a bachelor of literature (BLitt) degree as the next rung up on the academic ladder, his subject to be "Mediaeval Lead-Glazed Pottery from the Eleventh to the Sixteenth Centuries." Although he twice failed to win "a research fellowship" at All Souls College, he managed to get a grant of £50 from Jesus College, but one senses that his heart was not really in the problems of lead-glazed pottery, however much they fascinated Bell.

Even though he left immediately for Rouen, to look "at mediaeval pots," Lawrence also dropped what must have been a bombshell for his friend E. T. Leeds and for Bell, who had envisioned him safely seated at a desk in the Ashmolean Museum in Oxford, examining potsherds on his return from France. "Mr. Hogarth is going digging, and I am going out to Syria in a fortnight to make plain the valleys and level the mountains for his feet:—also to learn Arabic," he informed them. "The two occupations fit into one another splendidly."

"The dangerous crises of self-development are permitted to come to pass under the protecting eye of an experienced initiate . . . who then enacts the role and character of the ancient mystagogue, or guide of souls," wrote Joseph Campbell in analyzing the development of the hero, and the need, at the crucial stages of the hero's life, for a wise, firm, and knowing mentor—one who sets the apprentice hero on the correct path and furnishes him with the knowledge and the weapons he will need, and who, above all, points to the great task that lies at the end of the many trials and terrors.

Nobody would have been more familiar with the role Merlin played in the life of King Arthur than Lawrence, whose appetite for medieval romance, myth, and poetry was voracious, and who would carry Sir Thomas Malory's *Le Morte d'Arthur* into battle with him. Henceforth, Hogarth would play that role in Lawrence's life.

In the meantime, it is clear, Lawrence was delighted to be freed from the pottery fragments in the Ashmolean, and sent to Syria. He sailed on December 10, 1909, for Beirut, and what would be the happiest years of his life.

CHAPTER FIVE

Carchemish: 1911–1914

We travel not for trafficking alone:
By hotter winds our fiery hearts are fanned.

> —James Elroy Flecker, "The Golden Journey
> to Samarkand"

David Hogarth, though he seems to have had a gift for remaining in the background, was one of those figures beloved in English popular fiction: the superbly well-connected don; a scholar who was also an intrepid traveler and "a man of action"; an Englishman who could speak French, German, Italian, Greek, Turkish, and Arabic fluently, and who was just as at ease negotiating with foreign governments and institutions as he was with those of his own country. Though married, and the father of a son, Hogarth was apparently not an enthusiast for domestic life; he was an inveterate and intrepid traveler, as well as a learned, witty, acerbic man, as much at home in high society as he was in the desert, a brilliant conversationalist in all his languages, and "respected throughout Europe" as well as in much of the Middle East. It comes as no surprise to learn that Hogarth and Sir Edward Grey, the British foreign secretary from 1905 to 1916, were at Winchester together and had remained in constant touch since their schooldays there.

When Lawrence went up to Jesus College in 1907 as an undergraduate, he was nineteen and Hogarth was forty-five and already a man of considerable accomplishments: a fellow of Magdalen College, he was the author of several well-received books; he had taken part in archaeological expeditions in Egypt, Crete, and Asia Minor; he had been director of the British School of Archaeology in Athens (an extremely prestigious post); he had served as a war correspondent for the *Times* during the 1897 revolution in Crete and the Greco-Turkish War—a hint that there was more to Hogarth's life than archaeology—and he would become keeper of the Ashmolean Museum in Oxford in 1909. Hogarth was one of those people who knew everybody worth knowing, and was welcome everywhere. A big, burly, sociable, broad-shouldered man, with a neatly trimmed beard, unusually long, powerful arms, and a dark, penetrating gaze, he was described by a woman who met him at a party as resembling "a cynical and highly-educated baboon." In rare photographs of himself and Lawrence together, he towers over Lawrence by a head. A member of what has come to be called in Britain the Establishment,* he was also an academic talent spotter, and the first to recognize in the young Lawrence the same quickness of mind, biting sense of humor, and sharp intellectual curiosity that had brought the young Hogarth himself a brilliant "First." He described Lawrence in a letter to Charles M. Doughty, the great explorer of Arabia, as "a boy of extraordinary aptitude both for archaeology and a wandering life among the Arabs." With great patience and tact he shaped the younger man's career, almost always as a presence in the background, sometimes without Lawrence's even being aware of it. As early as 1909, Hogarth remarked to E. T. Leeds, one of his archaeological assistants at the Ashmolean, about Lawrence, who was then just back from his first visit to the Middle East: "That's a rather remarkable young man: he has been in parts rarely visited by Western travelers in recent years."

Perhaps inevitably, Hogarth has been treated as a kind of Edwardian

---

*The equivalent of *les mandarins* in France—that is to say, men (and nowadays women) who move at equal ease in the worlds of academia, government, big business, finance, and the arts as a kind of invisible permanent ruling class.

equivalent of John Le Carré's spymaster George Smiley by some of Lawrence's biographers, as if he had recruited his young protégé for Britain's secret service while Ned was still bicycling in a schoolboy's shorts over to the Ashmolean with his finds, but this is to overemphasize that side of Hogarth's life, as well as to underestimate Lawrence's lifelong aversion to moving to anybody's pace or orders but his own. Still, Hogarth was certainly one of that informal circle of learned and adventurous men and women who passed information on to the government, in his case about the Balkans and the Near East, though he was not by any stretch of the imagination a spymaster who recruited and trained undergraduates. In the days before World War I, professional spies were employed by the continental powers against one another, but the British, particularly in the far reaches of the empire, relied on an informal and above all amateur web of explorers, archaeologists, adventurous businessmen, and travel writers for information. Given the secretive nature of the Ottoman Empire and its increasingly feeble hold over large areas of its territory, British explorers, adventurers, archaeologists, students of religion, and Arabists proliferated in the great empty spaces of Syria and Arabia, to the alarm of the French, who themselves had designs on Lebanon and Syria; and it would have been unlikely for some of these people not to have gathered such information as they could for friends in the government and the diplomatic service, without feeling that they were, in any organized way, "spying."

Certainly Hogarth encouraged the young Lawrence to combine his interest in the Middle East with his passion for archaeology; and Hogarth may also have been sensitive enough to guess that Lawrence would benefit from a long period away from home and away from the pressures placed on him there by his mother. Not that Lawrence would necessarily have confided all this to Hogarth, however sympathetic a listener he was, but there was no need for him to; Hogarth, Lawrence would later write, was "the only man I had never to let into my confidence—he would get there naturally."

While Lawrence was finishing his research in Rouen, Hogarth had just returned from Turkey, where he had been discussing with the Ottoman authorities British interest in the ruins of the ancient Hittite city of Carchemish, then a mound of rubble covered by sand, dirt, and the debris of later cities overlooking the Euphrates near Jerablus. The Hittites—unlike the ancient Egyptians—were an archaeological problem of great importance to scholars because there were few excavated Hittite sites and their language remained undeciphered. The Hittites had lived in a broad, crescent-shaped area of Anatolia and northern Syria, stretching as far to the south along the Mediterranean as modern Lebanon and as far to the east as the border of modern Iraq. The history of their kingdom began about 1750 BCE and came to an end about 1160 BCE, when internal strife, and warfare with the Egyptians to the south and the Assyrians to the east, brought about the collapse of what had once been a great empire. The British had a great interest in the Hittites, in part because dazzling new discoveries of whole cities seemed likely to be made in the area (in contrast to what was now the patient, painstaking excavation of Egyptian tombs), and in part because here, as elsewhere, rivalry between Britain and Germany played a major role. Hugo Winckler's discoveries at Bogazköy in Anatolia in 1906–1907 had put the "Hittite problem" on the map—until then there was some doubt that the Hittites had ever existed—and it now became an urgent matter of academic prestige for the archaeology department of Oxford and the British Museum in London not to lag behind the University of Berlin. The British had known about the mound at Jerablus since the eighteenth century, and had made several attempts to dig there, revealing the presence of immense ancient ruins buried under the shattered remains of a Greek and a later Roman city. But these excavations were being made in what one archaeologist described as "a dreary and desolate waste" in the Syrian desert north of Aleppo, and between that desolation and the difficulties raised by the hostile local inhabitants and the Turkish authorities, work did not progress swiftly. Now, doubts in the British archaeological world that the Hittites had existed gave way to the conviction that the mound at Jerablus was of greater importance than the one Winckler was working on at Bogazköy, and must be excavated systematically as soon as possible.

Hogarth, with his knowledge of Turkish, Arabic, and the area, was naturally an enthusiast for a project that combined patriotism and scientific knowledge. He had already visited the site in 1908, and pronounced favorably on it to the British Museum, which had applied for permission to dig there to the Imperial Ottoman Museum in Constantinople; authorities there let the matter rest for two years, owing to civil unrest, rebellion, and the overthrow of the sultan.

In 1910, after Turkey had settled down in the firmer hands of the "Young Turks," the British ambassador in Constantinople was asked to raise the matter again, and this time, permission was granted. Hogarth's choice of Lawrence was a natural one. Lawrence had clearly demonstrated a flair for digging up relics of the past, as well as for bargaining for them; he had bought a number of Hittite seals for Hogarth during his walking tour of the Holy Land; he was physically tough and fearless; he had a smattering of Arabic; he was a keen amateur photographer; and he had actually come very close to Carchemish while he was in Syria. Lawrence himself, when he heard about Hogarth's trip to Constantinople in 1910, had asked his old friend E. T. Leeds, at the Ashmolean, if there was any chance of his being included in the party going to Jerablus with Hogarth.

This raised any number of difficulties, since Lawrence was receiving a scholarship from Jesus College to support his research on medieval pottery for a BLitt degree, which, on the face of things, seemed incompatible with excavating a Hittite site in Syria. But despite Leeds's doubts, Lawrence demonstrated his lifelong ability to get his own way. Hogarth agreed to take Lawrence, and then, with superb diplomatic skill, managed to secure for his young protégé a "senior demyship," a kind of research fellowship, at his own college, Magdalen,* which meant that the British Museum would not have to pay anything but Lawrence's living expenses at the

---

*As a result, no fewer than three Oxford colleges have a claim on Lawrence: Jesus, where he spent his three undergraduate years; Magdalen, because of his four-year demyship; and All Souls, where he was made a fellow after the Paris Peace Conference. During his four years as an archaeologist in the Middle East he often wore the white blazer of the Magdalen College Boat Club, to which, as somebody who never rowed, he was not strictly speaking entitled.

site. This was not an inconsiderable feat—Lawrence's demyship would bring him £100 a year for four years (about the equivalent of $12,500 a year today).

With equal skill Jesus College was placated by the suggestion that Lawrence would not only continue his research on medieval pottery but extend his survey of crusader castles in Syria, enabling him to expand his BA thesis into a book; and the British Museum was informed (a little optimistically) that his services were necessary to the expedition because of his command of Arabic, his familiarity with the area, and his knowledge about pottery. All this was the academic equivalent of a carom shot at billiards, and speaks volumes about Hogarth's talent for manipulation, and Lawrence's ability to claim convincingly many different skills at the same time. If Lawrence's parents had any doubts, Hogarth no doubt dealt with those as well—he seems to have gotten along well with both of them—and moved swiftly to send Lawrence to Syria to improve his Arabic, for which so much had been claimed.

Lawrence sailed for Beirut at the beginning of December 1910, hardly more than two months after Hogarth's return from Constantinople, leaving in his father's hands the problem of the printing press that Vyvyan Richards and Lawrence were to have founded together. On the way to Beirut, Lawrence managed to visit Athens and Constantinople for the first time. Like many visitors to Greece, he was puzzled by how little the modern Greeks resembled the ancient ones, and compared the former unfavorably with the latter. The voyage, Lawrence complained, was very slow, and the meals were huge and endless (it was a French ship, of the Messageries Maritimes).

By December 10, he was able to write home from Constantinople, where he had an unexpectedly long stay when the engines of his ship broke down, leaving him free to do rather more sightseeing than he had expected. He reported home cheerfully that "the cholera has ceased to all practical purposes," and he was probably the only tourist in the city's long history to have found Constantinople "very clean." He praised the "disorder" of the city, the noisy and colorful variety of its open-air markets, and the fact that there were hardly more than "twenty yards of straight street" in all of Stamboul. He attempted to interest three Canadian priests whom he had befriended in the pleasures of sightseeing in Constantinople, but they found everything very dirty, prompting Lawrence to express the broad-minded point of view that would enable him to lead the Bedouin in warfare: "They were always talking of *quel salété*, of the dirt & disorder of things, of the lack of shops and carriages and what they were pleased to call conveniences (which are more trouble than they are worth). They seemed too narrow to get outside their civilization, or state of living. . . . Is civilization the power of appreciating the character and achievements of peoples in a different stage from ourselves?" This was a question that Lawrence was to answer for himself, over the next few years, with his attempt to live like a Bedouin and even to exceed the capacity of the Bedouin for living on the borderline of human existence.

Lawrence arrived in Beirut shortly before Christmas—it had taken him the best part of a month to travel from Britain to Lebanon—and moved immediately to Jebail, the ancient Greek city of Byblos, where he was to attend the mission school and "perfect" his Arabic.* His teacher, Fareedeh el Akle, who was still alive in 1976, was more realistic about her pupil's knowledge of the language than Hogarth had been. She praised his exceptional intelligence, and his determination to master the language, but pointed out that "in a short time he could speak and write a little," which is significantly less than the command of Arabic that Hogarth had attributed to him. It is curious that this supposedly "crash course" consisted of only "one hour [a day] on a red sofa in the large hall," though Lawrence surely also did a lot of reading and practiced his Arabic on the streets of Jebail. Fareedeh el Akle not only admired her young pupil, but appreciated his keen interest in the Arabian people, and "the spiritual

* How good Lawrence's Arabic became is still a matter of dispute among his biographers. He himself did not make exaggerated claims for it. He was eventually able to speak it reasonably well (though he was weak on grammar), and to recognize the major regional differences of speech, but he did not claim to be able to pass as an Arab.

side of his character." Once, when she was talking to Lawrence about some matter of spiritual significance, he replied, "Help comes from within, not from without," which might stand as the definition of his peculiar, lonely strength throughout his life. The inner strength of all the Lawrence boys was extraordinary, perhaps the most important quality they inherited from parents who had, by their own action, virtually cut themselves off from the rest of the world without any apparent regret.

Toward the end of her long life, after being questioned by John Mack, a biographer of Lawrence who was also a professor of psychiatry at Harvard Medical School, Fareedeh wrote to a friend, "Lawrence seems to me like an oyster which has, through pain and suffering, all through life developed into a pearl which the world is trying to evaluate, taking it to pieces layer by layer, without realizing the true value of the whole." There is some truth to this, even today. Lawrence's detractors and admirers alike tend to dissect his personality into thin slices, separating the soldier from the scholar, the hero from the teller of tall tales, the victim of neuroses from the man of action, and in the process losing sight of just what an attractive and interesting *person* he was, even at his most infuriating. Fareedeh clearly recognized this, and understood early on that Lawrence was always more than the sum of his parts. Provocative as Lawrence could be, there was about him a certain sweetness of disposition, a spiritual quality, and above all a sense that he was a special person, destined for greatness, even though it was not yet clear what kind it would be.

Lawrence remained at Jebail studying Arabic until mid-February, keeping up a steady flow of correspondence with his family and friends. The entire Lawrence family seems to have been engaged in writing an endless series of letters and postcards, so that Lawrence seems to have known as much about what was going on at 2 Polstead Road as if he had still been living there, and there was hardly a detail of his own life in Jebail on which he did not report home at length. Apparently his parents were in the habit of showing his letters to Hogarth, since Lawrence asks them to stop doing so, perhaps fearing that Hogarth would be bored by the humdrum details of his life at Jebail, and that his correspondence with Hogarth ought to be kept on a higher level than worries about Thomas Lawrence's health, or promises of coins and stamps for Arnie's collection.

A long letter from Vyvyan Richards reminds Lawrence uncomfortably of the promise to go into business with him. Richards, who seems to have been unable to take a hint, was in the process of planning to build "the hut" where they would live together, and Lawrence asks his father to send Richards some money on his behalf, but in rather lukewarm terms, surely aware that his father will be reluctant to do any such thing.

On January 24 he responds to his mother's copy of a long letter from Richards—Lawrence describes it as "huge"—attempting to deal with the practical problems Richards is raising about the project. Lawrence asks his father to bear in mind that printing, as he and Richards envision it, is "not a business but a craft," which pretty well sums up Thomas Lawrence's objection to the scheme, and argues that he and Richards cannot be expected to "sit down to it for so many hours a day, any more than one could paint a picture on that scheme," although in fact that is exactly what printers and painters do.

By February 18 he was back in Beirut again, to meet Hogarth. Those who think of the Middle East as uninterruptedly hot should bear in mind that Lawrence reported the railway line between Beirut and Aleppo was blocked by "snow 30 feet deep for 7 kilometers," a factor which would play a part in the later stages of his campaign against the Turks in 1917–1918. Hogarth, who had been delayed by bad weather in Constantinople, arrived accompanied by his assistant R. Campbell Thompson, a "cuneiformist" and specialist in Semitic languages, whose presence Lawrence managed mostly to ignore in his letters home; Hogarth's "archeological overseer" Gregorios Antoniou, a Greek Cypriot who had supervised the excavating on Hogarth's previous expeditions, joined the party in Beirut. They were stuck there for some days, since snow continued to fall in the mountains while a ferocious storm prevented them from sailing, but they finally managed to get on a vessel bound for Haifa and from there went on by train to Damascus, on one of the railway lines that Lawrence would later spend much time and effort blowing up. They passed on their way Nazareth, which, Lawrence wrote for his mother's benefit, was "no uglier than Basingstoke," and journeyed on to Deraa, the vital railway junction where Lawrence would be taken prisoner, beaten, and suffer his worst and most painful humiliation. They lunched at the station buffet, which "was flagrantly and evidently an exotic" and served French food in an eastern decor. Hogarth dazzled Lawrence by speaking, with equal fluency, "Turkish & Greek, & French, & German, & Italian & English," and even Lawrence remarked on how weird it was "to be so far out of Europe." This was no longer the rocky, hilly landscape of the Holy Land, which had once been fertile under Roman rule, and over much of which he had walked on foot. Alongside the railway line lay "the Lejah, the lava no-man's-land, and the refuge of all the outlaws of the Ottoman Empire . . . almost impassible, except to a native who knows the ways." One senses Lawrence's fascination with that vast, empty space—he had glimpsed from the train the fabled "great Hajj road," the pilgrim way over which Doughty had approached on camel to the very outskirts of Mecca. That evening they reached Damascus, and from there, via Homs, went to Aleppo.

Lawrence wrote home from Aleppo that he found Thompson "pleasant," by which he seems to mean that Thompson was no competition for Hogarth's attention, and drops the news that he may not get back to England "this year," that is to say for at least another nine months. Hogarth's preparations for the excavation included, Lawrence notes with approval, nine kinds of jam and three kinds of tea; between the three men they carried the complete works of Shakespeare (Thompson), Dante (Hogarth), and Spenser (Lawrence), as well as large quantities of pistachio nuts and "Turkish delight." Lawrence was in a part of the world where his taste for sweet things and his dislike of alcohol were shared by most of the local population. Aleppo he found muddy and filthy, though he seems to have enjoyed the souk, since he was always on the hunt for local pottery and brassware that might please his mother. His brother Frank was apparently practicing pistol shooting, and Lawrence advises him to shoot without taking aim: "The only practical way is almost to throw your bullet like a stone, at the object." This is excellent advice for somebody with good eyes and a steady hand, and from one who knows what he is talking about— those who saw Lawrence in action during the war marveled at his marksmanship, including the Bedouin, who set great store by it.

The winter weather was so bad that they did not arrive in Jerablus until March 10, having made the journey from Aleppo by camel and horse (eleven baggage horses, ten camels), except for Lawrence, who walked. The only local industry was the raising of *Glycyrizza glabra*, a desert plant resembling fennel, from the roots of which licorice is extracted; and the headman of the nearest village was also the agent for the licorice company, who had put the company's house at the disposal of the British archaeologists. The village consisted of about forty fairly new houses—it was clearly something along the lines of what we would call a "company town"—with a good water supply, about half a mile west of a bend in the great Euphrates River, and about three-quarters of a mile south of the great mound of Carchemish, which loomed over the countryside. To the northwest the snow-covered summits of the Taurus Mountains were clearly visible, and the wind from them reduced the daytime temperature to the low forties. Provision for sleeping in the open on the roof of the one-story house, however, suggested that conditions in the summer might be radically different. (Lawrence included in his letter a helpful sketch plan of the house.)

To say that Lawrence found himself in his element would be putting it mildly. He was far from home, and fully occupied day and night. Indeed, he did not write home for another ten days, being busy with establishing their living quarters. For the moment, Lawrence seems to have been in charge of the food supply (with two servants to prepare it), and was pleased to find excellent goat's milk and an ample supply of lentils; how pleased Hogarth and Thompson were is unrecorded. Gregorios the Cypriot, Hogarth's man Friday, had the task of rounding up about 100 men to do the digging, while Thompson surveyed the site, Hogarth wrote up the results for the British Museum, and Lawrence did the drawing and "squeezing" of the inscriptions.* Lawrence was also charged with putting up doors and shelves, the kind of hand work he delighted in, invariably producing something finer than what was expected or required. Indeed his transformation of their living quarters soon became something of an obsession—oddly enough, for a man who would spend many years of his life in the desert or in barracks, he had a passion and a real talent for domestic improvement and decoration. As for the digging, they began in the area where the British had stopped work thirty years ago, and soon uncovered "a great entrance staircase" and a number of large bas-relief slabs. The work was difficult, involving the movement, without machinery, of huge rocks, slag, and shattered stone fragments of a later city, and went slowly. The *kaimakam* (police chief) of the Biridjik district, prodded by the government in Constantinople, had provided a small, tented garrison of Turkish soldiers to guard the archaeologists from any local hotheads, and Lawrence noted with interest the numerous deficiencies in these soldiers' equipment and training. At the end of a letter home, he adds briefly that they are expecting a visit from a "Miss G. Bell," the desert explorer, archaeologist, traveler, and author of *Between the Desert and the Sown*, then forty-two years old and already a famous and glamorous figure.

In his letters home from Carchemish Lawrence sounds like a man who has at last found his place in the world. Increasingly, he joined Gregorios in directing the men as they labored to move huge stones, some weighing many tons. He "devised a derrick" to help pull upright fallen statuary, repaired equipment, learned how to make his own paint, and wrote home to have another pair of boots made and sent out to him, "with slightly thicker soles" and leather laces, since the rocky terrain was already wearing out his present boots.

Hogarth was preparing to return to England, where he would publish the results to date in the *London Times*; he was taking Gregorios with

---

* A "squeeze" was then the accepted method for recording an inscription on stone. A sheet of paper of medium weight, not unlike blotting paper or papier-mâché, was soaked, applied to the stone, and forced into the crevices and markings with a brush and allowed to dry, then removed very carefully.

him, effectively leaving Thompson and Lawrence in charge of the site. Since Thompson was basically a language expert, that would put Lawrence in charge of the dig—no small responsibility for a young man of twenty-two. To replace Gregorios as overseer of the workforce, Hogarth selected a local man, Sheikh Hamoudi, surely a good choice, since he was "tall, gaunt . . . long-armed and immensely powerful," boasted that he had in his youth "provoked other men to fight for the sheer pleasure of killing them," and "admitted to six or seven murders." Hamoudi was to become a great friend and admirer of Lawrence's, and taught him much that would come in handy later, when Lawrence was dealing with the blood feuds and intertribal violence that were endemic in the Arab army.

Lawrence seems to have devised ways of keeping the workforce happy and active, by encouraging contests of one team against another in raising large stones, rather like a tug-of-war, and by instituting a system of small additional payments for each object found, though no matter how hard they dug, layer after layer of the ruins of the Roman city remained between them and the Hittite city below. Hogarth was disappointed, though realistic—some digs worked out; others didn't—but Lawrence continued to be almost irrationally happy. Between Thompson and himself, they managed to get rid of an incompetent and intrusive Turkish "commissaire," whose job it was to ensure that the Turkish Museum got its correct share of the finds; and to Lawrence's joy they were witnesses to a lively, romantic desert abduction, when a "black-bearded . . . & picturesque" young man galloped up on a horse, picked up a girl who had been washing at the spring, "set her before him on his horse, and galloped out of the village, offering to shoot anyone that stood in his way." They were cousins, and her parents had refused to give her to him. Her male relatives immediately mounted and sped after the eloping couple. A few days later there was an unrelated double marriage, in which "the whole people turned out, the men afoot, or on horse in such as had them, the women perched in threes and fours on the humps of camels: everybody in the most brilliant colours, new or clean."

This was a long way from Oxford, indeed about as far as Lawrence could get, and far outweighed Thompson's regret that they had not so far unearthed something like the Rosetta Stone, a stone or seal with writing in Hittite and in Assyrian cuneiform, without which most of what they were unearthing in the way of epigraphical specimens would remain unreadable. In the same letter, on May 16, Lawrence took the trouble of drawing the Carchemish "mound" and the surrounding countryside, in three-dimensional detail. He ends the letter with the reassuring note that the countryside has been peaceful, since "the Kurd chief of Kiranshehir was poisoned . . . by the *Vali* [governor] of Aleppo," a nice comment on ethnic politics in the Ottoman Empire.

On May 23, he reported home on the long-awaited arrival of Gertrude Bell, who at first took a rather high-handed approach to the work of her two young rivals in archaeology, but as the day went on was eventually dazzled and silenced by the sheer breadth of Lawrence's erudition. He thought her "pleasant," but "not beautiful (except with a veil on, perhaps)." Already a celebrity, Bell had traveled in the Jebel Druze against the wishes of the Turkish authorities, camped in Petra, and conducted her own expedition across the Syrian desert all the way to Baghdad, boldly pushing deeper into the life of the desert tribes than any European woman had ever gone (though her most daring journeys were still ahead of her). She was bold, fearless, impatient, formidably well educated, a chain-smoker in an age when women did not smoke in public, inured to hardship, and never at a loss when faced with Turkish interference with her plans or Arab hostility toward a foreign woman traveling alone.

Bell was disappointed not to find Hogarth; she had ridden across the desert from Damascus on her mare to see him, accompanied by her servant Fattuh, and dressed in her desert explorer costume: a long, divided khaki skirt and a linen jacket, with an Arab head cloth wrapped around her hat. She was prepared to be skeptical about the excavations carried out so far, but was immediately struck by Lawrence, about whom she wrote in her diary, "an interesting boy, he is going to make a traveler." Lawrence appears to have dressed for the occasion—for news of Bell's approach had preceded her—in his Magdalen blazer, white shorts, red

Arab slippers with upturned pointed toes, and a crimson woven Arab belt with extra-long tassels hanging over the left hip, which indicated that he was a bachelor.

After lunch, the three of them proceeded to the mound, where Bell observed the men excavating and condemned the methods being used as "prehistoric" (she was notoriously outspoken and critical), compared with those of the Germans. Lawrence maintained that the German methods, while they looked neater, involved a great deal of reconstruction, but eventually they made peace over dinner, and parted friends and mutual admirers when she retired to the tented camp Fattuh had set up for her. They would remain friends until her death, despite many furious arguments. On her departure, at five-thirty in the morning, Bell was dismayed that the villagers gathered to jeer at her—she did not realize that they assumed she had come to Carchemish to marry Lawrence. In order to calm them Lawrence had explained that she was too plain and old for him.

Hogarth was not certain that it was worth continuing the dig at Carchemish for a second season, but, always looking out for Lawrence's interests, suggested that he might benefit from a season or half a season of "tomb digging" for the great Flinders Petrie, the dean of Egyptian archaeology and the head of the British School of Archaeology in Cairo. This would represent a substantial step up in Lawrence's professional qualifications as an archaeologist, a career about which Lawrence remained nevertheless unsure—he toyed with the idea of becoming a newspaperman or a novelist, and continued to speculate on how best he might find a local source of fine vellum, to be "stained [purple] with Tyrian die," for the artistic binding of the books that he and Richards were still planning to print. Meanwhile, Hogarth, never one to delay once a plan had occurred to him, wrote about Lawrence to his colleague Petrie: "Can you make room on your excavations next winter for a young Oxford graduate, T. Lawrence, who has been with me at Carchemish? He is a very unusual type. . . . If he goes to you he would probably come on foot from north Syria. I may add that he is extremely indifferent to what he eats or how he lives. He knows a good deal of Arabic. . . . I can assure you that he is really worth while."

Lawrence did not learn until early in June that the excavation in Carchemish was to go on until August, though perhaps without a second season. By now the level of the Euphrates was falling, exposing sandbanks and islands, and the area was experiencing a plague of locusts, one of which he dried and sent to his youngest brother, Arnie. There was also an invasion of vast numbers of fleas and biting sand flies as the weather warmed. The constant company of Thompson seems to have been getting on his nerves—"any little thing upsets [him]," Lawrence remarked.

Lawrence was making something of a name for himself by producing miracle cures with such things as ammonia and Seidlitz powders, a popular nineteenth-century remedy for stomach distress which fizzed and bubbled furiously when added to water, and which terrified the Arabs, who had never seen such a thing. One of the two "water boys" was persuaded to take half a glass, and this is the first mention in Lawrence's letters of his name: Dahoum.

Dahoum means "darkness," and may have been an ironic nickname, in the same spirit that the friends of a very short man might call him "Lofty," or a very tall man "Tiny," since Dahoum seems in fact to have had rather light skin for a boy of mixed Hittite and Arab ancestry (his family actually lived on the Carchemish mound). He has been described as "beautifully built and remarkably handsome," but in photographs taken of him by Lawrence (and in a pencil sketch made of him by Francis Dodd, when Lawrence brought Dahoum and Sheikh Hamoudi home to Oxford in 1913) he looks not so much beautiful—his face is a little fleshy for that, very much like the faces on the Hittite bas-reliefs that Lawrence was uncovering—as good-humored, intelligent, and amazingly self-possessed for such a young man. It is possible that Dahoum's real name may have been Salim Ahmed—he was also referred to at least once as Sheikh Ahmed too, but that may have been one of Lawrence's private jokes. In any event, Dahoum, who was fourteen when Lawrence met him, would play a role of increasing importance in Lawrence's life, and became one of the many bonds which would tie his life firmly to the Middle East, in peace and in war, over the next seven years.

As the heat increased, Lawrence took to sleeping on the mound, over-looking the Euphrates, and getting up at sunrise to help Sheikh Hamoudi pick the men, and deal with the infinite problems of blood feuds and rivalry between those who shoveled, and thought of themselves as an elite, and those who merely carried baskets of dirt and rocks. Daily, Lawrence was learning not only colloquial Arabic, but the complexities of Arab social relationships, and the dangerous consequences of getting these wrong, or offending Arabs' sensitivity.

On June 24, he wrote home to say that the British Museum, disap-pointed in the results so far, had ordered work shut down in two weeks, and that he intended to take a walking tour of about a month. He added a warning, "Anxiety is absurd." If anything happened to him, his family would hear about it in time. Dahoum had apparently been promoted from one of the two water boys to "the donkey boy," and Lawrence described him as "an interesting character," who could "read a few words (the only man in the district except the liquorice-king) of Arabic, and altogether has more intelligence than the rank-and-file." Dahoum, he mentions, had hopes of going to school in Aleppo, and Lawrence intended to keep an eye on him. Lawrence deplores the intrusion of foreign influ-ence, particularly French and American, on the Arabs, and adds: "The foreigners come out here always to teach, whereas they had much better learn." In a postscript he adds that he has now decided to spend the win-ter walking through Syria (his new pair of boots has arrived), perhaps settling in one of the villages near Jerablus for a time, possibly in the house of Dahoum's father.

This information may not have alarmed the Lawrence family, but it should have. There was no more talk of working under Petrie in Egypt, let alone any mention of Richards and his printing press. Lawrence and Thompson were to go off and briefly examine another Hittite mound at Tell Ahmar, at Hogarth's request, and after that Lawrence proposed to go on by himself, walking to those crusader castles he had not already seen. On top of his next letter, written on July 29, from Jerablus, his mother wrote: "This letter was written when he was almost dying from dysentery."

Lawrence's letter home gives no hint of this—on the contrary, he writes, "I am very well, and en route now for Aleppo," and describes his itinerary so far. The letter is unusually short for him, however—surely a bad sign—and in fact, on the day before, he wrote in his diary, "Cannot possibly continue to tramp in this condition," and collapsed in the house of Sheikh Hamoudi. Hamoudi looked after Lawrence as best he could—though not without a note from Lawrence absolving him of responsibility in case his guest died. This was intended to protect Hamoudi from the Turkish authorities, who would certainly have punished him if a foreigner had died in his care.

Lawrence's mother was not wrong—he came very close to dying, and owed his life to the patient and determined care of Sheikh Hamoudi and the donkey boy Dahoum. By the first days of August Lawrence was beginning to recover, though he was still very weak, and sensibly concluded that his walking tour could not be completed, and that he would have to go home. His illness in 1911 set a pattern that would persist for the rest of Lawrence's life—he ignored wounds, boils, abrasions, infections, broken bones, and pain; paid no attention to the precautions about food and drinking water that almost all Europeans living or traveling in the East made sure to take; suffered through repeated bouts of at least two strains of malaria; and kept going as long as he could even when dysentery brought him to the point of fainting. He lived at some point beyond mere stoicism, and behaved as if he were indestructible—one of the essential attributes of a hero.

As Lawrence slowly regained his strength, he used the time to encourage Dahoum's "efforts to educate himself," and wrote to his friend Fareedeh el Akle at the American mission school in Jebail for simple books on Arab history for his pupil—if possible, books untainted by western influence or thinking. In the meantime he practiced his Arabic on Dahoum; and with a curious habit of anticipating the future, which creeps into his letters and diaries, he wrote to Hogarth that "learning the strongly-dialectical Arabic of the villages would be good as a disguise" while traveling.

While Lawrence lay ill in Jerablus, Hogarth was busy in London, deftly guiding the British Museum toward supporting a new season of digging at Carchemish, since the Turkish government was unlikely to allow the British to start excavation on another Hittite site before this one had been fully exploited. Apparently impressed by Hogarth's letters to the *Times* about Carchemish, Lawrence began what was to become a lifelong habit of writing to the editor of the *Times* about matters that displeased or concerned him. He broke into public print for the first time with a savagely Swiftian attack on the way the Turkish government was allowing important antiquities and archaeological sites to be torn down by developers. "Sir," he began: "Everyone who has watched the wonderful strides that civilization is making in the hands of the Young Turks will know of their continued efforts to clear from the country all signs of the evil of the past." Remarking on a plan to destroy the great castle of Aleppo for the benefit of "Levantine financiers," and on plans to do the same at Urfa and Biridjik, he went on to attack the Germans who were building the Berlin-Baghdad railway, and predicted that "the [Hittite] ruins of Carchemish are to provide materials for the approaches to a new iron girder bridge over the Euphrates," signing himself, "Yours, &c., Traveller." The *Times*, always quick to publish even the tamest of letters—and this one was anything but tame—under a provocative headline, published it on August 9, below the headline "Vandalism in Upper Syria and Mesopotamia," predictably eliciting an infuriated reaction from the German consul in Aleppo. Taunting the Turks and attacking the Germans for their activities in the Ottoman Empire was to become a habit with Lawrence in the years remaining before the outbreak of war.

On August 3 Lawrence began his trip home. He arrived in Beirut on August 8, and to his great delight met the poet James Elroy Flecker and Flecker's Greek wife, Hellé, who were to become his close friends over the next few years. Flecker was the acting British vice-consul in Beirut;

he had attended Trinity College, Oxford, where he had been, or felt he was, a misfit, although he had been a contemporary, friend, and rival of the poet Rupert Brooke. John Maynard Keynes, who had met Flecker while visiting friends in Oxford, wrote about him to Lytton Strachey: "I am not enthusiastic about Flecker,—semi-foreign, with a steady languid flow and, I am told, an equally steady production of plays and poems which are just not bad." There may be a trace of what might now be called gay bitchery in this comment, as well as a degree of genteel anti-Semitism—both Keynes and Strachey were members of a rather refined group of extremely bright, ambitious young homosexuals. Flecker labored under numerous erotic and familial difficulties, none of which he was able to reconcile or resolve: he had been educated at a school where his father was the headmaster, and as if that were not difficult enough, his father was a ferociously Low Church, evangelical Protestant who was half Jewish. Flecker's swarthy looks made his intense Englishness seem adopted rather than natural, and he rebelled against his parents in every way, running up reckless debts, and indulging himself by writing extravagantly garish poetry and striking exaggerated aesthetic poses that alarmed them. Only by dint of a heroic, last-ditch effort was Flecker able to squeak through the examination into the consular service (a large step down from the more socially and intellectually distinguished diplomatic service). In the process, he did nothing to please either his parents or the Foreign Office by falling in love with a forceful young Greek woman, who braved the issue of his ill health—he was already suffering from tuberculosis—to marry him. More or less exiled to a subordinate post in Beirut, Flecker paid more attention to his career as a poet than to his consular duties.

In Lawrence he found not only a friend but an admirer. Lawrence was deeply impressed by Flecker's poetry,* the best of which was written after Flecker was exposed to the color and drama of eastern life, and felt as much at home in the Fleckers' apartment in Beirut as he would a few

---

* Flecker was by no means a negligible poet—his work "The Golden Journey to Samarkand" made it into the *New Oxford Book of English Verse*, and many of his poems were much admired and praised in their day.

years later in that of Ronald Storrs, in Cairo. Indeed Lawrence photographed Flecker elaborately dressed in a Bedouin robe and headdress—though despite his dark complexion and an inherent love of dressing up in costume, Flecker does not look nearly as comfortable in Arab clothing as Lawrence. Flecker is also a good example of one of Lawrence's most endearing characteristics: once he became your friend he was your friend for life, and once he admired your work he was a supporter of it forever.

It is a measure of how ill Lawrence had been that he returned to England via Marseille and went on from there by train to Oxford—this route was much quicker (and more expensive) than traveling by sea from Beirut to England. At home, he recuperated under the watchful eye of Sarah, and faced the difficulties so common to talented young men of his age. In his case it was not so much that he couldn't decide what to do with himself as that he had too many choices and self-imposed obligations. Hogarth, he learned, had secured the funds for a second season of excavation at Carchemish; Flinders Petrie had accepted him for a stint of

*Lawrence's photograph
of James Elroy Flecker.*

tomb digging in Egypt; Vyvyan Richards was still eager to proceed with the printing press scheme; Jesus College expected to hear more about Lawrence's BLitt thesis on medieval pottery; and Lawrence himself was deeply mired in his plan to bring out his expanded BA thesis on castles and fortifications as a book, a project that was doomed for the moment by the number of his drawings and photographs that he deemed essential to the text.

Although the doctors were strongly against Lawrence's return to the Middle East, that of course did not deter him. Thompson, he learned, had declined to return unless his wife could accompany him, a suggestion that horrified everyone; and Hogarth replaced him with a young archaeologist, Charles Leonard Woolley, an assistant keeper of the Ashmolean Museum. Woolley would go on to a long and distinguished career; he would not only be knighted but serve as the inspiration for Agatha Christie's *Murder in Mesopotamia*. Lawrence and Woolley became and remained friends— Woolley was primarily interested in the discovery of big buildings and monuments, while Lawrence worked with the men, honed his knowledge of Arabic, and took care of the pottery finds and the photography.

Lawrence defied the doctors and set out again for Jerablus at the end of November, to report on the rumor that the Germans planned to build their railway right through the mound at Carchemish. When this proved to be untrue (the railway would pass uncomfortably near it, but not through it), he journeyed on to Egypt to join Petrie's current dig at Kafr Ammar, on the Nile south of Cairo, but not without enduring a terrifying carriage accident on Christmas Day, when the driver toppled the carriage and the horses off a bridge and into a stream. In a letter home on January 2 he comments darkly (and correctly) about conditions in the Ottoman Empire: "Great rumors of war and annexation:—not to be believed yet, but such a smash is coming out here."

He wrote next from Cairo, giving his family his new address in Kafr Ammar in Arabic script, so they could copy it out and add it to each envelope. The actual digging disgusted him, and prompted one of his darker descriptive passages: "It is a strange sight to see the men [dragging] out a mummy, not glorious in bright wrappings, but dark brown, fibrous, visibly rotting—and then the thing begins to come to pieces, and the men tear off its head, and bare the skull, and the vertebrae drop out, and the ribs, and legs and perhaps only one poor amulet is the result. . . . I'm no body snatcher, and we have a pile of skulls that would do credit to a follower of Genghis Khan." He found the Nile sluggish, and the brown sails of the boats on it depressing to look at.

A week later Flinders Petrie* and his wife arrived, and it is hard not to guess that the uncongenial nature of the work preconditioned Lawrence to dislike her. "I don't like Mrs. Petrie," he wrote home flatly after meeting her for the first time (this was unusual for Lawrence); as for Petrie, who was hugely dignified and full of himself, Lawrence seems to have displayed his dislike of tomb robbing by "taking the mickey" out of Petrie in small ways, perhaps not his most endearing trait. Lawrence turned up for digging in football shorts and a white Magdalen College Boat Club blazer, prompting Petrie to remark that they weren't here to play cricket. As one of Lawrence's biographers pointed out, the joke was on Petrie, who did not realize that cricket isn't played in football shorts (not that Lawrence played either cricket or football). Also, and perhaps more woundingly, flaunting the Magdalen blazer may have been Lawrence's way of reminding Petrie that unlike Lawrence he "was not an Oxonian, but merely Professor of Egyptology in the *petit bourgeois* University of London." Petrie, whose long white beard made him rather resemble God the Father in Michelangelo's ceiling fresco in the Sistine Chapel, may have been sharp enough to guess the intention of Lawrence's choice of clothing, but the Petries nevertheless showed him a remarkable degree of kindness and courtesy during his time there, and Lawrence thawed toward them.

Over time, despite his dislike of digging up mummified bodies (and a general distaste for Egypt, both the people and the way they spoke Arabic),

---

* Sir Flinders Petrie (as he became) was one of the first archaeologists to achieve worldwide celebrity, a trend that would reach its peak with the excavation of King Tutankhamun's intact tomb by Howard Carter in 1923. Lawrence himself would contribute something posthumously to the later (fictional) character of the armed archaeologist-adventurer hero, of which "Indiana Jones" is the most famous example.

Lawrence came rather reluctantly to admire Petrie's abilities. Petrie had discovered the first mention of Israel in Egyptian recorded history by deciphering the Merneptah stele, an accomplishment that won him international acclaim; and by linking the styles of pottery shards, he developed a new and more exact method of chronology for excavation sites, something from which Lawrence would benefit in his task of classifying Hittite pottery at Carchemish.

Petrie emphasized that all archaeological research "lies in the noting and comparison of the smallest details," advice from which Lawrence could surely benefit, and with which he agreed. In the end Lawrence not only learned a lot from Petrie, as Hogarth had surely intended, but came to like and respect him, despite their unpropitious first meeting. As for Petrie, he offered Lawrence £700, a not inconsiderable sum, toward the expense of two seasons investigating several sites on the Persian Gulf, which Lawrence was very tempted to accept if the resumption of the Carchemish dig fell through.

However, during Lawrence's one-month stay in Egypt—he may be the only visitor to pass through Cairo without bothering to see the Pyramids—Hogarth had unexpectedly tapped into a wealthy source for carrying forward the Carchemish digging. By the time Lawrence arrived back there early in February, the matter of financing was settled, and the opportunity to dig for Petrie vanished for the moment. Perhaps this was just as well, for Lawrence's commitment to a career in archaeology was never total. Lawrence was happy at Jerablus—happier than he would ever be in his life again—but he was never tempted by the academic life.

The world of caravans, camels, desert, and Bedouin nomads would hold Lawrence to the Middle East for the next three years, except for brief visits home, and spare him the decision about what career to follow, until at last the outbreak of World War I thrust him into the career for which he had been training himself all his life.

Lawrence arrived at Aleppo to find the Turkish authorities making difficulties about the resumption of work at Carchemish; nor had the money arrived with which to begin a new house for the archaeologists, nearer to the site. The years 1911 to 1914 were difficult ones for foreigners in Turkey—the country's political instability combined with a series of humiliating military defeats and territorial losses for the Ottoman Empire in Libya at the hands of Italy, and in the Balkans at the hands of Serbia, Greece, Montenegro, and Bulgaria, intensified the siege mentality of the Turkish government and its hostility to foreigners, and encouraged fear of the Russians and, therefore, a closer relationship with Germany. In the course of the nineteenth century Turkey had seen itself deprived of all its North African possessions, from Egypt to Morocco, and all its Balkan possessions except for a tiny enclave around Constantinople; of course, this made the Turks all the more determined to hold on to their Arabian possessions.

Lawrence kicked his heels in Aleppo for nearly two weeks, happy to be out of Egypt, buying small antiquities for Hogarth and the Ashmolean Museum, bargaining for a long camel-hair cloak for himself ("such as Bedouin sheiks wear: Baghdad made: very warm and beautiful"), and keeping himself going by borrowing from the British consul until money arrived from the British Museum. He spent much time searching for an armorer who still made chain mail as it had been made at the time of the Crusades, for the benefit of a friend in Oxford who shared his interest in armor. He wrote home often—in one letter, he expresses satisfaction that his brother Frank is keeping up with his shooting, and urges Frank "to do a little revolver work: it is harder than a rifle to learn, and more often necessary," a typically offhand remark that separates Lawrence from other archaeological assistants, few of whom would have felt that revolver marksmanship was a necessity. He seems to have been reading a lot—Maurice Hewlett's *Richard Yea-and-Nay*, a historical novel about Richard I, for the ninth time, Lawrence claimed; and William Morris's "Victorian-Icelandic-Anglo-Saxon-German epic poem" *Sigurd the Volsung*. This is a revealing choice of books. Hewlett was a prolific English writer of romantic historical fiction; he was a friend of Ezra Pound and of J. M. Barrie, the author of *Peter Pan*, and was famous and successful in his time, though he is largely forgotten now. His novel about Richard Coeur de Lion is a frankly hero-worshipping and meticulously detailed portrait of one of Lawrence's favorite medieval kings. Morris's hero, Sigurd, is the central figure of Norse myth and legend, the dragon slayer and hero of the Volsunga Saga, and Wagner's inspiration for the *Ring* cycle. Morris transformed Sigurd into a noble Victorian hero, a kind of fantasy *preux chevalier*, in what one biographer of Lawrence calls "a transparently Oedipal tale."* Both books are about the trials and tribulations of a hero as he passes from one dangerous adventure to another toward his fate: betrayal by a woman. It is hard to imagine anyone reading Hewlett's novel nine times, unless he identified in some way with Richard I. As for Sigurd's doom-laden (and pagan) story, it seems unlikely that Thomas and Sarah Lawrence would have shared their son's enthusiasm. As is so often the case with Lawrence, his interests and enthusiasms seemed to be drawing him toward a life in the heroic mold, for the moment still in the form of literary fantasy, even while on the practical, day-to-day level he pursued archaeology.

Once he arrived in Jerablus, after a three-day walk over rough country, followed by a recalcitrant mule train carrying the expedition's supplies, Lawrence was like a man back in his element. Physical discomfort, danger, and exhaustion acted on him like a tonic. He gathered a workforce; had the foundations for the expedition house dug; and argued over the ownership of the mound with a greedy local landowner who claimed it, and with a Turkish police lieutenant who ordered him to stop the digging. By the first week in March he was back in Aleppo, to pick up Woolley—there was a certain amount of excitement in the foreign community, since all Italians were being expelled from Turkey because of the war in Libya, and it was therefore possible to buy their collections of antiquities at

---

*John E. Mack, the author of *A Prince of Our Disorder: The Life of T. E. Lawrence*, was a professor of psychiatry at Harvard University, and perhaps as a result was apt to see the oedipal myth at work everywhere. What is more remarkable about *Sigurd the Volsung* is Morris's determination to infuse nobility into pagan stories of lust, betrayal, and murder and transform them into a high-flown romantic tale, a kind of quest for the Holy Grail, but without Christianity.

bargain-basement prices. Then, a week later, Woolley and Lawrence went to Biridjik together, to confront the *kaimakam* over the order to stop the digging and the interference from the local landowner.

Lawrence might easily have resented Woolley's presence, since Woolley was senior to him, and a more experienced archaeologist, but fortunately Woolley behaved exactly the right way for an Englishman confronting an Asian official, and told the *kaimakam* that he would shoot on the spot anyone who "interrupted the digs." He apparently spoke with enough high-handed vigor and righteous British indignation to cow the *kaimakam*, who had, of course, arranged the various attempts to stop the digging in the hope of extracting a bribe for himself. Woolley thereby won Lawrence's instant and lasting respect and friendship. Those who thought Lawrence was mild saw only his short stature, his slight figure, and the boyish shock of unruly fair hair, and failed to notice the icy blue eyes and the large, firm jaw: he was quite capable of acting just like one of Kipling's pukka sahibs when aroused, and he thoroughly approved of Woolley's boldly threatening the Turkish police chief in the chief's own office, as well as Woolley's parting shot: that he was declaring war not against the Turkish government, but only against the *kaimakam*.

Woolley acquired further merit in Lawrence's eyes by admiring Lawrence's pottery finds (and agreeing with most of Lawrence's theories about them) and showing a preference for Syrian over Egyptian cooking. Since Woolley could not speak or understand the local dialect, he needed Lawrence to translate for him, as well as deal with the workforce—not always an easy task, since almost every adult male was armed, and every find was proclaimed with a fusillade of shots. Even the cook, "the staid Haj Wahid," worked with a Mauser pistol stuffed into his sash and a Martini-Henry rifle by his bedroll, and at one point fired ten shots through the goat-hair roof of the tent in celebration; the holes then had to be darned.

By the beginning of April—despite the fact that no building permit had as yet arrived from Constantinople—the stone expedition house was almost completed. Consisting of eleven rooms, "two of them very large," the Carchemish house was to occupy a good deal of Lawrence's time and attention over the next two years. It had an impressive courtyard with a graceful stone entrance, and although the house was built of rough-dressed stone rather than adobe, in photographs it very much resembles a largish and rather fashionable home in Santa Fe. This is particularly true of the interior, with its hanging wall rugs; white plaster walls with deep, graceful niches for books and antiquities; carved wooden doors; and beamed ceilings, which look just like the rough-hewn vigas used in New Mexico.

By mid-April Lawrence and Woolley had settled into the new house and were waiting for the arrival (and the approval) of Hogarth. Despite a formal visit from the *kaimakam*, who had been ordered to apologize to them, Lawrence continued his campaign of harassing the Turkish authorities, picking the lock of the storeroom in which the "poor little [Turkish] Commissaire" kept the antiquities that had been excavated, and in general doing what he could to stoke the discontent in the local workforce against the nearby German railway builders. For the moment, all this was still on the level of undergraduate pranks, but the Middle East being what it was (and is), there would soon be an escalation to violence and the use of firearms. Even Woolley, who came to admire and love Lawrence, was aware of his "essential immaturity" about matters like this. That impression was no doubt accentuated by the fact that Lawrence looked, as Winifred Fontana, the wife of the British consul in Aleppo, remarked, "about eighteen." Another person who met Lawrence in Aleppo at that time described him as a "frail, pallid, silent youth," though that remark contrasts with Mrs. Fontana's description of him as "a young man of rare power and considerable physical beauty." Much as Lawrence spurned physical relationships with any women (or men), a number of women were strongly attracted to him over the years.

In a long letter home at about this time, Lawrence brings up the possibility, no doubt alarming to his family, that he may go off into the desert to seek out the primitive and nomadic Soleyb, survivors of the pagan predecessors of the Arabs; spend "a spring & summer with them"; then write a book, along the lines of Doughty's *Arabia Deserta*, devoted to this mysterious people. Lawrence expresses his belief that his book (or books) "would be better, if I had been for a time in open country," a very different and more demanding ambition than turning his BA thesis into an illustrated book. Lawrence may have lost interest in the elusive Soleyb on learning that they lived on raw antelope meat, though this is not the kind of consideration which would necessarily have held him back—more likely, his growing interest in archaeology and his responsibilities at Carchemish pushed this scheme into the background.

Lawrence's letters to his friend Leeds, back at the Ashmolean, are often rather franker than his letters home. Admittedly, in writing to Leeds Lawrence attempts to turn every event, however trying and difficult, into a funny story—one learns, for instance, that he and Woolley had prudently taken spare clothes and tinned food with them when they went to confront the *kaimakam*, since there was a good chance they might have been thrown into prison, and that Woolley had to brandish his pistol again, "when the police tried to hold up his donkeys." Lawrence was running footraces with the younger and nimbler workers, and painstakingly removing a splendid Roman mosaic floor from a plowed field near the excavation site and reconstructing it as the floor of one room in the expedition house. Since this consisted of 144,000 tesserae (small vitreous tiles) "weighing over a ton," it was no simple or easy task. In May the eagerly awaited visit of David Hogarth took place: "A breathless hush of expectation. . . . We're all dressed in our best, sitting in our empty, swept, and garnished rooms, awaiting the coming of the C H I E F."

Hogarth's nine-day visit to the site proved satisfactory—it is typical of Hogarth's amazing ability to be in the right place at the right time and, more important, to know the right people, that on his way out to visit Carchemish he met in Berlin with the kaiser and obtained from his imperial majesty "his explicit promise to make all right for us with the *Baghdadbahn* people, if there is any trouble," in Lawrence's words. Thus the German railway engineers were persuaded to carry away much of the spoil and rubble from the excavation site to use in building the bridge over the Euphrates and in bedding the tracks, thereby saving the British Museum a good deal of money, and speeding up the dig for Woolley and Lawrence.

Among the many things Lawrence learned from Hogarth, perhaps the most important was to go to the top unhesitatingly in any matter that interested or concerned him. Despite a reputation for shyness and a desire to remain in the background, as a young civilian in Cairo in 1914 Lawrence was apparently able to reach the formidable Field Marshal Kitchener to urge on him the importance of taking Alexandretta; he successfully bypassed many layers of military command to deal directly with General Allenby in 1917–1918; although only an acting lieutenant-colonel, he made his arguments about the Middle East directly to Lloyd George, Wilson, and Clemenceau at the Paris Peace Conference in 1919; and he made his case for reforms in the RAF directly to Air Chief Marshal Trenchard in the 1920s. It must be said that Lawrence seldom used either his fame or his remarkable ability to reach some of the busiest and most powerful people in the world to his own advantage; he used both only in pursuit of causes he deemed worthwhile, or to deflect policies that he thought were ill-advised.

Hogarth was sufficiently impressed with what had been done at Carchemish so far—and by the numerous signs that the remains of a great Hittite city would eventually be uncovered—that he recommended to the British Museum that Woolley's pay be increased, and that Lawrence be given a salary of fifteen shillings a day for the next season's digging. In the meantime, Lawrence was using Dahoum to help him reassemble and classify the growing collection of pottery fragments, and teaching Dahoum to act as his assistant in the darkroom. In June, Woolley stopped the dig and went home to England, leaving Lawrence on his own, to spend the summer months traveling through Syria with Dahoum as his companion.

Lawrence's friendship with Dahoum has been the subject of a good deal of speculation over the years, but it seems very unlikely that there was anything improper or scandalous about it—Vyvyan Richards's comment that Lawrence was totally without sexual feelings or temptation probably holds as true for his relationship with Dahoum as it held for Richards. Whether Lawrence was totally without such feelings or savagely repressed them for most of his life is a different question. Given his belief that his parents should never have had children, and his melancholy feeling that his father had given up great estates, a position in society, and a title for a transitory and guilty pleasure, Lawrence may well have begun early on in childhood to suppress in himself even the faintest hint of sexuality—a feat to which his unusual degree of willpower and determination would have lent themselves. The stormy relationship between Lawrence and his mother, and his refusal to be dominated by her formidable will, may have contained a complex, self-destructive reversal of the Oedipus complex: Lawrence not only refused to give in to his oedipal fantasies but suppressed *all* his sexual instincts completely to do so. This would be a psychological analogue of a "scorched earth" strategy, in which he constantly refused to surrender to sexual urges of any kind until his refusal became a fixed part of his personality, and the source of much of his strength.

Those who were closest to Lawrence and Dahoum, such as Leonard Woolley, have all emphasized that the close friendship between them was perfectly innocent; indeed had this not been the case, there would almost certainly have been a strong reaction among the local Arabs, and either Woolley or Hogarth would have felt obliged to deal with it. If Lawrence had had a physical relationship with Dahoum, it seems unlikely that he would have brought Dahoum home to Oxford to meet his family, as he would do in July 1913, or that he would also bring Sheikh Hamoudi, an unapologetic killer and not by any stretch of the imagination a tolerant soul, or that Hamoudi would have accompanied them had there been anything improper about their relationship.

That Lawrence *loved* Dahoum is certainly true, and sensing in Dahoum a degree of ambition rare in most Arabs at that time and place, he did his best to provide for Dahoum's education, and to offer him a broader view of the world. Lawrence's definition of love was decidedly not carnal—the boundaries he was crossing with Dahoum were those of race, religion, class, and age (Lawrence was seven or eight years older than Dahoum), not sexual. Whether Lawrence had sexual feelings toward Dahoum we cannot know. Certainly, he never expressed such feelings, though perhaps if he had ever allowed them to emerge, they would have been directed at Dahoum. To nobody else in his life was he ever so close, and with nobody else was he as happy.

In some ways, Lawrence's concern for Dahoum was fatherly; in other ways it was that of an older brother. Certainly he saw in Dahoum the kind of natural nobility he later found among his Bedouin followers, uncorrupted in his view by European or British influence and largely untainted by Turkish overlordship, the equivalent of Rousseau's *homme naturel*. That this was in some ways a romantic fantasy is certain—Dahoum was attractive, intelligent, sympathetic, and honest, and all those who met him liked him. On the other hand, he was not a Semitic version of an Arthurian hero as imagined by William Morris—but that was a fantasy Lawrence would follow right through the war to its tragic end, and even afterward, when he wrote *Seven Pillars of Wisdom*. Lawrence would seek throughout his adult life the company of men, and if, in that world, he found a kind of comfort, it was only during the few years he spent with Dahoum that he ever found somebody he loved who could share it.

One does not know how the matter appeared to Dahoum—he was only fourteen when Lawrence (then age twenty-two) met him, and he would have had very little experience of Europeans; but young men mature early in the Arab world, and as a result it is sometimes Lawrence who appears younger than his protégé. Dahoum cannot have been blind to the fact that Lawrence's friendship raised his status, as well as opening up for him a world of literacy and education that would have been unimaginable to most poor north Syrian Arab boys in the Ottoman Empire. A degree of self-interest may well have been present in Dahoum. Lawrence was his opportunity for a way out of his small village, and out of a future of herding goats or harvesting licorice root for the local *agha*, and he seized it eagerly; but this does not mean he did not care for Lawrence in return, and it is possible that he may have risked his life for Lawrence during the war. In one of a famous pair of photographs taken at Carchemish, Lawrence is shown wearing Dahoum's Arab robes, laughing as he tries to put Dahoum's headdress on correctly; the other photograph shows Dahoum in the same place and pose, wearing his own robes and headdress, looking straight into the camera, and smiling broadly. What is most significant about the photograph of Dahoum is that he holds lovingly in both hands, with undisguised pride, a nickel-plated Colt Model of 1903 .32-caliber "Pocket Hammerless Automatic Pistol," not a weapon he could have afforded to own unless Lawrence gave it to him. Possession of a modern firearm was almost mandatory for any self-respecting Arab male, and Dahoum's pleasure in holding the Colt is unmistakable. It hardly matters whether Lawrence gave Dahoum the pistol, or simply lent it to him for the photograph; either way, this was a princely gesture in a society where men did not give away or lend their firearms willingly, and Dahoum's face is lit up with unfeigned pleasure.

Lawrence enjoyed the years he spent working at Carchemish not just because of the constant presence of Dahoum. Lawrence and Woolley, though in many respects an odd couple, got along well; the expedition house was one of the only two homes that Lawrence would build and decorate to satisfy his own taste; and he was living among the Arabs, whom he came more and more to like and respect. In addition, he could arrange his days and nights to please himself, reading until late into the night, going without sleep or food when he felt like it, working in exhausting bursts according to whim. He was a commanding presence among the Arabs and something of a celebrity among the rare European visitors— as well as being a gadfly to the Turkish authorities and the German railway engineers without any interference, for on this subject, Woolley and Lawrence were of one mind, whatever the kaiser may have told Hogarth.

Lawrence notes in a letter home that he has not received a letter from Richards since November of the previous year—a sign perhaps that Thomas Lawrence's pessimism on the subject of the hand press has at last sunk in. In another letter, he orders a new pair of boots, always a sure sign that he is planning a long journey on foot. Lawrence never fails to fill his family in on the process of educating Dahoum—another sign that the relationship, however intense it may be, is blameless. In mid-June Woolley was to go home to England—the months from June through August were commonly thought to be unbearable for a white man in Syria, though of course this notion did not deter Lawrence—and on June 20 he writes home to say that he and Woolley have already reached the port of Alexandretta with fifteen cases of Hittite pottery to load on board Woolley's ship, and that they avoided Aleppo because of an outbreak of cholera. Having brought up the matter of cholera, surely alarming to Sarah, Lawrence writes home three days later from Baron's Hotel in Aleppo— the danger of cholera apparently forgotten—to say that he wants at least three pairs of regular socks and one pair of white wool, and that people come from far and wide to offer him *antikas* of every kind, which he is buying for Hogarth, for himself, for the British Museum, and for the Ashmolean. He notes that it is a time of unusually intense confusion and upheaval in the Ottoman Empire, since Turkey and the Balkan states are at war. (This war would end just in time for World War I to begin, and would strip Turkey of its remaining European territory.) Lawrence exults in the fact that "for the foreigner [this country] is too glorious for words: one is the baron of the feudal system." This is a reference to the German railway builders, who, apparently in awe of the kaiser's message as it filtered down to them after his talk with Hogarth, had ordered their workers to stop work on the bridge while Lawrence bathed in the Euphrates, so as not to inconvenience him. It also refers to the Turkish government's eagerness to keep the citizens of all the major European powers resident in the Ottoman Empire as happy as possible at a moment when the Turkish army was being humiliatingly defeated in the Balkans. Turkey was a police state humanized by inefficiency and corruption, but even so when an order was given in Constantinople it eventually made its way down to even such remote places as Jerablus, and for the moment the British archaeologists were the beneficiaries.

To Leeds Lawrence wrote, more frankly, about the epidemic of cholera, and about braving the heat and the epidemic to spend a day in the bazaars, "buying glue and sacking and wire gauze and potatoes and embroidery and Vaseline and gunpowder . . . and bootlaces and Damascus tiles." In fact, Lawrence had bought up the entire supply of glue in the province (some twenty-six pounds of it) for his Roman tile floor. Although he obtained fulsome letters of introduction to the governors of all the towns he proposed to visit from the newly obliging *vali* at Aleppo ordering all *kaimakams, mutessarifs, mirdirs,* and other "government officials to see that I am well lodged, well fed, provided with transport, with guides, with interpreters and escorts," and despite his request for new boots and socks from home, the long tramp he had proposed to take with Dahoum never took place.

Instead he plunged into caring for the cholera victims in the villages around Aleppo and Jerablus, as the epidemic spread rapidly. It seems to be about this time that Lawrence took to wearing Arab robes, perhaps because he thereby seemed less threatening or less unfamiliar to those suffering from the disease, which in those days was fatal nearly 90 percent of the time. He wrote to England for medical advice, and soon he was treating people in the surrounding villages despite the risk to himself. Indeed, he did fall sick himself, with malaria; and he soon found that he had to deal not only with cholera but with an outbreak of smallpox, for which he successfully vaccinated the local children. Giving these vaccinations was very daring, since had the children died, he would certainly have been held responsible.

He managed to get away with Dahoum to the American mission school in Jebail, to work on his Arabic and improve Dahoum's reading skills; and briefly to Lebanon, where the Fleckers, lonely in their summer home, were delighted to have somebody well educated to talk to. In those days, consular duties were not so pressing as to keep the vice-consul in Beirut during the summer, and the Fleckers had rented a cottage in the mountains with "a big garden, where the pomegranates were in full bloom," though the views of the sea and the colors of the garden did not serve to cheer poor Flecker up. He was still in debt; he was—correctly—pessimistic about passing his examination in Turkish; and his tuberculosis was getting worse. It may be on the occasion of this visit that "carelessly flung beneath a tree," he talked to Lawrence "of women's slippers and of whipping." The subject ought to have interested Lawrence, whose personality already inclined toward a degree of masochism, but he may not have wanted to share his interest with Flecker, whom he liked but did not see as a soul mate.

He was busy with other things—preventing the Germans from taking (despite the kaiser's promise to Hogarth) valuable Hittite material from the Carchemish mound for building their bridge, instead of the rubble they were supposed to remove; and carving a beautiful and very impressive winged sun disk into the lintel above the front door of the expedition house. The sun disk showed unexpected skill on Lawrence's part at stone carving—it was almost five feet from wing tip to wing tip—and was also a typical example of tongue-in-cheek humor, since visitors, even learned ones, invariably admired it as a splendid Hittite relic. Lawrence was particularly pleased when German archaeologists were taken in by it.

It is possible to feel in the letters he wrote during the summer of 1912 a strong preference for adventure over scholarship and a growing reluctance to return home to take up a formal academic career. The very idea of England, with its rich green fields and woods, seems increasingly foreign to him, as if the desert had finally claimed him. He wrote to his older brother, Bob, "I feel very little the lack of English scenery: we have too much greenery there, and one never feels the joy of a fertile place, as one does here when one finds a thorn-bush and green thistle. . . . England is fat—obese." There are few references to his plan for expanding his BA thesis on medieval castles, and fewer still to the BLitt on medieval pottery that Jesus College supposed him to be working on. He may, in fact, have settled rather deeper into Arab life than he or Hogarth had intended. He wrote to his youngest brother, Arnold ("Worm"), about a battle he had witnessed from the mound, in which two Arabs shoveling sand into boats for the railway were surprised by a long line of Kurds advancing toward them, to take their boats. The Kurds opened fire with their pistols, and the two sand diggers took off, leaving behind two other Arabs, one of whom "swam for it," while the other was captured and stripped of his pistol and clothes. The Kurds then used the remaining boat to try to cross the river, but the Arabs massed on their bank of the river and opened fire, eventually driving the Kurds off and chasing after them.* Since most of the shooting was done at 400 yards, an impossible range for most pistols, a lot of ammunition was wasted and nobody was hurt. Lawrence remarks, "Wasn't that a lovely battle?" but there is a certain glee to his account of the incident, which will be echoed from time to time in his early days with Feisal, when battle was still a new experience.

In August his third bout of malaria drove him back to the comparative comfort of Beirut and the mission school in Jebail, where a Miss Holmes was able to look after him. He reports to his family: "I eat a lot, & sleep a lot, and when I am tired of reading I go and bathe in the sea with Dahoum, who sends his salaams." His reading list, as ever heavy and

---

*Conflict and bloodshed among Syrian Arabs, Mesopotamian Arabs, and Kurds, as well as between Shiite and Sunni Arabs, do not represent a new phenomenon in the area.

impressive, includes Spenser, Catullus, Marot, the Koran, Simonides, and Meleager. For lighter reading he had a novel about the Crusade of the Children, and Maurice Hewlett's *Remy* (Lawrence is probably referring to *The Song of Renny*), which, despite Lawrence's enthusiasm for *Richard Yea-or-Nay*, prompts him to write, "I think that Hewlett is finished."* Miss Holmes apparently managed to force a midday siesta on a reluctant Lawrence, and he reports home with evident pride that "she has fallen in love with *Sigurd*," an acid test to which all of Lawrence's English-speaking friends appear to have been put at this time.

By the beginning of October, Woolley had returned and digging was resumed—Lawrence's work gang fired some 300 shots into the air to celebrate the new season and Woolley's return, alarming the German railway engineers in the nearby camp, who supposed that an insurrection was taking place. The countryside was in an uproar in any case, since the Turks were busy trying to round up recruits for the army as the Balkan wars dragged on, and the Kurds were threatening to rebel, as they always did when there was any hint of weakness in Constantinople. In a letter to Leeds, Lawrence mentions casually that he has suffered two broken ribs in a scuffle with a belligerent Arab—he treats this incident with his usual disdain for injuries of any kind. Hints of various other scrapes with the authorities and the local Arabs are scattered throughout his letters. It seems likely that at some point he was briefly imprisoned by the Turks, and that at another point he and Woolley were involved in a lawsuit from a local landowner, which Woolley solved in his own swashbuckling manner by threatening the judge. (Under the "capitulations," foreigners in Turkey were more or less immune from Turkish law.) It is certain that Lawrence was involved in an illicit and secret plot (Lawrence describes it as "the iniquity of gun-running") to smuggle rifles ashore from a British warship into the British consulate in Beirut, so that the staff members could protect themselves in the event of an anticipated Kurdish rising if the Turks could not (or would not) protect them. The plot involved Law-

---

*Not quite. Hewlett had another twelve years of life and thirteen more books to go, before his death in 1923.

rence, his friend "Flecker, the admiral at Malta, our Ambassador at Stanbul, two [British naval] captains, and two lieutenants, besides innumerable cavasses [consular guards and porters], in one common lawbreaking." This gleeful flouting of Turkish sovereignty, involving high British naval and diplomatic figures and masterminded by a young Oxford scholar and archaeological assistant, helps to explain the apparently effortless transition of Lawrence from deskbound intelligence officer to guerrilla leader in 1917. Lawrence also reports that he has been firing an expensive Mannlicher-Schönhauer sporting carbine, possibly presented to him as a reward for his part in the "gun-running" incident, and "put four shots out of five" with it into "a six-gallon petrol tin at 400 yards"; this is very fine shooting by any standard. He also reports having invented a number of special tools of his own design to help move heavy stones, and having taken up the risky use of dynamite to demolish Roman concrete remains and get at the Hittite ruins below them. It is easy to see that many of the elements that made Lawrence an effective military leader were already in place as early as 1912; it is almost as if Lawrence were training himself for what was to come, but of course he was not.

He and Woolley took the precaution of making friends with the local Kurdish leaders; indeed Lawrence hoped to steer the Kurds toward the German railway camp in case of trouble, but the Kurds remained disappointingly quiet. None of this excitement slowed down the steady stream of Lawrence's letters home. He relied on his older brother, Bob, a pupil of the great physician Sir William Osler at Oxford and now a medical student at Barts, for medical advice that would help him treat the Arabs— it had been Bob who gave Lawrence the instructions for vaccinating the local children against smallpox, and who recommended the use of carbolic acid and ammonia for the workers' boils and wounds. Even to Bob, though, Lawrence's tone is faintly paternal, a blend of advice and warnings on every subject under the sun. Indeed, much as Lawrence disliked receiving advice from his mother, he was never hesitant about giving it out. This was to be a lifelong characteristic—though there were exceptions, such as Bernard Shaw, whose advice on grammar and punctuation

Lawrence heard patiently, but mostly ignored; and Hogarth, the one person whose opinions Lawrence instinctively trusted. Lawrence was one of those difficult people who nearly always had to find their own way of doing things, and he turned a deaf ear to any differing opinion, however eminent the source. He would always prefer to fail by doing something his own way than to succeed by doing it somebody else's way: Lawrence never yielded willingly to anybody. Some of the most terrifying episodes in *Seven Pillars of Wisdom* are those in which Lawrence describes his experiences as a largely self-taught demolitions expert, casually dealing with guncotton and detonators, and using his own rule of thumb to determine how much explosive he needed to use to destroy a train or demolish a bridge. Typically, Lawrence presents these scenes as comedy, and notes that the bigger the bang, the more the Arabs were impressed. This was no doubt true, but he risked death time after time as rails, rocks, and pieces of locomotives rained down around him.

Lawrence's travels around Syria from 1911 to 1914 and his friendship with some of the Kurdish leaders in 1912 gave him a far better picture of the secret Arab societies and of the unrest boiling under the surface of Turkish rule than he is usually given credit for having. Although skeptics about Lawrence have since questioned his claim that he "dipped deep into" the councils of the Armenian and Kurdish secret societies, there is proof of this: on the way back to England for a brief holiday in December 1912, he stopped to give a detailed report of what he knew to the American vice and deputy consul-general in Beirut, F. Willoughby Smith, who encapsulated it in a long memorandum to the consul. Lawrence brought to Smith's attention the fact that the Turks had poisoned one of the principal Kurdish leaders, and that he had been shown a secret hoard of "eight to ten thousand" rifles and large stocks of ammunition in a crusader castle. The report is detailed, demonstrates that Lawrence had gained the full confidence of the Kurdish leaders, and goes on to mention that young Kurds who were conscripted to serve in the Turkish army were under orders to desert as soon as they had been issued a rifle—an interesting way of turning the Turks' conscription to the benefit of their enemies! Smith gives Lawrence and Woolley full credit, which seems to confirm that Lawrence was already dabbling in Middle Eastern politics, not as a British spy (if he had been a spy, he would hardly have passed what he knew on to the *American* vice-consul), but as an unusually adventurous supporter of the Arab cause. That Lawrence's judgment about such matters was very sound for an archaeological assistant is borne out, for example, by his frequent mention of the fears of the Armenian community and the Armenians' attempts to arm themselves. (Those fears were certainly proved well founded when the Turks set out to subject the entire Armenian population to genocide in 1915.)

Lawrence had a way of getting involved in matters far beyond the ordinary demands of field archaeology, like smuggling rifles into the British consulate. Echoes of Lawrence's adventures are strewn throughout his letters—it is possible, for example, that he and Dahoum were thrown into a Turkish prison as deserters from the Turkish army (Lawrence must have been in Arab clothes at the time), and were badly beaten there. Lawrence's contacts with the Kurdish revolutionaries (and to a lesser extent, the Armenians) seem to have been more in the nature of a high-spirited adventure than of serious intelligence work, but had the full approval of Woolley, who realized that in the event of an uprising in the area around Carchemish the two Englishmen would be at the mercy of the Kurds. Good relations with the Kurdish leaders were therefore a necessary precaution; Woolley even went so far as to arrange for the settlement of a three-generation blood feud between two of the most important Kurdish sheikhs—"Buswari and his great enemy Shalim Bey"—in the expedition house, with himself as the impartial referee, passing out chocolates to the party of "9 great Kurds."

Visitors to the excavation site were startled to see that the watchman was a villainous-looking, heavily armed Kurdish brigand, whom Lawrence had chosen because his reputation alone would keep away other marauding Kurds in the event of an uprising. Any doubts about what such an uprising might entail had been erased when Lawrence visited the nearby towns of Nizib and Biridjik, in Arab clothing. He found the body of an Armenian Christian doctor still lying in the street in Nizib, two days after the doctor had been shot by Kurdish militants; and he described the Kurdish hill villagers as "running around with guns and looking for another Christian to kill." Clearly, Lawrence's habit of wearing an Arab robe and a headdress was already more than a casual affectation; in certain circumstances it was a means of survival, long before Feisal asked him to put such clothing on in 1916.

Lawrence's short return home took place in part because there was a gentlemanly dispute simmering between Hogarth at the Ashmolean in Oxford and Kenyon of the British Museum in London over which institution should get first choice of the antiquities Lawrence was buying or (more rarely) unearthing in Carchemish; in part because funding for further digging was again in doubt; and in part because Lawrence's speculations regarding a Kurdish uprising had the no doubt unintended effect of raising, in the minds of Hogarth and Kenyon, questions about his and Woolley's safety. Certainly the Ottoman Empire seemed to be falling to pieces as the Balkan wars exposed all its weaknesses. Before his departure for home, Lawrence commented on the total unreliability of the postal system, the wolves attacking herds by night in close proximity to the dig, the erratic and brutal attempts to enforce military conscription, and the fact that steamships were no longer reliably entering Turkish ports. Lawrence had hoped to bring Dahoum, Sheikh Hamoudi, and perhaps Fareedeh el Akle (his Arab teacher at Jebail) home with him, but the uncertainty about whether to continue the dig had left him short of funds.

As usual, Hogarth performed the required miracle, smoothed over the difficulties with the British Museum, and found funding to resume the dig at Carchemish. Lawrence returned in the third week of January—after a pause of a few days in Egypt, where he made an amicable visit to Petrie's new site (and "was lucky enough not to find Mrs. Petrie there," as he ungraciously remarked). In Cairo he visited the famous museum and found a Hittite cup mislabeled as Persian. He made a huge fuss, demanding that a correction be made, and when the keys to the case could not be found, insisted on having it opened by the museum carpenter with a "hammer & screwdriver," showing once again how quickly he could take on the identity (and attitude) of a pukka sahib toward the "natives" when it suited him to. To be sure, he did not like Egyptians, but still, there is a certain mismatch between Lawrence in this mood and Lawrence as the champion of Arab freedom. His increasing admiration for the Arabs did not, for instance, make him more tolerant of Negroes, Indians, or Levantine Jews.

He wrote home in February from Aleppo, where the Armenians, in no doubt about what was coming, were "arming frantically" and where there were "snow-drifts, & ice & hail & sleet & rain." He managed to reach Beirut, but the railway north was blocked by snow in the mountains, and Lawrence was unable to get on a steamer from Beirut to Alexandretta in time to ensure the shipment of the many cases of antiquities piled up there for the Ashmolean and the British Museum. He drew on his friendship with the British consul, who arranged with the Royal Navy to have Lawrence, accompanied by Dahoum, taken to Alexandretta by a British cruiser, HMS *Duke of Edinburgh*—this kind of amazing good fortune seemed to happen only to Lawrence. On board the cruiser Dahoum was popular with the officers—he seems to have had considerable personal charm. In Alexandretta, another British cruiser took on board all the packing cases— the number of British warships and naval personnel with time on their hands off the Turkish coast is explained by the prevailing fear that the Turkish government might at any moment permit or encourage a massacre of foreign residents (including British subjects), to draw attention away from its defeats in the Balkans. In this matter, as in the buying of antiquities, Lawrence seems to have acted with a certain swagger.

While he was in England, he had ordered a canoe (from Salter Brothers, the famous boatbuilders in Oxford) and had it sent out to Beirut. In it, he hoped to explore the farther reaches of the Euphrates River during the spring—this is another example of Lawrence's lordly way when it came to those things that really interested him, and also of his determination to make his time at Carchemish, which would now stretch out for at least another year, as pleasant as possible. Carchemish, despite the occasional brawls and confrontations with the authorities, was "a place where one eats lotos* nearly every day." There, Lawrence, in the company of his friend Dahoum, could arrange his life as he pleased, without any interference, provided that he carried out the basic duties of his profession to the satisfaction of Hogarth, whose approval was unfailing.

By the middle of March, despite cold weather and storms, Lawrence already had his canoe in the river, was teaching Dahoum to paddle it, and was luxuriating in the number of objects he and Woolley were at last beginning to produce in quantity. The list is endless: Hittite bronze work and carved slabs of basalt, Phoenician glazed pottery, Roman glass. In addition, the excavation was at last beginning to uncover greater portions of the Hittite city itself. Lawrence and Woolley worked without friction, and to any reader of Lawrence's letters, it seems at least possible that Lawrence might easily have settled down into the role of an archaeologist and adventurer in the Middle East, if it had not been for World War I. On the other hand, it is hardly possible not to read into his letters a foreboding that some kind of breakup or collapse was impending— that he was enjoying his "lotos-eating" days in the knowledge they would soon be ended. Perhaps for that reason, his interest in crusader castles and in writing a great book about the major cities of the Middle East had apparently gone the way of the thesis on medieval pottery. One senses that he already knew none of these things was going to happen. Certainly the Ottoman Empire in 1913 was, of all the uneasy places in the world, the one in which fearsome threats, anger, and hatred between the subject races of the empire and their masters, and a terrifying mixture of cynicism, corruption, and brutality at the top, seemed most likely to produce a conflagration. Turkey was balanced at the edge of an abyss, having lost all its possessions in North Africa and Europe; its

* A pleasing, narcotic fruit on which the *Lotophagi*, referred to in the *Odyssey*, Book IX, fed. It produced apathy, and, in the case of Odysseus's shipmates, "as each tasted of this honey-sweet plant, the wish to bring news or return home grew faint in him." (*The Odyssey of Homer*, trans. T. E. Shaw [Lawrence of Arabia] [New York: Oxford University Press, 1932], 122.)

rulers were determined to hold out for the highest price in the event of war between the great powers rather than risk neutrality and being left out of the spoils of victory, and they were always acutely aware that the majority of Turkey's population consisted of subject races—Arabs, Armenians, Kurds, Jews, Christians—who had in common nothing except a desire to get rid of the Turks as overlords and masters. Lawrence, who understood the situation better than most, can hardly be blamed for enjoying himself in his own way for as long as possible.

As the fame of Carchemish increased, so did the number of visitors, some of them American, whom Lawrence much preferred to Germans. At the end of April, having been told by the local boatmen that with the Euphrates in full flood he "couldn't shoot the railway bridge" in his canoe "without upsetting," he naturally took "a Miss Campbell, staying with us," down the racing river, and back up again, drawing a rare note of concern from his father, the expert yachtsman. Lawrence had apparently fitted "a square-rigged sail" to the canoe, and he pointed out in his own defense that even if it did upset, all he had to do was swim back to shore towing it—though he did not say whether Miss Campbell, in the long skirt of the day, would have enjoyed the experience.

In the same letter, Lawrence rather vaguely sketches out his future plans—he hopes to go to "Asia Minor" in July and August, to pay a two-week visit to England in early September, and to return to Carchemish with his brother Will. He reports that he has been asked by the Turks to dig for "Arab glazed ware" in Mesopotamia, a signal honor, given their distrust of foreigners, and a sign that Lawrence's reputation as a specialist in pottery was growing in the scientific community—indeed, in mid-June he mentions that he is sending 11,000 pottery fragments back to Leeds at the Ashmolean, to be sorted and reassembled. He also boasts that it is already 109 degrees indoors in a darkened room, although the floor has been sprinkled with water—"a pleasant, healthy warmth," as he puts it. But then Lawrence's notion of comfortable warmth was very different from that of most Europeans: he relished heat, the hotter the better, and the only sensual indulgence he permitted himself throughout his life was frequent very hot baths, which he also recommended to his family as a precaution against influenza.

His interest in shooting remained strong—sensibly, perhaps, in view of the seething among the local Kurds—and he reported back to his brother Frank, also an excellent shot, that in a contest with a visiting British diplomat he had put five shots out of seven into a *medjidie* (a Turkish coin about the size of a fifty-cent piece) "at 25 yards with an automatic colt" (presumably the nickel-plated .32 Colt Dahoum is holding in the photograph Lawrence took of him). This is remarkably good, considering that Lawrence was "fast shooting without dropping the hand," that is, emptying the magazine rapidly rather than carefully target-shooting, and putting three shots out of ten into an orange box at 1,200 yards with his Mannlicher carbine. Not many people could hit *anything* at a range of 1,200 yards with a carbine, and this certainly represents a standard of marksmanship not usually found among Oxford scholars— as well as a sign that Lawrence's growing skill and interest in archaeology were unlikely to land him behind a desk at the Ashmolean Museum.

He adds, at the end of this letter, "Hope to bring 2 Arabs with me this summer," and he did so, both as a reward to Sheikh Hamoudi and Dahoum for saving his life when he was suffering from dysentery, and perhaps also because of the fuss and interest he knew they would cause in Oxford, where they lodged in the garden cottage at 2 Polstead Road. Already there had been protests from both his parents about his casual mention that at Carchemish Friday was his Sunday—that is, Lawrence had adopted the Muslim and Jewish holy day of the week, rather than trying to impose the Christian day on his workforce or simply taking Sunday off to observe it by himself. His parents surely took this as a sign of religious backsliding. The shortness of his visit home—he was there only ten days—and the proximity of Hamoudi and Dahoum, neither of whom spoke a word of English, were perfectly calculated, as his mother must have guessed, to prevent any serious questions from her about his life-style, his future intentions, or his current religious belief.

What the two Arabs thought of Oxford is hard to know, but Oxford was fascinated by them. They learned to ride a bicycle, and caused a stir by cycling through the Oxford streets in their eastern robes. Dahoum had his portrait drawn by Francis Dodd, a friend of Bell's; the process sparked in Lawrence a lifelong passion for sitting for portraits, far more than it did Dahoum, who shows his usual self-possession in the finished drawing. They met Janet Laurie, but were not impressed by her slim figure, the Arab taste being for plumpness in women.

No doubt one reason for bringing Dahoum and Sheikh Hamoudi home with him was that Lawrence wanted to make it clear to his mother and father that his future lay in Syria, not in England. The two men not only were his friends, but deeply respected Lawrence. More than that, he had assumed at Carchemish the role of a hakim, a man of wisdom—different from a sheikh, who is the practical day-to-day leader of a tribe or clan; or a mullah, who is a religious leader and Muslim clergyman. Hakim is one of the ninety-nine names of Allah in the Koran; and a hakim is one who settles disputes and the finer points of law and custom, and whose objective judgment can be relied on by all around him. In short, in the area around Jerablus Lawrence had become famous and admired, despite the fact that he was a foreigner and a Christian. He had all the attributes of a desert hero: he was immensely strong, despite his small size—he described himself as "a pocket Hercules"—an outstanding shot, physically tireless, generous, absolutely fearless, and yet gentle in manner. His self-imposed Spartan regimen gave him yet another bond with the Arabs, who made do with a little flour and a few dates out of necessity. Unlike most Englishmen, Lawrence could survive on their meager diet and walk barefoot where they did. And he could get them to work together without threats or the use of force, in contrast to the German officials, who, to Lawrence's rage, made full use of the whip, indeed considered it indispensable.

For the same reason that he brought his two friends home to Oxford—he would have added Miss Holmes, from the American mission, whose presence would have been reassuring to Sarah, had he been able to—he urged one of his brothers to come out and visit him; he suggested it in turn to Will, Frank, and Arnold. He was proud of the position he had achieved among people so very different from himself, and wanted his family to see it. His mother suspected that he had lost his religious faith, and this was true. Lawrence, once he left the family home and the daily Bible readings, never showed any further sign of interest in Christianity, or any other religion; it was a struggle his mother had lost by default, but being who she was she would never give up on saving her second son's soul as long as he lived. Her eldest son, Bob, would eventually become her partner in faith, a missionary doctor; her younger sons would at least pay lip service to their mother's intense Christianity for as long she lived; but her beloved Ned had managed to slip from her grasp in the one area that most concerned her. He had also succeeded in that most difficult of tasks for every young person—making a contented life for himself on his own terms, not those of his parents.

By the end of August, Lawrence and his two friends were back at Carchemish. Dahoum and Sheikh Hamoudi were transformed overnight into celebrities by their voyage to England, but Lawrence was disappointed to find that in his absence the local villagers had been digging up fourteenth-century Arab graves in search of gold, and carelessly destroying much valuable glassware and pottery.

In September, Lawrence's brother Will arrived, on his way to India, where he was taking up a teaching post, and Lawrence had, at last, an opportunity of showing a member of his family the immense scale of the work he was doing, and his position as a local celebrity. Fortunately, Will's letters are as long and as full of detail as Lawrence's—all five of the Lawrence brothers were prodigious letter writers. Will was enchanted by Beirut and, like most visitors, thought Damascus "the most beautiful town" he'd ever seen. Also like most European visitors, he was overwhelmed by the abundance of fruit and flowers—"peaches and nectarines and apples and grapes . . . sunflowers and roses"—and the friendliness of the people. On September 16 he reached Aleppo, where Lawrence and Dahoum met him. "Ned is known by everyone," Will noted, "and their enthusiasm over him is quite amusing." Lawrence took the opportunity of introducing his brother to "Buswari of the Milli Kurds, here, a marvel-ously-dressed and dignified person who's invited me to go over to his tribe and see some horse-racing and dancing." By September 17 Will was at Carchemish, overwhelmed by the number of Lawrence's friends—Armenian, Christian, and Kurd—and by the ubiquity of his fame. Bus-wari, of course, was one of the two Kurdish leaders who had settled their blood feud in the expedition house, and one of the grandest and most important figures in the area around Aleppo.

Will's stay at Carchemish was slightly blighted by the fact that Law-rence was down with a fever—presumably a recurrence of malaria—but he described the mound and the expedition house in tones of awe, and was amazed by the number of people who came to visit Lawrence: "a lieutenant Young, making his way out to India via Baghdad, an American missionary Dr. Usher, going back to Lake Van, and the people from Aleppo the Altounyans." The Altounyans were an enormously wealthy Armenian family: the father a doctor with his own hospital (staffed by English nurses) in Aleppo; the son a graduate of Rugby School and Cam-bridge; and the daughter, Norah, "very English." Young was, among other things, a crack shot, and spoke fluent Arabic and Farsi. Lawrence's abode near the site of the ancient Hittite city was more like a court than a schol-ar's residence—people called on him constantly, and indeed it had become necessary to expand the expedition house to twenty-two rooms. Although Lawrence continued his deliberately meager diet, guests were served omelets for breakfast, and lunches and dinners with many courses.

Since Lawrence wasn't up to a visit to Buswari Agha's tented encamp-ment, Young and Will went off together—Buswari had sent his son with splendid horses and an escort of armed retainers for the six-hour ride. They were treated to a lavish dinner of highly spiced minces (which gave Will stomach troubles that plagued him all the way to India) in a carpeted tent so big that half of it could hold more than 100 men for dinner (the other half was curtained off as the harem). They were entertained by music and men dancing, and slept in the position of honor, next to the harem curtain. The next day they watched a colorful and savage version of polo, which sounds very much like *buzkashi* in Afghanistan and is played with a slaughtered sheep's carcass instead of a ball. This was followed by another highly spiced feast. Will was able to report to his parents: "You must not think of Ned as leading an uncivilized existence. When I saw him last as the train left the station he was wearing white flannels, socks and red slippers, with a white Magdalen blazer, and was talking to the governor of Biridjik in a lordly fashion."

"A lordly fashion." This is an interesting choice of words on Will's part, for it is exactly the life that Lawrence reproached his father for having abandoned. He lived in Carchemish as he imagined his father must have lived in Ireland—as a grand squire, an important person in the county, a gentleman. At the time Will was in Carchemish, their father was, by coincidence, on one of his secretive trips to Ireland, where he had, though Will did not of course know it, a wife and four daughters. From time to time, the subject of Thomas Lawrence's trips to Ireland comes up in Lawrence's letters home, as when he reacts to a remark in a letter from Will that their father "was still in Ireland," to which Lawrence comments, "Why go to such a place?" If we are to believe Lawrence, he had already learned at the age of nine or ten why his father was obliged to visit Ireland from time to time, and if so this seemingly innocent question may be a way of annoying his mother from a distance.

Unknowingly, Will had stumbled on the exact point that kept Lawrence in Carchemish, that put him at odds with his parents, and that separated him from his brothers. It is a pity Lawrence never knew that Will had described his way of life as "lordly," since this would no doubt have given him a certain sardonic pleasure, but they would never see each other again.

Throughout the autumn the dig at Carchemish proceeded at a rapid pace; more and more decorated wall slabs, monuments, basalt doorways, and sculptures were being unearthed, enough to make it clear that Lawrence and Woolley were uncovering one of the most important archaeological sites in the Middle East. As winter comes, Lawrence reports that they have purchased five tons of firewood ("olive tree boles . . . which burn most gloriously"), and that he has been presented with a young leopard, which serves in the role of watchdog. The expedition house had been enlarged, and it is pleasant to imagine how luxurious it must have seemed, with the olive wood blazing in the burnished copper fireplace, the Roman mosaic on the floor, the innumerable precious rugs (Lawrence's Armenian friend from Aleppo, Dr. Altounyan, was a renowned collector and connoisseur of Oriental rugs), and the leopard stretched out in front of the fire as the two Englishmen ate their dinner, or sat in their easy chairs and read. Lawrence had busied himself, with the help of the multitalented and ubiquitous Lieutenant Young, in carving gargoyles out of soft sandstone to decorate the building. One of these, modeled after Dahoum, had caused considerable fuss among the Arabs,* since, like Orthodox Jews, they were forbidden to make or keep "graven images," let alone sit for any. In fact the drawing that Dodd had made of Dahoum in Oxford, which was hung in the house, caused trouble enough among Muslims who saw it, though one visitor to the house expressed unusual tolerance by remarking, "God is merciful, and will forgive the maker of it."

It was an idyllic life—when he was not piecing together stone fragments, or collecting rugs to decorate the house or send home, Lawrence went hawking with the magnificent Buswari Agha at his desert camp, and astonished the Kurds by shattering four glass bottles with four shots at sixty yards. Unsurprisingly, the leopard was proving to be more of a nuisance than Lawrence had anticipated, and the piecing together of Hittite statuary from hundreds of fragments, ranging from several tons to pieces the size of a penny, was exhausting and time-consuming. That Lawrence intended to stay at Carchemish for as long as was necessary is

---

* Woolley, who subsequently became critical of Lawrence, claimed that the villagers were scandalized because Dahoum had posed naked for Lawrence; but there is no proof of this, and since Young was present at the time, as well as any number of visitors, Arab and European, it seems unlikely. The carving of gargoyles, naked or not, would have been enough to scandalize the villagers, and would still do so in many parts of the Middle East, including Saudi Arabia.

indicated by the fact that he at last took the step of writing to tell his friend Vyvyan Richards that he could not join the printing enterprise. "I cannot print with you when you want me," he wrote. "I have felt it coming for a long time, and I funked it."

By mid-December, however, a new and more exciting job had turned up—one that Lawrence, with his thirst for adventure, could hardly resist. The project had powerful sponsors, including Field Marshal the Earl of Kitchener himself, and was one for which Lawrence was unusually well suited. Throughout the 1870s and early 1880s, the British Palestine Exploration Fund had carried out a meticulous, one-inch-to-the-mile map survey of western Palestine, which ended on a line drawn "from west to east, through Gaza and Beersheba, to Masada on the Western Shore of the Dead Sea." Kitchener himself had at one point led this survey, drawing up the first modern map of the Holy Land and even establishing the borders of future states such as Lebanon and Syria. The work, which was ultimately published in eight volumes, had intense military as well as biblical importance. In 1913, as the Germans intensified their diplomatic effort to bind Turkey to what would soon become known as the Central Powers (i.e., Germany and Austro-Hungary) in the event of war; and as the Turkish leaders hemmed and hawed and upped their price, attempting to negotiate simultaneously with both sides, Kitchener, now the British agent and consul general (the equivalent of a viceroy) in Egypt, felt an urgent concern to have the survey completed, especially in the Sinai peninsula, from Beersheba to Aqaba, since in the event of war with the Ottoman Empire the Turkish army would certainly attempt to cross this area and seize or block the Suez Canal.

In order to secure the permission of the Turks for the British to carry out this ambitious survey on their soil, it was thought advisable to stress its biblical significance; thus the work would be done under the auspices of the Palestine Exploration Fund, and so far as possible the presence of serving British officers of the Royal Engineers would be balanced out by the presence of scholarly archaeologists. Mapping the Sinai, for example, might be accomplished on the pretense that the archaeologists were seeking to find the exact path that Moses and the Jews took on their forty-year journey from Egypt to Canaan.

All attempts to map uncharted areas of the world have multiple purposes. The Palestine Exploration Fund was not in any way a mere fig leaf for the British army or the government of Egypt. There was genuine scholarly interest in extending the survey of the Holy Land beyond the Gaza-Beersheba line to the south and east; and had a Sinai expedition in fact turned up archaeological finds indicating the presence and the exact route of the Jews, it would have been a historical and religious discovery of major importance, not just to Christians, but to Jews and Muslims as well. The Turkish government was neither naive nor entirely convinced by all this biblical packaging; but then again, not all the members of the Turkish government were eager to conclude an alliance with Germany, and even those who were so inclined felt a need to keep the goodwill of the British government for as long as possible—certainly for long enough to attempt to extract the best terms from one side or another in the event of war. Under the circumstances, permission to map the Sinai seemed like a small but friendly concession to a major power, and Turkish permission was forthcoming.*

At home, the War Office, the Foreign Office, and the Palestine Exploration Fund moved with astonishing speed, ignoring regular channels and using instead the "old boy" network, always the most efficient way of getting anything done in Britain. Colonel Hedley, the head of the Geographical Section of the War Office (in charge of all mapmaking for the army), had, by one of those convenient coincidences, just been elected to the Executive Committee of the Palestine Exploration Fund; he was therefore able to explain the objective of the expedition to the other members within five days of the Turks' communicating their agreement to it to the British ambassador in Constantinople. It almost goes without

---

*In fact, given the use that was made during Allenby's advance on Gaza, Jerusalem, and Damascus of the very accurate maps for which Lawrence was in large part responsible, the Turks might have been better off turning down the Palestine Exploration Fund's proposal, rather than merely trying to obstruct it.

saying that Hogarth was also a member of the Palestine Exploration Fund committee and recommended that one of them "approach Kenyon" of the British Museum. Kenyon replied almost immediately: "Hogarth concurs in the idea of lending our men from Jerablus to the P. E. F. [Palestine Exploration Fund] survey . . . and suggests that, as time is short, *both* should go. Their names are C. L. Woolley and T. E. Lawrence. The former is the senior man, with rather wider experience; the latter is better at colloquial Arabic, and gets on very well with natives. He has, I think, more of the instincts of an explorer, but is very shy. . . . Hogarth can tell you more about them, if you wish." Once again, Hogarth, who seems always to have been in the right place at the right time, had pushed forward the name of his protégé, and moved Lawrence from the land of lotos eating into that of exploration and high strategy.

From 1875, when Disraeli, with the help of the Rothschilds, purchased Khedive Ismail Pasha's shares in the Suez Canal Corporation for £4 million, to 1956, when Britain and France went to war with Egypt over Nasser's nationalization of the canal, the protection of the canal had always been regarded as one of the most vital of British interests. The canal was the priceless link between Britain and its vast colonial possessions and dominions in the East. The fear that in the event of war the Turks might attack the canal as a surrogate for the Germans was one of the main reasons for British control of Egypt and the Sudan. Mention of *any* threat to the canal or any improvement to its defenses therefore invariably produced an instant response, so it is hardly surprising that despite the relatively slow communications of the period, the holiday season, and the normal languor of government and private committees, Woolley and Lawrence (accompanied by Dahoum) arrived in Beersheba on January 9, 1914, after having spent Christmas in Carchemish, and got to work immediately.

From Beersheba south and east there were no roads or railway. Quite apart from the difficulties of the terrain, which were considerable, the Turks wanted nothing that might encourage the British to advance north from Egypt in the event of war, and the British would have regarded any attempt to build roads or a railway as a threat to the canal. "The place is an absolute wilderness," Lawrence wrote home about the Sinai. "Not even any Arab tribes there: empty, they say." Gaza was, in those days, "a picturesque little crusading town of about 20,000 people: a fine xiith Cent. Church." Nothing appeared to have been prepared for them, although a telegram informed them that Captain (later Colonel) S. F. Newcombe of the Royal Engineers was on his way with a caravan of camels. Woolley and Lawrence bought themselves tents, "camp outfit, hired servants, etc. (all on credit, since the P.E.F. had sent our money to Jerusalem)," and made their way to Beersheba with their gear on a donkey, to wait for Newcombe. Lawrence noted that already, "the Turkish Gov. is exceedingly shy of us, and is doing its best to throw all possible difficulties in our way"; this problem would grow worse throughout the expedition. Whatever had been decided about the map survey in Constantinople, here, only a few miles from the Egyptian border, the police recognized a foreign, Christian intrusion when they saw one, and acted accordingly.

Fortunately, Lawrence and Newcombe liked each other at once, and their friendship would last throughout the war years and beyond. Lawrence's attitude toward professional soldiers was, and would remain, ambivalent. From an early age he felt he had mastered the art of war— very few professional soldiers had anything like his broad knowledge of military history and literature, his ability to inspire others, his endurance, or his sense of terrain and topography. Whatever Lawrence's preference for the methods of Marshal de Saxe over those of Napoleon, he would not have disagreed with the latter's comment, "In war, as in prostitution, the amateur is often better than the professional." As time would show, Lawrence was something of a self-taught genius in tactics and strategy, and he already knew it; this knowledge must have made it all the more difficult for him to accept that he could never have been a regular officer in the post-Edwardian British army. Oxford might be willing to blur or ignore the family background of its scholars, but at Sandhurst, the social conventions were more rigorously enforced, and by people who could read *Debrett's Peerage and Baronetage*. Illegitimacy was not necessarily a bar to a commission in the British regular army—the future General Sir Adrian Carton de Wiart, VC, KBE, CB, CMG, DSO, brilliantly caricatured by Evelyn Waugh as Brigadier Ritchie-Hook in *Officers and Gentlemen*, was widely believed to be illegitimate, though on the other hand it was also rumored that his father was the king of the Belgians, so Carton de Wiart was a very different proposition from one of the five illegitimate sons of an Anglo-Irish landowner. Even leaving to one side Lawrence's height, as somebody who was born out of wedlock to a servant he would very likely not have been accepted into Sandhurst as a cadet, or into most of the regiments of the British army as an officer. It never ceased to gall him that men with nothing like his talent or knowledge became regular officers and rose to high rank. This is not to say that Lawrence had ever wanted to go to Sandhurst; he simply did not want to be patronized by those who had gone there. With regulars whom he didn't like, or whose hostility he rightly or wrongly suspected, no matter how high their rank, he often adopted an attitude of know-it-all superiority and impertinence bordering on insubordination. On the other hand, with those who knew their business and recognized that he knew his, he often formed close and long-lasting friendships, despite great differences of rank. These men included such very dissimilar military figures as Young, Newcombe, Wingate, Lieutenant-Colonel Alan Dawnay, the future Field Marshal Lord Wavell, Allenby, and of course Marshal of the Royal Air Force Lord Trenchard.* Throughout most of his life, Lawrence remained a military man manqué—the runaway boy soldier would become a decorated lieutenant colonel, and in the end, an aircraftman first class (the equivalent of a private), sitting on his bunk in a barracks, writing ambitious (and sensible) schemes for the improvement of the Royal Air Force to his old friend, the chief of the Air Staff.

Newcombe turned up in Beersheba to greet Woolley and Lawrence with a caravan of a dozen camels. He had supposed that Woolley and

---

*Young, Newcombe, Wingate, and Allenby the reader has already encountered. Dawnay was a tall, lean, perfectly dressed Guards officer, who would become one of Lawrence's devoted admirers in 1918 (photographed together they looked like Mutt and Jeff), as did A. P. Wavell, and Trenchard later on.

Lawrence would have a heavy load of equipment, and was surprised to find that they could carry everything they needed on a donkey. He seems to have been expecting a pair of scientific graybeards from the British Museum, and so may have been equally surprised to meet two healthy young men, fit and armed. Newcombe had five surveying teams at work, and collated their findings himself every night. Lawrence, who already supposed himself to be an expert on the subject, would learn a lot about practical mapmaking from Newcombe in the six weeks of the expedition. From the very beginning the archaeological results were disappointing. However long the Jews had wandered in the Sinai, they had been a nomad people, and left no more trace of themselves behind than the modern Bedouin did. Even places that were mentioned as important in Exodus proved to have no ruins older than the Byzantine or Roman period. When they got to Kadesh (from which Moses had sent envoys to the king of Edom asking for passage for his people, and where Miriam is buried), Lawrence wrote, typically, "[It] is a filthy dirty little water hole, and we more than sympathize with the disgust of the Children of Israel when they got here." Isaac's well at Rehoboth, although nearly 300 feet deep, showed no signs of ancient origin; and Zephath, one of the cities of the Canaanites attacked by Joshua, was unfindable. Everywhere Lawrence looked, the land was wasted and abandoned, although he believed, correctly, that if some of it was plowed and irrigated it could be rendered as fruitful as it had been in Roman times. Even the normally ebullient Woolley was pessimistic about finding any trace of biblical cities, let alone of Moses's route from Egypt. The complete absence of any local food crops made them dependent on what little they carried with them, plus an occasional pigeon that they managed to shoot. At one point they failed to make contact with their baggage caravan and wandered through the desert in search of their tent camp, while the Turkish police, alerted to their disappearance, searched ineffectually for them. Eventually, Woolley and Lawrence split up, Lawrence and Dahoum accompanying Newcombe to the southeast across the Sinai toward Aqaba, over what even Lawrence describes as very "rugged" country.

At Aqaba, the Turks lost patience with what had been described to them as a biblical expedition; or perhaps it simply became clear to the men on the spot that Lawrence and Woolley were merely the window dressing for a team of British military topographers. Newcombe was not dismayed—Aqaba had already been surveyed—but Lawrence was annoyed, and decided to tweak the noses of the *kaimakam* and his policemen. For his own amusement he had wanted to visit the ruins of a crusader fort on the island of Geziret Faraun, a few hundred yards from the shore at Aqaba. When the *kaimakam* refused to allow this, Lawrence constructed a crude raft out of old gasoline cans, and he and Dahoum paddled it out to the island, despite the presence of large sharks, for which the Red Sea is well known. As a result, he and Dahoum were marched out of town under escort. They eventually managed to shake off the escort in the steep, rocky defiles that rose behind Aqaba—very close to the route down which Lawrence would lead the Howeitat in 1917. Skeptics who attribute the capture of Aqaba to the plans or local knowledge of Auda Abu Tayi or Sharif Nasir almost always overlook the fact that the countryside around Aqaba and the approaches to it from inland were familiar to Lawrence because he had been there only three years before, and on foot, and had later mapped it from an aerial survey. Aqaba's defenses and its weaknesses were well known to him and, with his almost photographic memory for topography, familiar. It was, as he described it, "a country of awful crags and valleys, impassible for camels, and very difficult on foot," and the Turkish policemen assigned to escort him were still wandering back into Aqaba exhausted days after Lawrence and Dahoum had left them behind.

The two made their way from Aqaba to the Hejaz railway, then "back to Mount Hor," where Lawrence visited Aaron's grave. From there they went to Petra, which impressed him as much as it still impresses the modern tourist, and where he found, encamped in the desert, two well-dressed "English ladies" typical of the intrepid British tourists of the period, who never hesitated to plunge off the beaten track. One of them was Lady Legge, and the other Lady Evelyn Cobbold—a forceful former

Mayfair beauty who was a daughter of the earl of Leicester, and an accomplished gardener, fisherwoman, and deerstalker, and who, after converting to Islam, would become the first Englishwoman to enter Mecca. Lawrence was able to borrow money from Lady Evelyn Cobbold to continue his journey. More important, on the way out of Aqaba Lawrence located the crossroads where lay the two great paths through the desert that had served the Jews in their flight from Egypt; these paths were still in use by Bedouin raiding parties. This knowledge would be of enormous value to him in 1917, as he and Auda Abu Tayi approached Aqaba across the desert.

Thanks to Lady Evelyn Cobbold, Lawrence made his way from Petra to Maan, waiting there for the train to arrive from Medina; and from there to Damascus, and back to Carchemish via Aleppo. At Maan, the Turks had threatened to arrest him, but he managed to disarm the police patrol and march them off, with their rifles under his arm, to their headquarters, where he staged a scene worthy of Woolley, extracting an apology from the chief of police. "A huge jest," he called it, but then Lawrence's sense of humor was different from that of most people. Even when he was *on* "the beaten track," as opposed to the desert, each of his journeys was an adventure; and not surprisingly, the Turkish authorities seldom knew how to deal with a determined, well-armed, indignant Englishman, dressed in Arab clothing, speaking Arabic, and apparently enjoying the official protection of both the British government and the Palestine Exploration Fund.

By the beginning of March Lawrence was back in Carchemish, much pleased to hear that Hogarth had raised enough money for a new season of digging—in fact, he had secured enough money from a donor to cover five more years—but irritated that permission had not yet been obtained from the Turkish government to renew the work. In the meantime, Lawrence continued to send home what seems, from reading his letters, a never-ending shipment of carpets. Possibly influenced by his Armenian friends the Altounyans, Lawrence had become something of a connoisseur of Oriental carpets, and bought them everywhere he went—by this time, 2 Polstead Road can hardly have had a single room without one or more carpets shipped home by Lawrence.

On March 21, Woolley and Lawrence resumed the dig at last—they had been busy brokering a peace between the German railway engineers and Buswari Agha, after their Kurdish workers went out on strike. As usual, the dispute had turned violent, and it even reached the pages of the *London Times,* under the headline "Riot on the Bagdad Railway," not unnaturally alarming Lawrence's family. A Circassian working for the Germans had shot a Kurd during the protest over wages; this led to a shoot-out between the German railway engineers and the Kurds, in which eight men were wounded, including a British subject and an Australian. Woolley and Lawrence intervened, negotiated a settlement (or "blood payment") of £70 for the family of the dead Kurd, and received the thanks of the Turkish government. (The British consul in Aleppo suggested that Woolley and Lawrence should receive decorations for their courage, and these were apparently offered but refused.) Lawrence dismissed the whole affair as "a mere trifle," which was no doubt what he wanted his mother to believe.

Hogarth, who arrived shortly after the shoot-out, praised Lawrence for his behavior "at much risk," and promised to reassure Sarah when he got home. He stayed three weeks, and was much impressed by the progress that was being made at Carchemish, in part due to Lawrence's vigorous dynamiting. In May, Stewart Newcombe arrived—Woolley had suggested to him that he should take an interest in archaeology, and that a trip to Carchemish to look at the railway line the Germans were building might be worthwhile. Newcombe had mentioned this suggestion to Lord Kitchener, who was all in favor of it. Newcombe and another British officer took a somewhat perfunctory look at the Hittite artifacts, then set off to the west to follow the railway route to the difficult country in the Taurus Mountains. They were unable to obtain much information, however, perhaps because they were only too clearly British officers, so Newcombe asked Woolley and Lawrence, who were planning to go home in June, to follow the same route on their way back to England. Lawrence planned to return to Carchemish in August 1914, but he was happy to spend a couple of weeks sightseeing in Anatolia with Woolley. They managed to get farther into the Taurus Mountains than Newcombe, perhaps because they were only too clearly a pair of archaeologists. They were certainly able to confirm that the railway tunneling in the mountainous areas was considerably behind schedule and that goods and passengers bound from Haidar Pasha, opposite Constantinople, to Baghdad would have to get off at Muslimie Junction, just north of Aleppo, and at Bozanti Khan, northwest of Adana, since the tunnels in both places were incomplete; thus there would be additional days of travel time and endless difficulties for troops, guns, and supplies being shipped to Iraq. Lawrence explained the two-week delay in his arrival home by telling his family that he was going down the Euphrates River with an army friend to see Baghdad, though in fact he would be traveling in the opposite direction overland with Woolley. No doubt it would have been difficult to explain why he was going on a long tour of the Taurus Mountains on the way home to England rather than simply taking the train to Beirut. Woolley would later explain, with what sounds like a certain degree of indignation, that it was "the only piece of spying that I ever did before the war," but it is difficult to see the survey of the Sinai as anything but a milder form of espionage.

By the first week of July Lawrence was at home in Oxford again, working with Woolley on the book that was intended to prove the survey of the Sinai had been on behalf of the Palestine Exploration Fund.* This turned out to be a bigger task than either of them had anticipated, in part because they had so little to show for their travels, and in part because Woolley's and Lawrence's styles of writing were very different, and neither was a natural collaborator. Furthermore, Lawrence's notes did not take into account the work of numerous previous travelers in the Sinai, so he was obliged to spend a good deal of time gathering material in the Oxford libraries, perhaps no longer an easy task for a man who was now used to being out in the open all day with a gang of laborers. For whatever reason,

---

* It would be published in 1915 as *The Wilderness of Zin*. There was also a brief report by Woolley in the 1914 Palestine Exploration Fund annual statement.

the work went slowly, and the only hint we have of any relief from it is that Lawrence had dinner at Hogarth's home with that intrepid traveler Gertrude Bell, and they exchanged many hair-raising tales about life in Syria, Mesopotamia, and Arabia. More interesting still was the amount of information she had gathered about the tribes who lived in the desert on either side of the Hejaz railway, including the Howeitat.

There is no evidence, despite their political sophistication, that they dwelled on the news that the heir to the throne of the Austro-Hungarian Empire and his wife had been assassinated by Serb nationalists at Sarajevo on June 28, 1914.

On July 28 an even more sinister event took place. Unsatisfied by the Serbians' reply to its ultimatum, Austria-Hungary declared war on Serbia; and in response, Serbia's patron, Russia, began the slow (by reason of its immense size and primitive road and rail system) process of mobilizing its army, the largest in the world. Alarmed, Germany declared war on Russia on August 2. On August 3, France, obliged by treaty to mobilize its army in support of Russia, found itself at war with Germany; and in accordance with the long-standing plans of the German high command, the German army invaded neutral Belgium so as to reach Paris by the shortest possible route. Standing in his office as the long summer day drew to a close, Sir Edward Grey, the British foreign secretary, said, "The lamps are going out all over Europe. I fear we will not see them lit again in our lifetime." The next day, August 4, obligated by a seventy-five-year-old treaty to defend Belgium's neutrality, a horrified and divided Liberal government declared war on Germany.

It only remained to be seen whether Turkey would still be neutral— and, if not, which side it would join.

Lawrence had planned to be back in Carchemish in August, and to work there for the next four or five seasons.

He would never return.

CHAPTER SIX

Cairo: 1914–1916

There was seen in the churchyard, against the high altar, a great stone four square, like unto a marble stone, and in the midst thereof was like an anvil of steel a foot on high, and therein stuck a fair sword naked by the point.

—Sir Thomas Malory, *Le Morte d'Arthur*

L ike that of almost every family in Britain, the Lawrence family's life was immediately transformed by the war. Frank, the next-to-youngest, slipped effortlessly and almost immediately into the Gloucestershire Regiment (popularly known as "the Glosters"), just as the Oxford University Officers Training Corps had prepared him to, and was rapidly commissioned as a second-lieutenant. Bob, the eldest, would join the Royal Army Medical Corps as soon as he graduated from medical school. Will, still working as a teacher in India, debated whether to join up over there, or come home. Like many other people, he expected that the war would be over in a few weeks, perhaps won by a great naval battle against the German high seas fleet; only gradually did he become aware that it would be a land war, with no end in sight.

As for Ned, he was at first sidelined, at a moment when young men were volunteering in very large numbers. Some of Lawrence's critics have wondered why he held back, but the reasons were perfectly simple. First of all, he did not see himself in the role of an infantry subaltern. Second, the War Office had raised the minimum required height for volunteers in an attempt to reduce the excessive number, and Lawrence, at five feet five inches, was well below it. Third, and most important, Field Marshal the Earl Kitchener was determined to have the Palestine Exploration Fund publish its book as quickly as possible.

Kitchener, who had been on leave in England, had been about to board a cross-Channel ferry on his way back to his post in Cairo when Great Britain declared war. A messenger halted him on the gangplank at the last moment with a request from the prime minister that he return to London at once. The Liberal government, divided about the wisdom of going to war in the first place, was notably short of warlike figures, except for the first lord of the admiralty, Winston Churchill, a former professional soldier and by far the most bellicose and self-confident member of the cabinet. Kitchener was offered and accepted, without any particular enthusiasm, a seat in the war cabinet as secretary of state for war. It was felt that his massive and formidable presence would reassure both the British public and Britain's allies that military affairs at least were in the right hands. The poster of Kitchener, with his penetrating eyes and impressive mustache, pointing his finger directly at the viewer over the caption "BRITONS—(Kitchener) 'wants you' Join your country's army! God save the king," at once became perhaps the most familiar image of World War I.

It soon became apparent that while Kitchener, the supreme imperial hero and autocrat, overshadowed the rest of the cabinet, his many years as a proconsul in Egypt had given him a certain resemblance to the Sphinx. He spoke seldom, and then in riddles that required considerable interpretation. He did not stoop to explain himself, and his enormous dignity and almost superhuman reputation discouraged his colleagues from asking questions. Whatever else he was, Kitchener was not a born

politician. He was not a clever debater at cabinet meetings, and he did not relish the give-and-take of political infighting, unlike his aggressive young colleague Churchill. The result was that the British army and the Royal Navy were directed in very different spirits. Kitchener's enormous, silent, intimidating presence at cabinet meetings was rather like that of the graven image of worship against which the Lord warned Moses on Mount Sinai.

Although Kitchener was in charge of the War Office, he did not by any means give up his concern for the Middle East; and everybody in the Middle East—including Sir Reginald Wingate, the *sirdar* in Khartoum; and Sir Henry McMahon, who had replaced Kitchener in Cairo—still looked to him for advice and direction. Others in the cabinet might be alarmed by the Germans' swift advance through Belgium, or by the ponderous slowness of Russia's mobilization, or even by the diminutive size of Britain's regular army, but some part of Kitchener's mind was still set on the Ottoman Empire and the Suez Canal. Despite a secret alliance with Germany, the Turkish government had not declared war, and was in fact vigorously negotiating with both sides in the conflict. Kitchener, who had spent much of his adult life in the Middle East, except during the years 1902–1909 when he was commander in chief in India, still hoped to keep Turkey out of the war, or bring it in on the Allies' side. He was therefore all the more determined not to admit that the Sinai map survey had been a military expedition, as opposed to an archaeological one. With his formidable memory and his capacity for detail, Kitchener continued to urge the book forward, thus effectively blocking Lawrence (and Leonard Woolley) from joining the army for the moment, and keeping them at their desks in Oxford.

Trying to placate the Turks was all the more important because even before Kitchener had joined the government, Winston Churchill had single-handedly made a decision that brought relations between Britain and Turkey almost to the breaking point. The Turkish navy was so enfeebled after the Russo-Turkish War of 1877 and the Greek-Turkish War of 1897 that the then first lord of the admiralty, the second earl of Selborne, on visiting Turkey's fleet in 1903, announced when he returned home, "There was no Navy!" The army was scarcely in better condition, and at the beginning of the twentieth century, Turkey took the extraordinary step of entrusting the modernization of its army to a German military delegation, and of its navy to a British one. To some extent, this can be seen as an attempt to have the best of both worlds—an army trained and equipped by the Germans, and a navy trained and equipped by the

British—but it was also symptomatic of Turkey's attempt to survive by means of a balancing act between the great powers. In order to play the role of a great power in the eastern Mediterranean and the Black Sea, Turkey would need modern warships, and it thus set out on an ambitious and expensive program to order more than forty ships from European shipyards, of which the two most important were the *Reshadiye* and the *Sultan Osman I.*

Laid down in 1911, these were battleships of the British *Dreadnought* class, among the most powerful and modern warships in the world; the *Reshadiye** was built by Vickers, and the *Sultan Osman I* by Armstrong. The Turks had spread their bet by commissioning each ship from one of the two great rival British arms firms, in the expectation that competition between the two firms would speed up delivery. These two great ships were a matter of intense and widespread national pride—the Turkish government, strapped for cash, had raised the £4 million (about $320 million in today's money) needed to build the ships by asking for public donations. From all over the Ottoman Empire people, even schoolchildren, had contributed toward their purchase, and larger donations were rewarded with a patriotic medal. Both ships were launched late in 1913, and in a charming ceremony the daughter of the Turkish ambassador to the Court of St. James's "christened" the *Reshadiye* by breaking a bottle of rose water against the bow, champagne being thought inappropriate for a vessel of a Muslim power. But as the months went by the Turkish government became increasingly alarmed by the long delays in fitting the ships' armament, and in endless gunnery and speed trials. By August 1914, however, the ships were at last ready for delivery, and Turkish crews were on hand to take them over and hoist the Turkish flag; but before they could do so, on August 1, 1914, armed British troops and naval personnel seized both battleships and raised the White Ensign on each stern.

---

*The *Sultan Osman I* had originally been ordered from Armstrong by Brazil, which found itself unable to meet the payments for construction. Turkey then took over the contract. The *Reshadiye* was built from scratch for Turkey, and included such special features as Turkish-style "squat" toilets. A third battleship was also on order.

As every day brought Britain closer to war, Churchill, determined not to let two modern battleships go into the hands of a government allied with Germany, had boldly made the decision to "requisition" the two great ships, which were immediately incorporated into the Royal Navy as HMS *Erin* and HMS *Agincourt*.

The reaction in the Ottoman Empire to this high-handed act was widespread anger—the ships had been paid for by public subscription, and Turkey was still a neutral country. "In Constantinople the seizure seemed an act of piracy," in the words of Martin Gilbert. Historians still debate the wisdom of Churchill's impulsive decision, but of course there was no easy answer. If Turkey was going to join the Central Powers anyway, then seizing its battleships was the right thing for the British to do; if there had been any chance at all of Turkey's joining the Allies or staying neutral, then it was clearly the wrong thing to do. As first lord of the admiralty, Churchill thought it was better to be safe than sorry regarding two powerful warships.

The act would almost immediately have grave and unforeseen consequences. In the first days of the war two fast, powerful German warships were in the Mediterranean, hotly pursued by a superior but slower British fleet. The German battle cruiser SMS *Goeben* and the smaller SMS *Breslau*, both under the command of Rear-Admiral Wilhelm Souchon, having failed to prevent the convoy of French troops from North Africa to France, steamed east and managed to outrun and evade the British fleet sent to sink them. "As the shadows of the night fell over the Mediterranean the *Goeben* increased her speed to twenty-four knots," wrote Churchill in Volume 1 of *The World Crisis*, ". . . shook off her unwelcome companions and vanished gradually in the gathering gloom." Having thrown off his pursuers, Souchon paused to take on coal from German freighters at Messina; then, instead of entering the Adriatic to seek shelter in an Austro-Hungarian port, as the British expected him to do, he set course instead for Gallipoli, where on arrival he urgently requested permission from the Turkish government to pass through the strait. After several hours of intense diplomatic negotiations the two German warships were permitted to enter the Dardanelles, and were led through the minefields by a Turkish destroyer. They were now safely in neutral waters, and on August 16 they anchored off Constantinople, where, to almost universal astonishment, both ships were immediately commissioned into the Turkish navy, their German crews raising the Turkish flag and changing into Turkish uniforms, with a fez to replace the uniform cap. Thus, in less than two weeks, the Turks had lost two battleships and replaced them with two German cruisers—one of the cruisers, the *Goeben*, almost the equivalent of a battleship in strength and speed. Practically speaking, this had no immediate effect on the war—although the German ships and their crews could easily dominate the antiquated Russian warships in the Black Sea—but it was a brilliant propaganda coup for the Germans, whose popularity in the Ottoman Empire soared as a result. To most people it seemed to ensure that Turkey would join the war immediately on the side of the Central Powers.

Disenchantment soon set in. Despite the Turkish flag and the fezzes, it began to dawn uncomfortably on some of the less pro-German members of the Turkish government that all of Constantinople was now threatened by the 12.5-inch guns of the *Goeben*. Still, Turkey showed no sign of entering the war as the great battles of the late summer of 1914 shook the nerves of all those who had believed that the war would be over in a matter of weeks. In the west, the vaunted attack of the German right wing through Belgium—intended to drive to the Channel, destroy the British Expeditionary Force, then cut south to separate the French armies of the north from Paris—came to an abrupt end within sight of the Eiffel Tower at the Battle of the Marne. From September 5 to September 12, this battle produced hundreds of thousands of dead on both sides and a bloody stalemate that would endure for four years. In the east, the equally vaunted "Russian steamroller," the avant-garde of an army of 6 million men, entered East Prussia and met with a bloody and decisive defeat at Tannenberg, between August 23 and September 2, exposing the incompetence of the Russian high command, as well as the fecklessness and indifference of the czar and his advisers. Illusions were shattered from one end of Europe to the other, among them any remaining shred of belief in Berlin that Turkey was a trustworthy or reliable ally.

Appeals to Turkey's loyalty having failed, another strategy was called for. On October 27 Rear-Admiral Souchon, who had been appointed commander of the Turkish fleet—an appointment largely intended as window dressing to please the Germans—sailed his two cruisers, supported by Turkish destroyers and torpedo boats, into the Black Sea. The Turkish government—which was now essentially a three-man cabal—may have supposed that Souchon merely intended to make a demonstration, but on October 29 the Turks received news that Odessa and Sebastopol had been shelled, and at least fourteen ships sunk, including a Russian minelayer and a British freighter. The French ambassador immediately asked for his passports,* while the British ambassador continued to negotiate with a deeply divided and hesitant Turkish government—some of its members still hoping to avoid what now seemed inevitable. Then, on October 31, at 5:05 P.M., the Admiralty at last signaled to all British naval vessels: "COMMENCE HOSTILITIES AT ONCE AGAINST TURKEY STOP ACKNOWLEDGE." The two German cruisers had turned out to be a poisoned gift; Admiral Souchon had used them to produce a fait accompli that outraged Russia and brought Turkey into the war at last.

Until early October 1914 Lawrence labored to complete the maps and illustrations for *The Wilderness of Zin*. He and Woolley had both made efforts to join the army, and Woolley, who was a good deal taller than Lawrence, eventually succeeded in getting a commission in the Royal Artillery and was sent to France, leaving Lawrence to finish the book. Newcombe, and no doubt the always well-informed Hogarth, advised Lawrence to be patient—when Turkey joined the war he would surely be needed in Cairo—and once *The Wilderness of Zin* was done, Hogarth found him a post in the Geographical Section of the General Staff (GSGS).

---

* Before declaring war an ambassador asked the foreign minister of the government to which he was accredited for the passports of his embassy staff and their families, signaling their imminent departure.

This cannot have been difficult—the department was run by Colonel Hedley, a member of the committee of the Palestine Exploration Fund, who was well aware of Lawrence's gifts as a surveyor and mapmaker, and was also eager to have him, since most of the officers serving in the GSGS had been sent to France. Lawrence was taken on as a civilian, and his casual manners and even more casual clothes did not endear him to officers working in the War Office. Hedley, who valued Lawrence's intelligence and skills, does not seem to have minded, but not everybody else was pleased to see a diminutive figure with an unruly shock of long blond hair, looking very much like an Oxford undergraduate, walking around the War Office in a position of some importance. Nor did Lawrence try to help matters by assuming an attitude of respect which he did not feel for senior officers, or by curbing his strong and unorthodox opinions. He was at once disheveled, opinionated, and cocky—not a combination of qualities likely to appeal to brass hats. It may be true that when Hogarth asked Hedley if Lawrence was being helpful, three weeks after his arrival at the War Office, Hedley replied, "He's running my entire department for me now," but not everyone was as happy about this as Hedley. When Hedley sent Lawrence off with some maps for General Sir Henry Rawlinson, GCB, GSI, GCVO, KCMG, who was the commander of the British IV Corps in France and another protégé of Kitchener's, Rawlinson "nearly had a fit," and sent him back to Hedley, saying, "I want to talk to an officer." Hedley was a professional soldier himself, and could read the writing on the wall; and, like Hogarth, he knew his way around. He put Lawrence's name in for a commission as a "Temp. 2nd Lieut.-Interpreter," which he received almost immediately, and which was gazetted in the Army List for November–December 1914. (Hedley, knowing all about Lawrence's time at Carchemish and the Sinai, probably assumed that Lawrence's Arabic would shortly prove more useful than his skill in drawing up maps.)

In later years, Lawrence, who loved to tell a good story, used to tell people that he had never been commissioned at all, that following Rawlinson's rebuke, he simply went out to the Army-Navy store at lunchtime and bought himself an off-the-rack uniform; but his army file makes it clear that he was commissioned on October 23, 1914, and that there was nothing irregular about this except the haste with which Hedley managed to bring it about. No doubt with a little more time Hedley could have managed to get Lawrence a higher rank, but his main objective was to get him into uniform quickly so he could keep on doing Hedley's donkey work in the GSGS. The only unusual aspect of Lawrence's commission beyond the speed with which it was obtained was that he underwent neither a physical examination nor any training. That he bought his uniform ready made at the Army-Navy store may be true, however, if we judge by photographs of him in uniform.

With Lawrence's exquisite gift for timing, he received his commission just a week before the Allied Powers declared war on the Ottoman Empire. Not only did Hedley recommend him "as an officer ideally suited for intelligence work in Egypt," but so did almost everybody else. Lawrence's abilities as a linguist and a surveyor, together with his travels through Palestine, Lebanon, Syria, Mesopotamia, and Turkey, made it certain that he would be sent to Cairo, where a new, larger, and more cosmopolitan intelligence staff was being swiftly assembled. Lawrence's companions on the Sinai survey, Newcombe and Woolley, were brought back from France, and a group of "Middle East experts" was picked to man the new department; it included Ronald Storrs, Oriental secretary of the British Agency in Cairo and a disciple of Kitchener, with whom Lawrence would make his first trip to Jidda; Colonel Gilbert Clayton, an experienced intelligence officer with close ties to Sir Reginald Wingate in Khartoum; Aubrey Herbert, a member of Parliament well known for his sympathy with and knowledge of the Ottoman Empire; George Lloyd, another member of Parliament with great experience of the Middle East; and Lawrence himself.

This rather extraordinary brain trust would eventually be joined by the ubiquitous Hogarth, and by Gertrude Bell. The British taste for last-minute improvisation—always contrasted with the grim efficiency of the Germans—is in part contradicted by the formation of the Intelligence

Department of General Headquarters, Cairo, which, though improvised, was made up of strong-willed and independent thinkers, with very different backgrounds and experience, each of them in his or her own way brilliant and well-informed, and—except for Clayton, who would become their indispensable leader—none of them a professional soldier. It is doubtful that the German army could have put together such a colorful and opinionated group of civilians to run its intelligence department, or would have paid any attention to them if it had.

Such diversity was unlikely to produce unanimity, nor was it expected to. Herbert and Lloyd were both Turcophiles of long standing, and while everybody wanted to defeat Turkey now that it had joined the Central Powers, there was less agreement on how to replace it. Voltaire wrote of God, *S'il n'existait pas, il fallait l'inventer* ("If He did not exist, we should have to invent Him"). Similarly, if the Ottoman Empire ceased to exist, it would have to be *re*invented—a daunting prospect, which would entail resolving the competing ambitions in the Middle East of Britain, France, and Russia, and at the same time attempting to satisfy the mutually hostile aspirations of Arabs (both Shiite and Sunni), Kurds, Armenians, Maronite Christians, Jews (both Orthodox and Zionist), and many others, all of them for the moment living, however unhappily, under Turkish rule. This vast and backward area was at once the strategically vital link between Europe, Asia, and Africa, and the birthplace of three of the world's great monotheistic religions; and Mesopotamia was already recognized as one of the world's largest reserves of petroleum, just as the navies of the great powers, led by Britain, were converting from coal to oil.

Storrs would later describe the intelligence group in a little poem, with his usual urbane wit, as:

> Clayton stability,
> Symes versatility,
> Cornwallis is practical,
> Dawnay syntactical,

Mackintosh havers,
And Fielding palavers,
Macindoe easy,
And Wordie not breezy:
Lawrence licentiate to dream and to dare
And Yours Very Faithfully, *bon à tout faire.*

It was not instantly apparent that Lawrence's role would be "to dream and to dare," and he may not have even realized it himself yet. He was, in fact, despite his eagerness to get back to the Middle East now that he was in uniform at last, delayed for weeks in London. The "general officer commanding" (GOC) in Egypt had wired the War Office for a map of the roads of the Sinai, which it didn't have, so Lawrence was put to the task of converting and expanding *The Wilderness of Zin* into a military document. He belittled his own work, and joked that he had to make up or invent much of it and that he would hate to be sent into a battle using his own maps, but it was finally done by the end of November. He complained that he had now written the same book twice, both times without pay—and on December 9 he and Newcombe finally took the train for Marseille, and from there sailed to Egypt.

He was preceded by a message from the director of military operations in the War Office to the GOC in Egypt, General Sir John Maxwell, introducing him as: "a youngster, 2nd Lt. Lawrence who has wandered about in the Sinai Peninsula, and who came in here to help in the Map Branch." Not every second-lieutenant is posted overseas with an introduction from one general to another, but even at this early stage of the war, with only one pip on his sleeve, Lawrence was being treated as someone of unusual importance.

Before leaving London, Lawrence had written to his brother Will, who was still in India, advising him to do nothing in a hurry—apparently in recognition of the fact that it was going to be a longer war than Will supposed—and mysteriously warning him, "Keep your eye on Afghanistan." Now, from Cairo, he wrote again to Will to say that he had been there for six weeks, "in the office from morning to night," trying to make sense of the news that was brought to him from all over the Ottoman Empire, and preparing "geographical essays" for general headquarters (GHQ). To the family he wrote quite a jolly letter, first to express gratitude for their sending his bicycle out to Cairo, then giving his somewhat outspoken opinions about his new colleagues, as well as revealing that he sees "a good deal" of General Maxwell, the GOC, whom he describes as "a very queer person, almost weirdly good-natured, very cheerful. . . . He takes the whole job as a splendid joke," an odd description of the general in command of the entire Middle East. Of the two members of Parliament, he describes Lloyd as "very amusing," and Herbert as "a joke, but a very nice one." He mentions a few more odd additions to the staff, including Père Jaussen, an Arabic-speaking French Dominican monk from Jerusalem; and Philip Graves, the correspondent for the *Times* of London. Lady Evelyn Cobbold, who had lent Lawrence the money at Petra, had just arrived "on her usual winter trip to Egypt," and invited him to dinner. In general it sounds as if Lawrence was having a very much jollier and more sociable life in Cairo than at home. The letter reads as if censorship of officers' mail was not yet being exercised efficiently, or perhaps the Intelligence Department had some way to get around it. What Lawrence did not mention to his family was his remarkably quick jump up the promotion ladder: he had been appointed an acting staff captain less than three months after he had been commissioned as a second-lieutenant.

Lawrence's dislike for Egypt, Cairo, and the Egyptians had not diminished, even though he seems to have settled in very fast this time. All members of the intelligence staff were quartered together at the Continental Hotel (at ten shillings a day) with a direct line to GHQ, at the Savoy Hotel, and Lawrence bicycled over to his job every morning. His army pay was £400 a year, so he was well off in Cairo. He saw General Maxwell frequently—the commander in chief does not appear to have been in any way a remote figure—but Lawrence's opinions were already his own: "So far as Syria is concerned it is France & not Turkey that is the enemy," he wrote home. This idea was to form the basis for much of what he did in 1917–1918, but it was far from British policy.

Indeed, British policy in the Middle East was hampered from the beginning both by France's historic claim to Lebanon and Syria, the origins of which went back to the time of the Crusades and included French support for the Maronite Christians of Lebanon; and by the fact that the British government in London and the government of India in Delhi had radically different ideas about the Middle East. Kitchener had always looked to the Arabs with the thought that given British support they might one day form a dominion or a colony under British rule, creating a British "block" or area that would stretch from the western border of Egypt through much of what is now Saudi Arabia, Israel, and Jordan, and extending south in Africa to include Sudan, which he himself had conquered, and of course the Suez Canal, which would then be protected by British possessions, rather than exposed at the extreme western end. To achieve this, it would be necessary to stoke the fires of Arab nationalism and separatism, which in the view of most people burned so low as to be invisible, since "the Arabs" scarcely even recognized themselves as such, and remained divided by region, by tribe, by clan, by religious differences, and by mutual enmity. The gap between the urbanized Arabs of Beirut or Damascus and the nomads of the Arabian Desert was so great as to seem unbridgeable, and the Turks had skillfully played one group against the other for centuries.

From the vantage point of the government in India a very different view prevailed. First of all, the largest single Muslim population in the world was in India, under British rule. Any attempt to ignite an Arab nationalist uprising in the Middle East could hardly fail to inspire Muslims in India to do the same. Worse still, the sultan of Turkey, impotent figurehead though he had now become, was caliph, the commander of the faithful, the successor of Muhammad, the spiritual leader of all Muslims everywhere, and the only person entitled to proclaim a jihad, or holy war, against the infidel. The last thing the government of India wanted on its doorstep was an Arab holy war. Moreover, the government of India, if obliged to fight the Turks, wanted to do so in Mesopotamia (now Iraq), and had in mind for it a full colonial government—in short, rule from Delhi. Properly farmed, it was believed, Mesopotamia could produce grain to help India through its periodic famines, and could be policed by the Indian army. Indeed, within days of the British declaration of war against Turkey the Indian Army Expeditionary Force (which had been at sea for nearly three weeks, waiting for news of the declaration) had landed to ensure the safety of British oil installations in the Persian Gulf. Shortly afterward this force took the city of Basra, where Sir Percy Cox was installed as chief political officer, and announced that all of Mesopotamia was now under the British flag and would henceforth enjoy "the benefits of liberty and justice," but not of course those of national independence.

Busy as he was with map work, and digesting intelligence reports into concise and useful documents for General Maxwell and Maxwell's staff—Lawrence described himself self-deprecatingly as "bottle-washer and office boy pencil-sharpener and pen-wiper"—his view of the Middle East was inherently that of Cairo, rather than Delhi. He did not see the Arabs as "natives," and he had no sympathy for traditional colonialism, whether British or French. He was well aware of events that were taking place in the Arab areas of the Ottoman Empire, since he, Woolley, and New-combe all worked together in one room, and ate all their meals together, so it would have been hard for them to keep secrets from each other, even had they wanted to. Since they worked for Colonel Clayton, they also had a broader knowledge than other staff officers of what was happening. Clayton not only was in charge of the army's Intelligence Department, which reported to General Maxwell, but also ran the Egyptian civilian intelligence service, which reported to the high commissioner, Sir Henry McMahon, and in addition was the representative in Cairo of the *sirdar* and governor-general of the Sudan, Sir Reginald Wingate. For a man with three masters—one of whom, Wingate, combined a high military position and a civil position—Clayton was a model of patience, tact, and objectivity; and unlike many "spymasters" he does not seem to have tried to keep those who worked for him out of the larger picture.

As a result, Lawrence was one of the best-informed persons in Cairo—he made, corrected, and "pieced together" maps; he interrogated Turkish prisoners of war; he kept a record of the positions and the movements of each division of the Turkish army; he wrote and produced (with Graves) the official handbook of the Turkish army for the use of officers; and he was in constant telegraphic communication with London, Paris, Saint Petersburg, and Khartoum. His keenness, energy, and capacity for hard work drew people's attention—as did his superior tone and his determination to impose his own opinion on other people, however much higher in rank or more experienced they were. Thus he set about changing the whole system for transliterating Arabic place-names on maps, stepping sharply on the toes of numerous experts, and causing considerable distress in the Survey Department.* The head of the Surveyor-General's Office in Cairo, Sir Ernest Dowson, had once said of Lawrence, "Who is this extraordinary little pip-squeak?" but quickly changed his mind and came to admire him, though adding that the young officer had a rare talent for annoying people when he chose to be difficult. Dowson saw a lot of him, since among other duties Lawrence almost immediately became the liaison between the Intelligence Office, the Survey Department, and the Egyptian Government Printing Press. There is no question that Lawrence was a busy and well-informed young man, so busy indeed that when his brother Will stopped briefly at Port Said on the way home to England to join the Oxford and Buckinghamshire Light Infantry as a second-lieutenant in March 1915, Lawrence was unable to meet him, and they were only able to speak by telephone. Will reported home in a letter mailed from Marseille that his brother Ned was now a staff-captain and that Egypt was "as quiet as a mouse," so their mother need have no concerns on his account.

Lawrence certainly knew that Arab nationalists had been in touch

---

* This is odd, since later, in writing *Seven Pillars of Wisdom*, Lawrence deliberately abandoned any attempt at systematic or consistent spelling of Arabic names, informing the copy editor, "I spell my names anyhow, to show what rot systems are" (Jonathan Cape edition of 1935, p. 25). But then, as Ralph Waldo Emerson pointed out, "A foolish consistency is the hobgoblin of little minds."

with British high officials in Cairo even before Turkey entered the war, suggesting the possibility of an Arab revolt financed and armed by Britain. This was a delicate subject, all the more so while Britain and the Ottoman Empire were still at peace. In the first place, just as the British government in India was strongly opposed to Arab nationalism because it might spread to Indian Muslims, the authorities in Egypt were reluctant to encourage anything that might bring Egyptians into the streets protesting against British rule in Egypt. In the second place, hardly anybody had a clear idea of how strong the various groups of nationalist Arabs were, or what they wanted, whereas French ambitions in the area were clearly understood. Clayton himself had had several interviews with Aziz el Masri, an Arab figure of some importance in Turkish politics, whose secret support for Arab independence had led to his exile in Egypt before the outbreak of war. He had been lucky to leave with his life, since he had been condemned to death by his former colleagues. Aziz el Masri (or, as Clayton referred to him, Colonel Aziz Bey) was an impressive figure, but since what he sought was an independent Mesopotamia, his ambitions were directly opposed to those of the British government in India, and all the more so once Indian army troops had occupied Basra. Indeed, two of his collaborators, including Nuri as-Said, a future prime minister of Iraq, were deported from Basra to India by Sir Percy Cox.

A more promising approach—that is, one less likely to be vetoed outright by India—had been made before the war, by Emir Abdulla—second son of Sharif Hussein, emir of Mecca—on a visit to Cairo. Abdulla's concern was that the Turkish government might attempt to depose, remove, or assassinate his father, and replace him with somebody more compliant. This was not an empty threat. One son, Emir Feisal, was in Constantinople, ostensibly as a deputy in the Turkish parliament, but in fact in a position of comfortable house arrest as a hostage for his family's loyalty; and Sharif Hussein himself had spent more than fifteen years in Constantinople with his family as a "guest" of Sultan Abdul Hamid II. The sharifian family was widely respected, even revered, both as being directly descended from the Prophet and for its role as guardian of two of the three holiest cities in Islam. Consequently, the family was an object of suspicion to the Turkish government, all the more so since Mecca, in the Hejaz, was so far removed from the centers of Turkish power that before the building of the single-line railway to Medina, the journey to Mecca could take weeks or months. Even after the completion of the railway, there was still a daunting journey of 250 miles on camel or on foot from Medina to Mecca across a forbidding desert dominated by predatory Bedouin. Abdulla's importance and diplomatic skill were such that he not only met with Ronald Storrs but may have met with Kitchener himself; but neither of them was able to offer any meaningful support so long as Great Britain and the Ottoman Empire were at peace (or to provide Abdulla with the half a dozen modern machine guns he wanted). The moment they were at war, however, Storrs suggested reopening the discussion with Abdulla; and Kitchener, now in London as secretary of state for war, agreed.

Abdulla, speaking for his father, sought British support against the Turks, and after a series of messages from Mecca to Cairo to London and back, it was given, on the condition that the sharif (and "the Arab nation") assist Britain in the war against Turkey. Kitchener not only had given his approval but had sought the approval of the prime minister and Sir Edward Grey, the foreign secretary, thus committing Britain in principle to arm and finance a revolt in the Hejaz against the Turks under the leadership of Sharif Hussein. The timing of the revolt and the exact meaning of the phrase "Arab nation" were left undefined for the moment; still, at one stroke, Great Britain had committed itself to the creation of an Arab state and to the leadership of Sharif Hussein and his sons. Kitchener went even farther. In his message to Abdulla, he not only alluded to an Arab state but as good as pledged Britain to support Sharif Hussein as a new caliph, replacing the Turkish sultan: "It may be," Kitchener wrote, falling into language as stately and opaque as that of Hussein himself, "that an Arab of the true race will assume the Caliphate at Mecca or Medina, and so good may come by the help of God out of all the evil which is now occurring."

Since Kitchener's utterances, not unlike those of the sharif, tended to be Delphic, it is hardly surprising that his message of October 30, 1914, has been a source of controversy for the past ninety-five years. That and the Balfour Declaration of 1917 are among the most fiercely disputed documents in the history of British diplomacy. It is clear enough, though, that British policy now promised "the Arabs" (without as yet defining who and where they were) a state carved out of the Ottoman Empire if they helped to defeat the Turks, and offered the sharif (and his family) a role of special political and religious importance within such a state, as well as suggesting that he should assume spiritual leadership of all Muslims everywhere (something that was hardly in the gift of the British government). Not surprisingly, these assurances were accepted with alacrity by the sharif, and very shortly afterward he offered the first proof of his allegiance to the Allies' cause.

Almost immediately after the outbreak of war between the Allies and the Ottoman Empire the sultan, though now hardly more than a figure-head, in his role as calpih proclaimed a jihad against the Allies. The proclamation appeared to have had little effect on Muslims in India, in North Africa, or even in Egypt. Although the sharif of Mecca had been expected to announce his adherence to the jihad, he showed no sign of doing so. His silence on the matter was deafening, and registered clearly in Constantinople and Berlin.

It may or may not be true that the British acquired their empire "in a fit of absence of mind,"* but certainly their policy for the Middle East was improvised in haste and as something of an afterthought, by men who were overwhelmed by the sheer size and ferocity of the war only three months after it had begun. However, when Lawrence arrived in Cairo, British policy, at any rate on the surface, appeared to coincide with his own view, except for the intrusion of the Indian army and government into Mesopotamia, which Lawrence opposed from the start. He plunged into his duties in Cairo with enormous enthusiasm—and daily expanded

---

* The famous line of Professor John Seeley, in *The Expansion of England* (1883).

them in every direction. He was convinced that British policy would lead to the creation of an independent Arab state, one that would, of course, include "his" Arabs, Dahoum and Sheikh Hamoudi among them, and would eventually include Syria, where he had spent the four best years of his life.

For a junior staff officer, he seems to have had no hesitation in writing long, opinionated reports on strategy. No sooner was he settled into the Continental Hotel than he prepared an essay on the advantages of seizing the port of Alexandretta (now Iskenderun). The attraction of the scheme was that it could be carried out, in Lawrence's opinion, with a relatively limited number of troops, would provide the Royal Navy with a major deepwater harbor in the eastern Mediterranean, and would at one stroke cut Turkey off from its empire in the south and bring British troops directly into Syria, instead of having the British fight their way north over the hilly and easily defended territory from Gaza to Jersualem. Kitchener, whether encouraged by Lawrence or not, took a similar point of view, but the Alexandretta scheme was doomed from the start. The French distrusted any move that would bring British troops into Syria, which France intended to have as its share of the Turkish empire, along with Lebanon; also, there was a competing plan, hatched in part by Churchill, to use the fleet to break through the Dardanelles, threaten Constantinople, and open up the Black Sea to Allied shipping.

Throughout the winter and spring of 1915, Lawrence energetically pushed the Alexandretta scheme, apparently without anybody in Cairo or London questioning why an obscure temporary second-lieutenant was dabbling in grand strategy. He went on to write a long, persuasive, closely reasoned report on Syrian politics, which was once again read at the highest levels, where it seemed to dovetail with Kitchener's opinions. Lawrence's impressive knowledge of Syrian secret political societies (any political discussion that involved opposition to Turkish rule had to be, by definition, secret), and of the desires of the very different peoples who lived in Syria, was well-informed, realistic, and compelling, as was his conclusion that a functional Arab state would have to include Damascus and Aleppo, and if possible the littoral area and ports of Lebanon, under an administration flexible enough to include desert dwellers and city dwellers as well as Maronite Christians. He doubted that there was any such thing as Syrian "national feeling," but thought that the binding force of a Syrian state would be the Arabic language, and foresaw the possibility that Lebanon might need to be treated separately because of its large Christian minority. Palestine, he concluded sensibly, would present a wholly different set of problems. Anybody reading these documents would have to conclude that Lawrence's four years at Carchemish and his travels throughout Syria and Lebanon had given him an extraordinary knowledge both of the Arabs' hopes and of the reality (and complexity) of the situation in the Arab-speaking parts of the Ottoman Empire.

In February, the Turks carried out their long-awaited attack on the Suez Canal, but it failed, since they had counted on an Egyptian uprising, which was not forthcoming. This was the attack that prevented Lawrence from meeting his brother Will. In March the Franco-British naval assault on the Dardanelles took place; it failed when six of the eighteen battleships engaged were either seriously damaged or sunk by mines, so that the hesitant naval commander, Admiral de Robeck—who had replaced the even less bold Admiral Carden at the last moment, when Carden had a collapse attributed to stress—decided to break off the attack. Many people—first and foremost Winston Churchill—have since argued that if de Robeck had not given in to his fears he could have pushed on to Constantinople, and that Turkey might have collapsed with an Allied fleet anchored off the Golden Horn. Instead, the result was that British, French, Australian, and New Zealand troops were landed on Gallipoli in April, to take the Turkish forts and allow the strait to be swept clear of mines—an attempt that dragged on until December 1915 and cost the Allies nearly 150,000 casualties, including more than 44,000 killed. The failure at Gallipoli caused the Turkish attitude toward the Allies to harden, and led to the genocide of the Armenians, since they represented the largest Christian population in the Ottoman Empire. It also resulted in the final shelving of the Alexandretta scheme, for which there were now neither sufficient troops nor sufficient shipping. Other results included a weakening of Kitchener's position as Britain's warlord, a setback to Winston Churchill's career (Gallipoli would raise questions about his judgment until May 1940), and Lawrence's growing conviction that Turkey would somehow have to be attacked on the periphery, rather than frontally.

In May came news of his brother Frank's death. Frank had been killed while leading his men forward "preparatory to the assault," as his company commander put it in a letter to Frank's parents, adding, in a note typical of the futility of trench warfare on the western front, "The assault I regret to say was unsuccessful." Lawrence's letters home after he received the news of Frank's death are odd. Writing to his father, he regretted that the family had felt any need to go into mourning: "I cannot see any cause at all—in any case to die for one's country is a sort of privilege." To his mother he wrote, "You *will* never understand any of us after we are grown up a little. *Don't* you ever feel that we love you without our telling you so?" He ended: "I didn't say good-bye to Frank because he would rather I didn't, & I knew there was little chance of my seeing him again; in which case we were better without a parting." The letter to his mother makes it clear that even over a distance of thousands of miles, the old conflict between them was continuing undiminished. Clearly, despite the pain of Frank's death, his mother was still anxious to be reassured that her sons loved her, and Lawrence was still determined not to say so. His disapproval of the fact that the family was mourning Frank and his slightly defensive tone at not having been able to say good-bye are typical of Lawrence's lifelong effort to cut himself off from just such emotions—a kind of self-imposed moral stoicism, and a horror of any kind of emotional display. "You know men do nearly all die laughing, because they know death is very terrible, & a thing to be forgotten until after it comes," he writes to his mother; this is neither consoling nor necessarily true. It is exactly the kind of romantic bunk about war that Lawrence himself was to dismiss in some of the more brutally realistic passages of *Seven Pillars of Wisdom*.

Some allowance must be made of course for the patriotic feeling and the willingness to endure pain and death that separate Lawrence's generation from those that followed it. These traits are exactly why Rupert Brooke's romantic war poems seem so much harder to understand or sympathize with than the bitter, angry war poetry of Siegfried Sassoon or Wilfred Owen. Even so, Lawrence's letters to his father and mother after Frank's death seem harsh, and full of what we would now think of as the false nobility of war—putting a noble face on a meaningless slaughter. Frank's own letters home are full of similar sentiments: "If I do die, I hope to die with colours flying." This kind of high-minded sentiment about the war was shared by millions of people, including the soldiers themselves, although by 1917 it was wearing thin for most of the troops, as bitter postwar books like Robert Graves's *Goodbye to All That* and Frederic Manning's *Her Privates We* demonstrate. Lawrence, who would become a friend and admirer of both authors, would in the course of time proceed through the same change of heart as they did; hence the savagery, the nihilism, and the sense of personal emptiness that run through *Seven Pillars of Wisdom.** Then, too, in May 1915, though Lawrence was in uniform, he was not fighting. However determined he may have been to be knighted and a general before he reached the age of thirty—he still had four years in which to accomplish these ambitions—he had not as yet made the first step toward active soldiering, and was beginning to feel a certain uneasy guilt. "Out here we do nothing," he complained to his mother. "But I don't think we are going to have to wait much longer." This was probably not a prediction she wanted to receive with the death of one son on her mind; nor was it accurate, since almost eighteen months would pass before Lawrence was in action.

Communications between Cairo and Mecca, in 1914 and 1915, may be likened to putting a letter in a bottle and throwing it into the Hudson River in New York City in the expectation that it will eventually reach the person to whom it is addressed in London. After the message from Kitch-

---

* The book's subtitle, "a triumph," is bitterly sarcastic, though seldom recognized as such.

ener promising British support for an Arab state was passed on to Mecca, a long silence ensued. This was partly because communications of any kind were dangerous—contact with the British was treason—and partly because Sharif Hussein was extremely cautious. He took the precaution of sending his son Feisal to Damascus and Constantinople, to meet with Jemal Pasha, the "minister of the marine," who had been put in charge of the campaign to attack Egypt and in general of the entire Arab population of the southeast, and with whom Feisal exchanged courtesies; and to meet more secretly with the Syrian nationalist organizations, to see whether they would support the sharif as their leader, and to try to define exactly what the borders of an Arab state should be. This was a mission that could have cost Feisal his life, but his gift for secrecy and for Arab politics exceeded even that of his elder brother Abdulla. His position, as well as that of his father and his brothers, was made more delicate by the fact that the French consul in Lebanon, François Georges-Picot, on returning to France after the declaration of war between the Allies and the Ottoman Empire, had left behind in his desk drawers a mass of incriminating correspondence with most of the major Arab nationalist figures, including messages implicating the sharif of Mecca himself. All this was now in the hands of Jemal Pasha, permitting him to play a sinister and protracted cat-and-mouse game with Arab political figures— with tragic consequences for many of those mentioned in the documents.

In the summer of 1915, after conversations with Arab nationalists who had made their way to Cairo, Sir Henry McMahon, with the blessing of Kitchener and the war cabinet, issued a declaration promising that after victory Britain would recognize an independent Arab state; for the moment, he did not define its borders. The fact that the British had unilaterally transformed Egypt, which was, in theory, part of the Ottoman Empire, into a "protectorate" with McMahon as "high commissioner" made Arab nationalists nervous about Britain's intentions, all the more so because the French made no secret of theirs.

It was hoped that the declaration of a future Arab state would calm these fears, and perhaps persuade the Arabs to take up arms against the

Turks, but all it produced was a note from Sharif Hussein to McMahon, which took almost a month to reach Cairo, and in which Hussein outlined the Arab demands for an independent state in great detail, repeating almost word for word what his son Feisal had heard in the secret talks with Arab nationalists in Damascus and Constantinople. These demands stunned McMahon. Great Britain was asked to recognize an Arab state that extended from the Mediterranean littoral in the west to the Persian Gulf in the east, and from the northernmost part of Syria to the Indian Ocean in the south (excluding Aden, which was already in British hands). In modern terms, this area would include Saudi Arabia, Iraq, Syria, Jordan, Israel, and Lebanon. Since, in the words of Hussein, "the entire Arab nation is (God be praised!) united in its resolve to pursue its noble aim to the end, at whatever cost," an affirmative reply was requested within thirty days of receipt of the message.

To say that McMahon was taken aback by this message would be putting it mildly. For one thing, the area included a number of powerful Arab leaders who were no friends of the sharif of Mecca, including his rival ibn Saud, who was under the protection of the government of India; for another, the British themselves had designs on Iraq, where British and Indian troops were already fighting the Turks, and on Palestine, which they regarded as necessary for the protection of the Suez Canal. After consulting the war cabinet and the Foreign Office, McMahon set out to write a temporizing note—no easy task, especially given the prevailing phrasing of notes to and from Mecca. His reply begins:

> To the excellent and well-born Sayyed, the descendent of Sharifs, the Crown of the Proud, Scion of Muhammad's Tree and Branch of the Quraishite Trunk, him of the Exalted Presence and of the Lofty Rank, Sayyed son of Sayyed, Sharif son of Sharif, the Venerable, Honoured Sayyed, his Excellency the Sharif Hussein, Lord of the Many, Amir of Mecca the Blessed, the lodestar of the Faithful, and the cynosure of all devout Believers, may his Blessing descend upon the people in their multitudes!

It continues in much the same impenetrable style. The sharif's notes, equally full of compliments, titles, blessings, and protestations of respect, are even more opaque, so that the sense has to be teased out of each beautifully crafted sentence like the meat from a nut, then parsed the way Orthodox Jews parse the Old Testament, repeating every sentence over and over again in search of its truest meaning.

Despite the flowery beginning, McMahon's first message poured cold water on the projected borders of "Arab lands," as defined by the nationalist groups in Damascus and by the sharif of Mecca. Stripped of its polite decoration, his reply was that discussion of the precise borders of an Arab state would have to wait until after victory. The sharif's reply to this, in September, took the form of a fairly sharp rebuke, though even an admirer of his, the pro-Arab historian George Antonius, remarks that it "was a mode of expression in which his native directness was enveloped in a tight network of parentheses, incidentals, allusions, saws and apothegms, woven together by a process of literary orchestration into a sonorous rigmarole." It was not sufficiently florid, however, to conceal the sharif's irritation at what he describes as McMahon's "lukewarmth and hesitancy," which was reinforced by the arrival in Cairo of an Arab officer, Muhammad Sharif al-Faruqi, a Baghdadi, who had crossed over to the British lines at great risk to convey the fact that the sharif's demands were essentially the same as those of the Arab nationalist groups, and not by any means those of the sharif alone.

After consulting London and his own experts, chief among them Storrs, McMahon replied on October 24 with a letter that was intended to start the immemorial Oriental process of bargaining, setting out Britain's offer in response to the sharif's overambitious asking price. McMahon consented this time to give Great Britain's pledge to the independence of the Arabs within the area outlined in the sharif's letter, but with certain important exclusions. These included the Arabs' recognition of Britain's "special interest" in Mesopotamia (oil); some form of joint Anglo-Arab administration for the *vilayats* (provinces) of Basra and Baghdad; and the exclusion of the areas to the west of Damascus, which were not "purely

T. E. Lawrence, by Augustus John.

T. E. Lawrence,
by Eric Kennington.

Hogarth, by Augustus John.

Clayton, by Eric Kennington.

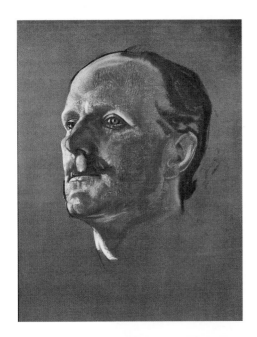

Ronald Storrs,
by Eric Kennington.

Allenby, by
James McBey.

Feisal, photograph by Harry Chase.

The rifle presented to Lawrence by Feisal. Note that Lawrence carved his initials, the date, and four notches in the stock.

Feisal's bodyguard and slave,
by James McBey.

Sharif Hussein,
photographed in Jidda.

Lawrence, photographed
by Harry Chase at Aqaba,
1918.

Abdulla, by Eric Kennington.

Auda Abu Tayi, by Eric Kennington.

T. E. Lawrence,
by Harry Chase.

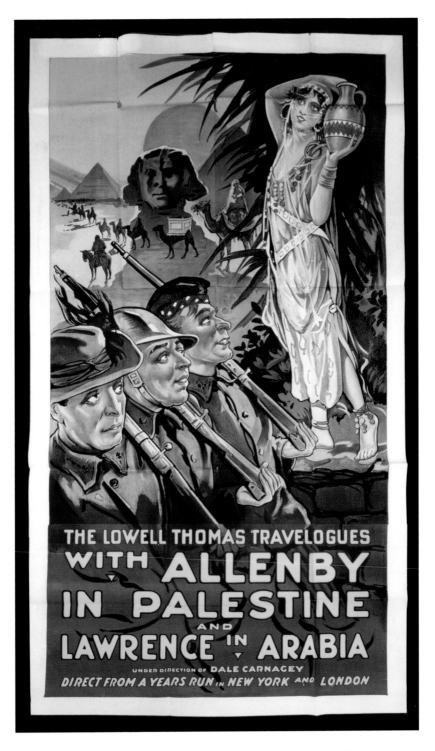

Poster for Lowell Thomas's "travelogue," this one probably for the Australian production. (Note the Australian soldier in the characteristic slouched hat, in the foreground. Note, too, that the future author of *How to Win Friends and Influence People* is still spelling his name "Carnagey.")

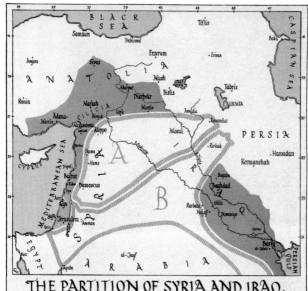

Left: Map of the partition of Syria and Iraq as devised in the 1916 Sykes-Picot agreement, by Tom Wrigley.

Below: Lawrence's plan for the partition of the Ottoman Empire, prepared by him for the Eastern Committee of the War Cabinet, in October 1918.

Arab," in other words Lebanon, where the Druses regarded themselves as under the protection of the British and the Maronite Christians as under the protection of France. Further exclusions included—a rather broad sweep—those areas in which Great Britain was not "free to act without detriment to the interests of her ally France," and those areas controlled by "treaties concluded by us and certain Arab Chiefs," a polite reminder that ibn Saud and several of the sharif's other rivals would not be included in Hussein's Arab state. Nowhere in the letter is Palestine mentioned, unless it is meant to be included in McMahon's guarantee that Britain would protect the holy places—by which he almost certainly meant the *Muslim* holy places, Mecca, Medina, and Jerusalem. On the other hand, since Palestine was not "purely Arab"—two Jewish communities were living there, one devoutly Orthodox, the other defiantly Zionist—and was indubitably to the west of Damascus, he may have meant to exclude it, or he simply took it for granted that the Allies were unlikely not to seek some form of control over the Christian holy places after the war.

Much bloodshed and strife might have been spared had Storrs and McMahon drafted the note of October 24 more precisely, but they were working under pressure from London. The Gallipoli expedition had all too clearly failed, the Turkish army was still within reach of the Suez Canal, and the invasion of Mesopotamia was going more slowly than expected, while on the western front losses were soaring for no gain in ground, and on the eastern front the Russian army was already showing signs of an impending collapse. If there is a chance that the Arabs can be drawn into the war, promise them whatever they want: this was essentially the message from London. After the war was won, such promises could always be renegotiated, or fine-tuned.[*]

The exchange of messages between the sharif and McMahon continued at a leisurely pace until January 1, 1916, with no major changes in the position of either side. Neither party was content with the agreement that had been reached: the Arabs were unsatisfied because they wanted

---

[*] This applied to many other agreements, including the Sykes-Picot agreement and the Balfour Declaration.

Syria above all, with its seacoast, as well as Palestine and Mesopotamia; the British were unsatisfied because this protracted negotiation had so far produced only Hussein's refusal to endorse the jihad, and because lurking behind McMahon and Hussein's correspondence like a guilty secret in a marriage was the fact that it had not yet been communicated to the French. This was how things stood on May 24, 1916, when the Arab Revolt finally began.

Attempts to reach an amicable accord between Britain and France* over sharing the Arab-populated areas of the Ottoman Empire once Turkey was defeated had been going on since 1914, despite the fact that the Turks seemed by late 1915 to be winning their war, and despite whatever agreements were being made by the British separately with Arab nationalists and Sharif Hussein. The views of the British and French on the future of the Middle East were so divergent, and their distrust of each other's ambitions in the area was so strong, that Kitchener and Foreign Secretary Sir Edward Grey eventually shifted the whole issue to a committee headed by an experienced diplomat and civil servant, Sir Maurice de Bunsen, no doubt in the hope that the matter could be shelved until a victory of some sort was won against the Turks. Though neither Kitchener nor Grey said it, they might well have echoed Talleyrand's famous instruction to his staff on taking charge of the Ministry of Foreign Affairs: *Surtout, messieurs, pas trop de zèle.* Unfortunately, this was to underestimate French interest in the subject, as well as the zeal of one committee member, Sir Mark Sykes.† Tall, wealthy, charming, handsome, well connected, ambitious, a member of Parliament, a baronet, and a successful author,

---

* Both the British and the French understood that Russia's ambitions would also have to be satisfied, and would at least include sizable gains in the Caucasus, equal representation in control of the Christian holy places in Jerusalem, and the biggest prize of all: Constantinople and Russian control over the exit from and entrance to the Black Sea—the supreme goal of Russian foreign policy since Catherine the Great.

† Sir Mark Sykes would reemerge as front-page news in 2008. He had died of the Spanish flu in Paris, in 1919, and been buried in a sealed, lead-lined coffin. With the permission of his family, his remains were exhumed in the hope of finding viral traces of the flu that could be used as a vaccine against newer forms of flu, such as avian flu H1N1.

Sykes was the perfect example of a supremely energetic and self-confident man placed where a cautious, slow-moving one would have been a better choice.

The sixth baronet, Sykes was both "a Yorkshire grandee," who inherited a great house and 30,000 acres (as well as the fortune to support them), and a sophisticated world traveler from an early age. His mother was a Cavendish-Bentinck, one of a great and influential family at the head of which was the duke of Portland, and which by many strands was related to the royal family. Effervescent, imaginative, impulsive, and generous, Sykes was, among other things, a gifted caricaturist, whose cartoons of the great and famous are often hilarious, but never malicious or unkind. He was one of that rarest of creatures, an upper-class Englishman who was at home everywhere, and almost completely without racial or religious prejudice. He had a particular affinity for Turkey—he wrote two travel guides to Turkey, and a history of the Ottoman Empire—and also visited Mexico, Canada, the United States, Egypt, and India, and served in the Boer War, where he may first have attracted Kitchener's attention. From the moment he took his seat in the House of Commons, he was recognized as a young man who could "fill the House," a witty and provocative speechmaker clearly destined for a political future full of glittering prizes. He once held Ronald Storrs in thrall in Cairo by speaking into Storrs's office Dictaphone "a twenty-minute Parliamentary Debate . . . with the matter as well as the manner of such different speakers as Lloyd George, F. E. Smith, John Redmond or Sir Edward Carson rendered with startling accuracy," as well as a parody of a Drury Lane melodrama, complete with music and sound effects.

Everybody liked and admired Sykes; he was the life of the party wherever he went. Indeed his only defect, like that of his friend Winston Churchill, was that while he enjoyed a good argument he always came away from one under the impression that he had won it and that he had converted the other person to his point of view. Kitchener sent Sykes, now a lieutenant-colonel of the Green Howards, out to the Middle East in the summer of 1915 on what would today be called a fact-finding tour. He charmed everyone he met, even the French, since he was "a devout Roman Catholic and a Francophile," and spoke perfect French. He traveled on to India, via Aden, where he had less success with Lord Hardinge, the viceroy. The government of India vigorously contested both the idea of the Arab Revolt and any promise to the Arabs of a future state. The government of India saw no signs in Basra that the Arabs wanted or would know what to do with self-government, and they proposed to run Mesopotamia as an extension of colonial rule in India. In the same spirit, they were backing ibn Saud with arms, support, and money, which, since he was the mortal rival of Sharif Hussein, put Delhi and London at loggerheads.

Sykes does not seem to have been deeply troubled by any of this—he was a man who could hold several passionate enthusiasms in his head at the same time without apparently noticing that they were contradictory. He was at once sincerely in favor of an Arab state and a wholly committed supporter of Zionism;* he was determined to give the French what they wanted, and at the same time in favor of McMahon's correspondence with Sharif Hussein. He was sympathetic toward both Turks and Arabs, as well as Armenians and Kurds. If Sykes was aware that the one point most Arabs agreed on, whatever their other differences, was that the heart of any viable Arab state must be Syria, and that under no circumstances would they accept French domination, given France's colonial record in North Africa, he managed to suppress this when he finally returned to London to report on his mission. It is typical of Sykes that he not only helped form the sentiment behind, and draft the language of the Balfour Declaration, but also designed the flag of the Arab Revolt, "a combination of green, red, black and white." (Variations of this design would become the national flags of Jordan, Iraq, Syria, and Palestine.) Sykes is an example of a fatal British ability to see both sides of a dispute in an area of the world where there are only absolutes.

---

* This was a fairly common delusion among the British at the time, right up to the Balfour Declaration in 1917. It was based on the assumption that—the Arabs and Jews both being Semitic peoples—the Jews would contribute to an Arab state their knowledge of international finance, science, and medicine, as well as the growing agricultural expertise of the Zionists. This was, and has since proved to be, overoptimistic.

It should not be supposed, however, that Sykes was a British Pangloss, who believed *Tout est pour le mieux, dans les meilleurs des mondes possibles.* Sykes had a good, if shallow, understanding of what was happening in the Middle East, but not of the complexity of interests involved. Lawrence, who liked him, would nevertheless describe him in *Seven Pillars of Wisdom* as "a bundle of prejudices, intuitions and half-sciences," and it was certainly true that Sykes was someone who leaped to the conclusion that he had understood a problem before the other person had even finished explaining it. He was, however, no fool; he brought back from his long journey, among other ideas, the perfectly correct conclusion that it was fatal to British interests in Arabia to have intelligence on that area split between so many competing departments. In Egypt, military intelligence reported to General Maxwell, the commander in chief of the Egyptian Expeditionary Force, and civilian intelligence reported to Storrs and McMahon. In Basra, military intelligence reported to the commander in chief of the Indian army in Delhi, and civilian intelligence to the viceroy in Delhi. In addition, Sir Reginald Wingate, the *sirdar,* had his own intelligence service in Khartoum. Sykes had the sensible idea of uniting all these services into a single "Arabian Bureau," in Cairo, of which he hoped to be named the chief.

In this Sykes was to be disappointed—the Arab Bureau, when it was formed, would come under Clayton, would have as its chief Lawrence's old mentor Hogarth, and would include both Lawrence and Gertrude Bell, while Sykes was sidelined for the moment to deal with the numerous complaints and problems of the French on behalf of the war cabinet, though he would remain a constant presence, in person or by cable, in Middle Eastern affairs. Of Sykes it may truly be said, in George Bernard Shaw's words, "There is nothing so bad or so good that you will not find Englishmen doing it, but you will never find an Englishman in the wrong. . . . His watchword is always duty, and he never forgets that the nation which lets its duty get on the opposite side to its interest is lost."

Sykes's return to London coincided most unfortunately with the decline in prestige of his patron, Kitchener. Among the civilian members of the war cabinet, the failure at Gallipoli and the stalemate on the western front were beginning to erode faith in Kitchener's infallibility. His reputation and his popularity with the general public made it impossible to get rid of him, but in the war cabinet he found himself increasingly isolated, and in the position of "the god that failed." Kitchener responded by increasing the length of his periods of silence, with the result that it was Sykes himself who was given the opportunity to present "every aspect of the Arab question" to the War Committee of the cabinet. He did this brilliantly—nobody was better at putting on a "bravura" performance than Sykes, unless it was Lawrence. In the eyes of many, Sykes became almost overnight *the* expert on the Arab question in London— after all, he had been in the Middle East and had met everyone concerned—despite the fact that many of his ideas were eccentric or failed to represent the experience of those on the spot, like Clayton, Hogarth, and Lawrence. A happy, wealthy, and contented man—he had among other things a large family of his own—Sykes was almost constitutionally unequipped to convey the stubborn refusal to compromise, the fierce dogmatism, or the ancient and ineradicable hatreds of the Middle East to an audience of British political figures. In Sykes's *tour d'horizon* the lion would lie down with the lamb: the views of Cairo, Khartoum, and Delhi would be reconciled; the ambitions of the French and the sharif of Mecca would both be met; and Britain would gain oil from Mesopotamia and control over Palestine to protect the Suez Canal.

Not surprisingly Sykes seemed to everybody just the right man to straighten things out with the French, so less than a week after his report to the War Committee, he was invited to attend a meeting of the "Nicolson Committee," a group of Foreign Office civil servants under the chairmanship of Sir Arthur Nicolson,* which had been attempting to thrash out the details of what the French actually wanted, or at least might be persuaded to accept. Sykes's presence, his charm, his sense of humor, and his knowledge of the Middle East, it was hoped, might reduce the acrimony

---

* The future Lord Carnock, father of the author Sir Harold Nicolson, politician, prolific author, and husband of Vita Sackville-West.

between the allies on this subject, and very soon Nicolson suggested that Sykes should sit down one to one with the "intransigent" French representative, the diplomat François Georges-Picot, and draw up a document outlining the claims of both countries.

To say that the Christmas spirit was lacking in these discussions would be putting it mildly. Although it would be only two months before the Germans launched the Battle of Verdun in an attempt to bleed the French army to death (the battle would last nine months and cost the French nearly 400,000 casualties), the French were already impatient with their British ally, which, they thought, was not pulling its weight in the war; and they were as well deeply distrustful of British policy. Picot was a master of detail and a determined negotiator, and virtually the product of French colonial ambitions. His father was a founding member of the Comité de l'Afrique Française, and his brother the treasurer of the Comité de l'Asie Française, both well-financed right-wing organizations with solid bourgeois support for the promotion of French colonialism. Picot himself had a deep, instinctive belief not only in France's *mission civilisatrice*, but in its imperative need to emerge from the war with a substantial gain in overseas territory as some compensation for the enormous sacrifices it was making. Quite apart from that, Picot, like many of the French, had an almost mystical belief in France's deep historical connections to Lebanon and Syria, going back nearly 1,000 years to the Crusades and continuing through Napoleon Bonaparte's conquest of Egypt. Syria and Lebanon were referred to as *La France du Moyen-Orient*, and in Paris it was widely assumed that the indigenous inhabitants of "France of the Middle East" were eagerly awaiting the imposition of French culture, laws, prosperity, and commerce. For a number of reasons rooted in the history of the Crusades, it was also assumed that "Syria" included not only Lebanon—You only had to look at the map, *voyons*, to see that Lebanon was nothing more than the Mediterranean coastline of Syria!—but Palestine. Had not Godefroy de Bouillon, after all, conquered Jerusalem and founded the Kingdom of Jerusalem in 1099, creating a state where 100,000 French-speaking soldiers ruled over 400,000 Muslims and Jews?

Had not the French built, during the next few centuries, the magnificent castles that Lawrence had been at such pains to study and photograph in Syria, Lebanon, and Palestine? The past spoke for itself, so far as the French were concerned—the French had led the way, and had paid for this land in blood and gold! Were their rights to be contested now by Arab nomads and sheepherders, or by the British, who had not arrived in force in this part of the world until the late nineteenth century?

Few people could have been found less well equipped to resist such arguments than Sir Mark Sykes, who had a genuine love for France, and whose strong point in any case was imagination and a concern for what we would now call the big picture. He did not, alas, have a head for details, or any willingness to argue about the meaning of every word in a text, let alone insignificant geographic features on a map. These, however, were Picot's strengths. He was tireless and well-informed; his mind was made up; and he had been sent to the negotiating table with strict, precise instructions from his government with which he was in wholehearted agreement—unlike Sykes, whose mission was merely to smooth things over with the French, and, if possible, slow them down.

"The Sykes-Picot Agreement is a shocking document . . . the product of greed at its worst, that is to say, of greed allied to suspicion and so leading to stupidity: it also stands out as a startling piece of double-dealing . . . [a] breach of faith." If even so moderate a pro-Arab historian as George Antonius, writing from New York, in 1938, only three years after Lawrence's death, can so describe the Sykes-Picot agreement, it can scarcely be wondered that Arab historians of the period today regard it as a betrayal equaled only by the partition of Palestine and the creation of Israel in 1947–1948. Few diplomatic documents in history have attracted such odium over so many decades. It now stands for most of the things Arabs resent about the Middle East as the region has evolved since 1918: the unnatural division of the Arabic-speaking area of the Ottoman Empire into relatively small states, with frontiers drawn carelessly (or sometimes cunningly) by western powers; the unequal distribution of natural wealth, including water and later oil; the opening up of Palestine to Jewish settlement (under the protection of the British flag); the imposition of royalty *à l'anglaise* on people who wanted democracy;* and much else besides.

It must be remembered, however, that when Sykes sat down with Picot the much-delayed revolt of the Arabs against the Turks had yet to begin, and there was still a good deal of doubt among the British that it ever would—or that it would amount to anything much if it did. A British army had been defeated by the Turks at Gallipoli; another British army was about to be surrounded by the Turks at Kut al-Amara; the French army was about to endure the martyrdom of Verdun, followed shortly afterward by the martyrdom of the British Expeditionary Force in the First Battle of the Somme. The possibility of persuading the sharif of Mecca to declare a revolt against the Turks and raise a few thousand ragged, if picturesque, Bedouin tribesmen to take Medina, if they could, was not foremost on the minds of those in power in London and Paris.

In *A Peace to End All Peace*, David Fromkin raises the possibility that Sykes and Clayton misunderstood each other, or that Clayton may even have attempted to deceive Sykes. This is not improbable. Clayton, after all, was a professional soldier and intelligence officer, as well as the *homme de confiance* of Sir Reginald Wingate in Cairo. He would certainly have been cautious in speaking to a wealthy and influential member of Parliament touring the Middle East on behalf of the government, even one who came dressed in the uniform of a lieutenant-colonel of the Green Howards. In fact, what really mattered was not the difference between Clayton's view of a future Arab state (that is, the view from Cairo and Khartoum) and Sykes's (that is, the view from London and Paris) but rather the assumptions they *shared*. For both of them, an Arab state, whatever its borders, would require an Arab king—a role for which they considered the sharif of Mecca admirably suited, since he was by any standards an

---

* The British had a touching faith in the value of royalty—hence their support of the princely states in India until 1947, and their eagerness to place Emir Feisal on the throne of Iraq and his brother Abdulla on the throne of Jordan; both of these "monarchies" were invented overnight on the British model. Ibn Saud, at least, turned himself into a king without British help.

imposing figure and a gentleman. They saw the Arab state, in other words, as resembling one of the larger principalities in India, with a British adviser hovering in the background among the gorgeous figures of the court; or as a clone of Egypt, with a British high commissioner pulling the strings behind a facade of "native" government. One reason why Sykes managed to make such rapid progress with the normally difficult Georges-Picot was that Picot's view of French Syria was very similar. He had in mind a native ruler very much like the one who was then sultan of Morocco, kept in power by a native army led by French officers, and kept in line by a French high commissioner who took his orders from Paris. That this was not the independent state the sharif, his sons, the Bedouin tribesmen, or the intellectuals and Arab nationalists in Damascus were expecting to get did not deter either of them.

Even Lawrence, who would do his best in 1918 "to biff the French out of Syria," did not at the time envisage a single Arab state like the one to which Sir Henry McMahon and the sharif had agreed in their correspondence. In any case, every British plan for the future of the Middle East bore within the text two escape clauses: the first was that the Arabs would have to fight the Turks and make a significant contribution to the Allies' victory; the second was that any agreement made by the British would be (in McMahon's words) "without detriment" to French claims, whatever these might be. The first had not yet happened, and the second was exactly what Sykes and Picot were trying to put down on paper.

What they came up with was very much like the famous description of a camel as a horse designed by a committee. The French received as a direct colonial possession the so-called Blue Area, including Lebanon, the port of Alexandretta, and a large chunk of what is now Syria and southern Turkey; the British received the Red Area, consisting of a good deal of what is now Iraq, from Basra to Baghdad; the A Area, consisting of what is now modern Syria and a large part of Iraq, would be reserved for a French-controlled Arab state; the B Area, consisting roughly of modern Jordan and southwestern Iraq, would be reserved for a British-controlled Arab state. Palestine would be shared by the French and British.

Even a glance at the map will show that the areas for the Arab states consisted basically of the leftovers, without ports on the Mediterranean or the Persian Gulf. As envisioned, the Arab states had no natural geographic boundaries; nor did they have any control over the great rivers or over the oil fields in Mesopotamia. The Middle East was carved up like a carcass by a careless butcher, with the Arabs being thrown the parts that nobody wanted to eat. By design, the Arab states, if they ever came to exist, would be isolated and separated; and by lack of foresight, the vast area to the south (what is now Saudi Arabia) was excluded from the map. Ibn Saud was at the time one of half a dozen ferocious rival warrior chieftains in the great desert; his capital at Riyadh was virtually unreachable. He kept the golden sovereigns he received from the government of India to prevent him from attacking the coastal sheikhdoms on the Persian Gulf, as well as the gold coins he received from the Turks to stop him from raiding Turkish outposts, locked in a wooden strongbox, bound in iron, in his tent, under the guard of his slaves. The idea that he might shortly emerge as the ruler over the world's richest supply of oil had not yet occurred to anyone, least of all himself. The wide swath of French influence, stretching from the Mediterranean to Mosul and the Persian Gulf, was due to the concern of the British about Russia—they assumed correctly that Russia would have to be cut in on the deal, and wanted the French to provide a buffer zone separating Russia from the areas to the south that protected the approaches to the west bank of the Suez Canal. It was hoped that a French zone would prevent any future attempt on the part of the Russians to march south and seize the canal, or would at least bring the French into the fight against them. Far from Picot's having cleverly squeezed Mosul and its oil fields out of a reluctant Sykes, Sykes had instead forced it on Picot.

It is a measure of the British government's relief that Sykes and Picot had achieved an agreement of any kind that the document was approved swiftly and without any particular difficulty, and Sykes was sent off to join Picot in Petrograd and secure the approval of the Russians. The Russian foreign minister, Sergey Dmitriyevich Sazonov, showed very little interest in the division of Arab-speaking areas of the Ottoman Empire, but insisted that Russia must have possession of Constantinople; must participate in the administration of Palestine, where there were ancient and important Russian Orthodox monasteries and privileges; and must receive a large chunk of the Turkish areas in the Caucasus. It seems to have been Sazonov who gave Sykes the notion that the Zionists might have something to say about Palestine, though since the czar was fiercely anti-Semitic, Sazonov may have been warning against this rather than recommending it. In any event the idea was to germinate in Sykes's mind—he was always, as Lawrence described him, "the imaginative advocate of unconvincing world movements." The notion was coupled with Sykes's sympathy for the underdog and his freedom from racial prejudice, and he soon encouraged a new and hitherto unexpected British intervention into the division of the Turkish empire, which would reemerge in the form of the Balfour Declaration in 1917.

A dawning concern that the Sykes-Picot agreement might not meet with approval outside France, Britain, and Russia led to the decision not to show it to Sir Henry McMahon for his comments before it was approved on January 5, 1916, or even afterward. It was placed in the Pandora's box of the Allies' secret agreements, and would not emerge until after the Bolshevik Revolution in 1917, when Lenin and Trotsky decided to publish in *Izvestia* and *Pravda* all the secret treaties to which the czarist government had been a party. Lawrence would claim in 1918, in Damascus, that he knew nothing about the Sykes-Picot agreement, but that is certainly untrue. Clayton knew about it, and the intelligence services Clayton headed in Cairo were run more in the spirit of an Oxford Senior Common Room than a secret government department. Keeping the actual text of the agreement from Cairo was elementary prudence, preserving what would now be called deniability—it would of course be easier for all those in Cairo to deny that they knew the contents if they hadn't seen it. Nor was Mark Sykes much good at keeping secrets—particularly when he thought he had brought off a diplomatic coup. Besides, Lawrence would later claim to have briefed Feisal on its contents. The truth seems to be that the general terms of the agreement were common knowledge by then. Those among the British who disagreed with it consoled themselves with the thought that it would be renegotiated, modified, or ignored once the Allies sat down to discuss the peace; but this consolation failed to take into account that the French, in their irritating, precise way, regarded every word of it as binding.

Lawrence's own view of the matter varied according to his mood. He did not take Sykes altogether seriously, and on the subjects of the Middle East and the Arabs' future he was inclined to regard Sykes as a lightweight. When he was exhausted by the physical and psychological stress of warfare in the desert, or by the endless difficulties of keeping the Bedouin together, he tormented himself on the subject, as in his note to Clayton from Wadi Sirhan: "I've decided to go off alone to Damascus, hoping to get killed on the way. . . . We are calling on them to fight for us on a lie, and I can't stand it." Of course Lawrence had a gift for self-dramatization, together with a need for self-punishment, but there is no doubt that this cri de coeur was genuine and would form the basis for many of the major decisions he made about his life after the war's end. No child of Sarah's could be free from a deep sense of guilt and personal responsibility, or forgive himself for obeying an order to lie about what he knew to be true. No matter how much he wanted to break free from her fierce religious beliefs, Lawrence could not—they were implanted too deeply in him to eradicate.

In his lighter moments, when things were going well, he could console himself, like many of his colleagues, with the thought that something was better than nothing—the Arabs would get one or more states, and would be better off in any case than they were under Turkish domination and misrule—but even this compromise was complicated by his determination to get the Arabs what he had promised them *despite* the Sykes-Picot agreement. Lawrence knew about McMahon and Hussein's correspondence, and noted a significant loophole in the Sykes-Picot agreement: it could be argued that if the Arabs themselves seized Damascus,

Aleppo, Hama, and Homs before the Allied forces, they might keep these cities under some form of Arab suzerainty, despite the French claim on Syria.

It became the idée fixe behind Lawrence's strategy, a secret that he withheld from all the British civil and military authorities, who would instantly have discouraged him. He, personally, would get Feisal and the Arabs to Damascus before the British or the French, and declare an independent Arab Syria before he could be stopped. Once that was done, he thought, the French would have to back down in the face of public opinion in Britain and the United States. This was the straw he clutched at, throughout 1917 and 1918.

Lawrence was kept busy with his intelligence duties; this was probably just as well, for he was informed in October 1915 that his brother Will, whom he had just missed seeing, had been listed as missing and presumed killed only a week after reaching the western front as an observer in the Royal Flying Corps. Lawrence wrote to his friend Leeds, at the Ashmolean Museum in Oxford: "I have not written to you for ever so long. . . . It's partly being so busy here, that one's thoughts are all on the jobs one is doing, and one grudges doing anything else . . . and partly because I'm rather low because first one and now another of my brothers has been killed. . . . I rather dread Oxford and what it may be like if one comes back. Also, they were both younger than I am, and it doesn't seem right somehow, that I should go on living peacefully in Cairo."

As 1916 began, there was nothing to suggest that Lawrence would ever get into combat. Work in Cairo was complicated by the fact that there were now three armies to keep informed: the former Mediterranean Expeditionary Force, commanded by Lieutenant-General Sir Archibald Murray, which had been evacuated from Gallipoli; the British "Force in Egypt," commanded by General Sir John Maxwell, which was responsible for defending the Suez Canal; and the Egyptian army, of which General Sir Reginald Wingate was the *sirdar*. Lawrence complained that there were at least 108 generals in Cairo, and while that may have been an exaggeration, there were certainly enough generals, together with their staffs, to make Lawrence remark to Leeds, "I'm fed up, and fed up, and fed up:—and yet we have to go on doing it, and indeed we take on new jobs every day." His daily intelligence bulletins would soon be converted into the famous *Arab Bulletin*, the brainchild of Hogarth, who came out to Cairo in the uniform of a temporary lieutenant-commander of the Royal Navy Volunteer Reserve to oversee intelligence matters, and brought with him Gertrude Bell, whose knowledge of the Arab tribes would prove invaluable. The *Arab Bulletin* was a secret news sheet that quickly grew into a regularly published magazine, of which only twenty-one copies of each issue were initially printed, and which contained the latest information on the Turkish army, as well all the news from inside the Ottoman Empire that could be gleaned from agents and from Turkish prisoners of war. Lawrence was working at least thirteen hours a day, seven days a week. In addition to his previous duties, he was responsible for collecting information about each of the eighty or so divisions of the Turkish army. The only one of them that was "really settled," he joked to Leeds (ignoring the censor), "the one we 'defeat' from time to time on the canal, is located in the Caucasus by the Russians, at Pardima by the Athens people, in Adrianople by Bulgaria, at Midia by Roumania, and in Bagdad by India. The locations of the other thirty-nine regular, and fourty reserve divisions are less certain." Lawrence was thus in regular touch with the intelligence services of all the Allied nations, and indeed was sent to Athens on a quick trip to help straighten out matters there. As for the Russians, who were fighting the better part of the Turkish regular army in the Caucasus, Lawrence apparently reached out on his own, on the basis of information obtained from the interrogation of the Arab deserter from the Turkish forces, al-Faruqi, "to put the Grand Duke Nicholas in touch with certain disaffected [Turkish] officers in Erzurum," thus making possible the successful Russian assault on this important fortress town in February 1916.

These were deep waters and confirm the fact that Lawrence was not only being treated as a wunderkind by his superiors in Cairo and in

London, but also being encouraged (or at any rate allowed) to expand his reach in every direction. His role in the multifaceted and confusing intelligence world in Egypt remained anomalous, however, even after March 1916, when Clayton and Hogarth simplified the competing intelligence departments in Egypt. The Arab Bureau was housed in a few rooms in the Savoy Hotel, and its mission was to study and develop British policy toward Arabia, a rather vague directive that allowed Hogarth to move and influence events throughout the Arab world, from Basra, where he sent Gertrude Bell to represent him, to Syria and, of course, Mecca, where Sharif Hussein was still promising a revolt and demanding money and weapons. Although Lawrence was unable to transfer himself from the uncongenial task of providing intelligence reports for the headquarters of the two separate British armies as well as the Egyptian army, and would not join the Arab Bureau until October 1916, he could hardly fail to benefit from Hogarth's presence; and he added to his already substantial list of tasks that of liaison between the various military intelligence departments and the fledging Arab Bureau, most of whose members were civilians, including two members of Parliament: Aubrey Herbert and George Lloyd, both friends of Sykes. The Arab Bureau was thus intended from the outset to be a fairly high-powered organization, with many back-channel connections to the War Office and the war cabinet. It would have considerably more clout than the military intelligence departments in Cairo and Ismailia. Its aim, as Sykes, Clayton, and Hogarth conceived it, was both to encourage the Arab Revolt, and to outmaneuver Paris and Delhi in determining British policy and postwar ambitions in Arabia. The first point was of great importance, since the British now had a substantial number of troops in Egypt who were contributing nothing significant to the war effort, and whom Sir William Robertson, GCB, GCMG, GCVO, DSO, the chief of the Imperial General Staff, and the French would rather have seen fighting Germans on the western front than sitting idly around Cairo and Ismailia.

General Maxwell's attempts to break through the Turkish lines and take Gaza had resulted in failure, and the British had suffered three times the casualties of the enemy—further proof, if any were needed, of the dogged powers of resistance of Turkish troops under the command of the brilliant German General Friedrich Freiherr Kress von Kressenstein,* whose masterly planning of the entrenchments and artillery around Gaza made it virtually impregnable. Kress had ingeniously combined trenches, machine gun nests, barbed wire, and large preexisting areas of native cactus into a formidable defense system. In addition, the presence of two British armies in Egypt made the French particularly unhappy, since they were deeply suspicious of British intentions in the Middle East, and feared that their ally would try to do them out of Syria by conquering it with British forces, kept in Egypt for just this purpose.

It was not just the Arab Bureau that was created in March 1916: events now began to move rapidly in the Middle East. On instructions from the Foreign Office, the £50,000 in gold coins that Sharif Hussein had been demanding as a down payment for the Arab Revolt was paid at last, and at the same time a large stockpile of rifles and ammunition was begun at Port Sudan, to be shipped across the Red Sea to Jidda as soon as the revolt broke out. The British Force in Egypt and the British Mediterranean Expeditionary Force (the latter survivors of the disaster at Gallipoli) were at last united into one army, henceforth called the Egyptian Expeditionary Force (EEF) and placed under the command of General Murray. Prodded by Kitchener, Murray decided it was wasteful to man a British defense line the length of the Suez Canal; he moved his forces forward to El Arish and began to build up a serious network of desert roads,† a narrow-gauge railway for supplies, and a water pipeline across the desert, without all of which he correctly believed no attack on Gaza could possibly succeed.

---

*Kress von Kressenstein shared his command for form's sake with a Turkish general, Tala Bey, and both were overseen from Damascus by Jemal Pasha, who was both the political and the military chief of the Syrian, Lebanese, and Palestinian portions of the Ottoman Empire.

† The key to building roads in the desert was to lay down wire netting, so that vehicles did not get bogged down in the sand—a huge job of physical labor that was performed for the most part by Egyptians.

Lawrence had not been forgotten in all these great changes. Both in Paris and in London, there were signs of the unusual respect in which this comparatively junior young officer—he was then twenty-seven—was held by those at the center of events. By one of the strange coincidences that often mark Lawrence's life, on March 18 he was awarded—much to his surprise and dismay, given his determination "to biff the French out of Syria"—the French Légion d'Honneur, and almost simultaneously he was picked, with Kitchener's approval, for not one but two delicate and secret tasks in Mesopotamia.

The first task was to assess and report back on the possibility of an Arab uprising there, a project that appealed to everybody in Cairo but was stubbornly resisted by the Indian government. Even though Lawrence carried with him a letter from Sir Henry McMahon to Sir Percy Z. Cox, the chief political officer in Basra, the very last thing Cox and the viceroy wanted to do was to light the flame of Arab nationalism in a part of the Ottoman Empire they hoped to secure for India. Although Kitchener himself was in favor of it, the idea of sending prominent Arab nationalist officers who either had been captured or had deserted from the Turkish army from Cairo to Basra, to link up with Arab nationalist figures there, was fiercely resisted in Delhi. Lawrence's role was to seek out these figures, most of whom were known to Gertrude Bell, and report back to Cairo on their potential, as well as to give Cairo a clearer picture in general of how intelligence was being gathered in Mesopotamia. Needless to say, this dual role—that of a critical outsider and a snooper—did not make Lawrence popular in Basra; nor did the fact that he was also supposed to tell the Royal Flying Corps and the Indian army intelligence staff in Basra that their method of using serial aerial photography to produce maps—another subject on which he had made himself an expert—was all wrong. At the best of times, Lawrence's manner of dealing with those who disagreed with him was likely—and often calculated—to provoke resentment, and in Basra he seems to have been at his worst, perhaps because officers in the Indian army were sticklers for pukka sahib dress and behavior, perhaps too because they were inclined to treat

Arabs as they would Indian "natives," with a mixture of racial superiority and brutality that shocked and offended Lawrence.

Lawrence's second task was more delicate still, and even more bound to create local resentment, since it involved the consequences of an embarrassing defeat. In 1915 an Anglo-Indian army under the command of Major-General Charles Townshend, KCB, had moved north from Basra with the intention of taking Baghdad, and came very close to doing so after a significant victory over the Turks at Ctesiphon, less than thirty miles away. At that point, however, the exhaustion of Townshend's troops, the precarious length of his line of communication to Basra, and the astonishing ability of the Turks to revive after a defeat forced Townshend back until he reached the small town of Kut al-Amara on the Tigris River, just over 200 miles from Basra, where the Turks very quickly managed to surround and besiege him.

Opinions differ as to whether Townshend might have captured Baghdad if he had pushed on boldly after his victory at Ctesiphon, or whether, once he started to retreat, he should have paused in Kut, but once he was there he was stuck. Since he could no longer feed the horses, he sent his cavalry south, and proceeded to fortify the town. His original force of 30,000 men was by then already reduced to less than half of that by death, wounds, and sickness—the area around Kut was a hellhole of humidity and heat, made even more intolerable by clouds of stinging black flies and malaria-carrying mosquitoes. By December 7, a week after their arrival, they were surrounded by Turkish troops under the effective command of the formidable Field Marshal Colmar Freiherr von der Goltz, an elderly but skilled German general (and a respected military historian), and the Turkish general Khalil Pasha, a nephew of the Ottoman minister of war Enver Pasha. They made three attacks on Kut in December, but eventually decided to dig siege works around the town and block the river to prevent supplies from reaching Townshend. From January through April 1916 the British made four gallant attempts to relieve Kut, all of which were driven back, costing nearly 30,000 British and Indian casualties, while the Turks lost less than 10,000. One of the Turkish casualties was

Field Marshal von der Goltz, who died of typhoid fever and was replaced by the Turkish commander of Mesopotamia, Khalil Pasha. In wretched, crowded, unsanitary conditions, with poor sanitation, every kind of disease raging, and no healthy drinking water, the British force was diminishing rapidly, and by April 22 it was clear that there was no option left except unconditional surrender. As for Townshend himself, he was beginning to lose either his nerve or his hold on reality.

Surrendering an Anglo-Indian army to the Turks was thought to be an unacceptable humiliation, particularly by the government of India, which feared the loss in native eyes of British prestige. The situation was made worse because the majority of Townshend's unfortunate troops were Indian and there were no illusions about what would become of the garrison once they were force-marched into Turkish prisoner-of-war camps. Townshend, in a fit of desperation, proposed that he be authorized to offer the Turkish commander £1 million in gold and the surrender of his forty guns in exchange for letting him and his troops "go free on parole." Surprisingly, though this suggestion infuriated Sir Percy Cox and British senior officers in Basra and Delhi, it found favor with Kitchener, who feared the loss of British prestige throughout Asia if Townshend surrendered. Townshend, as it turned out, perhaps through wishful thinking, had overrated the willingness of Khalil Pasha to negotiate; and what Kitchener had in mind was a two-pronged approach, which involved stirring up Arab desertion and resistance within the Turkish army to put more pressure on the Ottoman government to offer reasonable terms. Since neither Cox nor anybody else in Basra wanted anything to do with either part of the scheme, somebody else was needed to carry it out.

The choice of Aubrey Herbert—Sir Mark Sykes's friend, a fellow member of Parliament, and a member of the Arab Bureau in Cairo—was a natural one. Herbert was a Turcophile, spoke Turkish, and knew most of the Turkish leaders personally; also, he was urbane, sophisticated, and cosmopolitan, the ideal person to offer Khalil Pasha what was, in effect, a £1 million bribe. Lawrence was chosen to accompany Herbert because he spoke Arabic. His chief role was to make contact with Arab nationalist officers in the Turkish army who might join with Arab nationalist figures in Basra and Baghdad to start a revolt—or at least shake Khalil's confidence in his Arab troops. Since this was exactly what Lawrence had done when he provided Grand Duke Nicholas with the names of dissident Arab officers before the Russian attack on Erzurum, it was no doubt hoped that he could perform the same trick twice. The original idea had been to send a senior Arab officer on parole in Cairo to cross the lines and open negotiations with Khalil Pasha, but Cox firmly squashed this, with the result that it was left to Lawrence to make his way up the Tigris on a steamer, a journey of six days, followed soon afterward by Herbert. Lawrence arrived to undergo a difficult interview with the commander of the relief forces, General Sir Percy Lake, KCB, KCMG, and then almost immediately succumbed to a fever, probably a recurrence of his malaria, made worse by the marshy, humid, sweltering air.

During Lawrence's illness, the last attempt to relieve Kut failed, as did an attempt on April 24 to breach the Turkish blockade of the Tigris with a river steamer loaded with supplies. By this time, Townshend had opened negotiations with Khalil Pasha for the surrender of his force. He had been hoping that General Lake would do the negotiating for him—the idea of offering Khalil £1 million in gold to let Townshend's forces go was a hot potato, which neither general wanted to touch; but in the end it was left to Townshend, who, in Aubrey Herbert's words, "fears he is going to be blamed whatever happens," a fear which was fully justified. Although Khalil was "extremely nice," as Townshend put it, he proved to be a difficult, wily, and cautious negotiator, so Townshend, perhaps hoping, if nothing else, to spread the blame, requested a safe-conduct for three British officers—Colonel W. H. Beach (the head of Indian army intelligence in Basra); Captain Aubrey Herbert, MP; and Captain T. E. Lawrence—to join him in Kut as his "delegates" in the negotiations. By April 28 Townshend had offered Khalil £1 million, and Khalil had courteously declined it, under orders from his uncle Enver Pasha in Constantinople, who saw here an opportunity for a propaganda coup even more rewarding than the money. Townshend then sought permission to raise the offer to £2 million. On April 29, having failed to materially improve any of Khalil's terms, Townshend destroyed his guns (thereby losing his last bargaining chip) and finally surrendered. By that time Beach, Herbert, and Lawrence were already on their way upstream for their meeting with Khalil, which was now pointless. As it turned out, Herbert's command of Turkish and Lawrence's command of Arabic proved unnecessary, since the conversation took place in French, but it produced no results, even when Colonel Beach raised the offer to £3 million.* Lawrence described the colonel in a letter home as "about 32 or 33, very keen & energetic but not clever or intelligent I thought." Lawrence complained that when he arrived back he would "be nailed within that office at Cairo," again, and asked his parents to have a new pair of brown shoes made for him, and to send his copy of Aristophanes—a sign that he was still unaware of how much his life was about to change.

Lawrence was sickened by conditions around Kut—it combined all the horrors of trench warfare on the western front with humid, intense heat, unburied bodies, and dense clouds of biting insects—and by the sheer futility of what he was doing there. Townshend's troops were force-marched across the desert to indescribably brutal prisoner-of-war camps, preyed on by raiding Arabs along the way. Nearly three-quarters of the British troops and half of the Indian troops would be worked or starved to death in captivity, whereas Townshend himself was held in luxurious quarters in a villa on the island of Malki.

In the early summer of 1916, it seemed, in fact, that the British effort in the Middle East was an abject failure. Despite the prevailing contempt for the Turks, and the many glaring deficiencies of their army and government, de Robeck's attempt to attack Constantinople by sea had failed, the British landing at Gallipoli had failed, and the British attack on Baghdad had ended in a humiliating debacle, as had every attempt to break through the Turkish lines at Gaza. Ramshackle though the Ottoman

---

* £3 million would be about $240,000,000 today. If it was to have been paid in gold, the current value would be in the billions!

Empire might be, it had successfully resisted every British attempt to defeat it—only the Russians, whose empire was hardly less ramshackle than that of the Turks, had put a dent in it so far.

Lawrence returned from Basra raging against the inefficiencies of the Anglo-Indian army and administration in Basra, and spent his time on the ship writing a long report criticizing everything from the quality of the lithograph stones used in printing maps to the method of unloading supplies on the docks at Basra. Indeed, the missive was so vitriolic that General Murray's staff insisted on toning it down before it was shown to him, which was probably just as well for Lawrence. The reorganization of the intelligence departments in Cairo was in full swing, and Lawrence found himself answering to three different departments again, neither in the Arab Bureau nor altogether out of it, and at odds with the staff and the demands of the Egyptian Expeditionary Force intelligence department, toward whom he took an increasingly haughty and insulting tone.

On June 5, two events of great importance occurred. One, which was front-page news all over the world, was the death of Field Marshal the Earl Kitchener, who was traveling to Russia on board the armored cruiser HMS *Hampshire* when it struck a German mine and went down in the North Sea, drowning Kitchener, his staff, and most of the crew. The other was the outbreak, at long last, of the Arab Revolt. Informed that a force of nearly 4,000 Turkish soldiers accompanied by "a German field mission led by Baron Othmar von Stotzingen" was going to march through the Hejaz to reinforce the Turkish force in Yemen, and shocked by the execution in Beirut and Damascus of twenty-one Arab nationalists, many of them known to Hussein and his sons, Sharif Hussein drew the conclusion that the Ottoman government intended to overthrow and replace him. The sharif himself fired the opening shot of the revolt, with a rifle, through a window in his palace, aimed at the nearby Turkish headquarters.

Thwarted on every other front in the war against Turkey, the British moved quickly. Abdulla had already warned the British on May 23 that the revolt was imminent, and as a result Hogarth and Storrs were already on their way to Hejaz, carrying £10,000 in gold sovereigns, as requested.

After innumerable delays and adventures, Storrs finally met with Zeid, rather than Abdulla, and was told that the revolt had already begun—or was about to begin, Zeid was not sure—and that his father required an immediate payment of £70,000 in gold, delivery of a long list of military supplies and equipment, and assurance that the annual pilgrimage of Indian Muslims to Mecca—on which much of Mecca's prosperity depended—would not be impeded by the British. Storrs noted that Zeid brought his entourage on board HMS *Dufferin*, including a pet gazelle "pronging playfully at strangers and eating cigarettes off the mess table."

The sharif's arrangements produced an overwhelming initial success— the Turkish garrison in Mecca surrendered; the Turkish force in Taif, where well-to-do Meccans went to escape the summer heat, was besieged (it did not surrender until September); and the Turkish garrison of Jidda, Mecca's port, surrendered after being bombarded from the sea by HMS *Fox*. Medina, it was optimistically forecast, would fall at any moment to the forces lead by the emirs Feisal and Abdulla. After nearly two years of promises, extravagant demands, and delays, the Arab uprising seemed at last to be under way.

Lawrence, though still deskbound, was delighted. "This revolt," he wrote home, "will be the biggest thing in the Near East since 1550." All the same, he was limited to such roles as overseeing the printing of maps, and designing stamps for the sharif of Mecca at the request of Storrs. The stamps were a political necessity. It was obviously impossible for Hejaz to continue using Ottoman stamps, and it was important to portray the Hejaz as an actual independent Arab state, rather than a former Ottoman province. Lawrence expended considerable energy and imagination on the project, hunting up Arabic designs in mosques, overseeing the engraving and the printing, and making plans "to have flavored gum on the back, so that one may lick without unpleasantness." The flavored gum turned out to be a mistake—Lawrence produced a fla- vor so tasty to the Arabs that they licked all the gum off and then couldn't stick the stamp to the envelope—but he was able to send a few samples home for his youngest brother, Arnie, noting that they might be valuable one day, and that "things are not going too well" in Arabia, despite the initial successes.

What was not going well was the attempt to take Medina, where the Turks had 14,000 troops, well provided with artillery and supplied by rail from Damascus, against whom the Arab tribesmen, mostly carrying antiquated rifles, could make no headway. The sharif, Lawrence noted in his letter home of October 10, "has a sense of humor," an opinion which he would soon change, but noted "his weakness is in military operations." Lawrence complained about the volume of his work, and the amount of interruptions he had to endure in answering telephone calls from the staff, with whom he was fighting a kind of bureaucratic guerrilla war in order to get himself transferred once and for all to the more congenial Arab Bureau. He does not mention the fact that within forty-eight hours he would be on his way to Jidda in the company of Storrs. Storrs wrote in his diary, "12. X. 16. On the train from Cairo little Lawrence my super-cerebral companion."

Just nine days later, Storrs waved good-bye to Lawrence at Rabegh, from where Lawrence was to ride into the desert for his first meeting with Feisal. "Long before we met again," Storrs wrote later, "he had already begun to write his page, brilliant as a Persian miniature, in the History of England."

CHAPTER SEVEN

1917: "The Uncrowned King of Arabia"

After Aqaba Lawrence appeared to some a different person. He was no longer an intelligence officer observing the war from a distance; he had become a warrior, already famous and much admired. He had not only fought and won a significant victory against the Turks—in contrast to the British defeat at Gallipoli and the shame of General Townshend's surrender at Kut—but also ridden far behind the enemy lines with a price on his head. He had discovered that his name, his impatience with routine, his unorthodox opinions about war, and even his appearance were weapons more powerful than guns, swords, and high explosives. When he thought that humility and modesty were called for, Lawrence could give an excellent performance of both. He had an Englishman's understanding of the value of those qualities and the degree to which they mattered to other Englishmen of his class, but there was not in fact anything remotely humble or modest about him, as Allenby had instantly perceived. Allenby possessed to the full that most important of skills in a good general, handling men; and throughout the next two years he handled Lawrence brilliantly. In a metaphor that is entirely appropriate to apply to a cavalryman, Allenby rode Lawrence on the loosest of reins, giving him his head, and allowing him to pick his own way forward over difficult ground. With a few notable exceptions, he gave Lawrence goals and directives, and allowed him to reach them in his own way.

Neither Lawrence nor the men he led and served would have been useful if handled in any other way. The Bedouin could be inspired by the right leader, and they could be bribed or shamed into doing great things, but they did not obey orders or submit to threats, so the discipline of a conventional army was beyond them: Lawrence relied instead on the strength of his own personality, and on his seemingly endless supply of British gold sovereigns.

Different as they were—Allenby was huge, overbearing, and notoriously abrupt and outspoken; Lawrence was, by comparison, tiny, soft-spoken, and inclined to be tactful, enigmatic, and often indirect—the two men became, at any rate in public and in their correspondence with each other, a kind of mutual admiration society. Their relationship survived the war, the publication of *Seven Pillars of Wisdom*, and even the fact that Allenby, perhaps the most successful and competent British general of World War I, found himself living in Lawrence's shadow, a supporting player in an epic where "Lawrence of Arabia" was the star.

Allenby was astute enough, from the beginning, to allow Lawrence direct access, an immense concession for a busy army commander, whom even major-generals approached warily through his chief of staff. To put this in perspective, it is as if an acting major commanding a small force of French guerrillas behind enemy lines had direct access to Eisenhower whenever he pleased in the second half of 1944. It was shrewd of Allenby to see that Lawrence would never be able to go through the normal chain of command, and also to understand, perhaps better than Lawrence himself, that Lawrence's curiously inverted vanity and sense of being "special" could be satisfied only by going directly to the top. For a long time Lawrence was accused of not taking his own rank seriously, and that is certainly true. In later years he always talked about "Colonel Lawrence" as if that were a separate person, whose legend kept on growing, marching on indestructibly while the real Lawrence sought to hide. But the truth was that Lawrence considered himself, from the first, above such commonplace things as rank. Once, he had expressed an ambition to be a general and knighted before he was thirty; now, neither of those ambitions, though both were within his grasp, was enough to satisfy him. He had become, instead, something much more: a hero on a grand, unconventional, and glamorous scale.

On his arrival in Cairo on July 10, 1917, after the capture of Aqaba, Lawrence told Clayton, his nominal superior officer, that there was much more he could do, if Clayton "thought I had earned the right to be my own master," a telling phrase, and produced a sketch map of his plans— ambitious enough to startle Allenby when he saw it. Lawrence proposed to use seven separate Arab "forces" to disrupt the Turkish railway system, from Homs and Hama, north of Damascus, to Maan in the south, and to threaten vital railway lines and junctions deep inside Lebanon and Palestine, throwing Turkish communications into confusion, and perhaps even seizing Damascus.

With his usual quick mind, Lawrence had guessed that Allenby's intention was to advance from El Arish to Jerusalem, though he could not have known that David Lloyd George, on sending Allenby out to replace General Murray, had said "that he wanted Jerusalem as a Christmas present for the British people." Allenby was determined to give Lloyd George what he wanted, and instantly saw the advantages of using the Arabs to disrupt Turkish communications and supply lines, rather than have them try once more to take Medina, and probably fail again. He had also been concerned, not unnaturally, about advancing on Gaza and Beersheba with his right flank "in the air," a position no competent general wants to find himself in. Despite the forbidding terrain and the lack of roads between the coastline of Palestine and the Dead Sea, an enterprising Turkish or German commander could still assemble a force large enough to strike westward against Allenby; and Lawrence was proposing to fill this vacuum with Arab irregulars, advancing north from Aqaba parallel to Allenby's line of march. Feisal's forces, whatever they might be—both Feisal and Lawrence were often wildly optimistic about numbers—would become Allenby's extended right flank, freeing him to feint at Gaza, then use all his strength to advance on Beersheba and outflank the Turkish lines.

Allenby did not necessarily expect Lawrence to succeed with these ambitious plans, but so long as Lawrence and the Arabs were active on his right and cut Turkish telegraph wires, he would be content. The Turks who were engaged in patrolling or repairing the single-line railway to Medina, defending Medina and Maan against Arab raiders from the desert, would be pinned down, unable to be moved quickly to threaten his right flank. For all practical purposes in the battle to come, they might as well not exist.

Lawrence moved fast to capitalize on his newfound position. He secured Allenby's permission to transfer his base from faraway Wejh to Aqaba—no easy task, because it involved securing Hussein's agreement to place Feisal and his Arab forces under Allenby's command, as well as squaring General Wingate in Khartoum, and drawing on the stores at Rabegh that had been intended for Abdulla's use. The shifting relationships between Sharif Hussein's sons, consistent only in their obedience to their stern father's authority, required a constant, careful study of the Hashemite family and its moods, a subject on which Lawrence was already an expert. It also involved something he did not regret: further friction with the French, who wanted to see the Arab army tied up trying to take Medina, as opposed to seeing it in a position to advance into Syria. Indeed Colonel Brémond and the French military mission were in Jidda for the main purpose of preventing this.

One by one, these difficulties were sorted out. Clayton wisely chose, with Lawrence's agreement, Lieutenant-Colonel Pierce Charles Joyce to take command at Aqaba, and turn it into a secure base for the Arab army, leaving Lawrence free to go inland without worrying about supplies and support. Joyce, who had been offended by Lawrence's unmilitary appearance and flippant manner when they had met briefly at Port Sudan in

1916, had become a convert, and would be a lifelong friend and admirer. On paper, Joyce was Lawrence's commander, but in fact he was the firmly planted anchor to Lawrence's ambitious schemes, a broad, six-foot-tall pillar of strength, common sense, and knowledge of how to get things done by the book and—more important—*despite* the book, in the army.

Lawrence was sent off at once to explain matters to King Hussein. The sharif had announced his newly assumed title as king of the Hejaz late in 1916, over the repeated objections of the British, who feared the effect this would have on ibn Saud as well as on the presumably more democratically-minded Arab nationalists in Syria. Lawrence boarded HMS *Dufferin*, which had been placed at his disposal, and stopped for one day in Wejh. There the RFC provided an airplane to fly him 100 miles inland to Jeida, "a little palm garden," where Feisal and Joyce were encamped. It is a mark of Lawrence's new status that naval ships and aircraft were now his for the asking. At Jeida, comfortable under the palms, he discussed with Feisal the best way of approaching his father, and also a new factor in the Arab army. Jaafar Pasha, a Baghdadi who was a former Turkish officer, had become Feisal's chief of staff and had also organized a number of Arab prisoners of war from the Turkish army into a uniformed group, quite separate from the Bedouin tribesmen who made up the bulk of Feisal's forces. Jaafar's regulars were professional soldiers, not irregulars, and while their number was still small, they would play an increasingly important role in the Arab army.

In Jidda, Lawrence met King Hussein, whom he described as "an obstinate, narrow-minded, suspicious character, little likely to sacrifice his vanity to forward a unity of control." This was putting it mildly— almost all the British, while they admired him as a "splendid old gentleman," found Hussein difficult to deal with, unreasonable, intolerably long-winded, and vain. The only exception was Ronald Storrs, who had been negotiating with the old man since 1914, and described him more generously as a "gracious and venerable patriarch . . . of unparalleled dignity and deportment," and whom the king in turn addressed familiarly as *ya ibni* ("my son") or *ya azizi* ("my dear").

Toward Lawrence, King Hussein seems to have been more than usually suspicious, perhaps because of Lawrence's youth, perhaps because
he feared Lawrence's growing influence over Feisal, perhaps because the
shrewd old man guessed that Lawrence's passion for the Arab cause was
deeply conflicted, that he did not so much want to give the Arabs what
they wanted as what the British wanted them to have. In any case Colonel
Wilson, General Wingate's patient and long-suffering representative in
Jidda, managed to talk Hussein around to the advantages of putting
Feisal under Allenby's command instead of his own; and with that the
king lapsed into a long and "discursive" description, "as usual without
obvious coherence," of his religious beliefs, a tactic he seems to have
used with British visitors to prevent them from asking questions he did
not want to answer. For their part, both Wilson and Lawrence were
embarrassed by the supposition that they knew more about the Sykes-
Picot agreement than the king did and by trying to put the best light on
it they could—wasted efforts, since the king by now surely knew more
about the treaty than he let on, and was better at dissembling than either
of them.

Lawrence seems to have made a quick, unauthorized visit to Mecca, a
city closed to unbelievers, certainly without the knowledge of the king or
Feisal, to shop for a gold dagger to replace one that he had given to a
Howeitat chief. For an Arab of Lawrence's rank to go without a curved
gold dagger in his belt was the equivalent of being "half-naked," and he
was determined to have the best and the lightest dagger that could be
made, one that would establish his sharifian status at a glance. Though in
general Lawrence disliked being tied down by possessions, there were
certain areas in which he was unapologetically extravagant, and in which
only the best would do: pistols, fine bookbindings, motorcycles, the art
he commissioned for *Seven Pillars of Wisdom*, and the famous dagger
were all examples of this. He would later write in detail about ordering
the dagger from a goldsmith named Gasein, "in the third little turning
to the left off the main bazaar," and once it was delivered, he would wear
it through the rest of the war, whenever he was in Arab dress. It would

become something of a trademark, and was often wrongly described as being the symbol of "a prince of Mecca," a title which did not exist, and which he never claimed.

The pleasure Lawrence felt at the king's rapid assent was marred by news from Cairo that Auda Abu Tayi and his Howeitat were in secret negotiations with the Turks, which, if they succeeded, would have meant the loss of Aqaba, and everything that Lawrence had planned. Lawrence's naval friend Captain Boyle provided him with a fast armed steamship, HMS *Hardinge*, to take him at flank speed north to Aqaba, where Nasir told him that the Turks had indeed already retaken several outposts and gave him a "swift camel" and a guide to take him to Auda's camp in the desert. Lawrence intended to surprise Auda, and did—he "dropped in on them," walking unarmed into Auda's tent, where the old warrior was in conversation with his confederates, just in time to join in their meal. After the ritual fulsome greetings of desert courtesy, Lawrence revealed that he knew about Auda's correspondence with the Turks, and was even able to quote phrases from the letters that had passed between Auda and the governor of Maan. Auda dismissed it all with a laugh—unbeknownst to him, he explained, one of his men who could read and write had sent a letter to the Turkish governor under Auda's seal, seeking out terms for his switching sides. The governor had agreed on a price, and to a demand for a down payment. When Auda found out about it, he caught the messenger with the gold in the desert and robbed him "to the skin," for his own benefit. It was a mere matter of business—brigandage being the main business of the Bedouin.

Behind this farce, however, Lawrence correctly divined that Auda had grievances strong enough to tempt him to seek out better terms from the Turks, one of them being that Lawrence was receiving more attention than Auda for the capture of Aqaba, and the other that the gold Auda had been promised was slow in coming. Lawrence explained in detail what was on the way—more gold, rifles, ammunition, food—and made "a down payment" on the gold that would be coming to Auda when Feisal arrived in Aqaba with the rest of the army. Like two old friends, they laughed over the incident, but it served as a lesson to Lawrence that even the best of the Bedouin were cold and crafty, and that it was foolhardy to make them wait for their money. Henceforth, sacks of gold sovereigns would always be the most urgent of his supplies, more important by far than high explosives, ammunition, or fuse wire.

Showing a capacity for duplicity that equaled Auda's, Lawrence then returned on the *Hardinge* to Cairo, where he declared that he had looked into the situation and that there was "no spirit of treachery abroad," and vouched for Auda's loyalty. In this Lawrence recognized a great truth; "the crowd wanted book-heroes," and would never understand the complexity of a man like Auda, who not only was moved by greed for gold, but, as a tribal leader, would always want to keep a way open to the enemy. Over the next two years Lawrence would have many occasions to deal with the combination of greed and caution that was a natural part of Arab politics, an instinctive survival mechanism that would emerge in moments of setback or defeat, and that had to be concealed at all costs from the simpler minds of the British leaders.

Lawrence's duplicity has been an issue for some who have written about him, and in fact a number of biographies are intended to debunk him wholly or in part. This is partly Lawrence's own fault. He sometimes embellished the truth, and he invariably placed himself at the center of events, but it must be said that when the British government finally released most of the papers and documents relating to Lawrence, almost everything he claimed was confirmed in meticulous detail. Sir Ernest Dowson, KBE, the director-general of the Egyptian Survey, who had clashed sharply with Lawrence over the transliteration of Arabic place-names on maps in 1914 and later became an admirer, remarked on his "puckishness," and went on to comment: "Many men of sense and ability were repelled by the impudence, freakishness and frivolity he trained so provocatively . . . and regarded him in consequence at the bottom as a posturing stage player whose tinsel exploits were the fruits of freely lavished gold." (Dowson also shrewdly observed that it was "idle to pretend he was not ambitious. He was vastly so. But, like all men of large calibre, he was ambitious for achievement rather than recognition.")

The fact remains that Lawrence loved to "take the Mickey out of someone" as the English say, particularly if that person was pompous, obstructive, or slow to give him what he wanted, and not everyone enjoyed being on the receiving end, or forgave him for the experience.

A sense of humor is often the most difficult thing to convey about great men. Winston Churchill, for example, certainly had a robust sense of humor, but it was very often at the expense of people who were in no position to answer back,* and reads badly in cold print. Something similar is true of Lawrence. With him, exaggeration was a form of teasing rather than boasting, and was usually aimed at those who were senior to him in rank and slow to recognize his ability. Once he had joined the ranks as a simple aircraftman or soldier after the war, he never did it to his barracks mates; he targeted only officers who had provoked him by some form of injustice to those mates.

Warfare and politics, of course, are a different matter; in both, duplicity is a weapon, and Lawrence used it expertly. During the war Lawrence was obliged to conceal from his Arab friends the ambitions of France and Britain in the territory the Arabs supposed themselves to be fighting for, as well as to conceal from his British superiors the problems of the Arab army. He was not Sarah's son for nothing, however—tactics and politics apart, in the things that mattered most to him he always told the truth, however painful for others or himself.

No sooner was Lawrence back at Aqaba—which was rapidly being transformed into an armed base, with a landing strip for the RFC and a stone jetty built by British sailors for unloading supplies—than a letter from Sir Mark Sykes brought alarming hints that the British government was secretly negotiating with the Ottoman government in the hope of Tur-

---

* To be fair, this was also true of Franklin D. Roosevelt, and of course vastly more true of Stalin, whose sense of humor was directed at his terrified subordinates, and was distinctly cruel and sinister in tone.

Middle Eastern diplomacy: Sir Mark Sykes's cartoon of himself negotiating with Sharif Hussein in Jidda.

key's accepting a negotiated peace. It was not only Auda who was putting out feelers to the Turks. In the absence of a significant British victory, a negotiated peace with Turkey was a constant temptation to a wily politician like Lloyd George. From the British point of view, it would have freed large numbers of troops in the Middle East to reinforce the British Expeditionary Force (BEF) on the western front in France for the one big attack that might perhaps bring the war to an end in 1917; and it would no doubt have negated all British promises to the Arabs. From the Turks' point of view, it would have enabled them to get out of the war with the minimum of loss to their empire, and to reexert Turkish hegemony over Arabs, Kurds, Christians, and Jews, and whatever remained of the Armenian population after the genocide.* Sykes, ever the enthusiast, claimed

---

* The lowest estimate for the number of Armenians murdered by the Turks in 1915 is somewhere between 1 million and 1.5 million.

to have returned to London and put an end to this attempt by facing down Lloyd George—a delusion, given the prime minister's habit of making promises he had no intention of keeping. Sykes was just as overconfident of his ability to handle Lloyd George as he was of his ability to handle Picot and King Hussein. As usual, Sykes was bubbling over with contradictory ideas: Lawrence should be given a knighthood for what he had accomplished so far, and must persuade the Arabs that they would be better off in the end under ten years of British rule, or "tutelage," as Sykes put it gracefully, before achieving independence. The French must be made to see that French colonial rule over the Arabs was out of the question—he would go to Paris himself and "slam" this to Picot. The British must stick together loyally with the French in the Middle East, and not let the Arabs divide them along the lines of "You very good man, him very bad man," in Sykes's cheery phrase, for despite his sympathy for every racial and ethnic group, there was still an element of the pukka sahib in him, which he was unable to altogether suppress.

There were many reasons for these well-meant contradictions on the part of the imaginative and mercurial Sykes. The bloody stalemate on the western front showed no sign of ending; the abdication of the czar in February 1917 had led to a precarious stalemate on the eastern front as Kerensky's government sought to keep Russia in the war, while the Russian people yearned increasingly for peace. The United States had been drawn into the war in April 1917 by the folly of Germany's declaration of unrestricted submarine attacks in the Atlantic; and the Americans' entry had brought with it Woodrow Wilson's stern warning against further colonial acquisitions by the European powers, and had enshrined the principles of "self-determination" and democracy as the basis for any postwar settlement. The Sykes-Picot agreement seemed to be exactly the kind of secret diplomacy that Wilson was warning against, and it no longer looked to the British, or even to Sykes himself, like an attractive solution to the problems of the Middle East.

Early in September Lawrence wrote a long letter to Sykes from Aqaba, objecting to the continuation of a policy that would, in effect, marginalize the Arabs, and anticipating in detail the effect the Balfour Declaration would have on King Hussein and Feisal. The letter is particularly interesting because it is couched in the form of a request to know exactly what he should tell Feisal about every point Sykes raises, and among other things predicts accurately how bitterly opposed the Arabs would be to Zionist attempts to purchase large amounts of land in Palestine, whatever efforts were made to sweeten the pill. Clayton, who was nobody's fool, in effect "spiked" Lawrence's letter, and instead wrote back to Lawrence that the Sykes-Picot agreement was as good as dead, so he (and Feisal) should stop worrying about it.

Lawrence's concerns on the subject cannot have been stilled by the arrival of a French contingent at Aqaba, under the command of Captain Rosario Pisani, an experienced French colonial officer. The French detachment was dwarfed by the 800 uniformed Arab soldiers under Jaafar, by the tribesmen who were coming in daily to join Feisal's forces, and by the British technicians, instructors, and supply personnel, but Pisani's presence and the French tricolor were a daily reminder that France's claims in the Middle East were not about to go away as easily as Clayton predicted.

It is in this light that one must consider the ambitious plans Lawrence made to demonstrate the fighting power of the Bedouin—he could not determine British policy, but he could perhaps undermine it by demonstrating just how effective the Arabs could be in the field. By their achievements he would enforce their title to the lands that they claimed—and that, at least in his own mind, he claimed for them. The sooner they moved north, into Syria, the better.

But "Syria" was, of course, merely "a geographical expression," as Metternich famously described Italy, and no two people agreed on what it was, or should be. Lawrence, for the moment stuck at Feisal's "base camp," now that Feisal had moved his headquarters to Aqaba, gave some serious thought to what lay ahead, and carefully studied the map. He had spent the better part of the war so far drawing up British army maps, and nobody was better at that most basic skill of warfare, the ability to look at a map and visualize what it means in terms of tactics, strategy, and lines of communication. He concluded that the war in the Hejaz had been won by the move to Wejh; that the threat to Mecca was over; and that the railway line to Medina should be cut just often enough to keep the Turks fully occupied repairing and defending it, but never so completely as to tempt them to abandon Medina, where they were, in effect, bottled up, half starved and reduced to eating their mules and camels, which might have carried them to Rabegh or Mecca. This was a program he could continue, and eventually delegate to others, as he moved north toward Maan, providing Allenby with the all-important flank on the right as he advanced on Jerusalem. At the same time, Lawrence needed to expand his contacts with anti-Turkish elements in Syria; the Hejaz was empty space, crossed only by the nomadic Bedouin, but as Feisal's army moved north it would be entering areas that were cultivated, where peasants worked the land and clung to their villages, and relied on roads, however primitive, to sell their produce. These Arabs depended on some form of order, and recognized that in their region, unlike the Hejaz, not everyone was automatically, even unthinkingly, Muslim.

Syria held ancient and long-established communities of Christians—Maronite, Greek Orthodox, and Arab Christians—and of Druses, Circassians, Kurds, Jews, Shia and Sunni Arabs, and many smaller, dissenting Arabic sects, as well as Algerian refugees who had fled from the violent French suppression of Abd el Kader's uprising in the mid-nineteenth century. While it was not exactly a melting pot so much as a mosaic of different groups, each with a unique ancient history of martyrdom, special privileges, and animosity toward neighbors in the next village or town, it was very unlike the Hejaz. Many of these Syrian communities—perhaps most of them—were unlikely to greet with enthusiasm the arrival of rapacious armed nomads led by a Meccan sharif.

Syria was also an area of great cities—Jerusalem, Beirut, Aleppo, Homs, Hama, and Damascus—each of which had an educated elite, or rather several competing elites, famous educational or religious institutions, and a thriving commercial life. Chains of mountains further divided Syria.

THE HEJAZ RAILWAY

KONIA

TARSUS

BAGHCHE Tunnel

JERABLUS

ALEXANDRETTA

NISIBIN 80 Miles

ANTIOCH

ALEPPO

CYPRUS

HAMA

HOMS

TRIPOLI

PALMYRA

BEIRUT

BAALBEK

RIYAQ

MEDITERRANEAN

DAMASCUS

SEA

BAGHDAD 260 Miles

HAIFA

SEA of GALILEE   The Hauran

YARMUK VALLEY

DER'A

N.

JAFFA

ES SALT

QAL'AT EL MAFRAQ

Jordan

JERICHO

AMMAN

'AZRAQ

JERUSALEM

GAZA

PORT SAID

RAFAH

DEAD SEA

Wadi Sirhan

ROMANI

BEERSHEBA

QATIYA

EL ARISH

ISMAILIA

MA'AN

JAUF

SUEZ

'AQABA

MUDAUWARA

TEBUK

HAIL 100 Miles

R E D

MEDAIN SALIH

WEJH

1914-1919

BRITISH   TURKISH

BROAD GAUGE ....

NARROW   ,, ...

RIYADH 430 Miles

Scale of Miles

50   0   50   100

S E A

EL MEDINA

YENBO

Also, the coastal areas of Palestine and Lebanon were sharply separated from the inland area, and indeed boasted of an entirely different culture and history; and the inland area was divided into smaller segments by rivers such as the Jordan and the Litani, and by valleys or wadis or by rugged hills. In the absence of paved roads (the small number of automobiles in the Ottoman Empire made it unrewarding to build paved roads, and much of Syria still depended on the remains of the roads the Romans had built), the railway system was the one link that made commerce other than the caravan and the mule train possible.

Reviewing all this from "a palm-garden" in Aqaba, Lawrence evolved a strategy, which was to move Feisal's army northwest into the desert beyond Wadi Sirhan, then directly north following the railway into the strategic heartland of Syria. Lawrence hoped to enlist along the way each of the tribes in the semi-cultivated area where the desert began, seventy-five miles east of the Dead Sea and the Jordan River, then climb 300 miles north up "a ladder of tribes," as he put it, until they reached Damascus, while at the same time constantly attacking the Turks' railway so that they could neither feed nor reinforce their troops.

Those who think of Lawrence merely as a dashing guerrilla leader overlook both the originality of his plan and his capacity for detail. He compared "camel raiding-parties" operating on the border between cultivated land and the desert to ships, able to attack at will and by surprise, then break off the fight and retire into the desert, where the Turks could not follow them. He hit on the essential advantage of the guerrilla: "tip and run" tactics, "using the smallest force in the quickest time, at the furthest place." This would of course negate the Turks' superiority in numbers and heavy weapons—a lesson that would later be put to good use by the British Long Range Desert Group in the Libyan Desert in World War II (as well as by Mao in the Chinese civil war, and by the Vietcong in Vietnam). Rather than seek a decisive battle, Lawrence was determined at all costs to *avoid* one; his object was to bleed the Turks to death by pinpricks, while forcing them to waste their troops trying to defend nearly 800 miles of railway line.

He worked out with great precision exactly what his guerrillas needed. They would ride female camels, and each man would carry half a bag (forty-five pounds) of flour "slung on his riding saddle," enough for six weeks. A camel needed to drink every third day, and the rider would carry at most a pint of water, to see him through the second day of marching from one well to another. This would give the force the capability of riding "a thousand miles out and home," covering anywhere between fifty and 110 miles a day. It was Lawrence's idea to arm as many men as possible with Lewis light, drum-fed machine guns, to be used as long-range, automatic sniper rifles, rather than in their conventional role, as well as a rifle, and to keep those who had automatic weapons "ignorant of their mechanism." If the gun jammed, they were not to waste time trying to clear it but throw it away, and use their rifle instead—speed was essential; attacks should be over in minutes. (Lawrence himself rode with a Lewis gun, from which he had removed the bulky cooling shroud, the butt secured in a leather bucket slung from his saddle, as well as the Lee-Enfield rifle that Feisal had presented to him, a bag containing 100 rounds, a pistol, and his dagger.) So far as possible, each man should be instructed in the basics of high explosives, though in practice it was usually Lawrence or one of the other British officers who did the delicate job of planting them and handling detonators.

The most difficult problem Lawrence faced he turned to his advantage. No tribe would fight in the territory of another, and it was impossible to mix men of different tribes in any raiding force. Instead, when he entered the territory of a new tribe, he would take on new men from that tribe, thus automatically giving himself a fresh force at regular intervals, and giving the men and their camels a chance to rest. A further benefit was that his force would change continually in size and composition, making it more difficult for the Turks to guess how strong it was or where it would strike. In every respect, this was the opposite of a well-trained, disciplined army of whatever size. Far from handling the weapons with respect, the men would toss them aside the moment they jammed; instead of being molded into a tightly bonded unit, the men would come and go interchangeably; it would be an army without ranks or any visible chain of command, and without written orders, since the tribesmen were for the most part illiterate.

As the Turks, reinvigorated by new supplies and the sound advice of General Erich von Falkenhayn, moved south in an attempt to retake Aqaba, Lawrence showed his command of modern warfare while Feisal was at Aqaba by using bombing raids carried out by the RFC to slow the enemy down, while the Howeitat, under Auda, blew up railway bridges and culverts in the opposite direction to distract the Turks' attention.

As for Lawrence, he decided to carry out a raid on the "Mudawara, the great water station in the desert eighty miles south of Maan," sixty miles inland, directly to the east of Aqaba. If Lawrence could blow in the well, the Turks would need "to add so many more water wagons to their trains" that they would be hard pushed to supply the garrison at Medina at all. Since the insulated cable and the exploder sent from Cairo had arrived without the right kind of detonators, Lawrence borrowed three from the captain of HMS *Humber* and successfully exploded one on the deck of the monitor, proving to himself that he had mastered the technique. Tinkering with explosive devices and mastering the art of demolition by trial and error would be one of Lawrence's more dangerous activities over the next two years.

Mudawara was guarded by a substantial Turkish garrison, so Lawrence added to his Arab forces "two forceful sergeant-instructors," one to display the capabilities of the Lewis gun and the other to do the same for the Stokes trench mortar. "Lewis," as the Lewis gun instructor was nicknamed, was an Australian; "Stokes," also nicknamed after his weapon, was "a placid English yeoman." It is a tribute to Lawrence's skill at leadership that he was able to persuade the Arabs to accept two red-faced uniformed European unbelievers as fighting companions, and also that he was also able to steer Lewis and Stokes through the hardships of living like Bedouin.

—

Lawrence and his small party rode out of Aqaba on September 7, in a temperature of 123 degrees, measured in the shade of palm trees by the sea. Inland, on the yellowish sand that reflected the sun, and among the red sandstone rocks, the temperature quickly rose far higher. They rode for two days at a slow pace, to accustom the sergeants to camel riding in the desert, and arrived at Auda's camp in Guweira just in time for the daily Turkish bombing raid—an occurrence not to be taken lightly, given the amount of high explosives Lawrence's camels carried, all of which could be detonated by a single red-hot bomb fragment.

Guweira was a small village, the site of an abandoned Ottoman fort, a few miserable buildings in a sea of fine yellow sand and small hillocks, set next to a black volcanic rock. Auda's encampment, however, was a mass of people and camels shaded only by a huge cloud of swarming flies, a gathering of hundreds of the Howeitat, many of them discontented with the fact that Auda kept for himself most of the money he was now receiving from the British. It was impossible even for Auda, who was in any case enjoying himself in his tent with a new young wife, to gather enough of the Howeitat for Lawrence's purpose.

Lawrence decided to go forward on his own, with his two sergeants and the small party of Arabs with whom he had left Aqaba, riding south to Wadi Rumm, where a party of Arabs friendly to Feisal was said to be encamped. The sun was so ferocious that even the Bedouin complained, so Lawrence "played about," pretending to enjoy himself, to keep their spirits up. But when they camped for the night one of the Arabs, a Harithi sharif named Aid, came to Lawrence, who lay sleeping on the ground wrapped in his robe, to say, "in a chilled voice, 'Lord I am gone blind.'" The sun reflecting off the sand had been so intense as to burn out his retinas.

With this grim reminder of the desert's danger, they rode on the next day through a steep valley with rose-colored cliffs 1,000 feet high, sometimes even rising to 2,000 feet, between great boulders the size of houses that had fallen from the heights. They crossed a valley so broad that in it "a squadron of airplanes could have wheeled in formation"; then, at sunset, they climbed a zigzag trail up the cliff to a ledge where they halted, near a spring around which were placed several villages of tents. Wadi Rumm was as beautiful as Petra, but the little party was not cheered by it. With the blinded Aid sunk in misery, Lawrence sought to persuade the other chiefs to join him, but such was their resentment of Auda that they refused. Lawrence decided to leave his two sergeants behind when one of the Arabs sympathetic to Lawrence guaranteed their life with his own—a necessary precaution, for feelings were running high and two infidels with not a word of Arabic between them were at grave risk without Lawrence to look after them. Having done his best for the sergeants, he rode back with one companion all the way to Aqaba, where he obtained from Feisal the promise of twenty more camels to carry the explosives, and the help of Sharif Abdulla el Feir, "his best man present," who would ride back to Rumm with Lawrence to quell the mutiny in Feisal's name.

Over the next few days Sharif Abdulla succeeded in patching things up, and the extra camels arrived, accompanied by four of Feisal's enormous black Sudanese slaves, each armed with a rifle, sword, dagger, and pistol. These slaves were fanatically loyal to their master, and were intended to protect Lewis and Stokes, two to each sergeant, until they returned safely to Aqaba.

This precaution shows the degree to which clan and tribal animosities threatened to undo the capture of Aqaba, as well as the degree to which the different tribes and clans were sensitive to their own feuds and rivalry, and always subject to the ever-present temptation to test whether the Turks, who were at least fellow Muslims, might outbid the British for their support. Lawrence, who would be remembered generations later as "the Englishman who brought the gold," distributed it lavishly, but that inevitably had the effect of making the Bedouin ever more greedy, a reality of desert warfare which he tried scrupulously to hide from his superiors.

On September 16 Lawrence led a motley and ill-assorted group of men out of Rumm, about 120 in all, including the two saddle-sore sergeants and their bodyguards, and the blind Sharif Aid, who was determined to go on. They camped for the night on a "strange flat of yellow mud," and ate "gazelle meat and hot bread," as Lawrence made his plans for the attack on Mudawara, which he expected to reach at the end of the next day.

In the morning they rode across a wide and varied plain of sand, limestone, and flint, only to find, when they halted, that the Turks had fouled the pool by throwing dead camels into it a few months ago. The water was covered in thick, oily green slime, and disgusting to smell or taste, but there was no help for it but to fill their water skins, despite the stench. If they took Mudawara, they would have access to water, but if they did not, they could not retreat without having first watered their camels and provided a water supply for themselves.

At dusk, they arrived close to the station at Mudawara, and Lawrence, the two sergeants, and the Arab leaders dismounted and crawled forward from sand mound to sand mound and through the deserted Turkish trench lines to a point from which they could see the buildings and the tents of the Turkish garrison. To Lawrence's disappointment, he did not see any way of rushing the station with his mixed force, in whose reliability he had been rapidly losing confidence. There was no good cover for Stokes and the mortar, or for Lewis and the machine gun, within the range of their weapons, and it seemed to Lawrence very likely that an attack would fail. There was never anything amateurish about Lawrence's battle craft. It is a measure of his innate professionalism that he never allowed enthusiasm or his gift for improvisation to cloud his judgment. He did not trust his force in a pitched fight with superior numbers, and with Sharif Aid blinded, he did not have an Arab leader who could rally the men once they started to suffer casualties, as they surely would. He decided to withdraw, blow up a Turkish train, and let his Arabs loot it; this, if nothing else, might raise their morale a bit, and lower that of the Turks.

The next morning he found a convenient spot along the line to lay the mine. At this spot, a short two-arched bridge crossed a gulley, about 200 yards from a ledge on which Stokes and Lewis could place "their toys" with a good field of fire in whichever direction the train approached, and from which they could retreat under cover if necessary. Lawrence was always careful with the lives of his men, Arab or British, and disliked spending them unnecessarily. The swashbuckling, "romantic" picture of Lawrence charging on his camel, along with his Bedouin tribesmen in their flowing robes wielding their gleaming curved sabers, caught the public imagination once he became famous, but he was first and foremost a gifted, practical soldier who knew what he was doing. Although his military training was minimal (unlike his omnivorous reading of classics ancient and modern about strategy), Lawrence might as well have attended Sandhurst as an officer cadet—from the very first he displayed the instincts of a born soldier. However wild and undisciplined the Arabs might be, Lawrence was as careful as any professional in choosing the right ground, selecting a field of fire, working out his logistics down to the last bullet and pint of water, and preparing an avenue of retreat in case it proved necessary. Guerrilla warfare it might be, with all the messiness that such warfare entails, but he waged it with the care and instincts of an exceptionally capable regular officer. He left nothing to chance, right down to the smallest detail; what is more, he served in the field as his own adjutant, regimental sergeant major, and quartermaster sergeant. This is all the more impressive when one considers that he had nobody to advise him, nobody on whom he could call for reinforcements, and no assurance that the Bedouin would obey him. There was also the certainty that if he was seriously wounded, he would die, and if he was captured alive in Arab dress by the Turks, he would be tortured, then executed as a spy.

He had the camels unloaded and led away to a position where they could graze unseen (first making sure that the Arabs scraped salt from an overhanging limestone ledge for them—Lawrence had the Napoleonic eye for detail that makes a great commander), then kneaded his blocks of gelignite into a viscous lump that half-filled a sandbag, and buried it in the stone ballast under the tracks. He then had to replace the stones carefully one by one, brush the whole area clean of footprints with the hem of his cloak, and unroll the heavy insulated cables. These turned out to be an unexpected headache—burying them left a break in the sand's thin, wind-created crust, and the stiff cables tended to rise in one place when they were buried in another. In the end, Lawrence had to weight the cables down with heavy stones to flatten them out, fill in the long trenches and smooth out the sand by brushing an empty sandbag over the surface, then use a bellows and his own cloak to create ripples in the sand that matched the rest. Finally, he had to remove every footprint for 200 yards from the mine to the ledge where the sergeants had placed their weapons. It took him two hours to lay the charge, and five hours to render everything invisible to the naked eye.

Salem, the most senior of Feisal's slaves, was given the honor of wielding the exploder, and Lawrence spent the afternoon teaching him how— it required a firm but not overhasty push to produce the right spark. As the sun began to set, they returned to where the camels should have been, only to find that the Arabs had moved up to a high ridge, where they were clearly outlined against the setting sun, attracting the attention of the Turkish outposts, and drawing a certain amount of nervous rifle fire. Lawrence seldom complained about the Bedouin—it was in their interest and his to portray them as natural fighting men with a born talent for desert warfare—but later, in *Seven Pillars of Wisdom*, he noted with disapproval how their contempt for the Turks made them incautious, and that unlike British soldiers they were restless and noisy while waiting, without the patience to stay put and remain quiet.

In the morning, as Lawrence had feared, a Turkish patrol marched out of the station in search of them. Lawrence ordered thirty of the Arabs to open fire and then lead the Turks as slowly as possible away from the railway tracks, where they might discover the mine, and into the surrounding sand hills. At noon, a stronger patrol appeared, and Lawrence was just about to order his party to pack up and retreat, leaving the mine behind in the hope of returning another day and setting it off under a train, when he saw the smoke of a locomotive in the distance. In an instant, he placed his Arabs behind a long ridge running parallel to the track, from which they could fire at the train at a distance of about 150 yards once it was derailed. He left one man standing up to watch the train's progress, in case it was full of troops and should suddenly stop to let them off for a rush attack, but to his relief, the train did nothing of the sort. Drawn by two locomotives—a welcome bonus for Lawrence—the train kept on coming. Turkish soldiers stuck the muzzles of their rifles out of the open windows, or sheltered on the roof of each carriage behind sandbags, prepared to fend off an Arab attack, but they clearly did not anticipate the full magnitude of what was to come.

As the second locomotive began to cross the bridge, Lawrence raised his hand and Salem the slave pushed the exploder. With a mighty roar, the entire train vanished in a huge explosion of black dust, 100 feet high and equally wide. "Out of the darkness came a series of shattering crashes, and long loud metallic clangings of ripped steel, while many lumps of iron and plate, with one wheel of a locomotive, whirled up suddenly black out of the cloud against the sky, and sailed musically over our heads to fall slowly into the desert behind." For a few moments there was absolute silence as the cloud of smoke drifted away; then the Arabs opened fire on the shattered carriages, while Lawrence, dodging under their bullets, ran back to join the two sergeants on their ledge. By the time Lawrence got to them, the Arabs were leaving their positions to rush for the train and loot it, while those Turks who had survived the explosion fired back desperately. He found Lewis and Stokes calmly going about their work, Lewis sweeping the Turks off the roofs of the carriages with his machine gun, and Stokes firing his mortar bombs over the carriages to the far side, where the Turks huddled on the embankment. Stokes's second shot made "a shambles of the group, and the survivors broke eastward as they ran. . . . The sergeant grimly traversed with drum after drum into their ranks till the open sand was littered with dead bodies," while the Bedouin "were beginning like wild beasts to tear open the carriages and fall to plunder. It had taken nearly ten minutes."

Lawrence had destroyed the bridge completely. All the carriages were smashed, including one that contained sick and wounded Turks, some of them dying of typhus. Lawrence found that the Turks "had rolled dead and dying into a bleeding heap at the splintered end" of this carriage.

One locomotive was smashed beyond repair; the other was less seriously damaged, but Lawrence calmly finished this one off by attaching explosive to its boiler and detonating it. The train had been full of troops, civilian refugees, and the families of Turkish officers. The Bedouin, "raving mad . . . were rushing about at top-speed bare-headed and half-naked, screaming, shooting in the air, clawing one another nail and fist," as they looted the living and the dead. The wives and the children of the Turkish officers gathered around Lawrence begging for mercy, and were then pushed out of the way by their husbands, who tried to seize and kiss Lawrence's feet. He kicked them away "in disgust," and went on to accept the surrender of a group of Austro-Hungarian officers and NCOs, artillery instructors, one of whom was seriously wounded. Lawrence, who had seen a large Turkish patrol leaving the station, promised that the Turks would be there with help in an hour, but the man died of his wounds, and Lawrence went on to deal with other problems, including a dignified and infirm old Arab woman, whose servant he managed to find—the old woman would later send him a valuable carpet from Damascus as a token of her gratitude. In the meantime, the Bedouin killed all but "two or three" of Lawrence's Austrian prisoners.

The raiding force evaporated into the desert, each man loading his camel with as much booty as it could carry. In the aftermath of the destruction of the train, Lawrence was obliged to go back and try to rescue Salem, who had been hit by a Turkish bullet, then stripped and left for dead by his Howeitat allies. Lawrence also attempted to retrieve the kits of the two sergeants, and with their help stalled the Turks by blowing up the remaining ammunition. He took care to finish off "out of mercy" those of the Arabs who were badly wounded, since "the Turks used to kill them in horrible ways." He returned with the sergeants to Aqaba on September 22, "entering in glory, laden with all manner of precious things," and with his usual care for those who served under him, made sure that once they got back to Cairo each of them was decorated by Allenby, and paid himself for their missing kit.

—

The account of the raid on the train at Mudawara in *Seven Pillars of Wisdom* is a literary set piece, one of the great pieces of modern writing about war: dry, businesslike, and ever so slightly ironic in tone, it is brilliantly underplayed, so that at first the only moments of horror the reader feels are when Lawrence enters the smashed carriage full of dead or dying Turks, when he is surrounded by the women pleading for their lives, or when the Austrians are killed after surrendering to him. But reading his account of the incident a second time, one realizes just how gifted a writer Lawrence was. The horror is there, all right, in tiny details, just as it is in the scenes of battle in Tolstoy's *War and Peace*, or in certain scenes in Hemingway's *A Farewell to Arms*. The spare, unemotional prose, unlike Lawrence's much lusher descriptions of landscapes and people, does not hide the reality of the incident—the dead and dying Turks; the shooting of the Arab wounded; the noise, smoke, bloodshed, fear, carnage, and wild looting, all of it over and done with in less than ten minutes in the implacable desert heat. The scene is a small masterpiece, like a sketch by Goya. Lawrence does not tell us what he felt, and does not for a moment try to present himself as heroic or sympathetic; nor does he attempt to infuse the scene with glory, or shock the reader with the blood and gore of battle. Painstakingly, he simply attempts to tell the reader exactly what happened.

Shortly afterward Lawrence wrote to Frank Stirling, a fellow intelligence officer in Cairo who would himself go on to become one of the British army's boldest adventurers and guerrilla leaders, and to carve out his own fame in both world wars (and in between them) as Colonel W. F. Stirling, DSO, MC, and also to write a lively account of his life in a memoir aptly entitled *Safety Last*. Lawrence wrote to him: "I hope this sounds the fun it is. . . . It's the most amateurishly Buffalo-Billy sort of performance." But that was intended to appeal to Stirling, a man straight out of A. E. W. Mason's *The Four Feathers* who was never happier than when bullets were whizzing past his head, and who would, oddly enough, become an adviser on the first attempt to make a film of Lawrence's desert campaign, and live on to survive being shot six times by a Palestinian terrorist.*

Lawrence wrote about the attack on the train at Mudawara in a very different spirit to his old friend Leeds at the Ashmolean Museum in Oxford, with whom he had no need to posture as a hero from *Boy's Own*: "I hope when this nightmare ends that I will wake up and become alive again. This killing and killing of Turks is horrible. When you charge in at the finish and find them all over the place in bits, and still alive many of them, and know you have done hundreds in the same way before and must do hundreds more if you can . . ."

Many of those who have written about Lawrence have felt the need to decide between these two very different ways of looking at warfare, and come to some conclusion about which one represents the authentic Lawrence: the self-congratulatory but faintly self-mocking heroic mode, unshocked by bloodshed; or the bitterly self-critical mode, with its deep sense of guilt about his own efficiency as a killer, and his fear that he has crossed a moral line and can never recross it to return to normal life. Of course allowance must be made for the fact that Lawrence, perhaps more than most people, altered the style of his letters to suit the recipient— indeed, even his most casual letters are artfully written to please; thus the tone of his letters to Bernard Shaw is radically different from that of his letters to Charlotte Shaw, for example. Then too, Lawrence had an eerie ability to adopt or project the appropriate version of himself for different people: thus he presented himself to Colonel Stirling, or to General Allenby, and indeed to most professional soldiers of whatever rank, as a daring and efficient soldier untroubled by the inevitable horrors of war, with the traditional British stiff upper lip of their class. To the more sensitive Storrs, he presented himself as a much more reflective and intellectual figure, a reluctant warrior. Later, to admirers such as the

---

* Stirling particularly admired Lawrence's courage and toughness, and was a good judge of both. When told of the attempt on Stirling's life, an Arab friend remarked incredulously, "Did they really think they could kill Colonel Stirling with only six shots?" (*Safety Last*, 243).

Shaws, Robert Graves, or Siegfried Sassoon, he emphasized his guilt and suffering; and to hardheaded political realists such as Winston Churchill, he stressed his own version of hardheaded political realism. Lawrence, like an experienced seducer, had a different persona for everyone whose affection or admiration he wished to conquer (toward those whom he did *not* wish to conquer he could be downright rude), and yet no persona of his was false—they all coexisted within him, and fought for dominance. Hence the confusion of most professional soldiers who had known and admired him during the war, such as Colonel A. P. Wavell (later Field Marshal the Earl Wavell, GCB, GCSI, GCIE, CMG, PC), at the many controversies surrounding Lawrence after the war, and indeed after his death, as well as the very different portraits of Lawrence drawn in the early biographies of him by authors who knew him well, and to whose books he contributed. Liddell Hart, Lowell Thomas, and Robert Graves might as well have been writing about three completely different people, Liddell Hart presenting the reader with a military genius, Thomas presenting a flamboyant and romantic scholar-hero, and Graves presenting a heroic adventurer in the tradition of Burton and Gordon.

Lawrence wrote of himself, "He who gives himself to the possession of aliens leads a Yahoo life, selling himself to a brute," a harshly self-depreciatory comment on his service among the Arabs; but he who alters his personality at will to appeal to everybody from illiterate Bedouin tribesmen to Lloyd George, Wilson, and Clemenceau, or from RAF aircraftmen to Air Chief Marshal Sir Hugh Trenchard, GCB, OM, GCVO, DSO, is surely no better off. Lawrence's chameleonlike ability to present different aspects of himself to different people has, over the years, led to confusion about who he was at the core and what he accomplished, and indeed created a whole anti-Lawrence school of history and biography, which is by no means confined to the Middle East, where his role in the Arab Revolt is consistently diminished in importance, for obvious reasons. But as those who knew him best, particularly his surviving brothers, constantly pointed out, Lawrence himself in fact changed very little, if at all, from his Oxford years to his years of fame, and remained recognizably the same person. Indeed in his letters to Hogarth there is never a hint of affectation: the tone is consistent from Lawrence's early forays to the Ashmolean Museum in Oxford with potsherds to Hogarth's death in 1927, and in his letters to other people about Hogarth afterward. Here, if anywhere, is the real Lawrence—here and in his letters to his family, his correspondence with Charlotte Shaw, and much of *Seven Pillars of Wisdom*.

The successful attack on the train at Mudawara led Lawrence to plan a series of attacks on the Turkish railway, cutting it often, and just badly enough to keep the Turks' attention focused on it, but never so badly or for so long that they might be tempted to give up their hold on Medina. Some of these attacks he carried out personally—using high explosives to damage the railway became something between an obsession and a hobby for Lawrence in the autumn of 1917—but increasingly the Arabs, taught by British instructors, could do much of this demolition work themselves, though it did not give them the pleasure, or the profit, of looting trains. Lawrence, who had eagerly absorbed everything that Major Garland, the demolitions expert, had taught him, encouraged them to create "tulips," using small amounts of explosive to blow up the rails, which then twisted in the air in a tulip shape. He also urged them to concentrate on blowing up the curved tracks, since these were in short supply and gave the Turks more trouble to replace. The Arab raiding parties could blow up miles of undefended track in desolate areas of the desert, keeping Turkish repair crews busy, and occasionally picking off a few soldiers when they came to repair the track.

In the meantime, Allenby was drawing up his plans, determined to succeed where generals Maxwell and Murray had failed. He replaced the staff with men of his own, bringing his own chief of staff over from France, and adding to it Lieutenant-Colonel Alan Dawnay, an immensely tall, thin Coldstreamer, who was Lawrence's kind of soldier—a banker, a poet, and a Greek scholar, with a surprising gift for unconventional tactics, given his conventional appearance. At first, he and Lawrence did not see eye to eye—"Dawnay," Lawrence remarked, "was a cold shy mind, gazing on our efforts with a bleak eye, always thinking, thinking"—but each man came to appreciate the other's special skills, and to overlook the contrast between Dawnay's perfect military appearance and Lawrence's habit of appearing out of nowhere barefoot and in flowing white robes.

A general who had made his name carrying out frontal attacks against the Germans on the western front, in the style approved and demanded by General Sir Douglas Haig, commander in chief of the BEF, Allenby nevertheless decided not to repeat the frontal attacks against Gaza that had failed under Maxwell and Murray. Instead, he would feint a frontal attack against Gaza, which was where the Turks would expect it, and support it with heavy artillery and a naval bombardment, while at the same time sending the bulk of his forces, led by the British and imperial cavalry, far to the right to attack Beersheeba and capture intact the vital wells there, then turn west and roll up the Turkish line from Beersheba to the coast. Alan Dawnay's older brother Guy, on Allenby's staff, was an enthusiast for "dirty tricks" in warfare, despite a formal manner and appearance. He busied himself building roads designed to mislead the Turks about the direction of the attack, raising dust by moving phantom divisions and corps, and he sent Major Richard Meinertzhagen, a soldier almost as unconventional as Lawrence himself, riding out too close to the Turkish lines to trick the Turks. As he galloped for home under fire Meinertzhagen dropped a satchel containing a forged set of maps and orders encouraging the Turks to expect that the attack on Gaza would be preceded by a feint toward Beersheba, and giving a date for the attack several days later than it would actually take place. Meinertzhagen, for some time a rival of Lawrence's, was a very different kind of man: tall, violent, a world-famous ornithologist* who took great pleasure in bash-

---

* Even as ornithologist Meinertzhagen played dirty. In his old age he was discovered to have acquired his enormous and famous collection of birds in part by stealing specimens from the collections that, as a respected and honored expert, he was invited to examine at museums. He also rewrote and retyped the content of his diaries years after the events he described, giving rise to the suspicion that much of it was false and self-serving.

THE NORTHERN THEATER

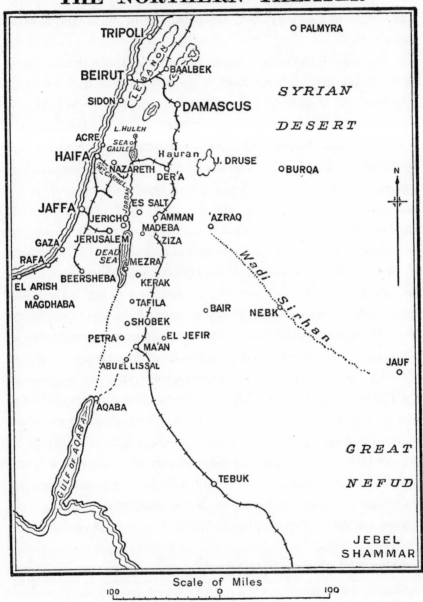

Scale of Miles

100   0   100

ing in the heads of cornered Germans with his "African knobkerri" instead of taking them prisoner, and who, unlike Lawrence, enjoyed deceiving his friends as much as his enemies. He and Lawrence eventually became friends of a kind, but neither altogether trusted the other.

While Lawrence was eager to help Allenby's attack, he had his own goal in mind: "the navel," as he called the vital junction of "the Jerusalem-Haifa, Damascus-Medina railways . . . the only common point of all their own fronts," the town of Deraa. He was convinced that he could seize Deraa, and thereby cut all Turkish lines of communication and supply, and that once he had it, Damascus would fall to the Arabs like a ripe fruit, before the British or, more important, the French could reach it. His great concern was that there would be only one chance to do it, for it involved persuading the Syrians to rise against the Turks; but the Syrians were not Bedouin who could retreat back into the desert and strike again; they were town dwellers, farmers, people with fixed abodes and families in place. If Feisal authorized them to rise in his name and was unable to hold Deraa or Damascus, the Turkish reprisals would be cruel, savage, and brutal, and directed against people and families who had nowhere to flee. There was no margin for error—the risings must take place to coincide with Allenby's attack on the Gaza-Beersheba line, but Allenby was still an untried factor, commanding troops who had twice failed to take Gaza. In the end, Lawrence reached the decision that it was too risky, and put Deraa in the back of his mind—though his strategic interest in the town and his decision to examine its railroad yard with his own eyes would lead very soon to the single greatest crisis of his life.

Instead, he decided to use what forces he had to attack the vital Turkish bridges at Yarmuk. The railway from Deraa to Haifa, Jerusalem, Gaza, and El Arish passed through the steep, winding valley of the Yarmuk River from a point about twenty miles east of Deraa to the southern tip of Lake Tiberias, and followed the twisting turns of the river as closely as possible, crossing and recrossing it where necessary "on a series of identical steel bridges each fifty metres, one hundred and sixty-two feet, in span." Of these bridges, the farthest west and the farthest east, numbers two and thirteen, would be the most difficult to repair—indeed impossible to repair in any reasonable length of time. If either of the two bridges was destroyed at the same time as Allenby's attack, the Turks holding the Gaza-Beersheba lines would be instantly cut off from supplies and reinforcements from Damascus, and forced to retreat—and the retreat would almost certainly turn into a rout if at the same time the population of Syria rose against them. A complete and decisive victory over the Turks could occur as soon as early November 1917, with incalculable effects on the war on the western front and in Russia.

Allenby gave Lawrence his blessing for the operation, which he requested should take place on November 5, "or one of the three following days," to coincide as closely as possible with his own attack. As at Aqaba, Lawrence's advantage was that the Turks didn't think it was possible, so the bridges were lightly guarded. Still, Lawrence would need to march his force 320 miles across the desert from Aqaba to Azrak, make that his base of operations, then cover more than 100 miles from Azrak to Yarmuk undetected, over rough terrain, securing the assistance of tribes along the way, any of which might prefer to sell their knowledge of the raid to the Turks. For that matter, any of those who rode with Lawrence could betray the raid. Though he writes about it almost without emotion, he was proposing to ride deep into country that was tightly held by the Turks, where there were plenty of people who were waiting for a British victory before committing themselves, and not a few who preferred a Muslim master to a European, Christian one.

Given the elaborate steel structure of the bridges he hoped to destroy, Lawrence appealed to the gunners on board HMS *Humber*, who made him up a network of canvas straps and buckles to quickly attach "a necklace of blasting gelatine" around the key girders. Since destroying the bridges would be a more precise job than destroying a train, the chief engineer at Aqaba, C. E. Wood, an officer of the Royal Engineers, agreed to come along, although he had been wounded in the head in France, was "unfit for active service," and had never ridden a camel. In case Lawrence was wounded or killed, Wood would act as his deputy and place the charges. Lawrence's friend from the Arab Bureau, George Lloyd, MP, who was visiting Aqaba, agreed to come along part of the way, more as a companion for Lawrence and out of curiosity than for any practical reason.

Lawrence added a company of Muslim Indian cavalrymen as a machine gun section, under the command of Jemadar* Hassan Shah; a carefully picked bodyguard of his own; and his two riotous young servants, Farraj and Daud, whom he described as "capable and merry on the road," but whom most others seemed to find troublesome, insolent, and too fond of practical jokes. Childhood friends, Farraj and Daud seem to have filled a role somewhere between body servant and court jester, and shared an intense and feudal loyalty to Lawrence.

A latecomer to the group, and something of a question mark, was Emir Abd el Kader, grandson and namesake of the man who had fought against the French occupation of his native Algeria from 1830 to 1847, and took refuge in the Ottoman Empire after his defeat. The great Abd el Kader had been an authentic hero throughout the Muslim world, and indeed was admired by many outside it. The French occupation of Algeria and the suppression of the Algerian insurgency had been lengthy, bloody, and violent, a protracted scorched-earth policy involving the destruction of villages, crops, and livestock. Against this, Abd el Kader fought a brilliantly conducted guerrilla war, and demonstrated a capacity for the chivalrous gesture altogether lacking in his French enemies. Many in Europe and America had regarded him as a hero, and once he reached Damascus his friends included many Europeans, including the British explorer and translator of that notorious classic of Victorian pornography *The Book of the Thousand Nights and One Night* Sir Richard Burton, and Burton's wife Isabel.

Abd el Kader lived on to save thousands of Christians from massacre at the hands of the Druses, to become a Freemason, and, ironically, to be awarded the Grand Cross of the Legion of Honor by France, as well as being honored by Abraham Lincoln and having a town in America named

Jemadar was the lowest commissioned rank in the Indian army, the approximate equivalent of a lieutenant.

after him—Elkader, Iowa. The family lived on in Damascus, and a number of Abd el Kader's loyal followers, either exiled by the French or fleeing Algeria as refugees, also settled in the Ottoman Empire, many of them in villages not far from the bridges Lawrence planned to destroy.

The grandson of Abd el Kader seems to have had from the beginning something of what we would now call a love-hate relationship with Lawrence. Later on, when writing *Seven Pillars of Wisdom*, Lawrence would describe him as "an Islamic fanatic, half-insane with religious enthusiasm, and a most violent belief in himself"; but there was no shortage of Islamic fanatics in the Arab Revolt, and King Hussein had been impressed enough by Abd el Kader when the latter visited Mecca to give him a blood-red banner and his blessing. Whatever his father thought, Feisal did not hide his own doubts about Abd el Kader from Lawrence. But Lawrence—a man who certainly shared "a violent belief in himself"— seems to have been more impressed with Abd el Kader than he was later willing to admit, and believed that this famous name would be useful in rallying the descendants of the Algerian exiles to the revolt when he got to the Yarmuk River.

Lawrence set off from Aqaba on October 24, and at first made slow progress—not surprisingly, given the number of people he had with him who were new to camel riding, which involves not only getting used to a completely different gait from that of a horse, but also accustoming oneself to the equivalent of a lady's sidesaddle. Some of his party fell behind and got lost, while Lawrence rode on at a leisurely pace chatting pleasantly with Lloyd—perhaps a mistake, since he might have done better to cultivate the excitable Abd el Kader, whose dislike of Europeans and contradictory desire to be accepted as Lawrence's companion and equal were both strong. Lloyd was a man Lawrence liked, and it is revealing that their conversation involved many of the things that were on Lawrence's mind at the time: the exact text of the Sykes-Picot agreement, which neither Feisal nor his father had yet seen; Lawrence's misgivings about his meeting in Cairo with the Zionist agronomist Aaron Aaronsohn, leader of a

British spy ring in Palestine, who had expressed the intention of acquiring "the land rights of all Palestine from Gaza to Haifa," a position that even then Lawrence recognized would cause many problems (the Balfour Declaration was just about to be published in London, though neither Lloyd nor Lawrence knew about it); even the basic question of whether the Allies would be justified in partitioning the Arab lands without the consent of the inhabitants. Lloyd would later express his fear that Lawrence was taking too great a risk—Lawrence planned to use his Indian machine gunners to fight the guards on the bridges and thus keep the Turks' attention fixed elsewhere while he laid the explosive charges, and his plans for escaping back to Azrak after the bridges had been blown seemed to Lloyd to leave too much to chance. Lloyd wanted Lawrence to ride a fast horse for his escape, but Lawrence was no horseman—an unusual gap in his father's attempt to provide his sons with knowledge of his own gentlemanly pursuits, like sailing and shooting, presumably because riding lessons for five boys would have been too expensive.

In the event, the stragglers eventually joined the main party in dribs and drabs, and they camped for the night in the extravagant landscape of Wadi Rumm, with its towering multicolored cliffs, where they were joined the next day by Abd el Kader, accompanying Sharif Ali ibn Hussein of the Harith and his men. This was not a good mixture; Abd el Kader may have resented being separated from Lawrence's party, and the two men were arguing furiously when they arrived, since Abd el Kader also resented the amount of attention paid to Sharif Ali. This was inevitable; Ali was a legendary figure, both as a warrior and as a leader, who "could outstrip a trotting camel on his bare feet, keep his speed over half a mile, and then vault with one hand into the saddle, holding his rifle in the other," as well as kneel down, put his arms on the ground, and rise to his feet lifting two men, one standing on each of his hands. Lawrence described him with admiration as "impertinent, headstrong, conceited . . . reckless [and] impressive," all adjectives which might have been applied to himself, except perhaps "conceited."

In Lawrence's account, the long journey from Aqaba to Azrak seems more like a sightseeing tour than a hardship, but they were still moving slowly day by day in deference to the saddle-sore Indians and British, and eating what were by Bedouin standards lavish feasts: rice cooked specially to Lawrence's taste by Farraj and Daud, and bully beef (the British army's equivalent of canned corned beef) and biscuits for the rest of the British. Their route was not without danger; as they crossed the railway it took them past Turkish blockhouses, close enough so that Lawrence called a halt and sent Lloyd's soldier-servant to climb up the pole and cut the telegraph wires. This created another grave problem for the Turks, since it obliged them to use radio messages, which the British could intercept and decode. In the distance, Lawrence could hear Turkish rifle and machine gun fire, a sign that Abd el Kader and Ali were encountering difficulties as they crossed the railway line a few miles away.

The next morning Lawrence continued to ride north, parallel to the railway line, so that he was able to give the train coming south from Maan an ironic, cheerful wave, as if he led a body of harmless, friendly Bedouin rather than a band of heavily armed train destroyers. Then they turned slightly to the west, away from the tracks, until they reached the flat plains around El Jefer, where they found Auda Abu Tayi uncomfortably camped.

Auda had been obliged to send his tents, his womenfolk, and his herds deeper into the desert, out of range of Turkish aircraft, and was living in a makeshift tent, really more of a rough lean-to in the brush, and quarrelling bitterly with his Howeitat tribesmen over the wages they claimed they had not been paid. He served his guests a feast of rice, meat, and dried tomatoes—even the abstemious Lawrence, who was usually indifferent to food, commented that it was "luscious"—but it seemed to Lawrence unlikely that Auda or his men would be in a mood to follow him to the Yarmuk gorge to blow up a bridge, with no prospect of loot. As they were drinking coffee, a cloud of dust was reported on the horizon from the direction of Maan, and assumed to be a regiment of mounted Turks venturing out to attack them. Auda quickly ordered his tents struck; Lawrence had his camels led into shallow gullies, and made to kneel to keep them out of sight; and Jemadar Shah deployed his Indian machine gunners with their Vickers and Lewis guns among the thornbushes. In the event, the dust cloud turned out to be Abd el Kader and Ali ibn el Hussein and his men arriving, so the tent was put back up and a second meal prepared. "They had lost two men and a mare in the shooting on the railway in the night," Lawrence noted, without surprise.

The next day Lloyd left to ride back from Auda's encampment to Aqaba with his soldier-servant, who was suffering from sunburn and opthalmia (as well as wood splinters in his hands and legs, from climbing the telegraph pole); Lawrence immediately missed Lloyd's company, as he went on to more "war, tribes and camels without end." Camels were a constant preoccupation. Once the Bedouin were encamped somewhere, they sent the camels far off to graze, so there were none close by Auda's encampment for Lloyd to ride back to Aqaba—one senses also, reading between the lines of Lawrence's account, that Auda and the Howeitat were not in a generous or cooperative mood, and were making difficulties even over such a small matter as the loan of a couple of camels for a British member of Parliament.

Lawrence needed to keep the Howeitat reasonably happy—they had supposed optimistically that the capture of Aqaba was the triumphant climax of their part in the war, rather than the beginning of a longer and more difficult campaign—since they were the first rung in the ladder of tribes that was to take him from Aqaba to Yarmuk. He therefore attempted to make peace between Auda and the tribesmen, and to urge them on to one more big effort. Finally, near midnight, Auda held up his camel stick for silence, and they heard from far away a noise "like the mutter of a distant, very lowly thunderstorm." It was October 27, and Allenby's attack on the Gaza-Beersheba line had begun with a prolonged artillery barrage against Gaza.

The sound of the guns had a strong effect on the Howeitat—here, at last, was some sign that the British were prepared to fight—and Lawrence remarked that the atmosphere in the camp became "serene and cordial," in contrast to that of the previous night. However, as Lawrence was about to mount his camel, Auda leaned close, brushed his beard against Lawrence's ear, and whispered, "Beware of Abd el Kader." There were too many people around for Auda to expand on this warning, and it is notable that even in his own camp, Auda did not feel able to speak freely. As in the French Resistance movement in World War II, treachery, double-dealing, and betrayal were facts of everyday life—Lawrence was behind the enemy lines from the moment he set foot out of Aqaba, and at the mercy of anybody who wanted to claim a reward or curry favor with the Turks. In any case, since he would need Abd el Kader once he arrived at Yarmuk if he stuck to his original plan, he seems to have decided to ignore Auda's warning—or it may be that he thought Abd el Kader was more of a buffoon than a threat.

The sound of the big guns firing on Gaza urged Lawrence on to greater speed and greater risks if he was to fulfill his promise to Allenby. The distance from Jefer to Azrak was nearly 150 miles, across flinty desert, broken only by steep, rocky escarpments and dry wadis; even on a modern map of the Middle East it is shown as a vast empty area, bisected only by oil pipelines. On the British War Office map of 1917 it is shown as beige-colored blank space, meaning that no European had ever surveyed it, or even seen it. Lawrence's Indian machine gunners could do at best thirty or thirty-five miles a day, so he was already falling behind schedule. From the way he writes about the journey in *Seven Pillars of Wisdom*, he might seem to have been enjoying the scenery, but inwardly he must have been seething with impatience.

No matter how empty the desert looked to a European, it was full of hostile strangers. At one point, near Beir, Lawrence's group came under attack from raiders firing indiscriminately over their heads. These turned out to be Suhkuri of the Beni Sakhr tribe, "a dangerous gang," as Lawrence described them; once they had ceased firing, at the sight of Ali, they explained that it was an immemorial Beni Sakhr custom to shoot at all strangers. Though these rough, surly customers were distinctly unfriendly, Lawrence and Ali went to the trouble of putting them at their ease, and their chief eventually arrived and put on a tribal show by way of apology. The show was a rough equivalent of a Moroccan *fantasia*, in which the tribesmen rode around Lawrence's group at a full gallop on their horses, firing their rifles into the air and shouting at the top of their voices, "God give victory to our Sharif!" in honor of Ali, and, "Welcome Aurens, harbinger of victory!" to Lawrence—perhaps merely a sign that his reputation was firmly established as a man with gold sovereigns to distribute.

One senses, in Lawrence's description, how strained and fixed his smile must have been, both because of the delay and because of the danger of being hit by a stray bullet. When the Beni Sakhr finally stopped raising the dust and wasting ammunition, Abd el Kader, apparently infuriated by their hailing of Ali and Lawrence, and not of him, and eager to demonstrate that he could put on as good a show, mounted his mare and rode around in circles, as in a dressage ring, followed by his seven servants, firing into the air with his rifle, until the Beni Sakhr chief asked that Lawrence and Ali put a stop to this before one of his own men was shot. This was not, as it happened, a remote possibility. Abd el Kader's brother, Emir Mohammed Said el Kader, "held what might well be the world's record for three successive fatal accidents with automatic pistols in the circle of his Damascus friends," according to Lawrence. This had led Ali Riza Pasha, the governor of Damascus, to remark, "There are three things notably impossible: one, that Turkey win this war; one, that the Mediterranean become champagne; one, that I be found in the same place with Mohammed Said, and he armed."

As Lawrence continued on across the desert toward Azrak, he still heard the thunder of the British guns, louder now. On October 31 "some 40,000 troops of all arms," were on the move to attack Beersheba, after an intense four-day artillery barrage, which had convinced Kress von Kressenstein that Allenby was about to launch another full-scale assault on Gaza. By the end of the day, after intense fighting and a brilliant and daring cavalry charge by the Fourth Australian Light Horse Brigade, whose troopers not only swept over two lines of Turkish trenches at the gallop, but then "dismounted and cleaned up with the bayonet the trenches over which they had passed," the Turkish left simply collapsed. "General Allenby's plan to mislead his enemy had been entirely successful"; he had taken Beersheba and, more important, the wells there, before the Turks were able to dynamite them. Fierce fighting would continue over the next few days, but the Gaza-Beersheba line, which had resisted the British since 1914, was broken, and the only question remaining was where—and if—the Turks could reestablish a line in Palestine.

At every stop on the way to Azrak, Lawrence received more disturbing news about the strength and disposition of the Turks in the Yarmuk gorge, from tribesmen and their chiefs who were reluctant to join him. There were three routes he could take, but as the paramount sheikh of the Serahin explained to Lawrence, none of them was good.

In one place the Turks had sent large groups of military woodcutters (wood was a constant preoccupation, since the Turkish locomotives south of Damascus were fueled by wood, it being impossible to add a further burden to the already overtasked railway system by shipping large amounts of coal), and Lawrence could not hope "to slip through undetected." In another place—Tell el Shehab—the villagers were enemies of the Serahin "and would certainly attack them in the rear"; in addition, the ground would turn muddy in the event of rain, and the camels would then be unable to cross it to get back to the desert. Finally, the villages of the Algerian descendants in the Jaulan that Abd el Kader claimed to control would certainly be hostile, and "nothing would persuade [the Serahin] to visit the one under the guidance of the other." Lawrence could not go forward without the Serahin—they were the last major tribe on his way—so he gave them a rousing speech, which won them over for the moment. The next day they marched for Azrak, where a Roman legion had once been garrisoned, leaving behind it in the desert monuments dedicated to Emperor Diocletian, and where "the ruins of the blue fort on its rock above the rustling palms" were "steeped in an unfathomable pool of silence and past history," an Arab Camelot of legends, mythic heroes, and "lost kingdoms."

Romantic as the legends surrounding Azrak might be, it was here that

Abd el Kader and his servants slipped away from the group. Lawrence had no doubt that Abd el Kader would betray him to the Turks; an equally difficult problem was that without him, two of the three approaches to the Yarmuk were essentially closed off, leaving only Tell el Shehab, from which a retreat might be impossible, and where the troops guarding the bridge would now be on the alert—for Abd el Kader knew all of Lawrence's plans. At this point, Lawrence had no choice but to go forward to Tell el Shehab—indeed, the only surprise is that he managed to so inspire the doubtful Serahin tribesmen that they went forward with him.

Yarmuk was a two-day ride from Azrak, and during those two days Lawrence's nerves and patience were further stretched by the need to pass judgment on two of his men who had tried to shoot each other in a quarrel while out hunting gazelle. Pushed once again into a position where only he could make a judgment without causing a blood feud, Lawrence ordered "that the right thumb and forefinger of each should be cut off," the traditional punishment. The fear of this drove the two men to make peace, in token of which each man was beaten around the head with the sharp edge of a dagger, so that the painful scar should become a permanent reminder of their obligation not to renew the quarrel. Under the circumstances Lawrence was lucky that a scouting party sent out by the Turks just missed his men as they were about to water their camels and fill their water skins for the last time before the ride to the bridge. They faced a ride of forty miles; then the laying of the charges; and, after the bridge was demolished, another forty miles of hard riding back into the desert—all of it to be done in the thirteen hours of darkness.

Some measure of just how dangerous the operation was, even had Abd el Kader not betrayed Lawrence, can be gleaned from the concern of Hogarth in Cairo, who wrote to his wife, apparently not mindful of censorship, or in a position to ignore it, "I only hope TEL will get back safe. . . . If he comes through it is a V.C.—if not—well, I don't care to think about it."

Hidden as best he could manage in a hollow by the railway line, Lawrence made a drastic, last-minute decision to rely on speed rather than force. The Indian machine gunners were still slow and clumsy riders, so he picked the six of them who were the best riders, and their officer, and reduced his firepower to one Vickers machine gun. He weeded out the least enthusiastic of the Arabs, particularly among the Serahin, whose zeal for the operation, never great to begin with, was rapidly diminishing; and with the help of Wood, who was to remain close by in case Lawrence was killed or wounded, he removed all the explosive from its wrapped packages, kneading it all into thirty-pound lumps, then placing each lump in a white sack that one man could carry downhill in the dark under fire. The fumes from the explosive gave both Lawrence and Wood a severe headache.

At sunset, Lawrence set off with his much-reduced company, and rode through the darkness, "very miserably and disinclined to go on at all." Along the way they bumped into terrified nocturnal travelers—a peddler and his two wives, a shepherd who opened fire on them, a Gypsy woman, a stray camel—and saw the flares of Deraa station, lit up for army traffic. The going in the dark was slow and difficult—this was not desert; it was cultivated land, and the camels "sank fetlock in," and began to stumble, slip, and labor, as a steady drizzle started to turn the ground to mud, just as the Serahin had warned. Shortly after nine o'clock they halted before a band of pitch darkness, with the sound of a waterfall in their ears—they had reached Yarmuk gorge.

They dismounted and made their way down a steep bank, gripping with their toes in the slippery mud—the reluctant Serahin chosen to carry the bags of explosive were particularly nervous, since a stray shot could set it off—and set off toward the bridge. They halted about 300 yards from it. Lawrence could look down at it from the edge of the gorge through his binoculars, and could clearly see a sentry standing in front of a fire, and a guard tent, on the far side. Followed by the "explosive-porters" he made his way down a steep construction path to where the bridge abutted, the river running far below it. All he had to do now was to climb the latticework of steel beams that supported the bridge, fasten each thirty-pound bag of explosive where it belonged, place the fuses and wires—all of this in the dark, without alerting the sentry—and then make his way with the wires back to where Wood waited with the exploder. If the sentry heard anything, the Indians were to rake the guard tent with their Vickers.

This daring and ambitious plan was thwarted at the last minute when one of the Indian machine gunners, slipping on the steep path down to the bridge, dropped his rifle. The Turkish sentry opened fire in return, blindly, in the dark; the Turkish guards came rushing out of their tent and opened fire; and the terrified "explosive-porters" dropped their sacks, which fell down the steep gorge toward the river, where it would obviously be impossible to retrieve them.

The retreat from the bridge was grim—every village on the way opened fire as Lawrence and his party passed it in the night, this being the standard practice when strangers were about. Also, the Serahin, angered by something Lawrence had said about their cowardice in dropping the explosives, paused to attack a group of peasants returning home late from the market at Deraa, stripping them of everything, including their clothes, and setting off from all sides outraged screams and volleys of rifle fire.

However sick at heart Lawrence might be at his failure, his Arabs were determined to come home with something in the way of loot; and since there was still one sack of explosive left, they wanted to blow up a train. Lawrence seems to have felt that this was unwise. For one thing, he had decided to send the machine gunners back to Azrak accompanied by Wood. (He hoped that Wood could enforce peace between the Indians and the Arabs, who hated each other even though both groups were Muslims.) Also, the party had run through its rations, having expected to dash back to Azrak once the bridge was blown, and so was not prepared for the day or two it might take to find a suitable place on the railway line and wait for a train. Still, Lawrence himself had no wish to return to Azrak without having accomplished anything.

He selected a stone culvert, in which he carefully concealed his bag of explosive, though he was hampered by the fact that he had only sixty yards of insulated cable with him—it was in short supply in Egypt—and would be uncomfortably close to the explosion when it occurred. Before the exploder could be attached, a train of freight cars went by, and Lawrence huddled, "wet and dismal," unable to blow them up. It rained hard, soaking the Arabs, but also discouraging the Turkish railway patrols from looking too hard at the ground as they went by, within a few yards of where Lawrence was hiding behind a tiny bush. The next to arrive was a troop train, and as it went by he pushed down the handle of the exploder, but nothing happened. As the carriages clanked by—three coaches for officers and eighteen open wagons and boxcars for the troops—he realized that he was now sitting in full view only fifty yards away from the train. Officers came out onto the little platforms at either end of their carriage, "pointing and staring." Lawrence feigned simplicity and waved at them, aware that he made an unlikely figure of a shepherd in his white robes, with twisted gold and crimson *agal* wound around his headdress.

Lawrence prepares to blow up a train full of Turkish soldiers and their officers.

Fortunately, he was able to conceal the wires and get away when the train drew to a stop and some of the officers got out to investigate—he "ran like a rabbit uphill into safety," and he and his Arabs spent a cold, hungry, wet, sleepless night in a shallow valley beyond the railway. In the morning, Lawrence managed to get a small fire going by shaving slivers off a stick of blasting gelignite, while the Arabs killed one of the weakest camels and hacked it into pieces with their entrenching tools.

Before they could eat the meat, however, the approach of another train was signaled. Lawrence ran 600 yards, breathlessly, back to his tiny bush and pushed the handle of the exploder just as a train of twelve passenger carriages drawn by two locomotives appeared. This time it worked. He blew his mine just as the first locomotive passed over it, and sat motionless while huge pieces of black steel came hurtling through the air toward him. He felt blood dripping down his arm; the exploder between his knees had been crushed by a piece of iron; just "in front of [him] was the scalded and smoking upper half of the body of a man." Lawrence had injured his right foot and in great pain limped toward the Arabs, caught in the cross fire as the Arabs and the surviving Turks opened fire on each other. He had suffered a broken toe and five bullet grazes, but was pleased, as the smoke cleared, to see that the explosion had destroyed the culvert and damaged both locomotives beyond repair. The first three carriages were badly crushed, and the rest derailed. One carriage was that of Mehmed Jemal Kuchuk Pasha,* the general commanding the Turkish Eighth Army Corps, whose personal chargers had been killed in the front wagon and whose car was at the end of the train. Lawrence "shot up" the general's car, and also his imam, a priest who was thought to be "a notorious pro-Turk pimp" (an unusually savage comment for Lawrence); but there was not much more he could do against nearly 400 men with only forty Arabs, and the surviving Turks, knowing they were under the eye of a general, were beginning to deploy as they recovered from the shock. The Arabs were able only to loot sixty or sev-

---

* Known as "Jemal the Lesser" to distinguish him from Jemal Pasha.

enty rifles, some medals, and assorted luggage scattered from the wreck-age—enough, however, for them to feel that it was an honorable episode.

Lawrence made an effort to gather up those wounded who could be saved, including one Arab who had received a bullet in the face, knocking out four teeth and "gashing his tongue deeply," but who still managed to get back on his camel and ride away. Someone had been farsighted enough to lash the bloody haunch of the slaughtered camel to his saddle, so once they were deeper in the desert, they halted and ate their first meal in three days, then rode back to Azrak, "boasting, God forgive us, that we were victorious."

For Lawrence, this was a humiliating episode. Derailing a general's train was not the kind of feat he wanted to bring Allenby. He guessed that the constant rain, turning everything to mud, would slow down the British advance in Palestine, and now regretted that he had been hesitant about sparking an Arab rising in Syria and had chosen to go for the Yarmuk bridge instead.

Lawrence took over the old fortress at Azrak, and made it his winter headquarters, so as to reach out toward Syria. Despite the icy cold, rainy weather, which rendered travel difficult, visitors poured in from the north to pledge their homage to Feisal, which Sharif Ali ibn el Hussein was happy to receive on his behalf; but Lawrence was not at his best in enforced idleness, or with the endless obligatory politeness of Arab greet-ings, or with the memory of his failure at the Yarmuk bridge tormenting him. From the small red-leather notebook in which he wrote down frag-ments of poetry that caught his attention, he searched for consolation and reread Arthur Hugh Clough's "Say Not the Struggle Naught Availeth":

> And not through eastern windows only,
> When daylight comes, comes in the light,
> In front the sun climbs slow, how slowly,
> But westward, look, the land is bright.

But it was irony he found, not consolation. Westward, in Palestine, the weather was the same as at Azrak; and since Lawrence could safely leave the greeting of Syrian dignitaries to Ali, he set out to do a reconnaissance with the swaggering, glamorous Talal el Hareidhin, sheikh of Tafas, "an outlaw with a price upon his head," who was familiar with the approaches to Deraa. For Deraa still fascinated Lawrence as an objective; if he could take the town and hold it, if only for a few days, he could cut off all railway traffic to Palestine, and as well give the Arab cause a victory that would not only satisfy Allenby, but go a long way toward convincing the British, and perhaps even the French, to accept an independent Arab state in Syria. His mind buzzed with plans to take Deraa, but he needed to see for himself the lay of the land, and above all the strength or weakness of the Turkish garrison there.

He decided to go there himself.

Probably no incident in Lawrence's life looms larger than Deraa, or is more controversial. His decision to go there is hotly debated, and often criticized, but Lawrence had always been as reckless when it came to his own safety as he was careful of the life of others—indeed he made a point of courting danger—and it is also hard to calculate the degree to which his failure to destroy the bridge at Tell el Shehab weighed on him. His admiration for Allenby was enormous, uncomplicated, and sincere—Allenby's huge, commanding presence made him seem to Lawrence like a natural feature, something immovable and irresistible, a mountain perhaps; and having failed to keep what he regarded as a promise to Allenby, he felt obligated to provide an acceptable substitute. Capturing Deraa would be as good as destroying the bridge at Tell el Shehab, or even better.

Talal could not have accompanied Lawrence into Deraa, even had he wanted to—he was a dashingly dressed and flamboyant figure, with "a trimmed beard and long pointed moustaches . . . his dark eyes made rounder and larger and darker by their thick rims of antimony," who had "killed some twenty-three Turks with his own hand," and was wanted by the Turks almost as much as Lawrence was. Talal appointed Mijbil, an elderly, ragged peasant, to guide Lawrence through the town, and Lawrence disguised himself by leaving behind his white robes and gold dagger, and wearing instead a stained, muddy robe and an old jacket.

It occurred to Lawrence that Abd el Kader would long since have given the Turks an accurate description of him, but this does not appear to have caused him any concern, though it should have. His intention was simply to walk through the town with Mijbil and see whether it would be better to rush the railway junction first, or to cut the town off by destroying the three railways lines that entered it. They made "a lame and draggled pair" as they sauntered barefoot in the mud toward Deraa, following the Palestine railway line past the fenced-in "aerodrome," where there was a Turkish troop encampment, and a few hangars containing German Albatros aircraft. Since Lawrence was looking for a way to attack the city from the desert, this approach made sense—the railway bank and the fence were impediments worth noting—but it must also be said that he could hardly have picked anyplace in Deraa more likely to be guarded with some care than a military airfield.

In any case, after a brief altercation with a Syrian soldier who wanted to desert, Lawrence was grabbed roughly by a Turkish sergeant, who said, "The Bey wants you," and dragged him through the fence into a compound, where a "fleshy" Turkish officer sat and asked him his name. "Ahmed ibn Bagr," Lawrence replied, explaining that he was Circassian. "A deserter?" the officer asked. Lawrence explained that Circassians had no military service. "He then turned around and stared at me curiously, and said very slowly, 'You are a liar. Keep him, Hassan Chowish, til the Bey sends for him.'"

Lawrence was led to the guardroom, told to wash himself, and made to wait. With his fair complexion, blond hair, and blue eyes he might, of course, have been a Circassian, and it was no doubt his boyish appearance and size that had attracted unwelcome attention. He himself had always admitted that he could not "pass as an Arab," but now his life depended on whether he could pass as a Circassian. He was told that he might be released tomorrow, "if [he] fulfilled all the Bey's pleasure this evening," which can have left him in little doubt about what was in store for him. Lawrence had the impression that the bey was Hajim (actually Hacim Bey), the governor of Deraa, but he could have been mistaken.

"The garrison commander at Deraa was Bimbashi [Major] Ismail Bey and the militia commander Ali Riza Bey." It seems unlikely that the governor of Deraa would have lodged in a military compound next to the airfield and the railway yard; and in Turkish the title "bey" had long since lost its original significance of "chieftain" and become a widespread honorific roughly equivalent to the use of "esquire" instead of Mr. in Britain: i.e., a member of the educated professional, officer, or senior civil servant class, a step above "effendi" and a couple of steps below "pasha."

That evening Lawrence was taken upstairs to the bedroom of the bey, "a bulky man sitting on his bed in a night-gown trembling and sweating as though with fever." The bey looked him over, and then dragged him down onto the bed, where Lawrence struggled against him as if they were wrestling. The bey ordered Lawrence to undress, and when he refused to, called in the sentry who was posted outside the door, ordered the sentry to strip Lawrence naked, and began "to paw" at him. Lawrence then kneed the bey in the groin. The bey collapsed in pain, then, calling for the other three men of the guard, had him held naked, spat in Lawrence's face, and slapped his face with one of his slippers, promising "that he would make me ask pardon." He bit Lawrence's neck, then kissed him, then drew one of the men's bayonets and plunged it into Lawrence's side, above a rib, twisting it to give more pain. Lawrence lost his self-control enough to swear at him, and the bey then calmed himself, and said, "You must understand that I know about you, and it will be much easier if you do as I wish."

Lawrence feared that the bey had identified him, and much of the horror that was to follow may have been enormously increased by his belief that at the end of the ordeal he would simply be hanged, as well as by his burning conviction that Abd el Kader was responsible for his being stopped in the first place, and by his sense of failure for not destroying the bridge at Tell el Shehab. All this was to become firmly fixed in Lawrence's mind, and would have unexpected consequences toward the end of the war.

His description of the incident in *Seven Pillars of Wisdom* is remarkable. Even in moments of horror—such as the attack on the train at

Mudawara, with the looting, pillaging, and cutting of throats; or the scalded trunk of a man that landed at his feet when he blew up Jemal Pasha's train—Lawrence's style is usually ironic and almost deliberately detached. But he writes about Deraa in an unflinching style that is at once physically detailed, intense, and lurid, almost pornographic, in the manner of William Burroughs or Jean Genet—indeed at certain moments, like the precise and even finicky description of the whip that was used on him, it is reminiscent of the Marquis de Sade, who reveled in such descriptions. It is clear that Lawrence, as in his brilliant, almost *pointilliste* descriptions of the desert landscape, is determined that the reader will understand *exactly* what he saw and felt. It is the one passage in the book, apart from a few attempts at humor, when he slips out of the skin of a man whose ambition it was to write "a great book," one that could take its place beside *Moby-Dick, Thus Spoke Zarathustra,* and *The Brothers Karamazov,* and relies on his own voice, without literary artifice:

> They kicked me to the landing at the head of the stairs, and there threw me on the guard-bench and stretched me along it on my face, pummelling me. Two of them knelt on my ankles, bearing down with their arms on the back of my knees, while two more twisted my wrists over my head till they cracked, and then crushed them and my ribs against the wood. The corporal had run downstairs, and now came back with a Circassian riding whip, of the sort which gendarmes carried. They were single thongs of supple black hide, rounded, and tapering from the thickness of a thumb at the grip (which was wrapped in silver, with a knob inlaid in black designs) down to a hard point much finer than a pencil.
>
> He saw me shivering, partly I think with cold, and made it whistle through the air over my head, taunting me that before the tenth cut I would howl for mercy, and at the twentieth beg for the caresses of the Bey, and then he began to lash me across and across with all his might, while I locked my teeth to endure this thing which wrapped itself like flaming wire about my body. At the instant of each stroke a hard

white mark like a railway, darkening, slowly, into crimson, leaped over my skin, and a bead of blood welled up wherever two ridges crossed. As the punishment proceeded the whip fell more and more upon existing weals, biting blacker or more wet, till my flesh quivered with accumulated pain, and with terror of the next blow coming. From the first they hurt more horribly than I had dreamed of and, as always before the agony of one had fully reached me another used to fall, the torture of a series, worked up to an intolerable height.

To keep my mind in control I numbered the blows, but after twenty lost count, and could feel only the shapeless weight of pain, not tearing claws, for which I was prepared, but a gradual cracking apart of all my being by some too-great force whose waves rolled up my spine till they were pent within my brain, and there clashed terribly together. Somewhere in the place was a cheap clock, ticking loudly, and it troubled me that their beating was not in its time.

I writhed and twisted involuntarily, but was held so tightly that my struggles were quite useless. The men were very deliberate, giving me so many, and then taking an interval, during which they would squabble for the next turn, ease themselves, play a little with me, and pull my head round to see their work. This was repeated time and again, for what may have been no more than ten minutes. They had soon conquered my determination not to cry, but so long as my will could rule my lips I used only Arabic, and before the end a merciful bodily sickness came over me, and choked my utterance.

At last when I was completely broken they seemed satisfied. Somehow I found myself off the bench lying on my back on the dirty floor, where I snuggled down, dazed, panting for breath but vaguely comfortable. I had strung myself to learn all pain until I died, and, no longer an actor but a spectator, cared not how much my body jerked and squealed in its sufferings. Yet I knew or imagined what passed about me.

I remembered the corporal kicking me with his nailed boot to get me up and this was true, for next day my left side was yellow and lacerated and a damaged rib made each breath stab me sharply. I remembered smiling idly at him, for a delicious warmth, probably sexual, was swelling through me: and then that he flung up his arm and hacked with the full length of his whip into my groin. This jerked me half-over, screaming, or rather trying impotently to scream, only shuddering through my open mouth. Someone giggled with amusement, but another cried, "Shame, you've killed him." A second slash followed. A roaring was in my head, and my eyes went black, while within me the core of my life seemed to be heaving slowly up through the rending nerves, expelled from its body by this last and indescribable pang.

By the bruises, perhaps they beat me further: but I next knew that I was being dragged about by two men, each disputing over a leg as though to split me apart: while a third astride my back rode me like a horse. Then Hajim called. They splashed water in my face, lifted me to my feet, and bore me, retching and sobbing for mercy, between them to his bedside: but he now threw me off fastidiously, cursing them for their stupidity in thinking he needed a bedfellow streaming with blood and water, striped and fouled from face to heel. They had laid into me, no doubt much as usual: but my indoor skin had torn more than an Arab's.

So the crestfallen corporal, as the youngest and best-looking of the guard, had to stay behind, while the others carried me down the narrow stairs and out into the street. The coolness of the night on my burning flesh, and the unmoved shining of the stars after the horror of the past hour, made me cry again. The soldiers, now free to speak, tried to console me in their fashion, saying that men must suffer their officers' wishes or pay for it, as I had just done, with still greater suffering.

They took me over an open space, deserted and dark, and behind the Government house to an empty lean-to mud and wooden room, in which were many dusty quilts. They put me down on these, and brought an Armenian dresser who washed and bandaged me in sleepy haste. Then they all went away, the last of the soldiers whispering to me in a Druse accent that the door into the next room was not locked.

I lay there in a sick stupor, with my head aching very much, and growing slowly numb with cold, till the dawn light came shining through the cracks of the shed, and a locomotive began to whistle in the station. These and a draining thirst brought me to life, and I found I was in no pain. Yet the first movement brought anguish: but I struggled to my feet, and rocked unsteadily for a moment, wondering that it was not all a dream, and myself back five years ago in the hospital at Khalfati, where something of the sort had happened to me.

The next room was a dispensary, and on its door hung a suit of shoddy clothes. I put them on slowly and clumsily, because of my swollen wrists: and from the drugs chose some tablets of corrosive sublimate, as a safeguard against recapture. The window looked north on to a blank long wall. I opened it, and climbed out stiffly. No one saw me, which perhaps was the reason why I had been shut up in so weak a place.

I went timidly down the road towards the village, trying to walk naturally past the few people already astir. They took no notice, and indeed there was nothing peculiar in my dark broadcloth, red fez and slippers: but it was only by restraining myself with the full urge of my tongue silently to myself that I refrained from being foolish out of sheer terror. The atmosphere of Deraa seemed inhuman with vice and cruelty, and it shocked me like cold water when I heard a soldier laugh behind me in the street.

By the bridge were the wells, with men and women already about them. A side-trough was free, and from its end I scooped up a little water in my hands, and rubbed it over my face: then drank, which was precious to me: and afterwards wandered aimlessly along the bottom of the valley for some minutes, towards the south, till out of sight of both town and station. So at last was found the hidden approach to Deraa for our future raiding party, the purpose for which Mijbil and myself had come here it seemed so long ago.

Further on a Serdi, riding away on his camel, overtook me hobbling up the road towards Nisib. To him I explained that I had business there, and was already footsore. He had pity, and mounted me behind him on his bony camel, to which I clung the rest of the way, learning the feelings of my name saint on his gridiron. The tribe's tents were just in front of the village, where I found Mijbil and Daher, very anxious about me, and curious to learn how I had fared. Daher had been up to Deraa in the night, and knew by the lack of rumour that the truth about me had not been discovered. I told them a merry tale of bribery and trickery, which they promised devoutly to keep to themselves, laughing aloud at the simplicity of the Turks.

We rested there the night, during which time I managed to get along towards the village, and to see the great stone bridge to the north of it, one of the most important in this neighbourhood. Then we took horse, and rode very gently and carefully towards Azrak, without incident, except that on the Giaan el Khunna a raiding party of Wuld Ali let us and our horses go unplundered, when they heard who I was.

This was an unexpected generosity, for the Wuld Ali were not yet of our fellowship; and their action revived me a little. I was feeling very ill, as though some part of me had gone dead that night in Deraa, leaving me maimed, imperfect, only half-myself. It could not have been the defilement, for no one ever held the body in less honour than I did myself: probably it had been the breaking of the spirit by that frenzied nerve-shattering pain which had degraded me to beast-level when it made me grovel to it; and which had journeyed with me since, a fascination and terror and morbid desire, lascivious and vicious perhaps, but like the striving of a moth towards its flame.

When allowance is made for Lawrence's post-Victorian avoidance of certain words, and for his dislike of the subject of sex in the first place, this is certainly one of the most horrifying descriptions of torture and male rape ever written, made even more horrifying by the knowledge that Lawrence, as so many of those who knew him confirm, hated being touched by anyone, under any circumstances. Even a friendly handshake, a pat on the back, or an affectionate embrace was torture to him, and here he was stripped naked, beaten savagely, fondled, kissed, and eventually buggered, to use the word he avoided using himself, all of it taking place in the shadow of the knowledge that if the bey's words meant what Lawrence supposed they meant, he would be hanged at the end of it all.

Those who are critical of Lawrence have argued that he exaggerated the incident, or even invented it altogether. But the episode was not improbable—the brutality of the Turks toward their subject races was a known fact, and the practice of anal rape, while by no means restricted to the Turkish soldiery and their officers, was a recognized peril of becoming a prisoner of the Turks in World War I, as in the many earlier Balkan wars—nor was it uncommon; indeed it remains one of the dangers of warfare in the Middle East. Lawrence, given his small size, pale skin, apparent youth, and seemingly delicate body, would have looked like an obvious victim for this kind of treatment (some of the portraits painted of him after the war emphasize the androgynous quality of his features, particularly the lips); indeed it had almost happened to him earlier, before the war, when he and Dahoum were arrested as deserters and imprisoned.

Bearing in mind that no pages of *Seven Pillars of Wisdom* were more often revised by Lawrence than those describing the incident at Deraa, or subjected to more criticism and soul-searching by his many literary advisers, including Bernard Shaw and E. M. Forster, the reader will have to decide whether they carry conviction or not. There seems no good reason why Lawrence would have invented the incident—on the contrary, it seems more like the kind of thing that he would have suppressed, had he not been determined to tell the whole truth even when it was distasteful and damaging to him. For he does not strain himself to come out of it with credit; it is not just his body but his spirit that was broken, and much of what happened in 1918, and what became of Lawrence later, after the war, would be incomprehensible except for Deraa.

He himself put it best, in 1924, in a letter to Charlotte Shaw, who by then had become a kind of alternative mother figure: "About that night, I shouldn't tell you, because decent men don't talk about such things. I wanted to put it plain in the book, & wrestled for days with my self-respect. . . . For fear of being hurt, or rather, to earn five minutes' respite from a pain which drove me mad, I gave away the only possession which we are all born into the world with—our bodily integrity. It's an unforgiveable matter, an irrecoverable position: and it's that which has made me forswear decent living & the exercise of my not-contemptible wits & talents.

"You may call this morbid: but think of the offense, and the intensity of my brooding over it for three years. It will hang about me while I live, & afterwards if our personality survives. Consider wandering among the decent ghosts hereafter, crying 'Unclean, unclean!' "

Considering that the Shaws had what used to be known as *un mariage blanc*—that is, they were legally married and lived together as man and wife, but Charlotte remained celibate—perhaps nobody could have been better suited to understand Lawrence's mortification and shame than she, who had all her life refused to have sex, or even to contemplate the possibility of childbirth. In this revulsion toward sex, she and Lawrence were very much alike, except that he had been violated, had given in under the pressure of pain, and had even felt, the ultimate horror, "a delicious warmth, probably sexual . . . flooding through me . . . a fascination and terror and morbid desire, lascivious and vicious perhaps, but like the striving of a moth towards its flame."

In short, he had not only been humiliated, tortured, and brutally raped, but to his horror had felt a sexual excitement that made his torturers mock him and filled him with shame. The ultimate abasement is not to be violated, after all, but to *enjoy* being violated, and Lawrence had discovered in himself at Deraa just what he had been at such pains all his life to avoid admitting.

Whole books have been written putting Lawrence posthumously on the analyst's couch, but it is hardly necessary to be a professional psychoanalyst to glean from Lawrence's description of the incident at Deraa and his later explanation to Charlotte Shaw—they were equally frank about their lives to each other—a fair understanding of what happened, and some sense of why Lawrence felt he had to atone for it. He had failed to

live up to his own standards, impossibly high as they might be—by giving in to pain and fear, by submitting himself to rape as an escape from
the pain, and by discovering that despite himself he felt a forbidden sexual excitement that he could not conceal from his torturers.

Those who have doubted the story point out that the governor of
Deraa, Hacim Bey, though brutal, was a notorious womanizer, and that if
he really knew he had Lawrence in his hands, he would never have dared
to let him go. But neither of these things is necessarily so. The bey, as we
have seen, could have been one of at least two other Turkish officers in
Deraa, and the phrase "I know all about you" could have meant many
things. The bey, whoever he was, may have meant, "I know all about what
kind of man you are, and what you like, so stop fighting against it"; indeed
this is far more likely than that he knew the man standing stripped before
him was Major T. E. Lawrence, CB. A Turkish officer who had such a
notorious figure as Lawrence in his hands and let him escape would have
been court-martialed and shot; besides, there was a substantial reward
on Lawrence's head.

Lawrence limped to safety, still suffering from the toe he had broken
while destroying the train; rode back to Azrak; concealed his wounds
and what had happened to him; and returned to Aqaba, where "he seemed
like a wraith, so white and remote . . . and crept away into a tent," and
where he learned that Allenby, ahead of schedule, had given the British
people what Lloyd George wanted for them as a Christmas present: Jerusalem.

Allenby had not yet entered Jerusalem, however, and he wanted Lawrence to be there when he did.

Years before, in 1898, Kaiser William II had visited Jerusalem, and had
caused the Jaffa Gate to be enlarged so that he could ride into the city,
in his glittering full uniform. At the time, a wit at the Foreign Office
had remarked, "A better man than he entered the city on foot," and
this thought must have occurred to Sir Mark Sykes, ever the imperial
stage manager, who telegraphed Allenby from London with the advice to

dismount, or get out of his automobile, and enter Jerusalem humbly on foot. Very likely Allenby, no mean stage manager himself, had already reached the same conclusion.

The Turks had abandoned Jerusalem, and for many, including Lawrence himself, the taking of the city by British and Commonwealth troops was "the most memorable event of the war." Allenby, with an unfailing genius for the big event, was determined to make the most of his capture of the Holy City, and left orders at Aqaba that Lawrence was to join him at once. Lawrence, not unnaturally, supposed that Allenby was going to give him hell for his failure at Yarmuk, but an airplane had been sent for him, and he was flown directly to Allenby's headquarters in the field, north of Gaza, still barefoot and in white robes. To his surprise, the interview with Allenby went better than he had imagined—the breakthrough at Gaza and Beersheba and the fall of Jerusalem had pleased Allenby so much that he didn't seem to mind about the bridge at Tell el Shehab. He had wanted the Turks to the east of the Dead Sea and the Jordan River to be harassed, preoccupied, and disorganized as he advanced from Beersheba, so that he could not be attacked on his right from the desert, and God knows Lawrence had achieved this, and with fewer than 100 armed men.

As a sign of his regard, Allenby insisted that Lawrence should be present as part of his staff when he entered the city, so Lawrence borrowed bits and pieces of uniform from the other staff officers, and resplendent with red staff collar tabs and a major's crown on each shoulder, he walked behind Allenby on December 11, through the Jaffa Gate and into Jerusalem.

Sykes had originally hoped to write Allenby's proclamation to the inhabitants of Jerusalem himself, and as a new convert to Zionism he wanted to include a few rousing words about the Balfour Declaration; but after due deliberation by the cabinet, Lord Curzon was asked to draft a more cautious message, merely promising to safeguard "all institutions holy to Christians, Jews and Muslims," and declaring martial law. Within hours after the city was taken, the pattern of the future was clear: the Ashkenazi Jews were exultant that Allenby had entered the city "on the Maccabean feast of Hanukah," though this timing had been wholly unintentional; the Arabs complained not only about that, but about their suspicion that the Jews were attempting to "corner the market" in small change; and Picot protested that the right of the French to have their soldiers, and theirs alone, guard the Holy Sepulcher was being ignored. Lawrence wrote his first letter home in more than a month to tell his family that he had been in Jerusalem, adding that he was now "an Emir of sorts, and have to live up to the title," and that the French government "had stuck another medal" onto him. This medal was a second Croix de Guerre, which he was trying to avoid accepting, no doubt in part because it would surely have involved being kissed on both cheeks by Picot.

Storrs, who had missed the official entry, arrived to take up his surprising new duties as "the first military governor of Jerusalem since Pontius Pilate," with the temporary rank of lieutenant-colonel. It was in this capacity that Storrs first met Lowell Thomas, the brash American journalist, documentary filmmaker, and inventor of the travelogue. Thomas was a former gold miner, short-order cook, and newspaper reporter with a gift for gab, who had studied for a master's degree at Princeton, where he also taught, of all things, oratory, and who had been sent by Woodrow Wilson, a former president of Princeton, to make a film that would drum up Americans' enthusiasm for the war and for their new allies, now that the United States had joined it—an early and groundbreaking attempt at a propaganda film. Thomas, his wife, and the cameraman Harry Chase set off for Europe, but one look at the western front was enough to convince them that nothing there was likely to serve their purpose, or to convince the American public that it was a good idea to send their sons to the war. They went on to Italy, but that was not much better—Italy was locked in battle with the German and Austro-Hungarian armies in circumstances that were almost as grim as the western front, and that would be described perfectly after the war, from firsthand experience, by Ernest Hemingway in A Farewell to Arms. There, however, Thomas learned about General Sir Edmund Allenby's campaign against the Turks in Palestine, which sounded like more promising material for a film, and particularly for an American public to whom biblical place names—

Jerusalem, Gaza, Beersheba, Galilee, Bethlehem—still had more reso-
nance than Verdun, the Somme, or Passchendaele.

Thomas, who had the American go-getter's ability to move like lightning when his interest (or self-interest) was aroused, quickly had himself
accredited as a war correspondent; and he arrived in Jerusalem, with
Harry Chase, in time to film Allenby's entrance into the city—a worldwide scoop. Sometime later, he was buying dates on Christian Street
when he saw a group of Arabs approaching. His "curiosity was excited by
a single Bedouin, who stood out in sharp relief from his companions. He
was wearing an agal, kuffieh, and aba such as are only worn by Near Eastern Potentates. In his belt was fastened the short curved sword of a prince
of Mecca, insignia worn by the descendents of the Prophet. . . . It was not
merely his costume, nor yet the dignity with which he carried his five
feet three, marking him every inch a king or perhaps a caliph in disguise . . . [but] this young man was as blond as a Scandinavian, in whose
veins flow Viking blood and the cool traditions of fiords and sagas. . . . My
first thought as I glanced at his face was that he might be one of the
younger apostles returned to life. His expression was serene, almost
saintly, in its selflessness and repose."

Wisely, Lowell Thomas sought out Storrs ("British successor to Pontius Pilate"), and asked him, "Who is this blue-eyed, fair-haired fellow
wandering around the bazaars wearing the curved sword of—?"

Storrs did not even allow Thomas to finish his question. He opened
the door to an adjoining room, where, "seated at the same table where
Von Falkenhayn had worked out his unsuccessful plan for defeating
Allenby, was the Bedouin prince, deeply absorbed in a ponderous tome
on archeology. Introducing us the governor said, 'I want you to meet Colonel Lawrence, the Uncrowned King of Arabia.' "

CHAPTER EIGHT

1918: Triumph and Tragedy

"Good news: Damascus salutes you."

—T. E. Lawrence, *Seven Pillars of Wisdom*

"Two names had come to dominate Cairo," Ronald Storrs wrote concerning the end of 1917: "Allenby, now striding like a giant up the Holy Land, and Lawrence, no longer a meteor in renown, but a fixed star." It is worth noting that despite the failure of the attack on the bridge at Yarmuk and the incident at Deraa (about which Lawrence had told nobody except Clayton and Hogarth, both of whom seem to have received a strictly sanitized version of the story), Lawrence's name was already being placed in conjunction with Allenby's, as if they were partners, rather than a full general who was the commander in chief and a temporary major who was a guerrilla leader. Lowell Thomas was not the only person to recognize that Lawrence was a great story—perhaps *the* great story of the war in the Middle East—as well as a genuine hero in a war in which individual acts of bravery were being submerged in the public's mind by the sheer mass of combatants. People hungered for color, for a clearly defined personality, for a hint of chivalry and panache rather than the endless casualty lists and the sheer horror of mechanized, muddy, anonymous death on a hitherto unimaginable scale. The desire for a hero was not limited to Great Britain—in Germany it would produce at about the same time the enduring cult of *Rittmeister* Manfred Freiherr von Richthofen, the famous Red Baron, the handsome, daring air ace, commander of the "Flying Circus," with his bright red Fokker Triplane and his eighty victories.

Lawrence's cult had started long before his arrival in Jerusalem; indeed it had its beginning among a much more critical group—his fellow soldiers. His flowing robes; his apparent indifference to fatigue, pain, and danger; his ability to lead desert Bedouin; and the fact that he appeared to be fighting a war of his own devising, with no orders from anybody except Allenby—all these gave Lawrence a legendary status well before the arrival of Lowell Thomas and Harry Chase. Lawrence had already mastered the art of seeking to avoid the limelight while actually backing into it—as his friend Bernard Shaw would write, years later: "When he was in the middle of the stage, with ten limelights blazing on him, everybody pointed to him and said: 'See! He is hiding. He hates publicity.' "

Storrs had unwittingly introduced Lawrence to the man who would shortly make him perhaps the world's first media celebrity and also the media's victim. This is not the only thing that happened in Jerusalem. Lawrence gleefully records that at an indoor picnic luncheon after Allenby's entrance into the city, François Georges-Picot announced to Allenby that he would set up a civil administration in Jerusalem, only to be fiercely snubbed by Allenby, who pointed out that the city was under military government until he himself decided otherwise. It was a bad day for Picot, who had been greeted everywhere on his way to Jerusalem (with the amiable Storrs as his traveling companion) as France's high commissioner for Palestine, and was now reduced to the role of a mere political officer attached to the French mission. To his fury he had been placed next to Brigadier-General Clayton in the order of precedence of those following General Allenby into Jerusalem.

Even more pleasing than this snub to the French was the fact that

Allenby had important plans for Lawrence in the next stage of his campaign. Given the weather and the number of casualties he had already sustained, Allenby intended to stay put for two months, and then, in February, advance north from a line drawn from Jerusalem toward Jericho and the mouth of the Jordan River. He wanted Lawrence to bring what was now being rather grandly referred to as the "Arab army" to the southernmost end of the Dead Sea, concentrating at Tafileh, both to discourage the Turks from launching an attack against the flank of the British army, and to cut off the supplies of food and ammunition that the Turks were sending the length of the Dead Sea. Lawrence agreed to this—the area was one where the tribes were friendly to Feisal—and suggested that after Allenby took Jericho, the headquarters and supply base of the "northern Arab army" be moved from Aqaba to Jericho and supplied by rail. He did not mention that this position would make it easier for the Arabs to reach Damascus before the British could get there, and he indulged in a certain amount of flimflam, which may not have fooled a man as astute as Allenby. The "northern Arab army" consisted of Jaafar's 600 or 800 former Turkish soldiers (their number depends on whom you believe), plus however many Bedouin tribesmen could be persuaded to rally around Lawrence and Auda Abu Tayi, but its importance far outweighed its size. The most important points were that the Arab army would henceforth be acting formally as Allenby's right wing, and that blowing up railway lines and locomotives would now take second place to advancing into Syria. Lawrence was in a position to ask for more mountain guns, camels, automatic weapons, and money. In addition, he requested, and got, the support of Joyce's armored cars, and a fleet of Rolls-Royce tenders to support them. In his raid from Aqaba to Mudawara to attack the station there, he had remarked on how much of the desert consisted of smooth, flat, baked mud, and it seemed to him certain that a car could be driven across it at high speed, so that as the Arab forces advanced north into Syria the cars would give him vastly increased mobility and firepower.

Shortly after his return to Aqaba he and Joyce would put this to the test by driving a Rolls-Royce tender equipped with a machine gun across the desert from Guweira to Mudawara, in some places at sixty miles an hour. The trip was so successful that they went back to Guweira; gathered up all the tenders, which carried water, gasoline, spare tires, and rations; and drove back to Mudawara to shoot up the station there, opening up a new phase in desert warfare that would be imitated in the Libyan Desert by the Long Range Desert Group from 1941 to 1943. The cars Lawrence used were not tanks, of course, and he could not use them to attack Turkish fortifications, but they helped to keep the Turks bottled up in their blockhouses and trenches, while the Bedouin rode where they pleased and destroyed stretches of undefended railway.

Lawrence's experience at Deraa, and the fact that Turks' price for him, dead or alive, had risen from the £100 they would pay for any British officer to "twenty thousand pounds alive or ten thousand dead" after the attack on the general's train, also persuaded him to enlarge his personal bodyguard. Its members were loyal only to him, "hard riders and hard livers: men proud of themselves and without family," as he described them, though they were often men whom other Bedouin regarded as troublemakers or worse, "generally outlaws, men guilty of crimes of violence." Chosen from different tribes and clans so that they would never combine against Lawrence, they were ruled and disciplined with "unalloyed savagery" by their officers. Their flamboyance and their total commitment to "Aurens" raised eyebrows among both the Arabs and the British. "The British at Aqaba called them cut-throats, but they cut throats only to my order," Lawrence would boast, and they would eventually grow to a force of ninety men, dressed "like a bed of tulips," in every color of the rainbow except white, which was reserved for Lawrence alone, and armed with a Lewis or Hotchkiss light machine gun for every two men, in addition to each man's rifle and dagger. This was a protective force far larger than that of any Arab prince at the time, as well as better paid, better armed, and better dressed (at the British taxpayers' expense), and it confirmed Lawrence's growing prestige. He also used his bodyguard as shock troops— more than sixty of the ninety would die in combat. They were recklessly loyal to him, and referred to him as "Emir Dynamite" because of his continuing interest in blowing up trains, rails, and bridges.

Implicit in Allenby's plans for 1918 was a fundamental change in the tactics of the Arab army from guerrilla skirmishing on the border of the desert to a full-fledged attack by the Arab "regulars" on Turkish-held towns. The Arabs would not only have to fight against Turkish troops, but take ground and hold it—something they had never done before, and that Lawrence had hitherto been determined to avoid. Lawrence saw at once that four small rural towns, which marked the border between cultivated land and the desert, represented the key to the next phase of the march toward Damascus. Maan was too far south, and too heavily garrisoned by the Turks, to interest him. But to its northwest, only a few miles from Petra, lay Shobek, with its store of wood for fueling the railway; the Arabs had taken Shobek once in October for a few days. Tafileh was next, "almost level with the south end of the Dead Sea. . . . Beyond it lay Kerak, and at the northern end of the Dead Sea, Madeba." Each of these towns was about sixty miles away from the next, and they formed a chain that the "northern Arab army" might climb up until it made contact with Allenby's army advancing on the other side of the Dead Sea to take Jericho.

A Turkish attempt to make a sortie out of Maan to protect Shobek had already been repulsed by the Arabs; one Turkish battalion, which lagged behind, had been cut to pieces by the Arabs—a taste of things to come. By January 1918 the Turks were effectively bottled up in Maan again, while the "motor-road" was completed—an astonishing feat in this part of the world—from Aqaba up through Wadi Itm to Guweira, from which the mudflats of the desert stretched out for many miles. Guweira became the advance base of operations. From it, large sections of the railway to Medina were now only an hour's drive away. The Turks could drive off camel-mounted tribesmen, but there was no way they could defend the railway against armored cars. Lawrence was, in the words of Liddell Hart, "at least a generation ahead of the military world in perceiving the strategic implications of mechanized warfare," and putting it into effect. Henceforth, cars and trucks began to play almost as important a role in Lawrence's plans as camel- or horse-mounted Bedouin, and when he finally arrived in Damascus it would be in his own personal Rolls-Royce tender, which he named "Blue Mist," seated next to a British Army Service Corps driver and surrounded by his own colorful bodyguard.

Few tasks in warfare are more difficult than combining a guerrilla army with a regular one to wage a conventional war, and doing so while continuing to fight. Lawrence hoped to take Tafileh, the most important of these towns, by tackling it "simultaneously from the east, from the south, and from the west." To do this it would be necessary to take Shobek first, cut the railway line between Maan and Amman, and then attack Tafileh from the east, out of the desert, using a combination of mounted infantry under the command of Nuri as-Said (a future prime minister of Iraq) and whatever tribal levies could be produced by the Abu Tayi and their rivals the Beni Sakhr. The mixture of tribes, of Arabs and British gunners and drivers, not to speak of the overwhelming presence of Auda, was bound to create difficulties. Although this was desert warfare, it was winter; and on the high plateau, more than 3,000 feet above sea level, winds howled in from the Caucasus bringing snow, ice, and freezing temperatures—conditions that were underappreciated in Khartoum, Cairo, and London. Among the regular, uniformed Arab troops, many of whom had been issued only one blanket and were dressed in tropical khaki drill, it would not be uncommon for men to freeze to death during the night; and even among the Bedouin, with their thick, heavy cloaks, men would still suffer frostbite or die.

In the first week of January, Lawrence had enough to keep him busy in Aqaba, as the elements of his plan were put into motion. The Bolshevik Revolution had brought the Sykes-Picot agreement out into the open, and, predictably, it was causing doubts among the Arab leaders. It inspired Jemal Pasha to write to Feisal, proposing "an amnesty for the Arab Revolt," and suggesting that an Arab state allied to Turkey might be more in the Arabs' interest than an outcome in which the Allies would carve up the Turkish empire, giving the British Iraq, the French Syria and Lebanon, and the British and the Jews Palestine. Feisal forwarded this letter to Cairo, no doubt as a proof of his loyalty, but Lawrence encouraged him to reply to it, and to keep up a secret correspondence—or perhaps felt unable to prevent this. Even though Arab leaders had already guessed what it contained, the Bolsheviks' publication of the terms of the Sykes-Picot agreement threatened to undermine such trust as had been built up between the Arabs and Britain; and Lawrence, as he was in any case bound to do, no doubt thought it better to let Feisal explore various options. It did not help much that London had finally decided to publicize the Arab Revolt. Bringing his usual white-hot enthusiasm to bear on the subject, Sykes cabled Clayton to "ring off the highbrow line" of dignified press releases about British respect for all faiths in the Holy Land. Sykes wanted a propaganda blitz that would appeal to everyone, from "English church and chapel folk" to "the New York Irish," not to speak of "Jews throughout the world." Sounding just like Lord Copper in Evelyn Waugh's *Scoop*, he demanded local color: "Jam Catholics on the Holy Places. . . . Fix Orthodox on ditto. . . . Concentrate Jews on full details of colonies and institutes and wailing places[!] . . . *Vox humana* on this part."

Clayton, an experienced and secretive intelligence officer, was hardly the right person to launch this flood of propaganda—on the contrary, his specialty was *avoiding* reporters—but gradually the British press, whipped on by Sykes, began to focus on the Middle East in the afterglow of the conquest of Jerusalem. Lawrence's fame began to spread far beyond Cairo and the office of the chief of the imperial general staff (CIGS) in London—a fact that would have a major impact on his life less than two months later, when Lowell Thomas and Harry Chase finally arrived in Aqaba to make Lawrence once and for all the central figure in the Arab Revolt and put him and the Arabs, at last, not only on the map but, more important, on film.

Lawrence spent the early days of January composing a long and sensible report on the situation, perhaps intended to take Clayton's mind off Feisal's correspondence with Jemal Pasha, though its conclusions about

Syria were such as to prevent it from being published in the *Arab Bulletin*; it was circulated only among senior British intelligence officials who could be trusted to keep it out of the hands of the French. Lawrence also dealt with a minor breach of discipline, albeit one that could have had serious repercussions, in a way that makes any careful reader of *Seven Pillars of Wisdom* realize just how tangled Lawrence's feelings on the subject of sex and corporal punishment were.

If we bear in mind that the incident at Deraa had happened only six weeks earlier, it is surprising to read that when an Arab youth of seventeen, Ali el Alayan, an Ageyl camel man of his bodyguard, was "caught in open enjoyment of a British soldier," by which Lawrence seems to have meant that the British soldier had been buggering the Arab or vice versa, Ali was tried in five minutes and sentenced to 100 lashes, as "appointed by the Prophet," which Lawrence reduced to fifty. The Arab boy "was immediately trussed over a sand-heap, and beaten lustily." Meanwhile Lawrence told the British soldier, Carson, "a very decent A.S.C.* lad," that he would have to turn him over to his officer, who was returning to Aqaba the next day. Carson "was miserable at his position"—understandably, since in those days, and indeed through World War II and for some years beyond it, a homosexual act committed by a member of the British armed forces was both a military and a criminal offense.

When the British NCO in charge of the cars, Corporal Driver, appeared and asked Lawrence to hush the matter up for the boy's sake before their officer returned, Lawrence refused. He was not shocked; nor did he condemn the act morally—"neither my impulses nor my convictions," Lawrence wrote later, "were strong enough to make me a judge of conduct"—it was simply a matter of Anglo-Arab justice. It was important that there be equity, he told the British corporal. He could not "let our man go free. . . . We shared good and ill fortune with the Arabs, who had already punished their offender in the case." The corporal, who was clearly experienced and reasonable, explained that Carson "was only a boy,

---

* The Army Service Corps (ASC) dealt with transport, supply, and vehicles; it became the Royal Army Service Corps (RASC) in 1918.

not vicious or decadent," and "had been a year without opportunity of sexual indulgence." He also, though with considerable tact, laid part of the blame on Lawrence, who, for fear of venereal disease, had posted sentries to prevent British troops from visiting the three hardy Arab prostitutes who plied their trade at Aqaba.

Corporal Driver, having made his point respectfully, returned in half an hour and asked Lawrence to come and have a look at Private Carson. Lawrence, thinking Carson was ill, or had perhaps tried to harm himself in dread of the disgrace to come, hurried to the British camp, where he found the men huddled around a fire, including Carson, who was covered with a blanket, looking "drawn and ghastly." The corporal pulled off the blanket, and Lawrence saw that Carson's back was scored with welts. The men had decided that Carson should receive the same punishment as Ali, "even giving him sixty instead of fifty, because he was English!" They had carried out the whipping in front of an Arab witness from Lawrence's bodyguard, "and hoped I would see they had done their best and call it enough."

Lawrence's reaction was odd. "I had not expected anything so drastic, and was taken aback and rather inclined to laugh," he wrote, and noted that Carson was eventually sent "up-country," where "he proved to be one of our best men." Reading between the lines, we can easily guess that a wink passed between Lawrence and Corporal Driver. The Arabs not only were satisfied by Carson's punishment but apparently assumed that Lawrence had ordered it; and certainly it was well within the old-fashioned traditions of British military discipline to keep an incident like this "within the family," rather than let it go to a court-martial, which would disgrace the whole unit.

What is harder to understand is why Lawrence included the story in his book at all—it feels out of place, squeezed in between a long description of how he selected his bodyguard and the plans for his campaign against Talifeh. It is preceded by a puzzling disquisition on sex in Arabia, in which Lawrence remarks that "the sacredness of women in nomad Arabia forbade prostitution" (yet there were three prostitutes in Aqaba), and argues that "voluntary and affectionate" sexual relationships among Bedouin were better than "the elaborate vices of Oriental cities" or—in an odd aside—"the bestialities of their peasantry with goats and asses."

Aside from the fact that stories about peasants having sex with their animals are common to every country and culture, it is hard to see how "the elaborate vices" of Oriental cities would be different from or worse than those practiced in the open air at Aqaba. Granted that frankness about acts and words that were still taboo was one of the things Lawrence sought to bring to literature later on, there is still something disturbing about a man who has recently endured a savage whipping himself feeling "rather inclined to laugh" at the spectacle of two young men just having been whipped. There is also an uneasy feeling of sexual ambivalence—or perhaps simply a lack of sympathy with or understanding of the sexual impulse, which seems to affect Lawrence whenever he writes about what was, for him, an uncongenial subject.

By the second week of January, Lawrence was on the move again. He rode out into the desert with his bodyguard to reconnoiter a ridge overlooking the railway station Jurf el Derawish, thirty miles north of Maan. Deciding that the position was a good one, he brought up Nuri as-Said, with 300 Arab regulars and a mountain gun. Under the cover of darkness, he cut the railway line above and below Jurf, and at dawn opened fire on the station with the mountain gun, silencing the Turkish artillery. Then the Beni Sakhr charged on camels from their position behind the ridge, where they had been hidden. The Turkish garrison, surprised and overwhelmed, surrendered when Nuri captured the Turks' own gun and turned it on the station at point-blank range. Twenty Turks were wounded or killed, and nearly 200 were taken prisoner—but the discovery of two trains in the station loaded with delicacies for the officers in Medina set the Arabs off on a prolonged burst of looting and gorging, and as a result they missed an opportunity to destroy another train as it approached the station.

During two days of extreme cold, heavy snow, and hail, the tribes around Shobek, near Petra, stormed and took the town. Hearing the news Nuri rode on to Tafileh through the night, and halting at the edge of the cliff above the town at dawn, he demanded that the town surrender or be shelled, even though his gun and his troops were far behind him. The Turks hesitated—they too had heard the news of the capture of Jurf and Shobek, but they were 150 men, and well armed. Then Auda Abu Tayi cantered out in full sight of them, his heavy cloak flowing behind him, and called out: "Dogs! Do you not know Auda?"

In Liddell Hart's words, "The defences of Tafila* collapsed before his trumpeting voice as those of Jericho had once collapsed before Joshua." Holding on to the place was harder, however, since the Arabs immediately began quarreling among themselves, and the majority of the townspeople who were Arab were divided in their loyalty to different clans. Lawrence arrived, and began to spread around gold sovereigns to induce peace, but he had hardly even begun to restore order when news reached him that a sizable Turkish force was marching from Amman to retake Tafileh, consisting of "three . . . battalions of infantry, a hundred cavalry, two mountain howitzers and twenty-seven machineguns . . . led by Hamid Fakhri Bey, the commander of the 48th Division." By late afternoon, the Turks had brushed aside the Arab mounted pickets guarding Wadi Hesa, "a gorge of great width and depth and difficulty" ten miles north of Tafileh, which, like almost every place in Palestine and western Syria, was part of biblical geography, cutting off the land of Moab from that of Edom. Lawrence had been elated by the capture of Jurf, Shobek, and Tafileh, but he was dismayed by the swift response of the Turks; he had assumed they would be too busy defending Amman to worry about retaking Tafileh.

In ordinary circumstances, the right thing for the Arabs to do in the face of a powerful Turkish advance would have been to withdraw, first destroying whatever they could in Tafileh, and carrying away as much booty as they could load on their camels. Instead Lawrence decided to fight a conventional battle, marking a new stage in the development of the

*Lawrence spells it Tafileh; Liddell Hart spells it Tafila.

Arab army. He was moved in part by the plight of the residents of Tafileh, whom the Turks would certainly punish severely for surrendering the town, and in part by a desire to prove to Allenby that the Arabs could fight and win a conventional battle.

Until now, Lawrence had been following his own maxim: "To make war upon rebellion is messy and slow, like eating soup with a knife," and his aim was to keep the Turks trying to eat soup with a knife for as long as possible. His model was Marshal de Saxe, who had written, "I am not in favor of giving battle, especially at the outset of a war—I am even convinced that an able general can wage war his whole life without being compelled to do so." Now, Lawrence, a convinced admirer of de Saxe, was following instead the formula of Napoleon: "There is nothing I desire so much as a great battle." He had not changed his opinion about de Saxe, whose maxims would remain the essential basis for all guerrilla wars on into the present, but he recognized the political reality, which was that the British, and especially the French, were unlikely to take the Arabs' claims to territory seriously until the Arabs had demonstrated an ability to hold their ground and beat the Turks in a conventional battle of positions. It was not that Lawrence's philosophy of war had changed; it was that politics, and its by-product, public relations—Lawrence had already learned something from Lowell Thomas—required something more than blowing up bridges and looting trains if the Arabs were to get Damascus. Since Lawrence considered it his job to get them Damascus, he made up his mind to fight the Turks at Tafileh.

In desert skirmishes Lawrence's command was direct and unchallenged; by contrast, the force at Tafileh had, if anything, too many leaders for its size. The overall commander of the march toward the Dead Sea was Feisal's younger half brother Zeid, "a cool and gallant fighter," who did not have much experience directing a battle but who, as a son of the sharif of Mecca (now king of the Hejaz), had the respect of all the tribes, and even of Auda. The uniformed regulars were under the command of Major-General Jaafar Pasha, a former officer in the Turkish army and now Feisal's chief of staff, a competent professional soldier. Lawrence's bodyguard was led by Abdulla el Nahabi, a fearless adventurer with a series of murders and assaults on his head, as well as a price. As for the Bedouin, the bulk of them were divided into two mutually hostile factions, since Auda's tribe and the Motalga were traditional blood enemies. By means of a lavish payment in gold, Auda was sent "back to his desert beyond the railway to contain the garrisons of the Turkish stations," thus removing one source of friction, but clearly the battle could not be won unless Lawrence took command of it, though he passed his orders through the Arabs' chief.

It is always difficult to compare battles, but to anybody interested in military history, once allowance is made for the difference in climate and scale, the topography of Tafileh bears a startling resemblance to that of Gettysburg. Lawrence, then, was in the position of Lee, and Hamid Fakhri Bey in the position of Meade, when Longstreet launched his attack against Cemetery Ridge on the afternoon of July 3, 1863—with the crucial difference that Lawrence succeeded.

Tafileh was a small town, hardly more than a large village, in a rugged, forbidding, but beautiful landscape. Prosperous in peacetime, with a population of fewer than 10,000,* it was famous for its green gardens; for its crops of olives, dates, and figs; and for its profusion of wells and hot springs. Set in a deep ravine, it was overlooked by what was almost a terraced cliff to the west, and by a gentler, triangularly rocky plain to the east rising about 3,000 yards from the town to a rock ledge about 2,000 yards in length. At its northern end, this ledge overlooked the road from Kerak, on which the Turks were approaching.

At the first news that the Turks were coming, Jaafar, with the instinctive caution of a trained professional soldier, had moved his men onto the high ground to the west of the town, the textbook solution to the problem. But Lawrence disagreed, both because there was plenty of "dead ground" in front of Jaafar, which would allow the Turks to work their way around his flank instead of attempting a direct frontal attack uphill, and

---

*About 35,000 today.

because abandoning the town to the Turks was a political and tactical mistake. The Bedouin disliked townsmen to begin with, and the population of Tafileh was mixed and therefore doubly offensive to them. The Ottoman government had force-marched to Tafileh nearly 1,000 Armenians who had escaped the massacre, as well as "a colony of freebooting Senussi from North Africa," part of the long-standing Turkish policy of settling areas with mutually hostile groups in order to give the local population a presence they would hate more than they did the Turks. Zeid and Jaafar thought the townspeople were probably pro-Turk, and would welcome the Turks back, but Lawrence disagreed, and to prove his point made his way into Tafileh by night. He found that the local people, whether Arab, Armenian, or Senussi, were united only by their hatred of the Turks, and terrified by the fact that the Arab forces had marched out of town and abandoned them to their fate. The town was in chaos and terror, as people, in Lawrence's vivid description, "rushed to save their goods and their lives. . . . It was freezing hard, and the ground crusted with noisy ice. In the blustering dark the crying and the confusion through the narrow streets were terrible." The Motalga further terrified the townspeople by firing their rifles into the sky to keep their spirits up as they clattered out of the town at a gallop, while the approaching Turks fired back in the darkness to demonstrate how close they were.

Under the circumstances, it seemed to Lawrence that the townspeople might be persuaded to fight in their own defense. As dawn broke he gathered up a score or so of the Motalga tribesmen and sent them forward with a few of the local peasantry to engage the Turks, who were deploying on the long ridge at the top of the triangular plain to the east of Tafileh. He then went off to find Zeid and persuade him that Jaafar was positioned on the wrong side of the town, and that the right place to fight a "pitched battle" was in front of the town, on the triangular plain, not on the hills behind. Fortunately, Zeid had already come to the same conclusion. Lawrence, when he wrote about the Battle of Tafileh, would dismiss the action as a military parody—"I would rake up all the old maxims and rules of the orthodox army text-book, and parody them in cold blood today"—

BATTLE OF TAFILEH

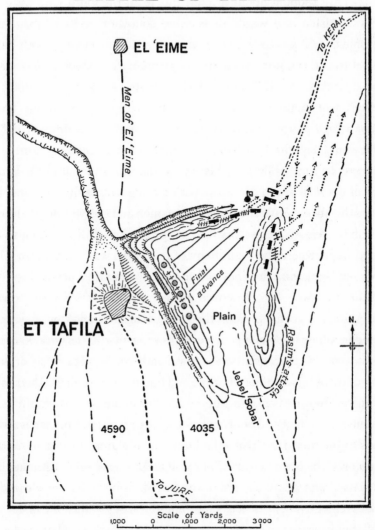

EL 'EIME

Men of El 'Eime

To KERAK

Final advance

Plain

ET TAFILA

Rasim's attack

Jebel Sobar

N.

4590

4035

To JURF

Scale of Yards
1,000   0   1,000   2,000   3000

but there is no evidence of this in the report he wrote after the battle. On the contrary, no less a judge than Colonel A. P. Wavell, the future field marshal, would describe it as "one of the best descriptions of a battle ever penned."

What strikes one most about Tafileh is that Lawrence could hardly have fought with more professional skill and personal daring, whatever he may have thought about it later; this is all the more true since his forces consisted of a wildly ill-assorted collection of Bedouin, armed townsmen, local peasants, and Arab regulars, none of them with much trust in the others, nor, except for the regulars, any experience of discipline. By rights, Fakhri Pasha, with three battalions of infantry, 100 cavalrymen, two mountain howitzers, twenty-seven machine guns, and a unit of armed police, should have been able to retake the town, and no doubt would have done so, had not Lawrence outmaneuvered him.

Lawrence sent Abdulla, a Mesopotamian machine gun officer, and some of his men ahead on mules with two Hotchkiss machine guns to engage the Turks, while the armed townsmen and the Motalga drove the Turkish horseman back across the triangular plain, from the first to the second ridge, where the main body of the Turks was forming up. They were slow to organize, for they had spent a night in the open and were so cold that they were "nearly frozen in their places." Zeid wanted to wait until Abdulla reported back on the strength of the enemy, but Lawrence elected to follow Napoleon's advice on how to win a battle: *On s'engage, et puis on voit.** He plunged into the town; gathered up gorgeously dressed bodyguards, who were busy looting; and told them "to recover their camels" and get to the eastern side of the ravine immediately. As for himself, he went on, barefoot and unarmed, climbing up a steep cliff, then walking across to the first ridge, where he found the remains of some Byzantine stonework, which would serve very well as "a reserve or an ultimate line of defense." Not many officers in the British army would have cared to walk barefoot over rocks, ice, snow, and the sharp stalks of wormwood plants, but Lawrence consoled himself with the thought that bare feet were surer on icy rocks than boots, and that "the climb would warm me."

Lawrence stationed Zeid's personal camel men and some of his own bodyguards on the ridge and told them to stay in full sight, so as to give the impression that the ridge was strongly held—Zeid's men were not enthu-

---

* "One attacks, then waits to see what happens."

siastic about his order, and he was obliged to harangue them in Arabic and give them his gold signet ring as a symbol of his authority. Then he walked forward alone across the plain toward the second ridge, where it joined the Kerak road where the enemy was forming up. He met Abdulla, coming back to say that he had had five men killed and one gun destroyed. Lawrence sent him back to ask Zeid to move forward with the Arab regulars as soon as possible, then continued walking forward under fire in full view toward the northernmost part of the second ridge, where the Motalga horsemen and the armed townsmen were still fighting fiercely. By now, the Turkish howitzers were firing at them, but their range was too short and the shells were falling instead on the plain all around Lawrence. He stopped and burned his fingers picking up a shell fragment to examine it, deciding it was from a Skoda eleven-pounder. He did not think the townsmen and the Motalga would hold out long under shell fire, and he could see that the Turkish infantry was moving from the road to the second ridge to outflank them. When he reached the townsmen they were out of ammunition, so he sent them back to the second ridge to get more, and told the dismounted Motalga horsemen to cover their retreat, giving them the sound advice "not to quit firing from one position until ready to fire from the next." The Motalga were amazed to see that Lawrence was unarmed and walking around among them as they tried to shelter behind a small, flinty mound while some twenty Turkish machine guns were firing at them. "The bullets slapped off it deafeningly, and the air above it so hummed and whistled with them and their ricochets and chips, that it felt like sudden death to put one's head over the top," Lawrence wrote.

He jokingly reminded the tribesmen of von Clausewitz's comment that a rear guard effects its purpose more by being than by doing, though this seems unlikely to have cheered them up, even if they had understood it. He then ordered the Motalga to hold out for another ten minutes before retreating, and left them, since he had to walk back across the plain under heavy fire, carefully counting his paces. He wanted to know the exact range to set the sights of his machine guns and his mountain gun, now that it was clear to him that the Turks were going to advance into his trap.

The Motalga held their position for almost ten minutes, as ordered, then mounted and galloped back across the plain. When they reached Lawrence, one of them lent him a stirrup so he could hold on as they raced back to the first ridge. There Lawrence lay down and rested in the sun as the Turks deployed along the ridge at the far end of the plain. Once the enemy were where he wanted them, he sent Rasim, "a Damascene, a sardonic fellow, who rose laughing to every crisis and shrunk around like a sore-headed bear . . . when things went well," to lead about eighty horsemen out of sight around the southern edge of the plain to attack the Turks' left flank. Lawrence reminded himself of the familiar military adage that an attack should be aimed at a point, not a line, and told Rasim to aim for the last man on the Turkish left. He moved men and guns up and down his ridge, clearly visible to the Turks so as to focus their attention on the ridge in front of them, instead of on their flanks. He had more than 100 men from the nearby village of Aima armed and sent them off to attack the Turkish left, then opened fire at the Turkish position on the far ridge with his mountain gun and his machine guns.*

The men from Aima, "who knew every blade of grass on their own village pastures," crept to within 300 yards of the Turks' right flank on the exposed ridge before they opened fire with their rifles and Lawrence's three light machine guns. Rasim had ten of his men dismount and move forward under cover with five automatic weapons, which "crumpled the Turkish left," then charged with his remaining horsemen. From his position on the ridge nearest Tafileh, Lawrence could see the curved swords of Rasim's horsemen flashing in the setting sun, at which point he ordered the rest of his men to charge uphill toward the Turks, on horse, on foot,

---

*Lawrence measured the distance at 3,100 yards by counting his paces; some of his critics have objected that the sights of a British Vickers machine gun were calibrated only up to 2,000 yards, but this ignores the fact that the Vickers was "effective" up to 4,500 yards, and like the British SMLE rifle of World War I, was designed to provide "long range volley firing" (also known as "indirect" or "plunging" fire) when needed. That is, the Vickers could be aimed and fired high in the air, so that the rounds would cover a great distance in an arc or parabola and plunge down on the enemy from directly above. Lawrence's text makes it clear that this was what he had in mind, and did.

and on camel. These men included the Armenian survivors of the massacre, who drew their knives in anticipation of cutting Turkish throats in revenge. The Turks were driven back into "the broken, precipitous paths, undergrowth, the narrows and defiles," behind them, where they and their general were massacred. It was, in the words of Liddell Hart, a victory "in the purest classical tradition. . . . It was Cannae, or still more, Ilipa,* adapted to modern weapons," a "gem" which placed Lawrence among "the Great Captains." It also bore out the truth of the duke of Wellington's remark: "Nothing except a battle lost can be half as melancholy as a battle won."

"In the end," Lawrence wrote, "we had taken their two mountain howitzers, very useful to us, their twenty-seven machineguns, two hundred horses and mules, and about two hundred and fifty prisoners. Of the rest above six hundred were killed, and they said only fifty got back, exhausted fugitives, to the railway. All the Arabs on their track rose against them and shot them as they ran. Our men had to give up the pursuit quickly, for they were tired and sore and hungry, and it was pitifully cold. Fighting a battle may be thrilling for the general, but terrible afterwards when the broken flesh that has been his own men is carried past him. It began to snow as we turned back. . . . The Turkish wounded had to lie out, and were all dead the next day."

Arab losses were about twenty-five killed and forty wounded. Lawrence reproached himself severely for these. Although he would never wear the ribbon or accept the decoration, he was awarded the Distinguished Service Order, only one step below the Victoria Cross, for which he had already been recommended.

Wavell's praise for Lawrence's account of the Battle of Tafileh was well earned. Better than any novelist, Lawrence succeeded in describing unflinchingly every moment and movement of the battle, and demonstrating that when called on to do so, he could direct his ragtag army in an orthodox way, while coolly exposing himself to danger.

* Scipio's decisive victory over Hasdrubal's Carthaginians in Spain.

As was so often the case with Lawrence, success was followed by a humiliating failure. One reason is that victory tended to undo the Arabs' shaky system of alliances, which was always at the mercy of the stronger pull of tribal and clan loyalty. Another was sleet—the foul weather and heavy mud that rendered the camels clumsy and helpless. Lawrence managed to send seventy Bedouin horsemen under Abdulla el Feir to raid the lake port near El Mezraa, at the southernmost end of the Dead Sea, where they overwhelmed a small group of Turkish sailors sleeping on shore, destroyed a motor launch and six lighters, and captured sixty prisoners and ten tons of grain. This interruption of the Turkish grain supply was in some ways more important than the victory at Tafileh, but Lawrence was still anxious to fulfill his promise to Allenby and move the Arab forces north toward Jericho.

He was restless and discontented at Tafileh—forced idleness was never good for Lawrence, and for once even he complained of the vermin. He finally set off for Guweira to meet with Joyce, Feisal, and Lieutenant-Colonel Alan Dawnay. Dawnay had been appointed by Allenby to create a "Hejaz Operations Staff" and to establish some kind of military order. Lawrence might have been expected to object to him—Dawnay was tall and thin; was a perfectly uniformed officer of the Coldstream Guards; and was the brother of Brigadier-General Guy Dawnay, who had come up with the plan of feinting at Gaza and putting the weight of the British attack on Beersheba—but something about Alan Dawnay's cold precision and "brilliant mind" appealed to Lawrence, who called him "Allenby's greatest gift to us."

Lawrence rode down to Guweira in foul weather; it was "freezing once again, and the slabby stones of the valley-slopes became sheets of ice." The camels balked at moving forward, and the men nearly froze to death, and all would have died if Lawrence had not pushed them mercilessly on. Even when they descended into the warmer air of the plain around Guweira, there was no relief. "The pain of the blood fraying its passage once more about our frozen arms and legs and faces was as great and much faster than the slow pain its driving out: and as we warmed we grew sensible that up there in the cold we had torn and bruised our unfeeling feet nearly to a pulp among the stones. We had not felt them tender while each step was deep in icy mud: but this warm salty mud scoured out the cuts, and in desperation we had to climb up on our sad camels, and beat them woodenly towards Guweira."

This passage seems to express Lawrence's state of mind, despite his earlier victory. Ostensibly, he had ridden to Guweira to pick up £30,000 in gold sovereigns with which to pay the tribes to the north; but one senses, reading his account in *Seven Pillars of Wisdom*, that he was briefly in need of friendly company—Joyce and Dawnay, and Feisal, whom he much preferred to his half brother Zeid—and that he was tired of dealing with Zeid and the recalcitrant tribesmen. He seems not to have been downhearted that Feisal's attack on the railway watering station at Mudawara had failed. Lawrence understood the lack of cooperation between the Bedouin tribesmen and the Arab regulars.

He spent three days with Joyce, Dawnay, and Feisal, then set off back to Tafileh, with an escort provided by Feisal. Lawrence split the gold coins into thirty canvas bags, each bag containing 1,000 gold sovereigns; two of these bags could be carried by a single camel. Even this was a heavy burden on the poor beasts, with the ice and frozen mud, and his return journey to Tafileh was as cold and difficult as the journey down. Once there, he found waiting for him a young British intelligence officer, Kirkbride, "a taciturn, enduring fellow," and leaving the gold in Zeid's care, he rode to Dana with the young man, then rode north on a reconnaissance mission of his own "as far as the edge of the Jordan valley," from where he could hear Allenby's guns attacking Jericho. It seemed to Lawrence feasible to bring the Arab army north of the Dead Sea, as he had promised, and he rode back to give Zeid the good news, only to find that Zeid, shamefaced, had been persuaded or browbeaten by the local sheikhs to pay them the gold Lawrence had brought from Guweira. Of the £30,000 in gold coins, he had nothing left, so the plan of advancing north was impossible.

Lawrence's reaction was very like a nervous breakdown. He was "aghast," and realized at once that this meant "the complete ruin of my plans and hopes." He decided on the spot to ride directly to see Allenby and offer his resignation. Admittedly, £30,000 in gold sovereigns* was a substantial sum, but Lawrence was used to handling thousands of pounds in gold coins at a time, and while he was himself scrupulously honest, he was aware that some of it was wasted, money down the drain. British gold was the lifeblood of the Arab Revolt; it had to be handed out in huge amounts; and Lawrence himself, who at times handed out thousands of pounds a week to the tribes, remarked that it was better (and, in the long run, cheaper) to open a bag and let a man take out as much as he could in a single handful than to dole it out coin by coin. Zeid's behavior had been weak and foolish, but that was no fault of Lawrence's. It was an overreaction for him to write that his "will was gone," and that he dreaded more pain, more suffering, more killing, "the daily posturing in alien dress," in short, the whole role that had been thrust upon him, and that he had reached out for so eagerly when it was presented to him at Rabegh a year and a half ago. Now he blamed himself bitterly for "that pretence to lead the national uprising of another race." He was clearly suffering from what was then called shell shock, and is now called post-traumatic stress disorder. He believed that he had lost his nerve, that he had "made a mess of things," and was determined to throw himself on Allenby's mercy.

He rode directly west, making a journey of more than eighty miles in twenty hours over terrible terrain in a countryside at war, where a party of five men on camels might easily be attacked by anyone, or shot by the British. At last he dismounted at Beersheba, thinking he had made his final camel ride, to learn that Allenby had just taken Jericho. By car and train he traveled north through the night to Bir Salem, where, to his surprise, Hogarth was waiting on the platform to greet him. Much as Lawrence may have been astonished by Hogarth's presence, Hogarth was not Merlin, and one may therefore suppose that somebody at Aqaba or at Beersheba passed on the message that Lawrence was on his way to Allenby in a desperate state of mind. Hogarth, and the Arab Bureau,

---

* Thirty thousand gold sovereigns would be worth about $9.6 million today.

would have been at pains to make sure that this meeting did not take place until Lawrence was put in a calmer state of mind, and nobody was better suited to this task than Hogarth. To be blunt, no one had more at stake either, for Lawrence was the most visible asset of the Arab Bureau, the brightness of his fame casting the rest of the bureau into shadow, where, as an intelligence agency shaping British policy in the Middle East, it was anxious to remain.

In any case, Lawrence, barefoot in his robe, cloak, and headdress, unburdened himself then and there on the station platform to Hogarth, equally disguised in the uniform of a naval officer. Hogarth listened patiently, as he always did. Lawrence complained that he was "a very sick man, almost at breaking point," that he was "sick of responsibility," that he had been given "a free hand," rather than an order, that "Cairo had put on him the moral responsibility for buoying up the Arabs with promises that might never be fulfilled," and that he had lost faith in the Arabs' ability to handle their own affairs even if those promises were fulfilled. His experience with the British troops manning the armored cars had reawakened his appreciation for his own countrymen, and taught him that vehicles might be as useful as camels for warfare in the desert. He wanted to be in "a subordinate position," handling machines, not people, "a cog himself in the military machine." In the words of Liddell Hart— and he was quoting from his conversations with Lawrence—"The harness of obedience was better than the self-applied spur of command." When Lawrence told Liddell Hart this, of course, it was years later and he was already serving in the ranks, so he may have been retroactively applying this thought to the events of February 1918, but perhaps the decision to serve "solitary in the ranks" had already formed itself in his mind. These moments of complete despair had occurred before in Lawrence's life—he had suffered one on his ride into Syria before Aqaba—and would recur frequently in years to come. Hogarth may also have realized, better than Lawrence himself, the cost of constantly playing the hero among people who were critical judges of heroism.

In any case, it was clear to Hogarth that his protégé was in bad straits, and very wisely he did not try to argue with Lawrence, but instead took him off to have breakfast with Brigadier-General Clayton, another of those strong, silent Englishmen who had won Lawrence's trust. An odd little group they must have made in the officers' mess over the toast and marmalade: the small barefoot major in his Arab costume, the neatly bearded Oxford don in his naval uniform, and the tall professional soldier. It would be interesting to know what the other officers in the mess thought of this unlikely trio, but by the time Lawrence had reached the breakfast table he had calmed down considerably. Hogarth may have advised him to forget about the £30,000 worth of gold coins; it was water under the bridge (and "a drop in the barrel as well," considering what the Arab Revolt was costing Britain every month), but in any case the subject did not come up again. Like the skilled producer he was, Hogarth had soothed his troubled star, and Clayton, playing *his* role, firmly pointed out that Lawrence was indispensable, that Allenby had great things in store for him—the kind of praise that Lawrence, for all his apparent lack of vanity and ambition, could never resist. Clayton added that General Jan Smuts of South Africa, even then the supreme fixer and stage manager of imperial Britain, had paid a visit to General Allenby on behalf of the prime minister to emphasize the crucial importance of victory over the Turks, and to promise reinforcements in men and weapons. These promises, like so many of Lloyd George's, were not to be fulfilled, since the Germans would launch their great spring offensive in a few weeks' time; but Allenby's mood was optimistic, and neither Clayton nor Hogarth wanted Lawrence to bring his personal loss of self-confidence to the attention of the commander in chief.

In the end Clayton bluntly told Lawrence that there was no question of "letting [him] off," and took him straight from the breakfast table to Allenby, who had for several days been sending airplanes out to find Tafileh and drop messages to Lawrence, ordering him to report in immediately. He was in no mood to listen patiently to Lawrence's problems, even had Lawrence cared to recite them. Smuts's visit had conveyed Lloyd George's burning desire to shift focus from the western front to the

Middle East and "to knock Turkey out of the war" as the first step toward victory, although the war cabinet and the CIGS were somewhat taken aback when Allenby replied that he would need an additional sixteen divisions to do it. In the end all he would get was one British division and one Indian infantry division from Mesopotamia, and one Indian cavalry division from France.

If Allenby was going to push his advance north against the Turks, he needed the Arabs to become, in effect, his right wing, taking on the Turkish Fourth Army to the east of the Jordan River. The Arabs would have to concentrate against one objective at a time, quite a different procedure from the irregular warfare they had waged so far. To accomplish that, Allenby needed Lawrence, who seemed to be the only person who could get the Arabs to fight in an organized way. Ironically, Lawrence's success at Tafileh had had the effect of making everybody at headquarters in Jerusalem overestimate the Arab army's ability to fight a conventional battle.

Allenby's overbearing optimism simply rode roughshod over Lawrence's self-doubts, and, with whatever reservations, Lawrence agreed "to take up again my mantle of fraud." No doubt he knew better than to show a glum face. Allenby thus persuaded Lawrence to accept a significant change in tactics. For Lawrence, the Arabs' great advantage over the Turks was space, the immense and empty desert. The Arabs could appear anywhere on its periphery in small numbers, attack the Turks, and then retire back into the desert, where the Turks could not follow them.

Now, Allenby wanted the Arabs to concentrate on the town of Maan and take it, cutting the railway south to Medina once and for all. Lawrence thought it could be done—or at least *said* it could be done—and even proposed a refinement of the plan. He suggested cutting the railway some miles north of Maan, so that in order to fight the Turkish garrison would have to come out into the desert, "where the Arabs would easily defeat [them]." This sounds like overconfidence on Lawrence's part, but given his admiration for Allenby, or perhaps out of relief that the subject of the missing £30,000 worth of gold hadn't come up, he may have laid it on a little thicker than he meant to.

In return, Lawrence had demands of his own. He would need at least 700 camels, to bring troops and supplies north from Aqaba—already, his purchases of camels in Arabia had driven up the price and reduced the supply—an immense increase in weapons, and, as usual, a lot more gold. More important, he wanted some assurance that the Turks would be prevented from bringing reinforcements down from Amman, with the obvious risk that the Arabs might be caught "between pincers," from Medina in the south and Amman in the north. Allenby agreed, and explained that he intended to take Salt, and could then destroy as much of the railway as necessary, south of Amman. Lawrence was doubtful about the wisdom of Allenby's plan—he knew the Arabs well enough to suspect that they would lose heart the moment the British fell back from Amman—but he seems to have kept this doubt to himself, though he hinted at his reservations to Allenby's chief of staff. Perhaps this was because Allenby was one of the very few people Lawrence found it impossible to resist.

The next day, February 28, Lawrence was invited to a corps conference, at which the plans were dealt with in more detail, and during which Lieutenant-General Sir Philip Chetwode, who commanded the XX Corps and would "direct the advance," asked Lawrence "how his men were to distinguish friendly from hostile Arabs, since their tendency was to be prejudiced against all wearing skirts." This was an odd—though sensible—question, to which Lawrence, who was of course in his white robe, replied, not very helpfully, "that skirt-wearers disliked men in uniform." This caused some laughter, but did not, of course, answer Chetwode's question. In fact, during the relatively brief time when the British and the Arab army came into contact, there were many unfortunate incidents in which British and Australian troops took Lawrence's Bedouin for hostiles, particularly because they tended to assume that all "natives" were thieves or cutthroats. Distrust of "wogs" was fairly widespread in the British army, but Lawrence's victory at Tafileh had made the Arab army briefly more popular, and had given it a certain credibility among the British that it lacked when it was chiefly engaged in looting trains, however important such looting was to the cause.

Confidence in the Arab army was high enough that Lawrence asked for, and got, permission to use the Imperial Camel Brigade, a handpicked unit composed of British yeomanry and Australians mounted on Sudanese camels. The yeomanry were British volunteer cavalry units, usually formed in rural areas, with the local farmers, or their sons or tenants, serving as troopers, and the local gentry, or their sons, as officers. Lawrence complained that both the camels and the men were too heavy to cover long distances in the desert, and insisted that the men and their beasts be slimmed down, and trained to subsist on the bare minimum of water. With them as "shock troops," he hoped to be able to threaten Deraa, when the time came, and fight the Turks as they attempted to retreat.

It was an ambitious plan, but despite the efforts of Lawrence, Alan Dawnay, and Joyce to supply such a widespread advance involving so many different elements, it failed to come off as planned. In the event, these plans were overshadowed by the German spring offensive on the western front in France, which breached the British line and sent the British army "reeling backwards on Amiens." This was Germany's last card, intended to drive the British back to the Channel ports; it used fifty additional divisions, which the Germans could withdraw from the eastern front now that the Bolshevik government had signed a peace. The Germans' hope was to win a victory, or at least a negotiated peace, before American divisions arrived in quantity in France. Even so convinced an "easterner" as Lloyd George was startled by the size and ferocity of the German attack—it began with the biggest artillery barrage of the war, 1.1 million shells fired in five hours—and by the horrifying prospect that after four years of trench warfare and millions of casualties the Germans might still manage to drive a wedge between the French and British armies, take Paris, and push the BEF to the sea.* In the circumstances, Allenby's plan to cross the Jordan River no longer seemed crucial, and

---

* By the time the *Kaiserschlact*, as Field Marshal Hindenberg and General Ludendorff had named their offensive (thus shrewdly saddling the kaiser with the responsibility for it), ground to an end in June, it had cost the Germans nearly 700,000 casualties, and the British and French almost 500,000 each.

very shortly he would be stripped of two complete British divisions (as well as numerous artillery, cavalry, and machine gun units), and with them his superiority in manpower and firepower over the Turks.

It is hard to guess Lawrence's state of mind in March 1918, while he was busy preparing for an advance which would not come off, and about which he was by no means confident. He spent some time in Cairo, where the Arab army now had its own little headquarters in the Savoy Hotel, and then returned to Aqaba, where he had to deal with a newcomer: Captain Hubert Young of the Indian army. Young, a fluent Arabic-speaker, had been designated as Lawrence's "understudy" now that Lawrence's indispensability had been recognized by almost everyone in Egypt. Lawrence went out of his way to be polite about Young, but the two men were a bad match, although they had gotten along well enough at Carchemish before the war. Young had deeply resented Lawrence's presence in Mesopotamia in 1916, and he was not very much more tolerant of Lawrence now, though in the interest of civility he did his best to hide his feelings. A look at Young's portrait in *Seven Pillars of Wisdom* is enough to tell the story: the touchy superiority, the suspicion in his eyes, the unmistakable look of a man who is standing on his dignity and fears he is about to be made fun of at any moment. It is by far the least appealing portrait in the book. Young at first remarked with some satisfaction that "Lawrence was only one of the many British officers who were helping the Arabs," but then came to what was, for him, the dispiriting conclusion that although Joyce was in theory the senior British officer and Lawrence's commanding officer, and Dawnay was officially the chief staff officer, "Lawrence really counted more than either of them with Allenby and Feisal, and used to flit backwards and forwards between G. H. Q. and Feisal's headquarters as the spirit moved him." The use of the word "flit" expresses perfectly Young's disapproval of Lawrence and his flowing white robes.

No sooner had Young arrived at Aqaba than he was to receive a further shock—instead of a neat chain of command in which Major Lawrence reported to Lieutenant-Colonel Dawnay and through Dawnay to their commanding officer, Colonel Joyce, it was announced that Lawrence himself had been promoted to lieutenant-colonel, and been awarded the DSO for Tafileh ("For conspicuous gallantry and devotion to duty"), so that he was now equal in rank to Alan Dawnay, and Young was put even more deeply in the shade. Lawrence later dismissed Young's role, relegating him to taking over "the transport, and general quartermaster work," but that is not how Young saw his job, then or later.

March or April 1918 (the exact date is uncertain) provided another irritation for Young in the form of the unexpected arrival of Lowell Thomas and Harry Chase. Young jumped to the conclusion that Lawrence had invited the two Americans to Aqaba in pursuit of publicity, whereas in

Young.

fact they had been allowed to go there by Allenby. Indeed Allenby himself made the suggestion to Thomas at a luncheon in Jerusalem for HRH the duke of Connaught (the seventh child and third son of Queen Victoria), who had come to confer on Allenby "the Grand Cross of the Order of the Knights of Jerusalem." The duke had hoped to decorate Lawrence too, but Lawrence took good care to be absent. It is a comment on Lowell Thomas's Yankee persistence, affability, and effectiveness that he had managed to get himself invited to the luncheon, where he was encouraged to go to Aqaba. Thomas's journey there would prove unexpectedly long and difficult—he and Chase "[sailed] fifteen hundred miles up the Nile into the heart of Africa to Khartum, and then across the Nubian Desert for five hundred miles to Port Sudan on the Red Sea, where we hoped to get accommodation on a tramp vessel of some sort." Although Allenby had given his blessing to the expedition, he did not apparently feel obliged to provide transportation, since Thomas and Chase could have taken a train from Cairo to Port Suez, and then been accommodated comfortably on a supply ship or a naval vessel from Port Suez directly to Aqaba, a journey of only a few days. The benefit of the roundabout route was that it allowed the pair to record on film Luxor and Thebes, a sandstorm in Khartoum, a visit to "Shereef Yusef el Hindi . . . the holiest man in the Sudan" (whose desert library, Thomas assured his American readers, apparently with a straight face, contained a volume of speeches by Woodrow Wilson), and a trip across the Red Sea on a steamer loaded with horses, mules, donkeys, and sheep, and a crew consisting of "Hindus, Somalis, Berberines, and fuzzy-wuzzies." At Aqaba, Thomas and Chase were sent ashore on a barge loaded with mules and donkeys, and when one of the donkeys "was kicked overboard by a nervous mule," it was immediately torn apart and devoured by two gigantic sharks. Lowell Thomas was not the inventor of "the travelogue" for nothing—all these incidents would play a role in the lecture and film show that would make "Lawrence of Arabia" world famous, so it is perhaps just as well that Thomas and Chase were obliged to take the long way around. Only a few hours after the donkey had been eaten by the sharks, "Lawrence himself came down the Wadi Itm, returning from one of his mysterious expeditions into the blue."

"To accompany Lawrence and his body-guard on an expedition was a fantastic experience," Lowell Thomas would write in his best-selling book *With Lawrence in Arabia*, though he never actually did go on such an expedition. "First rode the young shereef, incongruously picturesque with his Anglo-Saxon face, gorgeous head-dress and beautiful robes. Likely enough, if the party were moving at a walking pace, he would be reading or smiling to himself over the brilliant satire of Aristophanes in the original. Then in a long, irregular column his Bedouin 'sons' followed in their rainbow-colored garments, swaying to the rhythm of the camel gait. . . . At either end of the cavalcade was a warrior poet. One of them would begin to chant a verse, and each man, all along the column, would take his turn to cap the poet's words with lines of the same meter."

This vision of the young "prince of Mecca," engrossed in a volume of the Greek classics (in "the original" Greek, of course) as he and his colorful bodyguard ride across the desert on "one of his mysterious expeditions into the blue," was one that Lowell Thomas would fix firmly in the popular mind—so firmly that even forty-four years later, when David Lean's award-winning film *Lawrence of Arabia* was released to international acclaim, the Lawrence it portrayed still owed much to the colorful reporting of Thomas and the inspired photography of Chase. There is a considerable difference between Lawrence's estimate of how much time Thomas spent with them and Thomas's own account. Jeremy Wilson, in his authorized biography of T. E. Lawrence, writes that Thomas "spent less than a fortnight with Feisal's army and saw Lawrence for only a few days." This is surely correct, but it leaves out the intensity of the time Thomas and Chase did spend with Lawrence, and their determination to get as many photographs, reels of film, and interviews as they could, as well as Lawrence's willingness to cooperate. Judging from the number of photographs Chase took (many of them artfully staged), and from Thomas's voluminous notes, Lawrence was not only cooperative but enthusiastic; and in one of the photographs showing Lawrence and Lowell Thomas together, Lawrence looks unusually relaxed and good-humored, not at all like a man being inconvenienced by two importunate Yankee journalists. Nor can Lawrence have been under any illusion that Lowell Thomas was going to write a series of thoughtful, fact-filled dispatches about the Arab army and the war in the Hejaz. Thomas was a showman, an inspired huckster in the tradition of P. T. Barnum, a lecturer who would prove every bit as successful as Mark Twain; and anybody meeting him, let alone someone as intelligent as Lawrence, would have known all that about him in five minutes or less. As for Chase, he was a Hollywood cameraman, not a documentary filmmaker—his job was to put glamour on film. Lawrence himself may have enjoyed pulling the leg of the gullible American, but if so, the American had the last laugh. Thomas may or may not have believed everything he was told, but in either case he managed to sell it, burnished with his own additions, exaggerations, romantic touches, and flamboyant prose, to an audience of millions.

With Lawrence in Arabia is artfully written; it suggests that Thomas was an eyewitness to Lawrence's desert operations, without actually saying so, a familiar journalistic trick. Lawrence himself wrote Thomas out of *Seven Pillars of Wisdom* altogether, and later made it clear that Thomas "was never in the Arab firing line, nor did he ever see an operation or ride with me." There is no question, however, that Lawrence posed for innumerable staged photographs then and later on, including one in which he is claimed to be lying in the sand beside his kneeling camel's neck, holding his Lee-Enfield rifle at the ready, a bandolier of .303 cartridges around his neck, as if there were Turks on the horizon. In another he (or somebody else) appears disguised, his face covered with an embroidered flowered veil, as "a Gypsy woman of Syria," in which costume he planned to go behind the enemy lines to spy out information—something Lawrence actually did later on. Oddly enough, Thomas went to some trouble to deny that Lawrence cooperated with Chase in these carefully staged pictures. "My cameraman, Mr. Chase," Thomas wrote, "uses a high-speed camera. We saw considerable of Colonel Lawrence in Arabia, and although he arranged for us to get both 'still' and motion pictures of Emir Feisal,

Auda Abu Tayi, and the other Arab leaders, he would turn away when he saw the lens pointing in his direction. . . . Frequently Chase snapped pictures of the colonel without his knowledge, or just at the instant that he turned and found himself facing the lens and discovered our perfidy."

Nobody looking at Chase's photographs of Lawrence could possibly believe this story. They are not casual "snaps"; they are quite clearly well-thought-out formal portraits or carefully faked "action" scenes, for which the subject's willing cooperation would have been essential; and in fact Lawrence would pose for more of them later on, in London, where studio lighting and a backdrop were required. It suited both Thomas and Lawrence to pretend that Lawrence was the unwitting victim of the photographer—from Thomas's point of view, it made the whole story more of a scoop; and from Lawrence's, it freed him from the accusation of seeking publicity—but it cannot be true.

Feisal, whose understanding of the value of American publicity was a good deal sharper than Lawrence's, played the good host, taking Thomas and Chase on a long trip out into the desert—providing more good footage for Chase of camels, Bedouin, and tents—and sent them on an excursion to Petra, "the rose-red city, half as old as Time," where Thomas wondered whether "we had not been transported to a fairy-land on a magically-colored Persian carpet." Chase's pictures would later appear in Lowell Thomas's show about Lawrence, as well as in future travelogues.

Everybody seems to have been aware of just how important it was to present a positive picture of the Arab Revolt to America. Thomas got Clayton and Hogarth to talk to him about Lawrence, despite the fact that as senior intelligence officers they might have kept their mouths shut. Thomas also interviewed people at Aqaba, where everybody may have embellished stories about Lawrence for Thomas's benefit. Bedouin tribesmen, many of whom believed that the Koran forbade photography, since it involved making a human image, nevertheless meekly allowed Chase to take their pictures, and Feisal provided masses of horsemen and camel riders, banners flowing and swords drawn, for action crowd scenes. Whether Lawrence was conscious of it or not, the few days he spent with Lowell Thomas and Harry Chase in Aqaba would eventually be instrumental in creating the legend of "Lawrence of Arabia."

Lawrence may not have realized that he had launched himself on a collision course with a new and potent combination of tabloid newspapers, press photography, and the cinema, but what he did in those few days at Aqaba would change his life far more than the mere acceptance of a few decorations and medals could have done. He had the good fortune—or perhaps the bad luck—to put himself in the hands of one of the most gifted and silver-tongued promoters of the twentieth century, a man who would be a star in media not even invented yet, and who would live on to 1981: a long life devoted to making himself and Lawrence household names.

It was at about this time, after Lawrence had left Thomas and Chase to continue their interviews and filming without him, that he rode north to Shobek, about twenty miles from Petra, and learned there of the death of Daud, the friend of Farraj, one of his two high-spirited servant boys. Farraj himself came to Lawrence with the news that Daud had frozen to death at Azrak.* In Lawrence's account of this, in *Seven Pillars of Wisdom*, there is a clear change of mood, as if some of the exuberance and joy he had felt in his relationships with the Arabs was being squeezed out by the war. Fearless as he may have been for himself, Lawrence was not indifferent to the death of others, particularly those whom he loved, or for whom he felt responsible. He wrote of Farraj and Daud that they "had been friends from childhood, going about hand in hand, for the happiness of feeling one another, and diverting our march by their eternal gaiety." He reflected on the "openness and honesty in their love, which proved its innocence; for with other couples we had seen how, when passion had thrust in, it had not been friendship any more, but a half-marriage, a shamefaced union of the flesh." The relationship between Daud and Farraj leads Lawrence on to another of those curious speculations about sexu-

---

*Jeremy Wilson points out that Lawrence changed their names in *Seven Pillars of Wisdom*—they were actually Othman (Farraj) and Ali (Daud).

ality, which occasionally puzzle the reader of *Seven Pillars of Wisdom* and make it clear that Lawrence's ideas about heterosexuality were a strange mixture of innocence, idealism, his mother's disapproving eye for the slightest sign of sexual arousal, and the awful example (from Lawrence's point of view) of Thomas Lawrence's having given up his fortune and place in society out of lust for his daughters' governess. "European women," Lawrence wrote, "were either volunteers or conscientious objectors in this war to govern men's bodies," whereas, "in the Mediterranean, women's influence and supposed purpose were circumscribed and the posture of men before her sexual."

It is hard to unravel exactly what this means, but it clearly ties in with Lawrence's assumption that women endured sex unwillingly in the European world, where as in the East "all the things men valued—love, companionship, friendliness—became impossible heterosexually, for where there was no equality there could be no mutual affection." Of course Lawrence judged eastern domestic life as an outsider, whose relationship with the Arabs was either at work in Carchemish, or at war, when they were far from home. Much as he liked to think he had become part of their lives, he was still excluded from what went on between husband and wife (or wives) and from gauging the degree to which Arabs were invisibly influenced by women or by the demands of domestic life. All that, in the Arab world, took place behind a curtain, but the intrigues of the wives and concubines of the Turkish sultan, and the degree to which a woman of the harem might conspire to put her own son on the throne in place of another, should have cured Lawrence of the notion that women in the East were necessarily without ambition, interest, or influence in public or business affairs, or always submissive to their husband. King Hussein may have been an imposing, if infuriating, figure, but who knows what his four wives had to say to him about the relative positions of their sons when he stepped behind the closed door of his private apartments? The voices of women went largely unheard in the Middle East until very recently in its history, but this does not mean that they did not have ways to make themselves heard in private, or that men did not seek their advice, approval, or judgment, as they do elsewhere—or did not have to endure the relentless questioning of a strong-willed mother, as Lawrence himself did. The notion that male Arab society provided a "spiritual union," which complemented "carnal marriage," and that "these bonds between man and man [were] at once so intense, so obvious, and so simple," is a nice tribute to Daud and Farraj, but a very doubtful generalization about marriage in the East, which, while it is certainly different in many ways from marriage in the modern, industrialized West, is perhaps not as different as outsiders may suppose.

Lawrence's plan for the spring campaign was at once ambitious and simple. He would support Allenby's raid on Amman with three separate operations: in the center, Jaafar's regulars, whose numbers were increasing, would seize the railway north of Maan; in the south, Joyce would attack Mudawara with the armored cars, and cut the railway line to Medina once and for all; in the north, Lawrence would join Allenby at Salt, raising the tribes all along the way. Although Lawrence himself still had doubts about whether Jaafar's men could really take Maan, he finally deferred to the optimism of Feisal and Jaafar, and temporarily returned to his position as "an advisor," though he "privately . . . implored Jaafar not to risk too great a disaster."

Conveying more optimism than he felt, Lawrence rode north with his bodyguard and "an immense caravan of . . . camels, carrying five thousand rifles, great quantities of ammunition, and food, for the adherents in the north," only a week after a furious blizzard had covered the ground with snowdrifts. In the last light of day, Lawrence rode alone close to the railway line and surprised a solitary Turkish soldier, who had left his rifle a few yards away while he took a nap. Lawrence had the soldier, "a young man stout, but sulky looking," covered with his pistol, but after a moment, he merely said, "God is merciful," and rode off, faintly interested to see whether the Turk would grab the rifle and shoot him. This is Lawrence at his best—not just the moment of mercy toward an enemy, but the moral courage (and perverted curiosity) to test whether the "Turk was man enough not to shoot me in the back." Note too Lawrence's careful distinction—the *right* thing for the Turkish soldier to do would of course have been to shoot Lawrence, but the *manly* thing for him to do was to spare Lawrence, as he himself had been spared. How many British officers would have felt that way? How many would have put their lives at risk to see what the outcome would be? It is one of the most interesting and consistent parts of Lawrence's character that he continually set himself these moral tests, in which he risked everything to see whether he could live up to his own ideals.

On the fourth day Lawrence arrived in the Atara region, just south of Amman, where the various clans of the Beni Sakhr were gathering, to take advantage of the "flood-ponds" of water and of the "succulent green-stuff" of the spring. Lawrence's opinion of those on whom he was relying tells its own story: "Mitfleh with honeyed words came out to welcome us, his face eaten up by greed and his voice wheezy with it." The plan was to cross the railway line and meet the rest of the Beni Sakhr at Themed. Turki, one of the tribal leaders, had agreed to serve Feisal while his brother continued to serve the Turks, to keep them from suspecting what was about to happen. Turki would take the four nearest railway stations south of Amman—Lawrence did not think this would be difficult—and bring their garrisons in as prisoners, giving them a safe-conduct to reach British prisoner-of-war camps; then the whole force would move toward Salt to make contact with the British. Salt would then become the center of operations for both the Egyptian Expeditionary Force and the Arab army, which could be supplied by means of a new road from Jericho, and both armies would take advantage of the chaos spread along the Turkish lines of communication south of Amman to advance toward the north and threaten Damascus.

The British often complained that the Arabs did not live up to what they had promised to do, but in this case it was the British who let the Arabs down badly. The weakening of Allenby's forces was fatal, and in addition, the Germans had sent out as many units and specialists as possible to stiffen Turkish resistance. Lawrence seems to have relaxed and enjoyed himself "with every hollow a standing pool and the valley-beds tall with grass and painted with flowers," while waiting for news. Both he and the Arab chieftains were worried about Allenby's intention to fall back on Salt after taking Amman, and they were right. A report that Allenby had taken Amman was followed almost instantly by the news that it was untrue, and more alarming yet, that he had lost Salt, was in full retreat, and might actually have to give up Jerusalem. The Beni Sakhr would be exposed to the Turks' revenge. The Turks were already using improvised gallows to hang those who had greeted the arrival of the British with too much enthusiasm. The Beni Sakhr prudently returned their 1,200 Turkish prisoners to the four railway stations from which they had been captured, after giving them back all their personal possessions and arms.

Lawrence decided to ride south to see Feisal, but not before examining for himself what had happened in Amman, and how strong its defenses were. He and Farraj eventually made their way into the town with three Gypsy women Lawrence had hired, dressed like them in long robes with flowered veils. Even so, they attracted the attention of the Turkish soldiers, who chased after them, imagining them to be prostitutes. They fled, though not before Lawrence reached the depressing conclusion that the British had not done enough to damage the railway seriously, and that Amman was too heavily defended to be taken easily. Dangerous as all this was, it was also a kind of high-spirited prank, one that Lawrence could play only with someone like Farraj as his companion.

The next day, on the way south, following the railway line, Lawrence's small group of Arabs saw a patrol of Turkish soldiers, perhaps eight in all. Lawrence saw no reason to bother with them—he could easily continue his march out of their sight or range—but his Arabs, including Farraj, wanted to attack and he let them do so. In the brief fight that followed, Farraj was shot, and fell from his camel. Lawrence found the boy "sunken in that loneliness which came to hurt men who believed death near." The Turkish bullet had passed through his spine, and he could not move. Then one of the Arabs shouted an alarm—fifty more Turkish soldiers were coming toward them, and a motor trolley could be heard on the line. The tribesmen tried to pick Farraj up, but he screamed in pain so terribly that they had to give up the attempt.

One senses Lawrence's sadness in this passage—perhaps the saddest and most moving in *Seven Pillars of Wisdom*. He could not leave Farraj there alive for the Turks to find. They treated European prisoners of war with cruel neglect, but they tortured Arabs unmercifully, sometimes mutilating them or burning them alive. "For this reason," Lawrence wrote, "we were all agreed before action to finish off one another, if too badly hurt to be moved away, but I had never realized that it might fall upon me to kill Farraj."

"I knelt down beside him, holding my pistol near the ground by his head, so that he should not see my purpose, but he must have guessed it, and clutched at me with his harsh, scaly hand. . . . I waited a moment, and he said, 'Daud will be angry with you,' the old smile coming back strangely to his grey face. I replied, 'Salute him from me,' and he gave the formal answer, 'God give you peace,' and shut his eyes to make my work easier."

The number of people with whom Lawrence had a lighthearted and intimate relationship is very small, and there were very few among the Arabs in the two years that he fought with them. However close he may have felt to Feisal, Feisal was a prince and a major political figure with ambitions to win his own crown. Even Auda, with whom Lawrence got along well, was an older man, shamelessly avaricious and ambitious. None of these were people with whom Lawrence could indulge in his own undergraduate high jinks, or who would have responded well to playfulness. Only with his two servants, Daud and Farraj, could he let that side of him appear, and now they were both dead, one by his own hand, the other because he had been left in Azrak to freeze to death. Of Dahoum, the only other young man with whom Lawrence felt totally at ease, little is known. All evidence suggests that Dahoum died of typhus in 1916, along with much of the workforce remaining at Carchemish, though some have speculated that he worked as a spy for Lawrence behind the enemy lines in Syria. Indeed, one of Lawrence's British machine gunners, Thomas Beaumont, claimed to have met Dahoum, and alleged that his real name now that he was "a grown man and past the nickname stage" was Salim Ahmed, but since Beaumont frequently made up stories about Lawrence to sell to the press later on, this is doubtful. In any case, Dahoum was unreachable to Lawrence. Daud and Farraj had played something of the same role as Dahoum for him, though on Lawrence's part there was never the same intensity of feeling that he had for Dahoum, who was almost certainly the only person that Lawrence loved in every possible way except sexually. Now he was alone.

When Lawrence arrived "in sight of Maan," on April 13, he found that Jaafar's Arab regulars had indeed captured a nearby railway station in the hope of tempting the Turkish garrison out into the desert to fight; but, carried away by their success, they had decided to make a full-scale assault on the town, despite the fact that they had neither the forces nor the artillery shells to carry it off. It was another military failure. The plan was too complicated, involving three columns: the center one composed of Arab regulars and Auda's horsemen; the northern one, of more Arab regulars under Jaafar himself; and the southern one, of armored cars and Egyptian camelry, under Dawnay, since Joyce had been evacuated to Egypt with pneumonia at the last minute. When the British had failed to take Amman and had retired beyond Salt, the attack on Maan should in any case have been canceled, but it went forward anyway and miscarried badly, in the absence of a single commander who could pull the disparate forces together. Feisal himself was present, but did not attempt to fill a role as a battlefield commander. Lawrence went forward to watch the battle from a Ford car, instead of riding his usual camel, and was disappointed to see that even his old warhorse Auda Abu Tayi had done little to help the Arab regulars—Lawrence soon realized that it was a mistake to mix regulars and Bedouin forces, though he did not forgive Auda. The next day, when Auda entered Feisal's tent, and said, "Greetings, Lurens," Lawrence merely replied coldly, "Greetings for yesterday evening, Auda."

Lawrence went south to join Dawnay in yet another attack on the railway station at Mudawara, which this time was captured by a joint Arab-Egyptian force, aided by British armored cars. The victory sparked an epic splurge of looting (in which Lawrence managed to walk off with the station bell), and prolonged fighting between the Arabs and the Egyptians over the spoils. Lawrence quelled the disorder without raising his voice, "like the hypnotic influence of a lion-tamer," according to one witness. As usual the Arab force disintegrated as the men made for home with their loot, but Dawnay took his armored cars and the Egyptians south and destroyed nearly eighty miles of railway track, as well as seven stations and numerous causeways and bridges, severing the link to Medina. The town was now isolated; the Turks were left there until they chose to surrender.

Lawrence proposed to move north and destroy another eighty miles of railway line north of Maan, thereby isolating it like Medina; but first he and Dawnay sailed to Egypt, to meet with Allenby, only to learn to their dismay that, on the vague promise that "twenty thousand tribesmen" would come to their support, the British were proposing to advance on Salt again. Lawrence was infuriated that Allenby's staff was dealing with the Arabs directly, instead of going through him, and he was right. The promised tribesmen did not appear, having been bought off by a higher bid from the Turks. The subsequent British attack against the well-prepared Turkish defense failed, and the British were obliged to retreat back to the Jordan valley.

Lawrence was neither surprised nor completely displeased. He felt this experience would teach Allenby's staff a lesson—that communications with the Arab tribesmen were best left in his hands—and would reinforce the importance of Feisal as the one Arab leader the staff could trust. As for Allenby, he decided to make a virtue of necessity, and made plans to attack the Turks up the coast, while keeping their attention fixed on Salt and Amman.

While he was in Egypt Lawrence took advantage of the moment by persuading Allenby to give him 2,000 riding camels, which were made available by the imminent disbanding of the Imperial Camel Brigade and which would hugely improve the mobility of Feisal's army. Lawrence also received a commitment to make more aircraft available to bomb Turkish strongholds and destroy their communications. By May 1918 Lawrence was already a master of "combined operations," as they would become known in the next world war, involving irregular camel-mounted tribesmen and horsemen, armored cars operating far out in the desert, regular infantry, artillery, and "ground attack" aircraft. He was, in fact, one of the first to use aircraft to support ground attacks directly, with the enthusiastic help of Brigadier-General Geoffrey Salmond, commander of the Royal Flying Corps in the Middle East.

From May through July the war in what is now Jordan went on in a steady succession of raids, train and bridge demolitions, and hit-and-run attacks against the Turks. While Allenby prepared for his big offensive—for he, like Lawrence, was determined to take Damascus in 1918—Lawrence continued to put his life at risk to keep the Turks on the defensive to the east of the Jordan River and the Dead Sea. Much of this action was small-scale but desperate fighting. He wrote about one example with unusual frankness in *Seven Pillars of Wisdom*: "When combats came to the physical, bare hand against hand, I used to turn myself in. The disgust of being touched revolted me more than the thought of death and defeat. . . . Anyway I had not the instinct to sell my life dearly, and to avoid the indignity of trying not to be killed and failing, rode straight for the enemy to end the business, in all the exhilaration of that last and terrific and most glad pain of death." In this case, it turned out that the "enemy" were friendly tribesmen: they had donned the clothes of Turks whose post they had rushed, and at the last minute they recognized "Lurens." It is interesting that Lawrence was able to write so clinically about his revulsion at being touched, as well as the fact that he "felt fear, disgust, boredom, but anger very seldom," or that "Only once or twice, when I was alone and lost heart in the desert, and had no audience, did I break down." Lawrence apparently felt no revulsion at killing, except when he had to execute a friend. Long ago, he had set out to cut a notch in the stock of his rifle for every Turk he shot, but he gave up after the fourth, either because he thought the notches boastful, or because this count no longer mattered to him—after all, he killed far more Turks with dynamite.

It is also interesting to note his awareness of the extent to which his courage required an "audience," which is something most men would not have admitted, and which perhaps explains the breakdown of his will at Deraa. Not many men can be this objective about their courage, or admit that they have areas of disabling fear. Every hero fears *something*, however unlikely or irrational, and Lawrence was no exception: he would rather have been killed than physically touched in any way by another human being. It is hardly surprising to learn that less than four years later Bernard Shaw would base the character of Saint Joan in part on Lawrence; indeed Sir Michael Holroyd writes in his biography of Shaw: "To some degree *Seven Pillars of Wisdom* may be read as a cross-referring work to *Saint Joan*: the two chronicles, Stanley Weintraub [a Shaw scholar] has suggested, providing a parallel between the saintly Maid and the ascetic Prince of the desert." Even Shaw's physical description of Joan in the play bears a startling resemblance to Lawrence's face: "an uncommon face: eyes very far apart and bulging as they often do in very imaginative people, a long, well-shaped nose with wide nostrils, a short upper lip, a resolute but full-lipped mouth, and handsome fighting chin." This is a perfect description of Lawrence's face in Augustus John's famous 1919 portrait, so much so that it reads like something of a private joke between Shaw and Lawrence, perhaps in payment for a number of suggestions Lawrence offered Shaw about the play.*

—

*From 1922, when Shaw first met him, Lawrence floats eerily into and out of Shaw's plays: not only as Saint Joan, but elsewhere: as Private Meek in *Too True to Be Good*, and even as Adolphus Cusins, Barbara's fiancé in *Major Barbara*. Cusins is a slight, unassuming Greek scholar who in the end decides to become an armaments king, and his description again might also serve for Lawrence: "He is afflicted with a frivolous sense of humor . . . a most implacable, determined, tenacious, intolerant person who by mere force of character presents himself as—and indeed actually is—considerate, gentle, explanatory . . . capable possibly of murder, but not of cruelty or coarseness." (New York: Random House, 1952, 228.)

The failure to take Amman had consequences. As the bloody stalemate on the western front showed no sign of ending, and the war in the Middle East seemed to have slipped into a similar stalemate, the British government, which had anticipated a surrender by the Turks, began once more to explore the possibility of a negotiated peace. Aubrey Herbert, Sir Mark Sykes's protégé in the Arab Bureau, met in neutral Switzerland with Mehmet Talat Pasha, one of the triumvirate who governed Turkey, and the man who had carried out the Armenian genocide. That the British government was willing to negotiate with the most ruthless of the Turkish leaders shows to what extent the fortunes of war had suddenly shifted in Turkey's favor. The Bolshevik government had been quick to sign a peace treaty with Turkey, freeing it from any further threat to the east and north; the United States had not declared war on the Ottoman Empire; and the French, while anticipating their share of the empire, had made only a minimal contribution to the war in the Middle East—just enough to stake their claim at the peace conference. When it came to Turkey, the British were on their own. They held Basra, Baghdad, and oil-rich Mosul, and Turkey might have been willing to give up the area that is now Iraq in exchange for peace—and a free hand to deal with the Arabs.

Inevitably the news of these negotiations made its way rapidly to the Middle East, further discouraging the Arabs' confidence in Britain. As a result Feisal's off-again, on-again secret negotiations with Jemal Pasha grew more intense and specific. If the British were willing to sell out the Arabs and negotiate with Turkey, why should the Arabs not seek the best terms they could get from the Turks? Lawrence seems to have been involved in the correspondence between Feisal and Jemal, or so Jeremy Wilson believes, arguing that "As contacts between the two sides were inevitable, it seemed best to know what was going on," and that Lawrence hoped in fact to control the correspondence. Given Lawrence's natural gift for duplicity and his close relationship with Feisal, it was perhaps inevitable for Lawrence to have become involved. In fact, he seems to have been alarmed both by the generosity of the terms Jemal was willing to offer and by Feisal's interest in them, and he took the extreme step of securing a copy of Jemal's latest letter "without Feisal's knowledge," and passed the information on to Clayton in Cairo.

Lawrence was also involved in an even more delicate matter: Feisal's reaction to the Balfour Declaration, which was almost more troubling to the Arab leadership than the Sykes-Picot agreement. Nowhere were the words of the declaration parsed with more attention than in the Middle East, where the deliberately ambiguous phrase "a national home for the Jewish people," so carefully crafted by Balfour and the cabinet* to steer a middle course between the Zionists' aspirations and the Arabs' fears, raised more questions than they had in London. In June Clayton arranged a meeting between Dr. Chaim Weizmann and Feisal "at Arab Head-quarters." Clayton had stressed that "It is important that [Lawrence] should be present" at the interview, but Lawrence was up-country with Nasir, so Joyce took his place.

No two men could have been more polite, or more careful to guard their real ambitions from each other, than Feisal and Weizmann (who combined an "almost feminine charm . . . with a feline deadliness of attack"). But behind their diplomatic discussions about respect for the holy places of other monotheistic faiths, and the benefits that Jewish scientific, industrial, and agricultural knowledge, as well as capital, might bring to a new Arab state, it was apparent that what Hussein and his sons wanted was the maximum Jewish investment with the minimum number of Jewish settlers. Feisal's goodwill toward the idea of a "Jewish national home" was dependent on his father's getting everything he had been promised in the McMahon-Hussein correspondence of 1915. The implementation of the Balfour Declaration would, in the eyes of the Arab leadership, therefore depend on whether the Sykes-Picot agreement was dropped or enforced. Hussein and his sons were anything but unsophis-ticated—they were very much aware of European and, more important,

* Even in the United Kingdom there was doubt. Asquith, the prime minister, noted in his diary on March 13, 1915, that "the only other partisan of this proposal [the Balfour Declaration] is Lloyd George who, I need not say, does not care a damn for the Jews or their past or their future." (Earl of Oxford and Asquith, *Memories and Reflections*, 1928.)

American sensitivity on the subject of Jews, a sensitivity which, being Semites themselves, they did not share. They were therefore carefully gracious about an event that they hoped would never happen, or, if it did happen, would take place under Arab political control. Lawrence would later meet with Weizmann in Jerusalem, and would conclude very realistically that whatever he said, Weizmann and his followers wanted a Jewish state, though Lawrence thought it might not happen for another fifty years. (Lawrence was off by twenty years, but he could hardly have predicted the effect the Holocaust would have on the creation of Israel.) Since the Zionists would come "under British colours," Lawrence was guardedly in favor of them, if only because he thought they might bring Jewish capital into Syria, and thereby thwart French business ambitions.

It is worth noting that even though Lawrence wanted the Arabs to win, and hoped by getting to Damascus first to invalidate the Sykes-Picot agreement, he never forgot that he was a British officer first and foremost, and like many intelligence agents and diplomats before and since he was adept at not letting the right hand know what the left hand was doing. In the end, it was the conflict between his loyalty to Clayton and Hogarth and his loyalty to Feisal and the Arabs that had the most traumatic effect on his character. No man ever tried harder to serve two masters than Lawrence, or punished himself more severely for failing.

On both sides, British and Turkish, there was a certain degree of betrayal in the air. Jemal Pasha, for example, not only was in correspondence with Feisal but sent him a personal emissary in the person of "Mohammed Said, Abd el Kader's brother in Damascus." Mohammed Said was the man who was so careless with his automatic pistol as to have killed three friends accidentally. Abd el Kader was the man who had deserted from Lawrence's force on the way to destroy the bridge over the Yarmuk, and whom Lawrence suspected of having betrayed his mission to the Turks, and of having been responsible for his being picked up shortly afterward at Deraa. Lawrence regarded both brothers as dangerous enemies, and cannot have been pleased to discover that Mohammed Said, of all people, was having secret discussions with Feisal.

The possibility of the Arabs' changing sides was in the end precluded by two things: the first was King Hussein's old-fashioned, honorable (and, as it turned out, unreciprocated) scruples about betraying his British ally; the second was the determination of Allenby, who was not nicknamed "the bull" for nothing, to attack again on the grandest possible scale in September. When Lawrence and Dawnay met with Allenby in July, they learned that he wanted them to keep the Turks' attention focused on Deraa and the Jordan valley while he attacked along the coast toward the end of September—almost the exact opposite of what he had done at Gaza and Beersheba.

Lawrence came up with a number of ways to do this, none of which made him popular with the staff at Aqaba. In particular, Young, who was working night and day to organize a supply line for the Arab regulars as they advanced, was now told to change his plan in favor of Lawrence's Bedouin irregulars. "Relations between Lawrence and ourselves," Young wrote, "became for the moment a trifle strained, and the sight of the little man reading *Morte d'Arthur** in a corner of the mess tent with an impish smile on his face was not consoling." No doubt the "impish grin" was partly at Young's expense—Young was busy drawing up a full tactical plan, with stop lines and exact times, for the benefit of irregulars none of whom had ever owned a watch, and who, if they found good grazing, were as likely as not to stop for a day or two and let the camels eat their fill. Young had changed his original opinion of Lawrence—"Lawrence," he wrote, "could certainly not have done what he did without the gold, but no one else could have done it with ten times the amount. No amount of pomp and circumstance would have won him the position he gained among Arabs if he had not established himself by sheer force of person-ality as a born leader and shown himself to be a greater dare-devil than any of his followers." Lawrence, for his part, had come to admire Young's

---

* There are conflicting accounts of Lawrence's camel-borne field library, but Liddell Hart, who got the information from Lawrence himself, reports that he carried with him Malory's *Morte d'Arthur*, the *Oxford Book of English Verse*, and the comedies of Aristophanes.

dogged effort to deal fairly with the Arabs, his bravery under fire and while laying explosive charges, and his orderly mind; but this is not to say that there was a bond of friendship between Lawrence and his "understudy."

No doubt it was galling for Young to see Lawrence calmly reading *Morte d'Arthur* while he himself struggled to load onto baggage camels in an orderly way drinking water; forage; and separate rations for the Arab regulars, the British armored car crews, the French gunners, the Egyptian machine gunners, and a unit of Nepalese Gurkhas (all of whom had different tastes in food, in addition to deep religious prejudice against beef on the part of the Gurkhas and against pork on the part of the Arabs and Egyptians). Young was under pressure because Allenby had moved the date of his attack forward by two weeks, and wanted the Arab army to attack "no later than September 16th." This meant that Young had to prepare two convoys of 600 camels each to carry the army's supplies "to Aba'l Issan,* seventy miles north of Akaba," where 450 of the baggage camels would have to be resaddled to serve as riding camels, with saddles that had not yet arrived from Egypt, and then move everything forward to form a permanent base at Azrak. Lawrence's indifference to all this was not just a pose to irritate Young, though it certainly achieved that effect. Lawrence received his orders straight from Allenby, so he knew that what Allenby really wanted was a demonstration at the right time— Allenby joked that if "three men and a boy with pistols" turned up at Deraa on September 16, they might be enough—rather than a carefully prepared textbook attack that arrived too late.

Because there was intelligence that the Turks were planning a raid on Abu el Lissal, which would badly disrupt Lawrence's attack on Deraa, Lawrence and Dawnay had arranged to "borrow" two companies of the remaining battalion of the disbanded Imperial Camel Brigade ("on the condition that they should avoid casualties"), march them from Suez to Aqaba across the Sinai (no mean feat to begin with), and from there send

---

* This is the same place as Abu el Lissal. Transliterations of Arabic place-names into English were, and remain, idiosyncratic.

them on to attack the watering station at Mudawara again, then make "a long stride" north to Amman, to "destroy the bridge and tunnel there, and then return to Palestine." This was a tall order for British soldiers, many of them yeoman cavalry, who were not born to the camel or the desert. Lawrence went down to Aqaba to greet them on their arrival, and as they gathered around a blazing campfire, he gave them a rousing speech, which impressed even so hardened an imperial adventurer as Colonel Stirling, the author of *Safety Last*, who called it "the straightest talk I have ever heard." Lawrence told them there was no need to worry about the Turks, but to keep in mind that they were entering "a part of Arabia where no white man had ever set foot," and had every need to worry about the Bedouin, who were "none too friendly," and would certainly think that the British troops had come to take their grazing grounds. They were "to turn the other cheek," and avoid any kind of friction.

Lawrence rode with them the next day through Wadi Itm to Rumm. This was just as well, since several of the tribesmen took the opportunity of sniping at the British, even though they were allies. He was moved by riding in the company of British soldiers, a novel experience which filled him with "homesickness, making him feel an outcast."

Once he had calmed the Howeitat at Rumm, who rumbled with discontent and anger at the presence of infidel soldiers, he rode back to Aqaba, then flew to Jefer to meet with that sinister old chieftain Nuri Shaalan and the Ruawalla sheikhs, whose goodwill he needed to reach Deraa. He settled their doubts with another rousing speech, this time "emphasizing the mystical enchantment of sacrifice for freedom," then flew back to Guweira, and from there to Aqaba, racked by guilt at having once again persuaded men to risk their lives in the knowledge that they would probably only exchange living under Ottoman rule for life in a French colony.

The news that the 300 troopers of the Imperial Camel Brigade, under Major Buxton, had retaken Mudawara, together with 150 Turkish prisoners, for a loss of seven of their own killed and ten wounded, cheered him up, and he joined them at Jefer, where they were encamped, this time riding in his Rolls-Royce tender Blue Mist,* with an armored car as an escort. From there they moved north, Lawrence riding far ahead of Buxton's troopers to "smooth the way" for them among the tribesmen, going all the way to Azrak, then returning to Beir to rejoin the troopers. Being among them again gave Lawrence "a mixed sense of ease and unease." He felt at home among these big men from the rural shires of Britain, but at the same time was conscious of being, in their eyes, both a legendary hero and an oddity. He was afflicted with what Liddell Hart describes as not merely the usual self-doubt, but a growing "distaste for himself," inevitable in one who accused himself of play-acting among his own admiring countrymen.

A few days later they reached Muaggar, only fifteen miles southeast of Amman, and within easy reach of the railway bridge and tunnel. Here they were discovered by a Turkish airplane. There were Turkish mule-mounted infantrymen near the bridge, and Lawrence, mindful of the fact that he and Dawnay had promised to avoid casualties among the Imperial Camel Brigade, seven of whose troopers had already been killed, decided to send them back to Azrak. They left enough evidence behind them of fires, "empty meat-tins," and crisscrossing armored car tracks to make the Turks fear that Amman would be attacked.

Leaving his explosives buried at Azrak for future use, Lawrence raced back across the desert to Abu el Lissal to put out a blazing row between King Hussein in Mecca and the officers of the Arab army in the field. This particular tempest in a teacup had been caused by the fact that Jaafar had received a British decoration and had been referred to as "the general commanding the Arab Northern Army," and King Hussein had thereupon announced in the official Mecca newspaper that no such rank existed. As a result of this insult, all the senior officers of the Arab army resigned, as did Feisal himself after receiving a "vitriolic" message from his father. The fact that most of these ranks were bogus in the first place did not reduce the tension between Abu el Lissal and Mecca. Feisal was

---

*A tender was an open car converted into the equivalent of what Americans call a pickup truck.

styled a lieutenant-general and corps commander by the British, even though on a good day, counting regulars and Bedouin irregulars together, he seldom commanded more than the equivalent of a division; Jaafar Pasha was styled a major-general, although the number of his regulars seldom exceeded that of a brigade; and everyone else was ranked accordingly. It was an army with a disproportionate number of senior officers, and hardly any trained junior officers or NCOs. Lawrence, who had a certain respect for Hussein's stubborn defense of his own prerogatives as a self-made king, and who was privy to both codes, adopted the novel technique of editing and altering Hussein's messages to his son, simply eliminating any paragraphs that would offend Feisal, thus saving honor and, more important, avoiding the disintegration of Feisal's army. Feisal very likely saw through this stratagem, but was wise enough not to question it. The episode also shows the degree to which Lawrence was involved in the politics and the differing ambitions of the sharifian family. For better or worse, he was not only Feisal's military adviser, but his friend, political counselor, and confidant, the young Thomas à Becket to the young Henry II, with the addition of all the danger of being a foreigner and an unbeliever. Lawrence could play the role of courtier in an eastern court perfectly: as he himself put it, "I could flatter as well as flutter." His position and his safety depended on Feisal's trust. He never lost it, and he sacrificed what would have been, to anyone else, a comfortable and well-rewarded career, with every prospect of a knighthood or better, to secure thrones for Feisal and for Feisal's older brother Abdulla.*

In the meantime, his objective was to get the Arab army and Feisal to Damascus before the British reached it. By the first week of September, "the desert had become a military highway, dotted with northern-moving columns that headed steadily for Azrak." Lawrence, who rode past the long columns in his Rolls-Royce, had achieved a kind of double deception:

*His position was not unique. Captain J. R. Shakespear played much the same role toward ibn Saud on behalf of the government of India. When Shakespear was killed in a desert skirmish, he was replaced by St. John Philby, the noted Arabist, ornithologist, and convert to Islam, and father of the master spy and traitor Kim Philby.

the Turks believed that he was aiming for Amman, reinforced it accordingly, and even sent a column farther south to recapture Tafileh; the British believed that he was obeying Allenby's orders to take Deraa and destroy the vital railroad junction. In fact, Lawrence had begun moving the bulk of the Arab forces away from Medina and the Hejaz, and from Aqaba and the sea, moving north unseen in the desert that only they could cross, toward Damascus. "The climax of the preaching of years had come, and a united country was straining towards its historic capital," Lawrence wrote, something of an overstatement.

In the meantime, every Turkish soldier sent toward Amman weakened the forces that faced Allenby in the north, and every raid, smashed railway line, or smashed bridge to the south and east kept the Turks looking in the wrong direction. Allenby was a master of bluff—he had used it to persuade the Turks that he would attack Gaza, instead of moving to his right and enveloping Beersheba, and now he used Lawrence to persuade them that the crucial blow was coming from the east side of the Dead Sea toward Amman. Lawrence had spent hundreds of thousands of pounds and countless hours in securing the cooperation, or at least the temporary neutrality, of the tribes from Aqaba to Damascus. In Liddell Hart's words, "He had removed the obstructions and paved the way," and this was already something of a miracle. His exact plans were unclear, even to his staff and his superiors. Essentially, he would play cat and mouse with the Turks, hitting them where they least expected; then retreating back into the desert, hoping to destroy the railway junction at Deraa; then moving north from there to take Damascus. But "it was ever [his] habit, while studying alternatives, to keep the stages in solution." In other words, his plans would remain flexible, and he would exploit opportunities as they arose, having secured a firm base deep in the desert at Azrak.

Ignoring the warning of Frederick the Great—"He who attempts to defend everything, defends nothing"—the Turks attempted to defend everything, in a huge arc from Medina to Maan to the Mediterranean, more than 300 miles long. Reacting violently to every pinprick on the periphery, the Turks were unable to maintain their lines of communication from one day to the next, thanks to Lawrence's constant sabotage of their railway tracks and bridges.

Allenby compounded their confusion west of the Dead Sea by "creating dust columns with mule-drawn sleighs moving eastward by day, while troop columns marched [back] westward by night," and by marching battalions toward the Jordan valley by day, then marching them back at night, so the Turks had the impression that Allenby's whole army—"12,000 sabres, 57,000 rifles, and 540 guns"*—was methodically moving, unit by unit, toward the east. Fifteen thousand dummy horses made of canvas "filled the vacant horse lines in the interior," forcing the enemy to conclude that the British were preparing to attack in force to the east and take Jericho. Lawrence contributed by buying up all the forage he could find east of the Dead Sea, paying in gold even as the price soared, hiding from nobody the fact that he was buying it to support the British cavalrymen when they crossed the Jordan and advanced northwest toward Damascus.

At dawn on September 14, two days before Allenby's attack was scheduled, the main body of the Arab forces, "about twelve hundred strong," marched out of Azrak toward Umtaiye, "a great pit of rain water fifteen miles below Deraa and five miles east of the railway to Amman." The day before, Lawrence had sent Captain Frederick Peake Pasha, commander of the newly formed Egyptian Camel Corps and an enthusiastic dynamiter, to break the railway near Amman; but Peake's guides led him straight to a portion of the railway that was guarded by Arabs loyal to the Turks, and he was obliged to withdraw without accomplishing his mission. Had Lawrence been present, he might have won these Arabs over, or bribed them, but he was not. He did not blame Peake, but since he was determined to keep the Arab forces to their schedule he set off for Umtaiye across the desert in the Blue Mist; found a suitable bridge for demolition; then drove back and informed everybody that he would destroy the bridge himself, a "solo effort [which] would be rather amus-

---

*Wavell meant, in modern terms, 12,000 cavalrymen, 57,000 infantrymen, and an artillery strength of 540 guns.

ing." Young remarked that "it did not sound at all amusing. It sounded quite mad," but then reflected that Lawrence's madness had after all enabled him to take Aqaba, and might serve him as well here.

The next day, September 16, Lawrence set out for the railway near Jabir in a Rolls-Royce tender "crammed to the gunwale with gun-cotton [an explosive] and detonators." He was accompanied by Colonel Joyce, ostensibly his commanding officer, but temporarily reduced to the role of an onlooker; and by Captain Lord Edward Winterton (the future sixth earl, and undersecretary of state for India), an officer from the disbanded Imperial Camel Corps, in a second tender, escorted by two armored cars. When they reached "the cover of the last ridge before the railway, Lawrence transferred himself and 150 lbs. of gun-cotton" to one of the armored cars, and drove straight to the bridge, while the other cars took on the Turkish redoubt protecting the bridge. After a brief firefight, in which two of the Turkish soldiers were killed and the rest surrendered, Lawrence set about the task of mining the bridge, fully justifying Wavell's description of him as "a fastidious artist in demolitions."

Despite his disappointment at being unable to remove, as a souvenir, a polished marble plaque with a florid inscription in Turkish, Lawrence proceeded to place his six charges "in the drainage holes of the spandrils . . . inserted zigzag, and with their explosion all the arches were scientifically shattered." This demolition was all the more satisfying because it would leave "the skeleton of the bridge intact, but tottering," so the enemy would "first have to tear down the wreckage before they could begin building a new bridge." Lawrence was never one to rush the business of placing explosive charges, even under pressure, as he was here, since Winterton and Joyce were waving frantically to signal that enemy patrols were on the way.

After the demolition, he had a moment of dismay when one of the springs of his Rolls-Royce broke, stranding him about 300 yards from the ruined bridge. It was, Lawrence later remarked, the first and only time a Rolls-Royce had broken down in the desert, inconveniently just as the Turkish patrols arrived, leaving him in despair at losing both the car and his explosives kit; but Lawrence and the driver got out, and decided to "jack up the fallen end of the spring, and by scantling [planks] on the running-board wedge it into nearly its old position." Rolls—the aptly named driver—and Lawrence managed to cut three pieces of wooden scantling to the right length—they had no saw, but Lawrence shot through each piece of wood with his pistol crosswise several times, until they could snap the end off each piece; then they jacked the car up, slipped the scantlings in to replace the spring, lashed them together with rope, and fastened them to the angle irons that held the running board. They then lowered the car back down onto the improvised spring, cranked the engine, and drove on.

Connoisseurs of Lawrence's prose about machinery—he would later go on to write in great detail about engines, for example in the justly celebrated "User's Guide and Notes to the 200 Class Royal Air Force Seaplane Tender"—will find a good example on page 720 of *Seven Pillars of Wisdom*. Lawrence notes that he and Rolls performed this emergency repair as several companies of Turkish infantry were approaching. Apart from his crystal-clear description of how to repair the Rolls-Royce—one almost feels that by following his instructions, one could do it oneself— the passage shows Lawrence's interest in and aptitude for fine machinery. This was another trait that separated him from other Englishmen of his class and generation, who were mostly happy enough to leave such things to the lower classes: chauffeurs and mechanics. Lawrence loved using his hands, and inventing his own ways of making machines work better; this was unusual, in those days, for a scholar and literary man.

Bouncing and lurching over the desert, they rejoined the main force (and his bodyguard) the next morning, September 17, "just as it was attacking the redoubt that guarded the bridge at Tell Arar." The Arab regulars stormed the Turkish redoubt, at which point Lawrence "rushed down to find Peake's Egyptians making breakfast. It was like Drake's game of bowls and I fell dumb with admiration." Lawrence, however much he admired their sangfroid, got them away from their breakfast fires and moving again, only to be attacked by Turkish airplanes. One British plane appeared, took on all eight of the Turkish airplanes, and drew them off, though the pilot had to crash-land; and with the kind of "British pluck" that usually appears only in boys' novels of the period, he removed his machine gun from the wreck, lashed it to a borrowed Ford car, and set off on his own to attack the Turkish troops.

While the Egyptians demolished the bridge, Lawrence and Nuri as-Said (commanding the Arab regulars) set off for the nearest railway station and attacked it, cutting "the telegraph, thus severing the main communication between the Turkish armies and their home-base, before proceeding to dynamite the rails and points and wreck the station and its rolling stock," all this despite the fact that Lawrence had been wounded by a bomb splinter in the arm. (This did not, apparently, discourage his habit of carrying in his pocket detonators that could have been exploded by a bullet or a piece of shrapnel.) Undaunted, he moved his force on to attempt once more to destroy his old target, the railway bridge over the Yarmuk River at Tell el Shehab. Once again, he failed—just as he was about to lay his charges in the dark, a train filled with German reserves halted there. Although Nuri suggested a nighttime bayonet charge, Lawrence, for once cautiously realistic, pulled back, circled around in the desert back to the Deraa-Amman line, and sent a party to distract the Turks by machine-gunning the station at Nisib. Then Lawrence set out to blow up the important bridge north of the station. He was in a hurry now, and when the members of his bodyguard balked at walking out onto the bridge with their loads of blasting gelignite in a sack cast over the shoulder—since the gelignite could be detonated by a single bullet and would then blow them all to pieces—Lawrence set them an example, calmly walking to the center of the bridge by himself to test whether the guards had gone to help defend the station. Once the bodyguards had followed him, he methodically packed his explosives into the bridge's critical structural points, placed the detonators, and laid the fuses, tumbling into the enemy's deserted redoubt to set off the explosions. These produced "a lurid blaze," shattering the abutment arch, sending "the whole mass of masonry sliding slowly down into the valley below," and showering him with enormous chunks of masonry.

The speed with which Lawrence moved and the unexpected direction of his attacks, along with his habit of "snipping" telegraph wires wherever he could, spread confusion at every level of the Turkish armies on both sides of the Jordan. The action convinced General Liman von Sanders, head of the German military mission to Turkey, and now de facto commander of the Turkish forces facing Allenby, whose headquarters was in Nazareth, that when Allenby's attack came, it would be directed away from the coast and toward the east.

At 4:30 A.M. on September 19, 385 guns opened fire on the Turkish front line in Palestine for fifteen minutes. This firing was followed by a full-scale infantry assault advancing behind a "creeping" artillery barrage that drove the startled Turks from their trenches. So firmly had the Turks been convinced that the assault would be toward the Jordan River that they had thinned out their infantry on the coastal plain, and their defenses quickly crumbled. Ironically, one redoubt held out against the repeated attacks of the small French detachment (approximately of brigade strength), but by 7 A.M. Allenby's forces had reached all their objectives. (Some divisions advanced "7,000 yards in 2½ hours," a rate of advance unthinkable on the western front.) By midday, the Turkish Eighth Army "had broken in hopeless confusion," and its demoralized remnants were streaming northwest under constant bombing attack by British aircraft.

Once the infantry had punched a hole in the Turkish line, Allenby poured his cavalry in, en masse, in the Napoleonic manner. For many of the British and Australian troopers, it was the first opportunity to use their newly sharpened sabers in combat. So swift were the Turkish collapse and the British advance that the Thirteenth Brigade of the British Fifth Cavalry Division clattered into Nazareth at dawn on September 20, almost forty miles north of its starting point, forcing an astonished General von Sanders, whose lines of communication had been so deftly cut by Lawrence, and who therefore had no idea of the extent of his army's disintegration, to flee from his headquarters—which was being defended by staff officers with carbines and by "clerks, orderlies, etc." firing from the windows—to avoid capture. By the end of the day the advance scouts of Allenby's cavalry were approaching the Jordan River, just south of the Sea of Galilee, while his infantry was wheeling away from the coast into the hills of Samaria, to take Nablus. Some idea of what conditions were like can be gleaned from the official military handbook for Palestine, which notes, "Nothing is known of the climate [of the Jordan Valley] in summer time, since no human being has yet been found to spend summer there."

"Early on September 21st," Liddell Hart wrote, "British aircraft sighted a large column [of Turks] winding down the steep gorge from Nablus towards the Jordan. . . . Four hours' continuous bombing and machine-gunning by relays of aircraft reduced this procession to stagnation, and inanimate chaos of guns and transport." Everywhere, the story was the same. The Turkish Seventh and Eighth armies, west of the Jordan, had for all intents and purposes ceased to exist except as isolated mobs of starving, unarmed men, desperate to surrender. The strongest Turkish force, the Fourth Army, east of the Jordan, was also rapidly losing cohesion. Lawrence had disabled the railroad, so the troops were forced to retreat on foot, without water, rations, or forage for the animals, and exposed to "constant pinpricks" by the Bedouin, who swept out of the desert to shoot and plunder the stragglers and the wounded. Haifa, with its vital port, was captured on September 23 by a bold cavalry advance around both sides of Mount Carmel, carried out by two Indian regiments of the Fifth (Imperial) Cavalry Division, the Mysore and the Jodhpur Lancers, with the addition of a squadron of the Sherwood Rangers, effectively placing every major city in Palestine in British hands.

At this point, the main danger to the Arab forces was from the air, since Allenby did not have enough aircraft to provide what would later come to be called "air cover" over the vast area of the Arab advance. The Arabs were still particularly sensitive to being bombed or machine-gunned from the air. This no doubt explains Lawrence's hastily improvised raid on an advance Turkish landing field on his way back to Azrak;

during this raid, his armored car was bombed, sending a shower of broken stone through the vision slit, wounding his hand, blowing off a tire, and nearly overturning the vehicle in a ditch. He complained of "feeling like sardines in a doomed tin," and remarked, "Of all dangers give me the solitary sort." But although he had gone five nights without sleep, he pressed on to provide cover for another railway demolition, then carried out a nighttime "running fight" between his armored cars and a Turkish train, racing alongside the track in the darkness "lit up by the green shower of tracer bullets."

On September 21 Lawrence reached Azrak, where an airplane landed early the next morning to bring him news of Allenby's victory on the west bank of the Jordan. He immediately suggested that Feisal should set in motion "the long-delayed general revolt in Syria." This was a significant decision. Both Feisal and Lawrence had discouraged any large-scale uprising in Syria, so long as there was any danger of the Turks' gaining the upper hand, as they had done in March and April, when Allenby had been driven back from Amman and Salt. Any rising under those circumstances would simply lead to savage and widespread executions by the Turks. This time, however, it was clear that the Turks had been completely defeated, and that the only question was whether the remnants of the Turkish Fourth Army could reach Damascus before the British cavalry or the Arabs did. To Lawrence, what mattered now was to take advantage of the loophole in the Sykes-Picot agreement, the somewhat ambiguous language acknowledging that the Arabs might keep those territories they themselves captured during the course of the war. A careful parsing of the documents would also reveal that everything in them was subject to French claims, and the French had already claimed Lebanon and Syria (including Damascus). Still, Lawrence hoped that if the Arabs captured Damascus and a Syrian government was installed there before the British arrived, the world—and particularly the United States—might accept a fait accompli and might also accept the British government's view, which was that the Sykes-Picot agreement was a "dead letter," and superseded by events. He hoped, too, that the fall of the imperial Russian government, the unexpected strength of the Arab contribution to victory, and Woodrow Wilson's demand for an end to secret treaties—and to European colonial acquisitions made without the consent of native populations—would prevail over the agreement. It was a slim reed on which to build a nation, as both Lawrence and Feisal recognized, particularly since urban Syrians were, as they still are, sharp and sophisticated traders, whereas rural Syrians were for the most part peasant farmers, few of them likely to greet with pleasure a government by King Hussein, or by his son Feisal.

In the morning, Lawrence flew directly to Ramleh, and drove from there to General Allenby's headquarters in Palestine, where he "found the great man at work in his office unmoved" by the magnitude of his victory. Allenby personally briefed Lawrence on the next stage of his advance—the Australian Mounted Division (Major-General W. G. Hodgson) and the Fifth Cavalry Division (Major-General H. J. M. Mac Andrew) would turn north of the Sea of Galilee and advance on Damascus, while the Fourth Cavalry Division (Major-General Sir G. deS. Barrow) would strike east to capture Deraa, and then turn north toward Damascus. From one point of view, all this was welcome news to Lawrence—Allenby would shortly reach Damascus, very likely forcing the Turkish government to sue for peace. From another point of view, it meant that Lawrence's hope of an independent Arab state in Syria depended on getting Feisal and the Arab forces into Damascus before Allenby's cavalry divisions arrived—a very narrow window of opportunity. Allenby, always well informed, was aware of this, and in fact strictly warned Lawrence against attempting an "independent coup" in Damascus; the Arab forces, Allenby told him, should cooperate with the British Fourth Cavalry Division to cut off the retreat of the Turkish Fourth Army, and let the British and Australian forces deal with Damascus and move on. On the subject of air cover, Allenby was more generous; he agreed to provide the latest Bristol fighters to operate from the airstrip Lawrence had created in the desert at Umtaiye, about forty miles south of Deraa, and since there was no fuel there, to provide a giant Handley-Page bomber, the first to reach the Middle East, to shuttle back and forth loaded with cans of gas.

Lawrence swiftly integrated the pilots and their aircraft into his strategy. He happily shared his young pilots' breakfast of tea and sausages,* cooked over an open fire, something of a deviation from his usual vegetarian meals, and watched them shoot down a German two-seater, the wreckage of which he would later pass, "noting the two charred German bodies." They flew back to Azrak, then traveled northwest with Feisal and that sinister old chieftain Nuri Shaalan—"packed into the green Vauxhall, which its British soldier, proud of his prince to drive, kept always spick and shining," no mean feat in the desert—to Um el Surab, about fifty miles from Deraa. At Um el Surab, Nuri as-Said had prepared a landing ground big enough for the Handley-Page bomber. Unfortunately, they had to turn away to settle yet another of the endless intertribal disputes and so missed the great airplane's landing. But later a single wild-eyed Bedouin riding in the opposite direction shouted that he had just seen "the biggest aeroplane in the world," a report which quickly spread throughout all the tribes south of Deraa, and impressed the Bedouin even more than the news of Allenby's victories. At Um el Surab they found the Handley, "majestic on the grass with the Bristols . . . like chickens beneath the spread of its wings." The sight prompted the Arabs to say, " 'Indeed and at last they have sent us the aeroplane, of which these little things were the asses.' " Even the most skeptical tribesmen were now convinced that the Turks were done for.

The Handley-Page contained enough gas, spare parts for the aircraft, and food for the air force personnel to enable Lawrence to have his own small air force east of the Jordan, and also to provide his cars with enough fuel to get them to Damascus. At night the big aircraft would be used to bomb Mafrak and Deraa, further disrupting the Turkish Fourth Army's line of retreat.

On September 23, Lawrence rested, and therefore missed the sight of

---

*These were the standard "bangers" of the British army. Lawrence occasionally ate meat, when it was a question of being polite to his Arab hosts, or when there was nothing else to eat but camel meat. On at least one occasion he expressed pleasure at a piece of gazelle roasted over an open fire. His vegetarian bent was not dogmatic.

old Nuri Shaalan charging the Turks on the railway line, as he "personally led his Rualla horsemen, galloping in his black broadcloth cloak with
the best of them." The next day Lawrence attacked the railway line again,
but this time he was driven off by unexpectedly vigorous and accurate
machine gun fire, from a German army unit, as it turned out. It did not
much matter; at that point the entire Turkish Fourth Army was in hopeless and disordered retreat, becoming a mob of hungry, thirsty, unarmed
stragglers, except for islands of discipline where small German units were
retreating with them. Turks began throwing away their rifles, and cutting the horses loose of the guns they were pulling in order to ride them.

This sight of all this misery stretching from south of Amman almost
to Damascus led to a sharp quarrel between Lawrence and Young, who
with his gift for the non-U* phrase or word held what he called a "pow-
wow" in Lawrence's tent, where the atmosphere was not improved by
Lawrence's languid flippancy and Young's belief that he was the one in
command. Young "still regarded him more as Feisal's liaison officer with
General Allenby than as a real Colonel in the army, a position which he
gave the impression of holding in great contempt." It would dawn on him
only later that Lawrence was under the opposite impression—that *he* was
in command of Young. Young felt that the Arabs had by now done all that
Allenby had asked, and that they should at all costs avoid putting themselves between Deraa and the Turkish line of retreat, since they were on
the flank of an army more than twenty times their strength. He felt that
the right thing to do was to "worry the Fourth Army as it passed . . . and
to wait for the 4th [British] division," to appear. As a regular officer, he
felt he knew more about this kind of thing than Lawrence, whose respect
for regular soldiers was in any case limited. Lawrence also seems to have
been at his most annoying—Young almost invariably brought out the

---

* The famous term describing non-upper-class usage—that is, lower-middle-class and
middle-class usage—that Nancy Mitford enshrined in the English language when she
wrote "The English Aristocracy" for *Encounter* in 1954. Whatever else he was, Lawrence was an Oxonian who spoke impeccable upper-class English. The word "pow-
wow" from a fellow officer would grate on his nerves as much as "serviette" for
"napkin."

worst in him—and was determined to cross the railway. He did not think the Turks would fight. More important, although Young might think that the war in Turkey was as good as won, Lawrence was determined to get to Damascus, whatever it cost—something he could hardly reveal to Young.

Lawrence won the argument by default, saying that he was going to sleep, since he intended to cross the railway line with his bodyguard at dawn and "reach Sheikh Saad by daylight," with or without the Arab regulars. Nuri as-Said, who commanded the Arab regulars, had been curled up in the tent pretending to be asleep; he merely asked, "Is it true?" once Young had "gone away grumbling," and when Lawrence said it was, nodded. At dawn they rode off with Lawrence's bodyguard and were soon joined by Auda, Nasir, Nuri Shaalan, and Talal, and their large bodies of irregular Bedouin. With Lawrence's blessing, Auda, Nuri, and Talal split up and each raided a separate place: Nuri and his men rode down the main road to Deraa and Damascus to pick up prisoners; Auda went to take the station at "Ghazale by storm, capturing a derelict train, with guns and two hundred men, of whom some were Germans"; and Talal took Ezraa, which was defended by Lawrence's old foe, Abd el Kader, and his Algerian followers. To Lawrence's regret Abd el Kader fled, but by the time the irregulars reassembled at Sheikh Saad, they were burdened with loot, machine guns, and prisoners. On September 27 an English aircraft flew low over them and dropped a message that Bulgaria had surrendered, the first of the Central Powers to do so. The Arab regulars arrived soon afterward, having taken nine hours to cover a distance that Lawrence and his bodyguard covered in three. With them were Young, whose feelings were still bruised; and Lord Winterton, who seems to have been at his happiest when raiding the railway, rather than attempting to keep the peace between his two quarrelsome superiors.

A British aircraft dropped a warning that two very large columns of Turks were moving toward Sheikh Saad—one of 4,000 and the other of 2,000. Lawrence decided to take on the smaller one, which was approaching Talal's village, Tafas. He moved off at once, leaving Young behind.

Because "kindly" Winterton had ordered Young's tent pitched beside his own "in a little dell some distance away from the Sherifian officers, thinking that I should like to be undisturbed," Young, who was so tired that "he could hardly keep [his] eyes open," fell asleep and woke up to an empty, silent camp, with just a few men left to guard the prisoners. He therefore missed the scene that would haunt Lawrence for the rest of his life.

Riding toward Tafas, Lawrence encountered "mounted Arabs, herding a drove of stripped prisoners towards Sheikh Saad . . . driving them mercilessly, the bruises of their urging blue across the ivory backs." These were the Turks of the police battalion at Deraa, being whipped savagely by Arabs whom they themselves had often whipped. Lawrence recognized some of them from his own punishment at their hands at Deraa, and he had "his own account" to settle with them. He rode on faster, hearing that a regiment of Turkish lancers had already entered Tafas, from which smoke was rising. As with Lawrence's description of his own torture in Deraa, it is best to present Tafas in his own words—this account and the execution of Gasim before Aqaba and the incident at Deraa are the three most extraordinary and grueling passages in *Seven Pillars of Wisdom*; and certainly the description of Tafas, along with the Battle of Tafileh, justifies placing Lawrence among the great writers about war.

> When we got within sight, we found their news true. They had taken the village (from which sounded an occasional shot), and were halted about it. Small pyres of smoke were going up between the houses. On the rising ground to this side, knee deep in dried thistles, stood a distressed remnant of the inhabitants, old men, women and children, telling terrible stories of what had happened when the Turks rushed in an hour before.
>
> It was too late to do anything but hope for the others, so we lay there on watch, crawling down through the thistles till we were quite near and saw the enemy re-form close column to march out in an

orderly body towards Miskin, cavalry in front and in the rear, infantry and machine-guns as a flank-guard, guns and transport in the centre. We opened fire on the head of their line when it showed itself beyond the houses. They made an active return from two field guns, unlimbered behind the village. Their shrapnel was over-fused, and passed above us into the rough.

At last Nuri came with Pisani. Before their ranks rode Auda Abu Tayi, expectant, and Talal nearly frantic with the tales his people poured out of the sufferings of the village. The Turks were now nearly quit of it, and we slipped down behind them to end Talal's suspense, while our infantry took position and fired strongly with the Hotchkiss, and the French high-explosive threw their rearguard into confusion.

The village lay there stilly before us, under the slow wreaths of white smoke, as we rode to it guardedly. Some grey heaps seemed to hide in the long grass, embracing the ground in that close way which corpses had. These we knew were dead Arab men and women: but from one a little figure tottered off, as though to escape from us. It was a child, three or four years old, whose dirty smock was stained red all over one shoulder and side. When near we saw that it was blood from a large half-fibrous wound, perhaps a lance thrust, just where neck and body joined.

The child ran a few steps, then stood still and cried to us in a tone of astonishing strength (all else being very silent), "Don't hit me, Baba." Abd el Aziz, choking out something—this was his village, and she might be of his family—flung himself off his camel, and stumbled, kneeling in the grass beside the child. His suddenness frightened her, for she threw up her arms and tried to scream: but instead dropped in a little heap, while the blood rushed out again over the clothes: and then, I think, she died.

We left Abd el Aziz there, and rode on past the other bodies, of men and women, and four more dead babies, looking very soiled in the clear daylight, towards the village whose loneliness we now knew meant that it was full of death and horror. On the outskirts were some low mud walls, of sheepfolds, and on one lay something red and white. I looked close and saw the body of a woman folded across it, bottom upwards, nailed there by a saw bayonet whose haft stuck hideously into the air from between her naked legs. She had been pregnant, and about her lay others, perhaps twenty in all, variously killed, but set out in accord with an obscene taste.

The Zaagi burst out in wild peals of laughter, and those who were not sick joined him hysterically. It was a sight near madness, the more desolate for the warm sunshine and the clear air of this upland afternoon. I said, "The best of you brings me the most Turkish dead," and we turned and rode after the fading enemy, on our way shooting down those who had fallen out by the road-side and came imploring our pity. One wounded Turk, half-naked, not able to stand, sat and cried to us. Abdulla turned away his camel's head: but the Zaagi crossed him, and whipped three bullets from his revolver through the man's bare chest. The blood came out with his heart beats, throb, throb, throb, slower and slower.

Talal had seen what we had seen. He gave one moan like a hurt animal, and then rode heavily to the upper ground and sat there a long while on his mare, shivering and looking fixedly after the Turks. I moved near to speak to him, and lead his mind away: but Auda caught my rein and stayed me. After some minutes Talal very slowly drew his headcloth about his face, and then seemed to take hold of himself, for he dashed his stirrups into his horse's flanks, and galloped headlong, bending low and swaying in the saddle, right at the main body of the enemy.

It was a long ride, down the gentle slope, and across the hollow, and we sat there like stone while he rushed forward, the drumming of the hoofs sounding unnaturally loud in our ears, for we had stopped shooting and the Turks had stopped shooting. Both armies waited for him, and he flew on in the hushed evening till only a few lengths from the enemy. Then he sat up in the saddle and cried his war cry, "Talal, Talal," twice in a tremendous shout. Instantly their rifles and machineguns crashed out together, and he and his mare, riddled through and through with bullets, fell dead among their lance points.

Auda looked very cold and grim. "God give him mercy: we will take his price." He shook his rein, and moved slowly forward after the enemy. We called up the peasants, now drunk with fear and blood, and sent them from this side and that against the retreating columns. Auda led them like the old lion of battle that he was. By a skilful turn he drove the Turks into bad ground, and split their formation into three parts.

The third part—the smallest—was mostly made up of German and Austrian machine-gunners grouped round three motor-cars, which presumably carried high officers. They fought magnificently and repulsed our attacks time and again despite our hardiness. The Arabs were fighting like devils, the sweat blurring their eyes, dust parching their throats: while the flame of cruelty and revenge which was burning in their bodies so twisted them about that their hands could hardly shoot. By my orders we took no prisoners, for the only time in the war.

At last we left this stern section behind us, though they said it held Sherif Bey, commanding the lancers: and pursued the faster two. They were in panic, and by sunset we had destroyed the smallest pieces of them, gaining as and by what they lost. Parties of peasants flowed in on our advance, each man picking up his arms from the enemy. At first there were five or six to every rifle: then one would put forth a bayonet; another a sword; a third a pistol. An hour later, those who had been on foot would be on donkeys. Afterwards every man would have a rifle, and the most other arms as well. At last all were on captured horses. Before nightfall the horses were heavy-laden, and the rich plain behind us was scattered over with the dead bodies of men and animals.

There lay on us a madness, born of the horror of Tafas or of its story, so that we killed and killed, even blowing in the heads of the fallen and of the animals, as though their death and running blood could slake the agony in our brains.

Just one group of Arabs, who had been to the side all day, and had not heard our news, took prisoners, the last two hundred men of the central section. That was all to survive, and even their respite was short. I had gone up to learn why it was, not unwilling that this remnant be let live as witnesses of Talal's price: but while I came, a man on the ground behind them screamed something to the Arabs who with pale faces led me down to see. It was one of us, his thigh shattered. The blood had rushed out over the red soil, and left him dying, but even so he had not been spared. In the fashion of today's battle he had been further tormented, bayonets having been hammered through his shoulder and other leg into the ground, pinning him out like a collected insect.

He was fully conscious, and we said, "Hassan, who did it?" He dropped his eyes towards the prisoners, standing there so hopelessly broken. We ranged our Hotchkiss on them, and pointed to him silently. They said nothing in the moment before we opened fire: and at last their heap ceased moving, and Hassan was dead, and we mounted again and rode home slowly (home was just my carpet at Sheikh Saad) in the gloom which felt so chill now that the sun had gone down.

However, I found that I could not rest or speak or eat for thinking of Talal, the splendid leader, the fine horseman, the courteous and strong companion of the road: and after a while had my other camel brought, and, with one of my bodyguard, rode out in the night towards Sheikh Miskin, to join our men who were hunting the great Deraa column, and learn how they had fared.

It was very dark with a wind beating in great gusts from the south and east, and only by the noise of shots it tossed across to us, and by occasional gun-flashes did we at length come to the fighting. Every field and valley had its Turks, stumbling blindly northward. Our men were clinging on tenaciously. The fall of night had made them bolder, and they were closing with the enemy, firing into them at short range. Each village as its turn came took up the work, and the black icy wind was wild with rifle shots and shoutings, volleys from the Turks, and gallops as small parties of one or other side crashed frantically together.

The enemy had tried to halt and camp at sunset, but Khalid had shaken them into movement again. Some had marched, some had stayed. As they went many dropped asleep in their tracks with fatigue: They had lost all order and coherence, and were drifting through the storm in lost packets, ready to shoot and run, at every contact with us or with each other, and the Arabs were as scattered, and nearly as uncertain.

Exceptions were the German detachments, and here for the first time I grew proud of the enemy who had killed my brothers. They were marching for their homes two thousand miles away, without hope and without guides, in conditions mad enough to break the bravest nerves. Yet each section of them held together, marching in firm rank, sheering through the wrack of Turk and Arab like an armoured ship, dark, high set, and silent. When attacked they halted, faced about, took position, fired to order. There was no haste, no crying, no hesitation. They were glorious.

After many encounters at last I found Khalid, and asked him to call off all possible Rualla, and leave this routed enemy to time and the peasantry. Heavier work, perhaps lay to the southward. There had been a rumour, at dusk, that Deraa was empty, and Trad with the rest of the Anazeh had ridden off to make sure. I feared a reverse for him, since there must still be men in the place, and more struggling towards it up the railway and through the Iibid hills, in hope of safety there. Indeed unless Barrow had lost contact with his enemy there must be that fighting rearguard yet to follow. Disaster in this eleventh hour was possible:—almost likely for the Arabs in their distracted situation, and I wanted Khalid to go help his brother with what fellows he could collect from the night battle.

He agreed at once, and after an hour or two of shouting his message down the wind, hundreds of horsemen and camel-men had rallied to him. On his way to Deraa he charged through and over several formed detachments of Turks, in the star-blink, and arrived to find Trad in secure possession. He had won it at dusk, taking the station at a whirl-wind gallop, jumping the trenches, and blotting out the scanty elements that still tried to resist.

Then, with the help of the local people, they had plundered all the camp, especially finding booty in the fiercely burning storehouses, which the German troops had fired when they left. They entered them and snatched goods from beneath their flaming roofs at peril of their lives: but this was one of the nights in which mankind went crazy, when death seemed impossible however many died to the right and left, and when others' lives seemed just toys to break and throw away.

Meanwhile Sheikh Saad passed a troubled evening, all alarms and shots and shouts, threatenings to murder the prisoners of the day as added price of Talal and his village. The active Sheikhs were out with me or hunting the Turks, and their absence and the absence of their retainers deprived the Arab camp of its chiefs and of its eyes and ears. The sleeping clan-jealousies had come to life in the blood-thirst of the afternoon of killing, and Nasir and Nuri Said, Young and Winterton, were up nearly all the time, keeping the peace.

I got in long after midnight, and found Trad's messengers just arrived with news of Deraa. Nasir left at once to join him. I had wished to sleep, for this was my fourth night of riding: but my mind would not be still enough to feel how tired my body was; so about two in the morning I mounted a third camel, and splashed out towards Deraa, down the Tafas track again, passing to windward of the dark village and its plangent, miserable women.

Nuri Said and his Staff were riding the same road, and our parties hurried along together till the half-light came. Then my impatience and the cold would not let me travel horse-pace any longer. I gave liberty to my camel, the grand but rebellious Baha, and she stretched herself out against all the field, racing the other camels for mile upon mile with great piston-strides like an engine, so I entered Deraa quite alone in the full dawn.

—

There have been disputes from time to time over whether Lawrence actually ordered the Arabs to take no prisoners, or was merely unable to stop them from killing the Turks and Germans they found, but the text makes it clear that he gave the order. Once this order was given, it became difficult, if not impossible, to rein in the tribesmen, and the killing was soon beyond his control. The bloodletting reawakened the feuds and the hostility between Arab clans and tribes, so that Young and Winterton had their hands full attempting to maintain peace at the encampment, while Lawrence rode on through the night to Deraa.

His bodyguard soon joined him there, and shortly afterward he ran into the first of Allenby's troops, Indian cavalry troopers of the Fourth Cavalry Division manning a neatly ordered machine gun post, who at first wanted to take Lawrence prisoner. This was the first significant meeting of Allenby's troops advancing eastward from Palestine and the Arab army marching north toward Damascus, and neither force was impressed with the other. To the British, the Arab irregulars seemed like armed and "liberated" natives running amok, while the Arabs were not impressed by the spit and polish of the Indian troopers or the severe discipline imposed on them by their officers. Lawrence remembers that when he rode on to meet Major-General Barrow, the meeting was something less than a success. To begin with, Barrow was a confirmed believer in strict discipline, who had published an article before the war in which he argued that fear of his superior officers was the best motivating force for a soldier, a point of view to which Lawrence was temperamentally opposed. Then, Lawrence thought Barrow had advanced too cautiously, stopping to water his horses too often, and saw no reason why Barrow should think it was his job to take Deraa when the Arabs already had possession of it. He took a certain pleasure in the fact that the presence of his camel made Barrow's horse "plunge and buck" as they rode together into Deraa.

Barrow's own memory of meeting Lawrence was dramatically different. First of all, Barrow denies that he rode into town with Lawrence at all, and says they met for the first time at the railway station, opposite the sharifian headquarters. Wherever they met, Barrow was already in a state of high indignation. He was shocked by the condition of the town and the Arabs' open looting. "The whole place," he wrote, "was indescribably filthy, defiled and littered with smouldering cinders and the soiled leavings of loot. Turks, some dead and some dying, lay about the railway station or sat propped against the houses. Those still living gazed at us with eyes that begged for a little of the mercy of which it was hopeless of them to ask of the Arabs, and some cried feebly for water.... In all this there was nothing that was uncommon in war. But a revolting scene was being enacted at the moment when we entered, far exceeding in its savagery anything that has been known in the conflicts between nations during the past 120 years and happily rare even in earlier times.

"A long ambulance train full of sick and wounded Turks was drawn up in the station. In the cab of the engine was the dead driver and a mortally wounded fireman. The Arab soldiers were going through the train, tearing off the clothing of the groaning and stricken Turks, regardless of gaping wounds and broken limbs, and cutting their victims' throats.... It was a sight that no average civilised human being could bear unmoved.

"I asked Lawrence to remove the Arabs. He said he couldn't 'as it was their idea of war.' I replied 'It is not our idea of war, and if you can't remove them, I will.' He said, 'If you attempt to do that I shall take no responsibility as to what happens.' I answered 'That's all right; I will take responsibility,' and at once gave orders for our men to clear the station. This was done and nothing untoward happened."

Lawrence seems to have felt that he got the best of Barrow, and thought he had confused the general by his "exotic dress and Arab companions." Reading Barrow's account of Deraa in the hands of the Arab army, one is not so sure. Barrow knew that Lawrence enjoyed Allenby's confidence, but his feeling seems to have been basically that of a major-general who thinks a temporary lieutenant-colonel is not doing his job properly. As for Lawrence's attitude toward Barrow, it may have been at least in part colored by his dislike of Indian troops; he confessed to sharing the Arabs' disdain for them: "At least my mind seemed to feel in the Indian troops something puny and confined . . . so unlike the abrupt, wholesome Beduin of our joyous Army," he wrote. But his "joyous Army" was busy looting and cutting the throats of the Turkish wounded, and what Lawrence dismissed as "subservience" may merely have been the behavior of trained, professional troops who knew the meaning of the phrase "good order and discipline." However, allowance should probably be made for what Lawrence had gone through in the past forty-eight hours.

Years later, after the war, when Barrow and Allenby were chatting in the study of Allenby's London house, Allenby, according to Barrow, "tapped *The Seven Pillars of Wisdom* in his bookshelf and said: 'Lawrence goes for you in his book, George.' I replied to the effect that I was not taking any notice of it, and he said, 'No, that would be a mug's game. Besides, we know Lawrence. He thinks himself a hell of a soldier and loves posturing in the limelight.' " Of course we have no way of knowing if this conversation took place in exactly those words, or the degree to which Allenby was merely putting Barrow, a fellow general who was a guest in his home, at ease; but one suspects it is another example of the fact that Lawrence's dislike of regular soldiers was reciprocated to some degree by most of them, and that even Allenby's unwavering support may have faded ever so slightly after the taking of Damascus.

In any case, the conversation between Barrow and Lawrence at the railway station in Deraa set the tone for the future relationship between the British and Arab armies now that they had at last met east of the Jordan. Lawrence left Deraa and camped out in the open for the night with his bodyguard, for the last time; then at dawn he set out for Damascus in his Rolls-Royce with Major W. F. Stirling, who was wearing khaki and an Arab headdress. The road was blocked by Barrow's rear guard, so Lawrence had Rolls, his driver, take the car to the old French railway, from which the Turks had stripped the rails, and they drove over the gravel ballast as fast as they could. At noon, Lawrence saw Barrow and his staff watering their horses, so he switched from the Rolls-Royce to a camel and rode over to annoy Barrow further. Barrow, it seemed, had expressed the natural belief of a cavalryman that the horse travels faster than the camel, and was astonished to see that Lawrence's camel had caught up with him. He asked when Lawrence had left Deraa. "I said, 'This morning,' and his face fell. 'Where will you stop tonight?' was his next question. 'Damascus,' said I gaily and rode on, having made another enemy."* Lawrence was perfectly right about that. Barrow would not forget him, and since he survived Lawrence long enough to serve in the Home Guard in 1940, and did not write his memoirs until the end of World War II, he managed to have the last word. In any case, Lawrence was about to infuriate a good many more people on his way to Damascus, and after he arrived there.

Lawrence continued to be irked by the methodical advance of Barrow's division, with forward scouts and a cavalry screen thrown out in the regulation positions, since he had been told there were no cohesive Turkish forces between here and Damascus—information which, even if he considered it true, he apparently did not pass on to Barrow. That it was actually *not* true seems borne out by the fact that about halfway to Damascus Lawrence found Nasir, Nuri Shaalan, Auda, and their tribesmen attacking a large column of Turks, who were putting up an orderly resistance. Since the Turks had mountain guns and machine guns, Lawrence drove back to seek support from Barrow's leading cavalry regiment. He encountered an "ancient, surly" colonel of the Indian army who very reluctantly "upset the beautiful order of his march" by sending a squadron to attack the Turks, only to withdraw them when the Turks opened fire. Since he had promised the Arabs British support, Lawrence was furious, and turned back to find one of Barrow's brigadier-generals, who sent in the horse artillery and the Middlesex Yeomanry, which succeeded in making the Turks abandon their guns and transport, and stream into the desert. There, "Auda was waiting for them, and in that night of his last battle against the Turks the deadly old man killed and killed, plun-

---

* In his memoir, *The Fire of Life*, General Barrow asserts he had no such conversation with Lawrence, and that since Indian cavalry regiments on the Northwest Frontier always had a certain number of riding camels attached to them, he was as familiar with camels as Lawrence was. On the other hand, Barrow may not have realized only a few hours after the scene between them at Deraa that Lawrence was pulling his leg.

dered and plundered, captured and captured, till dawn came and showed him his work was finished." These were the last remnants of the Turkish Fourth Army, and when Auda had put an end to them, all meaningful Turkish resistance from Damascus south ceased.

Lawrence spent the night in Kiswe, only a few miles from Damascus; and the next day he consulted with Nasir and Nuri Shaalan, and "decided to send the Rualla horse galloping into town," to alert Feisal's supporters and Ali Riza Pasha, the governor of Damascus, who was a secret supporter of Feisal's, that the Arab army was on its way. Allenby had told Lieutenant-General Sir Henry Chauvel, who commanded the Desert Mounted Corps, to let the Arabs go into Damascus first if possible, and with that in mind Chauvel had ordered the Australian Mounted Division to swing around the city and cut the railway line leading to Aleppo in the north and to Beirut in the west. During the day British and Arab forces mixed together outside the city, and Lawrence was anxious that an Arab government should be in place before any British troops entered Damascus. That night he succeeded in sending another 4,000 mounted tribesmen into the city, to support the Rualla sheikhs; then he waited, sleepless, through a breathlessly hot night, illuminated by fires and explosions in Damascus as the Germans blew up their ammunition dumps and stores. At dawn he drove to a ridge and looked out over the city, afraid that he would see it in ruins. Instead, he saw a green oasis of silent gardens shrouded in early morning mist, with only a few columns of black smoke rising from the night's explosions. As he drove down toward the city, through green fields, a single horseman galloped up the road toward him. Seeing Lawrence's head cloth, the horseman held out "a bunch of yellow grapes, shouting: 'Good news: Damascus salutes you,'" and told him that his friends held the city.

Lawrence had urged Nasir and Nuri Shaalan to ride into the city before him. He was then temporarily halted by an importunate Indian army NCO who attempted to take him prisoner, and finally drove into Damascus along the long boulevard on the west bank of the Barada River toward the government buildings. People were packed solid along the road, on the pavement, on the roofs and balconies of the houses, and at every window. Many shouted Lawrence's name as they glimpsed the small Englishman in a dark cloak and a white robe and headdress with a golden *agal*, seated beside his driver in the dusty open Rolls-Royce. "A movement like a breath, in a long sigh from gate to heart of the city, marked our course," Lawrence wrote, and it was perhaps the proudest moment of his life, the culmination of what had begun just two years earlier when he set out to meet Feisal in the desert.

Whatever pleasure Lawrence may have allowed himself to feel at the taking of Damascus, or at the cheers from those in the crowds who recognized him, was soon erased by the scene that met him at the town hall. The building was mobbed by people dancing, weeping, and shouting for joy; but once he had pushed his way inside to the antechamber, he found a noisy chaos of political rivalry and old feuds boiling over. The leading figures among the Damascenes and the Bedouin were seated at a crowded table, with their followers behind them, all of them armed, all in furious dispute. Seated at the center of the table was Lawrence's old enemy Abd el Kader and his brother Mohammed Said, on either side of the respected old anti-Turk hero Shukri Pasha el Ayubi, who had been arrested and tortured by Jemal Pasha in 1916. Abd el Kader was shouting at the top of his voice that he, Shukri, and his brother had formed a provisional government and proclaimed Hussein king of the Arabs, even though until yesterday the brothers had been with the Turks. The two brothers had brought their Algerian followers with them and used them to break into the meeting and seize control of it.* Since Lawrence believed that Abd el Kader had betrayed his attempt to destroy the bridge over the Yarmuk and also given the Turks a description of himself that had led to his being stopped at Deraa, he was infuriated; but before he could do anything about it, a furious fight broke out in front of the table, chairs went flying,

---

*To put this in perspective, the number of the brothers' Algerian followers in and around Damascus may have been as high as 12,000 to 15,000 people (David Fromkin, *A Peace to End All Peace*, New York: Holt, 1989, 336).

Triumph: Lawrence, in the Blue Mist, arrives in Damascus.

and a familiar voice shouted in such violent rage that it silenced the whole room. In the center of an angry mob of their followers Auda Abu Tayi and the Druse chieftain Sultan el Atrash, old enemies, tore and clawed at each other until Lawrence "jumped in to drive them apart." Sultan el Atrash was pushed into another room, while Lawrence dragged Auda, "blind with rage," into the empty state room of the town hall. Sultan el Atrash had hit Auda in the face with a stick, and Auda was determined "to wash out the insult with Druse blood." Lawrence managed to calm Auda down, and to hustle Sultan el Atrash out of town. He then decided to make Shukri the temporary military governor of Damascus until Ali Riza Rejabi returned and Feisal arrived and sorted matters out. When he announced this to Abd el Kader and his brother, they "took it rather hard, and had to be sent home," though not before Abd el Kader "in a white heat of passion" had lunged at Lawrence with a drawn dagger, only to be stopped from using it by the intervention of Auda. Lawrence briefly contemplated having the two brothers arrested and shot, but decided that it would be a mistake to begin Arab rule in Syria with a political execution. The entire town was now in a combination of frenzied celebration and open political agitation, with the two brothers and their Algerian followers clearly bent on seizing control before Feisal or the British reached Damascus.

The arrival of Lieutenant-General Chauvel added to Lawrence's burdens. Like General Barrow at Deraa, Chauvel was shocked and appalled by the disorder in Damascus, anxious to assert order as quickly as possible, and infuriated to discover that the city appeared to be in the hands of a comparatively junior officer dressed in Arab clothing. Some of Chauvel's Australian horsemen had entered the city the day before, on October 1, despite Allenby's order, and Chauvel therefore believed that he, not Lawrence and the Arabs, had taken Damascus. He expected to make "a formal entry" into the city, with a parade the next day; and it is clear enough from Lawrence's account of their conversation that Lawrence not only attached no great importance to Chauvel's wish, but was pulling his leg—something that Chauvel no doubt recognized, though he was not amused. He considered himself honor-bound to receive the formal surrender of the city from the *wali*, the Turkish military governor. Lawrence told him that Shukri Pasha was the man, but did *not* tell him, until later in the day, that the "original" Turkish *wali* had fled and that he, Lawrence, had only just appointed Shukri to replace this man. When Chauvel learned this, he felt that he had been tricked, and warned Lawrence that he "could not recognize the King of the Hedjaz in this matter without further instructions."

In retrospect, it might have been wiser to bring Feisal into Damascus sooner, but there was also something to be said for Lawrence's idea of keeping him away while the local politicians and the tribesmen fought it out. Feisal's object was to make his entrance only after Lawrence and those political figures Feisal trusted had (to paraphrase Isaiah 40) prepared the way. The Turks' neglect of the city had to be put right; an effort had to be made to clean up garbage, round up and disarm the remaining Turkish soldiers, remove the signs of widespread looting and the corpses in the streets, and restore such vital public services as electricity, fire brigades, and hospitals. Above all, the activities of Abd el Kader and Mohammed Said, now amounting to a small-scale rebellion, had to be dealt with, since they were exhorting people to reject a government contaminated by its relationship with a Christian power—the British. The fact that Syria was going to be taken by the French was not yet widely known.

On October 2, Chauvel marched some of his troops into the city and placed a company of Australian light horsemen at the railway station and the town hall. Their presence was enough to restore a certain degree of order to the city, though it left Lawrence with the problem of finding forage for 40,000 horses. Still, the political situation remained obscure. Ali Riza Rejabi, a more energetic figure altogether, replaced Shukri as military governor, and promptly sided with Abd el Kader and his brother. Lawrence thought this was likely to give rise to trouble with both the British and the French.

That evening, as Lawrence heard the muezzins recite the call to evening prayer, he thought about the falseness of his position: "I had been born free, and a stranger to those whom I had led for two years, and tonight it seemed that I had given them all my gift, this false liberty drawn down to them by spells and wickedness, and nothing was left me but to go away." His departure would be sooner than he may have expected. In the meantime, Abd el Kader and his brother Mohammed Said staged their rebellion at midnight, encouraging their followers and dissident Druses to arm themselves and "burst open shops." At first light, Mohammed Said was arrested, but Abd el Kader fled into the countryside, to hide among his followers. Lawrence "itched to shoot him," but decided to wait until both brothers were in custody.[*]

---

[*] Abd el Kader would eventually be shot by sharifian police outside his home in Damascus on September 3, 1919—a classic instance of the cliché "shot while attempting to escape." Mohammed Said lived on to become a supporter of French rule in Syria.

At lunchtime, an Australian army doctor complained to Lawrence of the appalling conditions in the Turkish military hospital. Lawrence thought he had covered all three hospitals in Damascus—the civil, the military, and the missionary—but the Turks had used their barracks as a hospital as well, and this had been overlooked. He rushed to the barracks—where the Australian guard at first refused to let him enter, thinking he was an Arab—then walked through the huge area "squalid with rags and rubbish." He eventually found a room crammed with dead Turkish soldiers: "There might be thirty there, and they crept with rats who had gnawed red galleries into them. . . . Of some the flesh, just going putrid, was yellow and blue and black. Others were already swollen. . . . Of others the softer parts were fallen in, while the worst had burst open, and were liquescent with decay." Beyond this room was a large ward, into which Lawrence had to advance over "a soft mass of bodies," a worse place of horror, in which long lines of men lay in their beds, dying of disease, thirst, and hunger and crying out softly, *Aman, aman* ("Pity, pity"). Most of them had dysentery, and their few clothes and dressings were stiff with caked filth. Lawrence tried, but failed, to interest the Australians in helping, then went upstairs into the barracks and found the Turkish commandant and a few doctors "boiling coffee over a spirit stove." He forced them, and a few of the less seriously sick of the Turkish soldiers, to dig a six-foot-deep trench in the garden, gather up the corpses, and dump them one by one into it. Some of the corpses could be lifted and carried on stretchers; others had to be scraped up off the floor with shovels. He finally left another British officer in charge of the work and went back to the Hotel Victoria at midnight, ill and exhausted. He had slept less than three hours before leaving Deraa four days ago. At the hotel, the first thing to greet him was a reprimand from General Chauvel because the Arabs had failed to salute Australian officers properly.

The next morning, October 3, he went back to the Turkish barracks and found that conditions were improving. The dead were buried; lime had been spread everywhere; the living were being washed, put into clean shirts, and given water—it was still a charnel house, but a measure of order and humanity was being restored. Just as Lawrence was leaving, a major of the Royal Army Medical Corps, an Englishman, strode up to him and "asked [him] shortly if he spoke English." Lawrence said he did, and "with a glance of disgust at my skirts and sandals" the major asked whether Lawrence was in charge. Lawrence said that in a way he was, and the major began to shout at him indignantly and almost incoherently: "scandalous, disgraceful, outrageous, ought to be shot." Taken aback by this onslaught, just as he was about to congratulate himself on having taken care of a hopeless situation, Lawrence involuntarily laughed, "cackled like a duck, with the wild laughter that often took me at moments of strain." He was unable to stop laughing, and the major, wild with anger, slapped him hard across the face "and stalked off, leaving me more ashamed than angry, for in my heart I felt that he was right, and that anyone who had, like me, pushed through to success a rebellion of the weak against their master, must come out of it so stained that nothing in the world would make him clean again."

In essence this was the feeling that would motivate Lawrence throughout the rest of his life: the belief not just that he had failed the Arabs by not getting them the state and the independence they had fought for, but that he was rendered, by what he had done, seen, and experienced, permanently unclean, unfit for the society of decent people, a kind of moral leper. It is important to realize that while Lawrence's behavior after the war seemed strange to many people, it is not at all unfamiliar to those who have fought in a war.

Lawrence was always able to function; indeed in many respects his greatest achievements were still ahead of him—but in some way he took on the guilt and the shame of everything he, and millions of others, had done. His wild, manic laughter in Damascus took place, perhaps appropriately, on the day he would leave behind the role of "Colonel Lawrence," which he had come to despise, and begin, with halting steps, a new life, under a variety of new names.

Early the same morning, Allenby arrived in Damascus at last, and stopped briefly at the Victoria Hotel with his staff. Feisal was due to arrive the same day by train, and at first there was some doubt about whether he and Allenby, who was anxious to push on and take Aleppo and Beirut, could meet. Feisal was planning a "triumphal entry" into Damascus, and the streets were already packed with people anticipating his arrival. Allenby was not interested in ceremonies, and ordered Major Young to find Feisal and tell him "to come and see me at once." Young went off to intercept Feisal in General Liman von Sanders's huge red Mercedes *Roi des Belges* limousine, which had been captured in Nazareth. By the time Young found him, Feisal had already left the train and mounted his horse, ready to ride into the city at the head of the mounted Arab regulars. When Young told Feisal that Allenby had only a few minutes and wished to see him, he rode off at the canter at once, so Young was obliged to trail after him in the big car. We have no way of knowing what Feisal thought at having his plans disrupted, but whatever his feelings were, Feisal must have realized that meeting Allenby was more important. Young took him up to Allenby's suite; Allenby and Lawrence were on the balcony awaiting Feisal's arrival, and when Allenby walked back into the room he and Feisal met for the first time.

Allenby's mood was far from cheerful; he had hoped to avoid the meeting until he received definite instructions from London about the political arrangements for Syria, and after the polite greetings, it was his unwelcome task to give Feisal the bad news that the Sykes-Picot agreement was by no means dead. Using Lawrence as his interpreter—though it appears likely that Feisal understood a good deal more English and a lot more French than he thought it politic to admit—Allenby plunged right in with the bad news: France "was to be the Protecting Power over Syria"; Feisal was to have "the Administration of Syria" on behalf of his father, but under French "guidance," and was not "to have anything to do" with Lebanon, which was reserved to France; and perhaps most unwelcome of all, Feisal was to exchange Lawrence as his liaison officer for "a French Liaison Officer at once."

Feisal objected "very strongly." He said that he preferred British to French assistance; that if Lebanon was not joined to Syria, "a country without a port was no good to him"; and that he "declined to have a French Liaison Officer or to recognize French guidance in any way."

Allenby then "turned to Lawrence and said: 'But did you not tell him that the French were to have the Protectorate over Syria?' Lawrence said: 'No Sir, I know nothing about it.' [Allenby] then said: 'But you knew definitely that he, Feisal, was to have nothing to do with the Lebanon?' Lawrence said: 'No Sir, I did not.' "

After this embarrassing exchange, Allenby laid down the law. Feisal, he pointed out, was a lieutenant-general under his command, and would have to obey his orders. After some further discussion, Feisal took his leave. It is possible that he and Lawrence may not have known of some of the more humiliating details of the French "protectorate," but Lawrence certainly knew all about the Sykes-Picot agreement and had passed on what he knew to Feisal. Indeed Feisal could have read the agreement for himself, once the Bolsheviks had published the document. Feisal understandably found it more diplomatic to deny any knowledge of a document which he had supposed was a "dead letter," and whose legitimacy he was bound to oppose. Given his admiration for Allenby, Lawrence must have found it difficult to say with a straight face that he knew nothing of the terms, which differed so dramatically from promises made to the Arabs.

That perhaps explains the bluntness of his dismissal. After Feisal's departure, Lawrence told Allenby that "he would not work with a French Liaison Officer and that since he was due for leave and thought he had better take it now and go off to England. [Allenby] said, 'Yes! I think you had!' and Lawrence left the room."

The next evening, Lawrence left Damascus, driven, for the last time, in the Blue Mist. His ambitions for the Arabs would have to be fought out in London and Paris now.

By October 24, he was home in Oxford, for the first time since 1914.

CHAPTER NINE

In the Great World

... that younger successor of Mohammed, Colonel Lawrence, the twenty-eight-year-old conqueror of Damascus, with his boyish face and almost constant smile—the most winning figure ... of the whole Peace Conference.

—James T. Shotwell, *At the Paris Peace Conference*

Despite General Allenby's abruptness, he and Lawrence had not lost their esteem for each other. Allenby may well have felt that Lawrence's departure from Syria would make it easier for Feisal to get used to the inevitable, in the form of a French replacement, but if so he was wrong. Throughout the coming peace talks in Paris Lawrence would remain—to the fury of the French, and the occasional exasperation of the British Foreign Office—Feisal's confidant, constant companion, interpreter, and adviser, the only European with whom Feisal could let his guard down. In Cairo, Lawrence gave Lady Allenby one of his most treasured mementos, the prayer rug from his first attack on a Turkish train. Allenby not only wrote to Clive Wigram,* assistant private secretary to King George V, asking him

---

*Wigram eventually became the first baron Wigram, GCB, GCVO, CSI, PC, private secretary to the sovereign from 1931 to 1936.

"to arrange for an audience with the King" for Lawrence, but at Lawrence's request made him "a temporary, special and acting full colonel," a rank that entitled Lawrence to take the fast train from Taranto to Paris instead of a slower troop train, and to have a sleeping berth on the journey. Allenby also wrote to the Foreign Office to say that Lawrence was on his way to London to present Feisal's point of view on the subject of Syria.

Lawrence's return therefore had a semiofficial gloss—far from coming home to shed his rank and be "demobilized," in the military jargon of the day, Lawrence arrived with the crown and two stars of a colonel on his shoulders and a string of interviews arranged at the very highest level of government. Although Lawrence claimed to have felt like "a man dropping a heavy load," there seems to have been no doubt in his mind, or Allenby's, that he was returning to Britain to take up the Arab cause.

Lawrence was exhausted, thin almost to emaciation, weighing no more than eighty pounds, as opposed to his usual 112. This is borne out both by Lawrence's older brother Bob, who was shocked by his appearance when he arrived home, and by James McBey's startling portrait of him, painted in Damascus, in which his face is as thin and sharp as a dagger, and his eyes are enormous and profoundly sad. It is the face of a man worn out by danger, stress, responsibility, and disappointment. The faintly ironic smile on his lips seems to suggest that he already suspects nothing he fought for is likely to happen. The confusion, chaos, jealousies, and violence in Damascus may already have convinced him that there was not going to be a noble ending to his adventures.

On the ship from Port Said to Taranto, Italy, Lawrence persuaded his fellow passenger and former fellow soldier, Lord Winterton, a member of Parliament, to write on his behalf requesting interviews with Lord Robert Cecil (the undersecretary of state for foreign affairs*) and A. J. Balfour (the foreign secretary). Lawrence also interrupted his journey in Rome for a talk with Georges-Picot about the French position in Syria. During

---

*Later the Rt. Hon. the Viscount Cecil of Chelwood, CH, PC, QC.

*Tragedy: Lawrence, exhausted, emaciated, and shorn of illusions.
Damascus, 1918.*

the course of this discussion Picot made it very clear, if there had been any doubt in Lawrence's mind, that France remained determined to have Lebanon and Syria, and rule them from Paris in much the same way as Tunisia, Algeria, and Morocco. There was a place for Prince Feisal as the head of a government approved by France, and under the tutelage of a French governor-general and a French military commander, but he should have no illusions about creating an independent sovereign state.

There occurred on this journey an incident that puzzled Lawrence's biographers while he was still alive and provided material for them long after his death. Either at Taranto, between the ship and the train, or at Marseille, where the train presumably stopped before going on to Paris, Lawrence saw a British major dressing down a private for failing to salute, and humiliating the private by making him salute over and over again. Lawrence intervened, and when the major asked him what business it was of his, he removed his uniform mackintosh, which had no epaulets and hence no badges of rank; revealed the crown and two stars of a full colonel on his shoulders; pointed out that the major had failed to salute *him*; and made the major do so several times. Lowell Thomas's version of this incident differs radically from Liddell Hart's: according to Thomas, Lawrence asks the railway transport officer (RTO) at the Marseille station, a lieutenant-colonel ("a huge fellow, with a fierce moustache"), what time his train leaves, is snubbed, and then takes off his raincoat to show that he outranks the pompous RTO. In Robert Graves's biography, Lawrence sees "a major . . . bullying two privates . . . for not saluting him," and neglects to return their salute until Lawrence appears and makes him do so. Whichever one of these stories is true, they all illustrate the same point, which is Lawrence's dislike of conventional discipline and of officers' abusing their power over "other ranks."

One point that the indefatigable Jeremy Wilson has clearly demonstrated in his exhaustive authorized biography is that there is always a germ of truth in every story Lawrence told about himself, though over the years Lawrence sometimes improved and embellished such stories. Taranto seems much more likely as the place where this occurred, first of all because there were more British troops at Taranto, but also because it had been only a matter of days then since General Chauvel's inopportune complaint in Damascus about the Arabs' failing to salute British officers, so the subject of saluting may still have been very much on Lawrence's mind. This was also the first time in more than two years that Lawrence was dressed in a British uniform and found himself among British officers and men. In the desert, he had neither saluted nor encouraged British personnel below his rank to salute him. Now he was back in the army. He was returning to a world where rank mattered and class distinctions were absolute, a world very different from the rough simplicity of desert warfare.

He arrived home "on or about October 24th," but spent only a few days with his family in Oxford before getting down to the business of securing Syria for Feisal and the Arabs. Only four days later, thanks to Winterton's letter of introduction, he had a long interview with Lord Robert Cecil, perhaps the most eminent, respectable, and idealistic figure in Lloyd George's government. Cecil was a son of the marquess of Salisbury, the Conservative prime minister who had dominated late Victorian politics; the Cecil family traced its tradition of public service back to 1571, when Queen Elizabeth I made William Cecil her lord treasurer. Robert Cecil was an Old Etonian, an Oxonian, a distinguished and successful lawyer, an architect of the League of Nations, and a firm believer in Esperanto as a universal common language. He would go on to win the Nobel Peace Prize, among many other honors. The fact that he was willing to see Lawrence on such short notice is a tribute not only to Lord Winterton's reputation, but to Lawrence's growing fame as a hero. Of course he was not yet the celebrity he would become when Lowell Thomas had established him in the public mind as "Lawrence of Arabia," but his service in the desert was already sufficiently well known to open doors that would surely have remained closed to anyone else. Cecil's notes on the meeting—in which he shrewdly comments that Lawrence always refers to Feisal and the Arabs as "we"—make it clear that Lawrence's ideas on the future of the Middle East were both intelligent and far-reaching, and were viewed with sympathy by one of the most influential figures in what would later come to be called "the establishment." The next day, Lawrence had an equally long and persuasive discussion with Lieutenant-General Sir George Macdonogh, GBE, KCB, KCMG, adjutant-general of the British army, and creator of MI7, an intelligence unit intended to sabotage German morale. Macdonogh, who was very well informed about the Middle East, afterward circulated to the war cabinet a long and admiring report on his discussion with Lawrence, the gist of which was that the Sykes-Picot agreement should be dropped, Syria should be "under the control" of Feisal, Feisal's half brother Zeid should rule northern Mesopotamia, and Feisal's brother Abdulla should rule southern Mesopotamia—in short, Lawrence converted Macdonogh.

Perhaps as a result of the "Macdonogh memorandum," Lawrence was invited to address the Eastern Committee of the war cabinet on October 29, only five days after he had arrived back in Britain. Deducting two days for the time he had spent with his family in Oxford, Lawrence had reached the highest level of the British government in seventy-two hours. Judging from Macdonogh's memorandum, he did so first by the lucidity and intelligence of his ideas, and second because what he had to say was viewed with intense sympathy. The British government believed, like Lawrence, that the Sykes-Picot agreement should be discarded; that Arabs and Zionists should cooperate in Palestine under the protection of a British administration; that Mesopotamia should be an Arab "protectorate," ruled from Cairo, not from Delhi; and that Arab ambitions (and British promises) in Syria should be respected. If Lawrence was not quite preaching to the converted, he was at any rate preaching to those who were prepared to convert. On the other hand, since there were still few signs that the war was about to end suddenly—in twenty-three days, in fact—the general feeling was that there was still plenty of time to bring the French around to this point of view. The British also believed that Woodrow Wilson would certainly denounce the Sykes-Picot agreement as a perfect example of secret diplomacy, which he wanted to end once and for all. Lawrence, who had after all stopped in Rome to talk directly to Picot, had a good idea of just how intransigent the French were likely to be; but perhaps sensibly, he does not seem to have raised this with either Cecil or Macdonogh.

In any event, Lawrence's appearance at the Eastern Committee of the war cabinet is almost as much of a puzzle for biographers as the story about the saluting incident at Taranto or Marseille. He himself once said that he "was more a legion than a man," a reference to the man from Gadara whose name was "Legion" because he was possessed by so many demons. Lawrence found no difficulty in presenting different versions of himself to people throughout his lifetime, hence the often wildly conflicting reactions to him.

The meeting was chaired by the Rt. Hon. the Earl Curzon, KG, GSCI, GCIE, PC, former viceroy of India, leader of the House of Lords, one of the most widely traveled men ever to sit in a British cabinet, and perhaps one of the most formidable and hardworking political figures of his time. A graduate of Eton and Balliol College, Oxford, he was in some respects everything that Lawrence was not: his career at Oxford had been glittering, both academically and socially; he was renowned for his arrogance and inflexibility (caused in part by the fact that a riding injury in his youth obliged him to wear a steel corset that inflicted on him unceasing, lifelong pain, and made his posture seem unnaturally stiff and straight). His attitude toward life was grandly aristocratic, so that he sometimes seemed more appropriate to the eighteenth than to the twentieth century.

As Lawrence later told the story, he sat before the committee while Curzon made a long speech, outlining and praising Lawrence's feats—a speech that for some reason Lawrence "chafed at." Lawrence may, as he later complained, have found this speech patronizing, particularly since he knew most of the members of the committee, but it is more likely that Curzon's grandiloquent manner simply rubbed him the wrong way. In any case, once Curzon finished, he asked if Lawrence wished to say anything, and Lawrence answered: "Yes, let's get to business. You people don't understand yet the hole you have put us all into."

Lawrence, writing to Robert Graves in 1927, added: "Curzon burst promptly into tears, great drops running down his cheeks, to an accompaniment of slow sobs. It was horribly like a mediaeval miracle, a lachryma Christi, happening to a Buddha. Lord Robert Cecil, hardened to such scenes, presumably, interposed roughly, 'Now old man, none of that.' Curzon dried up instanter." Lawrence then warned Graves, "I doubt if I'd publish it, if you do, don't put it on my authority. Say a late member of the F.O. [Foreign Office] Staff told you."

There are many questions about this account, some of which are obvious. First, why would Curzon ask if there was anything Lawrence wished to say, since Lawrence's whole reason for being there was to speak to the committee? Second, it is hard to imagine Lord Robert Cecil, the most gentlemanly of men, speaking to anyone "roughly." The spectacle of Curzon sobbing at a meeting of a committee of the war cabinet would certainly have startled the other members, and in fact, after Graves's biography of Lawrence was published, Cecil wrote to Curzon's daughter, Lady Cynthia Mosley,* denying that the incident had ever happened: "I feel quite certain that your father never burst into tears, and I am even more certain that I have never addressed him in the way described under any circumstances." As for Curzon's speech about Lawrence, Cecil wrote: "Colonel Lawrence listened with the most marked attention, and spoke to me afterwards in the highest appreciation of your father's attitude."

Of course Cecil may have felt it was his obligation to be polite to Lady Cynthia about her father, but nobody else who was present at the meeting seems to have commented on the incident, and this fact raises a certain amount of doubt about Lawrence's story. Indeed, given how influential Curzon was, and the importance of Lawrence's meeting with the committee, why on earth would Lawrence have gone out of his way to attack him?

Against this must be set the rumor that Curzon burst into tears in 1923 when Lord Stamfordham, the king's private secretary, informed him

---

*She was then married to Sir Oswald Mosley, Bt., still a rising young politician and not yet the founder and leader of the British Union of Fascists.

that George V had decided to choose Stanley Baldwin instead of Curzon as prime minister, after Bonar Law announced his retirement. If Curzon could burst into tears on that occasion, then he could presumably have burst into tears in front of Lawrence and the members of the Eastern Committee of the war cabinet; but even so there is a certain gloating quality in Lawrence's letter to Graves, which makes one uncomfortable. In addition, Lawrence's suggestion that Graves should attribute the story to "a late member of the F.O. Staff" when he himself is the source of it seems rather devious for a man who set such high standards for himself.

In Scottish courts there used to be a verdict falling between "guilty" and "not guilty," namely "not proven." Lawrence's story about Curzon bursting into tears seems to fit into that category perfectly.

The day after Lawrence's appearance before the Eastern Committee of the war cabinet, he was involved in an even more controversial meeting at a much higher level. Allenby's letter to Clive Wigram had produced a private audience with the king, who was in any case, given his interest in military affairs, curious to meet young Colonel Lawrence. Allenby had also recommended Lawrence for the immediate award of a knighthood, a Knight Companion of the Order of the Bath (KCB), which was one step up in the senior of the two orders that Lawrence had already been awarded. Lawrence had already made it clear to the king's military secretary that he did not wish to accept this honor, and that he merely wished to inform the king about the importance of Britain's living up to the promises made to King Hussein, but whether this information was passed on accurately is uncertain. It seems unlikely that two men as realistic as General Allenby and Lord Stamfordham would have hidden from the king Lawrence's unwillingness to receive any form of decoration—perhaps the most important part of Stamfordham's job as a courtier was to ensure that the king was spared any kind of surprise or embarrassment, and Allenby was an ambitious man who would not have wished to offend his sovereign.

Once Lawrence arrived at Buckingham Palace, he learned that the king intended to hold a private investiture, and present him with the insignia of his CB and his DSO. It seems very likely that this was the king's own idea, that he intended it as a thoughtful gesture toward a hero. Once he made up his mind to do it, neither Stamfordham nor the military secretary attempted to confront him over the matter—George V's stubbornness and sharp temper were well known, and when he had made up his mind to do something he was not easy to divert. Thus Lawrence was ushered in to see the king and left to explain himself that he would not accept any decorations or honors, either old or new.

We have Lawrence's account of what he said to the king, in a letter he sent to Robert Graves with corrections he wanted Graves to make in his biography: "He explained personally to his Sovereign that the part he had played in the Arab Revolt was, to his judgment, dishonourable to himself and to his country and government. He had by order fed the Arabs with false hopes and would be obliged if he were relieved of the obligation to accept honors for succeeding in his fraud. Lawrence now said respectfully as a subject, but firmly as an individual, that he intended to fight by straight means or crooked until the King's ministers had conceded to the Arabs a fair settlement of their claims."

"In spite of what has been published to the contrary," Lawrence added to Graves, "there was no breach of good relations between subject and sovereign." In later years, the king, who liked to improve a good story as much as Lawrence, would tell how Lawrence unpinned each decoration as soon as the king had pinned it on him, so that in the end the king was left foolishly holding a cardboard box filled with the decorations and their red leather presentation cases. In fact the king seems to have been more curious than offended. Lawrence explained, with his usual charm, that it was difficult to serve two masters—Emir Feisal and King George— and that "if a man has to serve two masters it was better to offend the more powerful."

At first the king was under the impression that Lawrence was turning down the KCB because he expected something better, and offered him instead the Order of Merit, a much more distinguished honor—it has been described as "the most prestigious honor on earth"—in the personal gift of the sovereign, founded by King George V's father and limited to a total of twenty-four members. (Past members have included Florence Nightingale, and subsequent ones Graham Greene, Nelson Mandela, and Lady Thatcher.) This was not an offer to be taken lightly, but Lawrence refused it, at which point the king sighed in resignation, and said, "Well, there's one vacant; I suppose it will have to go to Foch."

The interview was cozy rather than formal. It had begun with the king "warming his coat tails in front of the fire at Buckingham Palace, the *Morning Post* in his hands, and complaining: 'This is a bad time for kings. Five new republics today.'" Lawrence may have consoled the king by saying that he had just made two kings, but this seems unlikely—Hussein had made himself a king without Lawrence's help, and Feisal had not yet been made one.* Lawrence had brought with him as a present for the king the gold-inlayed Lee-Enfield rifle that Enver Pasha had presented to Feisal, and that Feisal later gave to Lawrence in the desert. The king, an enthusiastic and expert shot and gun fancier himself—apart from stamp collecting, guns were his favorite pastime—was delighted with the rifle, which remained in the royal collection of firearms for many years until it was presented to the Imperial War Museum, where it is now a prized exhibit.

Later, Lord Stamfordham, in a letter to Robert Graves from Balmoral Castle, the royal family's summer residence in Scotland, confirmed most of Lawrence's account of the interview, and since Stamfordham and Lawrence dined together amicably at one point afterward, it does not seem likely that George V was offended—Stamfordham would hardly have dined "amicably" with somebody who had offended his sovereign. The two people at court who *were* offended were the queen and the Prince of Wales (the future King Edward VIII and then the duke of Windsor), both

---

*Lawrence had what appears to have been a streak of what the French call *l'esprit de l'escalier*, that is coming up with the clever last word too late, when one is already on the staircase after having left the room, and then incorporating it into later accounts of the conversation.

of whom resented what they interpreted as discourtesy to the king, a resentment that Edward expressed strongly all his life.

During the course of the conversation, Lawrence expressed the opinion that all the members of his majesty's government were "crooks," not an uncommon opinion so long as Lloyd George was prime minister. The king was "rather taken aback" but by no means shocked or offended—his own opinion of Lloyd George was no better than Lawrence's. "Surely you wouldn't call Lord Robert Cecil a crook?" he asked, however, and Lawrence had to agree with the king that Cecil was certainly an exception.

In his letter to Graves, Stamfordham also made an interesting point: Lawrence had explained to the king "in a few words" that "he had made certain promises to King Feisal, that these promises had not been fulfilled and, consequently, it was quite possible that he might find himself fighting against the British Forces, in which case it would be obviously impossible and wrong to be wearing British decorations."

One might have thought that if anything was going to shock the king it would be Lawrence's suggestion that a British officer wearing the king's uniform might have to take up arms against his own country, with or without his decorations, but the king seems either to have taken that in his stride, or to have decided that it was merely self-dramatizing nonsense, as indeed it was.

All things considered, Lawrence's talk with the king was not nearly as controversial as it has often been described, but it was nevertheless surely a tactical mistake on Lawrence's part. First of all, while Lawrence was within his right to decline new honors, he could not "turn down" those he already had, something the king understood better than Lawrence. For that matter Lawrence could just as easily have accepted the decorations without a fuss, then neglected to wear them afterward, and it would have made no difference at all. More important, the story made its way around London quickly, and usually it took the form of Lawrence being rude to the king, though he had not in fact been rude. This perplexed or outraged many people who might otherwise have admired Lawrence, or been helpful to him in getting the Arabs what they wanted.

Churchill was among them, until Lawrence had an opportunity to explain to him in private what had really happened. In those days, at least, nobody ever benefited in the long run from having been thought rude to the royal family—as Churchill knew well, since his beloved father, Lord Randolph Churchill, had learned that lesson after offending King Edward VII.

Lawrence spent the next few days preparing a long paper on the Middle East for the war cabinet's committee, in which he succeeded in presenting both his own views and those of Feisal as if they were the same. In fact, Lawrence was prepared to accept a far higher degree of British involvement, direct and indirect, in Arabian affairs than either Feisal or his father would have wished; it was France (and direct French rule) Lawrence wanted to keep out of the Middle East, not Britain. He clung firmly to the heart of the matter—an independent Arab state in Syria, with Feisal as its ruler, under some kind of British supervision; a British-controlled Arab state in what is now Iraq; and "Jewish infiltration" in Palestine, "if it is behind a British as opposed to an international façade." He was effectively recommending repudiation of the Sykes-Picot agreement, and firing two warning signals: one of them idealistic, "the cry of self determination" that the United States would be likely to approve; the other practical, the information that Feisal would be willing to accept increased Zionist immigration in Palestine *only* if it remained under British control, but not if Palestine was placed under international control as the Sykes-Picot agreement provided.

Lawrence delivered this document to the Eastern Committee on November 4, and went on to meet with Winston Churchill, then minister of munitions, who had presumably not yet heard about Lawrence's meeting with the king. This was to be the beginning of one of the most significant of Lawrence's postwar friendships with older and more powerful men. Churchill not only was impressed by the young colonel, but would go on to become Lawrence's lifelong supporter. Perhaps nobody would describe better the effect Lawrence had on his contemporaries than Churchill at the forthcoming peace conference: "He wore his Arab robes, and the full magnificence of his countenance revealed itself. The gravity of his demeanor; the precision of his opinions; the range and quality of his conversations; all seemed enhanced to a remarkable degree by the splendid Arab head-dress and garb. From amid the flowing draperies his noble features, his perfectly chiseled lips and flashing eyes loaded with fire and comprehension shone forth. He looked like what he was, one of Nature's greatest princes."

If Lawrence could inspire Churchill—a hardened politician; a former soldier himself who had ridden with the Twenty-First Lancers in the last major cavalry charge of the British army at the Battle of Omdurman in 1893, Mauser automatic pistol in hand; and the grandson of a duke—to gush like a smitten schoolgirl, it is hardly surprising that lesser men were bowled over even before Lawrence's legend took hold. Apart from Churchill, Lawrence made an instant and lifelong friend of Edward ("Eddie") Marsh, Churchill's devoted and brilliant private secretary. Through Marsh, Lawrence met many of the literary figures who became his friends over the years, including Siegfried Sassoon. For somebody who already had the reputation of being reclusive, Lawrence had a genius for friendship—he was a master of what would now be called networking, and an indefatigable correspondent.

On November 8, Lawrence took the step that would bring him onto the world stage as something of an independent power. He sent an "urgent message" to King Hussein in Mecca, informing Hussein that there would be "conversations about the Arabs" in two weeks' time in Paris, and advising him to send his son Feisal as his representative. Much as Hussein disliked and mistrusted Lawrence, he must have realized immediately the value of sending Feisal, rather than one of Feisal's older brothers, since Feisal and Lawrence were credited in the European and American press with the capture of Damascus. Certainly Hussein already realized that his claim to be "king of all the Arabs" and likewise his claim to the vast amount of territory promised to him by Sir Henry McMahon in 1915 were going to be a hard sell in Paris, let alone in Riyadh, where his rival ibn Saud, with the backing of the British government in India, was already moving to take control of the entire Arabian Peninsula.

It should be noted that Lawrence, with the skill of a natural "insider," was already well informed about the negotiations between Britain and France. On November 9, the Foreign Office released an Anglo-French declaration that embodied some of his suggestions, though couched in such vague and optimistic prose that it seemed to envisage both "native governments" and colonial rule. The British were in a difficult position. McMahon and Hussein's correspondence of 1915 directly contradicted the Sykes-Picot agreement of 1916 (as well as the Balfour Declaration of 1917), and while these conflicting promises to the Arabs, the French, and the Jews could be swept under the rug so long as the war continued, victory would instantly bring the British face-to-face with the unwelcome reality of having promised more in the Middle East than they or anyone else could deliver.

On November 8, only a day after Lawrence's message to King Hussein, the subject of the Middle East was suddenly overshadowed by the surrender of the Austro-Hungarian Empire. On November 9 the kaiser abdicated. And on November 11, "the eleventh hour of the eleventh day of the eleventh month," Germany itself asked for an armistice.

Those in charge of Britain's foreign and colonial affairs were suddenly faced with a range of issues more serious and pressing than the Middle East. What was to be the future of Germany? What was to replace the defeated Austro-Hungarian Empire, which was already beginning to crumble into a number of small, mutually hostile would-be states? Who was to receive the German colonies in Africa, and on what terms? Could a viable European peace be constructed without the participation of the Russians, now controlled by a Bolshevik regime that repudiated all treaties and preached universal revolution? Clamorous advocates for new states like Poland and Czechoslovakia were already appearing, maps and draft constitutions in hand; in the Balkans the Romanians were already demanding almost a third of Hungary as their reward for joining the Allies; the Serbs, on whose behalf the war had begun, were greedy to seize as much territory as possible and create a multinational Yugoslavia; and Zionists were pressing for the rapid implementation of the Balfour Declaration.

More important than all these problems was the fact that the president of the United States was planning to join in the peace talks himself, bringing with him a host of unwelcome ideas, including a "general association of nations." The New World was embarking on an effort to remake and reform the Old. "Even the Good Lord contented himself with only ten," Clemenceau grumbled, when he read Woodrow Wilson's Fourteen Points with the skeptical eye of an old-fashioned French nationalist who already knew what he wanted: Alsace; Lorraine; the Rhineland; formidable, crippling reparations; client states in the east to hold Germany in check; and, of course, last but not least, Syria, Lebanon, Mosul with its oil, and a share in the Holy Land.

At the same time, the prospect of President Wilson's participation in the peace talks, together with a formidable American delegation,* made his majesty's government more inclined to collaborate with the French. Only by standing together, arm in arm, *bras dessus, bras dessous*, could the two principal European powers hope to resist what they both saw as Woodrow Wilson's starry-eyed idealism and naïveté.

In the meantime, reports and advice on the Middle East continued to pour in to the Eastern Committee. Both Clayton and Hogarth sent long, detailed recommendations, basically echoing Lawrence's views. They were quickly countered by an equally long memorandum from Sir Arthur Hirtzel of the India Office, outlining the views of the government of India. These amounted to a sharp reminder that what really mattered was the oil deposits of Mesopotamia, rather than the Syrian Desert, and a warning that it was not worth jeopardizing British interests in Mesopotamia for the sake of nebulous promises that may have been made to Hussein and his sons. Hirtzel expressed polite scorn for Lawrence, whose

---

* It would include a remarkable number of intellectually brilliant figures, from President Wilson's powerful adviser and éminence grise Colonel Edward House to such future foreign policy heavyweights as John Foster Dulles and Walter Lippmann.

contempt for the Indian government and the Indian army on his brief visit to Baghdad in 1916 during the siege of Kut had not been forgotten or forgiven: "Without in the least wishing to deprecate [Lawrence's] achievements and his undoubted genius, it must be said about him that he does not at all represent—and would not, I think, claim to represent—the local views of Northern Mesopotamia and Iraq; of the latter, indeed, he has practically no first-hand knowledge at all."

Hirtzel also warned strongly against Lawrence's proposal to place one of Hussein's sons on a throne in Baghdad as king of Iraq, and another on a throne in Mosul to rule over the Kurds,* and suggested that if Britain raised objections to France's ruling over Lebanon and Syria, the French would hardly be likely to accept British rule over Iraq.

Even the joy of victory did not prevent Stéphen-Jean-Marie Pichon, the French foreign minister, from administering a sharp rap on the knuckles to the British Foreign Office, reminding them that so far as France was concerned, the Sykes-Picot agreement was still in force and that France expected to receive everything it had been promised. Pichon reminded the British Foreign Office of France's "historic duty towards the peoples of Syria," just in case the members of the Eastern Committee had forgotten, or might have plans to denounce the Sykes-Picot agreement to President Wilson as exactly the kind of secret diplomacy that the Fourteen Points were intended to prevent.

Much as the British might deprecate the exaggerated territorial claims of King Hussein, or the ambitions of Syrian nationalists, when it came to the Middle East there was more sympathy for the Arabs in London—partly because of Lawrence—than for the French. Lawrence's capacity for communicating enthusiasm was now concentrated on the task of getting Feisal to the Peace Conference, despite strong French opposition.

---

* Although Lawrence's plan may have been overgenerous to Hussein and his sons, it nevertheless recognized the difference between northern and southern Mesopotamia, and would have resulted in an independent Kurdish state and solved at least one of the fundamental divisive issues that plague modern Iraq.

"THE CURE"

European diplomacy: A diminutive Lawrence tries to restrain Feisal from being tempted by France at the Peace Conference. Cartoon by Sir Mark Sykes.

In this, he succeeded triumphantly. By November 21, when he attended the next Eastern Committee meeting, Feisal's participation was now considered indispensable by most of the members. "You do not want to divide the loot," Jan Smuts warned the committee; "that would be the wrong policy for the future." What Smuts meant, of course, was that the British should not be *seen* to be dividing the loot, least of all in cooperation with the French. They should, in the words of Curzon, "play [Arab] self-determination for all it was worth . . . knowing in the bottom of [their] hearts that we are more likely to benefit from it than anybody else." Lord Robert Cecil argued for the presence of a friendly Arab prince and felt "it was essential that Feisal and the British government have the same story." This carried the implication that Lawrence, the only person who knew Feisal, should be present to coach his friend on a common "story," one that would—it was hoped—satisfy the Americans without alarming the French.*

From November 8 to November 21, Lawrence had not only looked after Feisal's interests but also placed himself as one of the central figures at the forthcoming Peace Conference—for by now nobody could doubt that "Colonel Lawrence" would be part of the British delegation. For a man who denied altogether having any ambition, Lawrence had played his cards as adroitly as Machiavelli.

In fact, Feisal and his exotic entourage, which included his personal slave and the newly promoted Brigadier-General Nuri as-Said, were already at sea, on board the cruiser HMS *Gloucester.* Just as Lawrence had been able, after Aqaba, to summon naval ships and airplanes when he needed them, now he had adroitly managed to have the Royal Navy deliver Feisal to Europe. This was not only proof of Lawrence's prestige, but a very visible statement of British backing for the Hashemite family and its pretensions. Unfortunately, this move had not been announced to the French government, perhaps owing to a failure of communication, perhaps by an oversight, or more likely because nobody wanted to take responsibility for doing so. When the French were finally informed by their secret services that Feisal would be landing at any moment in Marseille from a British cruiser, they were predictably outraged.

Lawrence was dispatched by the Foreign Office at once to extinguish the fire, and arrived in Marseille, via Paris, with orders to smooth things down and get Feisal to Paris, or, if necessary, to London, with as little fuss as possible. Although the French claimed that Lawrence wore his white robes to greet Feisal, this seems not to have been the case. In photographs of their meeting, Lawrence is in British uniform, but he had borrowed the Arab headdress and *agal* of a Meccan officer. He gave further offense to the French by not wearing the ribbons of a *chevalier* of the

---

* Readers may find an echo of the kind of thinking expressed by members of the committee in scene IV of G. B. Shaw's *Saint Joan,* in which the (English) chaplain exclaims to the (French) bishop of Beauvais, "How can what an Englishman believes be heresy? It is a contradiction in terms."

Legion of Honor or his two Croix de Guerre. He was regarded in Paris as Feisal's "evil genius," and as a sinister agent of the British secret services. Colonel Brémond—France's former military representative in Jidda and Lawrence's old bête noire—was ordered to intercept Feisal and Lawrence posthaste, and inform them of France's displeasure. Regarding Lawrence, Brémond's instructions were uncompromising: "You must be quite candid with Lawrence, and point out to him that he is in a false position. If he is in France as a British colonel in British uniform, we welcome him. But we don't accept him as an Arab, and if he remains in fancy dress, he is not wanted here."

A brief tussle took place at Marseille; the British wanted Feisal to travel directly to Paris; but the French, playing for time, had quickly arranged a leisurely tour of the major battlefields, including Verdun—no doubt to show him how much greater France's sacrifices had been in the war than those of the Hejaz—as well as a number of factories, to impress him with France's wealth. Lawrence accompanied Feisal as far as Lyon, where Colonel Brémond finally caught up with them. The French warning regarding Lawrence was read to them, and Lawrence, possibly choosing this occasion to return his cross of the Legion of Honor to Brémond, bowed to French pressure and left Feisal to travel on to Paris alone. Throughout this trying episode Feisal behaved with a degree of dignity and patience that won him great admiration, but did nothing to change minds in Paris about Syria and Lebanon.

The French hoped that by keeping Feisal away from Paris they could persuade the British to confirm the Sykes-Picot agreement before the American delegation arrived in Paris. The two European powers could then present President Wilson with a fait accompli on the subject of the Middle East: a British Mesopotamia, a French Syria (including Lebanon), and some sort of face-saving arrangement in Palestine that would satisfy Britain, France, and American Zionists, for in Paris and London the Jews were—mistakenly—thought to have great influence over the American delegation. In large part because of Lawrence's skillful propaganda, the British still felt themselves under obligation to Feisal, and deeply uncom-

fortable with the Sykes-Picot agreement. British troops were still occupying Syria, Lebanon, and Palestine, and were stubbornly (and perhaps
unrealistically) prepared to play what would turn out to be a losing hand,
supporting Feisal and his father against the French.

As is so often the case in politics, unforeseeable events conspired to
make Feisal's case for an independent Arab government in Syria even
less promising than it had been. While Feisal was still being kept busy
touring French factories (displaying a dignified, polite, but remote smile
of interest), the French prime minister, Georges Clemenceau, arrived
in London on what was supposed to be a ceremonial visit. At seventy-
eight, the oldest of the Allied leaders, Clemenceau was a man of great

*Lawrence at the Paris Peace Conference, as part of Feisal's delegation. Feisal's
Sudanese slave and bodyguard, towering over everbody else, is on the right.*

intelligence, biting wit, and ferocious energy, nicknamed *le tigre* for his savage and unforgiving political skill, whose uncompromising leadership had saved France from defeat. Stocky, powerful, speaking excellent English (in his youth he had taught French and riding for a time at a girls' school in Connecticut), with piercing eyes and a bristling walrus mustache, his hands always clad in gray cotton gloves to hide his eczema, Clemenceau was an imposing figure, perhaps the most feared politician in France. Only the prolonged bloodletting of Verdun, the disaster of General Nivelle's offensive, and the widespread mutinies in the French army that followed it could have brought Clemenceau back to power in 1917. Now, after victory, he was faced with making a peace that would justify or repay France's sacrifices. Among the Allies, the only leader whom he considered his equal was David Lloyd George, but the two men loathed and distrusted each other, perhaps because they were cut from the same cloth.

As the two leaders stood together in the French embassy in London Clemenceau, who had no gift for polite small talk, and was determined to cement good relations between France and Britain before Wilson arrived, bluntly asked Lloyd George what he wanted. Lloyd George quickly replied that he wanted Mesopotamia, and all of Palestine, "from Beersheba to Dan," as well as Jerusalem. "What else?" Clemenceau asked. "I want Mosul." "You shall have it," Clemenceau replied. This appeared to be a burst of generosity, but it was followed by a request for Britain's agreement, in return, to "a unified French administration in the whole of Syria, including the inland area reserved for an independent Arab administration."

Lloyd George knew his Old Testament—"from Beersheba to Dan" was the territory granted by Abimelech to Abraham, and claimed by David as the southern and northern limits of his kingdom—but "Dan" was to provide numerous difficulties for the lawyers and mapmakers at the Peace Conference, since it had vanished altogether from modern maps of Palestine. (It was just north of the Sea of Galilee, and just southeast of the Litani River and the present border between Israel and Lebanon. From

South Hill, in Delvin, County Westmeath, Ireland, the home
Thomas Chapman abandoned when he left his family for Sarah.

Janet Laurie, at about the
time Ned proposed to her.

Sarah, about 1895, at Langley Lodge, Hampshire,
with four of her five sons. Ned, in a sailor suit, is
seated at the left.

Gertrude Bell, in her desert riding costume.

Cairo, 1917. At left, Lawrence, for once in uniform;
center, Hogarth; right, Alan Dawnay.

Aqaba, as it was when Lawrence captured it.

Photograph by Lawrence of Feisal's camp at dawn.

The vanguard of the Arab army arrives in Yenbo. Feisal is the figure on the black horse with a white blaze, to the right, in the lead, preceded by his slaves on foot. The figure behind him in white, mounted on a camel, is Lawrence.

Photograph by Lawrence of the Arab army on the move. Note the furled banners.

DECEMBER 1917:

Right: Allenby enters Jerusalem on foot.

Below: British and French officers congratulate each other after the entry into Jerusalem. Lawrence, in a borrowed uniform, is the short figure, third from left.

A Turkish train and railway station
after Lawrence wrecked them both.

FRAMES FROM THE FILM FOOTAGE
LOWELL THOMAS AND HARRY CHASE
SHOT IN AQABA, 1918:

Arab cavalry deploying.

Lawrence's armored cars,
attacking the railway line
between Maan and Medina.

The bridge
at Yarmuk.

Emir Abdulla, the future king of Jordan, reviews troops. The figure between the two British officers may be Lawrence; the tall officer on the right is Allenby.

Lawrence, in 1918. The dagger is the one he bought in Mecca, and later sold to put a new roof on his cottage.

T. E. Lawrence and Lowell Thomas pose together in Arab dress for Harry Chase. This photograph was probably taken after the war, in England (note the grass and the shrubbery in the background).

March 20, 1921: the imperial conference at Cairo. Figures immediately below the Sphinx's head are, left to right, Winston Churchill, Gertrude Bell, and Lawrence.

Two of England's most famous and celebrated figures:
Nancy Astor and Bernard Shaw, surrounded by admirers.

Bernard and Charlotte Shaw—a rare glimpse
of them together, and apparently at leisure.

Nancy Astor, in a characteristically energetic and combative pose.

Lawrence, barefoot, standing on a float of a seaplane.

Clare Sydney Smith

Lawrence in RAF uniform, at Cattewater, about the time he became a friend of both Smiths.

Lawrence relaxes with Clare (seated, far right), with two of her friends, and dogs.

Clare and Lawrence, then Aircraftman Shaw, in the *Biscuit*. Clare is at the wheel.

Lawrence, at the wheel, puts the *Biscuit* through
its paces at high speed, towing a water-skier.

WHAT 50 YEARS ON STAGE HAS TAUGHT ME—MARIE TEMPEST

DAILY SKETCH

THINGS I HATE BY **BERNARD SHAW**

No. 8,131 [Registered as a newspaper.]   MONDAY, MAY 20, 1935   ONE PENNY

TOO BIG FOR WEALTH AND GLORY

Lawrence the Soldier Dies to Live for Ever

Having lingered for six days, Lawrence of Arabia (Mr. T. E. Shaw) died in hospital at Bovington Camp, Dorset, yesterday from injuries received when he crashed with his powerful motor-cycle at Moreton. He was 46. In the year 1914 Lawrence was excavating Hittite ruins near Carchemish on the Euphrates. Two years later he organised and virtually commanded the Arab Army that gave such powerful help to the British campaign in Palestine. In this rôle he became famous the world over as Lawrence of Arabia (right) Scorning notoriety and wealth, he declined an offer of £10,000 to appear in a film.

Front page of the *Daily Sketch*, announcing Lawrence's death.

Eric Kennington's bust of Lawrence for the memorial in the crypt of St. Paul's Cathedral, London.

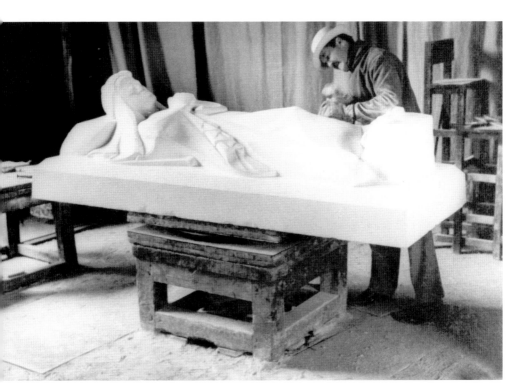

Eric Kennington works on his effigy of Lawrence.

Eric Kennington's effigy of Lawrence, in St. Martin's Church, Warcham, Dorset.

the point of view of Lloyd George, the important thing was that this area included Jerusalem.)

Lloyd George did not immediately inform the cabinet of his spur-of-the-moment gentleman's agreement with Clemenceau, no doubt because he knew that some cabinet members would object. Nor was Clemenceau anxious to let his foreign minister, Pichon, know that he had just given away the oil of Mosul and the city of Jerusalem to the man who was known in Britain, not for nothing, as the "Welsh wizard." Clemenceau soon came under attack from French imperialists and rightists for having betrayed France; and Lloyd George had inadvertently agreed to keep in place just those clauses of the Sykes-Picot agreement that most of his cabinet thought should be dropped or modified.

The day after this extraordinary example of impulsive personal diplomacy, Lawrence arrived back in Britain from France and went straight to see Lord Robert Cecil, to tell him about Feisal's unfortunate reception in France. Cecil, as always sympathetic to Lawrence, immediately sent a note to Lloyd George asking him to meet with "Colonel Lawrence (the Arabian)" [sic], who wished to warn him of Clemenceau's plans to undercut British and Arab aspirations in the Middle East. Because Lloyd George, unbeknownst to Cecil, had already agreed to those plans, the prime minister carefully avoided meeting with Lawrence, who was instead fobbed off with an invitation to attend his third session of the Eastern Committee, three days later. The opinion of the members was still strongly against the Sykes-Picot agreement—even Lawrence's old opponent Lord Curzon spoke scathingly about the arrangements for Syria, describing them as "fantastic" and predicting (correctly) that they would be a source of "incessant friction between the French and ourselves, and the Arabs as third parties."

Clearly, Curzon, like Cecil, had not yet been told of the prime minister's bargain with Clemenceau; but A. J. Balfour apparently *had*, for to everyone's surprise, since he seldom appeared at the committee, he spoke at length, emphasizing that Britain could not possibly repudiate the Sykes-Picot agreement, and that France's claim to Syria and Lebanon must be respected to the letter. Balfour's manner was famously languid and aloof, and even his friends complained that while he seemed urbane, he was ice-cold, but on this occasion he was unusually frank. If the Americans "chose to step in and cut the knot," that was their business, "but we must not put the knife into their hand." Balfour was foreign secretary, and while it could not be said that he enjoyed Lloyd George's confidence, he was the senior Conservative member of the coalition government, and Lloyd George would almost certainly have revealed to Balfour what he still regarded as a coup, a triumph that gave the British everything they wanted in exchange for Syria and Lebanon, where they had nothing to gain. Those whose political instincts were sharp (and Lawrence was certainly among them) must have guessed that the government had in effect abandoned Feisal to make the best deal it could with the French.

On the other hand, the British, being British, were anxious to put a good face on things, and with that in mind the Foreign Office hastened to add Lawrence's name to the members of the British delegation to the Peace Conference as an "advisor on special subjects," in addition to being "a member of Feisal's staff." Thus Lawrence was placed in much the same ambiguous position at the Peace Conference as he had been in Arabia in 1917. Once again he was called on to manage Feisal on behalf of the British government, while at the same time attempting to secure for Feisal what he already knew Feisal wouldn't get.

Lawrence himself would describe the postwar experience hauntingly in *Seven Pillars of Wisdom*, speaking for many of his generation who shared his bitterness: "We lived many lives in those whirling campaigns, never sparing ourselves: yet when we achieved and the new world dawned, the old men came out again and took our victory to re-make in the likeness of the former world they knew. Youth could win, but had not learned to keep: and was pitiably weak against age. We stammered that we had worked for a new heaven and a new earth, and they thanked us kindly and made their peace."

Feisal arrived in Britain on December 10. It is not certain whether

Lawrence went to Paris to meet him, in uniform, or met him on the dock at Boulogne in his white robes, looking—according to Colonel Brémond—"like a choir boy" as he came down the gangplank of a British destroyer under gray skies. Since Brémond's job, as long as Feisal was on French soil, was to stick as close to him as a watchdog on behalf of the French, it seems likely Brémond was correct.

Lawrence stayed with Feisal and his entourage at the Carlton Hotel in London, acting as Feisal's interpreter, and dressed in a British officer's khaki uniform, with an Arab headdress. Two days after Feisal arrived, he and Lawrence called on the foreign secretary, A. J. Balfour, to whom Feisal expressed his determination to fight the French if they tried to take control of Syria—a threat that failed to shake Balfour's majestic calm. Later in the day Feisal had a cordial meeting at the Carlton Hotel with Chaim Weizmann, the Zionist leader who had journeyed to Aqaba to meet with Feisal in June 1918. This time Lawrence was the interpreter, and he made sure to impress on Feisal the importance of good relationships with the Zionists, especially because of American public opinion. Feisal was very conscious of this. One of the formal dinner parties in his honor was given by Lord Rothschild; and the *Jewish Chronicle* commented favorably on his meeting with Weizmann. During that meeting, Feisal had stressed his belief that there was plenty of land for Jewish settlement in Palestine, and Weizmann had said that the Jews would finance and carry out large-scale public works and agricultural improvement to the benefit of both peoples, and that as many as 4 million or 5 million Jews could settle there without encroaching on Arab land.

Lawrence and Feisal would be together in Britain for almost three weeks, during which time the government did its best to keep Feisal busy. The activities included a journey to Scotland to attend a number of "civic functions," among them a formal visit on board the British battleship HMS *Orion*, where Feisal and Lawrence were photographed seated glumly on the deck, Feisal looking bored and dejected, and Lawrence, a tiny figure in British uniform beside him, appearing cold, and also furi-

ous at what must have seemed to him an irrelevant waste of time. The two of them are flanked and dwarfed by the ship's captain and a rear-admiral smiling for the camera, the admiral apparently the only happy person in the group. Efforts to keep Feisal amused seem to have been no more successful in Britain than they had been in France, especially since it cannot have escaped his attention that he was being excluded from substantive discussions. The visit to Scotland was no doubt primarily intended to keep him out of London and away from the attention of journalists; this perhaps explains why he and Lawrence look more like the victims of a hijacking than honored guests.

Lawrence tried to present Feisal's case by writing a long piece on Arab affairs for the *Times*, displaying, not for the first or last time, both his skill at dealing with newspaper editors and his skill at writing polemics. He gave a condensed but spirited account of the Arabs' sacrifices and risks during the war; drew attention to the fact that Feisal, like himself, had had a price on his head; and listed the promises made to them by the British—but despite British sympathy for the Arabs, the article does not seem to have been successful. Feisal was later invited to an investiture at Buckingham Palace at which the king decorated him with the chain, ribbon, and star of a Knight Grand Cross of the Royal Victorian Order, and at which Lawrence wore his white robes and headdress with a gold *agal*. Reading between the lines suggests that Lawrence's presence at the palace in white robes caused a certain amount of fuss with the king's military secretary beforehand; but the king, who by now must have been resigned to Lawrence's ways, does not seem to have raised any objection himself, whatever he may have thought of a British officer appearing at court in Arab dress.*

On January 3 there was another meeting with Weizmann, and during its course, Feisal, Weizmann, and Lawrence drew up one of the most remarkable and controversial documents in the modern history of the Middle East. In some ways, it was the most important result of Feisal's visit to Britain. Just as the Sykes-Picot agreement represents the great betrayal of the Arab Revolt, the agreement negotiated between Feisal and Weizmann on January 3, 1919, with Lawrence's help, was the first attempt to define the relationship between Arabs and Jews in Palestine. It embodied many of Lawrence's ideas on the subject, and it remains even today, for most Arabs, a blueprint of what they hoped would take place. It is perhaps one of the most interesting "might have beens" in modern Middle Eastern history.

It is not a lengthy document, and some of its nine articles are still being fought over today, both at the conference table and on the ground. Article I establishes that Palestine will be separated from the "Arab State," by which Feisal, Weizmann, and Lawrence meant what is now Syria and Lebanon, and controlled with "the most cordial goodwill and understanding" by duly accredited agents of the Arab and Jewish

---

* This is remarkable, since King George V, like his father, was a notorious stickler for correct dress, both military and civilian, and had an eagle eye for the slightest impropriety or flaw, as well as a very short fuse in this regard.

territories—in other words, it already presupposes a partition of Palestine into two separate territories. Article III envisages drawing up a constitution. Article IV permits Jewish immigration "on a large scale, and as quickly as possible, to settle Jewish immigrants upon the land through closer settlement and intensive cultivation of the soil," while preserving the existing rights of Arab peasants and tenant farmers, and "assisting them in their economic development." Article V provides for absolute freedom of religion, and prohibits any "religious test" for "the exercise of civil or political rights." Article VI guarantees that Muslim holy places will remain "under Mohammedan control." Article VII provides that "the Zionist Organization will use its best efforts" to provide the means for developing the natural resources and economic possibilities of Palestine. Article VIII—perhaps the key to the entire agreement—binds the two parties to act in "complete accord and harmony" at the coming peace conference: in short, to present a united front toward the British and the French.

The agreement can be summed up as proposing joint Jewish-Arab control over Palestine, with Britain playing a role as the guarantor and final arbiter of any disputes between the two parties, and with no limit on Jewish immigration. Feisal had already conceded that Palestine could contain 4 million to 5 million Jewish immigrants without harm to the rights of the Arab population. Since the population of Israel today is approximately 7.4 million, of which just over 1 million are Muslim, it is not so very far from what Feisal had in mind in 1919.

It is important to note that the agreement proposes neither an Arab nor a Jewish state, but rather a state under joint Arab-Jewish control, with absolute religious freedom for all, and that no limit is set on Jewish immigration. This would have produced an incalculably different history for both Palestinians and Zionists, as opposed to the ultimately doomed attempt of the British to rule Palestine under a "mandate," from 1920 to 1948, and to set tight limits on Jewish immigration.

Feisal was already aware that the chances of putting this agreement into practice were rapidly diminishing, since when he signed it he added, in graceful Arabic script above his signature, a handwritten "reservation," which Lawrence translated and wrote out in English, for attachment to the agreement: "If the Arabs are established as I have asked in my manifesto of Jan. 4th* addressed to the British Secretary of State for Foreign Affairs, I will carry out what is written in this agreement. If changes are made, I can not be answerable for failing to carry out this agreement. Feisal ibn Hussein."

In short, the title deed to a joint Arab-Jewish Palestine was conditional on the Arabs' getting an independent Arab state in Syria with Damascus as its capital, and including Lebanon and its ports, without which any such state would have been strangled at birth. Indeed Feisal had already remarked that Syria without Lebanon would be "of no use to him." It was already clear to both Feisal and Lawrence that this was not likely to happen; so, as idealistic as the agreement with Weizmann may seem, it can also be read as a bold attempt to win Jewish support (and particularly *American* Jewish support) for Feisal's claim to Syria, as well as Jewish financing for the Arab state. Lawrence was, at the time, steeped in realpolitik. He would later write to his comrade in arms Alan Dawnay that Feisal didn't need financing from France: " 'He'll say that he doesn't want their money, because by then the Zionists will have a centre in Jerusalem, and for their concessions they will finance him (this is all in writing, and fixed, but don't put it in the press for God's sake).' . . . Lawrence went on to say that the Zionists are not a Government, and not British, and their action does not infringe the Sykes-Picot Agreement. . . . 'They will finance the whole East, I hope, Syria and Mesopotamia alike. High Jews are unwilling to put much cash into Palestine only, since that country offers nothing but a sentimental return. They want 6%.' "

Thus the price for unlimited Jewish immigration to Palestine was to be Jewish financial assistance, and Jewish support for Feisal's claim to Syria. Like Balfour, Lloyd George, and many other people in Britain, Lawrence hugely overestimated the influence and wealth of the Jews, in

---

*This is certainly a slip of Lawrence's fountain pen, since Feisal's memorandum to Balfour was written on January 1.

America and elsewhere. Within less than fourteen years, most of Europe and America would turn a blind eye to the fate of the Jews. Even Weizmann, of all people, understood the Jews' lack of power. The importance of Zionism was not symbolic; the pressure that made Jews in Poland, Russia, and eastern Europe consider seriously the prospect of resettling in a strange, distant, and hostile land and climate was a product of poverty, intense discrimination, and fear. Rich philanthropists like Lord Rothschild might make the Zionist settlements in Palestine possible, but those who undertook the long journey there were for the most part poor and desperate.

In the end, neither the Arabs nor the Zionists would have much effect on the Paris Peace Conference. In the long memorandum to Balfour, which Lawrence had drafted, Feisal ended by begging "the Great Powers . . . to lay aside the thought of individual profits, and their old jealousies" and to think of the Arabs "as one potential people, jealous of their language and liberty, [who] ask that no step be taken inconsistent with the prospect of an eventual union of these areas under one sovereign government." The "Great Powers," of course, did nothing of the sort, and instead shared the Arab lands between themselves, with frontiers rough-hewn by European bureaucrats and statesmen. The effect was, more or less, to guarantee that there would never be "one sovereign power" in the Middle East.

The Paris Peace Conference of 1919 was the largest, most ambitious, and most comprehensive attempt to remake the world in the history of mankind. It began on January 18, 1919, and continued for more than a year, during which Paris was filled with the huge staffs of more than thirty national delegations, as well as thousands of people from all over the world lobbying for every imaginable cause. The Peace Conference took on itself such matters as the international regulation of air travel (then still in its infancy) and the attempt to define fishing rights in the open seas, still a subject of fierce controversy between nations today; but its two major challenges were to remake Europe in the aftermath of Germany's defeat and the collapse of the Austro-Hungarian Empire, and to deal with the former possessions of the Ottoman Empire in the Middle East.

The Peace Conference was under siege, from the very beginning, by an incredible array of issues, some of them defying any rational solution or compromise, and by demands for justice from every possible national, racial, or linguistic group. None presented themselves with more dignity or with a better-prepared case than the Arabs, led by Feisal in his robes as an emir and a sharif, and Lawrence omnipresent beside him, either in British uniform with an Arab headdress or, on more formal occasions, in white robes, with his curved gold dagger. From the outset, the French Foreign Office made difficulties. Feisal was left off the list of official delegates until the British protested on his behalf, and even then he was allowed to represent only the Hejaz. In addition, his mail was opened and his cables were intercepted and deciphered by the British, and every possible obstacle was placed in his path by the French.

The British delegates were housed in three hotels: the Majestic and the Astoria, with the overflow relegated to the Hotel Continental, a thirty-minute walk away from the other two. Lawrence was allocated a small room there, which, in the tradition of French hotels of the day that were not in the *grand luxe* class, had no bath. Having to use the one bathroom on his floor of the hotel was always a trial to Lawrence, whose only self-indulgence was taking long, very hot baths. By inference, his room had no telephone, either—Lieutenant-Colonel Richard Meinertzhagen, CBE, DSO, Lawrence's rival as a daring intelligence officer, had the room below Lawrence's at the Continental (with a bath), and reported that when Lawrence wished to communicate with him at night, he would thump on the floor to alert Meinertzhagen, then lower a message or a sheaf of manuscript on a string to Meinertzhagen's window. When Meinertzhagen wished to communicate with Lawrence at night, he would thump on the ceiling—not such a problem for Meinertzhagen, since he was very tall. According to Meinertzhagen, Lawrence continued to wear the badges of a full colonel on his uniform, even though that rank had been given to him only for the duration of his trip home in 1918. When

Lawrence asked if he could take a bath in Meinertzhagen's room late one night, there were "red weals on his ribs, standing out like tattoo marks," presumably where the Turkish bey at Deraa had plunged and twisted a bayonet between Lawrence's ribs.

Meinertzhagen and Lawrence had what might best be described as a wary relationship, and the veracity of Meinertzhagen's diaries, which he revised, edited, and retyped later in life, is not necessarily to be relied on, though some of his account rings true. He referred to Lawrence affectionately as "little Lawrence," and Lawrence described him as "a silent, masterful man, who took as blithe a pleasure in deceiving his enemy (or his friend) by some unscrupulous jest," which is what a lot of people said or thought about Lawrence. Meinertzhagen claimed to be the inventor of the famous "haversack ruse": he had ridden close to the Turkish lines in 1917, pretended to be wounded, and galloped away, dropping his haversack, which contained £20, faked love letters, and a falsified map and war diaries, all intended to persuade the Turks that Allenby's attack would be aimed at Gaza. Meinertzhagen's role at the Peace Conference was, in some ways, analogous to Lawrence's—though not Jewish, he was the expert on, the true believer in, and the spokesman for Zionist aspirations, as Lawrence was for the Arabs (a street in Jerusalem is now named after Meinertzhagen). He was wealthy and well connected; was a cousin of Beatrice Webb (a cofounder of the London School of Economics); had attended Harrow with Winston Churchill; and had once shot and killed the leader of a Kenyan tribal uprising while shaking his hand at a meeting to negotiate a truce.

Meinertzhagen, though his own nature was overbearing—his sheer size and his reputation for killing prisoners by smashing their heads in with his knobkerrie alarmed most people—seems to have understood and liked Lawrence very much. His analysis of Lawrence's character is at once sympathetic and penetrating: "his mind," he wrote, "was pure as gold. Indelicacy, indecency, any form of coarseness or vulgarity repelled him physically. . . . He had perfect manners if consideration for others counts and he expected good manners from others. . . . The war shattered his sensitive nature. He was shaken off his balance by the stresses, hardships and responsibilities of his campaign. These all went to accentuate and develop any little eccentricities of his youth."

He and Lawrence shared a taste for schoolboy pranks. Meinertzhagen claims that they hid themselves at the top of the stairs of the Astoria Hotel, unfurled rolls of toilet paper, and dropped them down in long strips on the heads of Lloyd George, Balfour, and Lord Hardinge, who were standing in the lobby, prompting Hardinge to remark: "There is nothing funny about toilet paper." Lawrence may have revealed to Meinertzhagen the fact that he was illegitimate, and the intimate details of his rape at the hands of the bey and the bey's men in Deraa. Meinertzhagen would probably have been a good choice of confidant, since he was unshockable: on the subject of illegitimacy he merely told Lawrence he was "in good company for Jesus was born out of wedlock." In late life Meinertzhagen claimed that Lawrence began to write the story of his involvement with the Arabs while he was in Paris.

Lawrence's pace of writing was remarkable—he wrote 160,000 words in less than six months, while putting in long days at the Peace Conference, or in meetings with Feisal and the British delegation, as well as enjoying a full social schedule. In the words of Gertrude Bell—who also became part of the British delegation, to lobby for Britain's control over what was to become Iraq—Lawrence was "the most picturesque" figure at the conference; also, he realized early on the need to win over journalists and members of the American delegation to Feisal's cause, and dined with them constantly.

Almost everybody who was at the Peace Conference seems to have noticed Lawrence. A typical example is Professor James Thomson Shotwell of Columbia University, a member of the American delegation, who wrote of Lawrence, after their first meeting: "He has been described as the most interesting Briton alive, a student of Mediaeval history at Magdalen, where he used to sleep by day and work by night and take his recreation in the deer park at four in the morning—a Shelley-like person, and yet too virile to be a poet. He is a rather short, strongly built man of not over twenty-eight years, with sandy complexion, a typical English face, bronzed by the desert, remarkable blue eyes and a smile that responded swiftly to that on the face of his friend [Feisal]. The two men were obviously very fond of each other. I have seldom seen such mutual affection between grown men as in this instance. Lawrence would catch the full drift of Feisal's humor and pass the joke along to us while Feisal was still exploding with his idea; but at the same time it was funny to see how Feisal spoke with the oratorical feeling of the South and Lawrence translated in the lowest and quietest of English voices, in very simple and direct phrases, with only here and there a touch of Oriental poetry breaking through."

Lawrence made many friends in Paris, among them Lionel Curtis, some of whose ideas about turning the British Commonwealth into a multinational, multiracial federation resembled those of Lawrence; and Arnold Toynbee, the historian. Even so, it is impossible to think of the time that Lawrence spent in Paris, however productive, as happy; indeed, if Meinertzhagen is to be believed, Lawrence was frequently (and "intensely") depressed. The ambiguity of his own role continued to disturb him—he was at the same time the most important (and most visible) part of Feisal's small "team," and a member of the British delegation, where Feisal was already seen as a lost cause.

Lawrence wrote home briefly on January 30, while waiting for his breakfast, to say that he was busy, and had dined only once at his own hotel since arriving in Paris (with his old friend and comrade in arms Colonel Stewart Newcombe). Certainly he saw everybody who mattered, starting with President Woodrow Wilson himself, into whose head Lawrence seems to have put the idea of a committee of inquiry into the wishes of the Syrians.* Lawrence assiduously cultivated American journalists, and gave them long interviews. With his startling good looks, his

---

* Lawrence was not the only one to float this idea with Wilson; another was Dr. Howard S. Bliss, president of the Syrian Protestant College (later the American University of Beirut). But it was shrewd of Lawrence to suggest a plan that would appeal to the democratic ideals of Wilson and would be sure to infuriate the French and alarm the British. If the Syrians, after all, why not next the Egyptians, or the inhabitants of Mesopotamia, or—worse yet, from the British point of view—the Indians?

youth, his reputation as a war hero, and his exotic headdress, he got enough attention and space in American newspapers to worry both the French and the more cautious of his colleagues in the British delegation. He fancied that he had persuaded Wilson, and the American public, to take responsibility for a free, democratic Arab state in Syria, instead of a French colony, but in this he was overoptimistic. Wilson, despite his belief in democracy and the self-determination of peoples, was wary of making any promises about America's becoming the godfather of an independent Arab state.

On February 6, Lawrence appeared in what was widely acknowledged as one of the most dramatic scenes of the Paris Peace Conference. Feisal's and Lawrence's appearance before the Council of Ten (the leaders of the Allied governments) to argue the case for an independent state in Syria had been widely anticipated, and was the subject of considerable back-stage maneuvering by the French. Unwisely, Lawrence had been telling people the story of how Feisal had addressed an audience in Scotland in Arabic by reciting the Koran to them, and then whispered to Lawrence to make up whatever he pleased as the English translation. This may have been true, since Feisal had been bored and irritated at being sent on a Scottish tour by the British government. When word of it had reached the French, they hoped to catch him out playing a similar trick in Paris. Therefore they provided themselves with a Moroccan civil servant to see if Lawrence's translation corresponded with what Feisal said. Fortu-nately, Lawrence had anticipated that the French would do something of the sort. He wrote out Feisal's speech in Arabic for him, then translated it into English for himself. Opinions differ as to what Lawrence wore for the occasion. Lloyd George wrote that he was dressed "in flowing robes of dazzling white," and Arnold Toynbee, the future author of the twelve-volume *A Study of History*, and a more reliable witness than the prime minister, recorded that Lawrence was "in Arab dress." Lawrence himself insisted that he was in British uniform with an Arab headdress. Feisal, at any rate, wore the white and gold embroidered robes of a sharif of Mecca, with a curved gold dagger at his waist and a gold-thread *agal* on his head-dress, impressing everybody, even the French, with his gravity, his melodic voice, and his dignified bearing. When he had finished his speech, Lawrence read it aloud in English, but several of the ten heads of government were still unable to understand what had been said. "President Wilson then made a suggestion. 'Colonel Lawrence,' he said, 'could you put the Amir Feisal's statement into French now for us?' " Lawrence then started again and read the whole speech aloud in flawless French. "When he came to the end of this unprepared piece of translation, the Ten clapped. Lawrence's spell had made the Ten forget, for a moment, who they were and what they were supposed to be doing. They had started the session as conscious arbiters of the destinies of mankind; they were ending it as the captive audience of a minor supplicant's interpreter."

The "minor supplicant's interpreter" had effectively upstaged "the minor supplicant" in the eyes of most of the delegates, but Feisal did not seem to mind. Photographs taken at the Peace Conference show him looking sad, like a man who already suspects that he is presenting a lost cause, whereas Lawrence, always standing tactfully a pace behind him, has his usual faint, cynical smile. Behind both of them, an unusual figure even at the Peace Conference, stands Feisal's tall, broad-shouldered black Sudanese slave and bodyguard in full Arab robes and cloak.

Despite Lawrence's "amazing" feat, Feisal's statement fell on deaf ears. The Italians, the Serbs, the Belgians, and the rest of the smaller Allied countries had no great interest in Syria—it was effectively a contest between Britain and France, with the United States as a neutral referee. Any hope of a united autonomous Arab state from the Mediterranean to the Persian Gulf was dead, since the British had occupied Mesopotamia and clearly intended to stay there; and to obtain increased British support Feisal voluntarily conceded Palestine, which the British were also occupying. He—or Lawrence, as his speechwriter—included numerous references to self-determination, in an effort to please Wilson. During the prolonged questions that followed, Feisal more than held his own against Clemenceau, pointing out, with superb tact, both how grateful he was for French military support and how minimal it had been; and when Clemenceau noted that French interest in Syria went back to the Crusades, he gently asked the French prime minister: who had won the Crusades?

A spokesmen in favor of French rule in Syria went on at such length that at one point Clemenceau angrily asked his foreign minister, Pichon, "What did you get that fellow here for anyway?" Wilson signified his own impatience with the proceedings by getting up and walking around the room. "Poor Lawrence wandered among Versailles' well-cut hedges, casting hateful glances at Arthur Balfour's aristocratic features and baggy clothes," commented an exiled czarist nobleman. Harold Nicolson, a member of the British delegation, remarked on "the lines of resentment hardening around his boyish lips . . . an undergraduate with a chin."

A hint that Lawrence's patience and good nature were fraying can be found in the interview he gave to Lincoln Steffens, the famous American muckraking journalist and progressive. By the time he saw Steffens, Lawrence may have had enough of American journalists, although Steffens was the kind of man Lawrence normally admired. Still, Lawrence was not without a certain streak of skepticism and snobbery on the subject of Americans, as well as a high degree of impatience with the professed moral superiority of Woodrow Wilson, especially in view of the Americans' reluctance to take on any commitments in the Middle East. Steffens, who called the interview "the queerest I have ever had in all my interviewing life," met with Lawrence in the latter's hotel room, and found the young colonel at his most difficult, argumentative, and ironic—very much a regression to the image of the languid poseur he had sometimes cultivated as an Oxford undergraduate. It didn't help, perhaps, that Steffens wanted to talk about the Armenians, whereas Lawrence wanted to present Feisal's case for Syria. Lawrence was far from disliking Armenians—the wealthy Altounyan family in Aleppo had been friends of his during his days at Carchemish—but he probably regarded the Armenians as a lost cause, since the Turks had murdered 1.5 million of them in 1915 without provoking the United States into breaking off diplomatic relations with the Ottoman Empire.* In any case, Steffens's somewhat holier-than-thou

---

* The United States' ambassador in Constantinople was Henry J. Morgenthau, Franklin Delano Roosevelt's neighbor in Hyde Park, New York, and eventually his secretary of the treasury. Morgenthau reported the massacres in full detail to the State Department, as well as the matter-of-fact admission of the Turkish leaders that the liquidation of the Armenians was taking place.

attitude brought out the worst in Lawrence, who suggested, deadpan, that the Armenians deserved to be killed off, and that the United States, with its particular combination of idealism and commerce and its experience at destroying the American Indians, was the best power to take on the task of completing what the Turks had begun. Steffens does not seem to have fully understood that Lawrence was pulling his leg, but what emerges from the interview more strongly than anything else is Lawrence's irritation with America's naive good intentions, particularly when they were coupled with its total unwillingness to take on the hard part of rebuilding a new world. Lawrence also played a curious cat-and-mouse game: Steffens was forced to put Lawrence's ideas into words, so that Lawrence could later deny having said them.

The United States was offered the mandate for Armenia at the Peace Conference and needless to say turned it down, condemning thousands more Armenians to death. Wilson also turned down all suggestions for an American mandate over Palestine, though Felix Frankfurter, then a professor at Harvard Law School, was rushed in to mediate a disagreement between Feisal and Weizmann over the number of Jews who could be admitted into Palestine every year. Lawrence not only was present but drafted Feisal's letter, which solved the dispute. Throughout March and much of April Feisal and Lawrence met with the French, the British, and the Americans, attempting to create a compromise for Syria that would be acceptable to the Arabs and the French. In the end the best they could do was to accept President Wilson's suggestion of "an inter-Allied commission of inquiry," if only as a delaying tactic. Lawrence wrote Feisal's letter to Clemenceau accepting the commission, and it conveys unmistakably Lawrence's gift for deadpan irony, as well as his bitterness, which Clemenceau can hardly have failed to notice.

The Spanish flu pandemic, which would kill between 100 million and 150 million people worldwide, raged from 1918 to 1920, and reached its peak in 1919. It was as if by some malignant stroke of irony the war had ended with a final, and even greater, human disaster. It killed Lawrence's ebullient friend Sir Mark Sykes in Paris in February (prompting Lloyd

George to remark rather ungraciously, "He was responsible for the agreement which is causing us all the trouble with the French. . . . Picot . . . got the better of him"), and on April 7 it killed Lawrence's father. A telegram from Oxford warned him that Thomas Lawrence was suffering from influenza and pneumonia, and Lawrence set off immediately for England to see him, but arrived too late. He returned to Paris, and did not tell anyone, not even Feisal, that his father had died, until a week later, when he requested permission to go home and see his mother. Feisal admired Lawrence's "control of personal feelings," and that assessment is fair enough, but Lawrence had long since made control of his personal feelings something of a fetish. He would certainly have deeply mourned the unexpected death of his father, and perhaps even more, dreaded being exposed once again to the emotional demands of his mother. Thomas Lawrence had tried, whenever he could, in his patient, gentle way, to diminish, control, or redirect those demands, but now he was no longer there to protect Ned from the full force of his mother's attempts to intrude into his life. He must have felt overwhelmed by his father's death, by his failure to secure Syria for the Arabs, and by the demands of his book, which forced him to relive the experiences of two years of war. He persuaded Feisal to return to Syria, rather than stay on in Paris watching his position erode, a decision Gertrude Bell endorsed. Lawrence himself decided to return to Egypt to retrieve the notes he had left behind in the Arab Bureau's files, and now needed.

Taking advantage of the fact that the Royal Air Force (upgraded from the Royal Flying Corps into a new and independent service in 1918) was about to send fifty big Handley-Page bombers to Egypt—the first sign that Britain was going to back up its occupation of Mesopotamia, Palestine, and what is now Jordan—Lawrence sought permission to fly out with one of the first squadrons. He left Paris on May 18 for what was intended to be a week's leave. Airplanes and the air force had always interested him, and he must have relished the opportunity of a long flight in the RAF's biggest bomber. He must also have welcomed the chance of getting away from Paris, where the French press had been running a series of hostile articles about him, accusing him of turning Feisal's head with notions of a united, independent Arab state; of being willing to do "a disservice" to his own country for his "sacred mission"; and of becoming "a second Gordon"*—all this carefully orchestrated by the French government.

On March 9, 1919, almost a year after his visit to Aqaba, Lowell Thomas opened his lecture—illustrated with motion pictures and tinted slides— in the Century Theater in New York. He played to packed houses. The lecture was originally titled *With Allenby in Palestine, Including the Capture of Jerusalem and the Liberation of Holy Arabia*, but it would shortly be changed to *With Allenby in Palestine and Lawrence in Arabia*, once Thomas realized that what the audience wanted most was Lawrence. The demand for tickets was so great that the lectures had to be moved to Madison Square Garden. Thomas promoted them with artful newspaper articles, and an advertising campaign that included giant photographs of Lawrence, in his robes and headdress, in the windows of the major department stores on Fifth Avenue, as well as a vivid full-color poster showing Lawrence charging on horseback, robes flowing, surrounded by "his" Arabs, curved sabers drawn and gleaming, against a background of the desert.

Lowell Thomas was a born publicist, huckster, and promoter, as well as one of the most successful lecturers in American history, with a phenomenal gift of gab and a naturally intimate relationship with his audience, however large, which equaled that of Mark Twain at the height of his career. Funny, folksy, and inspirational by turns, Thomas could keep people on the edge of their seats with suspense, bring tears to their eyes with sentiment, and make them hold their breath with drama. On the subject of Lawrence he not only did himself proud but had Harry Chase's photographs and films to back him up. It is hard for us to understand the impact of his show (which changed, and was more ambitiously staged,

---

*For reasons best known to themselves the French regarded the late Major-General Charles Gordon, CB, "Gordon Pasha," who was killed by the Dervishes at Khartoum in 1885, as the ultimate anti-French British imperialist hero-adventurer.

with every performance), but at its center was something people had never seen before: a real-life drama captured on film, in which the central figure was not an actor, but a real hero: T. E. Lawrence. Thomas enthusiastically proclaimed him "Lawrence of Arabia . . . a young man whose name will go down in history beside those of Sir Francis Drake, Sir Walter Raleigh, Lord Clive, Charles Gordon, and all the other famous heroes of Great Britain's glorious past." Even today, reading the typescript of Thomas's lecture, which accompanied the film and slides, is an extraordinary and thrilling experience, so sweeping were his eloquence and his enthusiasm for his subject.

While Lawrence watched Feisal's hopes begin to fade at the Paris Peace Conference, across the Atlantic he was about to become famous on a scale beyond anything he, or anyone else, could have imagined. *With Allenby in Palestine and Lawrence in Arabia* would be seen by more than 2 million people in the United States, and by even more in the United Kingdom and the British Commonwealth, when Thomas eventually took his lecture and "picture show" on a world tour.* The London theatrical impresario Percy Burton saw the show in New York and was so overcome that he immediately offered to bring it to London; and after spirited bargaining Thomas, who insisted on opening it at the Royal Opera House in Covent Garden, where no film had ever been played before, agreed to postpone his tour of American cities in favor of Great Britain. By then, it was already clear that the show was going to be a phenomenal success. In the end it would make Lowell Thomas a millionaire (he made a profit of $1.5 million on the show, the equivalent of at least $16 million in today's money), and set him on the first steps of the path that took the former cub reporter from Cripple Creek, Colorado, to a motion picture, radio, and television career that would last for more than sixty years. It also transformed T. E. Lawrence permanently into "Lawrence of Arabia."

---

* Demand was so great that Lowell Thomas was forced to hire an "understudy" to give some of the lectures in his place. He chose for the job a gifted young speaker named Dale Carnegie, who would himself go on to world fame and fortune as the author of *How to Win Friends and Influence People*, and founder of the Dale Carnegie Institute.

Lowell Thomas's show is hard to recapture accurately, since it was continually being changed. He modified it for different audiences; in Great Britain he frequently referred to Lawrence as "the prince of Mecca" (a nonexistent title conferred on him by Thomas) and "the uncrowned king of Arabia"; in the United States he described Lawrence more democratically as "the George Washington of Arabia"; in Australia he took special care to praise the role of the Australian Light Horse in the capture of Damascus. Thomas himself was not just a bold and talented producer but also a gifted narrator, with a sonorous delivery, relieved by the occasional joke, that would make him a star—indeed an institution—for the rest of his life. The show included not only the film that Chase had shot of Lawrence and the Arab army at Aqaba, as well as hand-tinted slides of Lawrence, but eventually exotically dressed young women dancing in front of a backdrop of color slides of the Pyramids to "eastern" music, braziers in which incense burned, and, for the London performance, the sixty-piece band of the Welsh Guards, as well as the "Moonlight on the Nile" scenery borrowed from Sir Thomas Beecham's production of Handel's opera *Joseph and His Brethren*.

Thomas, who had grown up in the time of Buffalo Bill's Wild West show, had a natural tendency to turn Lawrence into a figure like Billy the Kid or Wild Bill Hickok, but wearing an Arab headdress instead of a Stetson and mounted on a camel instead of a horse. Thomas was a pitchman— subtlety (like irony) was unknown to him—but still, the core of it all was the documentary film footage he and Chase shot of the Arab army advancing across the desert, its men mounted on camels and its banners flying. Audiences were fascinated by the glimpses Thomas offered of the apparently shy, slight, modest hero in a white robe—"He had a genius for backing into the limelight," Thomas would later say of Lawrence, as their relationship cooled, and Lawrence began to feel that he was being exploited and vulgarized, and to resent the fact that he could not appear on the street without being recognized and mobbed.

Lawrence's charisma (a concept cheapened by overuse today, but apparently only too appropriate for Lawrence) was never in doubt. In

London, *With Allenby in Palestine and Lawrence in Arabia* would open, just as Percy Burton had promised Thomas, at the august Royal Opera House, in August 1919. It was later moved, at the suggestion of the king, to the Royal Albert Hall, which could accommodate a much larger audience, and then to the Queen's Hall—its run in the United Kingdon alone was extended to six months, instead of the two weeks that Percy Burton had planned. Thomas also toured it in the provinces, including such cities as Birmingham, Manchester, Glasgow, and Edinburgh; and everywhere it played to packed houses. Audiences listened breathlessly as Thomas told them, for example, that he had watched while Lawrence blew up a Turkish train, and that "a number of Turkish soldiers who were about attempted to capture Lawrence, but he sat still until they were a few yards from him, then whipped out his Colt revolver, and shot six of them in turn, after which he jumped on his camel and went off across the country." Lawrence, Thomas revealed to his audience on a lighter note, was now "in hiding, but he had received 27 offers of marriage in all."

A command performance was held for the king; and the queen saw it twice, the second time with Princess Mary, the duchess of Albany, and the earl and countess of Athlone as her guests. At the end of the performance the queen "summoned Mr. and Mrs. Thomas . . . to her box . . . and congratulated Mr. Thomas on his eloquent descriptions and his wonderful pictorial record of the campaign." The king of Spain saw it and "expressed himself as delighted," and Prime Minister David Lloyd George saw it twice. Winston Churchill saw it, and sent Thomas a warm letter of congratulations on his "illustrated lecture," as did General Sir Edmund and Lady Allenby. A handbill for the London production of what eventually came to be called *With Lawrence in Arabia and Allenby in Palestine* shows a photograph of Lawrence in full Arab regalia brooding over the desert, above the caption: "$250,000 REWARD! DEAD OR ALIVE! FOR THE CAPTURE OF THE MYSTERY MAN OF THE EAST." Below that is a boldface headline: "THE MOST AMAZING REVELATION OF A PERSONALITY SINCE STANLEY FOUND LIVINGSTONE." At the bottom of the page is a boxed quote from no less a fan than Prime Minister Lloyd George: "Everything that Mr. Lowell

Thomas tell us about Colonel Lawrence is true. In my opinion, Lawrence is one of the most remarkable and romantic figures of modern times." Thomas, who compared Lawrence to such legendary heroes as "Achilles, Siegfried, and El Cid," as well as to a changing list of real ones (depending on which country he was lecturing in), invented the illustrated travelogue. However, this was not a word he thought did justice to his show, which was as much a circus as a documentary—a fact that perhaps explains its enormous success.

Unaware of the approaching tidal wave of publicity, Lawrence himself had been on his way to Cairo to collect his war diaries when the Handley-Page bomber he was in crashed on landing at Rome. The pilot had committed the grievous (and elementary) error of landing *with* the wind, rather than against it. Unsure whether he could stop before the end of the runway, he attempted to take off again for another try. The wing clipped a tree and the aircraft crashed, killing the pilot and copilot. Lawrence and two air force mechanics survived, though Lawrence fractured either a collarbone or a shoulder blade—the British air attaché reported first the one, then the other. He was kept in a hospital for a few days, then moved to the British embassy. The ambassador, Lord Rennell (one of whose sons would marry Nancy Mitford and appear gloriously caricatured in several of Evelyn Waugh's novels as the scapegrace "Basil Seal"), tried but failed to keep Lawrence in Rome for a few weeks of recuperation. This attempt was, of course, a waste of time. A few days later Lawrence resumed his journey to Cairo in another Handley-Page bomber. The journey amply demonstrated the limitations of air travel in 1919, as well as the dashing, cheerful amateurishness of the infant Royal Air Force. The aircraft made emergency landings in Taranto, Valona (Albania), Athens, Crete, and Libya because of various mechanical and navigational failures. Lawrence did not reach Cairo until late in June. The crew members were awed by Lawrence's sangfroid as they crossed the Mediterranean—a first for the Royal Air Force—and given the primitive navigational aids and undependable engines of the time, this awe was well deserved.

Once they were out of sight of land, Lawrence slipped a note in the pilot's hand: "Wouldn't it be fun if we came down? I don't think so!"

He managed to keep writing his manuscript even in flight—later he would claim that one chapter of *Seven Pillars of Wisdom* was written while he was flying to Marseille, and that the rhythm of the prose was set by the beat of the Rolls-Royce engines. The frequent landings at primitive airfields put him out of touch with anybody who wanted to reach him, so it was not until he reached Crete that St. John Philby told him open warfare had broken out between ibn Saud and King Hussein. "Jack" Philby (who was, as noted earlier, the father of Kim Philby, the notorious Soviet double agent at the heart of MI6) played much the same role relative to ibn Saud that Lawrence played relative to Feisal, though for a longer time. Indeed Philby, who had attended Trinity College, Cambridge, with Jawaharlal Nehru and was a cousin of Field Marshal Montgomery, eventually converted to Islam and took an Arab woman as his second wife. He was also the man chiefly responsible for opening up Saudi Arabia to the American oil companies. It was a singular embarrassment to Philby that Britain was financing both sides of the war—the government of India was backing ibn Saud, while the British Foreign Office was backing Hussein. In fact the Foreign Office had been trying to reach Lawrence to ask him to mediate between Hussein and ibn Saud, but by the time he arrived in Cairo it was too late. Ibn Saud's tribes, fanatical followers of the puritanical Wahhabi sect, had caught Hussein's army (literally) sleeping, still in their tents, and had all but destroyed them.

Among Hussein's mistakes was giving command of his army, such as it was, to his second son, Abdulla, a skillful diplomat but not much of a soldier. It is interesting to speculate how different the future of Arabia might have been had Feisal and Lawrence been in command of the sharifian forces—but the immediate effect was to increase the British sense of obligation toward Feisal. After all, the Hashemites would shortly become a royal family without a country or a capital, in part because the Indian government's candidate for control of the peninsula had defeated London's. Lawrence, when he learned about Abdulla's defeat, did not appear to be all that surprised or upset. King Hussein had always seemed to him vain and obdurate, and Hussein had never tried hard to conceal his dislike of Lawrence; also, Abdulla had always seemed to Lawrence a reluctant, ineffective warrior. In any case Lawrence's interest was in a modern Arab state in Syria and Lebanon, not a feudal state in the Hejaz, still less a Wahhabi state in Riyadh. Let ibn Saud rule over the vast, empty space of Arabia, so long as Feisal ruled in Damascus—this was Lawrence's point of view. That wealth beyond any calculation lay buried beneath the sand had not yet occurred to anyone. Ibn Saud still kept the gold sovereigns he received from Delhi via Philby in an ironbound wooden chest closed with a big padlock, in his tent, guarded by one of his slaves. The notion that only twenty-six years later President Franklin D. Roosevelt would interrupt his journey home from Yalta solely to pay his respects to ibn Saud would have seemed far-fetched in 1919.

By the time Lawrence returned to Paris, the Inter-Allied Commission of Inquiry on Syria had already fizzled out. The French refused to join it, and announced in advance that they would pay no attention to its recommendations. In deference to the French, the British refused to join it, and as a consequence it consisted only of two Americans: Dr. H. C. King, a theologian and the president of Oberlin College; and C. R. Crane, "a prominent Democratic Party contributor." Neither of them was particularly well suited to decide the fate of Syria. King and Crane spent ten hot, weary days in Damascus, and came to the conclusion that the Arabs "were not ready" for independence, but that French or British colonial rule would be morally unjust. On their return to Paris they recommended that the United States occupy Syria and guide it toward independence and democracy. By that time nobody was listening, least of all President Wilson.

Since there was nothing for Lawrence to do in Paris except go through the files of the British delegation reading unflattering comments about himself, toward the end of the summer he returned to Oxford, where his old mentor David Hogarth, and Geoffrey Dawson, the editor of the *Times*, had arranged a research fellowship for him at All Souls College. This entitled him to a set of rooms and £200 a year while he worked on his book and returned to work on "the antiquities and ethnology, and the history (ancient and modern) of the Near East." All Souls, a college that has no undergraduates, was and remains a kind of worldly sanctuary for Oxonians who have retired from public life to pursue their studies or write their memoirs. Election to a fellowship of the college is considered a great honor. With his usual efficiency and command of the Oxford establishment, Hogarth had provided Lawrence with a way to get on with his life and write his book.

In the meantime, the Foreign Office and the War Office disputed over which of them was responsible for Lawrence, and whether he was now a Foreign Office official dressed in the uniform of a lieutenant-colonel, or a lieutenant-colonel temporarily assigned to the Foreign Office as part of the British delegation to the Peace Conference, or possibly only an adviser to Prince Feisal. He was blamed by many for "our troubles with the French over Syria," and one official, Sir Arthur Hirtzel, at the India Office, expressed the vehement hope "that Lawrence will never be employed in the Middle East again in any capacity." Correspondence about whether Lawrence had been or should be "demobilized" went back and forth. An exasperated officer in the Department of Military Intelligence in Paris cabled to the War Office, "Colonel Lawrence has no Military status in Paris he is however a member of British delegation under foreign office [sic] section it is also believed he is a plenipotentiary from King of Hedjaz but has not yet presented his credentials his status in Army not known here but he continues to wear uniform with badges of rank varying from full Colonel to Major." A handwritten note on yet another attempt to clear up the matter reads: "I have tried again and again to get the F.O. to say whether Col. Lawrence is their man or not," and bounces the question on to Allenby. Finally, an abrupt letter from Egypt addressed to Major T. E. Lawrence, CB, DSO, clears the matter up once and for all: "I am directed to inform you that having ceased to be employed on the 31st July 1919, you will relinquish your commission and be granted the rank of Lieutenant-Colonel, a notification of which will appear in an early gazette." Much correspondence and many handwritten calculations ensue in Lawrence's army file about the size of his "gratuity" on being demobilized, which seems to work out at £213. Some of the correspondence is marked "Submit to King," which suggests that King George V was not so offended by Lawrence's refusal to accept his decorations that he was indifferent to the way Lawrence was treated on being demobilized. As for Lawrence, it is uncertain to what degree he cared or even knew—he was in the habit of tearing up, returning, or ignoring letters addressed to him with his rank and decorations.

Lawrence, thanks to his friendship with Geoffrey Dawson, was able to get his point of view printed frequently in the *Times*, to the embarrassment of the Foreign Office and the anger of the French. Lawrence argued that the Sykes-Picot agreement needed to be revised in the light of present realities, that this revision should be done with the inclusion of the Arabs, and that the various pledges the British government had made to the Arabs should be spelled out in detail. In the meantime, Syria continued to be occupied by British troops; this gave the British government some leverage over the situation, since what the French wanted was to replace them with a French occupation force as soon as possible. Moreover, the French wanted it done with appropriate ceremony, in order to impress on the Syrians the fact that their well-being now depended on France. The Union Jack must be pulled down in Damascus and Beirut, with "God Save the King" played for the last time, with pipers, and with all the panoply of British military ceremony, followed by the raising of the French flag and the playing of the "Marseillaise." To this, after much correspondence, Lloyd George eventually agreed, and by the end of the year, France would be firmly in control of Lebanon, and rather less firmly in control of Syria. Feisal, who, on Lawrence's recommendation, had stayed in Damascus rather than returning to Paris to endure further humiliation at the hands of the French,* now journeyed to Britain, where

---

* This may not have been the best advice. Feisal might have done better to return to Paris and negotiate with the French, rather than stay in Damascus, where he came more and more under the influence of Syrian nationalist hotheads preaching resistance to France.

he was told that he should make the best deal he could with France, and that the British government could take no further responsibility for events in Syria and Lebanon.

Feisal does not appear to have met with Lawrence while they were both in Britain, and Lawrence's letter to Curzon offering to "use his influence with Feisal" was ignored.

CHAPTER TEN

"Backing into the Limelight": 1920–1922

Any soldier's return home after a long war is bound to be traumatic, and Lawrence's was no exception. It was perhaps no accident, but more in the nature of a Freudian slip, that his last major written work would be a translation of the *Odyssey*. Neither he nor Hogarth could have believed that he would settle cozily into life at All Souls, dining at the "high table" in evening dress and black academic gown, chatting with dons and other fellows in the Common Room over a glass of port, and pursuing the research he had dropped in 1914, on the antiquities of the Near East. Hogarth could slip seamlessly back into the life of a scholar, but Lawrence's war years had been too tumultuous for that, and his devotion to scholarship, or at any rate to the academic life, had been only skin deep to begin with. The war had not taken him away unwillingly from what he loved, but instead offered him a much more intense and dramatic life, as well as a chance to play a significant role in grand events. He was not going back to a desk at the Ashmolean Museum, with a sigh of relief, to study potsherds, and as for archaeological research in the field, neither the British nor the French government would tolerate the presence of "Colonel Lawrence," a magnet for Arab nationalism and discontent, digging among the ruins of Carchemish, or anywhere else in the Middle East.

All Souls was a refuge of sorts from the outside world, but it was no great distance from there to Polstead Road, where Lawrence's mother continued to try to dominate his life. For five years Lawrence had been spared his mother's intense interest and, as he saw it, her unreasonable emotional demands, as well as the hothouse atmosphere of life in the Lawrence household. Sarah Lawrence had not only very high and unforgiving standards of behavior, but an elephant's memory for slights, or occasions when her will had been flouted. It would be easy to suppose that Lawrence exaggerated his mother's controlling personality, but those of his friends who met her, including Charlotte Shaw and Lady Astor—the former married to one of the more difficult personalities of late nineteenth-century and mid-twentieth-century Britain, and the latter no shrinking violet herself—seem to have been terrified of this tiny, and by then elderly, woman. Evidently, Sarah Lawrence always said *exactly* what was on her mind, without any attempt to sugarcoat it. By the early autumn of 1919 she had accumulated enough tragedy in her life to expect some emotional support from her second son, who was, of course, either unwilling or unable to provide it. Polstead Road cannot have been a place Lawrence wanted to visit, but now he was only a few minutes' bicycle ride away, and without the tempering influence of his father.

Without Thomas Lawrence present, his widow was free to explore many of the animosities and old complaints that Ned had been spared over the years. An example was her fierce quarrel with Janet Laurie, who had fallen in love with Ned's taller and more handsome brother Will. When the war broke out, it seems that Will, who clearly intended to marry Janet despite his mother's opposition, wrote to ask Janet if she thought he should come home and join up, and she, after much hesitation, wrote back and told him that "it might trouble him later if he did not." This was true, given Will's honorable nature, but once he had been listed as missing, and then declared dead, his mother either heard about or read Janet's letter (more likely, the latter), and blamed Janet for his death. There was a terrible "row," and the two women did not speak again until 1932. To do Sarah justice, as a devout Christian she finally sought Janet's forgiveness, and received it, but in 1919 Sarah's bitterness over Will's death was still raw.

Hearing in detail about such issues was exactly why Lawrence had left home in the first place. He was the least judgmental of men, and besides, he was still fond of Janet and would have been reluctant to take his mother's side or even to hear it. Also, his own attitude toward the death of two of his younger brothers was modeled on Roman fortitude. When Frank was killed, Lawrence had written to his mother urging her to "bear a brave face to the world about Frank. . . . [His] last letter is a very fine one & leaves no regret behind it. . . . I didn't say good-bye to Frank because he would rather I didn't, & I knew there was little chance of seeing him again; in which case we were better without a parting." This was stoic, but not exactly sympathetic or consoling. Lawrence would doubtless have felt the same about Will.

Lawrence's depression may be gauged by his mother's recollection that he sometimes sat for hours at home, staring into space; he did the same at All Souls, to the consternation of the other fellows. At times he broke out of his depression to play undergraduate pranks, or so the poet Robert Graves, a returning officer turned undergraduate, remembered. According to Graves, Lawrence climbed a tower at All Souls to hang the Hejaz flag from its peak, kidnapped a deer from the Magdalen College deer park, and rang the station bell he had captured from Tell Shahm from his window at night. These incidents would not have been out of the ordinary for an undergraduate, but Lawrence was at the time a thirty-one-year-old retired officer, and All Souls was not a place that looked with fond amusement on high jinks by its fellows. The pranks may be seen, not so much as cheerful rebellion against authority, but more likely as an attempt to revert to the happier, easier undergraduate state of mind that Lawrence had known at Oxford from 1907 to 1910. But that world had vanished forever. Oxford in 1919 was a place where the undergraduates were for the most part ex-officers, many of them old before their time. In every college dons were busy putting up a plaque with a long list of those who had been killed from 1914 to 1918. It was as if a whole generation had simply disappeared. Lawrence did not fit in at All Souls any more easily than he did at home.

He was still working on his manuscript, but without any conviction that it should ever be published. It was a giant, self-imposed task; and whereas most people write in the expectation of seeing their books published and reviewed, Lawrence seemed to be writing to get the war, and his role in it, out of his system. Perhaps for that reason, he included material that might be judged libelous or even obscene, by the strict standards of the time.

On August 14, 1919, Lowell Thomas's "illustrated travelogue" opened at least at the Royal Opera House in Covent Garden. Lawrence had not been affected by Thomas's success in New York—in the days before radio or television, let alone instant telephone communication, New York was far away, and a theatrical success there was merely a curiosity on the opposite side of the Atlantic. But in London Thomas made Lawrence, overnight, by far the most famous and acclaimed British hero of World War I, and what is more, a *live* hero, who lived only a short train ride from London. Lawrence had cooperated willingly with Thomas and Chase at Aqaba, on what he thought was a "propaganda film" for the American government, made under the orders of Colonel House, President Wilson's closest adviser. Even so, he gave the two Americans only a few days of his time, and was notably reticent. He saw no harm in pulling Thomas's leg, or in having a little fun at his expense, and cannot have imagined that the film would ever be made, or indeed that he would live to watch it, still less that it would be enlarged into a kind of three-ring circus. His colleagues at Aqaba had had their fun with Thomas too, telling him tall tales and burnishing Lawrence's legend. Aqaba was a dull, infernally hot place, and the opportunity of amusing themselves at the expense of two earnest Americans was not to be missed.

None of this is to suggest that Lowell Thomas was taken in—he was anything but credulous—but he was a *showman*, looking for a great story and, if possible, for a British hero who could be made appealing to an American audience (not an easy task, given the constraints of the British class system). He saw no profit in skepticism, and never hesitated to turn a good story into a better one, and Lawrence was first and foremost a good story, set against a great background. Thomas made the most of it.

Although Lawrence has been criticized for cooperating with Thomas, he could hardly have foreseen that a documentary film would fill London's biggest halls and theaters to capacity six nights a week and two matinees, let alone that the Metropolitan Police would have to be called out in force night after night to handle the huge crowds. On the night the Allenbys attended the show, Lowell Thomas reported that "Bow Street was jammed all the way from the Strand to Covent Garden . . . and we turned away more than ten thousand people." Lowell Thomas's wife, Fran, wrote to her parents that the show was having "a colossal success," and she was not exaggerating. Lawrence himself saw it five or seven times (depending on whose account we believe), apparently without being recognized except by Fran Thomas, who noted that "he would blush crimson, laugh in confusion, and hurry away with a stammered word of apology." That Lawrence was not initially offended at being turned into what he called "a matinée idol" seems clear enough. He wrote a nice letter to Thomas, adding that he thanked God the lights were out when he saw the show, and invited the Thomases to Oxford for a sightseeing tour.

Thomas had not only put Arabia on the map but made T. E. Lawrence a perennial celebrity. The normally staid *Daily Telegraph* summed it up nicely: "Thomas Lawrence, the archaeologist, . . . went out to Arabia and, practically unaided, raised for the first time almost since history began a great homogeneous Arab army." The *Telegraph* predicted that, thanks to Thomas, "the name Lawrence will go down to remotest posterity besides the names of half a dozen men who dominate history."

Lawrence would have had to be superhuman not to feel a glow at all this fame and praise. However much he pointed out that he had *not* been unaided, that he was only one of a number of British officers helping the

Arabs, his modesty only increased his popularity and fame. Here was no boastful hero, but a shy, modest, unassuming one, willing, even eager, to give credit to others. Lowell Thomas, in fact, stated how difficult it was to interview Lawrence about his own feats, then went on to publish in *Strand Magazine* a series of hero-worshipping articles about Lawrence, which, together with his lecture, he would soon transform into an internationally best-selling book.

"In the history of the world (cheap edition)," Lawrence complained to his old friend Newcombe about Lowell Thomas, "I'm a sublimated Aladdin, the thousand and second Knight, a Strand-Magazine strummer."

It is against this background that one must view Lawrence's life in 1919: as an ex-soldier struggling with a huge and difficult book; as a diplomat whose effort to give Feisal and the Arabs an independent state had failed; as a man who, to quote Kipling, "had walked with kings, nor lost the common touch," and was now stranded in his rooms in an Oxford college, or at home under the thumb of a demanding mother, all the time besieged by admirers, well-wishers, celebrity hunters, and cranks.

Lawrence tried to take up some of his old interests—he wrote to his friend Vyvyan Richards about resuming their old plan for setting up a printing press together to produce fine, limited editions of great books. It says much for Richards's affection for Lawrence that he was still open to this pipe dream after an interval of so many years; and it is hard not to believe that at this point Lawrence was simply casting around for some escape from the demands of his book, which was constantly growing in complexity, and from the rapidity with which his real accomplishments were being overshadowed by Thomas's romantic image.

It is possible that the completion of *Seven Pillars of Wisdom* might have solved many of these problems—he had already written more than 200,000 words—but since at the time Lawrence didn't expect to publish it, the book remained, in a sense, a perverse blind alley. One of Lawrence's peculiarities as a writer was that despite his immense gifts, he believed firmly that writing was a skill which could be learned like demolition, and he was constantly on the lookout for people who could teach him the formula for writing poetry or constructing a sentence. More often than not, such suggestions, however sensible, were ignored. Like Charles Doughty, whose *Arabia Deserta* he so much admired, Lawrence seems to have invented his own prose style, which is at once archaic and lush, and becomes simple only when he is writing directly about the fighting. The descriptions of landscapes are magnificent, but throughout the whole long book—it grew to some 400,000 words at one point, and was eventually cut to about 335,000 for the so-called Oxford text of 1922, which is now regarded as definitive—there is a sense of a man perhaps trying too hard to produce a masterpiece. This need not necessarily be a bad thing—neither *Ulysses* nor *Finnegans Wake* is an easy book to read, after all; and D. H. Lawrence, whose books T. E. Lawrence admired (although in *Lady Chatterley's Lover* D. H. Lawrence made fun of a certain "Colonel C. E. Florence . . . who preferred to become a private soldier"*), worked hard to produce a prose style distinctly his own. Still, there can hardly be a book in the history of English literature that was ever more thoroughly rewritten, revised, and agonized over line by line than *Seven Pillars of Wisdom*, and the pity of it is that it shows. It was a labor, not so much of love as of need, duty, and pride, and—more than that—another self-imposed challenge.

Whatever its merits, the first draft of the book, containing all but three of the eleven sections, much of Lawrence's research material, and many of his photographs, was either lost or stolen from him in Reading Station late in 1919—a catastrophe that can only have added to his depression. Although the full text of *Seven Pillars of Wisdom* would never be published in any conventional way in Lawrence's lifetime (he went to enormous trouble and expense, as we shall see, to produce his own limited subscription edition, and to protect the copyright in Great Britain and the United States), Lawrence had occasionally handed the manuscript to his friends for their suggestions or corrections—at least four people seem to have read it in handwritten form. That explains why he

---

*This brings to mind Noël Coward's famous remark after seeing David Lean's film *Lawrence of Arabia*: "If Peter O'Toole had looked any prettier they would have had to call it *Florence of Arabia!*"

sent or gave his only copy to Lieutenant-Colonel Alan Dawnay, who was then posted to the Royal Military College at Sandhurst. Lawrence went down to get his friend's opinion and corrections, and to go back to Oxford with the manuscript. So many versions of what then happened have been related, some of them fanciful, that it has become part of Lawrence's legend. These include the possibility that Lawrence may have "lost" the manuscript deliberately, in other words, abandoned it; that it was stolen by an agent of the British or French secret service to ensure it would never be published; and that the incident was totally fabricated by Lawrence, presumably out of morbid vanity or to add a note of drama to the writing of the book. All these theories are unlikely—Lawrence was genuinely distraught, and Hogarth was horrified when he heard of the loss.

The truth is quite simple: Lawrence had neglected to bring a briefcase with him to carry the manuscript, so Dawnay lent him an "official" one. Such a briefcase does not resemble a bank messenger's bag, as has been suggested, but is made of black leather, with the royal coat of arms stamped on the front flap in gold—quite an impressive-looking object. Obliged to change trains at Reading, Lawrence waited in the station café, and when his train was called he boarded it without picking up the briefcase, which he had placed under the table. Despite great efforts, the case was never found or returned.

It may of course be true that Lawrence had a subconscious desire to lose it, though this seems rather far-fetched; and it certainly seems odd that a thief would pick up the briefcase, examine the contents, and not think in terms of returning it for a reward—but then, we have no way of knowing whether the manuscript had Lawrence's name and address on it. In any event, it vanished. Lawrence's initial reaction was hysterical laughter, perhaps to avoid tears. Of course it may seem odd today to give the only copy even to so trustworthy a friend as Alan Dawnay, but in those days the only way to copy a handwritten manuscript was by photographing every page. Hence most writers either typed a copy and a "carbon" or hired a typist to do it. Oxford must have been full of such typists, given the number of theses and manuscripts being written there, but

Lawrence may not have wanted to be bothered hiring one, or may have felt it was too expensive.

There seems to have been no doubt in his mind that he would start from scratch and write it all over again, and Hogarth urged on him the importance of doing just that. By this time, Lawrence seems to have been fed up with All Souls, or more likely with his mother, since he spent more of his nights at Polstead Road than at All Souls, and he accepted the offer of Sir Herbert Baker, a distinguished architect he had met, to lend him the top floor of a building Baker rented in Westminster for an office. Sitting down to reconstruct a whole book would be a grueling and daunting task for anyone, but Lawrence made it an exhausting and physically punishing marathon, perhaps because only by turning it into a physical and mental challenge could he force himself to do it at all. He wrote at an incredible pace, producing "95% of the book in thirty days," sometimes writing thousands of words at a sitting, and eventually completing more than 400,000 words. At one point he wrote 30,000 words nonstop in twenty-two hours, possibly a world's record. It is almost impossible to keep straight the number of parts that Lawrence wrote—he called these parts "books," and their number varies from seven to ten. Some of the books he would revise again and again over the next six years, particularly Book VI, which describes the incident at Deraa.

Probably no part of *Seven Pillars of Wisdom*, even the pages about Deraa, gave Lawrence more trouble than the dedication of the work, which he went to endless pains to get right. He not only wrote it over and over again, but—unsure whether it was prose or poetry—gave it to his young friend Robert Graves, already an admired war poet, to help him turn it into blank verse, and submitted it to at least one other poet for advice. Despite changes made by Graves, it is what it is, neither fish nor fowl, at once awkward and deeply moving:

To S.A.

I loved you, so I drew these tides of men into my hands
and wrote my will across the sky in stars

To earn you Freedom, the seven pillared worthy house,
    that your eyes might be shining for me
        When we came.

Death seemed my servant on the road, till we were near
        and saw you waiting:
When you smiled, and in sorrowful envy he outran me
        and took you apart:
        Into his quietness.

Love, the way-weary, groped to your body, our brief wage
        ours for the moment
Before earth's soft hand explored your shape, and the blind
        worms grew fat upon
        Your substance.

Men prayed me that I set our work, the inviolate house,
    as a memory of you.
But for fit monument I shattered it, unfinished: and now
The little things creep out to patch themselves hovels
        in the marred shadow
        Of your gift.

The identity of S.A. has stirred up controversy ever since the book first appeared in print, partly because Lawrence was deliberately mysterious. It has been suggested that the dedication is to Sarah Aaronsohn, a courageous Jewish spy who committed suicide after being captured and tortured by the Turks; or to Fareedeh el Akle, Lawrence's teacher of Arabic. Since Lawrence never met Sarah Aaronsohn, and since Fareedeh el Akle lived on to great old age denying that Lawrence had dedicated the book to her, neither theory is plausible. Lawrence himself further confused the matter by saying that S.A. represented both a person and a place; but it seems self-evident from the context that the dedication is to

Dahoum, his friend in Carchemish before the war, and that it expresses not only Lawrence's love for Dahoum but his bitter regret that Dahoum did not live to see the victory.

The first four lines also suggest a very unusual degree of grandiloquence for Lawrence: "I drew these tides of men into my hands" and "wrote my will across the sky in stars" are an usually direct claim to Lawrence's authorship and leadership of the Arab Revolt, in contrast to his usual practice of giving full credit to other people. If they represent his real feelings—as they may, since the dedication is evidently to Dahoum—this is one of the few places where Lawrence lets his real self and his pride show through, an unexpected moment when the hero appears without apology or disguise.

Like many great works of literature *Seven Pillars of Wisdom* is a product of an intense obsession, driven first by Lawrence's need to explore and explain his own role in the Arab Revolt, and second by his need to portray the revolt as an epic, heroic struggle, full of larger-than-life figures (Auda Abu Tayi, for instance) and noble motives (those of Feisal particularly). Also as with many of the world's great books, the author was unwilling to give it up, or stop changing and revising it. *Seven Pillars of Wisdom* remained a work in progress until 1927, and even today is still available in two different versions. Although Lawrence was scrupulously accurate about himself, in this book he approached the Arabs in much the same spirit as Shakespeare approached the English in *Henry V*, determined to make his readers see them as he did—as glorious figures, inspired by a great ideal. When parts of the story did not reflect this, he played them down as much as possible.

The top floor of Baker's building was unheated, so Lawrence worked through the nights in a "flying suit," believing that cold, hunger, and lack of sleep would concentrate his mind. The room had neither a kitchen nor running water, so he lived off sandwiches and mugs of tea bought at street stands, and he washed at public baths, a London institution that has pretty much vanished.

In his authorized biography, Jeremy Wilson points out, correctly, that Lawrence got a head start by incorporating into his manuscript all the reports of his actions he had written for the *Arab Bulletin*, and that he decided to alleviate the comparative dryness of these reports by inserting long and sometimes lyrical descriptions of the landscape. This explains the curious shifts of tone in the finished book, from reportorial to lyrical. Wilson suggests that the second version—the version Lawrence wrote under such intense, self-imposed pressure—was deliberately intended to underplay the British role in the Arab Revolt, so as to build up Feisal's claim to Syria. When he wrote the lost first draft, in Paris and on the way to Egypt and back, Lawrence may still have had some hope that the French would relent, or that the British (and perhaps the Americans) would force them to, but by the winter of 1919–1920 he can have had no such illusion, so the second draft may have been written more as a propaganda document than the first. As Wilson puts it, "the book had now assumed a strongly political role"—though what use it would have been to the Arab cause if it was not going to be published remains unclear. In any case, from the beginning, Lawrence had tried carefully to put the spotlight on the Arabs, without in any way diminishing the enormous contribution made by British money, arms, specialists, officers, and men, and by the Royal Navy. We cannot examine the first draft of *Seven Pillars of Wisdom*, but in every subsequent version of the book Lawrence seems notably fair-minded toward the Indian machine gunners, the British armored car personnel and drivers, and above all Allenby and his staff, though they are overshadowed by the greater glamour of the Bedouin tribesmen. Still, the book was Lawrence's story, and his story was among and about the Arabs.

Lawrence was awash with contradictory impulses. He wanted the book to be read by those whose judgment, experience, and suggestions for changes he respected, but not to be published and reviewed in the normal way. It was as if he hoped to protect himself against criticism, allegations that he was wrong, or arguments that he had changed the emphasis of events in the Middle East to put himself in the limelight and show the

Arabs in a better light than they deserved. He toyed with the idea of publishing what he called a "boy-scout" version of the book in the United
States, sharply condensed, and with all the controversial material left
out. He even went so far as to start negotiations for it with F. N. Doubleday, the Anglophile American book publisher, whom he had met in
London—indeed his correspondence with Frank Doubleday (whose
nickname, coincidentally, was "Effendi") should be sufficient to dispel
any notions that Lawrence was indifferent to money, or had no head for
business. Among the dozen or so alternative ideas he had for the book,
once it was completed, he considered printing one copy only and placing
it in the Library of Congress to ensure copyright, or offering one copy for
a sale at a price nobody would pay, $200,000 or more. The idea of an
abridged edition would eventually be realized with *Revolt in the Desert*,
in 1927, but overall the curious history of *Seven Pillars of Wisdom* is one
of the more tangled and complicated episodes in book publishing.

The immediate reason for the negotiations with Frank Doubleday was
that Lawrence needed the money to build a house on his land in Epping
and to open the private press with Vyvyan Richards. The rest of Lawrence's ideas represent imaginative ways to protect the copyright and
prevent the text from being pirated without enabling people to actually
buy and read the book. Throughout his life, Lawrence did his best to prevent people from reading the unexpurgated text, either because he
shrewdly grasped that nothing creates more interest than a famous book
readers can't buy, or because he disliked the whole business of publication and the reviews that accompany it. Despite a reputation for innocence and eccentricity in business matters, which he was careful to
maintain, the curious thing is that in the end Lawrence by and large
managed to get his own way.

Had Lawrence been willing to allow *Seven Pillars of Wisdom* to be
published in the normal way, perhaps accompanied by a numbered
deluxe edition, there is no doubt that it would have been a huge best
seller, and would have made him a fortune. But money was always sec-
ondary to Lawrence, whose attitude toward the whole subject was a curi-

ous blend of his father's and his mother's. His father, he knew, had "lived on a large scale," on his estate in Ireland, and although Lawrence says that his father never so much as wrote out a check, Thomas Lawrence's correspondence shows that he not only had a sound head for business but made sensible provision for his sons. Whatever mysteries may still have surrounded Thomas Lawrence, his death must have dispelled most of them. Indeed one subject over which Lawrence revealed a certain amount of bitterness was the fact that the Chapman family did not reach out to him once he became famous, and that his fame did not persuade them to accept him as one of their own.

Lawrence should have been comparatively well off. His "gratuity" on leaving the army was apparently difficult to calculate, given the many changes in his rank, and the fact that the paperwork followed far behind his travels even to EEF headquarters in Cairo, let alone back to the War Office in London. Thus, in 1919, a puzzled War Office official, wrestling with underpayments and overpayments, came to the tentative conclusion that if Lawrence had been a temporary major and "Class X staff officer," he was owed £344, minus overpayments of £266, which would have given him a gratuity of £68 on relinquishing his commission. If he had been paid as a lieutenant-colonel, the gratuity should be £213; if he was being paid as a lieutenant-colonel *and* a Class X staff officer, his gratuity should be £464. A further calculation by a higher authority lowers this figure to £334. Some of this confusion is due to the exigencies of wartime service, some to the traditional inefficiency of the Paymaster Corps, and some no doubt to Lawrence's own lack of interest in such details. A note in the file points out, for example, that there is no record that Lawrence was ever commissioned in the first place. Lawrence himself remembered receiving a gratuity of £110, which seems on the low side, but in any case he had accumulated almost £3,000 in back pay. His scholarship from All Souls was worth about £200 a year, and he had a set of rooms at the college, and meals, had he cared to make use of them.

Thomas Lawrence had left £15,000 to be divided among his sons, with the expectation that more would be coming in, in the form of a legacy from his sister, and also provided comfortably for Sarah Lawrence. After the death of Will and Frank, this legacy would have given Lawrence £5,000, plus the £3,000 in back pay. If Lawrence had put the entire £8,000 away in some tidy investment, it would have been the equivalent of about $600,000 in terms of today's purchasing power, and should have produced an income equivalent to about $20,000 a year. When added to his scholarship from All Souls, this would have given him the equivalent of about $35,000 a year today—not bad for a man with abstemious habits, no dependents, and virtually no living expenses.

Perhaps because he had overestimated how much he would receive from his father's estate, Lawrence spent a good deal of his accumulated back pay buying land at Pole Hill for the house and printing press he intended to build there. Investing in farmland was not the wisest thing to do, since the land was primarily of interest only to Lawrence himself. As for the money his father had left him, Lawrence soon found himself in what would have been for anyone else a difficult moral position. Neither Will nor Frank had lived to inherit a share of the £15,000 Thomas Lawrence had left his sons, so when Lawrence discovered that Janet Laurie was in desperate need of money, he gave her the £3,000 that would have been Will's share. This was apparently in accord with Will's wishes. Lawrence later wrote that Will had left "a tangle behind" with respect to Janet, without making it clear exactly what kind of tangle it was. Lawrence should have been in a position to know, since Will had made him his executor, and it certainly seems possible that although Janet became engaged to another man after Will went to war, he may still have believed she would marry him eventually, despite Sarah's opposition. That Sarah's opposition survived Will's death is at any rate clear enough—as late as 1923 Lawrence was unwilling to admit even to his friend Hogarth what he had done with the money.

It is to Lawrence's credit that he respected Will's wishes, despite the fact that shortly after the war Janet married Guthrie Hall-Smith, who was a war hero and then an impecunious artist. She asked Lawrence to give her away at the wedding, but after agreeing, he backed out, feeling that the difference in height between them would make him look "silly," or, perhaps more important, concerned that word of it would get back to his mother. His generosity toward Janet thus left him with virtually no capital, and drastically reduced his income.

This did not prevent him from buying rare, hand-printed books and paintings, including one of Augustus John's portraits of Feisal (which Jeremy Wilson estimates may have cost him £600, roughly the equivalent of $45,000 today). Nor did it prevent him from commissioning artists to draw and paint the portraits and illustrations for *Seven Pillars of Wisdom*, an extended effort that took years and cost far more than he could afford. It resulted in Lawrence's becoming one of the most important patrons of British artists in his day, a kind of modern Maecenas, but without the requisite fortune.

He enjoyed sitting for portraits, and was constantly invited to do so. He was amused and delighted when the portrait Augustus John painted of him in his white Arab robes and camel-hair cloak was sold at auction to the duke of Westminster for £1,000, a record price. Lawrence called it "the wrathful portrait," presumably because of the red cheeks John had given him, for his expression in the painting is in fact straightforward and benign.

He returned to Oxford in April with much of the book in hand, and set about cutting the text for the "boy-scout" edition he had discussed with Doubleday. He eventually put this to one side, since he was adamantly opposed to publishing the book in Britain, where it could of course be expected to sell the most copies. In any case, he was soon occupied again with events in the Middle East, which were deteriorating just as he had predicted. Since nothing had been settled in Paris, discussion of the "mandates" was moved to a new conference at San Remo, a small Italian seaside resort. In comparative obscurity, now that the Americans had made it clear that they would take on no responsibilities in the Middle East, the British and French divided the whole area even more drastically than the Sykes-Picot agreement had proposed. Apart from the vast Arabian wasteland, which was left for ibn Saud and King Hussein to dispute between themselves, the British were awarded the mandates for Palestine and Mesopotamia, and the French the mandates for Lebanon and Syria.

No provision was made for an inland, independent Arab state of any kind, although a large area had been set aside for just that purpose by Sykes and Picot. Lawrence worked hard to arouse opposition to this brutal carving up, and he had a good deal of support, in the newspapers and among politicians on both sides of the House. Lawrence, despite his claim to dislike publicity, had a positive genius for getting it. Much as he would suffer, over the next fifteen years of his life, from constant speculation and headlines in the press about him, he was as adept at running a press campaign as he had been at leading the guerrillas. He was even willing to be referred to as "Colonel Lawrence," in order to get published. He managed to get his opinions about the Middle East into almost every newspaper, from the *Times* and *The Observer* to *The Daily Mail* and *The Daily Express*. At one point Lawrence, in a bitter outburst, compared British rule in Mesopotamia unfavorably with Ottoman rule. At another, imitating Swift's *A Modest Proposal*, he suggested that if the British were determined to kill Arabs, Mesopotamia, where "we have killed about ten thousand Arabs this summer," was the wrong place to start, since the area was "too sparsely peopled" to maintain such an average over any long period of time. He also remarked sarcastically that fighting the Arabs would offer valuable "learning opportunities" for thousands of British troops, thus adding the War Office to the list of British bureaucracies he had offended. In both Syria and Mesopotamia local uprisings rapidly got out of control, just as he had predicted, and were put down with brutal force. By the summer of 1920 Feisal had fought and lost a pitched battle against the French army in Syria, with heavy losses to the Arabs, and had been obliged to leave the country. He had been placed forcibly, but with formal *politesse*, on board a special train at the orders of the French government, and dispatched to Alexandria, in Egypt, together with his entourage, consisting of an armed bodyguard of seventeen men, five motorcars, seventy-two of his followers, twenty-five women, and twenty-five horses, rather to the dismay of his British hosts, who complained that "one never knows how many meals are required for lunch or dinner." At the same time the British found themselves attacked on all sides in Mesopotamia, and threatened with growing unrest in Egypt.

Lawrence's views were straightforward: that responsibility for affairs in the Middle East should not be divided between the Foreign Office, the War Office, the Colonial Office, and the India Office, because such a division was a recipe for disaster; that attacking the Arabs merely for attempting to get what the British had promised them was a fatal mistake; and that keeping more than 50,000 British troops in what was now coming to be referred to as "Iraq" to hold down a country that would have been peaceful and prosperous if given a reasonable degree self-government was morally wrong and financially suicidal.

Far from being extreme, Lawrence's was the voice of reason and common sense, and his fame added a certain weight to his advice, as did the support of people like Charles Doughty, the author of *Arabia Deserta*; Wilfred Scawen Blunt, the Arabian traveler and poet; George Lloyd; David Hogarth; Arnold Toynbee; Lionel Curtis; and many others. Lawrence even won over St. John Philby and Gertrude Bell, despite the fact that they supported ibn Saud rather than King Hussein and the Hashemite family in the contest for power over Arabia and the Hejaz. Indeed Lawrence made a forceful case in the newspapers against the idiocy of supporting both sides in the struggle, with the India Office financing ibn Saud and the Foreign Office King Hussein. Objections were raised in the Foreign Office, particularly by Lord Curzon, about these "calculated indiscretions" by someone who had been part of the British delegation to the Peace Conference, and might still be under some obligation to the Foreign Office, but Lawrence's campaign in favor of Feisal and an independent Arab state seems to have struck most people as moderate, sensible, and, as Curzon clearly feared, very well-informed.

Given the fact that Lawrence was merely one person whose only resources were his pen and his name, he made amazing headway in changing the British government's ideas about the Middle East. The idea of Lawrence as a shy or reclusive neurotic is sharply contradicted by his energetic and largely successful attempt to redefine British policy in 1920. He seems to have known, met with, and written to almost everybody of consequence, including the prime minister and the editors of the leading newspapers.* Some idea of the aura of celebrity that clung to Lawrence can be gained from the introduction to his perfectly sensible piece in *The Daily Express*: he is described once again, in the unmistakable, gushing prose style of Lord Copper's *Daily Beast*, as the "daring," "almost legendary" "Prince of Mecca" and "the uncrowned king of Arabia," a "slight and boyish figure . . . with mind and character oozing through his eyes . . . and an unquestionable force of implacable authority."

Lawrence succeeded in marshaling behind his ideas a wide variety of influential figures, enough certainly to outweigh the objections of Curzon, whom he thought of, perhaps unfairly, as his bête noire, and the Foreign Office. That was in part because the attempt to rule Iraq as if it were an extension of India was so clearly a failure, and in part because there was no appetite in Britain for the wholesale slaughter of Iraqi civilians by British troops, or for the large amounts of money needed to police Palestine and Iraq, and to suppress the Arabs' desire for a national identity. The British had been obliged, thanks to the Sykes-Picot agreement and Lloyd George's impulsive bargain with Clemenceau, to let the French rule and garrison Lebanon and Syria, but they were not under any obligation to follow the French example.

Although 1920 was a difficult year for Lawrence—he had lost his manuscript and had seen his hopes for Feisal and for a fair settlement in the Middle East crushed—his achievements had been nevertheless remarkable. He had rewritten *Seven Pillars of Wisdom* from scratch, and was now

---

* This was a mixed blessing, as Lawrence would soon discover. In 1920, he was making use of the newspaper editors for his opinions about the Middle East, but very shortly, once he decided to step out of the limelight, they would be intruding into his life in pursuit of ever more sensational (and often inaccurate) stories about him.

revising it in painstaking detail, as well as working hard on a pet project of his: to find a publisher for Doughty's *Arabia Deserta*, which had long been out of print. He wrote a long introduction to the new edition of *Arabia Deserta*, which would be his clearest and most eloquent description of Bedouin life and Arab culture. In addition to all this, he had widened his circle of friends, not only among artists but among writers, poets, politicians, and journalists, to a degree that was to play a very important role in his life; for just as Lawrence was a prolific writer of enormously interesting letters—his correspondence represents a vast and varied literary masterpiece in some ways even more impressive and interesting than his books—he had a particular genius for friendship. When he was a loner, as he would be for the rest of his life, his friends played much the same central emotional role in his private life that family, marriage, and children play in the lives of most people. There is a tendency to write about Lawrence as if he had been a lonely man living the secular equivalent of life in a monastery—but none of this is remotely true of the real Lawrence, whose friendships were enduring and important and cut across the lines of class and rank in a very un-English way. In none of his letters does Lawrence "talk down" to his friends in the ranks, or flaunt his superior education or heroic reputation. The tone of his letters is nearly always the same—he is highly personal, at ease, solicitous, frank about himself, and eager to hear the other person's news. His critics have taken exception to some of his letters as inappropriate or impertinent—such as those he wrote to Air Vice-Marshal Oliver Swann on entering the RAF as a recruit—but this is to ignore the fact that at heart Lawrence was indifferent to rank, and wrote in the same easy, natural style to everyone. The list of people whom he met in 1919 and 1920 and who remained his friends for life is enormous, and includes (among many others) Augustus John, Sir William Rothenstein, Robert Graves, Lionel Curtis, Eric Kennington, and Edward Marsh. For Lawrence there was no such thing as casual friendship—*all* his friendships were important to him, and all those who became his friends felt in some way permanently connected to him, whatever role he chose to play in the complicated drama of his life as Lawrence *after* Arabia. For in many ways, the best and most productive years of Lawrence's life were still to come. He adamantly refused to shape himself as "Colonel Lawrence" or to allow his life to be defined only by the two years he had spent fighting in the desert.

He was, in fact, about to embark on one of the most important adventures of his life—one that would, in many ways, shape the Middle East as we know it today. Lawrence's press campaign against the government's policies in the Middle East not only had been successful, but had been followed with close attention by the prime minister, David Lloyd George, who watched with rising concern the cost of putting down Arab and Kurdish rebellions in Iraq (estimated at £20 million there alone), of separating Jews and Arabs in Palestine, and of trying to prevent Emir Abdulla, Feisal's older brother, from attacking the French in Syria. Lloyd George even discussed Lawrence's ideas directly with him, bypassing Curzon; this was just as well, since Lawrence's first suggestion to the prime minister was "to relieve Curzon of the responsibility." But as Lawrence later told Liddell Hart, "Lloyd George made it clear that he could not remove Curzon from the Foreign Office, [so] the alternative was to remove the Middle East from him. This possibility, once planted in Lloyd George's fertile mind, soon fructified." Thus Lawrence had made the step from the peaceful cloisters of All Souls to 10 Downing Street, advising the prime minister behind the scenes on Middle East policy, and moving it in the direction he wanted.

Certainly Lloyd George appreciated at once Lawrence's suggestion that British policy in the Middle East should be placed in the hands of one man, and what is more knew exactly in whose hands to place it. Winston Churchill had rejoined the government as minister of munitions in 1917, after commanding an infantry battalion on the western front for several months following the inquiry into the Dardanelles campaign. Early in 1919, he became secretary of state for war and secretary of state for air, in which roles he presided, among other matters, over the British effort to crush the rebellion in Iraq. The experience left him with an interest in the Middle East and a firm belief that the RAF could control large areas at a fraction of the expense (and bloodshed) of ground troops.

Lloyd George had always treated Churchill with the respect most sensible people reserve for a fused hand grenade. They were friends and rivals, both of them fiercely ambitious for power. Of the two, Churchill was the more volatile, and at this point by far the more politically vulnerable, and Lloyd George, for all his fabled Welsh charm, did not conceal from his old friend the fact that only his personal intervention had persuaded the reluctant members of the Liberal and Conservative coalition to allow Churchill back into the government at all. Churchill was in the cabinet on suffrage, and at the pleasure of the prime minister, never a man to confuse good intentions with political self-interest. In any case, Lloyd George concluded that Churchill was the obvious man for the job—a choice which had the additional advantage that if Churchill failed, the prime minister could lay the entire responsibility on him.

Churchill was no expert on the Middle East, although he had strong opinions about it. He had "a virgin mind" on the subject, he told one of his advisers—but unlike his rivals in the cabinet, he relished the opportunity to shape the future of a vital portion of the globe. Doubts did not trouble him; nor did the vested interests of the Foreign Office, still less previous promises made to the Arabs, in which he had played no part. His partiality toward Zionism was strong and sincere, but like Lloyd George he saw his task as preserving above all vital British interests—protection of the Suez Canal, the oil fields of Iraq, and the safe air route to India across Arabia from Cairo to Baghdad—while cutting sharply the enormous expense of keeping large numbers of British troops in the Middle East. Being who he was, Churchill had, beyond these practical goals, the imagination, the courage, the vision, and the boundless self-confidence to undo what Britain had reluctantly agreed to at the Paris Peace Conference, and create a new reality in the Middle East, at least so far as the British were concerned. To make it clear that responsibility for the Middle East would no longer be shared between the Foreign Office, the Colonial Office, and the War Office, Churchill proposed to set up a "Middle East Department." Not surprisingly, his first significant step was to persuade T. E. Lawrence to become his political adviser and his emissary to the Arabs—though Churchill may not have been aware that Lawrence was the one to recommend *him* to Lloyd George for the Middle East.

Oddly enough, Lawrence initially hesitated. Churchill's omnipresent private secretary and their friend Eddie Marsh first broached the idea to Lawrence in December 1920, but Lawrence initially showed little enthusiasm, perhaps because he knew it meant returning to the role of "Colonel Lawrence." This was, of course, to underestimate the persuasive powers of Winston Churchill. Lawrence took his first step toward joining Churchill's team by sounding out Feisal, who was in London at the time to protest against the French occupation of Syria. Confirming Churchill's confidence in him, Lawrence managed to get Feisal to promise a willingness to make a new start from the Arab side. Feisal agreed to put aside for the moment his objections to French rule in Lebanon and Syria, acknowledging the inability of the British government to alter French policy in the Middle East—and to settle for a Hashemite presence in Iraq and what is now Jordan, where his brother Abdulla was at present de facto ruler of the local Bedouin tribes. Though it was not appreciated at the time, the most significant concession Lawrence wrung from Feisal was that his father would give up any claim to rule Palestine. This had the advantage, from Feisal's point of view, of leaving the explosive issue of a Jewish "national home" in the hands of the British, who would very soon come to regret the responsibility, and the promises they had made to the Zionists.

Lawrence had planned to make a journey to some of the principal sites mentioned in *Seven Pillars of Wisdom* with Eric Kennington, the distinguished war artist, who had caused a sensation in London with his modernist depictions of troops in the trenches. The paintings appealed to Lawrence as a contrast to the more formal portraits he planned to have painted, and he was reluctant to cancel the trip. (After Lawrence's death Kennington carved both an effigy of Lawrence in the medieval style, and the bust of him, a copy of which is placed in the crypt of St. Paul's Cathedral.) Lawrence was simultaneously tempted and repelled by the thought of returning to the Middle East, but he swiftly developed for

Churchill the same intense mixture of affection, loyalty, and respect that he had for Allenby, and eventually he allowed himself to be won over, as Churchill had been confident he would be. Lawrence attempted to set as a prior condition that all Britain's promises to the Arabs should be met, but Churchill refused to do this. Lawrence gave in—indeed he can hardly have expected that Churchill would agree to totally abandon the Sykes-Picot agreement, and undermine both Britain's and France's positions in the Middle East.

Lawrence's success with Feisal before he had even accepted a job, and almost a month before Churchill formally took office, demonstrated just how valuable he would be. For all his occasionally erratic or emotional decisions, Churchill was an experienced politician, who wanted to be in a position to claim that he had listened to more than one opinion. Lawrence's role as political adviser and emissary to the Arabs was vital to the success of Churchill's mission, but he carefully balanced Lawrence's pro-Arab views by adding to his staff Sir John Shuckburgh as assistant undersecretary; an experienced civil servant, Lawrence's old chief Sir Gilbert Clayton, as military adviser; Hubert Young, once appointed as Lawrence's understudy during the Arab Revolt; and Richard Meinertzhagen, who had been Lawrence's confidant at the Hotel Continental during the Paris Peace Conference. Clayton, with his background in military intelligence and his knowledge of Egypt, was the perfect man to prevent friction between the War Office and the ebullient new secretary of state for the colonies. Young—who had clashed with Lawrence in 1917 and 1918, had been co-opted by the Foreign Office, and over time had been converted to Lawrence's views on Middle Eastern policy—might be trusted to keep Lord Curzon from interfering. Meinertzhagen, whose fervent and uncritical enthusiasm for Zionism was almost unique among British officers, could be trusted to reach out to the Jewish communities in Palestine and to represent their point of view forcefully. Churchill would soon add to this group Gertrude Bell, whose knowledge of Iraqi politics and personalities would be of great value. Although Lawrence had irritated Gertrude Bell with his newspaper campaign in favor of Feisal and his doubts about ibn Saud, they had been friends for too long not to patch up their differences. As for Young, he and Lawrence had long since made peace; and Lawrence was under the impression that he himself and Meinertzhagen were friends. Indeed, it may not have been until much later that Meinertzhagen began to revise his diaries to represent a very different view of "little Lawrence," remarking that Churchill's attitude "almost amounted to hero worship," and that Lawrence was "a most remarkable man, with a most remarkable record, but as unscrupulous as he is dangerous. His meek schoolboy expression hides the cunning of a fox and the intriguing spirit of the East. . . . We all know that Lawrence is a humbug, though as able as a monkey." He was later to change his mind again; after Lawrence's death, he wrote, "I cherish his memory." But whatever Meinertzhagen really thought of Lawrence, the two of them worked together well enough under Churchill.

Lawrence became a civil servant on February 18, 1920, at a salary of £1,600 a year—about $120,000 a year in today's terms. He had asked for only £1,000, but Churchill dismissed this at once as too modest, and said, "We'll make it £1,600," enough to enable Lawrence to fund Kennington's journey to the Middle East alone to do the drawings for *Seven Pillars of Wisdom*. Lawrence had decided not to spend any of his salary on himself beyond the bare necessities, since he did not think it was right to accept money for trying to invent a solution to a problem he had helped to cause. Lawrence then sat down in a room at the Colonial Office, which he shared with Young, and on their first day together, they drew up the agenda for the meeting Churchill planned to hold in Cairo. "Talk of leaving things to the man on the spot," Lawrence wrote; "we left nothing."

As John Mack points out in *A Prince of Our Disorder*, it had always been Lawrence's habit to work through older and more powerful figures, influencing them in the direction he wanted them to go, but remaining in their shadow and carefully not seeking any personal credit. He had worked that way with Hogarth, with Clayton, and with Allenby—it was only in the desert, with Feisal, that he had stepped hesitantly into the limelight himself, tempted by the opportunity he was offered to carry out in practice his own theories about warfare, and to test his own courage and endurance in the hardest conditions imaginable. Even there, when he was in Feisal's presence he did his best to stay in the background, as the adviser and liaison officer, not the bold guerrilla leader, always careful to suggest by indirection, until eventually he and Feisal began to think as one, and each could predict what the other would say or do. He quickly achieved the same kind of relationship with Churchill.

Lawrence and Young not only drew up the agenda for Churchill's meeting in Cairo, but so far as possible tried to provide both the questions and the answers, to ensure that there should be no surprises or disagreements. Lawrence's recommendation to Churchill was succinct: "You must take risks, make a native king in Iraq, and hand over defence to the RAF instead of the Army." Lawrence's experience working in tandem with the air force in the desert had given him a good understanding of how a comparatively small number of aircraft could produce a disproportionate effect on relatively primitive tribal forces. He saw very clearly that the object should never be to invade or occupy territory with troops—a waste of time, manpower, and money against nomadic or seminomadic people—but to threaten punishment from the air and, only when necessary, carry it out. Relatively speaking, it was even humane; aircraft could drop leaflets on the rebellious natives warning that they would return to bomb a specific target the next day, and so long as there was someone on the ground who could read, women, children, herds, and flocks could be removed to safety. Air Marshal Sir Geoffrey Salmond, KCB, KCMG, DSO, who had commanded the Royal Flying Corps in the Middle East during the war, and Air Chief Marshal Sir Hugh Trenchard, GCB, OM, GCVO, DSO, the "founder of the Royal Air Force" and its first chief of the air staff, knew Lawrence, and were in sympathy with his ideas, as well as eager to prove that a few squadrons of aircraft could "police" a whole country. The result was that from its creation in 1921 to the end of the renewed British occupation during World War II, Iraq was a proving ground for Lawrence's visionary ideas about air power; and for several decades the principal RAF base at Habbaniya, outside

Baghdad, was one of the largest military airfields in the world. Lawrence had no trouble persuading Churchill of his views, and still less in suggesting who the "native king" of Iraq should be.

In his book about Lawrence, the military historian Basil Liddell Hart wrote: "Lawrence can bear comparison with . . . Napoleon in that vital faculty of generalship, the power of grasping instantly the picture of the ground and situation, of relating the one to the other. He generated too the same electric current of command." While this is high praise, coming from such a distinguished critic of strategy, what Liddell Hart did not point out was that Lawrence's genius for diplomacy and politics was, if anything, more striking. He anticipated by more than fifty years Henry Kissinger's "shuttle diplomacy," using aircraft to fly from one leader to another throughout the Middle East in intensive bursts of negotiation and persuasion, restlessly pursuing consensus before second thoughts had time to sink in among his interlocutors. It was not just that he was a young man in a hurry—he was perhaps the first person to appreciate that speed, in diplomacy as in warfare, was a vital weapon, and that keeping up the pressure was the best way to produce agreement.

Lawrence worked in the Middle Eastern Department of the Colonial Office for just over a year, yet in that short time he not only managed to help create the borders of modern Iraq, and place his friend Feisal on its throne as its first king, but also managed to create a kingdom in all but name for Feisal's brother Abdulla in what was then known as Trans-Jordan and later became the Kingdom of Jordan. He tried and failed to make a negotiated peace between King Hussein and ibn Saud, and was instrumental in persuading the British to give a measure of independence to Egypt, while maintaining a British military presence strong enough to ensure British control of the Suez Canal until 1956.

The transformation of the warrior into the diplomat was immediate and successful, beyond even Churchill's hopes. Lawrence even allowed himself to be described in his diplomatic credentials as "Our most trusted and well-beloved Thomas Edward Lawrence Esquire, Lieutenant-Colonel in Our Army, Companion of Our Most Honourable Order of the Bath, Companion of Our Distinguished Service Order," exactly those honors he had refused to accept from King George V, who must have chuckled when he saw and signed the warrant. Lawrence dressed as a civilian during this period of his life in the Middle East, looking a bit ill at ease without a uniform or his robes, in a formal dark suit, often worn with dusty desert boots. In one famous photograph he is shown mounted on a camel in front of the Sphinx, looking a good deal more comfortable than Winston Churchill and Gertrude Bell on either side of him. In most group photographs he seems anxious to get as far to the edge of the picture as possible. The curious thing is that even without the flowing robe, the headdress, and the gold dagger, and despite the fact that he is almost always the shortest person in the photograph, Lawrence's face still attracts the eye instantly. There remains something commanding about the eyes and the thrust of the powerful jaw that contradicts the meek pose and the nondescript three-piece suit, with the trousers always a few inches too short.

The velocity of his movements throughout the Middle East is astonishing even today, particularly when one keeps in mind that air travel then involved sitting in the open cockpit of a biplane and landing on the RAF's improvised, dusty air strips in the desert. A quick glance at Lawrence's journey is revealing. On February 16, 1921, he had a further meeting with Feisal to discuss Iraq and Trans-Jordan. On February 18, he joined the Colonial Office, and together with Young drew up the agenda for the Cairo meeting. On March 2, he left for Egypt. On March 12 the meeting began there, at the Semiramis Hotel in Cairo. The next day Churchill sought the cabinet's approval to offer the throne of Iraq to Feisal, on terms discussed between him and Lawrence. On March 24 Lawrence cabled Feisal to leave London for Mecca, "by the quickest possible route," then left Cairo to meet with Abdulla in Amman. On March 9 he arrived in Jerusalem. On April 21 he flew to Cairo to meet Feisal, and by May 11 he was back in London. He spent the summer and autumn going back and forth on critical diplomatic missions to King Hussein in Jidda, to Abdulla in Amman, and to the imam of Yemen.

The first difficulty Lawrence faced was not so much Feisal's initial reluctance to exchange his claim to the throne of Syria for that of Iraq—the latter had originally been promised to his brother Abdulla—although this was a factor, but Churchill's need to have it appear that the people of Iraq had called Feisal to the throne. Churchill's requirement was much harder to stage-manage, particularly given the doubts of Colonel Arnold Wilson, the stiff-necked acting chief political officer in Iraq, under whose orders the Iraqi rebellion of 1920 had been brutally repressed. Wilson remained skeptical about Feisal's appeal to the Iraqis, and about the Hashemite family in general, and his skepticism was initially shared by Gertrude Bell. Lawrence quickly managed to convert Bell to his point of view—his cheery self-confidence usually brought that about. The problem of Wilson, a firm believer in the use of force and in the inability of the Arabs to govern an area like Iraq, was solved by knighting him, then replacing him with the more malleable Sir Percy Cox.

Gertrude Bell was assigned—among many other more important tasks, including persuading the initially reluctant Shiites and the Jews of Baghdad to accept a Sunni king—the job of devising a national flag, drawing up a code of court etiquette, and selecting a recognizable national anthem. (The last proved impossible, so the initial choice was the music of "God Save the King," without the lyrics.) Deciding on Iraq's borders was a more difficult question. The western border with Syria was fixed by a previous agreement with the French, the southern border was an invisible line in the sand between Iraq and the vast empty desert ibn Saud claimed, and the eastern border was that of the old Ottoman Empire with Persia; but to the north was the territory inhabited by Kurds, Arabic-speaking non-Arabs, supposedly of Indo-European descent, who passionately desired an independent Kurdistan. Unfortunately for them, the grand prize of Iraq from the British point of view was Mosul, right in the middle of the Kurdish homeland, with its rich oil deposits. Accordingly, commercial interests and realpolitik combined to create a country with a Shiite majority, a Sunni king, a disappointed Kurdish minority, and a small but wealthy and cosmopolitan class of Jewish merchants in Baghdad.

As a condition of accepting the throne of Iraq—and British guidance and protection for some time from behind it—Feisal needed a quid pro quo for Abdulla—hence the amount of time Lawrence spent in Amman. Abdulla's move there "with 30 officers and 200 Bedouins" had alarmed the French, and he and Lawrence spent some time calming down the tribes, who were eager to make raids into Syria; they also had to calm the Syrian political figures who had fled from Damascus to Amman as France tightened its grasp on the country. Lawrence wrote to his mother that "living with Abdulla in his camp . . . was rather like the life in war time, with hundreds of Bedouin coming & going, & a general atmosphere of newness in the air. However the difference was that now everybody is trying to be peaceful." Unfortunately this was not how the French reacted to the threat of tribal disorder to their south.

Lawrence and Abdulla had always had a wary relationship, ever since their meeting in Jidda in 1916, and Abdulla had been particularly "suspicious of his influence among the tribes." In his memoirs, written long after Lawrence's death, and only a year before he himself was assassinated by a Palestinian extremist in Jerusalem, Abdulla wrote, "He was certainly a strange character. . . . Lawrence appeared to only require people who had no views of their own, that he might impress his personal ideas upon them." But Abdulla acknowledged Lawrence's genius and "valuable services," and believed, as General Wingate did, that Lawrence's most courageous feat was not the taking of Aqaba but his "adventurous reconnaissance" behind enemy lines to Damascus in 1917 to meet with the military commander of Damascus, for which Wingate had recommended him for "the immediate award" of the Victoria Cross.

Even without his robes and headdress Lawrence continued to have a mesmerizing effect on the Bedouin. Churchill's bodyguard, Inspector W. H. Thompson of Scotland Yard, a policeman not given to flights of fantasy, described Lawrence's effect on a crowd of initially hostile Arabs: "Lawrence was the man. No Pope of Rome ever had more command before his own worshippers. . . . Colonel Lawrence raised his hand slowly, the first and second fingers raised above the other two for silence and for blessing. He could have owned the earth. He did own it. Every man froze in respect, in a kind of New Testament adoration of shepherds for a master. . . . We passed through these murderous-looking men and they parted way for us without a struggle. Many touched Lawrence as he moved forward among them. Far off, drums were beating, and a horse neighed. A muezzin's cry fell sadly among us from a single minaret in the mosque. . . . Lawrence was so greatly loved and respected that he could have established his own empire from Alexandretta to the Indus. He knew this too." In fact, Lawrence had long since renounced any such ambitions, if he ever had them; but the reactions of the tribes to his presence in Amman as they cried out "Urens, Urens, Urens," and fired off fusillades of shots in his honor, was enough to persuade Abdulla to take him seriously and to listen carefully to his proposals for a mini-state in Trans-Jordan, and for restraining the tribes from making raids into Syria, which would produce a violent reaction from the French.

Lawrence reassured Churchill, "I know Abdullah: you won't have a shot fired," and he was right. Abdulla was a better diplomat than a warrior, "shrewd and indolent," and by slow stages he persuaded the British to offer him the "temporary" governorship over Trans-Jordan, which he then elevated to a principality and finally to a kingdom, with an army— the famous "Arab Legion," led and trained by the British—to back him up. Lawrence was enthusiastic about Abdulla's ruling over Trans-Jordan, and would spend some time there as the "chief political officer for Trans-Jordania." He was one of the political architects, if not the chief political architect, of the Hashemite Kingdom of Jordan. Already in 1921 there were considerable misgivings about Lawrence's solution to the problem of how to reward Abdulla for giving up any claim he had to the Iraqi throne in favor of his brother Feisal. The Balfour Declaration had prudently not attempted to define the exact frontiers of Palestine, but both historically and biblically it had always included the area to the east of the Jordan, as well as the west bank. Approximately three-quarters of the territory to which the Zionists aspired was now a separate country, under the rule of an emir and sharif of Mecca, with Jewish settlement forbidden there—an area moreover which potentially could have sufficient water and could be ideal for settlement and modern farming, but which would remain a sandy wasteland. The reaction of Lawrence's fellow political adviser Colonel Richard Meinertzhagen was apoplectic and immediate, and echoed the feelings of the Zionist leadership: "The atmosphere in the Colonial Office is definitely hebraphobe, the worst offender being Shuckburgh who is head of the Middle East Department. Hubert Young and little Lawrence do their best to conceal their dislike and mistrust of Jews but both support the official pro-Arab policy of Whitehall and frown on the equally official policy based on the Balfour Declaration; the latter is the only policy I recognize. I exploded on hearing Churchill had severed the Transjordan from Palestine. . . . Lawrence was of course with Churchill and influenced him. . . . This reduces the Jewish National Home to one-third of Biblical Palestine." Meinertzhagen described himself as "foaming at the mouth with anger and indignation," not necessarily a figure of speech where Meinertzhagen was concerned, but his protests were mild compared with those of the Zionists themselves, in Palestine and in the United States. The Israelis' belief that Jordan is, or ought to be, the Palestinian state, and that the West Bank and the Gaza Strip were always intended to be part of the Jewish state, thus goes back to 1921, and the creation of Trans-Jordan. If Lawrence had been unaware of that before the eight days he spent with Abdulla, calming the tribes and persuading Abdulla to accept the "governorship" of Trans-Jordan, he certainly became aware of it the moment he reached Jerusalem.

Churchill's daring initiatives were not all that disturbed the inhabitants of Palestine, who now suddenly found themselves living in a much smaller country than either the Jews or the Arabs had expected. Although Palestine was still occupied by the British army, and Lawrence's old friend Ronald Storrs had been rushed into khaki to serve as Jerusalem's military governor, a civilian high commissioner had been appointed in 1920, and the choice had fallen on Sir Herbert Samuel, the former home secretary, who was a Jew and an ardent Zionist. Even before his appointment was final, Arabs responded with "consternation, despondency, and exasperation," feelings shared for once with the Christian population of Palestine—Catholic, Russian Orthodox, Greek Orthodox, Armenian, and Protestant—as well as with the Orthodox Jews, who believed that any attempt to encourage Jewish immigration was impious until and unless God arranged it. Samuel arrived at Jaffa, in a white diplomatic uniform, and was greeted by a seventeen-gun salute. Then he was taken to a reception in Jerusalem, where the chief military administrator he was replacing handed him "a typewritten receipt for 'one Palestine taken over in good condition,' which Sir Herbert duly signed."* Below his signature, however, he cautiously wrote, "E.&O.E.," letters which, on commercial documents, stand for "Errors and Omissions Excepted." Samuel was happily unaware that even the unflappable and unmilitary Storrs was holding "a loaded and cocked Browning pistol in his left hand" as they sat together in the back of the open car on the way to the reception. Storrs was well informed of the Arabs' hostility toward Samuel, though in the event, Samuel was notably evenhanded and fair. Although he too was strongly opposed to the creation of Trans-Jordan, he got along well with Lawrence, who took him on a sightseeing trip to Petra. At one point, as Churchill, Samuel, and Lawrence stood surrounded by a crowd of chanting, shouting Arabs, Churchill took off his hat to thank them for their prolonged cheers. "What are they saying?" he asked Lawrence. "Death to the Jews," Lawrence explained quietly.

Samuel did his best to control the fear and anger that were already beginning to mar the relationship between the Jews and the Arabs in the Holy Land. He had wisely persuaded the king to issue a friendly message to the Christian, Arab, and Jewish inhabitants of Palestine, in English, Arabic, and Hebrew, which Samuel had printed on parchment in gold ink and distributed to the notables of every community. He was unfailingly courteous, sensible, and good-natured, in marked contrast to his Turkish

---

* Storrs (the source of this quotation) got it slightly wrong. In fact, it read, "Received from Major-General Sir Louis J. Bols, K.C.B.—One Palestine, complete." Samuel (by then in his nineties) was incensed when this chit, intended as a good-natured joke, was offered for sale at auction in New York, and went for $5,000. (Tom Segev, *One Palestine, Complete*, New York: Holt, 1999.)

predecessors, and immediately began to reform everything he saw. He set up a reliable police force; created an honest court system (perhaps the most visible sign throughout the empire of British institutions being successfully transplanted); and encouraged the building of roads, modern sanitation, and schools for the Arab communities (the first thing that Jewish communities invariably built was a school)—all of which the Turks had neglected shamelessly. Streets signs and road signs were written out scrupulously in English, Arabic, and Hebrew; British officials were encouraged to learn Hebrew and Arabic; and new trilingual postage stamps were designed, much to the pleasure of King George V (an avid stamp collector). Lawrence made it his business to establish a good working relationship between the high commissioner and Abdulla, which Abdulla cemented by presenting Samuel with a "beautiful bay Arab mare" from his own stable—he was famous throughout the Middle East for his stud of thoroughbred Arab horses. Despite all this, however, Jewish immigration and Jewish land purchases continued to provoke unrest in the Arab population, and undermined the Arabs' respect for British rule.

Kennington, who had been traveling through the Middle East making sketches and paintings, turned up to find his client filled with mixed emotions now that he was back in the desert. Like Inspector Thompson, he was amazed at the affection the Bedouin felt for Lawrence; visiting Abdulla's camp, he described the tribes riding in to greet Lawrence: "Their cries became a roar, Aurens—Aurens—Aurens—Aurens! It seemed to me that each had a need to touch him. It was half an hour before he was talking to less than a dozen at once. Re-creating the picture, I see him as detached as ever, but with great charm and very gracious. I thought he got warmth and pleasure from their love, but now know his pain also, for they longed for him to take them again into Damascus, this time to drive out the French. Easily self-controlled, he returned a percentage of the pats, touches and gripping of hands, giving nods, smiles, and sudden wit to chosen friends. He was apart, but they did not know it. They loved him, and gave him all their heart."

Kennington's comment was shrewd and correct. For Lawrence the pain was real and intense—he *was* "apart," a man in a European suit, unarmed, no longer a part of the Bedouin's world. The two years he had spent in the desert, leading them and fighting alongside them, with all the accompanying deprivations, cruelties, and horrors, was an Eden to which he could never return, a comradeship far more intense than anything civilian life could provide. Other soldiers, perhaps most, found a replacement for the bonds of war in domestic happiness, marriage, family, and children, but none of these was a possibility for Lawrence, who took as his motto "the Greek epitaph of despair": "Here lie I of Tarsus, never having married, and I would that my father had not."

In April, Lawrence met with Feisal in Egypt, to go over Feisal's conditions for accepting the throne of Iraq, which was to be offered to him after a carefully rigged election. His chief rival for power in Iraq, Sayyid Talib, the political boss of Basra—whose choice for the throne was the Naqib of Baghdad, an elderly and widely respected Sunni religious figure—was invited to tea by Sir Percy Cox, the chief political officer. With a typically British manifestation of old-fashioned politeness combined with brutal realpolitik Sayyid Talib was arrested after tea and deported to exile in Ceylon, leaving Feisal as the only viable candidate for an office many Iraqis considered unnecessary. Not everyone in the Middle East shared the British faith in monarchy as a universally appropriate political solution.

During the last three weeks of April and the first week of May, Lawrence flew back and forth between Feisal in Egypt and Abdulla in Trans-Jordan, tactfully easing both brothers into accepting their new roles, and overcoming their objections to what they feared might be perceived as British puppet monarchies. Abdulla's doubts were soothed in part by a down payment against his annual subsidy of £5,000 in gold and the fly-past of a squadron of RAF aircraft, in which Lawrence participated, intended to reassure Abdulla that the British could support him if he was threatened by the French. Feisal was reassured by a substantial subsidy and the promise of British help, if needed, "against his own people," a request that showed a good deal of realism on his part about the future relationship of the Iraqi people to their monarch, as well as a British promise to mediate between his father and ibn Saud. In case mediation didn't work, it was hoped that bribery might do the trick, and ibn Saud was paid £100,000 in gold to leave King Hussein in possession of the Hejaz and the holy cities of Medina and Mecca. Lawrence displayed a degree of tact, persuasion, and sheer dogged persistence that would have qualified him for a knighthood had he not already turned one down.

As usual, Lawrence communicated directly and at length with Winston Churchill, now back in London; with Lord Curzon at the Foreign Office; and with General Allenby in Cairo—in a stream of well-written messages, full of good suggestions and vivid descriptions of personalities and events. Lawrence was, in fact if not in title, a proconsul, making major decisions on his own, and explaining them later to the person who seemed most likely to approve. Lawrence later wrote to Robert Graves, unusually for him, "I take most of the credit of Mr. Churchill's pacification of the Middle East upon myself. I had the knowledge and the plan. He had the imagination and courage to adopt it." This was, as it happened, a bold but accurate claim: Lawrence had a central role in shaping the borders of the modern Middle East and in placing Hashemite monarchs on the hitherto nonexistent thrones of Iraq and Jordan. Nothing, after all, is fated: the British started with many obligations (a guilty one toward Feisal, and another, less guilt-ridden and more self-imposed, toward the Zionists), yet Lawrence, without ever appearing in the foreground, managed to impose his own ideas on everyone, and shape the area according to his own vision. Afterward, when Lawrence had left the scene, Zionists complained that a large part of what should have been Palestine had been given to Abdulla; many Iraqis complained that they had received a Sunni monarchy rather than a republic; Arabs everywhere complained that France and Britain had shared the Middle East between them and carved it up into client states; and the British complained that they had been burdened with the costs and responsibility of maintaining peace and order from Baghdad to Cairo, and from Amman to Suez, as well as with the impossible task of mediating between the Palestinian

Arabs and the Jews. Lawrence believed, as he wrote to Charlotte Shaw, that Britain was "quit of the war-time Eastern adventure with clean hands," though what he really meant was that *he* was quit of it with clean hands, and this much is certainly true. He had done his best to undo the Sykes-Picot agreement, and had placed two of Hussein's sons on semi-independent Arab thrones—he could hardly have done more.

He was not quite "quit of it" yet, however. After a brief spell in London in May, Churchill sent him back to the Middle East, to Jidda, to undertake the impossible, which was to persuade King Hussein to agree in writing to all the various and conflicting arrangements that had been made by the Allies in the Middle East since the end of the war. Given that Hussein would not budge from the exact language of his correspondence with McMahon in 1915, that he had proclaimed himself king of "all the Arabs" everywhere (and would shortly, and ill-advisedly, declare himself caliph as well), and that he regarded ibn Saud as an upstart and the British mandate for Palestine as unacceptable, this was not a task which even Lawrence welcomed, happy as he was to get away from his desk at the Colonial Office.

Nor was he, in this case, necessarily the right man for the job, even though he was given "special, full" plenipotentiary powers by his old adversary, Curzon, "empowering" him "to negotiate and conclude, with such Minister or Ministers as may be vested with similar power and authority on the part of His Majesty the King of the Hejaz, a treaty between the United Kingdom and the Kingdom of the Hejaz." There was a slight thaw between Lawrence and Curzon, perhaps because Lawrence had been obliged to ask Curzon to prevent the publication of Lowell Thomas's adulatory biography in the United Kingdom, on the rather flimsy grounds that it might contain material that would embarrass the government or constitute a breach of the Official Secrets Act. Curzon, whose view of the matter seemed to be one of lèse-majesté, allowed a letter to be sent in his name on Lawrence's behalf to Hutchinsons, the London publisher, and managed to set back the publication of *With Lawrence in Arabia* by four years. In fact, Thomas had merely included some passages from the

Arab Bulletin, which he had been allowed to copy in Cairo. The publication of government secrets did not concern Lawrence so much as the possibility that Thomas's enthusiastic buildup of him would be taken by King Hussein, Abdulla, and Feisal as a denigration of their own roles in the Arab Revolt—and the fact that by now he was tired of Thomas's praise, and of the money Thomas was making off his legend.

Narrow-minded, old-fashioned, stubborn, and infuriating, King Hussein had never liked or trusted Lawrence the way he had Storrs, and he was still deeply suspicious of Lawrence's relationship with Feisal. The threat to the Hejaz from ibn Saud and his fanatical Wahhabi followers had frightened the old man into a stricter application of sharia law, including the cutting off of a hand for theft; chained prisoners clanked mournfully in the dungeons beneath his residence. Still, what Churchill and Curzon wanted from the king was not a more democratic rule over his subjects, but merely his signature, freeing them of further obligations and of future complaints that the British had acted without the consent of the Arabs. Lawrence was free to use any means at his disposal—at various points in the interminable negotiations, conducted at a snail's pace in the intolerable humidity and heat of Jidda, he offered Hussein a yacht, a fleet of airplanes, and a visit from the Prince of Wales, all to no effect. At one point he secured Hussein's agreement to fifteen of the nineteen articles in the draft treaty, and he remained confident that the king's signature could probably be purchased if the price was high enough, but this was overoptimistic. Hussein alternated between long periods when he appeared to be listening sensibly to Lawrence, and moments when he lost his temper, shouted, or walked out of the room, leaving his son Zeid to continue the negotiations in his place. At one point, he called for his curved dagger and threatened to commit suicide; Lawrence replied calmly that then negotiations would have to be carried on with his successor. It seems very likely that Hussein was already suffering from the effects of senility—certainly Abdulla and Feisal, though still respectful toward their father, thought so—but he may also, in the Oriental manner of bargaining, merely have been stringing out the negotiations for as long as he could to see just how high the British were willing to go.

Lawrence arrived in Jidda at the end of July, only to discover that soon after his arrival Hussein had to break off the talks to return to Mecca and go on a pilgrimage. Lawrence used that period for an extended journey to visit the imam of Yemen, an even more difficult man to negotiate with. The imam had been, however reluctantly, on the Turkish side throughout the war, and now wished to extract the highest possible price for pledging his loyalty to Britain and promising not to attack the British port of Aden. Lawrence judged that Aden could probably defend itself, if necessary. He may be one of the few summer visitors to Aden—popularly believed to be the burial place of Cain and Abel—who found the place "attractive," and he spent a good deal of time there, and on board ship working on his revisions of *Seven Pillars of Wisdom*. He offered the imam a Ford motorcar as a gesture of peace, and wrote a long, detailed, thorough, and positive report on the commercial possibilities of Aden, which he foresaw as the thriving free port and banking center it later became. Reading Lawrence's report on Aden to Sir John Shuckburgh in the Colonial Office, one is struck again by the breadth of his remarkable talents, and by his strong practical streak; he was not just a hero, a guerrilla leader, or a gifted strategist—he had a remarkable eye for the commercial development of what we would now call the third world. His report on Aden makes one aware of just how valuable he might have been as a senior official of the Colonial Office, had he been willing to stay there beyond the year that he promised Churchill. It also makes one regret that Lawrence did not accept Churchill's offer to make him high commissioner of Egypt when that post fell vacant—he would have been very good at it, and both the British and the Egyptians would have benefited from his combination of tolerance and common sense.*

---

* There is a good deal of dispute about whether Churchill actually made Lawrence this offer or not, since the post was not at Churchill's disposal—Egypt came under the Foreign Office, not the Colonial Office. But such a detail would not have prevented Churchill from suggesting the appointment to Lawrence in a moment of enthusiasm, and in any case the prime minister, Lloyd George, later made much the same sugges-

Lawrence took a steamer back to Jidda, where he resumed his negotiations with King Hussein on August 30, in an atmosphere of high domestic drama, since the king's sons had formed a kind of committee to carry on the negotiations, and reported every night to the queen, who then lectured King Hussein about what he must do. Not surprisingly in these conditions, the king sulked and threatened to abdicate. Negotiations ground to a halt in mid-September, when Curzon cabled Lawrence to proceed as rapidly as possible to Jerusalem, since Abdulla was raising problems about staying on in Trans-Jordan.

Lawrence, depressed by the weeks of fruitless negotiations with Hussein in Jidda, and with the imam of Yemen, was reluctant to begin all over again with Abdulla; but after meeting with Sir Herbert Samuel for several days, he traveled on wearily from Jerusalem to Amman. He and Samuel had agreed that the best outcome for everybody would be for Abdulla to step down, and then for Trans-Jordan to be reintegrated with Palestine; but once Lawrence reached Amman he seems to have caught his second wind, and he became more optimistic about Trans-Jordan's survival. With considerable difficulty, he persuaded Abdulla to stay put.

Lawrence was obliged to stay in Amman until mid-December, acting as Abdulla's chief political officer; vigorously reforming the local police and the collection of taxes; and facilitating the lagging formation of the Trans-Jordan Arab Legion, Abdulla's "native army," which was under the command of Lawrence's old friend Frederick Peake, "Peake Pasha," of the Egyptian army's Camel Corps. It may be that the presence of a friendly comrade in arms helped Lawrence to snap out of his depression. Peake remarked on Lawrence's "depressed [and] incommunicative" state when he arrived in Amman, and thought he was "weighed down" with exhaustion and the disappointments of trying to create new states from the debris of the Ottoman Empire, but also noted that like many another war veteran he cheered up when he was with his old desert cronies. Lawrence

---

tion. Both men, of course, may have made the offer secure in the knowledge that Lawrence would turn it down, but certainly neither of them would have been held back by the fact that it was Curzon's toes they were stepping on.

took one look at Peake's recruits and intervened at once to get them what they needed. "Peake cannot show his men in public till they are reasonably smart and till they have rifles," he complained to the Colonial Office, with a trace of his old cheeky humor, "for in Trans-Jordan every man of military age carries a rifle as a mark of self-respect, and Peake's, the so-called Military Force, is the only unarmed body of men in the country."

Lawrence not only set up the political structure over which Abdulla would rule until his death and over which a great-grandson, Abdulla II, now rules, but chose his own successor, St. John Philby. As it turned out, this was an unusual but inspired choice. Lawrence and Philby had disagreed sharply over many things, since Philby was the closest adviser of ibn Saud and an outspoken opponent of King Hussein; but Philby was not just a gifted Arabist and a courageous explorer—he was also a skilled administrator and a forceful personality, whom Lawrence trusted to build solidly on the foundations he himself had laid in Amman. Philby, not normally an uncritical admirer of Lawrence's, commented: "I leave all business to Lawrence. . . . He must carry on while he remains here, and I am well content to let him do so. He is excellent, and I am struck with admiration of his intensely practical, yet unbusinesslike, methods." These "unbusinesslike" methods included destroying the passports of people Lawrence didn't trust, as well as any files that he thought might be incriminating. Lawrence was a much better administrator than he is usually given credit for, although his methods were never those of a conventional bureaucrat.

In the meantime, Lawrence did his best to get Abdulla to persuade his father to sign the draft treaty; but sympathetic as Abdulla was to the need to do so, he could not sign in his father's place. By the end of the year, Lawrence was back in London, with only a few months left of his service in the Colonial Office, and at a rather low ebb. He had exhausted most of his money on the gift to Janet Laurie and on commissioning illustrations for his book, and now felt that the text wasn't yet good enough to print. He was tired, ill (possibly from a return of his malaria), and unwilling to move back into his rooms at All Souls. He toyed with the idea of setting up his own press, but without much conviction—by now, he did not have enough capital left to start a business on even a very modest scale. In his letters he refers to money he expected to receive that had not come in, and probably never would. This refers to the fact that his father's younger sister Caroline Chapman, who had intended to leave a sum of £20,000 to her brother, with the intention that the money should be divided between his sons, died shortly after her brother, in 1920. Since Thomas Chapman had predeceased her, and she had not made any change in her will to provide for this—she was too ill to do so—the money went to his four daughters instead, a severe blow to Lawrence. He had no intention of continuing to serve at the Colonial Office, but if not that, then what?

This is perhaps the moment to put Lawrence's achievements in the Middle East in perspective. Our current problems have made it fashionable to ask what Lawrence would have done or said about events there today, or to hold him responsible for what often seems to be a dangerous and ungovernable mess. In much the same spirit, Lawrence's name is frequently evoked by generals and armchair strategists as the United States struggles to develop an effective strategy against terrorism and guerrilla warfare in the area—indeed whole books have been written about Lawrence either as the guiding spirit of insurgency or as the key to developing successful counterinsurgency tactics. Probably no comment on guerrilla warfare is more frequently quoted (often out of context) than: "To make war upon rebellion is messy and slow, like eating soup with a knife."[*]

Lawrence's military reputation is remarkable, since he was both a successful guerrilla leader and a battlefield commander, a combination rarely encountered in warfare. Most people picture him as a man in flowing white robes on a camel, but he very quickly learned to incorporate armored cars and aircraft into his thinking, and he became an innovator in what we would now call combined operations.

His campaign to destroy the Turkish railway system south of Damas-

[*] "Evolution of a Revolt," T. E. Lawrence, *Army Quarterly and Defence Journal.* October, 1920, p. 8.

cus also had the unintended effect of introducing the Arabs to the use of high explosives, a weapon hitherto unknown to them, and today's improvised explosive device (IED), the roadside bomb, and the suicide bomber are all a part of Lawrence's legacy. He understood better than anybody else in his generation the effect of surprise on the morale of an enemy—the explosion when it is least expected, placed by unseen hands where it will do the most harm, and its value in weakening the resolve of a much bigger and better-equipped army. This is a running fight of David against Goliath, with Goliath's attention constantly distracted, so he is not only unable to give a knockout blow, but unable even to decide where to aim it.

Lawrence was not, of course, alone in destroying the hold of the Ottoman Empire over its Arab subjects; nor was he the sole architect of what replaced it. He could not have foreseen that the rise of Nazi Germany would change Jewish immigration to Palestine from a thorny issue for the British into an explosive humanitarian need, or that the discovery of vast deposits of oil would make some Arab regimes on the eastern periphery of the Middle East—Iraq, Saudi Arabia, the Persian Gulf emirates—fabulously rich, while leaving the more densely populated and more politically advanced states like Egypt, Syria, and Lebanon comparatively poor. Lawrence was conscious of the potential for oil, but during the 1920s Texas and California were still the world's largest producers, and in the Middle East the biggest deposits were thought to be in Iraq and Persia, both of which were to a greater or lesser degree British client states. That ibn Saud would emerge not only as the preeminent national figure in the Middle East, but as the owner of its largest oil deposits, was not something Lawrence could have imagined in 1922.

As for Palestine, Lawrence, like Feisal, envisaged Jewish settlement there as taking place within an Arab framework. He did not doubt that the Jewish "national home" of the Balfour Declaration would one day become a Jewish state—Weizmann never made a secret of the Zionists' ultimate ambition, though he carefully sugarcoated the pill when talking to Arab leaders—but Lawrence assumed, like many other people, that the Jews would make a useful commercial, industrial, and agricultural contribution as partners within a larger Arab world, and that Jewish nationhood would be a long time coming.

Although Lawrence is blamed by Arabs today for aggrandizing his role in the Arab Revolt, and for leaving the Arabs with two states created mainly to provide Abdulla and Feisal each with a throne, a larger Arab state was not within his power or his vision. He saw Abdulla and Feisal as stabilizing influences, and with some reason—the great-grandson of Abdulla still rules in Amman; and the grandson of Feisal reigned as the third king of Iraq until he and his family were murdered in a military coup in 1958 that ended the monarchy and brought the Ba'ath Party (and eventually Saddam Hussein) to power.

Lawrence's ideas for the Middle East were, always, ahead of his time. On a map that he prepared in 1918 for the British government, he sketched in color his ideas about how to divide the Arab portions of the Ottoman Empire in order to respect the geographical, tribal, religious, and racial realities of the Middle East. It is, of course, an Anglocentric view, which respects British strategic needs and ignores the claims of the French but pays due attention to ethnic realities on the ground. On the other hand, Lawrence tackled head-on some of the problems that are still plaguing the region, like the claims of the Kurds for an independent nation, and the need to find a place for the Armenians. His plan for Syria made it a much larger state than it is today, spread in an arc from the Mediterranean to the Persian Gulf, and including Trans-Jordan, with, to its east, a smaller Iraq, and an independent Kurdistan. He created an Armenian state around Alexandretta, and a smaller Lebanon, recognizing the need for a separate state there to deal with a sophisticated and partly Maronite Christian population. Palestine, too, he carefully separated, in recognition of its special problems. His sketch takes into account the distinct differences between tribal areas and settled areas; between Sunni and Shiite Muslims; between Arabs and Levantines; between Kurds and Armenians—differences which the French and British governments preferred to ignore, and which still today are the cause of bloodshed, border disputes, and endless political strife. Rather than trying to create states by drawing straight lines on the map, he tried to create states or indigenous areas based on the religion or the racial and cultural identity of the people living there, and so far as possible to take into account geographical features and water resources. His concept was not perfect, but it looks a good deal more sensible than what emerged in 1921, or what exists today. It would have given Syria a piece of the Persian Gulf oil revenues, and allowed the Kurds to keep their own oil, thus spreading wealth around the Middle East, rather than putting most of it in the hands of the most politically backward and autocratic regimes in the area. As a piece of imaginative mapmaking it is a remarkable document, and by itself ought to be enough to dispel the popular image of Lawrence as a guerrilla leader with romantic and impractical ideas.

Lawrence was only thirty-three when he returned to Britain at the end of 1921, with only two months left of the year he had promised Churchill. He had won the approval of everyone, even Curzon; he had been instrumental in the creation of two Arab nations; and he had helped to secure Britain's presence in the Middle East. He had accomplished more in a year than anybody, even Churchill, could have expected, and there is no doubt that a great career of some sort was his for the taking. He could, for that matter, have returned to Oxford—All Souls was used to celebrity fellows who maintained a separate and successful career in politics and government in the great world outside Oxford, and Lawrence's friend Lionel Curtis was one of them. A life as a diplomat, an adviser to the government on the Middle East, an Oxford academic, and an author was open to Lawrence—not only open, but expected of him.

He had already made up his mind, however, to go in a very different direction, and take the steps that would put an end not just to "Colonel Lawrence" but to T. E. Lawrence himself.

As with a stage magician at the end of an amazing performance, his last and most remarkable trick would be to vanish from the stage as the curtain began to fall.

CHAPTER ELEVEN

"Solitary in the Ranks"

O n August 30, 1922, Lieutenant-Colonel T. E. Lawrence, CB, DSO, enlisted in the ranks of the Royal Air Force as a recruit, under an assumed name.

Joining the RAF "in the ranks" was not a hasty decision on Lawrence's part, unusual as it seemed to most people. There was a long tradition in Victorian and Edwardian Britain of officers and gentlemen enlisting in the ranks, but usually to expunge some sort of social or military disgrace—the "gentleman ranker" is a constant figure in Kipling's *Barrack Room Ballads*: "He's out on active service, wiping something off a slate—And he's left a lot of little things behind him."

In this, as in every other way, Lawrence was, of course, an exception to the rule. He had the education and upbringing of a gentleman, but illegitimacy was a bar to full membership in the "ruling class,"* something about which he feigned indifference but to which he was, in fact,

---

*An exception was made for the acknowledged illegitimate children of members of the royal family. King William IV's nine illegitimate children received titles and were ranked in precedence above a marquess. All of them attended the king's coronation in 1830, and one of them later became a favorite aide-de-camp to King William's niece and successor, Queen Victoria.

very sensitive. He had done nothing disgraceful, and he was rapidly becoming Britain's most famous war hero. His experience as a boy soldier might have helped him make up his mind, although he may have supposed that service in the ranks of the infant RAF would be very different from serving in the old prewar British army—though if this was the case he would shortly be disappointed.

The exigencies of battle on the western front had eventually made it necessary to commission a large number of "other ranks" (the British equivalent of American "enlisted men") and NCOs during the war, but the social gulf between officers and men remained wide, and once the war was over, it became unbridgeable again. Those who joined the armed services in the ranks in peacetime did so largely because they had failed in the civilian world, or because they were running away from something—they tended to be a rough and touchy lot, often bearing emotional scars inflicted by the British class system, and suspicious of anybody whose speech, bearing, and behavior seemed "posh."

This was true even in the RAF, despite Air Chief Marshal Trenchard's desire to recruit and train future skilled "technicians," who could be trusted to look after the intricacies of aircraft and aircraft engines. "Airmen" got the same kind of rough treatment as recruits did in the older services: "square bashing," the universal phrase for parade ground drill; endless (and often pointless) polishing and cleaning; fatigue duty, much of it intended to be exhausting and loathsome; and constant petty harassment from officers and NCOs. At just over five feet five inches and 130 pounds, and at the age of thirty-three, Lawrence was not by any stretch of the imagination a typical recruit; and given his well-educated speech and his gentlemanly manners he could hardly have expected to fit in easily with his fellow recruits, or to "muck in with his mates" on Saturday nights at the local pub. All barracks contain one or two odd specimens,* and men who clearly have a secret to hide, but Lawrence was odder than most.

* The author served in the RAF from 1951 to 1953, and recruit training then (at RAF Padgate) did not seem all that different from training in Lawrence's time.

His interest in the RAF, however, was unfeigned, and he was a good friend of Air Marshal Geoffrey Salmond and Air Chief Marshal Trenchard, both of whom admired him and were sympathetic to his desire to get into the RAF. Lawrence could easily have joined as a wing commander (the equivalent of a lieutenant-colonel), and no doubt even have learned to fly, but that was never his intention. Writing to Trenchard immediately after his return from the Middle East, Lawrence made it clear that he wanted to serve in the ranks, and warned Trenchard that he did not think he could pass the physical examination. He also suggested that he wanted to write a book about "the beginning" of the RAF, and that such a book could be written only "from the ground," not from the viewpoint of an officer.

Lawrence did succeed in writing a worm's-eye view of recruit training "from the ground up," but *The Mint*, which would not be published until 1955, long after his death, is hardly the full portrait of the RAF that Trenchard had wanted. It seems reasonable to guess that Lawrence's suggestion of using his experiences as a recruit as the material for a book was at least in part intended to make the otherwise inexplicable wish of a famous, decorated former lieutenant-colonel to serve in the ranks as an aircraftman second class (AC2) under an assumed name seem more plausible. Gathering material for a book about the RAF no doubt sounded sensible enough to Trenchard, particularly since *Seven Pillars of Wisdom*, though by no means finished, was already being talked about as a major literary work; it was more sensible at any rate than Lawrence's desire to shed his identity and vanish into anonymity.

Much has been made by some biographers of service in the ranks of the RAF as the equivalent of a secular monastery, and of Lawrence as seeking an expiation of sorts there, but that seems far-fetched. The only thing Lawrence had to expiate was his failure to abrogate the Sykes-Picot agreement, and he felt he had emerged from that with "clean hands" after the creation of Trans-Jordan and Iraq. The truth seems to be that Lawrence had simply reached a dead end on his return to Britain at the end of 1921. He had no wish to be a civil servant, or an academician; like his father, and surely in imitation of his father's example, Lawrence held an old-fashioned gentleman's view that working for a living was beneath him; he had run through what money he had and faced a lot more work on *Seven Pillars of Wisdom*. All these considerations contributed to his feeling of being trapped, and Lawrence, when trapped, nearly always chose to cut the Gordian knot by means of a single, sudden, startling major decision, rather than a series of small compromises. He even offered to join Colonel Percy Fawcett's Amazon expedition in search of the "Lost City of Z," which ended in the disappearance of Fawcett and his party. It is possible that the return to the Middle East had disturbed Lawrence's equilibrium, as had the continuous and exhausting revision of *Seven Pillars of Wisdom*, which forced him to reread obsessively his account of the incident at Deraa, so that far from putting such matters to rest, he was constantly reliving his worst moments of grief, shame, and guilt.

Then too, Lawrence had lost faith in himself, and felt a need for some kind of structure to replace it. He had had, perhaps, too much freedom since the taking of Aqaba, and wanted to exchange it for an orderly, disciplined routine, in which he would not have to be responsible for other people and, above all, would no longer have to give orders. He was willing, even eager, to *take* orders, but not to give them anymore; his orders had led too many men to their deaths—a few of them men he loved—or had killed civilians, some of them guilty of no greater crime than having bought a ticket on one of the trains he destroyed. Lawrence had a lifetime's worth of such responsibility, and the chief attraction of serving in the ranks was that he would never have to give an order to anyone again. Certainly most of these conditions could have been met in a monastery, but Lawrence does not appear to have had any religious convictions, let alone a vocation. All those morning prayers and Bible readings in Polstead Road had had the opposite effect to what his mother intended.

There was a tendency among Lawrence's contemporaries to see his decision to shed his rank and join the RAF as a form of penance, but he always denied that. His service in the RAF, once he was past recruit training, would prove to be the happiest time of his life, with the exception of the years he spent before the war in Carchemish.

For nearly ten months Lawrence had been instrumental in making kings, creating countries, and drawing the borders of new nations and territories; he was almost as legendary a figure in peacetime as he had been in the war. But it was, at the same time, exactly the way this role appealed to his vanity, his thirst for fame and praise, his need to be at the center of things, his ability to move and influence even the most powerful of men, that he distrusted most in himself. Lawrence never underrated his powers, but "Colonel Lawrence" the kingmaker appalled him almost as much as "Colonel Lawrence" the war hero.

Throughout the first seven months of 1922 Lawrence was like a man who has painted himself into a corner. For a while he stayed on at the Colonial Office, unwillingly, as Winston Churchill's "adviser"—Churchill was as reluctant to let him go as Lawrence was determined to leave— while at the same time he labored diligently, but without pleasure, on the seemingly endless task of revising *Seven Pillars of Wisdom*. As with all the other problems the book presented, he had devised an extraordinarily difficult way of ensuring that it would not be lost or stolen again. Instead of having the pages typed as he rewrote them, he sent them in batches to the *Oxford Times*, where, he had discovered, the printers could set them in columns of newspaper type more cheaply than the cost of a typist. However, he rendered his life and that of his printers more difficult by sending them unnumbered, random pages, so there was no chance of anybody's reading the book consecutively, and by leaving the most controversial sections of the book until last. That way, when the entire book was set in type, he could put the sheets in the right order himself, number them by hand, add the front matter, and have them bound into five sets of proofs. He would laboriously correct the copies, thus creating the first and most valuable of the many versions and editions of *Seven Pillars of Wisdom*. He may have looked increasingly hungry and shabby— not surprisingly, since he had to use the Westminster public baths to wash, and he worked through every night on a diet of chocolate bars and mugs of tea. He wrote later that he haunted the Duke of York's Steps at lunchtime to catch friends making their way from the War Office to their club on Pall Mall, in hopes of being invited to lunch—a sad glimpse of what his life must have been like in the first half of 1922.

Still, Lawrence did not have a totally reclusive life during this period in London. He was involved constantly with painters, publishers, poets, printers, and writers, and seems rather to have enjoyed the air of mystery that hung around him even then. One of his acquaintances, Sydney Cockerell, curator of the Fitzwilliam Museum in Cambridge and a kind of literary and artistic gadfly, took him, quite by chance, to pick up George Bernard Shaw's portrait by Augustus John from Shaw's London home. It was thus, casually, in March 1922, that Lawrence met Shaw, who, together with his wife Charlotte, would play an important role in Lawrence's life over the next thirteen years. It would be incorrect to say that Shaw was at the height of his fame—his fame burned at a bright, steady level from before the turn of the century to his death in 1951, and burns on even today, more than half a century later, and nobody ever gloried more in his own fame. Lawrence's fame was equally bright, though he, unlike Shaw, was dismayed by it. In any case, a first contact was made that Lawrence would pursue diligently, in a campaign as carefully planned and executed as any of his military campaigns. The resulting friendship was one of most extraordinary and literarily productive of the twentieth century.

Churchill finally gave in and allowed Lawrence "to leave the payroll of the Colonial Office on July 1st, while retaining him as an honorary advisor." Churchill had known about Lawrence's desire to join the ranks since January, and while he was sympathetic, it was hardly something he understood at heart, having lived on a firm basis of late Victorian class distinction as a grandson of one duke and cousin of another. Trenchard had in any case consulted him, as well as his own secretary of state, about Lawrence's wish to join the RAF, and with a more tolerant view of human behavior, had expressed his willingness to accept Lawrence as a recruit. Churchill was considerably more skeptical about "Colonel Lawrence's" chance of slipping into the RAF unnoticed, but he was willing to let Lawrence try. Trenchard went so far as to give Lawrence a privilege to which no other airman was entitled—at any time, if and when he chose to, he could leave the RAF, no questions asked and no obstacles placed in his way. Thus Lawrence was entitled to enter the RAF under a name of his own choosing, and to leave it if at any time he decided it had been a mistake; Trenchard could hardly have been fairer or more generous, as Lawrence gratefully recognized.

Lawrence dramatized his entrance into the RAF in writing *The Mint*, with its famous opening lines: "God this is awful. Hesitating for two hours up and down a filthy street, lips and hands and knees tremulously out of control, my heart pounding in fear of that little door through which I must go in order to join up. Try sitting for a moment in the churchyard? That's caused it. The nearest lavatory, now. . . . A penny; which leaves me fifteen. Buck up, old seat-wiper: I can't tip you and I'm urgent. Won by a short head. . . . One reason that taught me I wasn't a man of action was this routine melting of the bowels before a crisis. However, now we end it. I'm going straight up and in."

In fact, Lawrence's entry into the RAF had been carefully choreographed well in advance, and there was no chance at all that he would be rejected. The overdrawn description of his fear before entering the RAF recruiting office, at 4 Henrietta Street, Covent Garden, makes artistic sense, since in writing it Lawrence chose to portray himself as everyman, a generic narrator, rather than as a former lieutenant-colonel and war hero. As a result, *The Mint* sometimes reads more like fiction than a memoir, or than the piece of documentary reporting that Lawrence had in mind. One reason why it fails as reporting is that the most important fact of all is largely missing: the narrator is not an anonymous, terrified civilian trying to sign up for seven years of service and five years in the reserve but Lawrence of Arabia posing as an airman. The fact that Lawrence had an escape clause from the RAF is not mentioned either. Even the looseness of his bowels "before a crisis" seems unreal—nowhere in

Seven Pillars of Wisdom does he mention this problem, even though he is often in situations that would terrify anyone.

From the beginning it was clear that Lawrence would be no ordinary recruit. Trenchard, the chief of the air staff, replied to his letter asking to join the RAF in the ranks, on January 11, 1922: "With regard to your personal point, I understand it fully, and you too, I think. I am prepared to do all you ask me, if you will tell me for how long you want to join, but I am afraid I could not do it without mentioning it to Winston and my own Secretary of State, and then, whether it could be kept secret I do not know. . . . What country do you want to serve in, and how? I would make things as easy as anything." As Lawrence's release from the Colonial Office approached, he was invited to have dinner and spend the night at Trenchard's house in Barnet, outside London, to talk things over; and Trenchard made one more appeal to Lawrence to join as an officer, which Lawrence declined.

Trenchard approached the task of getting the most famous man in Britain into the RAF as an ordinary aircraftman with his usual common sense. Lawrence came up with the name John Hume Ross himself. He wanted a short name, and when his youngest brother Arnold mentioned a friend of their mother's, Mrs. Ross, he chose that. On August 14 Trenchard had Lawrence come to see him at the Air Ministry, and introduced him to Air Vice-Marshal Oliver Swann, the member of the Air Council for Personnel, who was to make the final arrangements. Swann was something less than a willing accomplice. Trenchard might enjoy breaking his own regulations, but Swann lived by them and was "considerably embarrassed" at the "secrecy and subterfuge." He "disliked the whole business," and particularly resented the letters he received from Lawrence, which expressed a breezy familiarity and equality that Swann considered inappropriate, and also told Swann a good deal more than he wanted to know about a recruit's life in the ranks. Swann soon came to dread Lawrence's letters. He would comment later, with the asperity of a man determined to set matters straight at last: "One would think from [his] letters that I was a close correspondent of Lawrence's, possibly even a friend of his.

But as a matter of fact . . . I disliked the whole business. . . . I discouraged communication with or from him."

Swann's orders left him in no position to argue, however. Trenchard's memorandum to him was simple and clear-cut:

> It is hereby approved that Colonel T. E. Lawrence be permitted to join the Royal Air Force as an aircraft-hand under the alias of
>
> John Hume Ross
> AC2 No. 352087
>
> He is taking this step to learn what is the life of an airman. On receipt of any communication from him through any channel, asking for his release, orders are to be issued for his discharge forthwith without formality.
>
> H. Trenchard
> CAS
>
> O. Swann
> AMP 16.8.22

Since this was dated only two days after Swann was introduced to Lawrence by Trenchard, it is apparently a written confirmation of what had been discussed at their meeting. Swann, a meticulous bureaucrat and a stickler for regulations, could not have been pleased that, apart from the hugger-mugger of slipping "Colonel T. E. Lawrence" into the ranks, something which Swann rightly feared might backfire on them all, Lawrence not only was given the right to opt out of service in the RAF but could do so at any time without going through the *correct* channels—i.e., from Lawrence to his sergeant, from his sergeant to his flight commander, from the flight commander to the station commander via the station adjutant, and from there on to the Air Ministry in London. Furthermore, Swann was to be the *only* person in the RAF, apart from Trenchard himself, who knew that AC2 No. 352087 Ross, J. H., was in fact T. E. Lawrence—so Swann was in the uncomfortable position of having to conceal the truth from his subordinates. Lawrence may have felt that this was great fun, and Trenchard may have shared that feeling, but

Swann did not, and was anxious to get Lawrence off his hands as quickly as possible. It could not have made him any happier to know that Lawrence was intending to write a book about his time in the air force, a book in which Swann and his subordinates might expect to appear.

Swann nevertheless arranged for Lawrence to present himself at the RAF recruiting office in Henrietta Street at 10:30 A.M. on August 22. (The date was later altered to August 30, at Lawrence's request, probably because he needed more time to complete the corrections on the proofs of *Seven Pillars of Wisdom*.) Lawrence was to ask for Flight Lieutenant Dexter, who would interview him and help him fill out the necessary forms. Dexter had been warned that "Ross" was entering the RAF "specially," but under no circumstances was Lawrence to tell Dexter who he really was.

Unhappily, Swann was the wrong man for planning this kind of transaction, and not at all suited for the role of Figaro. As Lawrence entered the recruiting office he was intercepted, as Swann should have guessed, by Sergeant Major Gee, who was not about to allow a seedy-looking prospective recruit to say which officer he wanted to see. Instead of taking Lawrence into Dexter's office, Gee took him straight to Flying Officer W. E. Johns, the chief interviewing officer, who was not in on the secret, and who did not like the look of Lawrence any more than the sergeant major did. Indeed Gee, who was standing behind Lawrence, made a signal to Johns to indicate that he suspected the recruit might be a man running away from the police: such fugitives often tried to join one of the armed services in a hurry, under an assumed name, to avoid prosecution. Johns, who kept in his desk drawer an up-to-date stack of photographs of men wanted by the police, was by no means an ordinary RAF officer. He would become the author of the hugely successful "Biggles" books, ninety-eight of them, about a fictional RAF pilot hero, which remained a mainstay of boys' reading material in Britain well into the 1950s. He edited the serious aviation magazine *Flying* but was forced out of his job by the government when he became an outspoken opponent of appeasement in the 1930s. He was not a man easily imposed on; nor was Sergeant Major Gee.

According to Johns, he questioned "Ross" sharply, and quickly ascertained that he had no copy of his birth certificate, and no references from previous employers. One might have thought the man who had traveled more than 300 miles across the desert behind enemy lines in 1917 would have provided himself with the necessary documents, or that Air Vice-Marshal Swann would have made sure he had them. Possibly Dexter had been warned not to ask for them, but Johns sent Lawrence packing to obtain these documents, and in the meantime he and the sergeant major examined the photographs from Scotland Yard and determined that "Ross" was not a wanted man. Johns was no fool, and he was thorough—he put in a call to Somerset House (the central registry of births and deaths) and discovered that no John Hume Ross had been born on the date given to him by Lawrence. When Lawrence returned later in the day with a sheaf of papers, Johns quickly realized that they were forged, and had Sergeant Major Gee show him firmly out the door.

The Air Ministry was only a few minutes' walk from the recruiting office, and Lawrence immediately went there to give Air Vice-Marshal Swann the bad news. Swann sent him back to the recruiting office in the company of a messenger from the Air Ministry bearing a black dispatch case with a copy of Trenchard's memo to Swann in it. Johns therefore became aware that it was now his job to get "Ross" into the RAF, and also that "Ross" was in fact Lawrence of Arabia. The secret, which Trenchard and Lawrence had hoped to keep for as long as possible, was already out, in the span of a few hours.

A further "stumbling block"* still awaited Lawrence: the medical examination. The RAF doctors were not impressed by Lawrence's physique, and at five feet six inches (they made him an inch taller than he actually was) and 130 pounds he seemed slightly too small for the RAF; he was also a few years too old. They were curious about his scars, too. He explained away the bayonet wounds between his ribs as barbed-wire scars, but the scars on his buttocks were harder to explain. "Hullo, what the hell's those marks? Punishment?" one of the doctors asked.

"No, Sir, more like persuasion, Sir, I think," Lawrence replied, not yet

---

* Johns's words. Since he was an accomplished writer of fiction, he may have overdramatized his role, but his account reads convincingly enough.

aware that for an aircraftman a clever or flip reply to an officer's question is always a bad idea—a lesson he would learn the hard way over the next few months.

The doctors, despite encouragement from Johns, eventually rejected Lawrence because his teeth failed to meet the RAF standard—a glance at the dental chart in Lawrence's RAF medical records does indeed reveal an amazing number of fillings and at least two bridges to replace missing teeth, perhaps more of a comment on the standards of British dental care at the time and the national passion for chocolate than on Lawrence. (Lawrence's dental chart shows seven teeth missing, and twelve teeth with significant decay, despite the notation that his "Oral Hygiene" was "Good.")

While Dexter shepherded Lawrence through filling out his application to join the RAF and took care of the standard education test—Lawrence could manage the essay, of course, but not the "square roots . . . and decimals"—Johns went off to explain his predicament to his commanding officer, who called the personnel office at the Air Ministry to ask what to do. When he had replaced the receiver he told Johns to get "Lawrence of Arabia" into the air force, or "you'll get your bowler hat." This was RAF slang for being dismissed from the service. Johns resourcefully found a civilian doctor who was willing to sign the medical form. Johns then signed the form himself, and "Ross" was officially declared fit for service in the RAF. His medical form rather modestly limits the "marks" on his body to "Scars both buttocks," overlooking the bayonet wounds on the ribs and a number of bullet scars; notes that he has perfect eyesight, as one would expect of such an expert shot as Lawrence; and gives his age as twenty-eight, whereas he was thirty-four.

Any pretense of secrecy vanished when Johns telephoned his opposite number, Flight Lieutenant Nelson, at RAF Uxbridge, the recruit training center, about fifteen miles from the center of London, "to warn him of who was on his way, for by this time Lawrence was making it clear that he had no time for junior officers." Johns took Lawrence to the station and chatted with him while he waited for the next train to Uxbridge.

They did not part friends. Johns remarked that Lawrence left him "with the memory of a cold, clammy handshake."

Lawrence left this slightly farcical episode out of *The Mint*, when he came to write it, and gives the impression that the medical examination at the recruiting office in London went more or less normally, and that the two RAF doctors were eager to pass him as fit. He may also have invented the description of his arrival at Uxbridge, in which he is one of six recruits who are met by a sergeant and marched from the railway station into camp. His description of his first night in the recruits' hut at Uxbridge rings true enough, however, to anyone who has entered the British armed forces. His fellow recruits were noisy, swore constantly, and smelled of beer, tobacco, and sweat.

Lawrence must also have been disoriented by this sudden immersion into lower-class life. He had a remarkable ability to get on with people who were very different from himself, but these had so far been Arabs and Bedouin tribesmen, foreigners rather than his own fellow countrymen of a different background. He was well brought up, fastidious, brilliantly educated, an ex-officer, however idiosyncratic, and a man whose quiet voice and unmistakable accent identified him immediately as a gentleman. He was also a man who hated to be touched, so he had a natural fear of barracks roughhousing—fistfights, towel-slappings, and all the normal physical horseplay of young men trying hard not to show they were afraid they might not prove tough enough for the rigors of recruit training, since the first weeks of training consisted of a deliberately harsh winnowing-out process, intended to eliminate those who were weak, rebellious, or unamenable to discipline, or who simply lacked esprit de corps.

For a man who had been imprisoned by the Turks, tortured, raped, and wounded countless times, Lawrence's reaction to his hut mates at Uxbridge is strangely prim: "As they swiftly stripped for sleep a reek of body fought with beer and tobacco for the mastery of the room. . . . The horseplay turned to a rough-house: snatching of trousers, and smacks with the flat of hard hands, followed by clumsy steeplechases over the obstacle of beds which tipped or tilted. . . . Our hut-refuge was become libertine, brutal, loud-voiced, unwashed."

Of course war and danger have a certain intoxicating glamour—certainly they did to Lawrence—whereas the prospect of weeks of sodden misery in a crowded hut full of noisy young recruits does not. Hardened as Lawrence was to danger, pain, and death, he had never been to an English boarding school, an experience that might as well have been designed to create a hard, self-protective shell against the small, daily abrasions of communal living, occasional physical violence, and unwelcome intimacy. In fact, Lawrence's description of life at Uxbridge often sounds like that of a new boy away at school for the first time; for example, he notes, with alarm, that "there had been a rumour of that sinful misery, forced games," and that "breakfast and dinner were sickening, but ample."

The next day, Lawrence was once more ordered to write an essay on his birthplace (which he had not seen since he was six weeks old); was submitted to fierce questioning about where he had been during the war (he came up with a story about being interned as an enemy alien in Smyrna, by the Turks); then, after waiting for two hours with forty or fifty other men (good training for the methods of the British armed services, which are usually described as, "Hurry up, and wait!"), he was sworn in at last, and became, officially, "AC2 Ross."

He describes his hut mates as a blacksmith from Glasgow (who fails his test job), two barmen, a former captain of the King's Royal Rifles, two seamen, a naval "Marconi operator," a Great Western Railway machinist, lorry drivers, clerks, photographers, mechanics, "a fair microcosm of unemployed England." Lawrence sums up this mixed bag accurately enough, pointing out that they are not the "unemployable," the bottom of the barrel, but merely those who have lost their jobs, or their way, or had financial or woman trouble of one kind or another. At the same time, it is not Kipling's army, or the French Foreign Legion; most of the men in Lawrence's hut have a trade of some kind, and hope to pursue it, or something similar to it, once they have finished the twelve weeks of "square

bashing" (drill), "bull" (polishing and shining their kit and their surroundings until their boots, their brass, and the barracks floor gleam
like mirrors), and fatigue duties, mostly filthy, demeaning, and back-
breaking hard labor, all intended to teach the raw recruit that his time
and his body belong to the RAF. Not surprisingly, given his age and background, Lawrence was at first slow at drill, hated PT (physical training),
and had no skill at turning his brown, lusterless boots into glossy black
ones that shone like patent leather.* But like most people he found that
there were others far less competent than himself, and that once the
recruits in his hut were uniformed and put into the training program,
their camaraderie, gruff sympathy, occasional good advice, and commitment to one another made the training program more bearable. There
were no winners or losers; it was not a competitive effort and so there
was no personal gain in being better turned out than the man next to
you; the entire purpose of the program was to perfect the *unit*, not the
individual, and to turn your "flight" (as a company is called in the RAF)
into a gleaming, responsive, perfectly drilled body of men on the parade
ground.

For somebody as individualistic as Lawrence, this was not easy to
learn. Sticking it out must have required all of his admittedly formidable
self-discipline, and this makes his effort to complete every part of his
recruit training even more impressive. He wrote about it from time to time
in some detail to Air Vice-Marshal Swann, under the mistaken impression that Swann wanted to know what the life of a recruit was like, or was
interested in improving the training program. In fact, what Swann wanted
most was not to hear from him at all. "I'm not very certain of myself,"
Lawrence wrote to Swann, after his first few days, "for the crudities,
which aren't as bad as I expected, worry me far more than I expected:
and physically I can only just scrape through the days. . . . If I can get able

---

*In the RAF, as in all the British armed services, this is a long, painstaking, time-
honored process involving black Kiwi boot polish, the handle of a service spoon heated
in hot water to just the right temperature, methylated spirits, spit, and many hours of
elbow grease, with a polishing rag.

to sleep, and to eat the food, and to go through the PT I'll be all right. The present worry is 90 per cent nerves. . . . Please tell the C. A. S. [Trenchard] that I'm delighted and most grateful to him and to you for what you have done. Don't bother to keep an eye on what happens to me." It may be imagined with what dread the unfortunate Swann opened these long letters. He was convinced that no matter how well it was handled, Lawrence's enlistment would blow up in his face, and at the same time his orders from Trenchard were precisely to "keep an eye on" Lawrence, something he could hardly do from his desk in London.

As it happened, the commanding officer of RAF Uxbridge, Wing Commander Ian Malcolm Bonham-Carter, CB, OBE, without knowing who Ross was, seems to have picked him out on sight as the wrong kind of airman. In *The Mint*, Lawrence reserves his harshest language for Bonham-Carter. It goes without saying that the worst thing a recruit can do is to attract the attention of the commanding officer in any way, but Lawrence succeeded in doing so almost immediately. It might have amused Bonham-Carter to know that he and "Ross" were both Companions of the Order of the Bath, but then again, probably not. In photographs Bonham-Carter is enormously good-looking, his uniform is perfectly tailored, and his expression is severe. He had a reputation as "a strict disciplinarian," but as Marshal of the Royal Air Force Lord Sholto Douglas, who had served with him, pointed out later—when *The Mint* was finally published—a disciplinarian was exactly the kind of man who was needed to run the recruit training depot. Bonham-Carter had been wounded in the war. He lost his left leg and the use of one arm, and sustained numerous other wounds, but often refused to wear a prosthetic limb, relying on crutches instead. It may be that Lawrence's hesitancy at PT drew Bonham-Carter's attention, for the commanding officer would drive over from his house to watch the recruits doing their physical training before breakfast at dawn, and would join in despite his wounds, doing the exercises as best he could while supporting himself against the cookhouse wall with one hand. Lawrence dismissed this as "theatrical swank"; decided that since Bonham-Carter was "always resentfully in pain," he was determined that the recruits should at least be uncomfortable; and complained that his presence forced the PT instructor to drag out the exercise "to its uttermost minute." Lawrence describes the commanding officer as "only the shards of a man," but he may have been exaggerating for effect: Bonham-Carter not only did the same physical exercises as the recruits but drove his own two-seat sports car, continued to fly, and would go on to serve during World War II as "duty air commodore" in the Operations Room of RAF Fighter Command. In any case, when Lawrence's turn came for duty as Bonham-Carter's "headquarters runner," the experience was so unpleasant that during a kit inspection of one of the huts Lawrence "found himself trembling with clenched fists," repeating to himself, "I must hit him, I must," but held himself back. He describes watching the commanding officer "pulled over on his face" when his two leashed dogs ran after a cat, and the airmen standing around "silently watching him struggle" to get back on his feet, but refusing to help, muttering, " 'Let the old cunt rot.' " Lawrence adds that at Bonham-Carter's next command the airfield "was ringed with his men almost on their knees, praying he would crash."

Lawrence also attracted the attention of the drill adjutant, Breese, a former regimental sergeant major of the Brigade of Guards, for whom drill was the equivalent of a religion, and who was responsible for the training of all the recruits once they had been separated into squads. Breese lived and breathed drill, and because he was an ex-Guardsman perfection was the only standard he knew. He announced to each new batch of recruits that any of them could come "and see him privately about any worries they had," and Lawrence unwisely chose to take this literally and avail himself of the privilege. He thus broke two of the most important rules of surviving as a recruit: first, keep out of sight of officers as much as possible; and second, approach an officer only through your own NCO, and with the NCO's approval. Breese, who had no idea who Ross was, asked him if he had "woman troubles," the usual reason for an airman's asking to see the drill adjutant, and was unpleasantly surprised when Ross indignantly denied it, and said "that what he wanted was a room where he could do some writing undisturbed." On his cot at night, Lawrence had been writing the notes that would become the first part of *The Mint*, and not surprisingly he found it difficult to concentrate in a crowded, noisy hut. Breese, taken aback, replied that with 1,100 recruits in the depot it was impossible to provide each of them with a study, but that he could use the NAAFI writing room whenever he liked, on his time off. Apart from the oddness of the request, something about Lawrence's manner—a kind of lofty sense of superiority and entitlement, just one step short of insolence, and clearly inappropriate to a mere recruit—may have put Breese on his guard, and made him decide to keep his eye on AC2 Ross.

The result was an unwelcome torrent of kit inspections for Lawrence. Breese claims to have admonished him for being untidy and "consistently dirty,* for being insubordinate to his hut sergeant, for refusing to obey an order about his kit, and for being consistently late on parade," although this seems unlikely, given the fact that Lawrence was on "the crack drill squad," as Jeremy Wilson points out, and also eager to please. When Breese asked Lawrence why he was late for one parade, Lawrence replied "that he had always felt a little tired in the early morning." If so, this is the kind of clever or smart-alecky remark that might have won him the admiration of his hut mates but was bound to infuriate an officer. Breese put him up on charges several times and finally tried to have him dismissed from the RAF for insubordination, but at that point Breese was sharply warned that Ross would have to stay.

Once, when a senior officer was inspecting the hut and noticed a copy of *Niels Lyhne*, a novel by the Danish novelist J. P. Jacobsen, "in the original" among Lawrence's possessions, he asked Lawrence why on earth he had joined the air force. Lawrence replied, "I think I had a mental breakdown, Sir." This reply immediately got him put up on a charge, though it

---

*This does not necessarily mean that Lawrence was physically dirty—unlike most of his fellow recruits he devoted much time and effort, and occasional small bribes, to seeking out ways to have a hot bath as often as possible. In the RAF "dirty" can imply nothing worse than a speck of tarnish on a cap badge or a smudged fingerprint on the polished lid of a shoe polish can.

later turned out that the officer was merely interested in the presence among the recruits of a man with such an unusual level of education.*

The cumulative effect of such incidents led to exactly what Air Vice-Marshal Swann had been afraid of. First of all, it was necessary to tell Breese who "Ross" really was and warn him off; then, to Breese's fury, Swann responded to a plea from Lawrence, spared him the last four weeks at Uxbridge, and packed him off to RAF Farnborough to be trained as a photographer, without having completed his drill course. Even thirty-two years later Breese was still fulminating about what a poor recruit "Lawrence of Arabia" had been, and regretting that, because of the interference of higher authorities, he had not been able to get Lawrence discharged from the service.

The liberal use of profanity in *The Mint*, and the description of Bonham-Carter, made it impossible to publish even decades after Lawrence's death, and it therefore received altogether unmerited notoriety as a "banned book." Most readers nowadays will be unlikely to find even the unexpurgated edition particularly shocking. *The Mint* is, in fact, an odd little book. The first two-thirds are about the horrors of recruit training; the last third (which Lawrence added later) is about the joys of serving on an RAF station with aircraft, and "how different, how humane" by comparison life was at the RAF Cadet College, Cranwell, when Lawrence was there three years later as an aircraft-hand. Just as his description of life at RAF Uxbridge seems too "savage" (to use his own word), so his description of life at Cranwell seems too idyllic. The book has long passages of praise to Trenchard, which Lawrence wrote knowing very well that Trenchard would be among the first to read the manuscript. "There are

---

* Although Lawrence had a remarkable gift for languages, and according to his youngest brother, A. W. Lawrence, could pick up the gist of any language very quickly, there is no other evidence that he knew Danish well enough to read it. This may have been a case of gilding the lily, on the part of Marshal of the Royal Air Force Lord Sholto Douglas, who was a friend and contemporary of Wing Commander Bonham-Carter, and whose dyspeptic opinion of Lawrence—also expressed to this author, who edited Sholto Douglas's memoir—was that "so far as the RAF was concerned, he was scarcely more than a nuisance," deliberately creating difficulties for the junior officers under whom he served. (Sholto Douglas, *Years of Command*, New York: Simon and Schuster, 1966, 144–145.)

twenty-thousand airmen better than us between [Squad 5] and Trenchard, the pinnacle and our exemplar: but the awe of him surely encompasses us. The driving energy is his, and he drives furiously. We are content, imagining that he knows his road." This reads uncomfortably, and improbably; unless the RAF has changed a lot since 1923, it seems unlikely that recruits would sit around the stove in their hut until late in the night swapping stories in "laughing admiration" and hero-worship of Trenchard. The hallmark of the British serviceman has always been a mocking and cynical disdain for those at the top, and the passages on Trenchard in *The Mint* merely read as if Lawrence hoped to balance out the scenes at Uxbridge, which Trenchard would certainly hate, by flattering him from time to time.

There is also a passage that still has the power to shock. While Lawrence is on parade at Cranwell to mark the death of Queen Alexandra, widow of King Edward VII, he remembers a visit he once made to her, when he was a famous and decorated war hero. She was not "a Saint, a Paragon," as the chaplain now describes her, he thinks, but "an unfortunate, a long-suffering doll." Lawrence recalls her as a "mummified thing, the bird-like head cocked on one side, not artfully but by disease, the red-rimmed eyes, the enamelled face . . . her bony fingers, clashing in the tunnel of their rings." This is one of the few times in the book when he refers to his previous life as the other persona he has left behind, "Colonel Lawrence," and it is surely the cruelest passage in *The Mint*. Even today, when the attitude toward the British royal family has changed, it seems out of place, like an attack on the wrong person.

Enlistment in the RAF had not been the only thing on Lawrence's mind in 1922. He was as determined to storm the literary world as he had been to enter the RAF, and he was probably the only person to whom it would have seemed that the two ambitions were not contradictory. He had sent one set of the corrected galley proofs of *Seven Pillars of Wisdom* run off by the Oxford newspaper printers to Edward Garnett, a gifted editor who had worked closely with Joseph Conrad and championed the work of

D. H. Lawrence, Ford Maddox Ford, and John Galsworthy. Garnett was now working as a consultant for the new publishing house of Jonathan Cape. He was a sensitive and gifted reader, with a sure touch for literary quality and a first-class sales instinct (a rare combination); he was good at building careers too, and played an important role in the lives of his authors. Garnett at once wanted to publish the book, but Lawrence shied away, writing to say that Garnett was the first person to read the book—but adding that his friend the artist Eric Kennington was already reading it. He accepted Garnett's handwritten list of notes, suggestions, and corrections, thus setting in motion an elaborate and long-drawn-out process of mutual seduction, as Garnett attempted to steer him to Cape. Garnett's praise of the book was enormously welcome to Lawrence, who—as the author of a 300,000-word book on which he had spent four years of his life—thirsted for recognition and praise. He revealed to Garnett that he had already received a sizable offer, sight unseen, from an American publisher for an abridged version of 120,000 words, but had said, "Nothing doing"—although the idea of an abridged, "boy's own" version of the book in fact intrigued him. Eventually, with much patient nudging and help from Garnett, he would produce such a version: the enormously successful *Revolt in the Desert*. Lawrence, despite his protestations of naïveté, had devised an extraordinarily successful way of dealing with book publishers: allowing them to read his book on the condition that they couldn't publish it. Similarly, he would later create a tidal wave of publicity for *Seven Pillars of Wisdom* among the public at large by ensuring that it was a book everyone wanted to read, but nobody could buy. Certainly his correspondence with Garnett is remarkably shrewd; he demonstrates a practical knowledge of book publishing economics while at the same time insisting that the book isn't for sale.

In the meantime, Lawrence had set out in pursuit of bigger fish than Garnett. Taking advantage of his one brief meeting with Bernard Shaw, Lawrence had written to ask Shaw to read *Seven Pillars of Wisdom*. His letter was a perfect mix of flattery and modesty: "I'd like you to read it . . . partly because you are you: partly because I may profit by your reading it, if I have a chance to talk to you soon after, before you have got over it." Nothing could have been more tactfully phrased, or more carefully baited, to lure Shaw into reading *Seven Pillars of Wisdom*; nor did it hurt that Lawrence, despite his modesty, was himself a celebrity. Shaw's ego and vanity were world-class—indeed by wittily mocking his own weaknesses, he had made himself ever more famous, and by 1922 he was at the height of his formidable powers, both intellectual and theatrical. Perhaps more important, he had succeeded—as two previous Anglo-Irish playwrights, Richard Brinsley Sheridan and Oscar Wilde, had done—in turning himself into a "character," whose doings and sayings were constantly publicized, and who was given wide license to say outrageous things because he was Irish and a self-proclaimed genius. As a theatrical reviewer he had been the talk of London for his wit and intelligence, and as a playwright he was, like Sheridan and Wilde, a huge success from the beginning, often confronting on the stage serious social problems that approached the limit of the lord chamberlain's tolerance (the Lord Chamberlain's Office was, until 1968, the official censor of the British stage). Queen Victoria's lady-in-waiting is supposed to have said, as she emerged from the theater after a performance of Shaw's *Caesar and Cleopatra*, shaking her head in disapproval, "How different, how very different, from the home life of our own dear Queen." Fiercely argumentative and intolerant of any opinion but his own, Shaw was the best known of the Fabian Socialists—he outshone Sidney and Beatrice Webb, with their compulsive gathering of statistics, and H. G. Wells, despite Wells's enormously popular novels, as the most articulate spokesman for socialism and social reform in Britain.

Shaw signified his willingness to read the book, so one copy was sent to him, and Lawrence, like any other author, chafed while waiting for his reaction. In the meantime, Lawrence had sent another copy to his friend Vyvyan Richards, who read it more promptly, and wrote a most confusing letter back about it: "It seems to me that an attempted work of art may be so much more splendid for its very broken imperfection revealing the man so intimately." This was probably meant as praise—at least Lawrence took it that way—though on its face it seems to mean that the book's faults revealed Lawrence's strengths. Lawrence replied at length, to say that he knew it was a good book, but felt that "it was too big for me: too big for most writers, I think. It's rather in the titan class: books written at tiptoe, with a strain that dislocates the writer, and exhausts the reader out of sympathy." This is a more perceptive judgment than Vyvyan Richards's, but luckily for Lawrence, he was a first-class writer about battle, and very good with the small, human dramas of war. When he stops trying to achieve the effect of a masterpiece, and lets his gift for description show through, his work rises to a level of its own, matched by no other nonfiction book on war in the twentieth century. In any case, Richards's praise, however qualified, was not what Lawrence was waiting for—he was awaiting Shaw's, which was distressingly slow in coming.

Doughty's *Arabia Deserta* was also on Lawrence's mind. He felt a great debt and affection toward Charles Doughty, and had been instrumental in getting the Medici Society and Jonathan Cape to bring that difficult and sometimes impenetrable classic, more often admired than read, back into print by agreeing to write an introduction for it—one of his best short pieces, and well worth reading for its own sake. Now, though he was a mere airman in training, Lawrence continued the campaign he had begun to obtain for Doughty a Civil List pension, reaching out to the prime minister, David Lloyd George. He wrote to Doughty, "Of the present Ministry three or four are Fellows of All Souls, and most of the others are friends of mine. The Duke of Devonshire, and Lord Salisbury, and Amery, and Wood and three or four others would be glad to serve you in any way you wished." In this generous service, he was successful. Doughty, who was old—and mostly forgotten and impoverished until Lawrence took up his cause—was overwhelmed by Lawrence's hard work on his behalf; and it says much for Lawrence's courage and determination that he used none of these friendships on his own behalf, but simply went on, not so much "solitary in the ranks" as, for the moment, *invisible* in the ranks.

But not for much longer.

—

Edward Garnett, despite Lawrence's reluctance to allow *Seven Pillars of Wisdom* to be published, was working painstakingly on the abridgment. This idea tempted Lawrence, both because it would remove from the book the more controversial passages he did not want the general public to read, and because it would almost certainly produce enough money to enable him to print a deluxe and very limited edition of the full text for his friends—something that Gertrude Bell had begged him to do while they were together in Paris during the Peace Conference.

In the meantime, Lawrence had been posted to RAF Farnborough, thanks to Air Vice-Marshal Swann's intervention, and arrived there on November 7, after a brief leave, which he cut short by two days, so anxious was he to get into the "real" air force. Farnborough was indeed the real air force—it was, among other things, home to several squadrons, and it contained research and experimental facilities and the RAF school of photography.

If there was one specialty in the RAF for which Lawrence was perfectly suited, it was photography. His father had not only taught him everything there was to know about photography, but made sure that he had the best and latest equipment; and with his natural interest in technology and crafts of any kind, Lawrence quickly became an expert. Some of the photographs Lawrence took in the Hejaz, during the war, are amazing—they belong among the classic images of warfare by photographers such as Robert Capa and David Douglas Duncan, and are all the more remarkable because Lawrence was a combatant, not a photojournalist, and because his equipment was by modern standards bulky and slow. His photographs of Feisal's encampment at dawn and of the Bedouin advancing toward Aqaba are still the two most emblematic and famous pictures of the Arab Revolt. In addition, Lawrence was one of the pioneers in the use of aerial photography in mapmaking and military intelligence. He devised his own system of laying out aerial photographs in a grid pattern to use them as the basis for a map, and taught pilots how to take the pictures he needed. Lawrence could have taught the class in

photography at RAF Farnborough—it is unlikely that any of the instructors there knew as much as he did, or had even a small fraction of his
practical experience. Trenchard was not wrong—Lawrence's refusal to
accept a commission in the RAF deprived the air force of the opportunity of learning something from a master of irregular warfare, and from
one of the few commanders who understood how to use aircraft to support ground troops or how to make practical use in the field of aerial
photography.

Still, the move to Farnborough was a happy one—so happy that it may
have increased Lawrence's confidence in the RAF to the point where he
became incautious. Here there was no square bashing; the NCOs were
mostly instructors; the airmen were either learning or carrying out their
"trades," as the RAF calls its different specialties. The predominant noise
on the station was that of aircraft engines warming up, not the yells of
drill corporals, the crash of boots on the parade ground, or the sharp,
metallic clatter of hundreds of men performing rifle drill. During his
leave Lawrence had purchased a motorcycle, a secondhand Triumph
with a sidecar—a new stage in the lifelong love affair with motorcycles
that would end only with his death. For the moment his duties at Farnborough were anything but onerous, a fact which very shortly got him
into serious trouble.

The November photography class had already begun, and in the usual
rigid way of the air force it was considered impossible for Lawrence to
join late and catch up with his fellow students, so he was put down for the
next class, which began in January. The notion of wasting an airman's
time was not one that occurred to anyone in authority in the RAF—his
time *belonged* to the RAF, to be wasted or used as his superiors and the
station schedule determined. For Lawrence, however, sweeping floors or
emptying the grate of the adjutant's stove while everybody else was
studying photography was insupportable. He wrote to Air Vice-Marshal
Swann, partly to thank Swann for getting him out of RAF Uxbridge early,
and partly to ask Swann to get him into the November class, or even an
earlier one, since, as Lawrence pointed out, "I'm already as good as the

men passing out. My father, one of the pioneer photographers, taught me before I was four years old." This was a mild exaggeration, but the letter exudes a certain overconfidence, as if Lawrence were writing to a family retainer rather than an air marshal, and can only have increased Swann's dislike of his role.

In the meantime, since nobody in authority in the RAF likes to see an airman sitting around doing nothing, Lawrence "was appointed to the Adjutant's office as an orderly," running messages and cleaning the office first thing in the morning—menial but not demeaning duty, for an airman without a trade. The adjutant of the photography school, Flight Lieutenant Charles Findlay, who seems to have been a decent sort, did not pay much attention to his new orderly: Lawrence did not seem to him in any way out of the ordinary. At some point Lawrence must have signaled his disapproval of this waste of his time to Swann, however, for about three weeks later the station commander, Wing Commander W. J. Y. Guilfoyle, called Findlay into his office to say that Air Vice-Marshal Swann had called to ask "why A/c2 Ross is not engaged in photographic training?"

Findlay began to explain that the pupils arrived "in penny packets," and had to be kept busy until there were enough of them to form a class, but the commanding officer cut him off short—he had already explained all that to Air Vice-Marshal Swann, but Swann "was not at all sympathetic," and insisted that "Ross's training must begin at once."

The two men were "frankly perplexed." "Who is this Ross? What's he like?" the commanding officer asked, and the adjutant suggested that he might like to see the airman himself. Ross was sent for, on the pretext of giving him a message to deliver. As Findlay described him, "His blue eyes were set in a long, finely chiseled face. His jaw was square. But the most outstanding features were his long, sensitive fingers." He was trim, erect, short, and while crisply respectful, his face conveyed none of the awe in which a recruit AC2 might be expected to hold his commanding officer on seeing him at close range. On the contrary, Ross gave the faint impression of being in command himself.

Once he had saluted and gone, the commanding officer "turned to the Adjutant with a look of amazement."

" 'Findlay! Do you know who I think he is? Lawrence!'

'Lawrence?'

'Yes, Lawrence of Arabia! I saw him once in Cairo early in the war, and this airman looks uncommonly like him.' "

The two officers had no idea what to do next. Guilfoyle's suspicion that AC2 Ross was Colonel Lawrence left him in the uncomfortable position of feeling that Air Vice-Marshal Swann had pulled a fast one on him, or had so little confidence in him that he had not seen fit to inform him of the real identity of one of his own airmen. Since he didn't know what else to do, Guilfoyle ordered Findlay to start Ross's instruction as soon as possible, even if he was in a special class of one, and to keep an eye on him for any clues as to whether he was really Lawrence. Lawrence immediately provided the clues. Recruits were given a mathematics test and were supposed to hand in their worksheets along with the answers to the problems. All Lawrence's answers were correct, but he turned in no worksheets. When reprimanded by the instructor, he said that he had worked them out in his head, and when given another problem, he worked that one out in his head too, and immediately wrote down the correct answer. The instructor in optics complained to Findlay that Ross knew more about the subject than he did, and the same thing happened when he was put in the "Neg. Room." As may be imagined, this did not make him popular with the instructors, and it added to the mystery surrounding Ross's special treatment. Perhaps Lawrence would have been wiser to feign a certain degree of ignorance, rather than, to put it crudely, showing off.

He made matters worse by replying flippantly to reprimands about his turn-out on guard duty, and by answering the orderly officer "in a foreign language," presumably Arabic, since the orderly officer would surely have recognized French; all this was bound to increase curiosity. It seems clear that Lawrence was suffering from overconfidence, brought on by the ease with which he had prodded Swann into getting him into a special class, and perhaps also by good news on the literary front.

For while Lawrence was astonishing (and provoking) his instructors, Edward Garnett was progressing rapidly with the abridgment of *Seven Pillars of Wisdom*. Lawrence was beginning, partly because of Garnett's shrewd knowledge of how to handle authors, to come around to approving the idea of an abridged volume of 120,000 to 150,000 words, preferably the former. Neither he nor Garnett had any doubt that the book would sell, so Lawrence was relieved of his worries about running up a considerable overdraft for an AC2 to pay the artists who were making the drawings and the paintings for the limited edition of the complete text, to which he was becoming more and more committed.

At the same time, his approach to Shaw had paid off in a most surprising fashion. At the end of October, impatient at having heard nothing, Lawrence wrote a brilliantly self-depreciatory little note to the great man:

> Dear Mr. Shaw,
>
> I am afraid you are rather making a labour of it, or you don't want to tell me that it's rubbish. I don't want to bore you (nice of me!), and if you say it's rot I'll agree with you & cackle with pleasure at finding my judgment doubled.
>
> Please laugh & chuck it.
Yours sincerely,
T. E. Lawrence

Unlike most such letters, this one very soon produced a lengthy reply, urging Lawrence to be patient and revealing that Charlotte Shaw had read the book with great admiration and had urged her husband to read it—more than urged, in fact. In his absence—he was "road tubthumping round England" for the forthcoming general election—she read every word of the awkward six-pound book, and on Shaw's return "she began ecstatically reading passages of it aloud to him." Shaw's letter to Lawrence, if allowance is made for the somewhat hectoring style he used to everyone, was thoughtful, encouraging, and full of advice, much of which Lawrence was to ignore, and it clearly opened up to Lawrence the possibility of friendship with the Shaws.

Of course forming a friendship with "G.B.S." was like letting the proverbial camel stick its nose inside the tent. Shaw was bossy, fussy, opinionated, indefatigable, irascible, determined not only to offer his friends advice but to ensure that it was followed in every detail. He was overwhelmingly generous with his time, despite his widespread commitments—a workload that would kill a horse; a firm determination to introduce to Britain not only socialism but a total reform of everything from English grammar, punctuation, and spelling to the way the British dressed, ate, and educated their children; and campaigning vigorously for such principles as wearing woolen garments next to the skin instead of cotton, total vegetarianism, and a radically different relationship between the sexes. On many of these subjects, Shaw sounded like a crank; on others, he wrote some of his greatest plays. But in any case his genius; the unstoppable flow of his eloquence; his sheer output of books, plays, letters, and pamphlets; and above all his willingness to argue with anyone about anything until whoever it was gave in out of exhaustion— all this made him seem to many like the Nietzschean superman improbably manifesting himself in England, as a fiercely bearded Anglo-Irishman.

The fact that Charlotte Shaw had read the book and liked it mattered very much indeed. The Shaws had what might best be described as an odd marriage: as noted earlier, from the very beginning they had agreed not to have sex. Charlotte had a deep-seated fear of sex and was determined never to have a child. Though it pained her often and deeply, it was part of the understanding between them that Shaw could have affairs, mostly with actresses, provided he did so with a certain amount of discretion. They got along very well together—Charlotte was wealthy and cultivated; they enjoyed each other's company; and they respected each other's opinions. Her enthusiasm for Lawrence's enormous book meant something to Shaw, and her determination that he must read it himself was not something he would ignore. Like Lawrence she was afflicted by "a fearful streak of conscience and sense of duty, complicated by a sensitiveness that is nothing less than a disease." In this Charlotte also resembled Lawrence's mother, who certainly had a "streak of conscience" and a fierce "sense of duty," though without Charlotte's "sensitiveness" or Charlotte's essential shyness, which was in such sharp contrast to Shaw's extrovert nature and his phenomenal capacity for rudeness when he chose to inflict it on people.

By mid-November, Lawrence had told enough people about his enlistment in the RAF to make further secrecy unlikely. Garnett knew, and this was probably safe enough, since he was that rarest of book editors, one who didn't gossip about his authors. But Lawrence would very shortly let Shaw know, and this was riskier. Also, for reasons best known to himself, Lawrence also informed his friend and admirer R. D. Blumenfeld, the editor of the *Daily Express*. Although Blumenfeld seems to have been uncommonly discreet for a newspaper editor, the *Daily Express*—Lord Beaverbrook's sensationalist daily—was not a place where any secret was likely to be kept for long. Lawrence had written for this newspaper when he was campaigning to make the British government live up to its promises to Feisal, and had developed a certain respect for Blumenfeld in the process. He may too, like many celebrities, have believed that if you fed the beast the occasional tidbit, it wouldn't bite you, but if so, he misunderstood the ethics of Fleet Street. Writing to Blumenfeld with the news that he was joining the RAF and adding, "This letter has got to be indiscreet. . . . Do keep this news to yourself," was either naive or self-destructive, or possibly both. Blumenfeld responded, from a nursing home where he was recovering from surgery, by offering Lawrence a job, possibly writing about British policy in the Middle East. Lawrence perhaps unwisely declined, in a breezy, personal letter that could only lead to trouble if it got into the wrong hands: "Your offer is a generous and kind one: and you will think me quixotic to refuse it: but I ran away here partly to escape the responsibility of head-work. . . . No, please don't publish my eclipse. It will be common news one day, but the later the better for my peace in the ranks." Some of Lawrence's biographers, including his authorized biographer, Jeremy Wilson, suggest that he consciously or subconsciously was seeking to bring to an end his service in the RAF, and of course this is possible; but one must bear in mind that he had only to go to a public telephone and call Air Vice-Marshal Swann, or send a postcard to Trenchard, to be released from the service.

Perhaps he wanted to achieve that end without having to bring it about himself, by forcing Trenchard and Swann to make the decision for him; on the other hand, one must set against this the fact that Lawrence, once he was discharged from the RAF, almost immediately enlisted in the army, then transferred back to the RAF as soon as he could—so clearly the military life, with its built-in foundation of discipline, order, and austerity, appealed to him. It seems more likely that Lawrence was suffering from what we would now call mood swings, perhaps as a result of his wartime stress, and that he rebounded from a deep depression and a sense of helplessness, which had engulfed him after he left the Colonial Office, to a dizzy height of overconfidence in his ability to eat his cake and have it too. After all, he had persuaded Swann to intervene on his behalf twice, he was on the brink of combining a military and a writing career, and he seemed to have everything he wanted—always a dangerous moment.

At the beginning of December Lawrence apparently made up his mind to publish the abridgment of *Seven Pillars of Wisdom*, informing Garnett that he in turn could inform Jonathan Cape of this decision, and selecting the literary agency Curtis Brown to represent him. Their task was obviously complicated by the fact that the idea of abridging the book had first been suggested to him by Frank Doubleday, the American publisher. By the first week in December Lawrence was already deep in negotiation with Cape—like so many authors, not letting the right hand know what the left one was doing, since he should have allowed Curtis Brown to do all this for him.

At this point Shaw's immense enthusiasm for the book, which he was still reading, was clear enough, to Lawrence's relief: "I know enough about it now to feel puzzled as to what is to be done with it," Shaw wrote to him. "One step is clear enough. The Trustees of the British Museum have lots of sealed writings to be opened in a hundred years. . . . You say you have four or five copies of your magnissimum opus, At least a couple should be sealed and deposited in Bloomsbury and New York."* Shaw

---

*He was referring to the British Museum Library and to the New York Public Library.

was concerned about several problems of libel (given his own writing, this was a subject he was familiar with), and suggested that an abridgment, leaving out the potentially libelous passages, would be a good idea. Lawrence must have glowed at Shaw's description of his book as a "magnissimum opus." And he was pleased that the great man not only took the book seriously, but favored an abridgment, which, between Lawrence and Garnett, was already moving forward quickly.

Between this whirl of correspondence, his motorcycle, his photography course, and the success of his campaign to get Doughty a pension, Lawrence may not have taken notice of the fact that reporters were appearing at RAF Farnborough asking questions about him. Not surprisingly, some were from the *Daily Express*, but there were also some from the biggest rival of the *Express*, Lord Northcliffe's *Daily Mail*—all the big Fleet Street dailies had spies in each other's editorial offices. On December 16, Wing Commander Guilfoyle, for whom Lawrence had already developed a strong but possibly undeserved dislike, was already writing to Air Vice-Marshal Swann that reporters had interviewed two of his junior officers, and on learning that "Colonel Lawrence" was unknown in the officers' mess, had started to wait outside the camp gate to waylay airmen as they came and went. "Do you think," Guilfoyle wrote stiffly, but not unreasonably, "that all this conjecture and talk is in the best interest of discipline?" Clearly, it was not, and there was worse to come.

Lawrence, in the meantime, found himself in another dilemma, this one at least not of his own making. Filled with enthusiasm for *Seven Pillars of Wisdom*, and acting with his usual conviction that he knew what was best for everybody, Shaw had brought the subject of the book up with his own publisher, Constable, urging the two senior partners to go after it boldly. Never one for understatement, Shaw, as he wrote to Lawrence, told them, "Why in thunder didn't you secure it? It's the greatest book in the world." Shaw urged Lawrence to open negotiations directly with Constable as soon as possible, with a view to publishing an edited version of the full text first, and an abridged version later (exactly the reverse of what Lawrence wanted to do), and he bullied the two senior partners of Constable into having a talk with Edward Garnett.

This put the fat in the fire, since Garnett had already discussed the book with Cape, whose reader he was, and discussions were already taking place between Cape and Raymond Savage, Lawrence's literary agent at Curtis Brown. Lawrence, whose intention was to bring out the abridged text first, and who had already authorized Garnett to bring the project to Cape, had to inform Shaw that all this was going on, and Shaw was, predictably, very put out. One reason for Lawrence's enthusiasm for the firm of Jonathan Cape was that both Cape and his partner G. Wren Howard were intensely interested in producing handsome books. Their ideas about book design, layout, and typography were less extreme than Lawrence's, but they were more likely than Constable to produce something close to what would please him. Since Cape is now a distinguished institution in British book publishing, not unlike Knopf in New York, it will surprise those who know anything about the publishing business that Shaw thundered back with a warning that Cape and Howard were "a brace of thoroughgoing modern ruffians," and that they probably lacked the capital to produce the book. He added, for good measure, on the subject of Lawrence's enlistment in the RAF, that "Nelson, slightly cracked after his whack on the head in the battle of the Nile, coming home and insisting on being placed at the tiller of a canal barge, and on being treated as nobody in particular, would have embarrassed the Navy far less," a comment that was undoubtedly correct. "You are evidently a very dangerous man," he wrote to Lawrence, with undisguised approval; "most men who are any good are. . . . I wonder what I will decide to do with you."

The truth was that Lawrence felt himself already committed to Cape, and his agent was already in discussion with Cape and Howard about the contract, so Shaw's unexpected charge into the middle of these negotiations put Lawrence in an embarrassing position with Cape, while Shaw, of course, felt foolish at having urged his own publishers to go after a book that was already as good as sold to somebody else. Over the years, this would become a pattern in the relationship between Lawrence and Shaw, yet Shaw, after an initial outburst, always forgave the younger man. From the outset, Shaw adopted the attitude of an exasperated and indulgent parent toward a wayward, difficult child. As if to demonstrate this, Shaw not only read all 300,000-plus words of the manuscript (Shaw estimated its length at 460,000 words, but this seems excessive); he also made copious, detailed notes, suggestions, and corrections, including a "virtuoso" essay on the use of the colon, semicolon, and dash, and the proposal that Lawrence drop the first chapter of the book and start with the second, which Lawrence eventually accepted, though he sensibly ignored most of the rest.

By the time Lawrence received this letter, however, his presence at RAF Farnborough had made the front page of the *Daily Express* in big headlines:

"UNCROWNED KING" AS PRIVATE SOLDIER

LAWRENCE OF ARABIA
Famous War Hero Becomes a Private

SEEKING PEACE
OPPORTUNITY TO WRITE A BOOK

The article inside was fairly innocuous by the standards of the *Express*, though written in its inimitable hyperbolic style—"Colonel Lawrence, archaeologist, Fellow of All Souls, and king-maker, has lived a more romantic existence than any man of the time. Now he is a private soldier." The next day a long and more detailed follow-up piece named him as AC2 Ross, placed him at RAF Farnborough, and gave details of his daily schedule, a sure sign that somebody had been talking to the *Express*'s reporter. Lawrence would afterward put the blame on the junior officers, rather than his fellow airmen, and say that one of them sold the story to the *Express* for £30 (more than $2,000 in contemporary terms), but this number sounds suspiciously like Judas's thirty pieces of silver, and in any case Blumenfeld was already onto the story. To put this in perspective: by 1923 Lawrence was Britain's most famous war hero, and a media celebrity on a scale that until then had been unimagined. It was as if Princess Diana had vanished from her home and had been discovered by the press enlisted in the ranks of the RAF as Aircraftwoman Spencer, doing drill, washing her own undies, and living in a hut with a dozen or more other

airwomen. Every newspaper now, from the most serious to the most sensational, rushed to catch up with the *Express*, briefly turning the area
outside the camp gates into a mob scene of reporters and photographers.

Trenchard and Swann were appalled, but since Trenchard did not
want to show that the clamor of the press could move him, he stuck to his
guns for the moment. Lawrence's "mates" took turns fooling the photographers by hiding their faces with their caps while entering or leaving the
camp; and Guilfoyle repeatedly pressed Swann to remove Lawrence,
earning Lawrence's disapproval. Despite that, Lawrence became friendly
enough with the adjutant, Flight Lieutenant Findlay, who was more sympathetic to his plight than the commanding officer. Findlay noted that
Lawrence was genuinely "keen" on photography, and eager to get on with
his course, but was "unreasonably" resentful at having to perform menial
duties and camp routine—an indication that Lawrence had not yet fully
understood what life was like at the bottom of the ranks. Findlay asked
him "why he had recorded 'Nil' on his Service papers in respect of the
item 'Previous Service,' " to which Lawrence replied jesuitically that John
Hume Ross had no "previous service." Much later—indeed, not until June
1958—Findlay recorded his impression of Lawrence. "Participating in
the life of the Royal Air Force was only a partial solution to his problem
at that time, and he appeared to be still trying to shake off something.
For what it is worth, a note I made at the time reads: 'I am convinced that
some quality departed from Lawrence before he became an RAF recruit.
Lawrence of Arabia had died.' The man with whom I conversed seemed
but the shadow of the Lawrence who was picked up by this whirlwind
of events to become the driving force of Arab intervention in the war. . . .
It was difficult to believe Ross was the same man. The only satisfactory
explanation must be that he was suffering from some form of exhaustion,
that the hypersensitive man had partially succumbed to the rough and
tumble of war . . . that he was . . . for the time being at least . . . a personality less intense."

This was a sympathetic but entirely incorrect reading of Lawrence's
character, though it was not out of line with what Lawrence himself pro-

fessed to believe—that he was no longer "Lawrence of Arabia," and was in the process of becoming someone else. One of his reasons for writing *Seven Pillars of Wisdom* had been precisely to put that whole experience behind him once and for all. Findlay refers to Lawrence's "assumption of mental leadership" as unsettling, as was his occasional resumption of the commanding role, which is probably what prompted Shaw to call him "a dangerous man." Findlay, even thirty-five years after the event, underrated his man.

Lawrence often made people uneasy, as if there were two separate personalities—the meek airman and the daring colonel—contending for control within him. Beatrice Webb, the astute and redoubtable Fabian social reformer, who together with her husband Sidney was among Shaw's closest friends, described Lawrence disapprovingly after meeting him as "an accomplished poseur with glittering eyes." Several people felt that Lawrence was a bad influence over Shaw, rather than vice versa (the majority view). "Already by the beginning of 1923," Michael Holroyd wrote in his magisterial four-volume biography of Shaw, "Shaw was advising Lawrence to 'get used to the limelight,' as he himself had done. Later he came to realize that Lawrence was one of the most paradoxically conspicuous men of the century. The function of both their public personalities was to lose an old self and discover a new. Lawrence had been illegitimate; Shaw had doubted his legitimacy. Both were the sons of dominant mothers and experienced difficulties in establishing their masculinity. The Arab Revolt, which gave Lawrence an ideal theatre of action, turned him into Luruns Bey, Prince of Damascus and most famously Lawrence of Arabia. 'There is no end to your Protean tricks . . . ,' " Shaw wrote to him. " 'What is your game really?' " This was a question Lawrence was careful not to answer, then or later.

It is revealing that Holroyd refers to Arabia as "an ideal theatre of action" for Lawrence, because Shaw himself, the supreme man of the theater of the twentieth century, seemed to believe that Lawrence's wartime self was a role that he could drop as quickly as he had picked it up, not recognizing that with Lawrence, as with himself, the role had taken over the man. "Bernard Shaw" (he disliked the name George, which reminded him of his drunken father) was an equally brilliant role, but it was not one Shaw could take off when he went home and resume the next day for the entertainment of his admirers. Neither he nor Lawrence was an actor who could change roles every night and twice on matinee days; like it or not, Shaw had over time *become* the role he had created for himself: the unorthodox, testy, argumentative agent provocateur and gadfly of British life and conventions, an amazing presence who combined some of the attributes of Shakespeare with those of *Monty Python's Flying Circus.* Only his death—in 1950 at the age of ninety-four—would release him from this role.

So it was with Lawrence. He could struggle against the role he had invented; hide in the ranks of the RAF or the army to escape from it; and attempt to sublimate it into meekness, modesty, and silence—but the powerful chin, the "glittering" bright blue eyes, and the hands, at once beautiful and very strong (as Findlay shrewdly noticed), gave him away even in the drabbest of uniforms. He was *not* a different man after the war, "a personality less intense," to quote Findlay. His personality, on the contrary, was remarkably consistent. His whole life had been, in a sense, a training program for heroism on the grand scale; the war had merely provided an opportunity for Lawrence to fulfill his destiny. His intense will and his determination to have things his own way were always remarkable. He had methodically pushed himself beyond his physical limits, as a child and as a youth long before the war. He had carefully honed his strength and his courage, forced himself to a lifelong repression of his own sexuality, punished himself for every temptation toward what other men would have regarded as normal impulses. Since boyhood his life had been a triumph of repression, a deliberate, calculated assault on his own senses. He would always remain, however reluctantly, a combination of hero and genius: "a dangerous man," indeed.

Only a day after the follow-up story in the *Express,* the rival *Daily Mail* published a story about Cape's negotiations to buy the rights to *Seven Pillars of Wisdom,* hardly a surprising leak, given the porous nature of book publishing. This news further alarmed the Air Ministry and the secretary of state for air, Sir Samuel Hoare, who had not been enthusiastic about having Lawrence join the RAF under an assumed name in the first place, and whose reservations now were vindicated, putting Trenchard in an awkward position. As for the commanding officer and the junior officers at RAF Farnborough, they now faced the difficulties of giving orders to a celebrity who was also the author of what would surely be a best-selling and widely debated book, a literary event of the first order.

Until this point, Lawrence's writing had not been a concern. The existence of *Seven Pillars of Wisdom* was known only within the limited circle of his friends. The public knew nothing about it, or about his intention to write a book describing the RAF "from the inside." Now both books were news, and big news at that. The heart of the problem Sir Samuel Hoare and Air Chief Marshal Trenchard faced was not just that Lawrence had made news but that he now *was* news. He no longer had to *do* anything to produce headlines.

Unfortunately, Hoare and Trenchard were not the only people this news story took by surprise. Lawrence's letter to Bernard Shaw explaining that he had decided to take his book to Jonathan Cape had not arrived by the time Shaw read the story in the *Mail*, and he was predictably outraged and baffled. Despite this initial reaction, however, he had calmed down by the time he responded to Lawrence (enclosing the clipping from the *Mail*): "The cat being now let out of the bag, presumably by Jonathan Cape with your approval, I cannot wait to finish the book before giving you my opinion and giving it strong. IT MUST BE PUBLISHED IN ITS ENTIRETY UNABRIDGED. . . . I REPEAT THE WHOLE WORK MUST BE PUBLISHED. If Cape is not prepared to undertake that, he is not your man, whatever your engagements to him may be. If he has advanced you any money give it back to him (borrowing it from me if necessary), unless he has undertaken to proceed in the grand manner."

Shaw had completely reversed himself on the subject of the abridgment, and now thought *Seven Pillars of Wisdom* should be published complete, perhaps in several volumes. He renewed his criticism of Cape in vehement terms, and had Lawrence cared to parse his letter carefully, revealed that he still had not finished reading the book, and was relying at least in good part on Charlotte's enthusiasm. Referring to the ten years he had spent on "the managing committee of the Society of Authors," Shaw pointed out that "there is no bottom to the folly and business incompetence of authors or to the unscrupulousness of publishers." As if all this were not alarming, Charlotte wrote an impassioned letter, the first of many: "How is it *conceivable, imaginable* that a man who could write the *Seven Pillars* can have any doubts about it? If you don't know it is 'a great book' what is the use of anyone telling you so. . . . I devoured the book from cover to cover. . . . I could not stop. I drove G.B.S. almost mad by insisting on reading him special bits when he was deep in something else. I am an old woman, old enough at any rate to be your mother. . . . But I have never read anything like this: I don't believe anything really like it has been written before. . . . Your book must be published as a whole. Don't you see that?"

Shaw himself wrote again a few days later, blending, as was his way, advice with abuse: "Like all heroes, and I must add, all idiots, you greatly exaggerate your power of moulding the universe to your personal convictions. . . . It is useless to protest that Lawrence is not your real name. That will not save you. . . . You masqueraded as Lawrence and didn't keep quiet: and now Lawrence you will be to the end of your days. . . . Lawrence may be as great a nuisance to you sometimes as G.B.S. is to me, or as Frankenstein found the man he manufactured; but you created him, and must now put up with him as best you can." He urged Lawrence to "get used to the limelight," and, so far as the book was concerned, reminded him that Constable was not only "keen" on it, but had "perhaps more capital than Cape," adding forcefully that it was a duty to publish the book unabridged.

Even before this barrage of correspondence reached Lawrence he had decided to give up on the abridgment of *Seven Pillars of Wisdom*, and to renege on his understanding with Cape—a decision reinforced when the chief of the air staff himself made an unprecedented visit to the camp, to warn Lawrence "that his position in the RAF was becoming untenable." Trenchard tried to soften the blow, telling Lawrence that he was "an unusual sort of person, inevitably embarrassing to a CO," but Lawrence disagreed, and felt that if Guilfoyle were a bigger man, he could ignore Lawrence's "lurid past," and treat him as an average airman. One result of all the publicity was that Lawrence tended to be treated in camp as if he were an exotic exhibit in a zoo, rather than an ordinary airman learning a trade, or so he felt.

Lawrence took Trenchard's visit to mean that he could not publish anything so long as he remained in the RAF, and he wrote to inform Cape of this. By now he had too much at stake to risk being discharged from the RAF: friendships; work that interested him; his powerful, glittering Brough "Superior" motorcycle, the Rolls-Royce or Bentley of motorcycles, with which he had replaced the more modest Triumph, handmade, idiosyncratic, powerful, precision-engineered, and very fast; even his blue uniform, sharply altered by the camp tailor to fit tightly like that of an "old sweat" or an NCO. Lawrence, it must be remembered, at the age of thirty-four had no home of his own, no family of his own, no lover, and almost no possessions; his only abode was a borrowed attic room in London, so to an extraordinary degree the RAF had become his life. The barracks, the parade ground, and the mess were all the home he had, or expected to have. The relationship between Lawrence and the RAF was neither reasonable nor explicable to civilians like Shaw—it was a love affair, albeit one-sided. He was desperate not to give all that up, and therefore decided to forgo publishing the book in any form for the time being.

Jeremy Wilson points out that the Shaws were partly responsible for this decision. It of course was exactly the opposite of what they had hoped to achieve, but by insisting that the book should be published in full, not as an abridgment, they had increased Lawrence's doubts on the subject. Certainly Lawrence might have wondered if his newfound friendship with the Shaws had been worth the price he had paid for it so far—but it may be too that for a man in Lawrence's fragile state of anxiety and emotional exhaustion, the pressure from all sides was simply too much for him to take. Not only was it more advice than Lawrence could cope with, but much of it was contradictory: the Shaws were pushing him to publish the full book, Trenchard was warning him that *any* book might bring about his dismissal from the air force, and on the sidelines his agent (Savage), his prospective publisher (Cape), and his editor (Garnett) all urged him to proceed at once with the abridgment. In the circumstances, it was understandable that Lawrence sought some security and peace of mind by giving up the book for the moment, but ironically, this did him no good at all. By the middle of January, Sir Samuel Hoare had reached the decision, as he later put it, that "the position, which had been extremely delicate even when it was shrouded in secrecy, became untenable when it was exposed. The only possible course was to discharge Airman Ross." Lawrence was abruptly sent on leave, then discharged, though not without protest: it began to dawn on Lawrence that he was losing not only the chance to publish the abridged book, which would have kept him in comfort, but his place in the RAF as well.

Flight Lieutenant Findlay was given the unwelcome task of breaking the bad news to him. Lawrence went to a small country hotel at Frensham, near Farnborough, "well-known for its large pond and bird life." From there, he wrote to Sir Samuel Hoare asking to be given the reason for his discharge. Trenchard replied on Hoare's behalf with a sympathetic personal letter. "As you know, I always think it is foolish to give reasons," Trenchard wrote, pointing out that once Lawrence was identified in the air force "as Colonel Lawrence, instead of Air Mechanic Ross," both he and the officers "were put in a very difficult position."

Before receiving Trenchard's letter, Lawrence had written to his friend T. B. Marson, Trenchard's personal assistant, asking to be given a second chance. He was still sure that he had "played up at Farnborough, and did good, rather than harm, to the fellows in the camp there with me," but this, of course, was part of the problem. Lawrence was still playing the role, even if unconsciously, of a leader of men, and the last thing that Guilfoyle or any other commanding officer wanted was one airman acting as a role model to his fellow airmen.

Trenchard moved swiftly (and perhaps mercifully) to put an end to whatever hopes Lawrence may still have had of being readmitted to the service, offering him a commission as an armored car officer, a job where his experience with and enthusiasm for armored cars would have been an asset, but Lawrence declined. He did not want a commission, and would not accept one. He returned to his attic above Baker's office in Barton Street, Westminster, and resumed his frugal life, to look for something to replace the RAF.

He was not short of friends to search out jobs for him. Leo Amery, now first lord of the admiralty, tried without success to find Lawrence a quiet job as a storekeeper at some remote naval station, and failing that as a lighthouse keeper, but the Sea Lords were not happy at the prospect of former Aircraftman Ross in either capacity. One job offer reached Lawrence from the newborn Irish Free State, where his experience with guerrilla warfare, demolitions, and armored cars would no doubt have come in handy. (Lawrence had met Michael Collins, the charismatic Irish revolutionary, military leader, and first president of the Irish Provisional Government, in London in 1920, and the two men seem to have admired each other—not surprisingly, since Collins's "flying columns" resembled Lawrence's hit-and-run tactics. By 1923, however, Collins had been murdered.) In the end Lawrence's friend Lieutenant-Colonel Alan Dawnay, who had served with him in the desert after Aqaba, managed to persuade the adjutant-general to the forces at the War Office, General Sir Philip Chetwode, GCB, OM, GSI, KCMG, DSO, who had commanded the Desert Column of the Egyptian Expeditionary Forces and later XX (Cavalry) Corps under Allenby, to slip Lawrence into the ranks as a soldier in the Royal Tank Corps.

Chetwode was something less than an uncritical admirer of Lawrence. He was the general who had asked at a staff conference in 1918, during which it was determined that Chetwode's corps should advance on Salt while Lawrence attacked Maan, "how his men were to distinguish friendly from hostile Arabs." Lawrence, who was in Arab robes himself, had replied "that skirt-wearers disliked men in uniform," producing a good deal of laughter, but not really answering Chetwode's perfectly sensible question. As for Lawrence, he repeated the story in *Seven Pillars of*

Wisdom in a way that could only make Chetwode look pompous or foolish to readers, though elsewhere he praised Chetwode's professionalism.
However, in 1923, Chetwode, who would rise to the rank of field marshal,
had of course not read *Seven Pillars of Wisdom*, and he shared the admiration everyone seems to have felt for Alan Dawnay, so perhaps it was the
fact that the request came from Dawnay that moved him to find a place
in the army for Lawrence.

When Dawnay had asked Lawrence what he was looking for, he had
replied, only half jokingly, "Mind-suicide"—that is, work involving a fixed
routine and no responsibility to give orders, or to make plans. Being a
lighthouse keeper might have had some appeal for Lawrence had the Sea
Lords been more willing to take a risk on him, but failing that, the army
seemed the quickest way to vanish back into the ranks. Unlike the RAF,
the army was not fussy about its recruits, and was more accustomed to
having men enlist under a false name. The Tank Corps would offer Lawrence a chance to tinker with machinery, or so he thought, and he enjoyed
that. Dawnay put Lawrence's case to General Chetwode; Chetwode
"sounded out" Colonel Sir Hugh Ellis, commandant of the Tank Corps
Center, and reported back to Lawrence that Ellis "sees no very great difficulty about it." So less than two months after his discharge from the
RAF, Lawrence was officially enlisted in the Royal Tank Corps for seven
years, plus five years in the reserve.

Before signing up, Lawrence had to find a new name, since "Ross" had
been outed. Although he told any number of people, including one of his
biographers, the poet Robert Graves, that he chose the first one-syllable
name he found in the Army List, the truth seems rather more complicated. He had called on the Shaws, probably to tell them of his intention
to join the army, and while there he encountered a visiting clergyman
who, supposing him to be a nephew of Shaw's, remarked on how much
like his uncle he looked. According to Shaw's secretary Blanche Patch,
Lawrence said at once, "A good idea! That is the name I shall take!" When
he signed on in the Tank Corps he gave his name as Thomas Edward
Shaw. This may or may not be true, but it seems very unlikely that Law-

rence's gratitude to and admiration for Shaw did not play some role in his choice of a name. In later years, people sometimes mistook him for Shaw's illegitimate son, and Lawrence's use of his surname seems to have amused Shaw himself, who would write, with his usual sharp wit, on the flyleaf of a copy of *Saint Joan*, "To Pte. Shaw from Public Shaw."

Private Shaw has been criticized for not denying the rumor that he was "Public Shaw's" son, but it seems hard to imagine how Lawrence could have announced to the world at large that the rumor was untrue. It would have caused another round of sensational front-page news stories and would also have raised a subject about which both men were sensitive. In any case, Bernard Shaw (who positively gloated over the rumor that Lawrence was his son) took a pleasure that was at once wicked and benign at the use of his name; and Lawrence, having at last found the name he wanted, never changed it again. He entered the army as 7875698 Private T. E. Shaw, "and was posted to A Company of the R.T.C. Depot at Bovington," as of March 23, 1923.

Unlike Lawrence's entrance into the RAF, this seems to have been a quick and simple enlistment. Lawrence may have learned the value of *not* "going to the top," since General Chetwode does not seem to have bothered consulting the secretary of state for war or the CIGS about the enlistment of the hero of Aqaba.

Lawrence's enlistment in the Royal Tank Corps (RTC) was a consequence of his misery, his sense of isolation, and his feeling of failure, after his discharge from the RAF. Like his fellow recruits at Bovington, he was there because he had failed, because he had no place to go, because he had fallen so far in his own estimation that he wanted to touch bottom: "mind suicide," as he called it himself. Nothing about the army changed his initial reaction to it: he loathed everything from the uniform to most of his hut mates. One measure of how much he disliked it is that he made no effort to secure a job he might have enjoyed, such as engine repair, but simply drifted into being a storekeeper after his recruit training.

It is clear that Lawrence was going through something like a nervous breakdown at the time of his second enlistment, and perhaps long before. The elements are hard to define exactly, but they included the huge task he had set for himself in rewriting *Seven Pillars of Wisdom*; what we would now call post-traumatic stress; a sense of displacement at his inability to find a settled and secure place for himself in civilian life; and, above all, his increasing discomfort at the gap between the public perception of him as a hero and his own intense feelings of worthlessness and self-contempt. Lawrence could suppress much of his angst when he was involved in something that interested him, but without a focus for his enormous energy, without something that could take his mind off himself, he was consumed by his own demons. Lawrence never reached quite the level of misery that George Orwell would describe ten years later in *Down and Out in Paris and London*, and he managed to keep up a social life that prevented other people from perceiving just how severely depressed he was; but between the time he returned to Britain from the Middle East and his enlistment in the Royal Tank Corps he went through a bleak period of confusion, self-reproach, and alienation that would have broken the will of a lesser man.

Lawrence's first impression of the RTC did not improve with time. Admittedly, he was predisposed to dislike it. "The Army is muck, stink, and a desolate abomination," he wrote, and he never changed his mind. Every day that he put on the khaki uniform merely made him more bitterly nostalgic for the blue-gray of the RAF.

Lawrence's friends in the great world never quite understood either of his enlistments—those who were civilians, or who knew the services only as officers, found it hard to understand the degree to which "other ranks" clung to the esprit de corps they felt for their particular regiment or service. Lawrence, after making a place for himself as an airman, found serving as a private soldier in the army a tremendous letdown. He complained that he felt "queerly homesick whenever I see a blue uniform in the street." With the exception of a couple of other men in his hut, Lawrence's fellow recruits appalled him. He complained to his friend Lionel Curtis—who, like Lawrence, was a fellow of All Souls—about their "prevailing animality of spirit, whose unmixed bestiality frightens me and hurts me. . . . This sort of thing must be madness and sometimes I wonder how far mad I am, and if a madhouse would not be my next (and merciful) stage. Merciful compared to this place, which hurts me, body and soul. It's terrible to hold myself voluntarily here: and yet I want to stay here till it no longer hurts me: till the burnt child no longer feels the fire."

In a letter to Trenchard, Lawrence was more composed, carefully comparing the army with the RAF in the spirit of an inspecting officer. The army, he reported, was more lavish than the RAF in providing food, bedding, hot baths, libraries, and fuel (presumably coke for the cast-iron stove in the hut), and the officers "speak and act with complete assurance, believing themselves better than ourselves: and they are: whereas in the RAF I had an uncomfortable feeling that we were better than the officers." In the the army, officers still enjoyed a natural and untroubled sense of class superiority. In the RAF, officers were uncomfortably conscious that many of the other ranks knew more about aero engines, or radios, or the intricate riggings of an aircraft, or even flying than any officer did, whereas, in the army the mere fact of holding the king's commission was enough to demand and receive respect from the other ranks; the gulf between officers and men was enormous.

To Curtis, Lawrence was franker: "It's a horrible life and the other fellows fit it." The endless drill and PT sapped Lawrence's strength—this was not just a matter of his wounds; he was also far older than the other recruits. Lawrence hated it all, and even the fact that "self-degradation" was his own game did not accustom him to "this cat-calling carnality seething up and down the hut, fed by streams of fresh matter from twenty lecherous mouths. . . . A filthy business all of it, and yet Hut 12 shows me the truth behind Freud." Lawrence—who, after all, had pioneered the use of armored cars in the desert—was also disappointed that there was no apparent interest in teaching the recruits anything about tanks. It was sixteen weeks of uninterrupted, soul-destroying "square bashing," gimlet-eyed inspections, and PT.

At the end of his training, he was assigned to an easy job as a clerk in the quartermaster's stores—very likely this was a sign that those who had gotten him into the army were still trying to protect him as best they could. He had plenty of time on his hands to work on the revisions of *Seven Pillars of Wisdom* and write letters. Once he was settled in the job, he moved his new Brough "Superior" motorcycle up to Bovington, provoking the envy and admiration of his fellow soldiers (who knew that it cost the equivalent of several years of a soldier's pay). He earned some relief from bullying by giving joyrides on it to a favored few. This too must have made Private Shaw seem like an unusual kind of soldier, both to the officers and to the men. Lawrence soon increased the curiosity by renting a nearby cottage called Clouds Hill, in Moreton, about a mile and a half from the camp, where he could get away from the army altogether when he had free time.

Built in 1808, Clouds Hill was more or less derelict. By coincidence Lawrence was renting it from "a distant cousin" of his father, a Chapman, for two shillings sixpence a week. Bit by bit Lawrence took on the task of making it habitable. He made a few friends in the Tank Corps; and to one of them, Corporal Dixon, who seemed comparatively well read, he even confided his real identity when Dixon asked him what he thought of all the stories about Colonel Lawrence, and whether he thought it was just "a stunt" on the part of the RAF to encourage recruiting. Dixon and a few other friends from Bovington helped Lawrence with the work that needed to be done; and by applying his own gift for building and decoration, he very shortly completed the basics. The cottage was small, damp (because of the overhanging trees), and secluded, and it would eventually become not just his hideaway from Bovington, but his only home. Like a snail's shell, it would gradually be reshaped exactly to Lawrence's Spartan ideas about living; indeed it became almost an extension of his personality.

One of the friends from Bovington was John ("Jock") Bruce, a tough, dour young Scotsman, about nineteen years old when Lawrence first met him. In a letter to Charlotte Shaw over a year later, Lawrence described him as "inarticulate, excessively uncomfortable," which is putting it mildly, since everybody else seems to have found Bruce more than a little menacing: a silent, hulking figure always intensely protective of Lawrence. "Bruce feels like a block of granite," Lawrence wrote to Charlotte, "with myself a squashed door-mat of fossilized bones between two layers."* This is a very striking description of Bruce, whose role in Lawrence's life would be precisely to make his friend and employer feel "squashed" by a giant, implacable, unmovable weight.

Long after Lawrence's death, Bruce claimed to have been introduced to him early in 1922, in circumstances that seem curious and unlikely even today. According to Bruce, Lawrence was still working at the Colonial Office and was looking for somebody to do "odd jobs" for him. Bruce claimed to have briefly met Lawrence at "the Mayfair flat" of "a Mr. Murray," presumably an acquaintance of Lawrence's. The son of a bankrupt milk distributor in Aberdeen, Bruce was there to be interviewed by Murray "for a position which was to become vacant presently," having been recommended for the job by his family doctor in Scotland, a friend of Murray.

In Bruce's account of this supposed "job interview," there is a louche sexual undertone. If Murray was interviewing Bruce for a job, one wonders why "Colonel Lawrence" (as he still was) would be watching from the sidelines. Bruce was no fool. "Lawrence did nothing without a purpose," he was to write later, "and using people was his masterpiece." Unkind as this judgment may sound, there is undeniably a certain amount of truth to it, at least so far as Lawrence's dealings with Bruce are

---

*There are a number of conflicting accounts of the relationship between Lawrence and Bruce, among them that of John E. Mack, professor of psychiatry at Harvard Medical School, who actually met Bruce while researching his Pulitzer Prize–winning biography of Lawrence in the 1970s; Jeremy Wilson's much more cautious and skeptical take on Bruce in his biography of Lawrence; and the frankly sensationalistic account given by Phillip Knightley and Colin Simpson in *The Secret Lives of Lawrence of Arabia*, based on their series for the (London) *Sunday Times*. Bruce also wrote his own account, on which Knightley and Simpson based theirs. Even reduced to the bare minimum of what everyone accepts took place between Lawrence and Bruce, it is still a disturbing story.

concerned. Not everybody fell under Lawrence's spell. For example, Harold Nicolson—diplomat, author, and husband of Vita Sackville-West—wrote of Lawrence unflatteringly: "His disloyalty reminded one of the boy who would suck up to the headmaster and then sneak to him about what went on in the school. Even when he became a colonel, he was not the sort of colonel whom one would gladly leave in the office when confidential papers were lying on the desk. So sensitive a man, it seemed to me, ought to have possessed a finer sense of mercy: when, in his gentle voice, he told tales of a massacre, his lips assumed an ugly curl." Much as Bruce was to fall and remain under Lawrence's spell, there is no denying that Lawrence was manipulative and deceptive in dealing with him over the years.

Forty-five years later, when Bruce sold his eighty-five-page typewritten account of their relationship to the *Sunday Times*, he described this meeting with Lawrence in detail; but like a great many other things in his story, this description is unverified, and much of it is improbable. He described how Lawrence put him through a series of tests, and, apparently satisfied, eventually revealed that he wanted Bruce to whip him from time to time, and would pay him what amounted to a retainer to do so.

The one certain truth in Bruce's account is that he took on the role of being Lawrence's chief administer of corporal punishment, but it is more likely that this did not begin until after Lawrence's enlistment at Bovington, and that Lawrence first met Bruce there, as a fellow recruit in Hut 12. Even Lawrence's youngest brother, Arnold, who was Lawrence's literary executor, became sadly and reluctantly convinced that Bruce was telling the truth about this.

Bruce's attempt to place Lawrence in the underground world of male sadomasochism in London, however, must be taken with a very large grain of salt. Admittedly, Lawrence had an interest in flagellation long before his treatment at the hands of the Turks at Deraa. He and his friend the poet James Elroy Flecker, an unapologetic masochist, had talked about the pleasures of being whipped when they were together in Lebanon *before* the war. Richard Meinertzhagen claimed that Lawrence behaved provocatively toward him in Paris, infuriating him to the point where he put "little Lawrence" over his knee and smacked his bottom. Lawrence, he reported, "made no attempt to resist and told me later that he could easily understand a woman submitting to rape once a strong man hugged her." Meinertzhagen, however was something less than a reliable witness, since he revised and retyped his diary entries years after the event. Arnold Lawrence compared his brother to a medieval penitent who sought punishment for his sins, real or imagined, and this was certainly an element in Lawrence's need to be whipped. Still, it is hard to draw the line between penance and pleasure, even for Lawrence.

Lawrence's desire to be whipped is not by itself a very shocking or very unusual feature of upper-class English life ninety years ago—indeed corporal punishment is something of a staple of English humor. This is not to say that sadomasochism in various forms is not equally prevalent in most national cultures—for instance, one thinks of Germany, Austria (Dr. Leopold von Sacher-Masoch was an Austrian), and France (birthplace of the Marquis de Sade himself)—but in England, the connection between whipping and sexual arousal has always been at once a source of snickering humor and an activity which is only barely repressed or hidden. At a time when prostitutes still advertised with a card thumbtacked to their front door, the number of those who offered "Lessons in discipline" never failed to provoke comments from foreign tourists. It would be idle to speculate on the reasons for this, except to note that among those of the upper middle class and the upper class who attended English boarding schools, whipping on the bare buttocks, whether inflicted by masters or by older boys, was not only common but usual—it was considered salutary and character-building—and it sometimes led to a certain confusion between pain and pleasure in later life.

Lawrence's mother, a believer in the old adage "Spare the rod, spoil the child," boasted of slapping young Ned on his bare buttocks, and appears to have singled him out for this punishment, since he was by far the most rebellious of her boys. Knowing what we do of Sarah Lawrence's nature, it seems doubtful that a beating inflicted by her would have been gentle. One imagines that she meant it to hurt, and that she believed the Lord would expect her to put her whole strength into each blow; she was not the woman to do things by half, particularly when it came to punishing wickedness or disobedience. It may be that early in Lawrence's life there was therefore a certain mingling of pleasure with fear and pain—and that however hard he tried to suppress any erotic arousal, he was not capable of eliminating it altogether. The connection between erotic arousal and his mother would certainly explain in part his lifelong flight from her desire for his love. As for the connection between his involuntary erotic arousal when being brutally beaten and sodomized by the Turks, that is not only obvious in Lawrence's own account, but also quite sufficient to explain his extreme dislike of being touched, as well as his lifelong determination to avoid any kind of sexual intimacy.

At this point in his life Lawrence apparently required infrequent sessions of severe pain inflicted by another man. What is more interesting than Lawrence's need for punishment, however, is the bizarre lengths to which he went in order to persuade Bruce that somebody else was *ordering* the punishment. It is useless to speculate on the degree to which the whippings may have produced erotic arousal or even ejaculation—i.e., pleasure as opposed to punishment—and neither Lawrence nor Bruce is alive to tell us. But it is quite clear that some measure of both was involved, and that Bruce was picked partly because Lawrence guessed he was reliable, and partly because, like Sarah Lawrence, he would not resort to half measures. Even in a photograph of the young John Bruce, there is something in the eyes and the broad, inflexible mouth that suggests he would consider it his duty to make every blow hurt as much a possible.

The degree of artifice, dissimulation, imagination, and careful planning over time, which Lawrence brought to bear on the task of recruiting Bruce to his purposes, is nothing short of astonishing, and suggests just why Lawrence was regarded as a genius at intelligence and clandestine warfare. In this case, the cover story was as bizarre as the end purpose. Lawrence knew exactly how to manipulate Bruce: money alone would never be his primary motive; Bruce needed to believe in the morality of

what he was doing; he needed to believe that he was enforcing punishment ordered by an older authority figure, and inflicting it on somebody
who deserved it.

In Bruce's account, Lawrence hatched a story that contained just
enough truth to sound plausible. He had borrowed from friends and
from "a merchant bank" money that he could not repay, and had gone to
a wealthy uncle, the "Old Man," who had inherited money that ought to
have gone to Lawrence's father. The Old Man "called him a bastard not fit
to live among decent people," who had "turned his back on God, lost an
excellent position at the Colonial Office, become financially involved
'with the damned Jews,' insulted a Bishop and insulted King George at
Buckingham Palace." That Lawrence was "a bastard" was true, and many
people did wrongly believe that he had insulted the king by refusing to
accept his decorations. The story about the bishop involved an altercation between the Anglican bishop of Jerusalem and Lawrence over Jewish immigration, which had led Lawrence to declare indignantly that the
bishop was not fit "to black Weizmann's boots." In short, Lawrence
trolled through his life to find and adapt to his purpose stories that might
persuade an elderly relative to punish him. More important, they were
stories about acts that Bruce might believe were both reprehensible and
true.

Lawrence claimed that his "uncle" was intent on saving the family
honor—one of the "threats" Lawrence invented was that if he didn't do
exactly as the Old Man demanded, down to the smallest detail, "a meeting
of the family would have to be called to see what was to be done with him."
This was well calculated to appeal to Bruce, who had a strong sense of family and who respected his milkman father in Aberdeen. The character
that Lawrence apparently created for the Old Man is interesting. So far
as one can judge, it resembled no male relative Lawrence knew, certainly
not his father, whom Lawrence remembers as having stopped once when
Ned was a child to upbraid a carter for whipping a horse. In reading
Bruce's account of what Lawrence had to say about his "uncle," it seems
more than likely that Lawrence built up his character from that of his

mother, and merely switched genders, since Bruce was more likely to accept a male authority figure. The Old Man's strict moral judgment, his unforgiving sense of right and wrong, his absolute conviction that he knew what was best for Lawrence, and his belief in the value of punishment, pain, and discipline are exactly the qualities that Lawrence found so difficult to accept in his mother. The criticism of his own conduct that Lawrence imputes to the Old Man is exactly what his mother would have said, and the Old Man's power to influence and interfere with Lawrence's life is what kept him away from home as much as possible.

The intensity with which Lawrence won Bruce's compliance and his determination that Bruce must agree to do whatever the Old Man told him to do are both impressive and frightening. Lawrence was creating a detailed and plausible fictional world, and assigning Bruce a role in a psychodrama, which would continue off and on until the end of Lawrence's life. Bruce later professed to have been shocked when Lawrence mentioned that the Old Man might call on him to inflict "corporal punishment," but this was surely face-saving on Bruce's part nearly half a century after the fact. It seems much more likely that Bruce guessed what Lawrence wanted from the beginning.

The first of the whippings Bruce claimed to have given Lawrence took place in Clouds Hill, the tiny brick cottage whose roof would soon be replaced. (Lawrence paid for the new roof by selling the gold dagger* he had bought in Mecca.) Lawrence was still elaborating on the fantasy that was intended to give him control over Bruce. The Old Man, he told Bruce, was disappointed because Lawrence had missed church parades, and had dispatched a birch† with which Lawrence was to be whipped. This time Lawrence backed up the request with "an unsigned, typed letter

---

* Lawrence sold the dagger to his friend Lionel Curtis, who donated it to All Souls College, where it still is.

† The "birch" was actually a bundle of twenty to twenty-four birch or elder twigs about twenty-eight to forty-eight inches in length, tied together at one end, the first six inches wrapped tightly with a strip of leather to form a handle, and was then in use as regulation punishment in British prisons. It was a big step up in severity from a schoolmaster's cane, but several steps down from a cat-o'-nine-tails.

which he said was from The Old Man," instructing Bruce that he was not only to carry out the whipping, but "to report in writing ... [and] to describe Lawrence's demeanour and behaviour under punishment." Bruce, the letter promised, would be paid for the whipping. These whippings (and the payments) would be continued at infrequent intervals over the next twelve years, and step by step the letters from the Old Man grew in terms of the complexity of his demands, his requests for accurate reports of Lawrence's reaction, and the loving details of the instruments of punishment to be used. Each of these letters was of course written with great care by Lawrence himself, prescribing down to the last detail the punishments that were to be inflicted on him. When the Old Man requested a reply from Bruce, Bruce handed his letter to Lawrence, for forwarding.

Lawrence, after his beating at Deraa, had been able to remember every detail of the "Circassian riding whip" which was used on him: "tapering from the thickness of a thumb at the grip (which was wrapped in silver, with a knob inlaid in a black design) down to a hard point much finer than a pencil." In the letters Bruce claimed to have received from the Old Man, Lawrence was just as precise, even fussy, in describing the details of what he wanted, how it was to be done, and what it was to be done with. It is, in fact, an amazing work of fantasy, backed up with carefully forged letters that were designed to convince Bruce, and succeeded. The letters may have been overkill—there is no evidence that Bruce needed anything like this much persuasion—but their tone is very revealing. It is that of "Colonel Lawrence," direct, explicit, a person of the officer class who expects obedience from a social inferior. Nowhere is it clearer that "Colonel Lawrence" was still alive and well, than in these bizarre letters. "Private Meek," as Bernard Shaw would call him in *Too True to Be Good*, treated Bruce with kid gloves—for Bruce was a difficult and demanding character. But the former lieutenant-colonel gave Bruce the commands, which, except for their subject matter, read like those a wealthy landowner might send to a farm manager. The letters Lawrence wrote as the Old Man are works of genius—with Dickensian skill, he managed to create, layer by layer, detail by detail, a crusty, demanding, difficult character whom one might almost expect to see in the next seat in a first-class railway compartment on the way "up" to London—neatly suited; his bowler hat, gloves, and umbrella beside him; with a regimental tie, a white mustache, and a monocle; reading the *Times* with furious concentration—a figure straight out of an Osbert Lancaster cartoon.

The combination of the cottage and Bruce made the army almost bearable for Lawrence, although he never grew used to wearing the hated khaki uniform or to the mindless violence and profanity of his fellow soldiers. He seldom spent a night in the cottage—he used it instead as a refuge during his ample spare time, and took a few friends there, like Bruce and Corporal Dixon. Over time, he added a phonograph, a radio, a library of books—in size, in austerity, and as a place to work it became the exact equivalent of the small cottage his parents had built for the young Lawrence in the garden of their house. It was not Lawrence's home in any conventional sense—as E. M. Forster pointed out, "it was rather his pied-à-terre, the place where his feet touched the earth for a moment, and found rest." The army made few demands on Lawrence and he was thus able to devote a good deal of time to the project of printing a limited edition of *Seven Pillars of Wisdom*. In addition he had his weekends free for a social life far more intense and well-connected than that of any other private soldier in the British army.

During this time, the Shaws became central figures in Lawrence's life, and Robert Graves introduced Lawrence to Thomas Hardy, who lived near Bovington, in Dorsetshire—"Hardy country," where many of his novels are set. The Hardys too became close friends, and their home, Max Gate, was another place of escape for Lawrence. Other friends in this period included the Kenningtons, the novelist E. M. Forster, the poet Siegfried Sassoon, Lionel Curtis, and John Buchan. Any portrait of Lawrence that fails to reflect his extraordinary gifts for friendship, conversation, and correspondence fails to reflect the man. Monastic and self-punishing as he might be, Lawrence was the very reverse of a military version of a cloistered monk; he was instead constantly on the move, constantly engaged with people, invited everywhere. Hardy, like Doughty, he came to admire and love. "Hardy is so pale," he wrote, "so quiet, so refined in essence: and the camp is such a hurly-burly. When I come back I feel as if I'd woken from a sleep: not an exciting sleep, but a restful one. . . . It is strange to pass from the noise of the sergeants company into a peace so secure that in it not even Mrs. Hardy's tea-cups rattle on the tray."

Still, it was not just the sight of the small, slim figure in khaki, puttees, and leather gauntlets arriving on his huge, glistening bike that alarmed his friends in 1923, but the impression he gave that he cared nothing for his life and was looking for a way to end it. The Kenningtons were disturbed by his "nihilistic" thoughts. Lawrence confided to Curtis, in a series of long, heartfelt letters, his "craving for real risk." To Shaw he confessed, "I haven't been in the mood for anything lately except high-speed motorbiking on the worst roads." Of course motorcycles always appear suicidal to those who don't ride one, and Lawrence was an excellent rider; nevertheless, he was riding perhaps the most powerful motorcycle one could buy in 1923, and boasted of the risks he took.* This was no pose. Lawrence's unhappiness—intensified by intense feelings of guilt—was deepening into despair, and his friends feared that suicide was possible. He wrote alarmingly to Hogarth, and even more alarmingly to Curtis, about his dislike of all animal life, especially his own, and of his antics on his motorcycle, when he "swerved at 60 M.P.H. onto the grass by the roadside, trying vainly to save a bird." Shaw was moved to write directly to Prime Minister Stanley Baldwin, urging him to give Lawrence "a position of a pensioned commanding officer in dignified private circumstances," and put to an end the "shocking tomfoolery" of Lawrence's

---

*The author owned a motorcycle from the age of seventeen to the age of sixty-six, including the two years he spent in the RAF. It was, in fact, reading about Lawrence as a boy (and hearing about him from the author's uncle Sir Alexander Korda and from H. Montgomery Hyde) that made him decide to buy a motorcycle and join the RAF.

service in the ranks, which he compared to "Belisarius begging for oboles in an ungrateful country," and warning darkly of the embarrassing consequences if Britain's most famous war hero took his own life. Baldwin was unable to do this; he took Lawrence's case up with Trenchard, though he failed to change Trenchard's mind about readmitting Lawrence into the RAF. Hogarth, who had been doubtful about the approach to Baldwin in the first place, wrote with slightly weary realism to Shaw: "Lawrence is not normal in many ways and it is extraordinarily difficult to do anything for him. . . . He will not work in any sort of harness unless this is padlocked on to him. He enlisted in order to have the padlocks rivetted on to him."

What saved Lawrence in 1923 was work: not in the army, where his job—"half-clerk, half-storeman"—hardly taxed his ability, but on his ever more complicated and expensive plans to get *Seven Pillars of Wisdom* printed and published as he wanted it to be. Lawrence's attitude toward his immense book alternated between a sense of failure and a glimmering of hope, sustained by those of his friends who had read it, and whose judgment resembled Siegfried Sassoon's, who wrote to him: "Damn you, how long do you expect me to go on reassuring you about your bloody masterpiece: It is a GREAT BOOK, blast you." E. M. Forster wrote to him in the same vein: "I can't cheer you up over the book. No one could. You have got depressed and muddled over it and are quite incapable of seeing how good it is."

In the latter part of 1923, hope took the upper hand. Lawrence decided to take on himself the printing and binding of a subscribers' edition of 100 copies of *Seven Pillars of Wisdom*, aimed at "the ungodly rich." The book would be lavishly printed and illustrated, and printed according to Lawrence's frequently eccentric or antiquarian opinions, and each copy would be bound in a different material or style. The book would cost thirty guineas; it would be ready in a year and a half; and Lawrence estimated that the total cost of producing it would be about £3,000. Since each subscriber would have to pay his or her thirty guineas up front, the book would be self-financed. This was an outrageously optimistic business plan. In the end it would cost Lawrence about £13,000* to produce the subscribers' edition, a crippling debt; and the number of copies went up considerably because he insisted on giving the book to those of his friends who could not afford the subscription and to people he loved or respected too much to accept money from them, such as Storrs, whose check he tore up. (Those who held on to their copies would have had a windfall—they could be resold instantly for many times thirty guineas, and the last one auctioned in the United States, in 2001, went for more than $100,000.)

For the next three years, Lawrence was constantly occupied with the problems of printing his book, as well as with elaborate subterfuges he concocted with the rival American publishers Frank Doubleday and George H. Doran (who would eventually merge in 1927 to form one company), intended to protect his copyright in the United States. Lawrence brought to his role as a publisher the same attention to detail and energy that he brought to everything he set his hand to, managing one of the most intricate and complicated jobs in the history of book production from his bunk in a barracks, or from the NAAFI reading room of a military camp. (The intricacy and complications were largely due to his own demands and prejudices about book design.) Of course, as is so often the case with Lawrence, he wanted to eat his cake and have it too. On the one hand, he wanted his friends to be able to read the book in the form of a sumptuous, private, limited edition; on the other hand, he wanted to avoid reviews and to prevent the general public from reading it at all.

Both Robert Graves and Bernard Shaw expressed concern about libelous material in the 1922 "Oxford" text—libel is always a big problem for authors in Britain, because of the strictness of British libel law as compared with that of the United States—but it does not seem to have been a fear of lawsuits that held Lawrence back from publishing his book in the

---

* About $1 million in today's money. A guinea was £1 and one shilling. Until the advent of decimal currency it was considered rather more respectable to charge in guineas than pounds—fashionable tailors, antique dealers, etc., always priced things in guineas. Thirty guineas was about the equivalent of $155 in the 1920s, or about $2,400 in today's terms.

normal way. Any British publisher would have had the text read for libel,
and a solicitor who specialized in libel law might have suggested comparatively small changes that would have protected Lawrence and his
publisher, rather than large cuts. More likely, the truth is that in writing
Seven Pillars of Wisdom Lawrence had, like most authors of a memoir,
expressed his own version of events, and was not eager to have it contradicted or debated in public. Much of the factual material in the book has
since been confirmed by the release in the 1970s of many if not most of
the documents, but throughout the book Lawrence, consciously or
unconsciously, attributed to himself decisions and actions that were
often initiated by others. No doubt, as he wrote, revised, and rewrote
Seven Pillars of Wisdom, getting with each revision farther away in time
from the events, he made himself increasingly the hero of the book. He
did not falsify events or invent them, as he has been accused of doing, but
he put himself at the center of the story, and by 1923 he was not anxious
to expose himself to criticism, or to objections from others who had
served in the Middle East.

The solution—a brilliant one—was to limit the readership to those who
were either friends (like Hogarth) or admirers (like Storrs and Allenby),
and who would not rush to write long, disputatious letters to the *Times*.*
Lawrence often had contradictory impulses. On the one hand, he wanted
to prevent *Seven Pillars of Wisdom* from becoming a collector's item; on
the other, by making almost every copy of the subscribers' edition different in some way—with variations in binding, and in the number and
placement of the illustrations—he inevitably produced a limited edition
that would keep bibliophiles busy and puzzled for decades.

---

* Lawrence was right to fear this. For example, when the abridgment of *Seven Pillars of
Wisdom, Revolt in the Desert*, was published in 1927, Sir Arnold Wilson, former civil
commissioner in Iraq and Lawrence's old antagonist, wrote that Lawrence was responsible for "the estrangement of Anglo-French relations in the Middle East . . . [and]
helped induce [Britain] to adopt a policy which brought disaster to the people of
Syria." Wilson also accused Lawrence of condoning homosexuality, of imputing
homosexuality falsely to the Bedouin, and of turning the Arab Bureau into "a cult of
which Lawrence is the chief priest and Lowell Thomas the press agent." (Wilson,
"Revolt in the Desert," *Journal of the Central Asia Society*, 14, 1927.)

In early to mid-1923, Lawrence was still waiting for Shaw's long-promised suggestions and corrections to the 1922 proof, and still circulating copies to those who had served with him and whom he respected for their comments. Colonel A. P. Wavell (the future Field Marshal) wrote back encouragingly, and the Hardys expressed their admiration. All this ought to have cheered Lawrence up, but failed to do so. He was weary of the book, sick of the Army ("A black core . . . of animality"), "brooding" on his own sense of dissatisfaction, unable to sleep more than an hour a night, and existing on one meal a day, usually breakfast; and although he was living in a hut with twenty-one other soldiers and a corporal, he felt as lonely as he had been in the attic on Barton Street in London. In an effort to keep his mind occupied, and produce an income beyond the army's two shillings nine pence a day, he asked Cape about the possibility of doing some translation from the French, estimating that he could probably produce about 2,000 words a day—a figure that was seriously overoptimistic. Cape proposed that he should translate J. C. Mardrus's 4,000-page *Mille et Une Nuits* (*The Arabian Nights*), a formidable task. In preparation for this, Lawrence agreed to translate a French novel, *Le Gigantesque*, about a giant sequoia tree, a book he came to dislike more and more as he translated it. He persisted with it, however—it was eventually published by Cape as *The Forest Giant*—but the effect was to deter Lawrence from taking on anything as challenging as *Mille et Une Nuits*. He took instead a French novel about fishes (even stranger than a novel about a tree), a book which he thought (correctly) English readers might not take to. When he was not translating, he and his friends worked on his cottage, repairing and altering it to his taste. He carved in the lintel over the front door of Clouds Hill two words from Herodotus best translated as "I don't care," or perhaps more to the point, "I couldn't care less."*

---

*This is from the tale about Hippocleides, suitor of the princess Agarista. Having drunk too much at dinner, Hippocleides "disgraced himself by standing on his head and beating time [to the music] in the air with his legs (the Greeks wore short skirts)." (John Mack, *A Prince of Our Disorder.*) At this unseemly display Agarista's father, angered, shouted, "You have danced away your wife!" to which Hippocleides responded,

When the Shaws were persuaded to visit Lawrence in his cottage, as the Hardys and E. M. Forster did, Bernard Shaw remarked, perceptively, that Lawrence's pretense of living "humbly with his comrades" as "a tanker-ranker" was misleading, and that surrounded by his army friends at Clouds Hill "he looked very much like Colonel Lawrence with several aides-de-camp."

Soon after meeting Lawrence, Shaw described him as "a grown-up boy," and there is an element of truth to this: both as regards Lawrence, many of whose interests and tastes (motorcycles, for example, or the tiny, cozy cottage, with sleeping bags coyly marked *Meum* and *Tuam*) remained boyish, and who scrupulously avoided any of the adult entanglements of love, marriage, and domesticity; and as regards Shaw's own relationship to him, which was that of an exasperated father. Lawrence had not only adopted Shaw's name as his own, but found in the name of the village where the Shaws lived, Ayot Saint Lawrence, a kind of portent. Lawrence's visits to the Shaws throughout 1922 and 1923 had made him, to all intents and purposes, almost a member of the family, and also gave him the unusual opportunity of sharing in the creation of one of Shaw's best plays, *Saint Joan*. His visits were curtailed when one of his fellow privates borrowed his motorcycle and crashed it, but he soon managed to acquire another Brough, and in the meantime remained in constant correspondence with both Shaws.

Occasionally, Public Shaw launched a Jovian taunt at Private Shaw: "I have written another magnificent play. When I finish a play, I write another: I don't sit down gloating in a spectacular manner over how the old one is to astonish the world. Yah!" Nevertheless, Charlotte sent Lawrence the draft acting script of *Saint Joan*, and Lawrence responded—

"I don't care." Lawrence himself translated it as "Wyworri?" Note that there is a strong sexual element to the story, since Hippocleides had shocked his prospective father-in-law by exposing his genitals. This subtext may be read into the inscription; and Lawrence, and the better educated of his visitors, must surely have been aware of it. An alternative translation might be "I'll do what I please, whatever you think of it," which seems closer to Lawrence's point of view.

boldly—with a long, detailed letter of suggestions to the great man. He answered via Charlotte, though he must have been aware that she would show the letter to her husband. He did not comment on the way Shaw had made use of his character and career in creating the part of Saint Joan herself. Like Lawrence, Joan had fought a powerful army to place a king "upon the throne of a nation-state"; like Joan, Lawrence had succeeded against the odds, and had then been dismissed (as she was martyred); like Joan, Lawrence combined unearthly courage with the ability to inspire men to follow him, and invented unorthodox military tactics that confounded the professionals; like Joan's, Lawrence's small size, humility, and modesty, whether real or feigned, did not prevent him from being the center of all attention wherever he went; and like Joan, he adopted a costume that separated him from his own countrymen—he went barefoot, in the robes of an Arab, and she wore the armor of a man. Even Joan's way of expressing herself in the play resembles Lawrence's—Shaw was nothing if not observant in pursuit of a character. In the words of Michael Holroyd, Shaw's biographer, "With their missionary zeal to mould the world to their personal convictions, Joan and Lawrence were two small homeless figures elected by the Zeitgeist and picked out by the spotlight of history." The comparison intrigued Shaw from his first meeting with Lawrence and gave him the key to creating a Shavian heroine who was at once saintly and proud, modern and medieval, as well as a deeply androgynous figure.

Lawrence was courageous enough to criticize one scene as "adequate" and another as "intolerable." But on the whole he liked the play, and he praised the fifth act as "pure genius," though several people have felt that *Saint Joan* would have ended better without it (among these were Lawrence Langner and the Theater Guild, producers of the play in New York, who were afraid the audience members would miss their last train home). Lawrence pointed out that Shaw "doesn't know how men who have fought together stand in relation to one another," and gave him some sensible suggestions. Once the play had opened, Lawrence went to see it in London, and wrote to Charlotte of Sybil Thorndyke's performance as Joan, "There isn't as much strength in Joan . . . as I had gathered in reading her," but added that since he had made the role and the text his, in his mind, "there was a little resentment at having others' interpretations thrust on my established ones."

Although Lawrence never enjoyed his years in the army as a private, one senses, in 1923 and 1924, not so much a softening of his attitude as an increasingly busy social and intellectual life that kept his mind off it. He was often in London, and was once even invited to a dinner to celebrate Armistice Day, given by Air Chief Marshal Trenchard. Lawrence accepted provisionally:

> I'd like to very much: but there are two difficulties already in my view:
> It is Armistice day, and I do not know if leave will be given.
> I have a decent suit, but no dress clothes at all.
> The leave I will ask for. . . . The clothes are beyond my power to
> provide: and I fear that Lady Trenchard might not approve a lounge
> suit at dinner. . . . Please ask her before you reply.

In the event, Lawrence attended the dinner at the Army and Navy Club in uniform, surely the only private soldier in the British army to be dining that evening with the equivalent of a four-star general. Again and again, there are instances of Trenchard's breaking the rules for Lawrence. He called General Chetwode, the army adjutant-general, to arrange for special leave for Lawrence, and called again, in a rage, because Lawrence, who was on the defaulters' list for having missed a parade in order to accept an invitation to tea from Thomas Hardy, was unable to meet him at the Air Ministry. Despite Lawrence's complaints, there was no lack of powerful friends smoothing his path, and no hesitation on his part in asking them to do so.

Nor was there a lack of glamorous job offers. Sydney Cockerell tried to persuade Lawrence to accept the post of professor of English literature at Tokyo University, a position of some prestige; and Trenchard gave him a chance to complete the official history of the Royal Flying Corps in the 1914–1918 war, since the author of the first volume, Sir Walter Raleigh, had died leaving four or five volumes to go. Hogarth had given the job a try, but he was suffering from "all sorts of minor ailments," as well as diabetes, and the air war was no great interest of his. Here, surely, was a job Lawrence could do superbly—and without having to leave England— but he turned it down, because he did not want the responsibility, and offered it instead to Robert Graves, who, with a wife, children, and a mistress, was in great need of money. But Graves also declined what Lawrence described as "a three-year job, worth £600–£800 a year," an optimistic guess, since the completion of the official RFC history would, in fact, take another twelve years.

Although Lawrence still shrank from the prospect of letting people read *Seven Pillars of Wisdom*, he had made the important step of putting its financing in the hands of Robin Buxton, a friendly banker, who as Major Buxton had led an Imperial Camel Corps unit of 300 men in support of Lawrence during the latter part of the war. Buxton was a rare type—an unflappable banker, endowed with energy, common sense, and a real affection for Lawrence; and Lawrence seems to have put together a "brain trust," consisting of Alan Dawnay, Hogarth, and Lionel Curtis, to advise him on how many copies to print and what to charge. He was, as usual, an infuriatingly difficult author. He wrote to Buxton: "I'd rather the few copies: I had rather one copy at £3,000 than 10 at £300, or 30 at £100 or 300 at £10. . . . I hate the whole idea of spreading copies of the beastly book." All this, of course, was still based on the notion that the whole job could be done for £3,000, which was hopelessly optimistic. At the same time, Lawrence decided that for moral reasons he should not make any money from the book, and gave up any claim to royalties. His choice of using the Oxford University Press to set the type was thwarted when it backed out, fearing the libel problems in the text. Lawrence eventually settled on hiring his own printer, an American named Manning Pike recommended by the artist Eric Kennington. Although this was his first attempt to design and set a book, Pike was a craftsman-artist after Lawrence's heart. Still, Pike soon became a martyr to Lawrence's cranky ideas about typography, a legacy of his passionate admiration for William Morris. Lawrence cut and changed the text to make paragraphs end on a page, to eliminate "rivers" of white space in the type, and to eliminate "orphans" (small pieces of text at the end of a paragraph). Lawrence's interest in typographical design soon became obsessive, and without a publisher like Cape or an editor like Garnett to control expenses, he began altering his text merely for the sake of its appearance on the page—Pike was, after all, in no position to contradict him. "The business will be done as crazily as you feared," Lawrence wrote to Shaw, and he was not exaggerating. Shaw's own ideas about spelling, punctuation, and typesetting were at least as cranky as Lawrence's, but his business sense was far sounder; he squeezed the maximum amount from his publishers, and was horrified that Lawrence proposed to forgo any profit from his book. Leaving his brain trust to find the necessary number of subscribers, Lawrence proceeded to have plates made of the illustrations and pay for the typesetting equipment Pike needed. He went through at least one more nerve-shredding round of revising the text, and then did so again as Pike began to produce proof sheets. This time he was aided, or perhaps hampered, by Shaw's detailed suggestions and advice (followed shortly by Charlotte's somewhat more timidly expressed ones), which finally arrived like a bombshell two years after Lawrence had first sent him the book:

Confound you and the book: you are no more to be trusted with a pen than a child with a torpedo. . . .

I invented my own system of punctuation, and then compared it with the punctuation of the Bible, and found that the authors of the revised version had been driven to the same usage, though their practice is not quite consistent all through. The Bible bars the dash, which is the great refuge of those who are too lazy to punctuate. . . . I never use it when I can possibly substitute a colon; and I save up the colon jealously for certain effects that no other stop produces. As you have no rules, and sometimes throw colons about with an unhinged mind, here are some rough rules for you.

When a sentence contains more than one statement, with different nominatives, or even with the same nominative repeated for the sake of emphasizing some discontinuity between the statements, the statements should be separated by a semicolon when the relation between them is expressed by a conjunction. When there is no conjunction, or other modifying word, and the two statements *are* placed baldly in dramatic apposition, use a colon. Thus, Luruns said nothing; but he thought the more. Luruns could not speak: he was drunk. Luruns, like Napoleon, was out of place and a failure as a subaltern; yet when he could exasperate his officers by being a faultless private he could behave himself as such. Luruns, like Napoleon, could see a hostile city not only as a military objective but as a stage for a *coup de théâtre*: he was a born actor.

You will see that your colons before buts and the like are contra-indicated in my scheme, and leave you without anything in reserve for the dramatic occasions mentioned above. You practically do not use semicolons at all. This is a symptom of mental defectiveness, probably induced by camp life.

But by far the most urgent of my corrections—so important that you had better swallow them literally with what wry faces you cannot control—are those which concern your libels. I spent fifteen years of my life writing criticisms of sensitive living people, and thereby acquired a very cultivated sense of what I might say and what I might not say. All criticisms are technically libels; but there is the blow below the belt, the impertinence, the indulgence of dislike, the expression of personal contempt, and of course the imputation of dishonesty or unchastity which are not and should not be privileged; as well as the genuine criticism, the amusing good humored banter, and (curiously) the obvious "vulgar abuse" which are privileged. I have weeded out your reckless sallies as carefully as I can.

Then there is the more general criticism about that first chapter. That it should come out and leave the book to begin with chapter two, which is the real thing and very fine at that, I have no doubt whatever. You will see my note on the subject.

I must close up now, as Charlotte wants to make up her packet
to you.

E. M. Forster too had written to Lawrence in detail, criticizing the
elaborate style, which Lawrence toned down considerably now that publishing the book was a realistic prospect. It was a moment that was at once
stimulating and deeply depressing for Lawrence, as if he were at once
summoning up from the past and finally burying the experiences of two
years of war, six years after it had ended. He had carried the burden of
Seven Pillars of Wisdom for so long that it must have seemed to him impossible to put it down.

It was soon apparent that there would be no shortage of subscribers—
indeed, Lawrence would have trouble keeping the number down to the
limit he wanted to set—and also that the entire project was going to prove
far more costly than he had supposed. The extraordinary workload he had
heaped upon himself, on top of a soldier's normal day, would have broken
the health of a far stronger man, and there is ample proof that he was sink-
ing deeper into depression. It is no accident that he had written confidingly
to Charlotte Shaw a kind of *de profundis*, explaining his experience at Deraa:

> I'm always afraid of being hurt: and to me, while I live, the force
> of that night will lie in the agony which broke me, and made me
> surrender. . . . About that night I shouldn't tell you, because decent
> men don't talk about such things. . . . For fear of being hurt, or rather
> to earn five minutes respite from the pain which drove me mad,
> I gave away the only possession we are born into the world with—
> our bodily integrity. It's an unforgiveable matter.

What he did *not* point out was that in the description of the incident
in *Seven Pillars of Wisdom* it is quite clear that the real horror was *not* the
pain, but the fact that he experienced pleasure at the pain; that his sexual
"surrender" was as "unforgivable" in his mind as it would be for a woman
experiencing pleasure from a gang rape. He certainly never mentioned
that he had gone to considerable trouble and some expense to reproduce

the moment, whenever the need overcame him. Jock Bruce was still in his hut at Bovington, and among the soldiers he invited to his cottage.

Lawrence's misery continued. He appealed once more to be allowed back into the RAF, but even a change in government did not help; the Conservative secretary of state for air, Sir Samuel Hoare, was adamantly opposed to having Lawrence back in the RAF. Hoare, who had known Lawrence well in Palestine and Jordan, feared the inevitable publicity, and may also have resented the direct appeal that Shaw made to Prime Minister Stanley Baldwin over Hoare's head, which suggested that Lawrence might take his cause to the newspapers. John Buchan put in a good word for Lawrence with Baldwin as well, but to no avail. Baldwin, a man who combined extreme political shrewdness with genuine indolence, must have felt besieged by Lawrence's friends, but true to form, he listened politely and did nothing.

To Buchan, Lawrence at least offered an explanation of a kind, writing to thank him for talking to Baldwin: "I don't know by what right I made that appeal to you on Sunday. . . . They often ask 'Why the R.A.F.?' and I don't know. Only I have tried it and liked it as much after trying it as I did before. The difference between Army & Air is that between earth & air: no less." Even Lawrence's pal at Bovington, Corporal Dixon, thought he was crazy on the subject of the air force, as did the sinister Bruce, but it made no difference; "I can't get the longing for it out of my mind," he wrote Buchan, and that was true. Lawrence's yearning for the RAF was not a matter of reason.

Meanwhile, Manning Pike was slipping far behind with his typesetting—Lawrence had committed his book to a man who was not only inexperienced but subject to "fits of extreme depression," and on top of that "had an unhappy marriage." Lawrence, sunk in depression himself, was obliged to cheer Pike up. At the same time, Buxton, Lawrence's banker, was reluctant to increase his overdraft. In the end, there seemed no other way out but for Lawrence to resign himself to staying in the Royal Tank Corps, and sell the rights to an abridged version of *Seven Pillars of Wisdom* to finance the printing of the subscribers' edition. Cape, despite Lawrence's earlier decision to withdraw from his agreement to the abridged version, offered Lawrence a comparatively modest advance of £3,000; and with whatever misgivings, Lawrence accepted it, and agreed to publication in 1927, giving himself enough time (and money) to complete the limited edition. Most, if not all, of the abridgment had already been made by Garnett, but of course it would now have to be redone in view of the changes Lawrence had made in the text of the complete book.

Lawrence might have continued to serve in the RTC and work on the two different versions of his book, however unhappily, but in May 1925 Lowell Thomas's *With Lawrence in Arabia* was at last published in Britain. It had been a huge success in the United States, and became one again in Britain, reviving curiosity about Lawrence at just the moment when he felt most defeated. The same old exaggerations, told in the jocular voice of an American pitchman, were made more unbearable for Lawrence because he had given Thomas so many of his stories and anecdotes in the first place. Overwhelmed, Lawrence wrote a plaintive letter to Edward Garnett, describing his book as "muck," and adding that this "gloomy view of it deepens each time I have to wade through it. . . . I'm no bloody good on earth. So I'm going to quit . . . [and] bequeath you my notes on recruit life in the recruits' camp of the R.A.F."

Garnett took this as a suicide threat and, thoroughly alarmed, wrote to Shaw, who once again took the matter to Stanley Baldwin, and pointed out that the suicide of one of Britain's most famous heroes because he had been refused permission to transfer from the army to the RAF would be a scandal. The last thing Baldwin wanted was a huge scandal—it was his fate to have to deal first with Lawrence and then with the far more embarrassing problem of King Edward VIII's wish to marry the twice-divorced Wallis Simpson and make her his queen. As a result, in August 1925 Private T. E. Shaw rejoined the Royal Air Force at last as 338171 AC2 Shaw.

CHAPTER TWELVE

Apotheosis

> He is all adrift when it comes to fighting, and had not
> seen deaths in battle.
>
> —T. E. Lawrence, commenting on Homer,
> in the note to his translation of
> the *Odyssey*, 1932

L awrence, like Homer's Odysseus, was home again. On July 16, 1925, Trenchard signed the order approving Lawrence's transfer from the army to the RAF for a period of five years of regular service and four years in the reserve. A week later Lawrence was ordered to report to RAF West Drayton for processing. All this was done far from the attention of the press. At West Drayton, he was immediately recognized. "A Flight-Sergeant came along. . . . 'Hello, Ross,' he greeted him, and was immediately corrected by a dynamo-switchboard attendant behind him who said: 'Garn, that ain't Ross . . . he's Colonel Lawrence.' "

After the usual medical examination, Lawrence was sent on to RAF Uxbridge in charge of a corporal. When he arrived there, on a Friday afternoon, nobody wanted to know anything about him, and nobody was willing to sign for him. He was "dragged in to the Headquarters Adjutant, the last hope. He glared. 'What are you?' I very stilly replied 'Yesterday I was a Pte in the R.T.C.' He snorted 'Today?' 'I think I'm an A.C. twice in the R.A.F.' Snort second. 'Will you be in the Navy tomorrow?' 'Perhaps,' said I. 'I can't sign for you. I don't want you.' 'I don't want anybody to sign for me.' 'Damned silly . . . who the hell are you?' At this point my feeble patience broke. 'If your name was Buggins, and I called you Bill . . .' Then he yelled with joy, recognizing my names for him . . . and gave me tea." (This from a long letter to one of Lawrence's pals from Bovington, Private E. Palmer, nicknamed "Posh.")

That night Lawrence was fully "kitted out," and at long last exchanged the hated army khaki for the beloved RAF blue, carrying back to his hut "two kit bags, a set of equipment,* great coat, bayonet, like a plum tree too heavy with fruit." Saturday he "squared" the camp tailors to alter his uniforms to the preferred tight fit and knife-edge creases. Sunday he spent "Blancoing" his webbing (it was issued in the same khaki color as the army's but had to be altered to RAF blue with a product called blanco) and polishing his bayonet. On Monday he took the train for RAF Cranwell, home of the Royal Air Force Cadet College, where candidates for a regular commission were trained. This was the RAF equivalent of the Royal Military Academy at Sandhurst and the Royal Naval Academy at Dartmouth. It was also a real aerodrome, where the cadets learned to fly. Like all airmen, Lawrence was really happy only with the comforting noise of engines revving up. Trenchard had chosen well. The commandant of the Air College was Air Commodore A. E. ("Biffy") Borton, who had flown with the RFC in support of Lawrence in the desert, and later commanded the air force in Palestine. It was Biffy Borton who had flown the big Handley-Page bomber that so awed Lawrence's tribesmen when it landed on a desert airstrip, and he instantly recognized Lawrence and

---

*A full set of equipment consisted of large pack, small pack, webbing belt, ammunition pouches, canteen and bayonet holders, rifle sling, and all the straps that held everything together; it had to be assembled in an exact pattern, brass buckles gleaming.

sent for him. Lawrence was not only back in the air force; he was under the command of a man whom he liked and trusted, and who admired him. The gloom of the past two years lifted ever so slightly.

Lawrence was posted to B Flight, as an aircraft hand. His immediate world consisted of a sergeant, a corporal, and fourteen airmen, who shared the same hut. Their job was to look after the six training aircraft used by the fifteen officers and cadets of B Flight. The work interested Lawrence, who loved machinery, and except for an early morning parade he spent most of his day in overalls working around the aircraft. Inevitably, there was a close relationship between the pilots and their ground crew—a pilot's life depended on the men who serviced his aircraft, so there was none of the distance that existed between officers and men in the army. Nor was any great secret made of the fact that AC2 Shaw was in fact Lawrence of Arabia. A good many of the airmen knew or guessed it, and Biffy Borton and his wife occasionally invited AC2 Shaw to their quarters for the evening, as did Borton's chief staff officer, Wing Commander Sydney Smith, and his lively and beautiful wife, Clare. The Smiths had known Lawrence in Cairo, and both of them liked and understood him. Clare shared Lawrence's passionate interest in music, and was able to maintain an easy and unforced relationship with him, in which neither his present rank nor his past glory was an issue. She may have been the only woman who actually flirted with Lawrence, an experience which he seems to have enjoyed.*

As for Lawrence, he himself was discreet, and never took advantage of his friendship with the Bortons and the Smiths, or with the college medical officer, an elderly wing commander who was a former surgeon to the king, and now quietly took on Lawrence as, in effect, a private patient. Normally, an airman who makes friends with officers is distrusted by other airmen, but Lawrence never lorded it over his mates or sought spe-

---

* Clare Sydney Smith would eventually write a touching book about her friendship with Lawrence, *The Golden Reign*. Nancy Astor (Viscountess Astor), the first woman member of Parliament, had a relationship with Lawrence that was certainly flirtatious—she was the only woman who rode pillion behind him on his motorcycle—but she was rather too formidable a personality to be described as a flirt.

cial favors. His own sergeant, Flight Sergeant Pugh, summed up his feelings about AC2 Shaw in words rarely heard from an NCO about any of his men: "He was hero-worshipped by all the flight for his never failing, cheery disposition, ability to get all he could for their benefit, never complaining. . . . Quarrels ceased and the flight had to pull together for the sheer joy of remaining in his company and being with him for his companionship, help, habits, fun and teaching one and all to play straight." Something of his old spirit, which he had shown when teasing Auda Abu Tayi, seems to have returned, touching the men who slept in Hut 105 at Cranwell.

Of course a service college is not an ordinary camp, even for the lowliest airman. At Cranwell the focus was on the cadets, not the airmen who looked after their aircraft—and it boasted amenities that included an excellent library (to which Lawrence would add a specially bound copy of the subscribers' edition of *Seven Pillars of Wisdom*), a weatherproof hut for his latest Brough "Superior" motorcycle, a noncommissioned aristocracy of sergeant pilots and sergeant technicians, and even a swimming pool. Lawrence and some of his mates would run to the pool "at first dawn" on summer mornings, "to dive into the elastic water which fits our bodies as closely as a skin:—and we belong to that too. Everywhere a relationship: no loneliness any more."

"No loneliness any more," expresses very precisely what Lawrence sought and found in the RAF; and while the bond between Lawrence and his air force mates was hard for friends like the Hardys, the Shaws, Winston Churchill, Hogarth, and Lionel Curtis to understand, it was vital to him. He was like the kind of schoolboy who goes home on a holiday from boarding school reluctantly, because his closest friends are his schoolmates. Lawrence corresponded with his mates when he was away, sending long, interesting letters, full of what he was doing; he even corresponded with some of the soldiers he had liked at Bovington, such as Corporal Dixon and Posh Palmer, and with those airmen who had been with him in Uxbridge. He made them small loans and did them small favors, and remained genuinely interested in their lives and open about his own life.

However widespread his friendships among the rich, the famous, the talented, and the politically powerful were, it was in the barracks, not the drawing room, that he found an antidote to his loneliness.

This is not to say that Lawrence could not switch from one world to the other. He would ride his Brough motorcycle (he had christened the first one Boanerges, "Sons of Thunder," and would continue naming the others Boanerges II, Boanarges III, etc.) down to London, or off to country

Lawrence takes delivery of a Brough Superior Motorcycle.
George Brough is on the left.

houses when he could get leave, always turning up in the uniform of an airman, to the astonishment of butlers and hall porters. He paid a visit to Feisal, now king of Iraq, in London, and they both went off for lunch at Lord Winterton's house in Surrey. Winterton, now undersecretary of state for India, had served with Lawrence in the advance on Damascus, but Lawrence tried to resist being drawn into nostalgic talk about the war. He "found Feisal lively, happy to see me, friendly, curious," as well he might be at the sight of "Aurens" in a simple airman's uniform—as much of a disguise, of course, as the Arab robes and headdress had ever been. Even in Lawrence's letter to Charlotte Shaw describing this visit, his ferocious self-renunciation is replayed with frightening intensity: "So long as there is breath in my body my strength will be exerted to keep my soul in prison, since nowhere else can it exist in safety. The terror of being run away with, in the liberty of power, lies at the back of these many renunciations of my later life. I am afraid of myself. Is this madness?"

Seldom has anybody stated more clearly his determination never again to be placed in a position of power over others. With all his formidable willpower Lawrence was determined to shackle the part of himself that had sought fame, glory, and greatness, and never allow it to rise again except in the pages of his book. Nobody knew better than Lawrence what he was capable of. He had executed a man in cold blood, suffered torture, killed people he loved, witnessed the ruthless murder of prisoners in the aftermath of battle. Nor was anybody more anxious to do penance. It was as if one of the great heroes of medieval times, one of those figures whose castles and tombs Lawrence had spent so much of his boyhood studying, had put aside his honors and retired in midlife to a monastery, tending to his herb garden and performing his humble chores, a simple brother, hoping not to evoke curiosity, pity, or interest. Yet, with the contradictory impulse that was so much a part of his nature, Lawrence was hard at work on two projects that were bound to stir up renewed interest in him: the completion of the thirty-guinea subscribers' edition of *Seven Pillars of Wisdom* (now planned to consist of 150 copies) and the abridged, popular version of the book, to be called *Revolt in the Desert*. Also, he had allowed

Robert Graves, who desperately needed money, to convert a proposed children's book about him into a full-scale biography.

Sometimes stormy, sometimes mundane, Lawrence's correspondence with Charlotte Shaw continued, while she and G.B.S. involved themselves in the formidable task of proofreading the subscribers' edition of *Seven Pillars of Wisdom*, which Manning Pike was struggling to set as Lawrence (and the Shaws) wanted it. Some hint of how demanding the job was can be gleaned from Lawrence's instructions to Charlotte about making insertions in the text.

> This bundle of proofs is sent, with an envelope, on its way to Pike. You were not satisfied with galley 18: so I have had it re-set, or its middle part, and the new piece is pinned on. . . . The rules are simple:
>
> i. Page always thirty-seven lines.
> ii. Each page begins with a new paragraph, and a small capital extending over three lines. Spaces for these are left in the new proof.
> iii. The last line of each page is solid, i.e. extends to the right hand margin.
> iv. No word is divided.
> v. Paragraphs end always after the half-way across the line.

Even in our own age of computerized typesetting, any one of these rules would present problems, particularly iii and iv, so it is hardly surprising that the work absorbed a huge amount of time and effort on the part of Lawrence and Charlotte and nearly drove Manning Pike crazy. It does not seem to have occurred to Lawrence that the completion of either of these two projects would bring the national press back to the gates of Cranwell in pursuit of the "uncrowned king of Arabia." But then, with Lawrence, one never knows. He does not seem to have been able to go for more than a year or two without bringing down on his head exactly the kind of attention he claimed to fear most. As Charlotte had once told her husband, "Something extraordinary always happens to that man."

Perhaps to alleviate Lawrence's depression, Charlotte kept up a stream of presents. Hardly any airman at Cranwell can ever have received more frequent packages: a novel by Joseph Conrad; a bundle of magazines, followed a few weeks later by two more books, and a few days later by more magazines, newspapers, and a copy of Liam O'Flaherty's *The Informer*; a week later, another novel; and shortly afterward a box of four books from an antiquarian bookseller and a gift basket of chocolates and cakes from Gunter's, the fashionable Mayfair tea shop. The gift basket from Gunter's arrived without a card, but Lawrence was in no doubt about who had sent it. This was a mutual though sexless seduction. Lawrence responded with long letters, sometimes gently teasing (a contrast to Bernard Shaw's cruel teasing), sometimes self-mocking (as when Lawrence likened the sumptuously illustrated and bound subscribers' edition to "a scrofulous peacock"); he also sent her further proofs from Pike, to be read over for misprints. Since poor Charlotte had weak eyes, her constant attention to the proofs of *Seven Pillars of Wisdom* is a further demonstration of her devotion to Lawrence, and his growing dependence on her. It would not be exaggerating to say that she mothered Lawrence—this was easier to do now that his mother and his eldest brother, Bob, had left to take up their own adventure as missionaries in China. For his part, he accepted being mothered by Charlotte, but there was more to it than this: they were also kindred souls, who could share with each other emotions and experiences that they could not have shared with anyone else—his reaction to the rape at Deraa, her fear of sex and childbirth—and that in Charlotte's case would have been brushed off or explained to her in Fabian or Freudian terms by her husband. It was as close to a love affair as either of them—two people who scrupulously avoided even the mildest terms of endearment in their thirteen years of correspondence—could ever have approached.

Like so many of Lawrence's friends, the Shaws learned to accept his appearance at their doorstep on his motorcycle, much as they disliked the machine. Lawrence had already survived two serious accidents while he was at Bovington, either one of which could easily have killed him. As the saying goes, "There is no such thing as a minor motorcycle accident." It was not so much that Lawrence was a bad or dangerous rider—George Brough, the designer and manufacturer of his motorcycles, would argue that on the contrary, he was a skillful and careful one—but he used his motorcycle as everyday transportation, often over long distances and poor roads in bad weather. Fallen leaves, puddles, and patches of ice can all cause a skid even at less than daredevil speeds; and in the 1920s and 1930s a motorcycle headlight was, by modern standards, dim and unreliable. (It was not for nothing that Joseph Lucas, founder of the major British manufacturer of automotive electrical equipment, was known to owners of motorcycles as the "prince of darkness.") Moreover, though Brough was something of a genius, his motorcycles were, for their day, large, heavy, and very powerful machines, a lot to handle for a slight man in his late thirties with a history of broken bones.

At an earlier stage of his life, Lawrence had traveled to far-off foreign places and had written to his family at home. Now, it was Lawrence who was in England while his mother and Bob were far away in China, which was impoverished, turbulent, dangerous, swept by competing warlords and by revolution, and at every level of society deeply hostile to European missionaries. It was now Lawrence who arranged for parcels to be sent abroad. He went to W. H. Smith's, the British chain of newsagents, where his uniform was greeted with suspicion, to take out subscriptions to the *Times* and the *New Statesman* to be sent to his mother in China; he also mailed packages containing items she had requested: Scott's journals, salts of lemon, and padlocks for her trunks. Lawrence's youngest brother, Arnold, and his wife were living temporarily at Clouds Hill—tight quarters for a married couple—while Lawrence spent Christmas Eve of 1925 alone in Hut 105 at Cranwell, correcting the proofs of his book and reading T. S. Eliot's collected poems, apparently content. On Christmas Day, he wrote to his mother, who had asked if he needed money, summing up his plans and his financial state:

> No thanks: no money. I am quite right that way just now. How I'll
> stand a year or so hence, when all the bills of the reprint of my book
> come in, I don't know. The subscribers (about 100) have paid £15
> each, to date. That is £1,500 more due from them. The expenses to date

are £4,500. The Bank has loaned me the rest, against security from me. To meet the deficit I have sold Cape (for £3,000 cash + a royalty) the right to publish 1/3 of the book after January 1, 1927. And there will be American serial & other receipts, too. Probably I'll come out of it well enough off.

For his mother's benefit, Lawrence oversimplified the immense task of printing the subscribers' edition of *Seven Pillars of Wisdom*. He also significantly underplayed the many difficulties he had imposed on Cape and his American publisher Doran over *Revolt in the Desert*, particularly by setting a limit to the number of copies of the abridgment that could be printed during his lifetime and thus eliminating for all practical purposes the possibility of a runaway best seller. In any case, he was determined not to benefit personally from either version of his memoir. This was high-minded but shortsighted—the two books would have made him a rich man, had he been willing to become rich. In this, as in other matters, Lawrence clung to his policy of renunciation. He very much wished to be recognized as a great writer, but—perhaps unlike all other authors—he did not want to profit from writing, or to endure (or encourage) the publicity that would inevitably accompany success.

The excellence of Lawrence's relationship with the airmen of his flight can be guessed by the fact that he hired a bus to take them all, including Pugh, to the annual air show at Hendon, just outside London. As the deadline—March 1926—approached, he also got two of his hut mates to help him in the laborious task of cutting the text of *Seven Pillars of Wisdom* for the abridgment, "as with a brush and India ink, [he] boldly obliterated whole slabs of text," at night in Hut 105, and cutting the first seven chapters entirely, thus deftly turning the account into a very superior adventure story. His cuts were not only bold but painstaking and supremely confident; he made almost no insertions, or "bridges," to link the text together, yet it reads so smoothly and seamlessly that one would never imagine it had been cut out of a much larger whole. No doubt Lawrence was guided to some degree by Edward Garnett's previous abridgment,

but his own version differed in some crucial ways. In particular, he eliminated the death of Farraj (which Garnett was reluctant to give up), partly
because it required too many pages to explain and partly, one guesses,
because the tone of *Revolt in the Desert* was considerably more upbeat
than that of *Seven Pillars of Wisdom*. Lawrence's shooting the wounded
Farraj to keep him from falling into the hands of the Turks was exactly the
kind of moral ambiguity that he wanted to keep out of the abridged book.

In truth, *Revolt in the Desert*, though it is dwarfed by *Seven Pillars of
Wisdom*, is a far more readable book. It opens with a bang at Lawrence's
arrival in Jidda—the first line is, "When at last we anchored in Jeddah's
outer harbour . . . then the heat of Arabia came out like a drawn sword
and struck us speechless," a very effective beginning—and it is by no
means an insubstantial volume. The 1927 Doran edition is 335 pages
long, or about 120,000 words. Interestingly, the author is identified on
the jacket, binding, and title page as 'T. E. Lawrence': the British-style
single quotation marks are Lawrence's way of suggesting that this person
was mythical rather than real. Lawrence had many misgivings about
putting his name on the subscribers' edition of *Seven Pillars of Wisdom*,
and at one point decided to use the initials T.E.S.; but in the end, he opted
to eliminate any mention that he was the author at all. Since all the copies are signed to the subscriber or to the person to whom he was giving
the book, putting his name on the title page seemed to him unnecessary.
This is perhaps the only case in literary history in which a major work
has appeared with no indication of who the author was. Although he was
still as opposed to bibliophiles as ever, Lawrence and his airmen aides
went to considerable trouble to make every copy of the subscribers' edition different, so that in some small way no two copies would be identical, thus keeping collectors busy for the next nine decades trying to spot
and identify the differences. Some, of course, were easy—Lawrence had
Trenchard's "partial" copy (it was missing a few illustrations) bound in
RAF blue leather, or as close as the bookbinder could get to that elusive
color. He wrote to Trenchard: "It is not the right blue of course: but then
what is the right blue? No two airmen are alike: indeed it is a miracle if

the top and bottom halves of one airman are the same colour. . . . I told the binder (ex-R.A.F.) who it is for. 'Then,' said he, 'it must be quite plain and very well done.' "

It was fortunate that Lawrence finished his labors when he did. In the spring of 1926, coming to the aid of a man whose car had been involved in an accident, he offered to start the engine and the man neglected to retard the ignition. The starting handle flew back sharply, breaking Lawrence's right arm and dislocating his wrist. Showing no sign of pain or shock, he calmly asked the driver to adjust the ignition, cranked the engine again with his left hand, then drove his motorcycle back to Cranwell. In Flight Sergeant Pugh's words, "with his right arm dangling and shifting gears with his foot, [he] got his bus* home, and parked without a word to a soul of the pain he was suffering." The medical officer was away, and it was the next day before he could see Lawrence, who still did not complain. "That is a man!" Pugh commented admiringly. Although Lawrence recovered from this injury, later photographs often show him clearly nursing his left arm and wrist, and it seems safe to say that it gave him pain for the rest of his life.

By 1926 it was clear that Lawrence's posting to Cranwell would soon have to end. One reason for this was RAF policy, which required that an airman must eventually be posted overseas—to India or Egypt for a period of five years, or to Iraq for two years (because of its vile climate). It would be impossible to send Lawrence to Egypt, where his presence would surely have a political effect—after all, he had been offered the post of British high commissioner in Cairo to succeed Allenby, and he was known to be in favor of greater independence for Egypt. Posting him to Iraq would be even more difficult; his friend Feisal was its king, and Lawrence's presence there would cause consternation, besides stimulating the Sunni tribesmen to who knew what dreams of war and plunder. Nobody had forgotten how the tribes had ridden in from the desert cry-

---

* "Bus," like "kite," is RAF slang for an aircraft, particularly a multiengine bomber or transport, and by extension also a motor vehicle of any kind.

ing "Aurens, Aurens" and firing off their rifles to greet him in Amman in 1921. That left only India, which was not an attractive proposition for Lawrence: he had done the government of India out of its ambition to occupy and control Iraq, and for that and other reasons was disliked by Indian officials, some of whom still bitterly resented the opinions he had expressed about them during his visit to Baghdad in 1916.

Trenchard offered Lawrence a chance to stay in Britain, but Lawrence was more realistic; the publication of *Revolt in the Desert*, of which 40,000 words would first be serialized in the *Daily Telegraph* (which had paid £2,000, or about the equivalent of $160,000 in today's money), and the release of *Seven Pillars of Wisdom* to the subscribers would make him headline news again, all the more so because *Revolt in the Desert* would be published in America at the same time. "It is good of you to give me the option of going overseas or staying at home," Lawrence wrote to Trenchard, "but I volunteered to go, deliberately, for the reason that I am publishing a book (about myself in Arabia) on March 3, 1927: and experience taught me in Farnborough in 1922 that neither good-will on the part of those above me, nor correct behaviour on my part can prevent my being a nuisance in any camp where the daily press can get at me. . . . Overseas they will be harmless, and therefore I must go overseas for a while and dodge them."

It was already clear that *Seven Pillars of Wisdom* would be oversubscribed: the list of subscribers included, among writers alone, Compton Mackenzie, H. G. Wells, Bernard Shaw, Thomas Hardy, and Hugh Walpole; and among other notable figures it included King George V (Lawrence contrived to return the check for the king's copy and make him a present of the book).* Lawrence declined to give the usual two copies to

---

*Lawrence printed 128 "complete" copies (with all the illustrations) for the subscribers, as well as thirty-six complete copies and twenty-six incomplete copies (the latter lacking some of the illustrations) to give away to friends, plus twenty-two copies without plates and certain textual omissions to go to the George H. Doran Company in New York, some to secure U.S. copyright, others to be offered for sale at the prohibitively high price of $200,000 a copy (about $3.2 million in today's money). Of these copies, Lawrence kept six. (*Letters*, 295, 466, quoted in Hyde, *Solitary in the Ranks*.)

the Bodleian Library in Oxford and the British Museum Library, as was required for copyright purposes, having already donated the original manuscript to the Bodleian. This was an infringement of the U.K. Copyright Act, but being Lawrence he got away with it.

His last weeks in England were spoiled by another serious motorcycle accident, in which his latest Brough was badly damaged, but Lawrence sustained only a cut on his knee. He had to rent out his cottage, collect the books he wanted to take with him, and make his good-byes to the Shaws and the Hardys. The farewell to Hardy was a sad moment for them both. Hardy was eighty-six, and neither of them expected he would live to see Lawrence's return. They stood on the porch at Max Gate in the cold weather, talking, and Lawrence finally sent Hardy into the house to get a shawl to wrap around his neck and chest. While Hardy was inside, Lawrence pushed his motorcycle quietly down to the road, started it up, and drove away, to spare Hardy the pain of saying farewell, and to spare his own feelings too, for he loved Hardy deeply. He sent his mother's copy of *Seven Pillars of Wisdom* to his brother Arnold, to look after it until she returned to England; and he wrote to her in China, chiding her gently for staying there despite the danger, and warning her and Bob of the futility of "endeavours to influence the national life of another people by one's own," a reflection not only of his dislike of Christian missionaries, but of his own experience with the Bedouin.

He sailed for India on December 7, 1926, on board the *Derbyshire*, an antiquated, squalid troopship, packed with 1,200 officers and men, as well as a number of their wives and children, in conditions that shocked him. "I have been surprised at the badness of our accommodation," he wrote to Charlotte, "and the clotted misery . . . on board." Conditions were so bad that Lawrence wrote a letter of complaint about them to his friend Eddie Marsh, Winston Churchill's private secretary, knowing that Marsh would pass it on. This became something of a habit with Lawrence— throughout his life in the RAF he made behind-the-scenes efforts to improve the lives of servicemen by bringing problems to the attention of those with the power to change things for the better. He persuaded Trenchard to drop many of the small regulations that plagued airmen's lives unnecessarily—reducing the number of kit inspections to one a month, for example, as well as allowing airmen to unbutton the top two buttons of their greatcoat (unlike soldiers), removing the silly "swagger sticks" they were supposed to carry when in walking-out uniform, and abolishing the requirement to wear a polished bayonet for church parades. Lawrence wrote detailed letters about anything that seemed to him unfair, antiquated, or just plain silly, and in a surprising number of cases won his point, substantially improving the life of "other ranks." Churchill was serving at the time as chancellor of the exchequer, and had already made the disastrous decision to return the pound to the gold standard, which many economists would later decide was the starting point of the great worldwide Depression; but at Lawrence's behest he paused long enough to inquire into the conditions of shipping British service personnel and their families. Lawrence had an uncanny knack for bringing to the attention of those in high office conditions about which they would not normally have been informed, and getting them to do something. This was perhaps the only aspect of his fame that he found useful. His correspondence is full of injustices he wants corrected, or idiotic regulations he wants abolished. He served as a discreet and entirely unofficial equivalent of what is now called an ombudsman, and was responsible for a surprising number of commonsense reforms, including the abolition of puttees for airmen and their replacement with trousers, and the replacement of the tunic with a high collar clasped tightly around the neck by a more comfortable tunic with lapels, worn over a shirt and tie. These interventions were seldom, if ever, for his own benefit; nor did he mention them to his fellow airmen. He was always a master of the skillfully handled suggestion that allowed other people to take the credit, just as Bernard Shaw re-created him in the role of the omniscient, omnipotent Private Meek in *Too True to Be Good*.

As it happens, the conditions of life on board the *Derbyshire* were shocking, though not unusual, and in describing them Lawrence provided unflinching descriptions of squalor and filth: the account of his experience as "Married Quarters sentry" is so painful as to be almost unreadable. His friend and admirer John Buchan said after reading it that it took "the breath away by its sheer brutality." Buchan considered Lawrence's power of depicting squalor uncanny, and said there was nothing in *The Mint* to equal it.

Swish swish the water goes against the walls of the ship, sounds nearer. Where on earth is that splashing. I tittup along the alley and peep into the lavatory space, at a moment when no woman is there. It's awash with a foul drainage. Tactless posting a sentry over the wives' defaecations, I think. Tactless and useless all our duties aboard.

Hullo here's the Orderly Officer visiting. May as well tell him. The grimy-folded face, the hard jaw, toil-hardened hands, bowed and ungainly figure. An ex-naval warrant, I'll bet. No gentleman. He strides boldly to the latrine: "Excuse me" unshyly to two shrinking women. "God," he jerked out, "with shit—where's the trap?" He pulled off his tunic and threw it at me to hold, and with a plumber's quick glance strode over to the far side, bent down, and ripped out a grating. Gazed for a moment, while the ordure rippled over his boots. Up his right sleeve, baring a forearm hairy as a mastiff's grey leg, knotted with veins, and a gnarled hand: thrust it deep in, groped, pulled out a moist white bundle. "Open that port" and out it splashed into the night. "You'd think they'd have had some other place for their sanitary towels. Bloody awful show, not having anything fixed up." He shook his sleeve down as it was over his slowly-drying arm, and huddled on his tunic, while the released liquid gurgled contentedly down its reopened drain.

The voyage from Southampton to Karachi took a month, and was sheer hell—"Wave upon wave of the smell of stabled humanity," as Lawrence put it, so awful that even India, which he disliked on sight, seemed to be a deliverance. He was sent to the RAF depot on Drigh Road, seven miles outside Karachi, "a dry hole, on the edge of the Sind desert, which desert is a waste of land and sandstone," a place of endless dust and dust storms, indeed, where dust seemed like a fifth element, covering everything, including the food. He was assigned as a clerk in the Engine Repair Section, where aircraft engines were given their regularly scheduled overhaul—easy work. The tropical workday at that time ran from 7:30 A.M. to 1 P.M., after which he had the rest of the day off. He spent most of his day in overalls; there was no PT; there were few parades; and his greatest problems were the lack of hot water to bathe in, and sheer boredom. Being on the edge of a desert filled him with both loathing and nostalgia—in the evenings, he could hear the noise of camel bells in the distance as a caravan made its way down Drigh Road. He did not leave the depot to go into Karachi; he had no curiosity about India at all. He spent his spare time sitting on his bunk reading the fifth volume of Winston Churchill's history of the war, *The Great Crisis*; writing letters; brushing up his Greek; and listening to classical music on the gramophone in his barracks, which he shared with fourteen other airmen.

In February, the pictures he had commissioned at such great expense for the subscribers' edition of *Seven Pillars of Wisdom*—oil paintings, watercolors, drawings, pastels, and woodcuts—were collected by Eric Kennington and put on display for the public at the Leicester Gallery, in London. Bernard Shaw contributed the preface to the catalog, declaiming, in his usual no-holds-barred style, "The limelight of history follows the authentic hero as the theatre limelight follows the *prima ballerina assoluta*. It soon concentrated its whitest radiance on Colonel Lawrence, alias Lurens Bey, alias Prince of Damascus, the mystery man, the wonder man," and calling *Seven Pillars of Wisdom* "a masterpiece." The gallery was packed for the two weeks of the show, with a long line of people waiting each day to get in. Although nobody but the subscribers could read the book, it was already creating a sensation. People eager to read it offered small fortunes in the classified ads of the newspapers for an opportunity to borrow one of the copies.

The center of this first, small storm of publicity meanwhile sat in the Drigh Road Depot, Karachi, keeping track of engine repairs as AC2 Shaw, almost as far removed from the limelight as it was possible to get. "I do wish, hourly, that our great Imperial heritage of the East would go the way of my private property. . . . However it's no use starting on that sadness, since coming out here is my own (and unrepented) fault entirely," he wrote to a friend. In March *Revolt in the Desert* was published; it sold, as Lawrence boasted to a friend, "Something over 40,000 copies in the first three weeks" in the United Kingdom alone, and would go on to sell 90,000 copies before Lawrence managed to get it withdrawn.* In America it was an even bigger success, selling more than 130,000 copies in the first weeks, and ensuring that Lawrence's debts and overdraft from the production of the subscribers' edition of *Seven Pillars of Wisdom* would be wiped clean. With money pouring in, Lawrence, still determined not to make a profit, founded an anonymous charity fund to educate the children of disabled or deceased RAF officers. The RAF Benevolent Fund, created by Trenchard, provided the same for all ranks, but Lawrence felt that since the majority of pilots killed in action were officers in those days, his fund would fill a special niche. No doubt it would have surprised Lawrence's fellow airmen in Room 2 of the barracks at the RAF Depot on Drigh Road, Karachi, not to speak of the officers there, that AC2 Shaw was sitting on his bunk, writing pad on his knees, giving away thousands of pounds; but as usual Lawrence was anxious to keep his benevolence, as well as his identity, to himself.

Through March and April the glowing reviews of *Revolt in the Desert* continued to arrive—Charlotte had thoughtfully subscribed to a clipping agency on Lawrence's behalf. The only reviewer who seemed to dislike the book was Leonard Woolf, husband of the novelist Virginia Woolf; he chided Lawrence sternly for imitating Charles Doughty's style ("so imitative . . . as to be near parody"), although even Woolf admitted to enjoying the book once he had overcome his irritation. It was typical of Lawrence's ability to cross class lines that he heard about Woolf's review from his old regimental sergeant major at Bovington Camp. Lawrence correctly pointed out to his friends that he had, for better or worse, created his own

*Perhaps more than any other single title, *Revolt in the Desert* ensured the survival and profitability of its U.K. publisher, Jonathan Cape.

style. With this one exception, the reviews he received would have pleased any author. The *Times Literary Supplement* called the book "a great story, greatly written." The *Times* called it "a masterpiece." *The Daily Telegraph* described it as "one of the most stirring stories of our times." From London came the flattering news that Eric Kennington had completed a new bust of Lawrence in gilt brass. A letter arrived from Allenby praising Lawrence for "a great work"; this was both a relief and a pleasure, given Lawrence's admiration for his old chief. John Buchan—author of *Greenmantle*, and the future Lord Tweedsmuir, governor-general of Canada—wrote to say that Lawrence was "the best living writer of English prose."

Although self-doubt was ingrained in Lawrence's nature, he could not help being pleased at the reception of his book, in both forms. He had accomplished exactly what he set out to do: to achieve fame as a writer while keeping the full text of *Seven Pillars of Wisdom* out of the public's hands. As was so often the case, he had neatly managed to fulfill what would have seemed to anyone else contradictory ambitions. Of course *Revolt in the Desert* rekindled his fame throughout the English-speaking world, though this time his story was conveyed in his own words, rather than in those of Lowell Thomas. Like it or not, he was now perhaps the most famous man of his time: his face, half-shrouded by the white Arab headdress with the golden *agal*, was instantly recognizable to millions of people; his status as hero was such that, of all the millions of men who fought in what was coming to be called the Great War, Lawrence would eventually become the one remembered by most people.

In the eyes of the world the hero had eclipsed the man. Without seeming to have desired it, Lawrence had reached a virtual apotheosis—it was as if the real person had been swallowed by the legend. Not only Bernard Shaw believed that if Britain had a Valhalla, Lawrence belonged in it. The immense success of his books, the mystery that surrounded him, his puzzling disappearance at the very moment when the English-speaking world was focused on his achievements—all this represented something of a miraculous feat itself. Not only had he managed to escape the press, but in India his presence went unnoticed. Unlike Uxbridge, Farnborough, Bovington, and Cranwell, the RAF depot in Karachi was a place where he remained for the moment merely AC2 Shaw, an ordinary airman meticulously keeping track of engine parts and attracting little or no attention.

Of course no legendary hero successfully disappears forever, as Lawrence surely knew better than anyone else. However modestly AC2 Shaw behaved, however carefully he did his job as a clerk, however quietly he kept to himself, there were still occasional signs that he was no ordinary airman. At Cranwell, the telegraph boy had been astounded by the number of telegrams he had to deliver every day to AC2 Shaw (at the time, ordinary people received a telegram only if there was a death in the family), as well as by the fact that Shaw always tipped him a shilling. At Drigh Road everybody was equally astounded by the number of letters and packages that AC2 Shaw received; books, gramophone records, gift boxes of food, manuscripts, play scripts, envelopes full of press clippings. Shaw spent most of his meager pay buying stamps to answer this constant stream of mail.

Among the letters of praise he received was one from his friend Trenchard, the chief of the air staff, recently promoted to marshal of the Royal Air Force. Trenchard was writing to his most unusual airman to say that he couldn't put down his copy of *Seven Pillars of Wisdom* (bound in RAF-blue leather), and that he had insured it and left it in his will to his little son. "When I opened your letter," Lawrence replied, "I gasped, expecting something of ill-omen. However, all's well. . . . There is no local press, and I arouse no interest in the camp." He dropped a quick hint in his reply that there was to be "another 'life' of me this autumn, written by a friend, the poet Robert Graves," a piece of news which must have made Trenchard sigh. One after the other, the books had flowed out: first Lowell Thomas's *With Lawrence in Arabia*, then Lawrence's own books, and now Robert Graves's biography.* Each one made headline news; there

---

* Lawrence had met Robert Graves when Graves came up to Jesus College, Oxford, as an undergraduate after the war (in which he had served with distinction as an infantry officer, and which he would later describe in *Goodbye to All That*). Graves had by then already achieved some fame as one of the British war poets, and he would go on to write more than 140 books before his death in 1985 at the age of ninety.

was no reason to suppose that Graves's would be an exception; and the last thing Trenchard wanted was to have Lawrence in the news again.

It would be a stretch to say that Lawrence was happy in his self-imposed "exile," as he called it, but he was relentlessly busy. At no point in his life did he write more letters. He spent nearly six months transforming his "notes" on his service at RAF Uxbridge and at Cranwell into a finished handwritten manuscript of *The Mint*, which he sent to Edward Garnett with instructions that it must not be published until 1950. He also accepted an American publisher's offer of £800 to make a new translation of Homer's *Odyssey*, a task for which he felt himself particularly well suited, since he had handled Bronze Age weapons as an archaeologist and had fought in a war close to that of the Greeks and the Trojans. He wrote to Eddie Marsh, thanking "Winston for his gorgeous letter," and adding, no doubt for Churchill's eyes, in an aside that sounds like a passage from *Greenmantle*: "The most dangerous point is Afghanistan. . . . The clash is bound to come, I think. . . . Do you know, if I'd known as much about the British Government in 1917, as I do now, I could have got enough of them [the people of the Middle East] behind me to have radically changed the face of Asia?"

To Trenchard, who was in part responsible for defending Iraq, and for preventing incursions into Trans-Jordan, Lawrence wrote in detail proposing a whole new policy for the Middle East. With his old self-confidence he also mentioned ibn Saud, whose advance was threatening Feisal and worrying Trenchard: "The fellow you need to influence is Feisal el Dueish. . . . If I were at Ur, my instinct would be to walk without notice into his headquarters. He'd not likely kill an unarmed, solitary man . . . and in two days guesting I could give him horizons beyond the Brethren [ibn Saud's Wahhabi fundamentalist warriors]. . . . Such performances require a manner to carry them off. I've done it four times, or is it five? A windy business . . . Beduin on camels will make a meal of any civilized camel-corps: or of infantry in the open: or of cavalry anyhow. Nor does a static line of defence avail. You need an elastic defence, in depth of at least 100 miles. Explored tracks for cars, threading this belt, approved landing grounds, sited pill-boxes of blockhouses, occupied occasionally and then fed and linked by armoured cars, and supervised from the air. . . . I could defend all E. Transjordan with a fist-full of armoured cars, and trained crews."

Since this was being written from his bunk by the RAF equivalent of a private to the RAF equivalent of a five-star general, it is fairly remarkable stuff, all the more so since it still remains good advice for dealing with desert raiders and insurgents, and indeed forms the basis for current strategy regarding similar enemies in Iraq and Afghanistan more than ninety years later. Trenchard certainly took it seriously, and recognized that Lawrence knew what he was talking about. He also knew that it would require a man with Lawrence's special courage to walk into an enemy leader's tent alone and unarmed, risking his life on the Muslim tradition of hospitality toward a guest.

It had not yet occurred to the powers that be in Drigh Road that AC1 Shaw (he had just been promoted to aircraftman first class, an automatic promotion which gave him no privileges, authority, or pleasure, but which he could not refuse) was in regular correspondence with Trenchard, Churchill, and Buchan about matters of state, or with Lionel Curtis about plans for transforming the British Empire into a commonwealth of equal states, or with the future Field Marshal the Earl Wavell about the future of tank warfare. Lawrence registered the death of friends: Hogarth, who, ironically, had been writing an entry on Lawrence for the *Encyclopaedia Britannica* when he died ("Hogarth is part, a great part, of Oxford, the concrete thing for which Oxford stood in my mind"); Thomas Hardy ("That day we reached Damascus," he wrote to Mrs. Hardy, "I cried, against all my control, for the triumphant thing achieved at last, fitly: and so the passing of T. H. touches me"); Gertrude Bell ("Gertrude was not a good judge of men or situations. . . . But depth and strength of emotion— Oh Lord, yes . . . A wonderful person. Not very like a woman, you know: they make much of her concern in dress:—but the results! She reminded me in one dress, of a blue jay. Her clothes and colours were always wrong").

Lawrence never left the depot itself—he described it as "a sort of voluntary permanent C.B." ("C.B." stands for a military punishment, "confined to barracks.") Unfortunately, that did not protect him. The air officer commanding the RAF in India was Air Vice-Marshal Sir Geoffrey Salmond, an old friend and admirer of Lawrence's since 1916. It was part of Salmond's duty to inspect every RAF station in India once a year—of course, his visit required prodigious preparation on the part of all the airmen—and following his inspection of Drigh Road Depot, he asked the commanding officer, Wing Commander Reginald Bone, CBE, DSO, "By the way, how's Shaw getting along?" Bone was puzzled. "Shaw? Shaw?" he replied. "I do not think we have here any officer of that name."

Air Marshal Salmond had dropped what is known in the RAF as a "clanger," or outside it as a "brick." Fortunately, he did not pursue the matter, but Bone kept an eye open for the mysterious AC1 Shaw and in time discovered that he was virtually the only person at Drigh Road not already in on the secret that AC1 Shaw was T. E. Lawrence.*

Bone was annoyed not to have been informed that one of his clerks was Lawrence of Arabia, and his natural tendency to take it out on Lawrence may have been increased by the fact that he had read and disliked Robert Graves's *Lawrence and the Arabian Adventure.* He sought out Lawrence, and as Lawrence put it in a letter to Trenchard's private secretary, Wing Commander T. B. Marson, another old friend, he "trod heavily on my harmless, if unattractive face."

Salmond quickly intervened to put a stop to this, presumably at the request of Trenchard, but the effect was that Bone was further embarrassed, and began to suspect that Lawrence was spying on him. Either because he had been informed by the camp post office, or because he had simply guessed correctly, he asked his adjutant to find out whether Lawrence was communicating with headquarters. The adjutant, who might

---

* By this time Lawrence had changed his name by deed poll to Shaw. Legally and officially he had abandoned the name which his father had chosen on leaving Ireland, and which Lawrence himself had made famous. It made little difference, of course—to most of the world he remained and would always remain "Lawrence"—but it at least removed the objection of some officers to the fact that he was serving in the ranks under a false name.

have proceeded with tact in view of the fact that the inquiry involved private letters between Airman Shaw and Marshal of the Royal Air Force Trenchard, was, in Lawrence's words, "bull-honest," and simply demanded to see the letters. Lawrence obediently showed him, among others, his latest letter from Trenchard, and another from Salmond, and so he "was sent for, cursed, and condemned to go up-country as a Bolshevik." This attack caused Salmond to reappear and read Bone the riot act, but it did not make Bone any happier to have such a well-connected airman on his station. Lawrence had mentioned in his last letter to Trenchard that he had been offered "$100,000 for a seven week lecture in the United States," and that he had turned down an offer of £5,000 for one of the five copies of the Oxford edition of *Seven Pillars of Wisdom*.* That Airman Shaw was turning down offers amounting to many times more than a wing commander would make in a whole service career can hardly have sweetened Bone's feeling about him.

Matters could hardly be expected to go on like this for long—Lawrence's presence was not only irritating his commanding officer, but also beginning to divide the officers: some thought he should be left alone, and others sided with Bone. This was certainly "contrary to the maintenance of good order and discipline," though the fault in this instance seems to have been more that of Bone than of Lawrence. Still, Lawrence was certainly an upsetting presence to several of his commanding officers; he was in battle, and he was a master of what we would label passive-aggressive behavior. (It is called "dumb insolence" in the British armed services, and is a chargeable offense.) Lawrence also had vast reserves of connections, patience, and unconcealed mental superiority to draw on in any struggle with authority, as well as the most important quality of all: innocence. There was no rule in *King's Regulations* that a marshal of the Royal Air Force and chief of the air staff might not write private letters to an airman, nor that the airman should not reply to such letters; still less was there any requirement that the airman should share their contents

---

* The figure of $100,000 in 1927 would be about $1.6 million today; £5,000 would be about $375,000.

with his commanding officer. Bone was on shaky ground, but it is always easy for a commanding officer to make trouble for a mere airman. As Lawrence had discovered at Farnborough, strict kit inspections and extra guard duty were the least he could expect.

The friction between the officers at Drigh Road on the subject of Lawrence is illustrated by the adjutant, Squadron Leader W. M. M. Hurley, who had been sent to ask Lawrence whether he was writing letters to headquarters. After getting to know Lawrence, Hurley offered him the use of the typewriter in the orderly room on Thursdays (a day off, in the relaxed working conditions of the British armed services in India), and soon got to know him even better. Hurley did not agree with the commanding officer's opinion about Lawrence at all. He admired Lawrence's scrupulously correct attitude toward his officers, and the fact that no matter how upset he was at the many small forms of military persecution he was subjected to, he never raised his voice. Hurley remarked too on Lawrence's appearance: "his head was everything, a noble feature indeed with a lofty forehead, very soft blue eyes and a strong chin. His body was small and wiry and must have framed a splendid constitution, when we consider the trials and the actual brutality which had been part of his share in the Arabic campaign."

Now and again the old Lawrence broke through the barriers behind which Airman Shaw had imprisoned him. On one occasion, when the officers were carrying out their annual pistol course on the firing range, Lawrence happened to be range orderly. At the end of the day, when only the adjutant, the NCO in charge of the station's armory, and Lawrence were left behind, Lawrence "suddenly and quietly . . . picked up a pistol and put six 'bulls' on the target," shooting far beyond the ability of any of the officers. On another occasion, when air routes from Karachi to Britain were being discussed by a survey party of the RAF, high political officers from the government of India, and the British resident in the Persian Gulf, AC1 Shaw was hurriedly brought into the meeting from the Engine Repair Section, in his overalls, to give his crisp opinion of the trustworthiness, character, and influence of the sheikhs along the route across

Iraq and Trans-Jordan. He did so, with a precision and an air of authority that astonished (and silenced) officers and civilian authorities alike.

Lawrence's fellow airmen were impressed by his willingness to take on guard duties over holidays, when everybody else wanted to go out drinking, and by the vast number of books he collected, including "William Blake, Thomas Malory, Bunyan, Plato, and James Joyce's *Ulysses*," as well as his own copy of the subscribers' edition of *Seven Pillars of Wisdom*, "which he kept in a small tin box under his bunk." He happily allowed Leading Aircraftman R. V. Jones, who had the bunk next to his, to borrow his own book; and Jones, who soon became a friend, later recalled that Lawrence, who had a gramophone and frequently received packages of classical records from Britain, also ordered the latest records of Sophie Tucker to appeal to the less highbrow taste of the airmen in his barracks.

By the beginning of 1928 Lawrence's mother and his brother Bob had left China, unable to continue their missionary work because of the hostility of the Chinese. Lawrence wrote to them, realistically, but without much sympathy: "I think probably there will be not much more missionary work done anywhere in the future. We used to think foreigners were black beetles, and coloured races were heathen: whereas now we respect and admire and study their beliefs and manners. It's the revenge of the world upon the civilisation of Europe." India, with its apparently subservient native masses and its small body of British rulers, made him feel this even more strongly. He was far ahead of his time in this, as in many of his other opinions, and once he was back in Britain he would unhesitatingly use his very considerable influence to change things to which he objected, such as the death penalty for cowardice. In the meantime, however, he was stuck in India, though even that did not prevent the London press from running fanciful and sensationalist stories about him. The *Daily Express*, for example, alleged that "instead of visiting Karachi . . . he goes when off-duty to the edge of the desert. . . . There he chats with the villagers, and joins in their profound Eastern meditations." Lawrence wrote to his friend R. D. Blumenfeld, the editor, ridiculing this kind of thing. He did not speak any of the local languages, he protested, and had never practiced meditation; but these stories found their way back to India and may have made Wing Commander Bone more determined than ever to get rid of Lawrence.

Lawrence himself was anxious to get away from Drigh Road, because he had good reason to believe that some of the officers there were gunning for him. He was always concerned about keeping his record clean, and he knew that nothing was easier for an officer than finding a reason to put an airman under arrest for a minor or imaginary crime, and thus leave a black mark on his record. He wrote to Trenchard, explaining why he had applied to Salmond for a posting "up-country," as the unruly mountainous region of the Northwest Frontier was then called, on what is now the border between Pakistan and Afghanistan. "A conversation between an officer and a civilian in a club after dinner was improperly repeated to me. . . . However this one was reported to have sworn he 'had me taped' and was 'laying to jump on me' when he got the chance. . . . So I'm going to run away to a squadron. They are small and officers mix with airmen, and aren't as likely to misjudge a fellow. I told Salmond I had private reasons. Don't think me a funk. At worst it's only overcautious."

Salmond sent Lawrence about as far away from Karachi as he could, to RAF Fort Miranshah, in Waziristan, where Lawrence arrived in August 1928. "We are only 26 all told," he wrote, "with 5 officers, and we sit with 700 Indian Scouts (half-regulars) in a brick and earth fort behind barbed wire complete with searchlights and machine guns." It would have been hard—perhaps impossible—for Salmond to find a more remote posting for Lawrence, but there were hidden dangers. Miranshah, a forward airfield of Number 20 Squadron, was less than ten miles away from the border between British India and Afghanistan—although the line was not only porous but meaningless to the local tribesmen, whose only loyalty was to their faith, clan, and tribe, and who raided impartially on both sides of the border. Afghanistan had been in a state of turmoil since time immemorial. "The graveyard of empires," Afghanistan was the gateway to India, and the locus of the "great game," in which, for more than a century, the British and the Russians had been vying with each other to control the country by bribery, secret intelligence missions, and occasional armed intervention. British and Russian agents traveled through the rough, mountainous, dangerous country in the guise of mountain climbers, botanists, or geographers, seeking out potentially friendly warlords and tribal leaders, drawing up maps, and gathering such political intelligence as could be gleaned from the bloodthirsty chaos that passed for politics in Afghanistan. In 1843, after invading the country and taking Kabul, its capital, an entire British army was defeated and slaughtered between Kabul and Gandamack. The only survivor was Dr. William Brydon, a regimental surgeon, who escaped captivity and rode to the gates of Jelalabad on a mule with the news of the disaster—the subject of a famous painting by Lady Butler. Nobody questioned the ferocity of the Afghan tribes or their determination to resist infidel foreigners in their country, but the British nevertheless fought two subsequent wars in Afghanistan, without achieving a clear-cut victory.

Shortly after Lawrence's arrival at Miranshah, a number of the Afghan tribes staged a rebellion against King Amanullah, who had been attempting to modernize the country by introducing reforms such as schools for girls, the abandonment of the *burka* for women,* and much else. The women of his court were even seen playing tennis in the gardens of the royal palace in Kabul, shamelessly wearing European tennis clothes. The result was a widespread and growing civil war, in the course of which Amanullah lost his throne. The first successor was the unlettered son of a water carrier; the next was Amanullah's sinister, cold-blooded former war minister and ambassador to France. It does not seem to have occurred to either Trenchard or Salmond that Lawrence's presence on the border might attract attention or cause trouble.

At first, life at Miranshah suited Lawrence. His duties as the commanding officer's orderly room clerk were not demanding; he got along well with the airmen and the small group of officers; and since this was a

---

* All this may sound familiar to the reader eighty-two years later.

working flying station, with aircraft landing and taking off, he felt himself to be back in the real RAF. He wrote a prodigious number of letters, many of them to Trenchard, who had read the manuscript of *The Mint*— it shocked him but did not prevent him from extending Lawrence's service in the RAF to 1935 before he retired as chief of the air staff. Indeed a small book on how to wage war against an insurgency could be put together from Lawrence's letters to Trenchard from Miranshah. Interestingly, both Trenchard, at the top of the RAF, and Lawrence, at its bottom, agreed that a policy of bombing tribal villages to enforce peace was more likely to do harm than good, by stirring up fierce resentment about civilian casualties.* However, such bombing was the whole purpose of the airfield at Miranshah.

At Miranshah there was little secrecy about the fact that AC1 Shaw was Lawrence—everybody knew it, and nobody cared much. "I think that the spectacle of a semi-public character contented in their ranks," Lawrence wrote to Trenchard, "does tend to increase their self-respect and contentment." Flight Lieutenant Angell, the commanding officer, liked Lawrence, who never showed him a letter without having first prepared a reply for his signature. The pace of life was leisurely, with plenty of native servants to do the cleaning and polishing, even for the airmen. Lawrence worked hard on his translation of the *Odyssey*, despite his irreverence toward its author and its characters. "Very bookish, this house-bred man," Lawrence wrote of Homer, and went on: "only the central family stands out, consistently and pitilessly drawn—the sly, cattish wife, that cold-blooded egoist Odysseus, and the priggish son who yet met his master-prig in Menelaus. It is sorrowful to believe that these were really Homer's heroes and examplars."

Lawrence did not feel oppressed by the fact that nobody was allowed beyond the barbed wire during the day, or out of the fort at night, since

---

* Those who favor this policy today (in much the same area where Lawrence was in 1928) should bear those doubts in mind. Whether by biplane or by drone, bombing people's villages and killing their wives and children will inflame, not put down, an insurgency.

he had no desire to see Waziristan. Nor was he bothered by the fact that the airmen slept with their rifles chained to a rack beside their beds, in case of a sudden attack. He went around bareheaded, to demonstrate that it was not necessary to wear a pith helmet, and often wore a shirt with the sleeves rolled up instead of his tunic. He was cheerful, hardworking, and fit; he had his books, his gramophone, and his records; he was not even disturbed by the news that somebody had bought the film rights to *Revolt in the Desert*, which almost guaranteed a lot of unwelcome publicity about who would play Lawrence in the film. He did not expect to return to Britain before 1930, at the earliest.

Unfortunately, by the beginning of December 1928, new rumors about Lawrence were making headlines in London. *The Daily News* reported that he was learning Pashtu in preparation for entering Afghanistan, either in support of or against King Amanullah. A few days later, even more sensationally, *The Empire News* revealed that Lawrence had already entered Afghanistan, met with the beleaguered king, "and then disappeared into 'the wild hills of Afghanistan' disguised as 'a holy man' or 'pilgrim,' " to raise the tribes in the king's support. In India, feelings ran high against Lawrence as a British arch-imperialist trying to add Afghanistan to the empire. A genuine holy man, Karam Shah, was attacked and badly beaten by a mob in Lahore when the rumor spread that he was Lawrence in disguise. In London, anti-imperialists in the Labour Party burned Lawrence in effigy during a demonstration held on Tower Hill.

The government of India was taken by surprise, since the Air Ministry had never informed it that Lawrence was serving there. On January 3, 1929, Sir Francis Humphreys, the British minister in Kabul, cabled Sir Denis Bray, foreign secretary of the government of India in Delhi, to point out that the presence of Lawrence as an airman on the border of Afghanistan created "ineradicable suspicion in the minds of the Afghan Government that he is scheming against them in some mysterious way." The Soviet, French, and Turkish ministers in Kabul were quick to spread these rumors, and in Moscow the Soviet newspapers carried stories that were soon spread around the world by left-wing newspapers, accusing Lawrence of being an imperialist agent responsible for the unrest in Afghanistan. Under the circumstances, Humphreys felt, the sooner Lawrence was moved as far away from Afghanistan as possible, the better. Air Vice-Marshal Salmond stoutly dismissed all this as "stupid," but in London the foreign secretary, alarmed by the spread of these stories, ruled that "Lawrence's presence anywhere in India under present conditions is very inconvenient," a superb piece of British understatement.

Trenchard and Salmond were overruled—Lawrence must be removed from India at once. Trenchard ordered Salmond to offer him a choice between Aden, Somaliland, Singapore, and coming home. Lawrence, indignant that he had been given only a night's notice, was flown out of Miranshah to Lahore, without his gramophone or his records, and from there to Karachi, where he was embarked as a second-class passenger in borrowed civilian clothes aboard the P&O* liner RMS *Rajputana*, with orders to report to the Air Ministry as soon as he arrived home.

In contrast to his journey out to India on a troopship, his journey home was comfortable. The ship was not crowded and he had a cabin to himself. In the meantime the furor about him continued to spread, causing the Air Ministry to question the wisdom of Lawrence's disembarking from the *Rajputana* along with the rest of the passengers onto the dock at Tilbury, where he was sure to be greeted by a mob of reporters and photographers. Instead, special arrangements were made to take him off secretly in a naval launch when the ship reached Plymouth Harbor; but the press was so intensely interested in Lawrence that this plan leaked, and when the ship arrived it was surrounded by dozens of motor launches and fishing boats hired by reporters and press photographers.

The Air Ministry consistently underrated both Lawrence's celebrity and the ingenuity of the press, and this was a good example of both. Wing Commander Sydney Smith, the commanding officer of RAF Cattewater

---

* The luxurious liners of the Peninsula & Orient Steamship Company were the preferred way of traveling to and from Britain to the British colonies in the East; they played much the same role as the French Messageries Maritimes.

(the nearest RAF station to Plymouth) and former chief staff officer at Cranwell (where he and his wife, Clare, had befriended Lawrence), was sent out on the launch in civilian clothes with instructions to escort him to London with the least possible publicity. But despite all the precautions, every moment of Lawrence's transfer from the *Rajputana* to the deck of the naval launch was caught on film, and would appear in newsreels and in newspapers the world over. It was even front-page news in *The New York Times*. In London, one headline above a front-page photograph summed up the situation from the point of view of the press and public: "GREAT MYSTERY OF COLONEL LAWRENCE: SIMPLE AIRCRAFTMAN—OR WHAT?"

Here was one of the first modern "media feeding frenzies"—a forerunner of those that would later be triggered by every event in the life of Princess Diana. The photographers with their long telephoto lenses

AC1 Shaw returns to England, 1929.

bobbed up and down in the swell of the harbor, while Lawrence, in his airman's uniform, descended slowly on a rope ladder thrown over the side of the *Rajputana*, then walked across the deck of the launch to its tiny cabin, hands in the pockets of his RAF raincoat in a most unmilitary way, with a faint, sardonic smile on his face. He seemed to be thinking, "All right, you bastards, you got me this time, but *next* time you bloody well won't!"

The comparison between Lawrence and Princess Diana is by no means far-fetched. They were both magnetically attractive—she was the most often photographed person of her generation, he the most often photographed, drawn, painted, and sculptured person of his; they both had a natural instinct for adopting a flattering pose in the presence of photographers and artists without even seeming to know they were doing it; they both played cat and mouse with the press, while complaining of being victimized by it; they both simultaneously sought and fled celebrity; they both—always a tricky task in Britain—managed to cross class lines whenever they chose to, she by making friends of her servants, he by serving in the ranks of the RAF and the army. Both of them were on the one hand intensely vulnerable, and on the other, exceedingly tough. Of course one recognizes the differences—Lawrence was an internationally acclaimed war hero, a scholar, and a writer of genuine distinction, perhaps even genius; and in the sixty-two years that separated their deaths in road accidents Great Britain changed radically (though not radically enough to save Diana's marriage or her life). But it will help modern readers to understand Lawrence's problems if they bear in mind that from 1919 to his death Lawrence was as famous, as sought after, as admired, and as persecuted by the press as Diana was. To this situation he added, by his own efforts to keep out of sight and the bungled efforts of the RAF to hide him, something of the mystery that surrounded Howard Hughes in Hughes's later, reclusive years. Lawrence, hidden away from the press in India or at RAF stations in England, provoked exactly the same unrelenting press interest as Hughes did when he was locked away in a hotel suite in Las Vegas, and the same kind of intense, almost prurient curiosity and speculation on the part of the public. Lawrence was perhaps the first in the long line of twentieth-century celebrities who became victims of their own fame. A journalistic tradition was born on February 2, 1929, when Lawrence was greeted at sea by the RAF wing commander and the Royal Navy lieutenant commander and taken ashore through a floating gauntlet of what would now be called paparazzi.

Not surprisingly, Wing Commander Smith was no more successful at avoiding press headlines than his successors in the role of "media handler" have been since then. To avoid the Plymouth railway station, which the press was sure to have staked out, Smith rushed Lawrence to Newton Abbott; but they were discovered as soon as they boarded the train to London, and when they reached Paddington Station in London the platform was crowded with an unruly mob of photographers and journalists, jostling and pushing to get close to Lawrence, who had been presented with a letter from Trenchard firmly warning him to say nothing. When Smith and Lawrence got into a taxi, they were followed by lines of cars and taxis full of photographers; meanwhile, their taxi driver, who may have been bribed by journalists, deliberately drove slowly and took them the longest way to the flat of Smith's sister-in-law on Cromwell Road. The wing commander rushed Lawrence into the flat in such a hurry that Lawrence literally bumped into Clare and almost sent her flying to the floor. *The New York Times* reported the car chase on its front page the next day under the headline: "LAWRENCE OF ARABIA HIDES IN LONDON: FLEES REPORTERS ON ARRIVING FROM INDIA."

The reporters could get nothing out of Lawrence, who was only quoted as denying that he was Lawrence, and saying, "No, my name is Mr. Smith." This didn't do him a lot of good. Whatever the expertise of the Air Ministry was in other areas, its ability to keep Lawrence's arrival a secret was zero, much to Trenchard's embarrassment. Lawrence grew increasingly concerned, for he was afraid that all this publicity would get him thrown out of the RAF. Nightfall finally enabled the Smiths to get Lawrence out of the flat by the back door and to the comparative safety of his old attic hideaway above Sir Herbert Baker's office. He then spent the weekend in the seclusion of the Trenchards' home, the last place the press would have looked for him.

He was right to be concerned about his future in the RAF. Trenchard was more amused than irritated by all these goings-on, but by this time questions about Lawrence were beginning to be asked in the House of Commons, and these posed a more serious problem for him. The accusations that Lawrence had stirred the tribes of eastern Afghanistan to rise against their king did not interest Labour members so much as why Lieutenant-Colonel Lawrence had ever been allowed to enlist in the RAF as an airman under a false name. Secretary of State for Air Sir Samuel Hoare replied to these questions reluctantly and with exceedingly bad grace, as was hardly surprising, since he had consistently been opposed to Lawrence's enlistment. Now, just as he had predicted, he was under attack for something he had resisted from the first. Hoare decided that Lawrence was now a nuisance and an embarrassment to the government.

Despite a weekend with the Trenchards, during which Lawrence must have received a lot of good advice, he elected instead to behave as if he were dealing with an insurgent tribal leader, walking alone and unarmed into the leader's tent. No sooner had Trenchard driven him back to London than Lawrence went to the House of Commons and asked to see Ernest Thurtle, the Labour member who had been the first to ask why Lawrence had been allowed to enlist under a false name. Thurtle had not been satisfied by Hoare's reply to his question in the House, and had given notice that he and his colleague James Maxton intended to pursue the matter further. Thurtle was, in his own way, as dedicated a man as Lawrence—an ex-serviceman with a particular interest in improving the life of servicemen in the ranks and making discipline more humane and sensible. He and Maxton must have been surprised when the object of their questions appeared in the lobby of the House of Commons, dressed in an airman's uniform, asking to see them. To do Thurtle credit, he was willing to listen to Lawrence's side of the story, and indeed sympathetic, once Lawrence made it clear that he was not an officer and a secret agent, but merely an airman burdened by more publicity, and more inaccurate newspaper reporting, than he could handle. Lawrence explained that any inquiry into his enlistment might have the unintended effect of deeply embarrassing his mother and his surviving brothers. He described to Thurtle "the marriage tangles of [his] father." Thurtle was not only mollified but convinced, and he and Lawrence thereafter became close friends, thus demonstrating the good sense of Lawrence's suggestion to Trenchard about how to deal with the murderous and obstinate Feisal el Dueish at Ur. Lawrence and Thurtle worked closely together on many of Lawrence's pet reform schemes for the armed services.

The famous Lawrence of Arabia appearing at the House of Commons in an airman's uniform did not go unnoticed; on the contrary, he caused a sensation, and Sir Samuel Hoare complained strongly to Trenchard, who called Lawrence into the Air Ministry and warned him sternly against any further appearances in Westminster. Lawrence apologized gracefully, though he asked if Trenchard could not find some way to shut up *The Daily News*, and Trenchard, patiently, asked him with gruff amusement, "Why must you be more of a damned nuisance than you need be?"

Lawrence walking around London in uniform was a constant target for journalists—as he wrote to E. M. Forster, "I am being hunted, and do not like it." Trenchard, who was anxious to get him away, moved quickly to have him posted to RAF Cattewater, near Plymouth, where Wing Commander Smith was the commanding officer. In the meantime, Lawrence received an unexpected and welcome present from Bernard and Charlotte Shaw: a new Brough "Superior" SS-100 motorcycle.* He arrived on this motorcycle at RAF Cattewater, where his friend Clare saw him pull up at the camp gates. "On it," she wrote, "was a small blue-clad figure, very neat and smart, with peaked cap, goggles, gauntlet gloves and a

---

*Lawrence was embarrassed by the excessive generosity of this gift, even though it turned out that some of his wealthy friends, like Buxton and Curtis, had also contributed toward it, and in the end decided to pay for it himself. Buxton, ever the astute banker, had managed to get Brough to agree to a discount (Lawrence was his most famous customer), so the final price was £144 four shillings and sixpence (£144/4s/6d), or about $7,500 in today's money.

small dispatch-case slung on his back." Lawrence was back in the RAF again, on a working station, serving under a commanding officer whom he admired and liked, and whose family made him one of their own. When Clare Smith wrote her description of Lawrence's years at RAF Cattewater, she called the book *The Golden Reign*, for Lawrence was the sovereign, casting over all their lives a glow of glamour, excitement, and adventure. It was as if he had been adopted by the Smiths and their children rather than merely posted to a new RAF station. This was perhaps as close to domestic bliss as Lawrence had ever been, and he loved every moment of it.

He was also about to enter on a period of his life when he found, at the same time, contentment of another sort. RAF Cattewater was a seaplane base, so boats, launches, and speedboats were a necessary part of its equipment, although the actual seaplane squadron had not yet arrived. It was here that Lawrence began a new career as a largely self-taught expert in the building and running of the RAF's high-speed rescue launches. During a six-year period Lawrence would make an extraordinary contribution to the revolutionary design of the boats that would be used to "fish" out of the water RAF pilots shot down over the Channel in the summer of 1940. Many of these men would owe their lives to the unconventional ideas, and the awesome ability to reach friends in high places in the Air Ministry and the government, of 338171 AC1 Shaw, T. E.

He described his new home in a letter to a friend: "Cattewater proves to be about 100 airmen, pressed pretty tightly on a rock, half-awash in the Sound: a peninsula really, like a fossil lizard swimming from Mount Batten golf links across the harbour towards Plymouth town. The sea is 30 yards from our hut one way, and 70 yards the other. The Camp officers are peaceful, it seems, and the airmen reasonably happy."

Safely out of London, Lawrence still kept up his connections to the great world, turning down Eddie Marsh's invitation to present the Hawthornden Prize to his friend Siegfried Sassoon, and writing in detail to Ernest Thurtle about his objection to the death penalty for cowardice—"A man who can run away is a potential V.C.," he noted, from experience.

He continued to write in detail to Trenchard about RAF reforms, objecting to spurs for the officers and bayonets for the men. To another friend,
an airman from Farnborough, he wrote with resignation, "I'm very weary
of being stared at and discussed and praised. What can one do to be forgotten? After I'm dead, they'll rattle my bones about, in their curiosity."

The cold of England ate into his bones—he "wished England could be
towed some thousand miles to the South," and at times he complained
that he was "so tired, and want so much to lie down and sleep or die." But
he soon began to cheer up as his work became more interesting. No
doubt he was also pleased to be serving as Wing Commander Smith's
clerk for the moment; he found himself instantly transformed into a kind
of junior partner in running the station, even suggesting that the camp's
name should be changed to RAF Mount Batten and drafting a letter to
the Air Ministry requesting the change. Smith signed the letter, and the
request was quickly granted.

Despite the absence of the seaplane squadron for the time being,
Smith was busy. Apart from running the camp, he was also the RAF's
representative for the organization of the next Schneider Trophy competition, scheduled for the first week of September 1929, at Calshot, near
Southampton. Named after a wealthy French industrialist—the trophy's
official name was *La Coupe d'Aviation Maritime Jacques Schneider*—this
was a speed event flown by seaplanes over a course of 150 miles. It was
first flown in 1912, and by the 1920s it had become one of the most glamorous and expensive contests in the world of aviation, and a test of the
major industrial nations' technology and aircraft design. The race had
begun as an annual event, but in 1928 the Aéro-Club de France decided
to change it to once every two years, in view of the increasing complexity
and sophistication of the designs, and the growing world economic crisis. If any nation should win the trophy three times in a row, it would go
to that nation in perpetuity. By 1929, the major contestants were Britain,
the United States, and Italy—Germany did not enter, because the German government had no wish to draw attention to its fast-growing aircraft industry. The fastest aircraft were often those designed by Reginald

J. Mitchell, of the Vickers-Supermarine Aviation Works. Mitchell would go on to design the "Spitfire," which was based in part on his Schneider Trophy aircraft and would become perhaps the most successful (and most beautiful) fighter aircraft of World War II.

The contest involved a huge amount of preparation on the part of the host nation, and Lawrence quickly took on much of the correspondence to and from Wing Commander Smith, as well as accompanying him to meetings, to take notes and look after the files. Since the British entries were largely government-financed (like those of the Italians and the Americans) and were run by the RAF, Smith was in charge of the British team. Thus Lawrence was involved in numerous meetings at the Treasury and the Air Ministry, during which he was occasionally recognized as the celebrated Lawrence of Arabia.

Lawrence was at the same time working hard to finish his translation of the *Odyssey*, and trying to decide whether it should be published under his name (given Trenchard's warning to keep Lawrence's name out of the press), or indeed whether he could ever finish it at all, given the scope and variety of his duties with the RAF. In addition to being the commanding officer's secretary-clerk, Lawrence was now a machine and workshop clerk and part of the motorboat crew. Bruce Rogers, the American book designer who had commissioned the *Odyssey* project, displayed a saintly patience with the delay; he sensibly decided to wait, writing Lawrence soothing letters, rather than trying to set deadlines that Lawrence couldn't meet.

There were occasional stories about Lawrence in the newspapers: the trashy scandal tabloid *John Bull* made his life more difficult by suggesting that he spent all his time at Mount Batten tinkering with his expensive motorcycle and translating Homer—exactly the kind of story Trenchard wanted to avoid. Still, Lawrence managed to get up to London on his motorcycle from time to time, and also managed to cut the journey to just over four and a half hours. This meant riding the big Brough over "the ton" (100 miles per hour) wherever he could.* Lawrence heard

* The author was stationed for a time in the early 1950s at the Joint Services School for Linguists in Bodmin, Cornwall, about thirty miles northwest of Plymouth, and fre-

Bernard Shaw read *The Apple Cart* aloud at the London house of Lord and Lady Astor, with a guest list of exactly the kind of people Trenchard wanted him to avoid. He soon found a soul mate in his hostess, Nancy Astor, Britain's first woman member of Parliament, and perhaps the most energetic, flamboyant, and outspoken woman in the country. She was originally Nancy Langhorne, from Danville, Virginia; and she and her sister reached fame as the original "Gibson Girls." After an unsuccessful marriage to Robert Gould Shaw II, she came to England and quickly married the immensely wealthy Waldorf Astor, Viscount Astor. Soon Nancy Astor became something of a national institution, known for her wit, her willingness to break social barriers and traditions, and her blunt outspokenness to opponents, including Winston Churchill. Her seat as a member of Parliament was Plymouth, virtually on Lawrence's new door-step. When she spied Lawrence in the streets of Plymouth, he reported to a friend, "A pea-hen voice screamed 'Aircraftman' from a car." Lawrence tried to escape, but she called Wing Commander Smith and "invited her-self" to RAF Mount Batten, where she not only tracked Lawrence down but persuaded him to give her a ride on his motorcycle. They immedi-ately became friends, much to the surprise of other people, for she was rich, reactionary, a militant Christian Scientist, and a dreadful bully. He described her to Charlotte Shaw as "one of the most naturally impulsive and impulsively natural people. Like G.B.S. [Charlotte's husband], more a cocktail than a welcome diet." (This was perhaps not the most flattering thing to say about Bernard Shaw to his wife.) Lady Astor became another of Lawrence's impassioned correspondents, arousing both disapproval and heartache in Charlotte. "I do not know when, or with whom, I have ever maintained for so long so hot a correspondence," Lawrence wrote Nancy Astor. "Clearly we are soul-mates."

For a man who gave the impression of being a confirmed misogynist, Lawrence had a surprising number of female soul mates: Charlotte Shaw,

---

quently rode his motorcycle up to London for the weekend in under six hours; he can vouch for the fact that on the roads in existence before the motorways were built, Lawrence was pushing it.

Nancy Astor, and Clare Smith. Clare had certain advantages—she was young, beautiful, always elegantly dressed, adventurous, and nearby. Extremely photogenic and gay, with a taste for saucy hats, she had the plucked, finely penciled eyebrows of the period, as well as the high cheekbones and vividly painted lips. In photographs she looks like a character in a Nancy Mitford novel. Lawrence spent a lot of time with her, at the Smiths' home—the RAF had saved money by converting a famous old Plymouth pub into the commanding officer's house—where he was encouraged to drop in whenever he liked. They also squeezed together in the tight seat of a tiny speedboat they had been given by a wealthy yacht owner; or they sunned themselves on the Smiths' porch. Clare loved warmth as much as Lawrence did. She called him "Tes," after his new initials, T.E.S., and he called her Clare and her daughter "Squeak." Clare noticed, among other things, how much he disliked shaking hands with anyone and how hard he tried to avoid it, holding his hands behind his back, and bowing slightly instead like a Japanese. However, he did not mind stroking dogs and cats— the Smiths' dogs, Leo and Banner, were devoted to him. Clare noted also that he never smoked, drank alcohol, or swore. The two shared a love of music, and he gave the Smiths his expensive electric gramophone, so that he and Clare could listen to classical records in the evenings, and taught her how to sing lieder in German. He especially enjoyed hearing Clare sing Schumann's *Frauenliebe und Leben*, but his favorite lied was Wolf's "Verschweigene Liebe." When Clare went shopping in Plymouth, she often brought him back a cake of Golden Glory soap, a transparent glycerin soap that he especially liked because it smelled sweet and didn't "make a mess of any bath." This curious domesticity between an airman and the commanding officer's wife was something that Clare seems to have accepted intuitively: "he lived a monastic life within the world of ordinary beings," she wrote. "Thus he was able to have a deep friendship for a woman— myself—based on the closest ties of sympathy and understanding, but containing none of the elements normally associated with love." He seemed, she thought, to have completely separated himself from the physical side of life, and indeed to be hardly even aware of it.

Her husband, far from disapproving of their relationship, which raised many an eyebrow in Plymouth, seems to have felt the same kind of affection for this strange and lonely man. When a well-intentioned friend told him that there was "a good deal of talk going on about your wife spending so much time with Mr. Shaw," Smith simply "roared with laughter." So did Lawrence, when the Smiths told him about it. The other airmen, and even the NCOs, seem to have had no problem with the close relationship that developed between Lawrence and the Smiths—RAF Mount Batten was small enough so that it was apparent to everybody that Lawrence never sought favors for himself, and that he was in some way a special figure, irrespective of rank—at once a problem solver and a natural leader to whom everybody came for advice. There was no secret about him at Mount Batten—the men knew he was Lawrence of Arabia and were proud to have him there, a celebrity and a person who seemed to live by his own rules. In a curious way, Lawrence had at last found happiness, perhaps for the first time since his life with Dahoum at Carchemish, or at least as much happiness as he was capable of enjoying, for he remained fiercely self-critical and ascetic.

As always, outside the gates of Mount Batten, the presence of Lawrence in the RAF continued to present problems. The Conservative government had been replaced by Labour and the new secretary of state for air, Lord Thomson, was no more disposed than his predecessor to have Lawrence in the ranks of the RAF. This was unfortunate, for the Schneider Trophy Race was bound to make Lawrence more visible, however much he tried to stay out of the limelight, and a full complement of the world's press would be covering it.

Lord Thomson was already irritated by Lawrence's presumptions to set Air Ministry policy. Britain was in the process of completing two giant "airships" in the summer of 1929. Every major nation was intrigued by the possibilities of these huge dirigibles, which many believed represented the future of long-distance air travel. That this was an illusion was not finally demonstrated until a great German airship, the *Hindenburg*, burst into flames on mooring at Lakehurst, New Jersey, in 1937. The two British airships were nearly 800 feet long, longer than the *Hindenburg*, and carried sixty passengers in private staterooms spread over two decks, with a cocktail lounge, a dining salon, a smoking room, and "two promenade lounges with windows down the side of the ship." In short, such an airship was a flying first-class ocean liner, with a range of 5,000 miles at sixty miles an hour. There were only three problems with the airship—the first was that there was no proof it could ever be made profitable; the second was that the hydrogen gas keeping it aloft, if mixed with air, was highly combustible; and the third was the question of how stable it might be in storms.

The air marshals were doubtful about the value of airships, which from a military point of view were in any case nothing new. The German zeppelins had bombed London in 1917–1918, and were found to be very vulnerable to antiaircraft fire and to determined fighter attack, since they were enormous, slow-moving targets. Still, Britain was naturally interested in any form of transportation that would make travel to the farthest portions of the empire a matter of only a few days; and the British were unwilling to concede the future to the Germans, who were planning scheduled flights to New York and Rio de Janeiro.

Lawrence entered the picture because he was convinced that an airship could overfly and explore the Rub al-Khali of Arabia—the so-called Empty Quarter, which no European or Arab had ever crossed—as part of its test flight to India, thus combining an aviation triumph with a notable geographical discovery. He urged this scheme on Trenchard, who was lukewarm on the subject and passed it on to Lord Thomson; but he also urged Bernard Shaw (who knew Thomson, a fellow Fabian) to make a personal appeal to the air minister. Unfortunately, Shaw was too busy to pay a call on Thomson and wrote to him instead, noting that Lawrence, with his knowledge of Arabia, would be a good person to add to the crew. As was so often the case with Shaw, his belief that any suggestion of his would be taken seriously rebounded, this time on Lawrence. Thomson replied to Shaw with enthusiasm about the idea of the airship as a means of making geographical surveys—he was a true believer on the subject of airships, which would very shortly cost him his life—but rejected Lawrence as a crew member: "As regards including Lawrence, or Private Shaw, as you have yourself described him, I will consider the matter. His passion for obscurity makes him an awkward man to place and would not improve his relations with the less subtle members of the crew." Lord Thomson's belief in Fabian socialism apparently did not extend to receiving suggestions from airmen, even when these were passed along to him by Bernard Shaw. Lawrence's habit of reaching out from the ranks to the great and famous was not likely to endear him to any civilian head of aviation, even though the suggestion that he should join the flight came from Shaw, not himself. In any case, Thomson clearly took it as a challenge to his authority.

On August 23, 1929, Trenchard inspected RAF Mount Batten, and took the opportunity for a private chat with Lawrence, "telling me off as usual," as Lawrence wrote to T. B. Marson, Trenchard's faithful private secretary, who had retired from the RAF to take up farming. Given that Trenchard himself would retire at the end of the year, he may have felt it necessary to warn Lawrence to be more careful about Lord Thomson in the future. If so, it was wasted breath.

That Lawrence upstaged Lord Thomson—and almost everybody else—during the Schneider Trophy Cup races was not entirely his fault. The press was more interested in Lawrence than in the pilots, let alone in Lord Thomson, and it did not help matters that Lawrence knew so many of the dignitaries present, or that they stopped to chat with him. Even Trenchard was annoyed to see AC1 Shaw in conversation with Lady Astor, but there was worse to come. Lawrence, leading from the ranks as usual, had organized some airmen to clean the slipway leading to the hangar where the Italian team kept their seaplanes. Marshal Italo Balbo—the famous Italian aviator,* minister of aviation, and at the time heir apparent to Mussolini—was in charge of the Italian team, and he knew Lawrence well. Balbo paused to chat with Lawrence in Italian, and

---

* At that time (and up until 1940) any large formation of aircraft was known in every air force in the world as a "Balbo," after the spectacular long-distance, large-formation flights Balbo had led to publicize Italy's aviation strength.

en passant asked if he could get the slipway cleaned up, since the rails were covered with scum. Lawrence proceeded to get that done in his usual efficient way, and was caught in the act by Lord Thomson, who wanted to know why a British airman was taking orders from an Italian air marshal, and passing them on to other British airmen as if he were an officer himself. There followed an animated discussion between Lord Thomson and Lawrence, which was unfortunately caught on film by the press photographers, and appeared in newspapers all over the world, to Thomson's great embarrassment. To use RAF slang, Thomson was clearly "tearing a strip off" Lawrence and did not forgive him.

The British not only won the race but set a new world speed record, and Lawrence, except for his brush with Thomson, had enjoyed being part of it. He was also delighted by the unexpected gift of the speedboat that he and Clare Smith would spend so much time on. A wealthy friend of Wing Commander Smith's, Major Collin Cooper, had made his motor yacht available to the RAF for the occasion, and Lawrence spent a good deal of time on board, tinkering with the temperamental engine of the tiny, two-seat Biscayne "Baby" American racing speedboat that it carried as a tender. Cooper was so impressed by Lawrence's efficiency and hard work that when the race was over he made Lawrence and the Smiths a gift of the speedboat. Clare and Lawrence renamed it *Biscuit*, no doubt because at rest it sat in the water looking like a low, flat, round object rather than a long, pointed one. The Biscayne "Baby" speedboats were a one-class racing design, built in Florida, powered by a six-cylinder, 100-horsepower Scripps marine engine, and capable of more than forty miles per hour. Designed after the pattern of Gar Wood's speedboats, the hard-chine hull had a very sharp V-shaped bow flattening out toward the stern, so that at high speed the boat raised its bow and planed over the water, rather than pushing through it. This design, partly thanks to Lawrence, would eventually be used for all the RAF high-speed rescue launches in Britain, and in the United States it was the basis for the famous PT boat, despite determined resistance by the navy in both countries. Major Cooper had the American speedboat delivered to RAF

Mount Batten, and Lawrence would spend much of the winter of 1929–1930 painstakingly stripping and rebuilding the engine and refinishing the hull.

In the meantime, his brush with Lord Thomson had consequences. He had applied to Trenchard for permission to accompany a friend on a seaplane tour of Europe as a member of the crew, and Trenchard had tentatively approved, provided Thomson agreed. The sight of yet another extraordinary request from AC1 Shaw to the chief of the air staff apparently infuriated Thomson, who instructed Trenchard to inform Lawrence that henceforth he was to stay in the country, was not to fly on any government aircraft, was to keep a low profile, and was forbidden to visit or even to speak to a distinguished group of people that included Winston Churchill, Lord Birkenhead (the former F. E. Smith, a pugnacious, brilliant, witty, hard-drinking Conservative political figure), Lady Astor, Sir Philip Sassoon (deputy undersecretary of state for air), and Sir Austen Chamberlain, KG (the autocratic former foreign secretary, winner of the Nobel Peace Prize and half brother of Neville Chamberlain). Bernard Shaw was outraged at being left off the list. Lawrence was "to stop leading from the ranks, and confine himself to the duties of an aircraftman."

Trenchard called Lawrence down to the Air Ministry and read him, as gently as possible, the riot act, warning him that any infraction of Thomson's rules would get him thrown out of the air force. Lawrence, it must be said, took all this calmly, no doubt counting on the fact that most people in the government and the House of Commons would not regard friendship with Lady Astor and Winston Churchill as grounds for a court-martial, but he did not want to embarrass Trenchard or create further difficulties for him. In the event, he was busy enough over the winter with *Biscuit* and Homer to stay out of trouble.

With the coming of better weather, Lawrence began to put the little boat to the test, and both he and Smith realized how far superior it was in design to the existing RAF rescue launches. Lawrence had painted it silver, and Clare Smith had the seats covered in navy blue cloth, with the initial S embroidered on both seat backs, so that they would serve for "Smith" and "Shaw." Lawrence taught Clare how to drive the little boat, and despite her initial fear, the two of them were soon covering long distances at high speeds. They took the boat upriver to have lunch with Lord and Lady Mount Edgcumbe—more friends of Lawrence's of whom Lord Thomson would surely have disapproved—and while being shown the famous twelfth-century manor house, Lawrence pointed out a priceless, museum-quality rug on which a hip bath had been standing. His expertise in Oriental rugs, begun at the Altounyan house in Aleppo before the war, had apparently not diminished over the years.

In the area of boat design at least, Lawrence's influence could be channeled through Smith to the Air Ministry, and very soon it began to affect the design of the next generation of RAF rescue launches. So long as Lawrence's contributions were indirect and did not make the front pages of the newspapers, he did not offend Lord Thomson. In any event, on October 5, 1930, Thomson died—a martyr to his belief in airships— when the R101, which Lawrence had hoped would explore the Arabian Desert on its way to India, crashed on a hillside in France, killing forty-eight men, including Lord Thomson, who had insisted on continuing the flight despite bad weather. For a time, this crash ended British interest in airships.

Lawrence's next brush with publicity was another tragedy, this time the crash of a seaplane—the RAF "Iris" III—in Plymouth Sound. Lawrence had been taking his morning coffee break with Clare Smith, in a sunny spot they liked for their "elevenses," when he saw a large seaplane descend toward the water as if to land; but instead of flattening out, it dived straight into the sea and disappeared. Before the seaplane crashed, Lawrence had realized that it was in trouble, and he ran to get the rescue boat moving. He not only organized the rescue, but dived into the sea himself to attempt to rescue any survivors. Of the twelve men on board, six were saved, though both pilots were among the dead. Lawrence knew at once what had happened: the senior officer on board was not qualified to fly such a large, complex seaplane—everybody at Mount Batten knew it—but once he was airborne his seniority gave him the right to insist on

taking control of the aircraft, and he had done so, with disastrous consequences. Lawrence, working through Lady Astor this time, made sure
the facts were known at the Air Ministry, and as a result it became RAF
policy that once an aircraft was airborne the pilot had command of it—
even if he was a sergeant and the senior officer on board was a wing commander or a group captain. Henceforth, the pilot was in complete
command of the aircraft, like the captain of a ship. Nobody on board, no
matter how high his rank, could overrule the pilot and take control. The
accident also demonstrated the importance of faster rescue launches, in
situations where minutes might save lives; this was one of Lawrence's
major interests and areas of expertise.

Lawrence was obliged to testify at the RAF inquiry, which posed no
problems for him, but also at a public inquest, where the press would be
present. Even without Thomson, Lawrence was concerned that he would
make headlines again, particularly if he was called on to criticize the officer who had taken over the controls. He was equally concerned that
Wing Commander Smith might be blamed for letting an officer go up
even though his incompetence as a pilot was widely known. Always the
gleeful trumpeter of doom, and eager to get Lawrence out of uniform
(where he did not think Lawrence belonged), Bernard Shaw wrote, "You
are a simple aircraftman: nothing but an eye-witness's police report can
be extorted from you. However, as you will probably insist on conducting
the enquiry, and as you will want to save your ambitious commander
from being sacrificed, the future, to my vision, is on the knees of the
gods. Pray heaven they sack you."

In the end, Lady Astor did her part splendidly—her friends the press
lords played down Lawrence's role (any other airman might have been
awarded a medal for his courageous effort to save lives), Smith was not
blamed for the incompetence of the pilot, and the need for faster rescue
launches was widely acknowledged. Shaw's gleefully dire prediction did
not come true. Writing to thank Lady Astor for her tactful and effective
intervention, Lawrence invited her upriver on *Biscuit* for a picnic. By this
time—March 1931—Lawrence himself was beginning to feel that his

best years in the RAF were coming to an end: Trenchard had left, and would shortly go on to a peerage and his next big job, as metropolitan commissioner of police; the Smiths, by now Lawrence's surrogate family, would move on to RAF Manston, where the wing commander, promoted to group captain, would take over as commanding officer.

As for Lawrence, he moved temporarily to Hythe, near Southampton, where he lodged in a cottage on Myrtle Road while working at the British Power Boats factory, to test and improve the prototype of the RAF 200 Class Seaplane Tender. He had made himself something of "a marine expert" (in his own words), and found in the person of Flight Lieutenant W. E. G. Beauforte-Greenwood, head of the Marine Equipment Branch of the Air Ministry, another sympathetic and appreciative commander, who knew how to make the most of Lawrence's growing (and self-acquired) skill at designing, handling, and servicing fast boats. Indeed, Lawrence knew so much about boats by now that Beauforte-Greenwood invited him to write the official handbook on the ST 200. Lawrence undertook this project with his customary zeal, and the handbook remains today perhaps the most concise and most instructive technical manual ever published. That discriminating judge of literature Edward Garnett described it as "a masterpiece of technology," perhaps the beginning of a new genre; and Lawrence himself boasted that "every sentence in it is understandable, to a fitter," and to a crewman as well, for he included instructions on how to handle the boat in the wind, or in high seas, and how to effect a rescue as quickly as possible. The handbook remained in use until the ST 200 Class boats were retired, well after World War II.

After the *Odyssey*, Lawrence put in good order a compilation of poems he had liked over the years: *Minorities*, consisting, with his typical taste for paradox, of minor works by major poets, or major works by minor poets. He had kept this in the form of a manuscript over the years, and gave it for a time to Charlotte Shaw. Some of the poems and poets in *Minorities* are not really minor, in fact. Lawrence included Arthur Hugh Clough's "Say Not the Struggle Naught Availeth," a poem that Winston

Churchill would quote to great effect in a speech on April 27, 1941, at one of the most difficult moments for Britain of World War II. Interestingly, Lawrence remarks that he had "read it at Umtaiye, when the Deraa expedition was panicking and in misery: and it closely fitted my trust in Allenby, out of sight beyond the hills." These were not so much "minor poems," in fact, as poems that had meant a lot to Lawrence at difficult points of his life.

From time to time he was tempted by further literary projects, among them a life of Sir Roger Casement, the Anglo-Irish British consular official who had been among the first to expose and document the atrocities that were committed in King Leopold of Belgium's Congo Free State—the background and subject of Joseph Conrad's *Heart of Darkness*—where it was routine to chop off the right hand of any native who was slow to collect or carry ivory and rubber. Casement was made a Companion of the Order of St. Michael and St. George for his revelations about the Congo, and was later awarded a knighthood for his extraordinary journey through the Amazon and his courageous attempts to protect the indigenous native population from slavery and mass murder at the hands of rubber planters. Casement was an adventurer very much like Lawrence, and something of a British hero for his humanitarian work, but in time he became one of the leading Irish nationalists and eventually resigned from the British Consular Service. Just before World War I he went to Germany, where, once the war had begun, he tried to recruit prisoners of war from Ireland for an "Irish Brigade" to fight the British. Early in April 1916 he was landed in Ireland, just three days before the Easter Rising, by a German submarine; he was captured by the British and tried for treason. The defense at his trial was hampered by references to Casement's "black diaries," which contained explicit descriptions of homosexual acts; these diaries almost certainly played a part in turning the jurors against him. He was found guilty and hanged in August 1916, despite pleas for clemency from W. B. Yeats, Sir Arthur Conan Doyle, the archbishop of Canterbury, and G. Bernard Shaw. Shaw had offered to write Casement's speech in his own defense at the trial, an offer that Casement turned down but should probably have accepted. (Casement became an Irish hero and martyr after his death, and in 1965 his body was exhumed from its lime-pit grave at Pentonville Prison, and repatriated to Ireland, where he was given a state funeral attended by more than 30,000 people.)

For many reasons, Casement would have been an excellent subject for Lawrence, and both Charlotte and Bernard Shaw pressed him to write this biography. But in the end Lawrence decided that unless the British government allowed him to read and quote from the "black diaries," it would not be an honest book; and no British government, Labour or Conservative, was likely to let Lawrence, of all people, see Casement's diaries, which many of his supporters believed had been forged by the intelligence services in order to ensure his execution. "As I see it," Lawrence wrote to Charlotte Shaw, "he was a heroic nature. I should like to write upon him subtly, so that his enemies would think I was with them till I finished my book and rose from reading it to call him a hero. He has the appeal of a broken archangel. But unless the P.M. will release the 'diary' material nobody can write of him." This was not likely to happen only fifteen years after an event about which emotions ran high on both sides, so Lawrence never began the book. He gave some thought to a kind of spiritual autobiography, and Charlotte Shaw was enthusiastic about the idea, but he never did more than talk about it. His translation of the *Odyssey* was the last work he wrote, and it seems fitting that when he went into a bookshop looking for something to read, the salesclerk tried to sell him *The Boy's Book of Colonel Lawrence* at a reduced price, since he was in RAF uniform. He told her that he knew the fellow, "and he was a wash-out."

Lawrence always managed to have the last word about himself.

By 1932, if he had been anyone else, Lawrence would have been wearing three stripes and a brass crown on his sleeves. Indeed, had he been willing to accept a promotion, he would have been yet another of those hugely competent middle-aged men on whom the RAF (like the Royal Navy) depends: the grizzled flight sergeant or chief petty officer who knows more about his area of expertise than any officer does, whether it is guns, marine engines, or anything else; who can repair anything; and whose word is law when it comes to his specialty. It had startled Lord Thomson to hear the NCOs at Calshot referring to AC1 Shaw as "Mr. Shaw," but they were merely recognizing that Shaw had the quiet authority of a man who knew how to get things done, and was reaching an age when he no longer looked like the glamorous young adventurer. He was still muscular and wiry, but photographs show that his hair was graying, cut now very short at the sides, though still long and unruly on top; his face had acquired a certain weather-beaten maturity; his body had filled in. He was not by any stretch of the imagination fat, but he was solid. With his strong jaw, powerful nose, and piercing eyes, he would have looked right at home in the sergeants' mess.

The sea made much the same appeal to Lawrence's imagination as the desert, with its emptiness and its sudden dangers. All things considered, he was where he wanted to be, and doing what he wanted to do. Much of his work around the boatyard he could do in civilian clothes, a sports jacket, baggy gray flannels, a sweater, and a scarf (Lawrence was never a natural collar-and-tie man). When Lawrence's new commanding officer showed up at Hythe, Lawrence sent himself home on leave, having already typed up the leave ticket for his signature.

With Lord Thomson's death, Lawrence's busy social life resumed much as before—he often visited Cliveden, the Astors' big country house, arriving for dinner on his motorcycle; and he kept up his correspondence with the great and famous. Harold Nicolson describes his arrival at a tea party in RAF uniform, looking "stockier and squarer . . . a bull terrier in place of a saluki." The notion of Lawrence as a lonely man is belied by his letters—he wrote to Edward Marsh, to Lord Trenchard, to Sir Edward Elgar, to C. Day Lewis, to Siegfried Sassoon, to John Buchan, to Lionel Curtis, and to Robert Graves. He met and liked Noël Coward (after being taken to a rehearsal of *Private Lives*), and sent Coward the manuscript of *The Mint* to read, a gesture of great intimacy and trust. Coward replied with a letter that begins memorably: "Dear 338171 (May I call you 338?)." Lawrence also began the lengthy correspondence with B. H. Liddell Hart that would eventually produce the best book about Lawrence as a military leader and innovator, *Colonel Lawrence: The Man behind the Legend.* He even corresponded with W. B. Yeats, one of the poets he most admired.

Jock Bruce had not altogether vanished from Lawrence's life, though he appeared less frequently, as if the intensity of Lawrence's demons was declining. According to Bruce, he was called down to whip Lawrence in 1929, when Lawrence returned from India, and again in 1930—he continued to receive his £3 a week, whether he was called on to apply the birch or not. Bruce claimed that the worst beating of all, a kind of marathon of torture, took place in the autumn of 1930, when Lawrence traveled all the way from Cattewater to Aberdeen with a new set of demands from the unappeasable Old Man. These included swimming in the North Sea ("The water was freezing cold and very rough," Bruce wrote, certainly a torture to somebody who hated the cold and disliked swimming as much as Lawrence did), and riding lessons, some of them bareback, which Lawrence hated, to be followed by a severe whipping. Oddly enough, Lawrence managed to write a long letter to Frank Doubleday, the American publisher, from the cottage Bruce had rented for all this punishment, making it sound like a jolly weeklong seaside holiday, and describing Jock Bruce, not inaccurately, as "the roughest diamond of our Tank Corps hut in 1923." Judging by the date, it is possible that this particularly sophisticated and elaborate series of punishments was intended to atone for the success of *Revolt in the Desert.* Nothing quite like it was repeated, although Bruce claims to have whipped Lawrence again in 1931, in 1935, and "six or seven times" after that. Charlotte Shaw was certainly aware of much of this—Lawrence was more frank about himself with her than with anyone else—though it seems doubtful that she passed any of it on to her husband, who was busy writing a play about Lawrence, *Too True to Be Good.* But then there was much about herself that Charlotte hid from her husband, including the sheer volume and intimacy of her correspondence with Lawrence, which, for once, deeply shocked the normally imperturbable Shaw when he discovered it after her death.

One has the impression that in some ways Lawrence's glamour as a hero was fading slightly. The public had come to accept him as "Aircraftman Shaw," and however odd his decision to serve in the ranks still seemed to many people, it was no longer news, even after Shaw's play opened. Lawrence paid a visit to Janet Laurie Hall-Smith, to whom he had once proposed marriage, and who was now a married woman and the mother of four children. It may be that Janet had asked for his help—her husband was a difficult man, whose ambition to be a great artist had failed, and who, in order to support his rapidly growing family, was stuck in a bank teller's job in the small seaside town of Newquay, in Cornwall, then a rather stuffy summer resort. Hall-Smith had won the DSO in the war, and he may have resented Lawrence's cavalier disregard for his own honors, as well as his fame and the fact that he had given Janet money early in her marriage, when the couple were virtually penniless. Janet herself had changed, not surprisingly, from the slim, tomboyish girl Ned had loved to a plump, matronly woman with more than her share of troubles; this may have dismayed Lawrence. In any event, as seen through the eyes of Janet's daughter Emma, Lawrence fades into insignificance. He had agreed to join the Hall-Smiths for "a beach picnic," but turned up very late, a "small man, made smaller, dwarfed, by the size of [his] motorbike," as Emma remembers him. Whereas the children are wearing bathing suits, Lawrence "is wearing a uniform of thick, scratchy material, heavy, clumpy boots, and knee-breeches. Our legs are bare, but his are bandaged from the ankles up, by what are called, we know, puttees. How horribly hot and uncomfortable he's bound to be, poor man, inside his layers of stuffy clothing." When her sister Pam says that she is Lawrence's godchild, he replies, with undisguised annoyance, that he has too many godchildren to count, mortifying the two little girls. "I didn't think he'd be so little," Pam says sadly, and the girls are doubly disappointed when their father and Lawrence appear to quarrel—Mr. Hall-Smith had hoped to achieve fame at last by painting his portrait, but Lawrence refuses and roars away on his motorcycle without saying good-bye to the girls.

Although Lawrence appears to have been quite good with the children of his friends, he was not always at ease with children he didn't know. For example, Anthony West, the illegitimate son of H. G. Wells and Rebecca West, describes meeting Lawrence, and being more impressed by his Brough motorcycle, "the best motorcycle out," than by Lawrence himself. He remembered Lawrence as a name-dropper who blushed easily. When his aunt—who, like his governess, falls almost instantly under Lawrence's spell—tells him that he should make allowances because Lawrence is an extraordinary person, the young West says uncompromisingly: "I didn't want to have to make allowances for him. . . . I wanted him to be a hero."

" 'Ah, yes—that—' said Aunt Gwen. 'One does. And that's his great problem. It's the problem all heroes have to cope with—when you've made your gesture you've got the rest of your life to live.'

" 'Do you think it's very difficult for him—being a hero?'

" 'Oh, yes, it's very hard work wearing a halo—or any other mark of distinction for that matter.' "

Aunt Gwen had a point—*the* point, in fact—whether she really said it, or Anthony West is speaking through her words: it *is* very hard work being a hero, much harder than becoming one; and although Lawrence spent the better part of his adult life, from 1918 to 1935, trying to escape from his own reputation, he never succeeded. Perhaps nobody with so enormous a reputation as his could have. Children, for whom he was a kind of mythic hero, sensed, perhaps more quickly than adults, the curious contrast between the heroic legend and the small airman with the diffident and curiously remote manner. Adults knew what Lawrence had been or done, and understood how hard he had tried to put all that behind him; children merely saw that he did not resemble what they thought of as a legendary hero like King Arthur and the knights of the Round Table, and were correspondingly disappointed.

Lawrence returned to RAF Mount Batten in 1931, but found it had lost its appeal now that the Smiths were no longer there. In addition, the Air Ministry decided to end "boat testing and experimenting" at Mount Batten, so Lawrence was left with nothing of any personal interest to do.

He did not find his commanding officer inspiring, either; and in March 1933 he "applied to be released from further service" as of April 6. Rather unimaginatively, his new commanding officer forwarded the application to the Air Ministry, with the note, "The discharge of this airman will cause no manning difficulty." The story leaked to the newspapers, which gave it full play, alarming the air member for personnel, Air Marshal Sir Edward Ellington, GCB, CGM, CBE, since everybody from Lord Trenchard on down assumed that Lawrence was being thrown out of the RAF. Until now, Lawrence had asked his many friends in high places to use their influence to get him *into* the RAF or to keep him there. Now the position was reversed: the Air Ministry, deeply concerned about bad publicity, was determined to keep him *in* the air force at any price. The secretary of state for air, the marquess of Londonderry, demanded to know why AC1 Shaw wanted to leave the RAF. Sharply prodded by Sir Philip Sassoon— member of Parliament, undersecretary of state for air, and a friend of Lawrence's—Air Marshal Ellington ordered Wing Commander Andrews, Lawrence's unfortunate new commanding officer at Mount Batten, to find out whether Lawrence had any grievances, and if so to remedy them at once.

However, Lawrence had no grievances, as such. He merely wanted a responsible job that interested him, rather than routine station duties; and he told his commanding officer that if there was any special job in which the chief of the Air Staff "could [find him] particularly useful" he would stay on—a modest enough request from an aircraftman to the chief of the Air Staff! Since Trenchard's successor was Lawrence's old friend Air Chief Marshal Sir Geoffrey Salmond, a solution was quickly found. Lawrence was posted to RAF Felixstowe, site of the Marine Aircraft Experimental Establishment, where he would wear civilian clothes in order to avoid publicity and travel around the various boatyards producing launches for the RAF, looking after the interests of the Air Ministry. "Lawrence of Arabia has decided to stay on in the Air Force," the secretary of the Air Ministry wrote to Trenchard, to reassure him, with a combination of relief and mild amusement. "As he knows a good deal about motor boats he has been given a fairly free hand to go round various motor boat firms in the country." Lawrence eventually found it more convenient to take a room in Southampton, rather than live at RAF Felix-stowe, and was therefore relieved of any of the normal duties of an air-man. As usual, Lawrence had gotten exactly what he wanted: a job in which he could help in the design, building, and testing of high-speed motor launches, but without the supervision of an NCO or an officer, or even the need to wear uniform. It was a position unique in the RAF, tailor-made for Lawrence. At the boatyards, where everybody knew who he was, he was referred to with respect as "Mr. Shaw."

The long-delayed publication in the United States of Lawrence's trans-lation of the *Odyssey* brought him a good deal of publicity, since his name was on it. The book was praised by the distinguished classical scholar C. M. Bowra, who "agreed with Lawrence's view of the *Odyssey* as a story." In general Lawrence received praise for his rendering of "scenes of action" and fighting, which, as in *Seven Pillars of Wisdom*, were his strong points as a writer. He had completed the translation on an elegiac note, writ-ing at the end of the manuscript: "This last page of my version of the ODYSSEY upon which I have spent almost as long as ODYSSEUS and trav-elled further, which has furnished me with luxuries for five years and so wholly occupied my hours off duty that I had no leisure to enjoy them . . ." Indeed, Lawrence's *Odyssey* is exactly that—*his* version, not a conven-tional translation, or a "crib" of the original, but rather a far more ambi-tious attempt to make the story accessible for a modern reader without trying to convey the poetic form of the original, and without the tire-some repetition of metaphors that had a specific emotional meaning for Homer's audience. In Lawrence's version, the *Odyssey* can be read like a novel, which of course it is, and the fact that his version of it is still in print today is proof he succeeded. Nobody, after all, understood better than Lawrence the difficulties facing a warrior and hero on returning home, or could write more feelingly about it: "surely I am not in clear-shining Ithaca? I think I have lighted on some foreign land, and you are telling me it is my Ithaca only in mockery, to cheat my soul."

Again and again, Odysseus reflects Lawrence's thoughts, and his predicament: that of a man forever trapped in his role as a hero, with whatever regrets and second thoughts about the war he has fought, whose return brings him no peace, since everything at home has changed. Oxford was Lawrence's Ithaca, but it had changed since 1914, and changed even more with the death of his father and of two brothers, and then, later, with the death of Hogarth. Lawrence had found no peace there, and placed himself in self-imposed exile. "Few men," he wrote about Homer, "can be sailors, soldiers and naturalists," yet Lawrence was all three: a gifted and fearless sailor (Jeremy Wilson notes that he took one of the ST 200 launches he had developed on a 740-mile journey from Calshot to Scotland through high seas and "appalling conditions" at "an average speed of 18.3 knots"); a brilliant and courageous soldier; and, as page after page of *Seven Pillars of Wisdom* shows, a writer about nature of no mean distinction, with amazing powers of observation and a remarkable fund of knowledge about geology, botany, and agriculture. Just as the young scholar and archaeologist had not hesitated to put his hand to generalship, and to invent his own tactics, so the task of translating into modern, idiomatic English one of the world's greatest classics had not prevented Lawrence from succeeding at giving the work his own special stamp. From time to time, we perceive that Lawrence is mocking both the gods and Ulysses for taking themselves too seriously.

B. H. Liddell Hart's book, the third major biography of Lawrence written during his lifetime, was published in 1934. Liddell Hart boldly affirmed that Lawrence was a military genius of the first magnitude. Lowell Thomas's book had come out first, in 1924, presenting Lawrence as a scholar turned warrior hero, and creating for hundreds of thousands of readers the portrait of "Lawrence of Arabia" that would persist and thrive despite every effort of Lawrence to contradict or obliterate it over the years. Lawrence's friend Robert Graves had attempted an altogether more serious biography, published in 1927, which Lawrence went to a good deal of trouble to correct in detail, but which still portrayed him as a popular hero, though Graves was far too intelligent to be an entirely uncritical admirer. Liddell Hart was in an altogether different category; a somewhat controversial celebrity himself, he had become, at an early age, the supreme judge and critic of war and generals in Britain, and certainly the first person to make military history both popular and taken seriously as a form of literature. Generals often wrote books about each other, or about the art of war, but these were either far too technical and abstruse for the average reader or, in many cases, self-serving and intended as frontal attacks on the character and abilities of the authors' rivals. Liddell Hart, from the beginning, sought to treat war as a science, and to write about it in prose that would be at once lively and completely accessible to the average reader. Although he reached only the rank of captain in the war, he evolved a series of theories and formulas about war that made generals and politicians come to him for advice. Liddell Hart could be waspish with those who did not agree with him, and he overwhelmed his opponents by a combination of industry—he was enormously productive—and the sheer breadth of his knowledge. His career as a self-anointed expert was helped by the fact that everyone in Britain from the king down recognized the 1914–1918 war as a military disaster that was only barely redeemed by victory and must never be repeated; hence anybody offering a way to eliminate trench warfare and frontal attacks from battle was bound to attract not only attention, but admirers and disciples. Thanks to Liddell Hart, even the generals who were responsible for the slaughter now discovered—like Molière's Monsieur Jourdain in *Le Bourgeois gentilhomme*, who learned to his astonishment that he had been speaking prose all his life—that they had been practicing, with whatever deficiencies, a fine and subtle art, rather than just sending hundreds of thousands of men stumbling forward through mud to their death. Liddell Hart was a formidable logician and analyzer of facts. Had the line "Elementary, my dear Watson!" not already been used, he could have made it his, for in many ways he resembled Sherlock Holmes, although his magnifying glass was turned toward tactics, lines of communication, and fortifications instead of cigarette ash and footprints. An adviser to prime ministers, ministers, and generals, and a philosopher of war, he experienced almost a comedown when he accepted the post of military correspondent at the *Times*.

In every way the opposite of Lawrence, Liddell Hart was tall, elegant, storklike, fond of the good things of life, and so fascinated by women that he oversaw the smallest details of the lingerie for both his wives, was exacting and deeply involved in the design of their corsets, and regularly measured the waists of his two daughters. He was in fact a walking encyclopedia on the subject of lingerie—or as one of his biographers, Alex Danchev, refers to it wittily, *"l'artillerie de la nuit"*—as knowledgeable about bras and merry widows and garter belts as he was about war. A perfectionist in all things, he was obsessed by the ideal of the feminine wasp waist, which was the *Schwerpunkt** (to borrow a phrase from German strategic thinking) of his sexual desire. Despite these differences, he and Lawrence got along very well; and Lawrence, in his many letters to Liddell Hart and in his lengthy written commentaries on the text, is perhaps franker about himself than he is with anyone else except Charlotte Shaw. He respected Liddell Hart as a scholar, and was pleased to be taken seriously as a strategic thinker. Their admiration and friendship were genuine.

Liddell Hart made contact with Lawrence as early as 1927, in one of his many guises as military editor of the *Encyclopaedia Britannica*—it was part of his strategy to command as many positions in the field of military commentary and journalism as he could—proposing that Lawrence should write the article on "Guerrilla Warfare." Lawrence, then in Karachi, declined to write the entry but suggested how it could be pulled out of *Seven Pillars of Wisdom*; and Liddell Hart proceeded to do this for the fourteenth edition of the encyclopedia, above the initials T.E.L. This began a learned correspondence between the two men, which continued over the next seven years. Anybody who doubts that Lawrence was an exceptionally well-read strategic thinker need only consult the correspondence between him and Liddell Hart in *T. E. Lawrence to His Biographers*,† which

---

*The *Schwerpunkt* was the central aim of German strategy, the focal point against which must be directed the maximum concentration of force to effect a breakthrough. The concept was characterized in World War II by General Guderian's comment, *Nicht kleckern, klotzen!* ("Don't fiddle around, smash!").

†London: Cassell, 1938.

Lawrence, standing on a bollard, with B. H. Liddell Hart.

itself provides something of a textbook in battle analysis and strategy. It was not until 1929 that Liddell Hart was finally persuaded by his agent David Higham to write a book about Lawrence. The book took him four years to complete—very unusually, since he typically dashed off books as quickly as he could, to keep his elaborate lifestyle afloat. The two men met frequently, and nothing ever dimmed Liddell Hart's admiration for his much smaller friend (in photographs taken of the two of them, Lawrence seems dwarfed by Hart's height, and in one of these photos he stands on a bollard to bring their heads to the same level). Liddell Hart called Lawrence "the Spirit of Freedom come incarnate to a world in fetters." This was insightful, for even though Lawrence had placed himself in a military world of tight restraints, he remained what Liddell Hart called an "anarch," always determined to reach his own conclusions and to do things his own way, though without forcing them on anyone else. Lawrence also told Liddell Hart, who was concerned about the daring way he rode his motorcycle, "It'll end in tragedy one day."

Still, there was no sign of gloom on Lawrence's part, as the inevitable date of his retirement from the RAF in 1935 approached. He was spending (overspending, in fact) on the rebuilding and modernization of Clouds Hill, in anticipation of living there full-time, and seeking translation jobs from publishers to provide a modest income for himself. He would have been gratified by the reviews of Liddell Hart's biography of him had they not reawakened people's interest, and had he not spoken so frankly to Hart about his parentage. He had said that "Lawrence" was a name as false as "Ross" and "Shaw," with the inevitable result that the newspapers sought to find out his real name, and came close to uncovering the secret of his illegitimate birth—about which he no longer cared, but which would have embarrassed his mother and his two surviving brothers.

The king, in a strange moment of insight, had once called Lawrence the happiest man in the kingdom, and perhaps it was true—he was doing what he wanted to do; he had exhausted his ambitions; he had no ties to anyone or anything. His mother and his brother Bob were back in China; his youngest brother, Arnold, was married and hard at work on a career as an archaeologist. Robert Graves, who knew Lawrence as well as anyone, claimed by way of defending his right to call himself Irish, "the rhetoric of freedom, the rhetoric of chastity, the rhetoric of honour, the power to excite sudden deep affections, loyalty to the long-buried past, high aims qualified by too mocking a sense of humour, serenity clouded by petulance, and broken by occasional black despairs, playboy charm and theatricality, imagination that overruns itself and tires, extreme generosity, serpent cunning, lion courage, diabolical intuition, and the curse of self-doubt which becomes enmity to self and sometimes renouncement of all that is most loved and esteemed." Whether these are Irish traits or not—

and Lawrence's claim to be Irish was not a strong one—perhaps nobody ever summed him up better, except that Graves left out Lawrence's curious mixture of vanity and modesty.

By the end of 1934, Lawrence was again facing the potential of huge publicity. The British Fascists were attempting to claim him as their own, despite the fact that he had turned down an invitation to one of their meetings with a jocular note suggesting that his only interest in them would be if they put an end to the popular press, and that he would dance on the grave of the *Daily Express, Daily Chronicle,* and *Daily Herald.* Since he signed his note, "Yours not very seriously, T. E. Shaw," it can be assumed that he had no interest in becoming a Fascist leader, a fact which was confirmed by no less an authority than the prospective British *Führer* and head of the British Union of Fascists, Sir Oswald Mosley. Lawrence was not about to exchange RAF blue for a black shirt, and he had no enthusiasm for Mussolini either.

Lawrence was now working in Bridlington, Yorkshire, on the North Sea, looking after the winter overhaul of the RAF launches and living in the Ozone Hotel. His enlistment in the RAF would at last come to an end in March 1935, but so long as he was still serving, he was determined to give the RAF value for its money. He worried about how he would support himself at Clouds Hill after he left the air force, and whether he would be able to afford his motorcycle. He described his predicament to Lady Astor: "In March 1935 the RAF takes away from me the right to serve it longer, and I relapse into a self-supporting life. My Cottage, 35/—a week, 24 hours a day. I am so tired that it feels like heaven drawing near." Job offers came in, including one as secretary to the Bank of England, though this was unlikely: it is hard to imagine him in a respectable City position, wearing striped trousers, a black coat, and a hat to work every day, neatly furled umbrella in hand. The truth was that he didn't really want a job or a position; he simply wanted to make enough money to live his own way. Despite his years of service in the army and the RAF his personality remained basically that of a bohemian and an artist.

He worried about the possibility that *Revolt in the Desert* might be made into a film; this had concerned him since 1928, when the trustees (of which he was not one) sold an option on the film rights. Lawrence was concerned not only about the publicity and the question of who would play him, but about the possibility of a ham-handed attempt to build a "sex interest" into the story, by creating a role for a female star. By now the rights had passed into the hands of Alexander Korda,* the Hungarian-born producer who had made Britain's first internationally successful film, *The Private Life of Henry VIII*, in 1933. This was the first British film ever nominated for an Academy Award for Best Picture, and its star, Charles Laughton, became the first British actor to win an Academy Award for Best Actor. Lawrence rightly feared that Korda was much more likely to actually make the picture than the previous owners of the rights. He went down to London to have it out with Korda, but found to his surprise that the film producer listened to him patiently and sympathetically, and appeared to agree. "I lunched with Alexander Korda, the film king," Lawrence reported to Charlotte Shaw: "He was quite unexpectedly sensitive, for a king: seemed to understand at once the inconveniences his proposed film would set in my path . . . and ended the discussion by agreeing that it should not be attempted without my consent. He will not announce its abandonment, because while he has it on his list other producers will avoid thought of it. But it will not be done. You can imagine how this gladdens me."

Korda would later speak with great fondness of Lawrence, and described him as "the nicest man I ever failed to do business with." What he had actually agreed to—a fine, but significant, point—was that the film would not be made without Lawrence's consent *until after his death*. Far from wanting to include a "sex interest," Korda had planned to base the script very closely on *Revolt in the Desert* and to have Leslie Howard play Lawrence. He wanted to have his brother Zoltan, who was about to make *Sanders of the River* (with Paul Robeson), direct the desert sequences;

* Alexander Korda (1893–1956) was the author's uncle. Zoltan Korda (1895–1961) was the middle brother; and the author's father, Vincent Korda (1897–1979), the youngest brother.

and to have his brother Vincent do the art direction. Korda liked Lawrence from the start (finding him *"très sympathique"*), and he also realized that making a film against Lawrence's wishes would bring down on him a host of protests from just the kind of Englishmen whose respect and friendship he wanted. In any case, Korda regarded the ownership of the film rights of important books as a kind of savings account. He was buying the goodwill of the authors—everybody likes to receive an unexpected check, hence Korda's purchase of the screen rights to Winston Churchill's two-volume biography of Marlborough. Also, if he was patient, sooner or later somebody else might eventually want to make a film of even the most improbable book, and he could then sell the rights at a profit. It was a form of saving for his old age, for a man who preferred gambling to saving. In any case, the more options he took on books, the more friends he made. Lawrence understood this intuitively; he wrote to Robert Graves, "Korda is like an oil-company which has drilled often and found two or three gushers, and has prudently invested some of its proceeds in buying options over more sites. Some he may develop and others not."

Lawrence enjoyed Bridlington, despite its melancholy ambience of an unfashionable summer resort in midwinter, and was comfortable at the Ozone Hotel, where he had a tower room looking out over the harbor wall to the sea. Officers seldom put in an appearance—one who did recalled him wearing a blue pullover, a scarf, an old sports jacket, and a pair of gray flannels. Lawrence ordered the few NCOs around with consummate tact, while they responded by calling him "Mr. Shaw," as did his formidable landlady. The equipment officer at RAF Catfoss, Flight Lieutenant R. G. Sims, had known Lawrence in Iraq, and Lawrence became a close friend of Sims and his wife, once more crossing what would have been for anyone else the rigid class barrier that separates other ranks from officers in the British armed forces. The Simses took Lawrence to concerts in Hull, and he became a frequent dinner guest in their cottage. Reggie Sims, as so many other people had, occasionally spotted the undiminished presence of Colonel Lawrence in AC1 Shaw, as on the day he came into a room where Lawrence was absorbed in studying a blueprint. For a moment Lawrence ignored his presence, then his head rose, and "his eyes blazed forth for a moment or two in what Sims took to be scorn or hate. Then there was a sudden half-smile of recognition. 'Oh, I am so sorry, Sir.' A. C. Shaw murmured apologetically, 'but for a moment I took you for a reporter.' "

His capacity for extracting awe and respect from his superiors was also undiminished. When a senior officer inspecting the boatyard had a question and was told he should ask Aircraftman Shaw, he snapped back, "When I want the advice of an A.C.1 I will ask for it!" The following night Lawrence and the senior officer—who in the meantime had agreed to an entire list of requests for tools and equipment Lawrence had requested— were seen dining together amiably. Nor had his habit of dining with the great and famous changed. He applied for weekend leave to accept an invitation to Lympne, the country house of Sir Philip Sassoon, where he dined in his airman's uniform, seated next to Lady Louis Mountbatten, whom he enlisted to persuade the undersecretary of state for air to take some hats out to Singapore, for Clare Smith, whose husband had been posted there, and who apparently had not been prepared for the elaborateness required of ladies at official functions in the colonies.* His past was always catching up to him, sometimes in improbable ways: he was obliged to interview an imposter who had been arrested for pretending to be Lawrence of Arabia; a woman wrote to the local police complaining that he was her husband who had abandoned her; the amateur theatrical society of Bridlington put on, with great fanfare, a performance of Shaw's *Too True to Be Good*, which Lawrence at first elected not to attend on the grounds that too many people in Bridlington already knew that "Mr. Shaw" was "Lawrence of Arabia" and would recognize him as "Private Meek." "They would have cheered, or jeered, probably: cheered, I'm afraid, so I funked it," he wrote to Charlotte, but then he changed his mind and went to see it with a party of RAF officers and their wives, laughed through the

---

*Photographs of Clare Smith generally show her wearing a smart beret with a diamond brooch, not at all the kind of hat expected of a group captain's wife in Singapore.

whole performance, and stood around afterward signing people's pro-grams—again the dichotomy between avoiding fame and relishing it that makes Lawrence such a puzzle. He applied for another weekend leave to spend two days being painted by Augustus John in his airman's uniform and peaked cap—a startlingly ambiguous portrait in which Lawrence's face and pose are those of a tough-minded general, while his uniform is that of a simple airman. Unlike most portraits of Lawrence in Arab dress, this one has a certain specific gravity; instead of looking weightless, here he looks solidly rooted, massive, more like a monument than a man. John, despite his famously blustery, aggressive nature, had a sixth sense as an artist, and may have already concluded that Lawrence's future was unlikely to be a quiet retirement in his Dorsetshire cottage, translating French novels and tinkering with his motorcycle.

The Simses gave a dinner party for Eric Kennington, one of Lawrence's favorite artists, when Kennington visited Lawrence at Bridlington. By this time it no longer seemed to matter to anyone that Lawrence was merely an AC1—and Lawrence, preparing himself for the inevitable, made a friend of Pilot Officer A. J. Manning, in command of the "arma-ment school" at Catfoss. He confided to Manning that he wanted to steer a middle course between being a pauper and having more money than he felt comfortable with. "He wanted to establish a balance, ensuring his independence," recalled Manning, who went on to become an air commodore.

To Robert Graves, who had written to say that the *Times* had asked him to update its obituary of Lawrence—not a premonition on anybody's part, but merely something that was done regularly for famous people—he replied cheerfully and at great length, urging that his work with Churchill in the Middle East after the war, and particularly his part in developing high-speed motor launches for the RAF, should not be put in the shadow of what he had done in Arabia during the war. "The conquest of the last element, the air," he wrote, "seems to me the only major task of our generation; and I have convinced myself that progress to-day is made not by the single genius, but by the common effort."

On Monday, February 25, 1935, dressed for once in uniform, Lawrence presented himself more formally to Pilot Officer Manning. "Aircraftman Shaw, sir, interview before discharge," said the flight sergeant as Lawrence came smartly to attention. After a brief chat, Manning signed the discharge form, ending Lawrence's career in the RAF.

Leaving behind the Brough motorcycle, Lawrence set off on a bicycle tour, dressed in his sport jacket and gray flannels and wearing a thick scarf, hoping thereby to avoid the press. He intended to reach Clouds Hill in stages, counting on the fact that few journalists would notice a middle-aged man in civilian clothes riding a bicycle on country roads—though it has to be said that not many men Lawrence's age would have attempted a bicycle trip of more than 200 miles in February. One of his gunners from the Arabian campaign, with whom he had been in correspondence for several years, had leaked the story that he was leaving the RAF, and *The Daily Express* ran a long article about it on February 17, thus alerting all the other newspapers to the story. Lawrence had had a few days of leave coming to him, and had taken his discharge early, hoping to avoid publicity, but a photographer still managed to get a picture of him on his bike, leaving Bridlington, with his hair still trimmed short on the sides, RAF-style, but, as usual, unruly.

Once on the road he was free. He had intended to ride south and visit Frederic Manning, the author of *Her Privates We*, one of the best novels written in the English language about the horror of life and death in the trenches. It could be published only in expurgated form during Manning's own lifetime (and under his serial number rather than his name), but even in that diminished form it had deeply impressed not only Lawrence, but Ernest Hemingway and Ezra Pound as well. Lawrence had come to like Manning—a lonely Australian who, like Lawrence, never married, led a withdrawn and solitary life, and was haunted by the war. Unfortunately, two days into his journey, Lawrence learned that Manning had died. "How I wish he hadn't slipped away in this fashion; but how like him," Lawrence remarked. "He was too shy to let anyone tell him how good he was."

Lawrence changed course for Cambridge to see his brother Arnold, who was at that time reader in classical archaeology at Cambridge University. From there he went by stages toward Clouds Hill, where, when he arrived, he found his way blocked by an unruly mass of reporters and photographers.

Horrified—he needed and had anticipated peace and quiet—he bicycled to London. Sir Herbert Baker had given up his offices on Barton Street, so Lawrence no longer had access to his old attic room; instead, he stayed in lodgings under (yet another) assumed name, while taking out membership in the Youth Hostels Association, since he vaguely intended to tour around the country by bicycle until interest in him had died down. He must have been aware that this was unlikely, for he wrote a letter complaining about the behavior of the press to the Hon. Esmond Harmsworth, who was chairman of the Newspaper Proprietors Association and the son of that most shameless of press lords Lord Rothermere. Stranded away from his only home, he missed the RAF enormously, and complained to Kennington that he felt like "a fallen leaf." He must have been given some reason to believe that the siege of his cottage had been called off, for he went back there and found it deserted, to his relief.

The relief was short-lived. Within a few days the press was back in force: reporters were hammering on his door and demanding that he appear and make a statement, and photographers were climbing to his roof and breaking the tiles in order to get a picture of him through the window. Infuriated, he made his escape through the garden, so fiercely hounded by the reporters that he gave one of them a black eye—the only record of any violence on Lawrence's part toward anyone since he reached Damascus in 1918.

Lawrence wrote a heartfelt letter to "Dear Winston," imploring him to intercede with Harmsworth, and bicycled over to see Churchill at Chartwell, his country house. Perhaps Churchill managed to deal with Harmsworth—he had, from long experience, a way with press lords—or perhaps the press had published enough about Lawrence's leaving the RAF to satisfy readers—but in either case, by the third week of March the siege ended, and Lawrence was left in undisputed possession of his own home. His nerves were badly shaken by the intensity of the press, and he was still undecided about what to do with himself now that he was a civilian again. For the moment, he collected his few belongings and the motorcycle he was no longer sure he could afford, and settled back into Clouds Hill, like a man waiting for the next act but in no hurry for it to arrive.

The Shaws had set out on a world tour, and his mother and his brother Bob had returned to China, but Lawrence kept up his industrious correspondence, both with the great world and with those who had served with him in the ranks. He tinkered with his house, feeling the slight bewilderment and loss of a familiar routine that comes over many people when they retire. He had expressed a wish to have a "porthole" in the bedroom of his cottage, and T. B. Marson, Trenchard's former private secretary, found him exactly what he was looking for in a ship breaker's yard, and sent it off to Lawrence by rail. Lawrence spent a good deal of time and effort cleaning it up and installing it in the wall, and scratched Marson's initials in the polished brass rim "in memory." Thanking Marson, he added: "All here is very quiet, but I am still calling the RAF 'we' in my talk. That is very sad." He had any number of pet projects he wanted to carry out in the cottage, and therefore may not have taken Nancy Astor seriously when she wrote to him, "I believe when the Government re-organizes you will be asked to re-organize the Defence forces. I will tell you what I have done already about it." She invited him to lunch at Cliveden, to meet Stanley Baldwin, who would shortly replace Ramsay MacDonald as prime minister in the coalition national government, but Lawrence gracefully refused both the invitation and any such job. "Wild mares would not take me away from Clouds Hill," he wrote to her, ". . . so do not commit yourself to advocating me."

Lady Astor's suggestion that he would soon be offered the job of reorganizing Britain's defenses should be taken with a grain of salt. As a member of Parliament and the wife of the immensely wealthy owner of *The Observer* she was in the habit of assuming that all her suggestions would be taken seriously. Except for Winston Churchill, there was nobody whose advice on matters of defense Stanley Baldwin was less likely to take seriously than Nancy Astor; nor did defense and foreign policy hold much interest for Baldwin to begin with—he was reported to sleep soundly through cabinet meetings whenever either of these subjects was discussed. His motto might have been peace at any price: not just peace in Europe, but also peace from Lady Astor's importuning him. Nor is it even remotely likely that Baldwin would have given Lawrence a place in reorganizing the national defenses, first of all because his policy was to let sleeping dogs lie, and second because Lawrence, like Churchill, represented exactly the kind of enthusiastic and publicity-attracting amateur strategist whom Baldwin most distrusted.* Baldwin's ambition was to rely as much as possible on solid Tory party figures and professional civil servants—the more cautious, the better—and until very late in the day he continued to believe that Hitler could be bought off by territorial concessions or would come to his senses like a reasonable man, as did Lady Astor, for that matter.

On May 12, 1935, Lawrence wrote what was almost certainly his last letter, to K. T. Parker, "keeper" of the Ashmolean Museum in Oxford, to express his pleasure that Augustus John's portrait of Hogarth would be hung in the Ashmolean—where, as a child, Lawrence had left pottery shards he had dug up, for Hogarth's scrutiny. "At present I am sitting in my cottage and getting used to an empty life," he wrote, but without any trace of self-pity or depression. Indeed, he ended the letter on a hopeful note.

He had, in the meantime, received a letter from Henry Williamson, an acquaintance who was the author of *Tarka the Otter*, a book Lawrence had greatly admired. Williamson was a member of the British Union of Fascists, but the purpose of his letter was not to convert Lawrence to Sir

---

* To his credit, Baldwin did authorize expenditure on what would come to be called radar and on the eight-gun monoplane fighter (the Spitfire and the Hurricane), but that was because they were presented to him in the most unobtrusive way by professionals he trusted. The task of "reorganizing" Britain's defenses was not put into the hands of one person until April 1940, when Prime Minister Neville Chamberlain, Baldwin's successor, most reluctantly made Winston Churchill chairman of the Committee of Service Ministers and Chiefs of Staff, in addition to his post as first lord of the admiralty.

Oswald Mosley's cause, but to get advice about a manuscript that had been entrusted to Williamson by V. M. Yeates, the author of *Winged Victory*, before his death. Yeates was also an author Lawrence admired— *Winged Victory*, a harrowing semiautobiographical account of a fighter pilot's experience of air combat during the war, was regarded as a classic by most readers at the time—so it is hardly surprising that Lawrence invited Williamson to have lunch with him at Clouds Hill. If there was anybody who knew everything there was to know about editing and publishing an account of war, it was Lawrence. There is no reason to believe that Lawrence was becoming more interested in Fascism, or that Williamson was coming to recruit him.

On the morning of Monday, May 13, Lawrence rode to the nearest post office, at Wool, the village just outside Bovington Camp, with a parcel of books he wanted to send to a friend. He also sent Williamson a telegram: "LUNCH TUESDAY WET FINE. COTTAGE ONE MILE NORTH BOVINGTON CAMP— SHAW."

In keeping with the mysteries that surround Lawrence's life, much has been made of this seemingly innocuous telegram, suggesting some urgency on Lawrence's part. But since Williamson had concluded his letter to Lawrence with, "I'll call in anyway on Tuesday unless rainy day," Lawrence's "WET FINE" had no such connotation. He was simply saying, in effect, "Come for lunch Tuesday, never mind the weather," a very sensible reply in England. The cryptic quality that some scholars find there is merely a reflection of the way people compressed telegram messages to the bare minimum of words and punctuation. Lawrence was not wealthy, and every word had to be paid for. Having completed his errands he got back on his motorcycle and set out for home, a trip of about a mile and a half.

The road between Bovington and Lawrence's cottage should have presented no special problems. It was and remains a narrow country road with several bends, but no sharp curves. The sides of the road are either steep or heavily wooded. There are three dips, deep enough so that any one of them might conceal an oncoming vehicle momentarily; and in 1935 the surface was still tar, on top of which loose gravel had been sprinkled. For obvious reasons this is not an ideal surface for a motor-cycle—loose gravel always presents a danger—but Lawrence knew the road well, and was an experienced rider. What appears to have happened was that he approached one of the dips in the road at about thirty-eight miles per hour or less (the motorcycle was found still in second gear after the accident), and did not realize that two local boys on bicycles were in front of him, since they were concealed in the dip. Instead of riding one behind the other, they were riding side by side, going in the same direc-tion as he was, so when Lawrence suddenly saw them, he had no easy way to get around them. He must have swerved sharply to avoid hitting them and braked hard at the same time, but he hit the rear wheel of one of the bicycles, at which point he lost control of his motorcycle; the brakes may have jammed, the bike may have skidded, and he was thrown forward over the handlebars. The bike fell away to the right, spinning in the loose gravel and gouging a mark in the road, while Lawrence landed on his head, then slid off the road, coming to a stop as his head hit a tree trunk. The first impact was hard enough to kill him, though it did not. He was unconscious, however, and bleeding heavily.

Probably no vehicle accident up until Princess Diana's has received more detailed scrutiny than Lawrence's. His death has been variously ascribed to a foreign or domestic assassination, or to some combination of death wish and speed, or suicide. True, Lawrence had written "In speed we hurl ourselves beyond the body," and he loved riding at high speeds, but it was subsequently established that he was going less than forty miles an hour when he was killed, so he was neither a victim of high-speed driving nor a successful suicide. As for the assassination theory, there seems no very good reason why either the British or the German intelli-gence service would have wanted Lawrence dead. Although *The Daily Express* would claim that he carried "the plans for the defence of England in his head," that too seems a typical Fleet Street exaggeration. Certainly Lawrence had *ideas* on the subject, but he was not privy to any secrets.

Though nobody said so at the inquest, his death was yet another proof that a motorcycle accident at *any* speed is dangerous. The helmets of the day were not scientifically designed to prevent head injury, and in any case Lawrence never wore a proper helmet—in extremely bad weather he sometimes wore a leather flying helmet, which would have offered no protection from impact. If he had landed on his side he might have suffered nothing worse than a few broken bones, but he was thrown forward and instead landed on his head, fracturing the skull.

The subsequent inquest and many further investigations by private individuals do not provide much more than this in the way of fact. A soldier, Corporal Catchpole, who heard the crash and ran to the site of the accident claimed to have seen a black car speeding away from the scene; the boys denied that they were riding side by side, no doubt warned by their parents not to admit that they had been breaking the law, though they were notorious for larking about on the road; and some people have speculated that the front brake cable in Lawrence's Brough may have snapped, although this seems unlikely: Lawrence was always conscientious to the point of fussiness about maintaining his bikes.

Catchpole flagged down a passing army lorry, and ordered the driver to take Lawrence and one of the boys, who had sustained minor injuries, to the Bovington camp hospital, the nearest medical facility, where Lawrence was quickly identified. After that the army took control, although Lawrence was a civilian and the accident had taken place on a civilian road. All ranks were warned that they were not to talk to newspapermen, and reminded that they were subject to the Official Secrets Act; newspaper editors were informed that bulletins about Lawrence's health would be issued by the War Office. As anyone could have predicted, this had the effect of increasing interest in Lawrence's crash, adding a note of mystery to what was simply a tragic road accident. Even without that, however, it was a major news story throughout the world. Arnold Lawrence was informed of the accident by the Cambridge police, and arrived the next day at Clouds Hill with his wife.

Lawrence lay unconscious in the hospital at the army camp he had disliked so much when he was exiled from his beloved RAF. Distinguished specialists in brain injuries were sent for; the king dispatched two of his own physicians, including the future Lord Dawson of Penn, and telephoned himself, asking to be kept informed. The Home Office, not wanting affairs left entirely in the hands of the military, sent two plainclothes officers from Scotland Yard, one to sit in Lawrence's room, while his relief slept on a cot outside in the corridor. To be fair, this was probably less from any fear of foreign agents or security issues than to prevent an enterprising newspaper photographer from finding a way in to take a picture of Lawrence on his deathbed.

Everything that could be done was done, given the limited facilities of the Bovington camp hospital; but as the doctors had concluded after examining Lawrence, the case was hopeless.

Lawrence lingered six days, never regaining consciousness, with his lungs becoming increasingly congested, and died just after eight in the morning on Sunday, May 19.

He was forty-six years old.

Postmortem examination revealed that Lawrence would have lost his memory and would have been paralyzed had he survived.

He was buried in the nearby churchyard of Moreton. His old friend Ronald Storrs (now Sir Ronald, and governor of Cyprus) was the chief pallbearer. The others were the artist Eric Kennington; Colonel Stewart Newcombe, who had known Lawrence since the Sinai survey before the war; a neighbor; and two service friends of Lawrence's, one from the army and the other from the RAF.

The small ceremony was quiet, despite a mob of photographers and reporters, and many of Lawrence's friends were present: Winston Churchill and his wife, Lady Astor, Mrs. Thomas Hardy, Allenby, Siegfried Sassoon, Lionel Curtis, Augustus John, Wavell, Alan Dawnay. As the coffin was lowered into the ground the soldier and the airman, on opposite sides of the grave, shook hands over it; and at the last moment a neighbor's little girl ran forward and threw a bunch of violets on the top of it.

Nancy Astor, in tears, ran to put her arms around Churchill, who was also in tears, and cried, "Oh, Winnie, Winnie, we've lost him."

The king's message to Arnold Lawrence would appear the next day in the *Times*:

The King has heard with sincere regret of the death of your brother, and deeply sympathizes with you and your family in this sad loss.

Your brother's name will live in history, and the King gratefully recognizes his distinguished services to his country and feels that it is tragic that the end should have come in this manner to a life still so full of promise.

Perhaps fortunately, because of his gifts of description, Ronald Storrs—who had taken the young Lawrence with him on his journey to Jidda in 1916, and had watched him wave good-bye from the shore at Rabegh, the day before his ride up-country to the meeting with Feisal and, in Storrs's words, to "write his page, brilliant as a Persian miniature, in the History of England"—was the last to see him before his burial.

I stood beside him lying swathed in fleecy wool; stayed until the plain oak coffin was screwed down. There was nothing else in the mortuary chamber but a little altar behind his head with some lilies of the valley and red roses. I had come prepared to be greatly shocked by what I saw, but his injuries had been at the back of his head, and beyond some scarring and discolouration over the left eye, his countenance was not marred. His nose was sharper and delicately curved, and his chin less square. Seen thus, his face was the face of Dante with perhaps the more relentless mouth of Savonarola; incredibly calm, with the faintest flicker of disdain. . . . Nothing of his hair, nor of his hands was showing; only a powerful cowled mask, dark-stained ivory against the dead chemical sterility of the wrappings. It was somehow unreal to be watching beside him in these cerements, so strangely resembling the *aba*, the *kuffiya* and the *agal* of an Arab Chief, as he lay in his last littlest room, very grave and strong and noble.

His plain, modest headstone merely describes him as "T. E. Lawrence, Fellow of All Souls College," as if even in death he was still resisting the rank of colonel and all his decorations. Below are inscribed the words:

> The hour is coming & now is
> When the dead shall hear
> The Voice of the
> SON OF GOD
> And they that hear shall live.

They were placed there, we may be sure, to please his mother, rather than from any wish of Lawrence's, who was at best a nominal Christian. At the foot of the grave is a smaller stone, in the shape of an open book, bearing the words "DOMINUS ILLUMINATIO MEA," which may be translated "The Lord is my light," but which can also mean "May God enlighten me."

The open book and the Latin phrase form part of the heraldic coat of arms of Oxford University, and it is perhaps the most fitting memorial to Lawrence, who grew up among the ancient walls and towers of Oxford, and whose character was formed by it more than by any other single element, perhaps the most extreme example of the scholar turned hero in the eleven centuries of its existence.

Life after Death

L awrence is in the select group of heroes who become even more famous after death than they were while alive. The Library of Congress lists more than 100 books about him, of which fifty-six are biographical, and that number does not include several children's books, two very successful plays, a major motion picture, and a television docudrama, as well as numerous Web sites devoted to his life and work. As Lawrence had feared, "the Colonel," as he sometimes called his former self in a spirit of derision, just keeps marching on, despite every effort on Lawrence's part to kill him off. Doubtless, if he had had his way, Lawrence would have been buried with the name T. E. Shaw inscribed on his headstone, but his brother Arnold stood firm in opposing that, and so it is as T. E. Lawrence that he lies in Moreton churchyard, and is commemorated by sculptures of various sizes in the crypt of St. Paul's Cathedral; at Jesus College, Oxford; at the City of Oxford High School; and in the tiny church of St. Martin's, near Clouds Hill, where Eric Kennington carved a life-size recumbent effigy of Lawrence in his Arab robes and headdress, his hands crossed over his Meccan dagger as if in prayer, very similar to the medieval effigies of knights, crusaders, and their wives that Lawrence had photographed in his childhood.

The limelight that Bernard Shaw had warned him about has never dimmed, and he remains as famous now as he was seventy-five years ago, and perhaps even more controversial. In part this is because there exists a flourishing Lawrence cult, fueled by the Lawrence legend, that has kept an apparently endless number of controversies going on the subject of Lawrence, many of them created, not always inadvertently, by Lawrence himself. As early as 1929 he had predicted, in a letter to a friend, "I am trying to accustom myself to the truth that I'll probably be talked over for the rest of my life: and after my life too."

After Lawrence's death his brother Arnold was bombarded by letters from admirers who saw Lawrence as the central figure of a new religion, in which they hoped Arnold might play the role of Saint Paul. Even before his death Lawrence was painted by "an Austrian-born religious artist named Herbert Gurschner" as a gently smiling, beatific religious figure in RAF uniform with a beggar's cloak like that of Saint Francis thrown over his shoulders, against a lush background of Egyptian religious symbols. His left hand is raised in a kind of casual blessing, and through the long, graceful fingers of his right hand run grains of golden desert sand.

Arnold sensibly resisted attempts to make his brother a religious symbol or a martyr, but the impulse was already there to turn Lawrence into many things he had never been. He has been celebrated as an antiwar figure, although Lawrence's feelings about war were ambivalent, to say the least. He has been made the hero of a novel portraying him as a thwarted homosexual who welcomes his own death, though nobody could have fought harder to be asexual than Lawrence, and there is no evidence that he wanted to die. He has been attacked as a total fraud and liar by one biographer, though the release of hitherto secret government files had by 1975 proved that Lawrence did everything he claimed to have done (and kept meticulous records), and that, if anything, he underplayed the importance of his role in the war and as Churchill's adviser on Middle Eastern affairs after the peace. He has been blamed by the Arabs for the

Lawrence as a religious cult figure, with a pilgrim's cape and sand running through his fingers. In the background, various mystical symbols. Painting by Herbert Gurschner, an Austrian-born religious artist, 1934.

existence of Israel, and criticized by the Israelis as pro-Arab. Insurgents such as Mao, Ho Chi Minh, and Che Guevara have claimed to follow his methods of guerrilla warfare; but anti-insurgency fighters, such as the United States Army today, also claim to use his tactics. He sometimes gets a bad press as a sadist because of the killing of Turkish and German prisoners after the Arabs discovered the massacre of Arab civilians in Tafas, in 1918, and as a masochist because of the whippings meted out to him by John Bruce. He is criticized as an imperialist who wanted the new Arab states to be within the British Empire, and as an anti-imperialist who disliked Britain's rule over India.

Given the secrecy in which much of his life was passed, it is hardly surprising that some people refused to believe he was dead at all, and that according to persistent rumors he was recovering from his injuries in Tangiers, and would return whenever England was in danger. There were numerous "sightings" of him, usually in Arab dress, in the Middle East.

As the years passed, and the heroes of the Great War slipped from the public memory, Lawrence became one of the few people who *could* be remembered from that terrible war—a stand-in, as it were, for all the others. He had not been one of the young officers who had gone to their death unflinchingly, leading their platoons over the top into German machine gun fire; nor had he been one of the legion of faceless men, the PBI or "poor bloody infantry," slogging through the mud and barbed wire. He was, in a curious way, classless; he had belonged to no regiment; he had fought according to his own rules; he was free from the cant and the naive patriotic enthusiasm that began to ring false to people in the 1930s; and he became, like Nelson, a pillar on which British patriotism rested, eccentric, perhaps, but undeniably a hero.

Even World War II did nothing to shake Lawrence's reputation. On the contrary, his tactics were followed to the letter very successfully by the British Long Range Desert Group (LRDG) in Libya in 1941 and 1942: *Seven Pillars of Wisdom* was their Bible, and Lawrence their patron saint. No less an authority than Field Marshal Rommel said, "The LRDG caused us more damage than any other unit of their size," praise from the enemy that would not have surprised Lawrence. His influence remained strong: his old friend and admirer A. P. Wavell was in command of the Middle East; and Lawrence inspired a number of bold imitators, chief among them Major-General Orde Wingate, DSO and two bars—the son of General Sir Reginald Wingate, the *sirdar* of the Egyptian army who had recommended Lawrence for the "immediate award" of the Victoria Cross in 1917. Unorthodox, courageous, and a born leader, Orde Wingate applied Lawrence's techniques, both in the Middle East and in Burma, with great success, becoming, like Lawrence, a great favorite of Churchill's. Most military figures from World War I seemed irrelevant during World War II, but Lawrence's reputation remained unscathed.

Lawrence's literary reputation grew steadily. After his death *Seven Pillars of Wisdom* was at last published in normal book form, using the text from the subscribers' edition rather than preferred "Oxford version" of 1922; it sold more than 60,000 copies in the first year and went on to become a steady seller in English on both sides of the Atlantic, and in many other languages. (*The Mint* was not published until 1955, and then it appeared in two versions: one expurgated and the other in a limited edition, with the barracks language intact.) The immense task of publishing Lawrence's letters proceeded, and these won him perhaps even more praise than his books, for the sheer quantity and the quality of his correspondence was extraordinary. He was the subject, as well, of much careful scholarship. With both his flanks—military and literary—secure, Lawrence might have continued as a respected English hero, except that it would not have been in character for him to do that, dead or alive.

The great crisis in Lawrence's reputation was caused by the publication in 1955 of Richard Aldington's controversial *Lawrence of Arabia: A Biographical Enquiry*. Aldington had set out to write a conventional, admiring biography of Lawrence, at the suggestion of his publisher, but as he researched the book he discovered that he neither liked nor trusted Lawrence, and came to the conclusion that Lawrence had systematically twisted the facts to create his own legend.

Aldington's book virtually destroyed his own health and his career as a writer. He was an odd choice for the thankless task of debunking Lawrence. He was not an investigative journalist, and he was far from being a mere crank; he was a respected, if minor, war poet, a novelist, a translator, a fairly successful biographer (of Voltaire, the duke of Wellington, and D. H. Lawrence), and a friend of such literary figures as D. H. Lawrence and Ezra Pound. A whole book has been written about Aldington's attempt to deconstruct Lawrence's legend—an attempt that began as a perfectly conventional exercise in biography rather than a deliberate attack on one of Britain's greatest heroes. Aldington, a prickly, quarrelsome, difficult character, may not even have realized that when he set out to write about Lawrence he had a chip on his shoulder—not just because Lawrence had achieved, it seemed almost effortlessly, the fame that eluded Aldington himself, but also because Aldington had served through some of the worst fighting on the western front, rising from the ranks to become a commissioned officer in the Royal Sussex Regiment. Aldington had been gassed and shell-shocked, and his experience of war made him contemptuous of Lawrence's role in what Lawrence himself described as "a sideshow of a sideshow"; he remarked disparagingly to a friend, "These potty little skirmishes and sabotage raids which Hart and Lawrence call battles are somewhat belly-aching to one who did the Somme, Vimy, Loos, etc." Not only did it seem to Aldington that Lawrence had had an easy war of it compared with those who fought in the trenches, but Lawrence had been rewarded with fame beyond even his own imagination, with decorations and honors that he had treated contemptuously and with the friendship of great and powerful figures. In short, whether Aldington realized it or not, his book about Lawrence was spoiled by his own envy of his subject from the very beginning; and the more deeply Aldington delved into Lawrence's life, the more bitter he became.

Aldington was one of those people who take everything literally— even his admirers do not credit him with a sense of proportion (or a sense of humor)—and the tone of his book about Lawrence was, from page 1, that of a man in a rage; it was a sustained 448-page rant, in which he attacked everything about Lawrence, apparently determined to blow up the legend once and for all. Much of it is minor stuff; partly, this is the fault of Lowell Thomas and Lawrence's other early biographers—his friends Robert Graves, the poet and novelist; and B. H. Liddell Hart, the military historian and theorist—who had written panegyrics to Lawrence without any serious effort at independent research or objectivity. Sooner or later, somebody was bound to come along and correct the balance.

It was Aldington's misfortune, however, to have unearthed proof that Lawrence and his four brothers were illegitimate, and to reveal it while Lawrence's mother was still alive. This struck most people, even those who were not admirers of Lawrence, as tactless and cruel.

Aldington was also the victim of an idée fixe: he believed that his whole case rested on whether or not Lawrence had told the truth in saying that he had been offered the post of British high commissioner in Egypt in 1922, when Field Marshal Lord Allenby seemed about to give it up in disgust. This dispute, into which Winston Churchill, then in his last year as prime minister, was drawn most reluctantly, sputtered on for ages, though it is obvious to anybody reading about the episode today that Churchill, then colonial secretary, in fact *did* suggest this appointment to Lawrence, though perhaps not altogether seriously, and that Lawrence, who never wanted the post, which was not in any case for Churchill to offer, later came to the conclusion that it had been offered to him genuinely. This was a reasonable belief, since Churchill was given to just that kind of impulsive gesture; and Lloyd George, then the prime minister, and himself notoriously impulsive about offering people high government positions without informing his colleagues in the cabinet, seems to have brought the subject up with Lawrence as well.

In any event, Aldington's book, when it was eventually published in 1955 after years of bitter quarrels with his own publisher, his long-suffering editor, and innumerable lawyers, brought down on him a landslide of abuse and criticism on both sides of the Atlantic. He succeeded in tarnishing Lawrence's image for a time, but at the cost of his own reputation and career—a sad object lesson in the perils of obsessive self-righteousness.

Aldington might have known better had he written a biography of Nelson instead of Wellington, for Nelson, despite character flaws that in some ways mirrored those of Lawrence, won a permanent place in the hearts of the British, while the victor of Waterloo, a cold and haughty aristocrat, never did. Nelson, like Lawrence, was a man who desperately craved attention and sought fame, who artfully cloaked vanity and ambition with humility, whose private life was something between a muddle and a disgrace, and who constantly appeared in the limelight without ever appearing to seek it. Like Lawrence he was small, physically brave to an extraordinary degree, able to endure great pain and hardship without complaint, and indifferent to food, drink, and comfort. Unlike Lawrence, he not only avidly sought honors, medals, titles, and decorations, but insisted on wearing them all even when doing so put his life at risk. However, both of them were cast from the same mold, heroes whose human weaknesses and flaws merely made them loved all the more, both by those who knew them and by those who admired them from afar. From time to time, in the more than two centuries since Nelson's death, people have written books attempting to put his myth in perspective, but to no avail—he remains as popular as ever, and hardly a decade goes by without the launching of a biography, a film, or a novel* (for example, there was a novel by Susan Sontag), adding yet another layer to his fame. So it is with Lawrence.

The release in 1962 of David Lean's monumental epic film *Lawrence of Arabia* as good as washed away Aldington's attempt to tarnish Lawrence's legend. One of the longest, most beautiful, most ambitious, and most honored films ever made, *Lawrence of Arabia* introduced a new generation to Lawrence the man and Lawrence the legend, and returned Lawrence to the kind of celebrity he had enjoyed (or endured) when Lowell Thomas first brought him to the screen in 1921.

---

* Perhaps the most popular film the author's Uncle Alex and his father ever made was *That Hamilton Woman*, starring Laurence Olivier as Nelson and Vivien Leigh as Lady Hamilton. Winston Churchill screened it innumerable times (it never failed to move him to tears), and took a print to Moscow as a gift to Stalin. As a result it was the only British film seen during World War II by Soviet audiences, and extended Nelson's heroic reputation to Russia.

The real hero of *Lawrence of Arabia* is neither Lawrence nor its director, David Lean, but its producer, Sam Spiegel, who not only persuaded Columbia Pictures to finance one of the most expensive films ever made, but who put it in the hands of a director notoriously resistant to the wishes of a studio, and quite as determined as Lawrence had been to have his own way.

The genesis of *Lawrence of Arabia* went back a long way, with many false starts and disappointments—enough to discourage anyone less resilient than Spiegel. When Lawrence died in 1935, Alexander Korda still owned the rights to *Revolt in the Desert.* He had agreed not to make a film so long as Lawrence was alive, but with Lawrence's death he was free to proceed. He had a star in mind to play Lawrence, the English actor Leslie Howard,* who had been a big success in Korda's *The Scarlet Pimpernel*; and he spent a good deal of time and money developing a script, written by Miles Malleson, who would go on to become a beloved English character actor, and edited by none other than Winston Churchill, then still in the political wilderness.

Korda's film was never made. Financing was difficult; more important, Korda, who was always sensitive to the opinions of those in government and in "the City," soon discovered that nobody wanted it made. A big film about Lawrence was bound to offend the Turks, who did not want to be reminded of their defeat; it would also anger the Arabs, who would not be pleased by the portrayal of the Arab Revolt as being led by a young English officer. Since it was hoped that the Turks might fight on the Allied side if there was another war, or at least stay neutral, and that the Arabs would stay quiet, it was discreetly suggested to Korda that it might be better to put the film aside for the moment. Nobody wanted to see angry Arab mobs burning down cinemas in Cairo, Damascus, Jerusalem, and Baghdad, or burning Lawrence in effigy again. Korda took the setback philosophically, and stepped neatly

---

*Leslie Howard, whose original name was Leslie Howard Steiner, was the son of an English-Jewish mother, Lillian Blumberg, and a Hungarian-Jewish father, Ferdinand Steiner.

from one desert film to another, sending his brother Zoltan off to make *The Four Feathers*, a film that could offend nobody but the Sudanese, about whose feelings few people cared in those days, and that turned out to be a huge hit.

Once World War II began, the film about Lawrence went to the bottom of Korda's large pile of optioned and purchased books; and after the war, events in the Middle East—anti-British rioting, assassinations, and the Arab-Isreali war—made the project seem even less appealing. Occasionally Korda floated rumors that he was planning to make it, now with Laurence Olivier as Lawrence, but that was only in the hope of interesting somebody who would take it off his hands. That person eventually turned up in the larger-than-life form of Sam Spiegel, a producer whose taste for the grand film was equal to Korda's, and who bought the screen rights to *Revolt in the Desert* over luncheon at Anabelle's, the chic club next door to Korda's offices at 144–146 Piccadilly. Spiegel bought the whole package: the book, the existing screenplay, all the preliminary sketches. (Over coffee, brandy, and cigars, he also bought the film rights to *The African Queen*, which prompted Korda, in a rare burst of poor judgment, to say, "My dear Sam, an old man and an old woman go down an African river in an old boat—you will go bankrupt.")

Perhaps the only person who could have brought *Lawrence of Arabia* to the screen was the indefatigable Spiegel, who made the impossible happen by sheer willpower and chutzpah on an epic scale. To begin with, because of the numerous Arab wars against Israel, the cause of Arab freedom and independence was not a popular one in Hollywood. Then too, Spiegel began by hiring Michael Wilson, an experienced screenwriter who had been blacklisted during the McCarthy era, to rewrite the original script—Spiegel hired blacklisted talent because it was cheaper, not out of political sympathy. Then, when Wilson's screenplay turned out to have an antiwar tone inappropriate to Lawrence, he hired Robert Bolt, an Englishman, to make it more triumphant. His first choice for Lawrence was Marlon Brando, whom he had hired for the lead in *On the Waterfront*; and on this assumption he was able to persuade Columbia

Pictures to finance the film, which, from the beginning, was planned as an epic that would appeal to both an American and an international audience. Spiegel managed to keep Columbia on the hook even after Brando turned down the role, as did Albert Finney, a British actor who was in any case hardly the big international star Columbia had been counting on. Finally, Spiegel got Columbia to accept Peter O'Toole, a comparative unknown, in the title role, as well as a British director, David Lean, known for his grandiose (and expensive) ideas and his determination not to be bullied by studio executives. Spiegel also hired a supporting cast of predominantly British actors, including Alec Guinness to play Feisal, and an Egyptian unknown, Omar Sharif. Nobody but Spiegel could have persuaded Columbia to finance this package, or to sit still through the interminable problems of filming on three continents, let alone to accept a film that was 227 minutes long, with a musical prelude and an intermission.

The result was a masterpiece. Nominated for ten Academy Awards, it won seven, including Best Picture and Best Director; it made (and continues to make) a fortune; and it appears constantly on lists drawn up by various bodies of the best movies of all time, and as number one on lists of the best epic pictures of all time. The director Steven Spielberg called it "a miracle," and so it is.

It is *not*, however, either the full story of Lawrence's life or a completely accurate account of the two years he spent fighting with the Arabs. Arnold Lawrence remarked, "I should not have recognized my own brother," when he saw the picture, and most people who had known Lawrence were horrified by it, even Lowell Thomas, which in his case was a bit like the pot calling the kettle black. Lawrence scholars feel even more strongly about it, and there exists a Web site on which each key scene of the film is compared with the reality of what happened. Still, even if this is a worthy endeavor, it misses the point. What Spiegel and Lean set out to do, after all, was to produce *entertainment*, as well as a film that would make money worldwide for Columbia—hence Spiegel's original choice of Brando for the role of Lawrence. As with George C. Scott's portrayal of

General George Patton, the object was to produce, not a faithful docudrama that would educate the audience, but a hit picture. O'Toole, like
Charles Laughton as Henry VIII or Helen Mirren as Queen Elizabeth II,
was an actor playing a role, not any more like the real Lawrence than
Shakespeare's Henry V necessarily resembles the historical soldier-king.
Lawrence of Arabia can be enjoyed for itself—criticizing it for its inac-
curacy is like arguing that *Gone with the Wind* does not provide the
depth of information and historical objectivity of Ken Burns's television
documentary on the Civil War: each has its merits, but the one is not a
substitute for the other.

Other portrayals of Lawrence on the stage or screen have not added
much. The respected British playwright Terence Rattigan wrote *Ross*, for
which John Mills was cast in the title role, but it tended to explore Lawrence's alleged homosexuality, to such a degree that Sam Spiegel
attempted to have it suppressed. (Knowing Spiegel, though, one could
guess that he was probably trying to appease Columbia Pictures and get
publicity for his own film, rather than expressing outrage.) A made-for-
television film about Lawrence at the Paris Peace Conference starred
Ralph Fiennes, but was a rather wooden docudrama about how the Arabs
were treated by the Allies—just the kind of issue Spiegel and Lean were
determined to avoid—though it has to be said that Fiennes at least *looked*
more like Lawrence than Peter O'Toole did.

Perhaps the one thing that Richard Aldington's book and David Lean's
film have in common is that they have raised the level of scholarship on
the subject of Lawrence, as Lawrence's admirers pored over his letters
and manuscripts in search of ways to refute Aldington's unflattering
portrait and Peter O'Toole's heroic portrayal. The release of British government documents in the 1960s and 1970s has, in the skillful and determined hands of Jeremy Wilson, the authorized biographer of Lawrence
and certainly the leading scholar of the subject, provided a much clearer
view of just how great Lawrence's accomplishments were in the war, and
how meticulous he was in describing all of it. The publication by Jeremy
Wilson of four expertly edited volumes of Lawrence's correspondence

with Bernard and Charlotte Shaw has also dramatically enriched our knowledge of what Lawrence was thinking and doing from 1922 to 1935, and also arouses, in any objective reader, considerable sympathy for him. Lawrence's account to Charlotte of what happened to him at Deraa, for example, makes it hard to accept the view that he invented the episode.

There are probably more people who know *of* Lawrence today than ever. At least two major biographies have appeared: one by Jeremy Wilson (1989), which is authoritative and formidably documented; and a psychological study by John E. Mack, MD* (1976), who was a professor at Harvard Medical School and a psychoanalyst. But people seldom know all that much *about* Lawrence, and many still see him, in their mind's eye, as Peter O'Toole, much the way people still think of Captain Bligh as Charles Laughton. Mack's book, whatever its merits, demonstrates the dangers of psychoanalyzing the dead, who after all cannot speak for themselves, and also the fact that Lawrence has, since his death, been taken over by numerous groups and turned into a gay hero, an anti-imperialist hero, or, even more improbably, a hero who betrayed the Arabs and encouraged increased Jewish immigration in Palestine. The fact is that Lawrence defies simplification and refuses to be pigeonholed, in death as he did in life. It is his complexity—his curious mixture of shyness and vainglory, of heroism on the grand scale and self-doubt about his own feats, of political sophistication and occasional naïveté—that makes him special. He was a hero, a scholar, a diplomat, a brilliant writer, endowed with enormous courage and capable of reckless self-sacrifice, and behind the facade that Lowell Thomas and the newspapers built up around him, also the kindest, gentlest, and most loyal of friends, and that rare Englishman with no class prejudices of any kind, as at ease in a barracks as he was in Buckingham Palace, in the desert, or at Versailles.

---

* Although Mack's book on Lawrence is in many respects fascinating—he was awarded the Pulitzer Prize for Biography for it in 1977—it suffered retroactively from his subsequent notoriety as a believer in and proselytizer for the personal stories of people who claimed to have been abducted by aliens and to have returned to tell the tale.

—

The difficulty with books about Lawrence is that most of them start with a definite thesis or fixed idea, or are aimed, whether consciously or unconsciously, either at correcting the wilder misstatements in Lowell Thomas's book (in the case of the earlier biographies like those of Graves and Liddell Hart), or at expunging the misleading portraits of Lawrence produced by David Lean and Aldington. The result is that while every fact, however minor, has now been examined, and psychoanalytical explanations have been provided for every facet of his character, the real Lawrence—and those qualities which made him a hero, a military genius, a gifted diplomat, the friend of so many people, and the author of one of the best and most ambitious great books ever written about war—has tended to disappear under the weighty accumulation of facts and the biographical disputes. Clearly, Lawrence had, throughout his life, an amazing capacity to inspire devotion, passionate friendship, fierce loyalty, and intense admiration, even from those who saw his faults as clearly as he himself did; and this is the Lawrence that needs to be re-created if we are to understand him and his remarkable hold on the imagination of people even three-quarters of a century after his death.

Then too, history has brought Lawrence back into the minds of those who are concerned with events in the Middle East. Not only did Lawrence introduce the Arabs to a new kind of warfare; his determination to "give them," as he saw it, an Arab state and his definition (and vision) of what that state should be are still at the center of every diplomatic dispute, war, insurrection, and political revolution throughout this vast area. Lawrence cannot be held responsible for the mess in the Middle East, any more than he was solely responsible for the Arab Revolt, which had already broken out before he arrived in Jidda, but everybody from Allenby down seems to agree that the revolt would never have succeeded to the extent it did without his vision and energy, and certainly he did his best throughout 1917–1918 and from 1919 to 1922 to give the Arabs the state they wanted. This, after all (despite lengthy Freudian explanations for his behavior), rather than his illegitimacy or the incident at Deraa, was the great moral crisis of his lifetime, which drove him to give up his name, his rank, and his decorations and join the RAF as a recruit under an assumed name.

Lawrence was at least partly responsible for the creation of present-day Iraq (with all its ethnic and religious contradictions) and Jordan, and he played a substantial role in the creation of Palestine as a separate entity. The British and French division of the immense Turkish empire that extended north and south from Syria to Yemen and east and west from the Mediterranean to the Persian Gulf—an area from which Lawrence had played a major, and admittedly flamboyant, role in driving out the Turks—was the primary guilt that Lawrence bore, and that explains much of his life from 1922 to his death in 1935.

He was partly instrumental in the creation of not one but *three* Middle Eastern kingdoms. Only one of these, Jordan, survives today in its original form; but much of the map of the Middle East was drawn by Lawrence, quite literally, as we have seen; and if he could not give the Arabs what they most wanted—a "greater Syria"—he at any rate helped to give them the states that now exist there, and, for better or worse, the dream of a larger, united Arab nation, which for a brief time led to the union of Egypt and Syria as the United Arab Republic, and which is still the motivating force behind much of the unrest and violence of Arab nationalism. Lawrence himself foresaw only too clearly what the price would be if the Allies failed to give the Arabs what they wanted—and had been promised—and the long-term consequences of letting the French take Lebanon and Syria as mandates—in effect, colonies—and letting the British take Palestine, Jordan, and Iraq. He did his best to persuade a reluctant Feisal to accept the Balfour Declaration, which promised the Jews a homeland in Palestine, but he understood that this acceptance was dependent on the Arabs' getting a meaningful state, and was unlikely to be achieved in the long run if the Middle East was carved up into small and mutually hostile units, under French or British colonial administration.

As it turned out, the brutal carving up of the Turkish empire was complicated by the fact that the great oil reserves were in the most backward areas, on the eastern fringe of the Middle East. These would have the effect of transforming remote desert "kingdoms" and "principalities" into oil-rich powers, while leaving the more highly developed, better educated, and more populous parts of the area—Egypt, Syria, Jordan, and Lebanon—impoverished. British and French policy (as strongly as each differed from the other) ensured that there would be no unitary Arab state as a major power in which oil revenues might be used to improve the lives of ordinary Arabs, and thwarted just those ambitions which Lawrence had been at such pains to arouse, and which led Lowell Thomas, with his usual touch of hyperbole, to describe Lawrence as "the George Washington of a United States of Arabia." Alas, after the Peace Conference, and the creation of Jordan and Iraq, Lawrence—knowing that he had done his best for the Arabs and that it was not good enough, and broken by shame and guilt at his own failure—resigned from public life and signed up as an airman, and the United States of Arabia was never born, with consequences that we are still facing today.

There is, therefore, every reason to examine objectively and clearly what Lawrence attempted to do, and to treat him not as an interesting neurotic with profound oedipal problems (though this may be true), but as both a visionary and a warrior; as a man who not only wrote an epic but lived one; and as a politician and diplomat, indeed a maker of nations, whose failure to get the Arabs what they had been promised had profound consequences for the world today, consequences that have not been played out yet, and whose outcome nobody can predict.

Few people have risen so high so quickly, or have voluntarily given up not only honors but power, and done so without regret or bitterness. Fewer still have been so famous and tried so hard to live obscurely. Lawrence found in the end peace of a kind in friendships, in literature, and in an unexpected gift for marine craftsmanship and engineering which has seldom been fully acknowledged, but to which many airmen in World War II would owe their lives.

However many books there have been about Lawrence, his is still a story worth telling, a life that needs to be described without prejudice and without a fixed agenda: a military "triumph," as he himself called it with a combination of pride, bitterness, and irony; an extraordinary and heroic epic; and a political failure whose importance we can only begin to reckon today as we pick among the ruins of Lawrence's hopes for the Middle East in search of a way forward.

Not surprisingly, Lawrence himself described his own genius best.

All men dream: but not equally.
Those who dream by night in the dusty recesses of their
Minds wake in the day to find that it was
vanity; but the dreamers of the day are
dangerous men, for they may act their dream
with open eyes, to make it possible. This I did.

Acknowledgments

My heartfelt thanks to my dear friends Marianna and Jay Watnick for their affectionate support.

I owe special gratitude to my friend and colleague from her days at Simon and Schuster, Phyllis Grann, whose suggestion it was that I should write about Lawrence in the first place, as well as for her editing of the manuscript; and to Lynn Nesbit for making all this possible. I also owe very special thanks to Hugh Van Dusen at HarperCollins, and to his assistant, Robert Crawford, for their unfailing help and enthusiasm; to Lucy Albanese of HarperCollins for her skill, taste, and patience; and to Diane Aronson for her very special and painstaking care.

I owe a special debt of gratitude to the incomparable Mike Hill, for his research, support, and friendship; to Kevin Kwan, *chocolatier par excellence*, for his brilliant picture research—and to Amy Hill, for once again taking on the task of designing one of my books. I am also deeply indebted to my assistant Dawn Lafferty, whose help has been unstinting, and whose calm in the middle of chaos has been a precious and invaluable gift to me, and to Victoria Wilson for reading the manuscript, and for her excellent and thought-provoking suggestions.

Close to home, I am profoundly grateful to John Ansley, Head of the Archives and Special Collections and of the Lowell Thomas Collection and Archives; and to Angelo Galeazzi, Project Archivist at Marist College, Poughkeepsie, New York, for giving me such valuable access to their films, photographs, and manuscripts, which contain a treasure trove of material about Lawrence, and for going to such trouble on my behalf.

I would also like to thank the following: Hugh Alexander, Deputy Manager, The Image Library, The National Archives, Kew, Richmond, U.K.; Katherine Godfrey, Archivist at the Liddell Hart Centre for Military History, King's College, London, U.K.; Colin Harris, Superintendent, Department of Special Collections, Bodleian Library, Oxford, U.K.; Penny Hatfield, Eton College, Windsor, Berkshire, U.K.; Jane Hogan, Assistant Keeper, Archives and Special Collections, Durham University Library, Durham, U.K.; Allen Packwood, Director, Churchill Archives Centre, Cambridge, U.K.; Lora Parker, Royal Agricultural College Library, Cirencester, Gloucestershire, U.K.; Peter Preen, Visitor Services Manager, Clouds Hill, Wareham, Dorset, U.K.; John and Rosalind Randle, Whittington Press; Gayle M. Richardson, Manuscripts Department, Huntington Library, San Marino, California; Daun van Eee at the Library of Congress, Washington, D.C.; Christine Warner, Oak Knoll Press; and John Wells, Department of Manuscripts and University Archives, Cambridge University Library, Cambridge, U.K.

My thanks to Will Bueche for so kindly making available to me many of the late Professor John E. Mack's notes and papers; and to Barry Singer of Chartwell Books, New York, the most eminent of "Eminent Churchillians," for so diligently seeking out books by and about T. E. Lawrence from all over the world.

To my dear friend Gypsy da Silva my thanks for being willing to answer questions at any hour of the day or night, and for always knowing the right answer.

And to "I Putti," my five schoolmates from Le Rosey, for their long-distance support and enthusiasm: Jean-Jacques Boissier; Max Cauvin, whose courage and good humor in adversity are an example to us all; Christian Delsol; Gabriel Villada; and Peter Wodtke, *chic types et chers amis*.

Finally, and above all, to my beloved wife, Margaret, for putting up with yet another time-consuming project and for the accompanying tidal wave of books, papers, and files overflowing through the house.

Notes

CHAPTER ONE "Who Is This Extraordinary Pip-Squeak?"

5 *"a most excellent dinner"*: Lawrence, *Letters*, Garnett (ed.), 206.

6 *"an odd gnome"*: Wilson, *Lawrence of Arabia*, 174.

6 *"Who is this extraordinary pip-squeak?"*: Aldington, *Lawrence of Arabia*, 127.

8 *"Into friendship with T. E. Lawrence"*: Storrs, *Orientations*, 218.

8 *"The first of us was Ronald Storrs"*: Lawrence, *Seven Pillars*, 37. Hereafter abbreviated SP.

9 *"revolver practice on deck"*: Storrs, *Orientations*, 200.

9 *"quite intolerable to the Staff"*: Lawrence, SP, 43.

9 *"But when at last we anchored"*: Ibid., 47.

10 *"Till now we have defended"*: Brown and Cave, *Touch of Genius*, 55.

11 *"Lawrence wants kicking and kicking hard"*: Wilson, *Lawrence of Arabia*, 331.

11 *"a holiday and a joy-ride"*: Lawrence, SP, 43.

12 *"like water, or permeating oil"*: Ibid., 37.

13 *"incoherent and spasmodic"*: Storrs, *Orientations*, 218.

13 *"None of us realized"*: Ibid.

14 *"a yellow silk kuffiya"*: Ibid., 201.

15 *"When Abdallah quoted"*: Ibid., 221.

15 *"was short, strong"*: Lawrence, SP, 48, 49.

17 *"Meeting today: Wilson"*: Storrs, *Orientations*, 221.

18 *"took a great fancy"*: Lawrence, SP, 59.

18 *"force of character"*: Ibid.

18 *"prophet"*: Ibid., 60.

18 *"staggered"*: Ibid., 59.

18 *"waving grateful hands"*: Storrs, *Orientations*, 221.

22 *Zeid, still a "beardless" young man*: Lawrence, SP, 60.

25 *"shelters of branches and palm leaves"*: Ibid., 64.

26 *"two inches thick"*: Ibid., 68.

28 *"dinner to the examiners to celebrate it"*: Wilson, *Lawrence of Arabia*, 67.

28 *"astonishingly wide"*: Liddell Hart, *Lawrence of Arabia*, 75.

28 *"schoolboy stuff"*: Ibid., 128.

30 *"a garrulous old man"*: Lawrence, SP, 70.

30 *"had been beaten out of Kheif"*: Ibid.

32 *"standing framed between the posts"*: Ibid., 75.

32 *"almost regal in appearance"*: Wilson, *Lawrence of Arabia*, 312.

33 *"I felt at the glance"*: Lawrence, SP, 75–76.

33 *"which were twisting slowly"*: Ibid., 76.

33 *"And do you like our place"*: Ibid.

33 *"like a sword into their midst"*: Ibid.

36 *"a desperate measure"*: Ibid., 77.

37 *"if their villages were spared"*: Ibid., 78.

38 *"They hunger . . . for desolate lands"*: Ibid.

39 *"view with favour the establishment"*: Knightley and Simpson, *Secret Lives of Lawrence of Arabia*, 117.

42 *"huge crags"*: Lawrence, SP, 95.

42 *"glassy sand mixed"*: Ibid., 96.

43 *"a salt wind"*: Ibid.

43 *"picturesque, rambling house"*: Ibid., 97.

43 *"travel-stained"*: Ibid.

45 *"cool and comfortable"*: Ibid., 99.

45 *spent his time reading Malory's* Morte d'Arthur: Ibid.

48 *hope "to biff the French:"* Knightley and Simpson, *Secret Lives of Lawrence of Arabia*, 81.

49 *"was much against my grain"*: Lawrence, SP, 103.

CHAPTER TWO Aqaba, 1917: The Making of a Hero

51 *"sacrament"*: Lawrence, SP, 104.

53 *"that invariable magnet of Arab good will"*: Ibid., 112.

54 *"to slip in and out"*: Ibid., 114.

55 *"Part of our booty"*: *Journal of the T. E. Lawrence Society*, Vols. 10–12, 9 (2000).

56 "Twenty-Seven Articles": Wilson, Lawrence of Arabia, 670.

56 "a magnificent bay camel": Lawrence, SP, 117.

56 "as a mass they are not formidable": Lawrence, Letters, Garnett (ed.), 217.

57 "Guerrilla warfare is what the regular armies": Callwell, Small Wars, 105.

57 "old rubbish": Lawrence, SP, 118.

58 "quiet, but in no other way mortified": Ibid., 117.

58 "While all goes well": Callwell, Small Wars, 66.

59 "and stamp out Feisal's army": Lawrence, SP, 121.

60 "the military art was one": Liddell Hart, Lawrence of Arabia, 370.

62 "It looked like a river of camels": Wilson, Lawrence of Arabia, 349.

66 "Our men were not materials": Mack, A Prince of Our Disorder, 211.

68 "a tall, strong figure": Lawrence, SP, 229.

72 "feeling that this need not": Ibid., 184.

72 "and gave him a few moments' delay": Ibid., 185.

73 "with the reckless equality": Ibid., 188.

74 "suffering a bodily weakness": Ibid., 191.

74 "woke out of a hot sleep": Ibid., 192.

78 "The cold was intense": Ibid., 212.

80 "I was about to take my leave": Ibid., 229.

82 "venture . . . in the true Elizabethan tradition": Liddell Hart, Lawrence of Arabia, 143.

82 "to capture a trench": Ibid.

83 "The weight is bearing me down now": Wilson, Lawrence of Arabia, 406.

86 "surly . . . stranger from Maan": Liddell Hart, Lawrence of Arabia, 146.

90 "Clayton, I've decided to go off alone": Wilson, Lawrence of Arabia, 410.

90 "Hideously green, unbearable": Ibid.

91 "he was very old, livid": Ibid., 413.

92 "quarrelling": Liddell Hart, Lawrence of Arabia, 154.

95 "A man who gives himself": Lawrence, SP, 11

98 "Our hot bread": Ibid., 323.

99 "By God indeed": Ibid., 325.

100 "Work, work, where are words?": Ibid., 328.

100 "when it became clear": Ibid., 330.

101 "The dead men": Ibid., 331.

109 He walked past the sleeping sentry: Ibid., 347.

110 "Allenby was physically large": Ibid., 348.

110 "He [Lawrence] thinks himself": Aldington, Lawrence of Arabia, 34.

110 "offering to hobble the enemy": Lawrence, SP, 348.

112 "a bumptious young ass": Wilson, Lawrence of Arabia, 331.

112 *Wingate praised Lawrence:* Ibid., 424.
113 *"Tell Mother":* Lawrence, *Home Letters,* 340.

CHAPTER THREE "The Family Romance"

115 *"To my sons":* Item MS English C6741, Special Collections and Western Manuscripts, Thomas E. Lawrence Papers, Bodleian Library, Oxford University; Orlans, Harold, "Ways of Transgressors," *Journal of the T. E. Lawrence Society,* Vol. 6, 120–33.
120 *Thomas Robert Tighe Chapman:* See Mack, *A Prince of Our Disorder,* 5–8; and Wilson, *Lawrence of Arabia,* 30–31, 941–944.
121 *"the Vinegar Queen":* Mack, *A Prince of Our Disorder,* 4.
122 *Sarah Lawrence:* Ibid., 8–11; and Wilson, *Lawrence of Arabia,* 31–32, 942–943.
123 *Sometime in 1885:* Wilson, *Lawrence of Arabia,* 943.
123 *"so gay and pretty":* Journal of T. E. Lawrence Society, Vols. 10–12, 29.
123 *"was the sort of woman":* Asher, *Lawrence,* 7.
124 *"T. E. got his firm chin":* Mack, *A Prince of Our Disorder,* 33.
124 *"No trust ever existed":* Ibid., 32.
128 *"a real love match":* Ibid., 13.
129 *"overpowering and terrifying":* Ibid., 8.
135 *As in most English families:* Ibid., 19.
135 *"quiet authority":* Ibid., 13.
138 *"he knew no fear":* Wilson, *Lawrence of Arabia,* 25.
138 *Lawrence claimed to have overheard:* Mack, *A Prince of Our Disorder,* 27.
139 *"a playground scuffle":* Wilson, *Lawrence of Arabia,* 27.
141 *"was placed in the First Class":* Ibid.
141 *Oxford was a good place:* Ibid., 28.
144 *His father—whose closest friend:* Ibid., 30.
147 *"a house telephone":* Aldington, *Lawrence of Arabia,* 44.
152 *"When . . . I suddenly went to Oxford":* Wilson, *Lawrence of Arabia,* 41.

CHAPTER FOUR Oxford, 1907–1910

155 *"as if he descended":* Mack, *A Prince of Our Disorder,* 62.
157 *"Quite frankly, for me":* Knightley and Simpson, *Secret Lives of Lawrence of Arabia,* 29.
158 *At the time he met Richards:* Mack, *A Prince of Our Disorder,* 60.
159 *His youngest brother, Arnold:* Ibid., 67.

159 *"I'm not a boy"*: Ibid., 20.

159 *"We could never be bothered"*: Aldington, *Lawrence of Arabia*, 36.

160 *"He is illuminated from inside"*: Mack, *A Prince of Our Disorder*, 14.

160 *She saw him as a beloved:* Ibid., 64.

161 *"worshipped Janet from afar"*: Ibid., 66.

162 *His mother vigorously denied:* Aldington, *Lawrence of Arabia*, 46.

162 *One friend told of Lawrence's:* Wilson, *Lawrence of Arabia*, 44.

162 *Lawrence's nearly drowning:* Aldington, *Lawrence of Arabia*, 48.

162 *A famous feat of Lawrence's:* Ibid., 49.

163 *It was also clear to Lawrence:* Wilson, *Lawrence of Arabia*, 44.

166 *In Doughty's opinion:* Ibid., 54.

167 *"a lightweight suit"*: Mack, *A Prince of Our Disorder*, 69.

167 *"a revolver"*: Aldington, *Lawrence of Arabia*, 62.

171 *"From Dan we passed"*: Lawrence, *Home Letters*, 97.

172 *"quite cool"*: Ibid., 89.

172 *"Nothing in life is more exhilarating"*: Churchill, *Story of the Malakind Field Force*, 172.

173 *"a person with nothing"*: Lawrence, *Home Letters*, 107.

174 "Sir John does not like": Ibid., 109.

174 *"village elders"*: Mack, *A Prince of Our Disorder*, 74.

174 *The robbery has caused:* Aldington, *Lawrence of Arabia*, 76.

175 *he apologized for the bloodstain:* Mack, *A Prince of Our Disorder*, 74.

176 *"a cry (if not from the housetops)"*: Campbell, *The Hero with a Thousand Faces*, 14.

176 *"thinned to the bone"*: Mack, *A Prince of Our Disorder*, 75.

177 *"in no way diminished"*: Ibid.

177 *Lawrence did not seem:* Aldington, *Lawrence of Arabia*, 68.

177 *"took a most brilliant First Class"*: Wilson, *Lawrence of Arabia*, 68.

177 *busy reading* Petit Jehan: Lawrence, *Home Letters*, 10.

178 *"a research fellowship"*: Wilson, *Lawrence*, 69.

178 *"The two occupations fit into one another"*: Ibid.

178 *"The dangerous crises"*: Campbell, *The Hero with a Thousand Faces*, 8.

CHAPTER FIVE Carchemish: 1911–1914

181 *"a man of action"*: Knightley and Simpson, *Secret Lives of Lawrence of Arabia*, 20.

181 *It comes as no surprise:* Mack, *A Prince of Our Disorder*, 102.

182 *When Lawrence went up to Jesus College:* Knightley and Simpson, *Secret Lives of Lawrence of Arabia*, 21.

182 *"a cynical and highly-educated baboon"*: Ibid., 20.

182 *"a boy of extraordinary"*: Ibid., 30.

183 *"the only man I had never"*: Mack, *A Prince of Our Disorder*, 369.

184 *"a dreary and desolate waste"*: Wilson, *Lawrence of Arabia*, 71.

186 *Lawrence sailed for Beirut*: Ibid., 76.

187 *"They were always talking"*: Lawrence, *Home Letters*, 122.

187 *"the spiritual side of his character"*: Mack, *A Prince of Our Disorder*, 77–78.

188 *"Lawrence seems to me"*: Ibid., 78.

189 *"sit down to it"*: Lawrence, *Home Letters*, 130.

189 *"archeological overseer"*: Wilson, *Lawrence of Arabia*, 78.

190 *"was flagrantly and evidently an exotic"*: Lawrence, *Home Letters*, 137.

190 *"Turkish & Greek"*: Ibid.

190 *"the Lejah, the lava no-man's-land"*: Ibid.

193 *"admitted to six or seven murders"*: Aldington, *Lawrence of Arabia*, 81.

193 *"set her before him"*: Lawrence, *Home Letters*, 154.

194 *Bell was disappointed*: Wallach, *Desert Queen*, 93.

195 *"stained [purple] with Tyrian die"*: Aldington, *Lawrence of Arabia*, 51.

195 *"Can you make room"*: Wilson, *Lawrence of Arabia*, 85.

196 *"beautifully built and remarkably handsome"*: Mack, *A Prince of Our Disorder*, 97.

197 *"an interesting character"*: Lawrence, *Home Letters*, 173.

198 *"I am very well"*: Ibid., 176.

198 *"efforts to educate himself"*: Wilson, *Lawrence of Arabia*, 95.

199 *Apparently impressed by Hogarth's letters*: Ibid., 92.

200 *"I am not enthusiastic about Flecker"*: Sherwood, *No Golden Journey*, 47.

202 *"Great rumors of war"*: Lawrence, *Home Letters*, 182.

203 *Lawrence turned up for digging*: Aldington, *Lawrence of Arabia*, 84–85.

203 *"was not an Oxonian"*: Ibid., 85.

205 *"such as Bedouin sheiks wear"*: Ibid., 192.

205 *He seems to have been reading*: Mack, *A Prince of Our Disorder*, 101.

208 *"essential immaturity"*: Ibid., 85.

208 *"frail, pallid, silent"*: Ibid., 81.

209 *"when the police tried"*: Lawrence, *Letters from T. E. Lawrence to E. T. Leeds*, 43.

209 *"explicit promise"*: Wilson, *Lawrence of Arabia*, 103.

210 *Lawrence was using Dahoum*: Ibid., 104.

211 *Those who were closest to Lawrence and Dahoum*: Arnold Lawrence (ed.), *T. E. Lawrence by His Friends*, 89.

214 *Lawrence notes in a letter home*: Lawrence, *Home Letters*, 210.

215 *"for the foreigner [this country]"*: Ibid., 218.

216 *He wrote to England for medical advice*: Wilson, *Lawrence of Arabia*, 107.

216 *"a big garden"*: Sherwood, *No Golden Journey*, 153.

216 *"carelessly flung beneath a tree"*: Ibid., 146.

217 *"I feel very little the lack"*: Lawrence, *Home Letters*, 230.

217 *He wrote to his youngest brother, Arnold:* Ibid., 226.

219 *"Flecker, the admiral at Malta"*: Mack, *A Prince of Our Disorder*, 85.

219 *"gun-running" incident:* Wilson, *Lawrence of Arabia*, 118.

220 *Although skeptics about Lawrence:* Graves, *Lawrence and the Arabs*, 36.

221 *"Buswari and his great enemy"*: Lawrence, *Home Letters*, 254.

222 *"running around with guns"*: Wilson, *Lawrence of Arabia*, 946.

224 *"a place where one eats lotos"*: Lawrence, *Home Letters*, 161.

225 *"couldn't shoot the railway bridge"*: Ibid., 255.

225 *"a pleasant, healthy warmth"*: Ibid.

226 *Already there had been protests:* Wilson, *Lawrence of Arabia*, 123–124.

227 *"a pocket Hercules"*: Lawrence to Edward Marsh, June 10, 1927. Lawrence, *Letters*, Garnett (ed.), 521.

228 *By the end of August:* Wilson, *Lawrence of Arabia*, 126.

228 *"the most beautiful town"*: Lawrence, *Home Letters*, 441.

230 *"You must not think of Ned"*: Ibid., 447.

230 *"was still in Ireland"*: Ibid., 256.

231 *"olive tree boles"*: Ibid., 274.

232 *"I cannot print with you"*: Wilson, *Lawrence of Arabia*, 132.

232 *"from west to east"*: Ibid., 137.

234 *"approach Kenyon"*: Ibid.

234 *"Hogarth concurs in the idea"*: Ibid., 138.

235 *"a picturesque little crusading town"*: Lawrence, *Home Letters*, 281.

238 *Newcombe was not dismayed:* Wilson, *Lawrence of Arabia*, 141.

238 *"back to Mount Hor"*: Lawrence, *Home Letters*, 286.

240 *On March 21, Woolley and Lawrence:* Wilson, *Lawrence of Arabia*, 143–145.

240 *A Circassian working for the Germans:* Ibid., 144.

241 *"the only piece of spying"*: Ibid., 147.

241 *More interesting still was the amount of information:* Ibid.

CHAPTER SIX Cairo: 1914–1916

248 *"In Constantinople the seizure"*: Randolph Churchill and Gilbert, *Winston Churchill, 1914–1916*, Vol. 3, 192.

248 *"As the shadows of the night"*: Churchill, *The World Crisis*, Vol. 1, 227.

250 COMMENCE HOSTILITIES: Geoffrey Miller, "Turkey Enters the War and

British Actions." December 1999, http://www.gwpda.org/naval/turk mill.htm.

251 *"He's running my entire department"*: Graves, *Lawrence and the Arabs*, 63.

251 *"I want to talk to an officer"*: Aldington, *Lawrence of Arabia*, 124.

252 *"as an officer ideally suited"*: Ibid., 126.

253 *"Clayton stability"*: Storrs, *Orientations*, 179.

254 *"a youngster, 2nd Lt. Lawrence"*: Wilson, *Lawrence of Arabia*, 154.

254 *"Keep your eye on Afghanistan"*: Lawrence, *Home Letters*, 300.

255 *"in the office from morning"*: Ibid., 301.

257 *"bottle-washer and office boy"*: Wilson, *Lawrence of Arabia*, 167.

257 *He was well aware of events:* Ibid., 169.

258 *"pieced together"*: Mack, *A Prince of Our Disorder*, 131.

259 *Abdulla's concern was that the Turkish government:* Wilson, *Lawrence of Arabia*, 164–165.

259 *One son, Emir Feisal:* Antonius, *The Arab Awakening*, 72.

260 *"It may be"*: Wilson, *Lawrence*, 165.

264 *"The assault I regret to say"*: Lawrence, *Home Letters*, 721.

264 *"You will never understand"*: Ibid., 304.

265 *"If I do die"*: Ibid., 718.

267 *"To the excellent and well-born"*: Antonius, *The Arab Awakening*, 167.

271 *"a twenty-minute Parliamentary debate"*: Storrs, *Orientations*, 229.

272 *"a devout Roman Catholic"*: Wilson, *Lawrence of Arabia*, 193.

273 *"There is nothing so bad or so good"*: Shaw, *Man of Destiny*, 87.

274 *"every aspect of the Arab question"*: Wilson, *Lawrence*, 235.

274 *"bravura"*: Ibid., 235.

275 *Picot was a master of detail:* Fromkin, *A Peace to End All Peace*, 190.

279 *It was hoped that a French zone:* Ibid., 192.

280 *"the imaginative advocate"*: Lawrence, SP, 38.

281 *"I've decided to go off alone"*: Wilson, *Lawrence of Arabia*, 410.

282 *"I have not written to you for ever"*: Lawrence, *Letters from T. E. Lawrence to E. T. Leeds*, 110.

283 *"I'm fed up, and fed up"*: Ibid., 109.

283 *The* Arab Bulletin *was a secret news sheet:* Wilson, *Lawrence of Arabia*, 242.

283 *The only one of them:* Lawrence, *Letters from T. E. Lawrence to E. T. Leeds*, 109.

283 *"to put the Grand Duke Nicholas in touch with"*: Wilson, *Lawrence of Arabia*, 242.

285 *The British Force in Egypt and the British Mediterranean Expeditionary Force:* Ibid., 252.

286 *"to biff the French out of Syria"*: Knightley and Simpson, *Secret Lives of Lawrence of Arabia*, 81.

288 *"go free on parole"*: Aldington, *Lawrence of Arabia*, 149.
289 *Lawrence arrived to undergo a difficult interview:* Wilson, *Lawrence of Arabia*, 268–269.
289 *Although Khalil was "extremely nice"*: Ibid., 272.
290 *"about 32 or 33, very keen & energetic"*: Lawrence, *Home Letters*, 326.
291 *"a German field mission led by Baron Othmar von Stotzingen"*: Antonius, *The Arab Awakening*, 191.
292 *"pronging playfully at strangers"*: Storrs, *Orientations*, 188.
293 *"Long before we met"*: Ibid., 221.

CHAPTER SEVEN 1917: "The Uncrowned King of Arabia"

297 *if Clayton "thought"*: Wilson, *Lawrence of Arabia*, 419.
297 *"he wanted Jerusalem as a Christmas present"*: Wavell, *Palestine Campaigns*, 96.
299 *"an obstinate, narrow-minded"*: Lawrence, SP, 351.
299 *"gracious and venerable patriarch"*: Storrs, *Orientations*, 213.
300 *"as usual without obvious coherence"*: Lawrence, SP, 352.
300 *"half-naked"*: Wilson, *Lawrence of Arabia*, 1079.
300 *"in the third little turning to the left"*: Ibid., 432.
302 *"no spirit of treachery abroad"*: Lawrence, SP, 353–355.
302 *"Many men of sense and ability"*: Arnold Lawrence (ed.), *T. E. Lawrence by His Friends*, 115.
302 *"idle to pretend"*: Ibid., 117.
305 *"You very good man"*: Wilson, *Lawrence of Arabia*, 441.
309 *"a ladder of tribes"*: Lawrence, SP, 367.
309 *"tip and run" tactics:* Ibid., 368.
311 *It is a tribute to Lawrence's skill:* Ibid., 367–383.
312 *"in a chilled voice"*: Ibid., 387.
312 *"a squadron of airplanes"*: Ibid., 388.
313 *"his best man present"*: Ibid., 392.
313 *"strange flat of yellow mud"*: Ibid., 398.
317 *"Out of the darkness"*: Ibid., 407.
317 *"a shambles of the group"*: Ibid., 408.
320 *"I hope when this nightmare ends"*: Lawrence, *Letters from T. E. Lawrence to E. T. Leeds*, 106.
321 *"He who gives himself to the possession"*: Lawrence, SP, 11.
325 *"African knobkerri"*: Ibid., 429.
325 *"on a series of identical steel bridges"*: Ibid., 432.
326 *"unfit for active service"*: Ibid., 433.

329 *"could outstrip a trotting camel"*: Ibid.

330 *"luscious"*: Ibid., 447.

331 *"They had lost two men"*: Wilson, *Lawrence of Arabia*, 450–455.

331 *"war, tribes and camels without end"*: Lawrence, SP, 450.

331 *"like the mutter of a distant"*: Ibid., 450.

332 *"Beware of Abd el Kader"*: Ibid.

333 *"held what might well be the world's record"*: Ibid., 453.

333 *"some 40,000 troops of all arms"*: Wavell, *Palestine Campaigns*, 117.

333 *"dismounted and cleaned up"*: Ibid., 123.

334 *"General Allenby's plan"*: Ibid.

334 *"nothing would persuade"*: Lawrence, SP, 462.

334 *"steeped in an unfathomable pool"*: Ibid., 464.

335 *"I only hope TEL"*: Wilson, *Lawrence of Arabia*, 455, citing D. G. Hogarth to his wife, November 11, 1917, Hogarth Papers, St. Antony's College, Oxford.

336 *The fumes from the explosive*: Lawrence, SP, 471.

338 *"pointing and staring"*: Ibid., 478.

339 *"ran like a rabbit"*: Ibid., 481.

339 *"in front of [him]"*: Ibid., 483.

340 *"gashing his tongue deeply"*: Ibid., 485.

340 *he searched for consolation*: Knightley and Simpson, *Secret Lives of Lawrence of Arabia*, 263.

341 *"an outlaw with a price"*: Lawrence, SP, 493.

341 *"a trimmed beard"*: Ibid.

342 *"a lame and draggled pair"*: Ibid., 495.

343 *"The garrison commander at Deraa"*: Knightley and Simpson, *Secret Lives of Lawrence of Arabia*, 217.

344 *"They kicked me to the landing"*: Lawrence, SP, 498–502.

349 *"About that night"*: Wilson, *Lawrence of Arabia*, 739; T. E. Lawrence to Charlotte Shaw, March 26, 1924, British Library, London, Add. MS 45903.

351 *"he seemed like a wraith"*: Liddell Hart, *Lawrence of Arabia*, 293.

352 *"the most memorable event of the war"*: Lawrence, SP, 508.

352 *"all institutions holy to Christians"*: Adelson, *Mark Sykes*, 245.

353 *"had stuck another medal"*: Lawrence, *Home Letters*, 345.

354 *"seated at the same table"*: Thomas, *With Lawrence in Arabia*, 3–6.

CHAPTER EIGHT 1918: Triumph and Tragedy

355 *"Two names had come to dominate"*: Storrs, *Orientations*, 318.
356 *"When he was in the middle of the stage"*: Arnold Lawrence (ed.),
    T. E. Lawrence by His Friends, 245.
358 *"twenty thousand pounds alive"*: Lawrence, SP, 520.
358 *"hard riders"*: Ibid., 526.
358 *"The British at Aqaba"*: Liddell Hart, *Lawrence of Arabia*, 207–208.
358 *He also used his bodyguard as shock troops*: Ibid., 209.
359 *"almost level with the south end"*: Ibid., 210.
360 *"simultaneously from the east"*: Lawrence, SP, 513.
360 *"an amnesty for the Arab Revolt"*: Wilson, *Lawrence of Arabia*, 469.
361 *"Jam Catholics on the Holy Places"*: Ibid., 467, from Sir T. B. M. Sykes to
    Sir F. R. Wingate, for G. F. Clayton, telegram 75, 16.1.1918. FO
    371/3383 fo. 14.
361 *Lawrence spent the early days of January*: Ibid., 475.
362 *"neither my impulses nor my convictions"*: Lawrence, SP, 529.
362 *"let our man go free"*: Ibid.
363 *"I had not expected anything"*: Ibid., 530.
364 *The Turkish garrison*: Liddell Hart, *Lawrence of Arabia*, 214.
365 *"The defences of Tafila"*: Ibid.
365 *"three . . . battalions of infantry"*: Ibid., 215.
366 *"To make war upon rebellion"*: Ibid., 135.
366 *"There is nothing I desire"*: Ibid., 133.
368 *"rushed to save their goods"*: Lawrence, SP, 538.
368 *"I would rake up all the old maxims"*: Ibid., 539.
370 *Not many officers*: Liddell Hart, *Lawrence of Arabia*, 217.
370 *"the climb would warm me"*: Army Quarterly, Vol. II, no. 1, April 1929, 26.
371 *"The bullets slapped off it deafeningly"*: Ibid., 28.
372 *"a Damascene, a sardonic fellow"*: Lawrence, SP, 149.
373 *"in the purest classical tradition"*: Liddell Hart, *Lawrence of Arabia*,
    382, 384.
373 *"In the end"*: Army Quarterly, Vol. II, no. 1, April 1929, 30.
373 *Arab losses were about twenty-five killed*: Wilson, *Lawrence of Arabia*,
    476.
374 *As was so often the case with Lawrence*: Liddell Hart, *Lawrence of Arabia*,
    220.
374 *"brilliant mind"*: Lawrence, SP, 579.
375 *"the complete ruin of my plans"*: Ibid., 568.
376 *"will was gone"*: Ibid., 572.
376 *"that pretence to lead the national uprising"*: Ibid., 571.

376 *"made a mess of things"*: Ibid.

377 *"a very sick man"*: Liddell Hart, *Lawrence of Arabia*, 233.

377 *"a cog himself"*: Ibid.

377 *"solitary in the ranks"*: Title of a book by H. Montgomery Hyde, *Solitary in the Ranks: Lawrence of Arabia as Airman and Private Soldier* (London: Constable, 1977).

378 *"letting [him] off"*: Lawrence, SP, 752.

379 *"to knock Turkey out of the war"*: Liddell Hart, *Lawrence of Arabia*, 224.

379 *In the end all he would get:* Ibid.

379 *"to take up again my mantle"*: Lawrence, SP, 572.

379 *"where the Arabs would easily defeat [them]"*: Liddell Hart, *Lawrence of Arabia*, 227.

380 *"between pincers"*: Ibid.

380 *"that skirt-wearers"*: Lawrence, SP, 574.

381 *"reeling backwards on Amiens"*: Wavell, *Palestine Campaigns*, 183.

382 Lawrence's *"understudy"*: Wilson, *Lawrence of Arabia*, 491.

382 *"Lawrence really counted more"*: Young, *The Independent Arab*, 143, quoted in Wilson, *Lawrence*, 491.

384 *"the Grand Cross of the Order"*: Thomas, *With Lawrence in Arabia*, 391.

384 *"[sailed] fifteen hundred miles"*: Ibid., 111.

384 *"Hindus, Somalis, Berberines"*: Ibid., 118.

384 *"was kicked overboard"*: Ibid., 120.

384 *"Lawrence himself came down"*: Ibid., 121.

385 *"To accompany Lawrence and his body-guard"*: Ibid., 183.

386 *"was never in the Arab firing line"*: Wilson, *Lawrence of Arabia*, 494, from T. E. Lawrence to E. M. Forster, June 17, 1925, King's College, Cambridge.

386 *"My cameraman, Mr. Chase"*: Thomas, *With Lawrence in Arabia*, 369.

387 *"the rose-red city"*: Mona Mackay, quoted ibid., 218.

388 *"openness and honesty in their love"*: Lawrence, SP, 581.

390 *"these bonds between man and man"*: Ibid., 582.

390 *"privately . . . implored Jaafar"*: Ibid., 584.

390 *"Turk was man enough not to shoot me"*: Ibid., 590.

391 *"Mitfleh with honeyed words"*: Ibid., 591.

393 *"For this reason"*: Ibid., 598.

394 *"a grown man"*: Knightley and Simpson, *Secret Lives of Lawrence of Arabia*, 163.

394 *"in sight of Maan"*: Liddell Hart, *Lawrence of Arabia*, 232.

394 *"Greetings, Lurens"*: Ibid., 234.

395 *"like the hypnotic influence"*: Ibid.

396 *"Only once or twice"*: Lawrence, SP, 630.

397 *"To some degree* Seven Pillars of Wisdom": Holroyd, *Bernard Shaw, 1918–1950: The Lure of Fantasy*, Vol. III, 86.

397 *"an uncommon face":* Saint Joan (New York: Random House, 1952), 62.

398 *Lawrence seems to have been involved:* Wilson, *Lawrence of Arabia*, 511.

399 *"without Feisal's knowledge":* Ibid., 512.

399 *"at Arab Headquarters":* Ibid., 513.

399 *"almost feminine charm":* Pakenham, *Peace by Ordeal*, 49.

400 *"under British colours":* Wilson, *Lawrence of Arabia*, 514.

400 *"Mohammed Said, Abd el Kader's brother":* Liddell Hart, *Lawrence of Arabia*, 254.

401 *"Relations between Lawrence and ourselves":* Ibid., 251.

401 *"Lawrence . . . could certainly not have done":* Young, *The Independent Arab*, 157.

402 *"no later than September 16th":* Ibid., 205.

402 *"three men and a boy":* Lawrence, SP, 462.

402 *"on the condition that":* Liddell Hart, *Lawrence of Arabia*, 250.

403 *"emphasizing the mystical enchantment":* Ibid., 257.

404 *"a mixed sense of ease":* Ibid., 258.

405 *"I could flatter":* Ibid., 262.

405 *"the desert had become":* Ibid., 263.

406 *"He had removed":* Ibid., 264.

406 *"it was ever [his] habit":* Ibid., 266.

407 *"creating dust columns":* Ibid., 274.

407 *"12,000 sabres":* Wavell, *Palestine Campaigns*, 195.

407 *"about twelve hundred strong":* Liddell Hart, *Lawrence of Arabia*, 268.

407 *"solo effort":* Ibid., 269.

408 *"crammed to the gunwale":* Ibid.

408 *"the cover of the last ridge":* Ibid., 270.

408 *"a fastidious artist":* Wavell, *Palestine Campaigns*, 203.

408 *"first have to tear down":* Liddell Hart, *Lawrence of Arabia*, 270.

409 *"rushed down to find Peake's":* Ibid.

410 *"the telegraph, thus severing":* Ibid., 271.

410 *"a lurid blaze":* Ibid., 273.

411 *"7,000 yards":* Wavell, *Palestine Campaigns*, 207.

411 *"had broken in hopeless":* Ibid.

412 *"clerks, orderlies etc.":* von Sanders, *Five Years in Turkey*, 282.

412 *"Nothing is known of the climate":* Ibid., 282, fn 184.

412 *"Early on September 21st":* Liddell Hart, *Lawrence of Arabia*, 275.

413 *"lit up by the green shower":* Ibid., 278.

414 *"found the great man at work":* Lawrence, SP, 753.

414 *Allenby personally briefed Lawrence:* Wavell, *Palestine Campaigns,* 216–217.

415 *"noting the two charred German bodies":* Lawrence, SP, 758.

415 *"packed into the green Vauxhall":* Ibid.

415 *" 'Indeed and at last' ":* Ibid., 759.

416 *"still regarded him":* Young, *The Independent Arab,* 243.

417 *"Ghazale by storm":* Lawrence, SP, 771.

418 *"When we got within sight":* Ibid., 775–780.

426 *"I asked Lawrence to remove":* Barrow, *The Fire of Life,* 211.

427 *"At least my mind":* Lawrence, SP, 784.

427 *"tapped* The Seven Pillars*":* Barrow, *The Fire of Life,* 215.

428 *"I said, 'This morning' ":* Lawrence, SP, 785.

428 *"Auda was waiting for them":* Ibid., 788.

430 *"A movement like a breath":* Ibid., 793.

431 *"jumped in to drive them apart":* Ibid., 794.

431 *"to wash out the insult":* Ibid., 795.

432 *"could not recognize":* Wilson, *Lawrence of Arabia,* 565.

433 *"I had been born free":* Lawrence, SP, 802.

433 *"burst open shops":* Ibid., 803.

434 *"squalid with rags":* Ibid., 805.

434 *"There might be thirty there":* Ibid.

435 *"asked [him] shortly":* Ibid., 809.

435 *"and stalked off":* Ibid.

436 *"triumphal entry":* Young, *The Independent Arab,* 255.

436 *"a French Liaison Officer":* Wilson, *Lawrence of Arabia,* 567–568.

437 *"declined to have a French Liaison Officer":* Ibid., 567.

437 *"turned to Lawrence":* Ibid.

437 *"he would not work":* Chauvel, quoted in Knightley and Simpson, *Secret Lives of Lawrence of Arabia,* 96.

CHAPTER NINE In the Great World

439 *"that younger successor":* J. T. Shotwell, *At the Paris Peace Conference* (New York: 1937), 121. Note that Shotwell, a member of the American delegation, was off by two years—Lawrence was in fact thirty at this time, though he did look far younger.

440 *"to arrange for an audience":* Wilson, *Lawrence of Arabia,* 572.

440 *"a man dropping a heavy load":* Ibid.

440 *profoundly sad:* Mack, *A Prince of Our Disorder,* 256.

442 *"a huge fellow":* Aldington, *Lawrence of Arabia,* 250–251.

443 *"on or about October 24th":* Wilson, *Lawrence of Arabia,* 573.

444 *"under the control" of Feisal:* Ibid., 575.

445 *"chafed at":* Graves and Liddell Hart (eds.), *T. E. Lawrence to His Biographers,* 108.

448 *"He explained personally":* Ibid., 106.

448 *"if a man has to serve":* Ibid., 107.

450 *"rather taken aback":* Wilson, *Lawrence of Arabia,* 578.

450 *"he had made certain promises":* Graves and Liddell Hart (eds.), *T. E. Lawrence to His Biographers,* 107.

451 *"if it is behind a British":* Wilson, *Lawrence of Arabia,* 579.

452 *"He wore his Arab robes":* Winston Churchill, *Great Contemporaries,* 157.

452 *"conversations about the Arabs":* Ibid., 581.

455 *"Without in the least wishing":* Ibid., 585.

455 *"historic duty towards the peoples of Syria":* Ibid., 584.

456 *"You do not want to divide the loot":* MacMillan, *Paris 1919,* 386.

456 *"it was essential that Feisal":* Wilson, *Lawrence of Arabia,* 586.

458 *"evil genius":* MacMillan, *Paris 1919,* 389.

458 *"You must be quite candid":* Aldington, *Lawrence of Arabia,* 256.

460 *As the two leaders stood together:* Wilson, *Lawrence of Arabia,* 589; Rose, *Chaim Weizmann,* 199.

461 *Curzon spoke scathingly:* Ibid., 590.

461 *"incessant friction":* Ibid., 591.

462 *"but we must not put the knife":* Ibid.

462 *"a member of Feisal's staff":* Ibid., 592.

462 *Thus Lawrence was placed:* Ibid., 410.

462 *"We lived many lives":* Lawrence, SP, 6

463 *"like a choir boy":* General Édouard Brémond, *Le Hedjaz dans la Guerre Mondiale,* 317, quoted in Aldington, *Lawrence of Arabia,* 257.

463 *"civic functions":* Wilson, *Lawrence of Arabia,* 593.

467 *"If the Arabs are established":* Weizmann, *Letters and Papers,* Vol. IX, Series A, reproduced images between 86 and 87.

467 *" 'He'll say that he doesn't' ":* Quoted in Knightley and Simpson, *Secret Lives of Lawrence of Arabia,* 120.

468 *"the Great Powers":* Wilson, *Lawrence of Arabia,* 597.

470 *"red weals on his ribs":* Meinertzhagen, *Middle East Diary,* 52.

470 *"a silent, masterful man":* Lawrence, SP, 429.

470 *"his mind":* Meinertzhagen, *Middle East Diary,* 39.

471 *"There is nothing funny about toilet paper":* Ibid., 40.

471 *"the most picturesque":* Mack, *A Prince of Our Disorder,* 264.

471 *"He has been described":* Shotwell, *At the Paris Peace Conference,* 231.

473 *"in flowing robes of dazzling white"*: Lloyd George, *Memoirs of the Peace Conference*, Vol. II, 673.

473 *with a curved gold dagger*: MacMillan, *Paris 1919*, 291.

474 *"President Wilson then made a suggestion"*: Toynbee, quoted in Mack, *A Prince of Our Disorder*, 267.

474 *"When he came to the end"*: Toynbee, *Acquaintances*, 182–183.

475 *"What did you get that fellow"*: MacMillan, *Paris 1919*, 391.

475 *"Poor Lawrence"*: Alexander Mihailovitj, *Nar Jag Var Storfuste Av Ryssland*, 314–315, trans. Gunilla Jainchill, quoted in Mack, *A Prince of Our Disorder*, 268.

475 *"the lines of resentment"*: Nicolson, *Peace Making*, 142.

476 *Wilson also turned down all suggestions*: Mack, *A Prince of Our Disorder*, 269.

477 *"control of personal feelings"*: Wilson, *Lawrence of Arabia*, 610.

477 *fifty big Handley-Page bombers*: Ibid., 611.

478 *"a second Gordon"*: Ibid., 608.

479 *proclaimed him "Lawrence of Arabia"*: Ibid., 622.

480 *The show included not only the film*: Mack, *A Prince of Our Disorder*, 274–275.

481 *"summoned Mr. and Mrs. Thomas"*: *London Times*, November 20, 1919.

483 *"Wouldn't it be fun"*: Mack, *A Prince of Our Disorder*, 271.

485 *"the antiquities and ethnology"*: Ibid., 277.

485 *"our troubles with the French"*: Wilson, *Lawrence of Arabia*, 617.

485 *"that Lawrence will never be employed"*: Ibid.

485 *"Colonel Lawrence has no Military status"*: NA General Staff WO M.I.2. B, July 21, 1919.

485 *"I have tried again and again"*: NA LA 1107, December 5, 1919.

487 *"use his influence with Feisal"*: Wilson, *Lawrence of Arabia*, 621.

CHAPTER TEN "Backing into the Limelight": 1920–1922

490 *"it might trouble him"*: Mack, *A Prince of Our Disorder*, 481.

491 *a terrible "row"*: Ibid.

491 *"bear a brave face"*: Lawrence, *Home Letters*, 304.

491 *At times he broke out of his depression*: Mack, *A Prince of Our Disorder*, 287.

493 *"Bow Street was jammed"*: Lowell Thomas to "Ronnie," March 29, 1956, Lowell Thomas Papers, Marist College.

493 *"he would blush crimson"*: Mack, *A Prince of Our Disorder*, 276.

493 *"Thomas Lawrence, the archaeologist"*: Wilson, *Lawrence of Arabia*, 624.

494 *"In the history of the world"*: Mack, *A Prince of Our Disorder*, 287.

495 *"Colonel C. E. Florence"*: Aldington, *Lawrence of Arabia*, 352.

496 *The truth is quite simple*: Wilson, *Lawrence of Arabia*, 627.

496 *an "official" one*: Ibid.

497 *"95% of the book in thirty days"*: Ibid., 628.

497 *At one point he wrote 30,000 words*: Mack, *A Prince of Our Disorder*, 84.

499 *"flying suit"*: Wilson, *Lawrence of Arabia*, 629.

500 *"the book had now assumed"*: Ibid., 630.

501 *"boy-scout"*: Ibid., 635.

501 *Among the dozen or so alternative ideas*: Mack, *A Prince of Our Disorder*, 284.

502 *His scholarship from All Souls*: Wilson, *Lawrence of Arabia*, 637.

502 *Thomas Lawrence had left*: Ibid., 637–638.

503 *Perhaps because he had overestimated*: Ibid., 637.

503 *Neither Will nor Frank had lived*: Ibid., 637–638.

504 *make him look "silly"*: Mack, *A Prince of Our Disorder*, 65.

504 *This did not prevent him from buying rare*: Wilson, *Lawrence of Arabia*, 641.

505 *"too sparsely peopled"*: Mack, *A Prince of Our Disorder*, 291.

505 *"learning opportunities"*: Ibid., 634.

506 *"one never knows how many"*: Storrs, *Orientations*, 505.

506 *Far from being extreme*: Mack, *A Prince of Our Disorder*, 293.

507 *Some idea of the aura of celebrity*: Wilson, *Lawrence of Arabia*, 633.

509 *"to relieve Curzon"*: Graves and Liddell Hart (eds.), *T. E. Lawrence to His Biographers*, 354.

510 *he had "a virgin mind"*: Young, *The Independent Arab*, 324.

511 *Churchill's omnipresent private secretary*: Wilson, *Lawrence of Arabia*, 643.

511 *Though it was not appreciated at the time*: Ibid., 644.

513 *"little Lawrence"*: Meinertzhagen, *Middle East Diary*, 55–56.

513 *Lawrence became a civil servant*: Graves and Liddell Hart (eds.), *T. E. Lawrence to His Biographers*, 143.

513 *"Talk of leaving things"*: Ibid.

514 *"You must take risks"*: Ibid.

515 *"Lawrence can bear comparison"*: Liddell Hart, *Lawrence of Arabia*, 384.

515 *"Our most trusted"*: Graves and Liddell Hart (eds.), *T. E. Lawrence to His Biographers*, 131.

517 *The western border with Syria:* Fromkin, *A Peace to End All Peace*, 503.

518 *"with 30 officers and 200 Bedouins":* Ibid., 504.

518 *"living with Abdulla":* Lawrence, *Letters*, Brown (ed.), 197.

518 *"suspicious of his influence":* Abdullah, *Memoirs*, 170.

518 *"He was certainly a strange character":* Ibid., 170–171.

518 *"Lawrence was the man":* Thompson, *Assignment Churchill*, 30.

519 *"I know Abdullah":* Fromkin, *A Peace to End All Peace*, 510.

519 *"shrewd and indolent":* Ibid.

520 *"The atmosphere in the Colonial Office":* Meinertzhagen, *Middle East Diary*, 99–100.

520 *"consternation, despondency":* Ingrams, *Palestine Papers*, 105.

521 *"a typewritten receipt":* Storrs, *Orientations*, 391.

521 *"E.&O. E.":* Samuel, *Memoirs*, 154.

522 *"Their cries became a roar":* Mack *A Prince of Our Disorder*, 304.

523 *"the Greek epitaph of despair":* Storrs, *Orientations*, 527.

523 *With a typically British manifestation:* Fromkin, *A Peace to End All Peace*, 508.

523 *"against his own people":* Wilson, *Lawrence of Arabia*, 650.

524 *"I take most of the credit":* Ibid., 651.

525 *"quit of the war-time Eastern adventure":* Mack, *A Prince of Our Disorder*, 314, attributed to Lawrence's notes in SP, 276.

525 *"to negotiate and conclude":* Wilson, *Lawrence of Arabia*, 655.

527 *Reading Lawrence's report:* Ibid., 660.

528 *Lawrence took a steamer:* Ibid.

529 *"for in Trans-Jordan":* Mack, *A Prince of Our Disorder*, 308.

529 *"I leave all business to Lawrence":* Ibid., 309, quoting from Philby's *Forty Years in the Wilderness*, 108.

530 *This refers to the fact that his father's younger sister:* Wilson, *Lawrence of Arabia*, 944.

CHAPTER ELEVEN "Solitary in the Ranks"

539 *He would laboriously correct the copies:* Jeremy Wilson, "Seven Pillars of Wisdom: Triumph and Tragedy," T. E. Lawrence studies Web site, telawrencestudies.org.

540 *"to leave the payroll of the Colonial Office":* Wilson, *Lawrence of Arabia*, 674.

541 *"God this is awful":* Lawrence, *The Mint*, 19.

542 *"With regard to your personal point":* Hyde, *Solitary in the Ranks*, 46.

542 *"considerably embarrassed":* Ibid., 48.

542 *"secrecy and subterfuge":* Swann, quoted ibid.

542 *"disliked the whole business":* Ibid.

542 *"One would think from [his] letters":* Lawrence, *Letters,* Garnett (ed.), 363.

546 *Johns resourcefully found a civilian doctor:* Hyde, *Solitary in the Ranks,* 52.

547 *"with the memory of a cold":* Ibid., 53.

547 *"As they swiftly stripped for sleep":* Lawrence, *The Mint,* 25.

550 *"a strict disciplinarian":* Hyde, *Solitary in the Ranks,* 57.

551 *"I must hit him, I must":* Ibid., 58.

551 *"Let the old cunt rot":* Ibid., 76–77.

551 *"and see him privately":* Ibid., 65.

552 *Lawrence had been writing:* Ibid.

552 *"consistently dirty":* Breese, quoted ibid., 66.

552 *"that he had always felt":* Ibid.

552 *"I think I had a mental breakdown":* Ibid., 62.

553 *"There are twenty-thousand airmen":* Lawrence, *The Mint,* 98–99.

554 *"mummified thing":* Ibid., 184–185.

555 *"I'd like you to read":* Lawrence, *Letters,* Garnett (ed.), 362.

556 *"It seems to me that an attempted work":* Wilson, *Lawrence of Arabia,* 686. See 1126, n 21, where Wilson gives the source as V. W. Richards to T. E. Lawrence, September 24, 1922, Bodleian Library transcript.

557 *"Of the present Ministry":* Quoted ibid., 688.

560 *"was appointed to the Adjutant's office":* Hyde, *Solitary in the Ranks,* 67–68.

560 *"why A/c2 Ross":* Ibid., 69.

560 *"was not at all sympathetic":* Ibid.

560 *"frankly perplexed":* Ibid.

560 *"His blue eyes were set":* Ibid.

561 *" 'Yes, Lawrence of Arabia!' ":* Ibid.

562 *"I am afraid you are rather making a labour of it":* Lawrence, *Letters,* Brown (ed.), 226.

562 *"road tubthumping round":* Holroyd, *Bernard Shaw,* Vol. III, 85.

562 *"she began ecstatically reading":* Ibid.

564 *"This letter has got to be":* Wilson, *Lawrence of Arabia,* 690.

564 *"Your offer is a generous and kind one":* Ibid., 691.

567 *"a brace of thoroughgoing modern ruffians":* Ibid., 695.

567 *"Nelson, slightly cracked":* Ibid.

567 *"You are evidently a very dangerous man":* Holroyd, *Bernard Shaw,* Vol. III, 85.

568 *a "virtuoso" essay:* Ibid.

569 *"unreasonably":* Hyde, *Solitary in the Ranks,* 74.

569 *"previous service"*: Ibid.

569 *" 'I am convinced that some quality' "*: Findlay, "The Amazing AC 2."

570 *"an accomplished poseur"*: Holroyd, *Bernard Shaw*, Vol. III, 88.

570 *" 'There is no end to your Protean tricks' "*: Ibid., 86.

572 *"The cat being now let out of the bag"*: Wilson, *Lawrence of Arabia*, 697.

573 *"How is it* conceivable, imaginable": Ibid., 699–700.

573 *"get used to the limelight"*: Ibid., 700.

574 *"that his position in the RAF"*: Ibid., 701.

575 *"the position, which had been extremely"*: Ibid., 706.

575 *"well-known for its large pond and bird life"*: Hyde, *Solitary in the Ranks*, 76.

575 *"played up at Farnborough"*: Ibid., 77.

576 *"how his men were to distinguish"*: Lawrence, SP, 574.

577 *"sounded out"*: Hyde, *Solitary in the Ranks*, 80.

577 *"sees no very great difficulty about it"*: Ibid.

577 *"A good idea!"*: Ibid., 80–81.

578 *"To Pte. Shaw from Public Shaw"*: Holroyd, *Bernard Shaw*, Vol. III, 88.

578 *"and was posted to A Company"*: Hyde, *Solitary in the Ranks*, 81.

579 *"queerly homesick"*: Ibid., 86.

579 *"prevailing animality of spirit"*: Ibid., 85.

580 *"speak and act with complete assurance"*: Ibid., 82.

580 *"It's a horrible life"*: Ibid., 83.

580 *"this cat-calling carnality seething"*: Ibid., 84.

582 *"inarticulate, excessively uncomfortable"*: Shaw letter, July 19, 1924; or Knightley and Simpson, *Secret Lives of Lawrence of Arabia*, 190.

582 *"Lawrence did nothing without a purpose"*: Knightley and Simpson, *Secret Lives of Lawrence of Arabia*, 168.

583 *"His disloyalty reminded"*: *Jerusalem Post*, 1961, quoted in Graves, *Lawrence and the Arabs*, 230.

586 *"called him a bastard"*: Knightley and Simpson, *Secret Lives of Lawrence of Arabia*, 174.

586 *"turned his back on God"*: Ibid.

587 *"an unsigned, typed letter"*: Hyde, *Solitary in the Ranks*, 88–89.

588 *"to report in writing"*: Ibid., 89.

588 *"Circassian riding whip"*: Lawrence, SP, 498.

589 *"it was rather his pied-à-terre"*: Hyde, *Solitary in the Ranks*, 93.

590 *"Hardy is so pale"*: Lawrence, *Letters*, Garnett (ed.), 429–431.

590 *"craving for real risk"*: Mack, *Prince*, 343.

590 *"swerved at 60 M.P.H."*: Lawrence, *Letters*, Garnett (ed.), 419–420.

591 *"Lawrence is not normal in many ways"*: Lawrence, *Correspondence with Bernard and Charlotte Shaw, 1922–1926*, Vol. I, 45.

591 *"Damn you, how long do you"*: Arnold Lawrence (ed.), *Letters to T.E. Lawrence*, 154.

591 *"I can't cheer you up"*: Ibid., 64.

594 *"A black core"*: Lawrence, *Letters*, Brown (ed.), 233.

594 *He persisted with it, however*: Wilson, *Lawrence of Arabia*, 719–720.

595 *"he looked very much like Colonel Lawrence"*: Arnold Lawrence (ed.), *T. E. Lawrence by His Friends*, 244.

595 *"I have written another magnificent play"*: Lawrence, *Correspondence with Bernard and Charlotte Shaw, 1922–1926*, Vol. I, 51.

596 *"upon the throne of a nation-state"*: Holroyd, *Bernard Shaw*, Vol. III, 86.

596 *"With their missionary zeal"*: Ibid., 88.

596 *"There isn't as much strength in Joan"*: Lawrence, *Correspondence with Bernard and Charlotte Shaw, 1922–1926*, Vol. I, 86.

597 *"I'd like to very much"*: Hyde, *Solitary in the Ranks*, 97.

598 *"all sorts of minor ailments"*: Ibid., 102.

598 *"I'd rather the few copies"*: Wilson, *Lawrence of Arabia*, 727.

599 *"The business will be done"*: Ibid., 731.

599 *"Confound you"*: Lawrence, *Correspondence with Bernard and Charlotte Shaw, 1922–1926*, Vol. I, 103–105.

601 *"I'm always afraid of being hurt"*: Wilson, *Lawrence of Arabia*, 739.

602 *"I don't know by what right"*: Lawrence, *Letters*, Garnett (ed.), 214.

602 *"fits of extreme depression"*: Wilson, *Lawrence of Arabia*, 754.

CHAPTER TWELVE Apotheosis

605 *"A Flight-Sergeant came along"*: Hyde, *Solitary in the Ranks*, 109.

606 *"dragged in to the Headquarters Adjutant"*: Lawrence, *Letters*, Garnett (ed.), 481.

608 *"He was hero-worshipped"*: Hyde, *Solitary in the Ranks*, 117.

608 *"to dive into the elastic water"*: Ibid., 113.

610 *"found Feisal lively"*: Ibid., 116.

610 *"So long as there is breath"*: Lawrence, *Correspondence with Bernard and Charlotte Shaw, 1922–1926*, Vol. I, 150.

611 *"This bundle of proofs"*: Ibid., 137.

611 *"Something extraordinary always happens"*: Ibid., 35.

612 *The gift basket from Gunter's:* Ibid., 150–6.

613 *"No thanks: no money"*: Lawrence, *Home Letters*, 360.

615 *"It is not the right blue"*: Hyde, *Solitary in the Ranks*, 127.

616 *"with his right arm dangling"*: Ibid., 121.

617 *"It is good of you"*: Trenchard Papers, November 20, 1926, quoted ibid., 124.

618 *This was an infringement of the U.K. Copyright Act*: Ibid., 126.

618 *"I have been surprised"*: Ibid., 132.

620 *"the breath away by its sheer brutality"*: Ibid., 133.

620 *"Hullo here's the Orderly"*: Lawrence, *Letters*, Garnett (ed.), 502–503.

620 *"Wave upon wave"*: Ibid., 502–503.

622 *"I do wish, hourly"*: Ibid., 506.

623 *Not only Bernard Shaw believed*: Hyde, *Solitary in the Ranks*, 135.

624 *At Cranwell, the telegraph boy*: Ibid., 128.

624 *"When I opened your letter"*: Ibid., 138.

625 *"The fellow you need to influence"*: Lawrence, *Letters*, Garnett (ed.), 599.

626 *"Gertrude was not a good judge"*: Ibid., 543.

628 *"was sent for"*: Hyde, *Solitary in the Ranks*, 143.

629 *"his head was everything"*: Ibid., 149.

629 *"suddenly and quietly"*: Ibid., 150.

630 *"William Blake, Thomas Malory"*: Ibid., 152.

630 *"which he kept in a small tin box"*: Ibid.

630 *"I think probably there will be"*: Ibid.

630 *"instead of visiting Karachi"*: Ibid., 154.

631 *"A conversation between"*: Ibid., 163.

631 *"We are only 26"*: Ibid.

633 *"I think that the spectacle"*: Ibid., 169.

633 *"Very bookish, this house-bred"*: Lawrence, *Odyssey of Homer*, end of "Note."

634 *A genuine holy man*: Wilson, *Lawrence of Arabia*, 845.

634 *On January 3, 1929*: Hyde, *Solitary in the Ranks*, 178.

634 *"ineradicable suspicion"*: Ibid.

636 *"GREAT MYSTERY"*: Ibid., 209.

638 *"No, my name is Mr. Smith"*: Wilson, *Lawrence of Arabia*, 846.

639 *No sooner had Trenchard*: Hyde, *Solitary in the Ranks*, 183.

640 *"the marriage tangles"*: Ibid., 184.

640 *"Why must you be"*: Ibid., 185.

640 *"I am being hunted"*: Lawrence, *Letters*, Garnett (ed.), 641.

641 *"Cattewater proves to be"*: Wilson, *Lawrence of Arabia*, 850.

641 *"A man who can run away"*: Lawrence, *Letters*, Garnett (ed.), 648.

642 *"I'm very weary of being stared at"*: Lawrence, *Selected Letters*, Garnett (ed.), 307.

643 *Lawrence heard Bernard Shaw read*: Wilson, *Lawrence of Arabia*, 854.

644 *"A pea-hen voice"*: Hyde, *Solitary in the Ranks*, 190.

644 *"invited herself"*: Ibid.

644 *"I do not know when"*: Lawrence, *Letters*, Garnett (ed.), 665.

645 *"Thus he was able to have a deep"*: Clare Sydney Smith, *The Golden Reign*, 37.

647 *Lawrence entered the picture*: Hyde, *Solitary in the Ranks*, 194.

647 *Unfortunately, Shaw was too busy*: Ibid., 195.

648 *"As regards including Lawrence"*: Ibid., 268.

648 *"telling me off as usual"*: Ibid., 197.

650 *"to stop leading from the ranks"*: Ibid., 199.

651 *"elevenses"*: Hyde, *Solitary in the Ranks*, 205.

652 *"You are a simple aircraftman"*: Arnold Lawrence (ed.), *Letters to T. E. Lawrence*, 180.

653 *"a marine expert"*: Hyde, *Solitary in the Ranks*, 209.

653 *"every sentence in it"*: Ibid., 210.

654 *"read it at Umtaiye"*: Knightley and Simpson, *Secret Lives of Lawrence of Arabia*, 260.

655 *"As I see it"*: Hyde, *Solitary in the Ranks*, 212.

655 *"and he was a wash-out"*: Lawrence, *Selected Letters*, Garnett (ed.), 324.

656 *"Dear 338171"*: Ibid., 473.

658 *Lawrence "is wearing a uniform"*: Emma Smith, *The Great Western Beach*, 244.

659 *"the best motorcycle out"*: West, *David Reese among Others*, 193.

659 *"Ah, yes—that"*: Ibid., 202.

660 *"The discharge of this airman"*: Hyde, *Solitary in the Ranks*, 218.

660 *looking after the interests of the Air Ministry*: Ibid., 220.

660 *"Lawrence of Arabia has decided to stay"*: Ibid.

661 *"agreed with Lawrence's view"*: Mack, *A Prince of Our Disorder*, 519–520.

661 *"surely I am not in clear-shining Ithaca"*: Lawrence, *Odyssey of Homer*, 190–191.

662 *Jeremy Wilson notes that he took*: Wilson, *Lawrence of Arabia*, 892.

666 *"It'll end in tragedy"*: Graves and Liddell Hart, *T. E. Lawrence to His Biographers*, 140.

666 *"the rhetoric of freedom"*: Ibid., 186–187.

667 *The British Fascists*: Wilson, *Lawrence of Arabia*, 916–917.

667 *"In March 1935 the RAF"*: Lawrence, *Letters*, Brown (ed.), 528.

668 *"I lunched with Alexander Korda"*: Ibid., 549.

669 *"Korda is like an oil-company"*: Ibid., 534.

669 *Lawrence enjoyed Bridlington*: Hyde, *Solitary in the Ranks*, 228.

670 *" 'Oh, I am so sorry' "*: Ibid., 230–231.

670 *"When I want the advice"*: Ibid., 232.

671 *"armament school"*: Ibid., 238.

671 *"The conquest of the last element":* Lawrence, *Letters*, Garnett (ed.), 368.

672 *"Aircraftman Shaw":* Hyde, *Solitary in the Ranks*, 241.

672 *"How I wish he hadn't":* Ibid., 234.

673 *Horrified—he needed:* Wilson, *Lawrence of Arabia*, 927.

674 *"All here is very quiet":* Hyde, *Solitary in the Ranks*, 245.

674 *"I believe when the Government":* Wilson, *Lawrence of Arabia*, 934.

674 *"Wild mares would not take me":* Ibid.

675 *"At present I am sitting":* Lawrence, *Letters*, Brown (ed.), 541.

676 *Having completed his errands:* Knightley and Simpson, *Secret Lives of Lawrence of Arabia*, 270.

678 *Lawrence lay unconscious:* Ibid., 272–273.

680 *"I stood beside him lying":* Storrs, *Orientations*, 530–531.

EPILOGUE Life after Death

684 *"an Austrian-born religious artist":* Brown, *Lawrence of Arabia*, 196–197.

Bibliography

MANUSCRIPT COLLECTIONS

B. H. Liddell Hart Papers, The Liddell Hart Centre for Military Archives, King's College, London.
Papers of T. E. Lawrence and A. W. Lawrence, University of Oxford, Bodleian Library, Oxford, England.
National Archives, Kew, Surrey, England.
Lowell Thomas Collection, James A. Cannavino Library, Marist College, Poughkeepsie, N. Y.
Thomas Edward Lawrence Papers, Huntington Library, San Marino, Calif.

BOOKS AND ARTICLES

Abdullah, King of Jordan. *Memoirs of King Abdullah of Transjordan.* London: Cape, 1950.
Adelson, Roger. *Mark Sykes: Portrait of an Amateur.* London: Cape, 1975.
Aldington, Richard. *Lawrence of Arabia: A Biographical Enquiry.* London: Collins, 1955.
Antonius, George. *The Arab Awakening: The Story of the Arab National Movement.* Philadelphia, Pa.: Lippincott, 1939.
Asher, Michael. *Lawrence: The Uncrowned King of Arabia.* London: Viking, 1998.
Barr, James. *Setting the Desert on Fire: T. E. Lawrence and Britain's Secret War in Arabia, 1916–1918.* London: Bloomsbury, 2007.
Barrow, General Sir George deS. *The Fire of Life.* London: Hutchinson, 1942.

Brown, Malcolm. *Lawrence of Arabia: The Life, the Legend.* London: Thames and Hudson, 2005.

Brown, Malcolm, and Julia Cave. *Touch of Genius: The Life of T. E. Lawrence.* London: Dent, 1988.

Callwell, C. E. *Small Wars: Their Principles and Practice.* London: His Majesty's Stationery Office, 1903.

Campbell, Joseph. *The Hero with a Thousand Faces.* Princeton, N.J.: Princeton University Press, 2004.

Churchill, Randolph Spencer, and Martin Gilbert. *Winston Churchill, 1914–1916: Challenge of War,* Vol. 3. Boston, Mass.: Houghton-Mifflin, 1966.

Churchill, Winston. *Great Contemporaries.* Chicago, Ill.: University of Chicago Press, 1973.

———. *Story of the Malakind Field Force: An Episode of Frontier War.* London: Longmans Green, 1901.

———. *The World Crisis,* Vol. I. New York: Scribner, 1931.

Findlay, C. "The Amazing AC 2." *The Listener,* June 5, 1958.

Fromkin, David. *A Peace to End All Peace.* New York: Henry Holt, 1989.

Gilbert, Martin. *Winston Churchill,* Vol. 3. London: Heinemann, 1971.

Graves, Robert. *Lawrence and the Arabs.* London: Cape, 1927.

Graves, Robert, and B. H. Liddell Hart. *T. E. Lawrence to His Biographers.* Garden City, N. Y.: Doubleday, 1963.

Greaves, Adrian. *Lawrence of Arabia: Mirage of a Desert War.* London: Weidenfeld and Nicolson, 2007.

Holroyd, Michael. *Bernard Shaw: The Lure of Fantasy,* Vol. III. New York: Random House, 1991.

———. *Bernard Shaw: Search for Love,* Vol. I. London: Chatto and Windus, 1977.

Hyde, H. Montgomery. *Solitary in the Ranks: Lawrence of Arabia as Airman and Private Soldier.* London: Constable, 1977.

Ingrams, Doreen. *Palestine Papers, 1917–1922: Seeds of Conflict.* London: J. Murray, 1972.

Knightley, Phillip, and Colin Simpson. *Secret Lives of Lawrence of Arabia.* New York: McGraw-Hill, 1969.

Lawrence, Arnold E. (ed.) *Letters to T. E. Lawrence.* London: Cape, 1962.

——— (ed.). *T. E. Lawrence by His Friends.* London: Cape, 1954.

Lawrence, T. E. *Correspondence with Bernard and Charlotte Shaw, 1922–1926,* Vol. I, Jeremy Wilson and Nicole Wilson (eds.). Fordingbridge, England: Castle, 2000.

———. *The Home Letters of T. E. Lawrence and His Brothers.* New York: Macmillan, 1954.

——. *Letters from T. E. Lawrence to E. T. Leeds*, J. M. Wilson (ed.). Andoversford, England: Whittington, 1988.

——. *Letters of T. E. Lawrence*, M. Brown (ed.). New York: Norton, 1989.

——. *Letters of T. E. Lawrence*, David Garnett (ed.). New York: Doubleday, Doran, 1939.

——. *The Mint*. London: Cape, 1955.

——. (trans.). *Odyssey of Homer*, New York: Oxford University Press, 1932.

——. *Selected Letters of T. E. Lawrence*, David Garnett (ed.). London: Cape, 1952.

——. *Seven Pillars of Wisdom: A Triumph* (complete 1922 text). Fordingbridge, England: Castle, 2003.

Liddell Hart, Basil. *Colonel Lawrence: The Man behind the Legend*. New York: Halcyon, 1937.

Lloyd George, David. *Memoirs of the Peace Conference*, Vol. II. New Haven, Conn.: Yale University Press, 1939.

Mack, John. *A Prince of Our Disorder: The Life of T. E. Lawrence*. Boston, Mass.: Little, Brown, 1976.

MacMillan, Margaret. *Paris 1919: Six Months That Changed the World*. New York: Random House, 2002.

Meinertzhagen, Richard. *Middle East Diary*. London: Cresset, 1959.

Miller, Geoffrey. "Turkey Enters the War and British Actions." December 1999, http://www.gwpda.org/naval/turkmill.htm.

Nicolson, Harold. *Peace Making: Being Reminiscences of the Paris Peace Conference*. Boston, Mass.: Houghton Mifflin, 1933.

O'Brien, Philip M. *T. E. Lawrence: A Bibliography*. New Castle, Del.: Oak Knoll, 2000.

Pakenham, Frank, Earl of Longford. *Peace by Ordeal: The Negotiation of the Anglo-Irish Treaty, 1921*. London: Pimlico, 1992.

Rose, Norman. *Chaim Weizmann: A Biography*. New York: Penguin, 1989.

Samuel, Herbert (Viscount Samuel). *Memoirs*. London: Cresset, 1945.

Seeley, Sir John Robert. *Expansion of England*. [N.p.] 1883.

Shaw, George Bernard. *Man of Destiny*. New York: Brentano, 1913.

Sherwood, John. *No Golden Journey: A Biography of James Elroy Flecker*. London: Heinemann, 1973.

Shotwell, James Thomson. *At the Paris Peace Conference*. New York: Macmillan, 1937.

Smith, Clare Sydney. *The Golden Reign*. London: Cassell, 1940.

Smith, Emma. *The Great Western Beach: A Memoir of a Cornish Childhood between the Wars*. London: Bloomsbury, 2008.

Storrs, Ronald. *Orientations*. London: Ivor Nicholson and Watson, 1937.

Thomas, Lowell. *With Lawrence in Arabia*. New York: Doubleday, 1967.

Thompson, W. H. *Assignment Churchill*. Farrar, Straus and Young, 1955.

Toynbee, Arnold. *Acquaintances*. Oxford: Oxford University Press, 1967.

von Sanders, Liman. *Five Years in Turkey*. Nashville, Tenn.: Battery, 2000.

Wallach, Janet. *Desert Queen: The Extraordinary Life of Gertrude Bell—Adventurer, Adviser to Kings, Ally of Lawrence of Arabia*. New York: Anchor, 2005.

Wavell, Archibald Percival. *Palestine Campaigns*. London: Constable, 1928.

Weizmann, Chaim. *Letters and Papers of Chaim Weizmann*, Mark W. Weisgal (gen. ed.), Vol. IX, Series A. Transaction Books, Rutgers University. Jerusalem: Israel Universities Press, 1977.

West, Anthony. *David Reese among Others*. New York: Random House, 1970.

Wilson, Jeremy. *Lawrence of Arabia: The Authorized Biography of T. E. Lawrence*. New York: Atheneum, 1990.

Young, Sir Hubert. *The Independent Arab*. London: Murray, 1933.

Illustration Credits

Museum, Negative No. IWM ART 1553; **page 4:** *top*: James A. Cannavino Library, Archives & Special Collections, Lowell Thomas Papers, Marist College, USA, *bottom*: Imperial War Museum, Negative No. IWM FIR 8255; **page 5:** *top left*: Imperial War Museum, Negative No. IWM 1567, *top right and bottom*: James A. Cannavino Library, Archives & Special Collections, Lowell Thomas Papers, Marist College, USA; **page 6:** *top left*: Harry Ransom Humanities Research Center, the University of Texas at Austin, *top right*: ©Seven Pillars of Wisdom Trust, *bottom*: James A. Cannavino Library, Archives & Special Collections, Lowell Thomas Papers, Marist College, USA; **page 7:** James A. Cannavino Library, Archives & Special Collections, Lowell Thomas Papers, Marist College, USA; **page 8:** *top*: from *The Arab Awakening* by George Antonius, *bottom*: National Archives, U.K.

BLACK AND WHITE

Page 1: *top*: from *A Prince of Our Disorder* by John E. Mack, *bottom left*: Bodleian Library, University of Oxford, MS. Photogr.c.126, Fol.2v, *bottom right*: from *"Lawrence of Arabia"* by Jeremy Wilson; **page 2:** *top*: Gertrude Bell Photographic Archive, Newcastle University Archaeology Team, *bottom*: James A. Cannavino Library, Archives & Special Collections, Lowell Thomas Papers, Marist College, USA; **page 3:** *top*: James A. Cannavino Library, Archives & Special Collections, Lowell Thomas Papers, Marist College, USA, *bottom*: Imperial War Museum, Negative No. IWM Q58838; **page 4:** *top*: Imperial War Museum, Negative No. IWM Q58754, *bottom*: Imperial War Museum, Negative No. IWM Q58863; **page 5:** *top*: Imperial War Museum, Negative No. IWM Q12616, *bottom*: from *Lawrence of Arabia: The Life, the Legend* by Malcolm Brown, published by Thames & Hudson Ltd; **page 6:** *top*: Hulton Archive / Getty Images, *middle and bottom*: film stills, James A. Cannavino Library, Archives & Special Collections, Lowell Thomas Papers, Marist College, USA; **page 7:** *top*: Imperial War Musuem, Negative No. IWM Q59641; **page 8:** *top*: General Photographic Agency / Getty Images, *bottom*: © Mary Evans Picture Library / Douglas McCarthy / The Image Works; **page 9:** *top and bottom*: James A. Cannavino Library, Archives & Special Collections, Lowell Thomas Papers, Marist College, USA; **page 10:** *top*: Popperfoto / Getty Images, *bottom*: Ernest H Mills / Getty Images; **page 11:** *top*: Hulton Archive / Getty Images, *bottom*: Bodleian Library, University of Oxford, MS. Photogr.c.126, Fol.83r/b; **page 12:** *top left*: photo by Sasha, from *The Golden Reign* by Clare Sydney Smith, *top right*: Bodleian Library, University of Oxford, MS. Photogr.c.126, Fol.57r/a, *bottom*: Bodleian Library, University of Oxford, MS. Photogr.c.126, Fol.64v; **page 13:** *top*: from *The Golden Reign* by Clare Sydney Smith, *bottom*: Bodleian Library, University of Oxford, MS. Photogr.c.126, Fol.89v/b; **page 14:** Bodleian Library, University of Oxford, N. 22891 b. 5, sc00a06661; **page 15:** *top*: National Portrait Gallery, London, *bottom*: courtesy of family of the artist; **page 16:** © Hulton-Deutsch Collection / Corbis.

Index

Note: Page numbers in *italics* refer to illustrations.

on Hamed's execution, 72–73
income from, 558, 598, 603, 617, 622
on Lawrence's army career, 49–50
Lawrence's contradictory impulses
  regarding, 500–501, 610
Lawrence's embellishments of truth in,
  593
Lawrence's maps in, 84
Lawrence's obsession over, 497,
  499–501, 538
Lawrence's writing of, 471, 483, 485,
  492, 494–501, 539–40
limited subscription edition, 495, 558,
  562, 589, 591–93, 601, 602–3, 610,
  611, 613, 614, 615, 617–18, 687
lost version of, 495–97, 500, 507
as major literary work, 537, 572, 622–24,
  687
on military strategy, 74–75, 332–33
negotiations with publishers on, 501,
  504, 554–55, 558, 565, 566–67,
  571–72, 592–93, 598–602, 614
on Nuri's appearance, 91
Oxford text (1922), 495, 687
on Paris Peace Conference, 462
places described in, 31
printing of, 539
publication of, 296, 617, 624, 687
and publicity, 555, 614, 617, 621, 634,
  668
quality of writing, 139, 319, 322, 369,
  409, 500, 557, 661, 662
reworking of, 495, 497, 499, 507–8, 527,
  538, 539, 579, 581, 593, 603, 611
serialization of, 617
Shaw's reading of, 555–57, 562–64,
  565–68, 574–75, 592, 594, 599–600,
  611
and Shaw's *Saint Joan*, 397
and Storrs, 8, 593
on Sykes, 273
on Tafas scene, 418–24
and Trenchard, 615–16, 617, 624
on war, 264–65, 396, 664, 686, 696
war experiences relived in, 477, 492,
  499, 538, 542, 570, 601
on Wilson, 11
on Wingate, 46–47
on Young, 382
Shakespear, J. R., 405n
Shakespeare, William, *Henry V*, 499, 694

Shakir, Sharif, 76–77
Sharif, Omar, 693
Sharraf, Sharif, 85–86
Shaw, Charlotte F.:
  and Deraa incident, 349–50, 601, 612,
    695
  Lawrence's friendship with, 120, 490,
    540, 595–96, 608, 611–12, 640,
    644–45, 653
  Lawrence's letters to, 143, 320, 322,
    349–50, 525, 601, 610, 611, 612, 618,
    644, 655, 657, 664, 668, 670, 695
  marriage of, 350, 563, 612
  personal traits of, 564
  and *Seven Pillars*, 562–64, 573–75, 599,
    611, 612
Shaw, George Bernard, 273
  and Casement, 654
  death of, 571
  fame of, 540, 556, 570–71
  genius of, 563
  and Lawrence's army enlistment, 578,
    591, 602
  Lawrence's correspondence with, 695
  and Lawrence's fame, 623, 650, 652
  Lawrence's friendship with, 120, 219,
    320, 356, 540, 563, 570, 590–91,
    595–96, 608, 640, 644
  marriage of, 350, 563, 612
  on St. Joan, 397, 457n, 578, 595–97
  and *Seven Pillars*, 349, 555–57, 562–64,
    565–68, 572–73, 574–75, 592, 594,
    599–600, 611, 617, 621
  and socialism, 563, 648
  and Thomson, 647–48
  Too True to Be Good, 588, 619, 657,
    670–71
  views on grammar, 563, 599–600
Shaw, Robert Gould II, 644
Shaw, Thomas Edward, Lawrence's name
  in RTC and RAF, 577–81, 603, 627
Sheikh Saad, as military goal, 417, 418, 424
Sheridan, Richard Brinsley, 556
Sherman, William Tecumseh, 60
Shobek, as military goal, 359, 360, 365
Sholto Douglas, Lord, 550, 553n
Shotwell, James Thomson, 471–72
  At the Paris Peace Conference, 439
Shuckburgh, Sir John, 512, 520, 527
Shukri Pasha el Ayubi, 430, 431, 432, 433
Simpson, Colin, 582n

Winterton, Lord Edward, 408, 417–18,
424, 425, 440, 443, 610
Wood, C. E., 326, 336, 337
Wood, Gar, 649
Woolf, Leonard, 622
Woolley, Charles Leonard, 211
and Carchemish site, 202, 206–9, 210,
214, 218, 219, 221, 224, 230, 240
and Palestine mapping expedition, 234,
235, 236–38
and World War I, 246, 250, 252, 257
World War I:
Allied Powers in, 10, 242, 252, 304,
305
Battle of the Somme, 45, 277
Battle of Verdun, 275, 277, 460
Central Powers in, 10, 13, 232, 233, 242,
249–50
Dardanelles campaign, 509
events in Europe overshadowing Arabia
in, 381–82
events leading to, 13, 204, 242
Gallipoli, 4, 29, 263–64, 277, 282, 285,
290, 295
and Kitchener, 244–46, 245, 262, 264,
265–66, 274
Lawrence as famed hero of, 492, 493,
536, 686, 687
Lawrence brothers in, 243–44
as military disaster, 663
and postwar peace, see Paris Peace
Conference
and postwar territorial demands,
453–54, 468–69
and Sarajevo assassination, 242
stalemate in, 398
surrender of Central Powers in, 417,
453
U.S. entry into, 305, 353, 381
World War II, 309, 698
Churchill's speeches in, 654
French Resistance movement in, 332
Spitfire aircraft in, 643

Yarmuk, Turkish bridges at, 325–28,
330–38, 340, 352, 355, 400, 410,
430
Yeates, V. M., 676

Yeats, William Butler, 73, 119, 654,
657
Yemen, imam of, 516, 527, 528
Yenbo:
Arab control of, 21
defense of, 56, 58–59, 60, 63
journey to, 42–43
strategic importance of, 49
Young, Hubert, 383, 416–18
and Allenby, 402, 436
and Arab army, 401–2, 416, 424, 425
and chain of command, 382–83, 416
in Churchill's Middle East Department,
512, 513, 514, 516, 520
and Lawrence's military actions, 408,
417–18
military traits of, 402
Youth Hostels Association, 673

Zaagi, 420
Zaal (raider), 92, 93–94
Zeid, emir (son of Hussein), 22, 526
and British gold, 292, 375, 376
and Mesopotamia, 444
retreating, 53, 56, 57, 58
at Tafileh, 366, 368, 370–71
Zionism:
and Aaronsohn, 328–29
and Balfour Declaration, 306, 399, 453,
454, 519–20, 531
and Churchill, 510
importance of, 468
and Jewish national home, 511, 520,
531–32
and Jewish settlement in Palestine, 451,
466, 467, 468, 531
Meinertzhagen as supporter of, 470,
512, 520
and Palestine, 280, 306, 328–29, 451,
458, 463, 466–67, 519–20, 524,
531
and Paris Peace Conference, 454, 458,
463, 468
Sykes as supporter of, 272, 280, 352
and Sykes-Picot agreement, 280, 399,
451, 453, 458, 467
and Weizmann-Feisal discussions,
399–400, 463, 465–68, 476